Statistical Methods in Data Science and Applications

Statistical Methods in Data Science and Applications

Editors

Niansheng Tang
Shen-Ming Lee

MDPI

Basel • Beijing • Wuhan • Barcelona • Belgrade • Novi Sad • Cluj • Manchester

Editors
Niansheng Tang
Yunnan University
Kunming
China

Shen-Ming Lee
Feng Chia University
Taichung
Taiwan

Editorial Office
MDPI
St. Alban-Anlage 66
4052 Basel, Switzerland

This is a reprint of articles from the Special Issue published online in the open access journal *Mathematics* (ISSN 2227-7390) (available at: https://www.mdpi.com/journal/mathematics/special_issues/statistical_methods_in_data_science_and_applications).

For citation purposes, cite each article independently as indicated on the article page online and as indicated below:

Lastname, A.A.; Lastname, B.B. Article Title. *Journal Name* **Year**, *Volume Number*, Page Range.

ISBN 978-3-7258-0747-5 (Hbk)
ISBN 978-3-7258-0748-2 (PDF)
doi.org/10.3390/books978-3-7258-0748-2

Cover image courtesy of Shen-Ming Lee

Contents

About the Editors

Nian-Sheng Tang

Nian-Sheng Tang was appointed a Full Professor of statistics in 2003. He has received several prestigious honors, including being recognition as a Yangtze River Scholars Distinguished Professor in 2013. He was elected as a member of the International Statistical Institute (ISI) in 2016. He served on the Board of Directors of the International Chinese Statistical Association (ICSA) and was honored with the ICSA Outstanding Service Award in 2018.

He was awarded by the National Science Foundation for Distinguished Young Scholars of China in 2012, he has received numerous grants from prestigious organizations, such as the National Key Research and Development Program of China, the National Science Foundation of China and Yunnan Province, and the Ministry of Education of China.

He has served on the Editorial Board of several esteemed journals, including Statistics and Its Interface, Journal of Systems Science and Complexity, Communications in Mathematics and Statistics. He serves as a standing director of the National Statistical Society of China, a standing director of the Chinese Society of Probability and Statistics.

His research interests span a wide range of statistical methods, including those in biostatistics, model diagnostic measures, missing data analysis, categorical data analysis, variable selection, high-dimensional data analysis, subsampling for big data, and Bayesian statistics. He has authored more than 200 research papers and has written four books.

Shen-Ming Lee

Shen-Ming Lee, a Professor at Feng Chia University since 1990, also served as a Visiting Professor at National Dong Hua University in 2004. He held administrative roles as Dean of the Business College (2005–2007) and the Finance College (February 2013–July 2013) at Feng Chia University. From 2015 to 2016, he was a Visiting Researcher at Academia Sinica, and from 2017 to 2020, an Adjunct Research Fellow at the Survey Research Center of Academia Sinica.

Throughout his career, Lee has been actively involved in various leadership roles. He served as Director of the Chinese Statistical Association (2005–2016) and continued as Supervisor (2016–2024). Additionally, he was appointed Chairman of Taiwan Intelligent Technology and Applied Statistics (2011–2013) and has been Director since 2014.

With over 80 papers in reputable journals and 3439 citations (according to Google Scholar 2024), Lee serves as a reviewer for esteemed statistics journals. His research interests span ecology population size estimation, missing data regression, statistical methodology for zero-inflated data, and randomized response design and analysis. Since 2008, he's conducted a long-term Feng Chia Night Market survey.

Recently, Lee has focused on developing statistical methods for Traditional Chinese Medicine constitution diagnosis, leveraging TCM constitution questionnaire data. Additionally, he excels in conducting surveys on food preferences and developing food recommendation systems, drawing on data from the Feng Chia Night Market.

Preface

As big data advances, the significance of data science is rapidly gaining momentum, igniting a surge of research across diverse disciplines, including mathematics, statistics, computer science, and artificial intelligence. Data science encompasses various methodologies involving modeling, computation, and learning processes to translate raw data into actionable insights, knowledge, and informed decision making. However, the intricacies inherent in big data, such as missing data, high- and ultra-high-dimensional datasets, response dependency, time series analysis, and distributed storage, present formidable challenges to existing theories, methods, and algorithms in data analysis. This challenge is particularly pronounced in fundamental statistical concepts, such as estimation, hypothesis testing, confidence intervals, and variable selection, spanning frequentist and Bayesian methodologies.

This book presents a comprehensive toolkit within the data science domain to address these challenges head-on. It covers a wide array of topics, including strategies for handling measurement errors or missing data, cognitive diagnosis modeling, constructing credit risk scorecards using logistic regression models, leveraging geographically weighted regression modeling, implementing privacy protection protocols in data mining, exploring clustering methods, and navigating the complexities of model selection for high-dimensional datasets. Additionally, we delve into predicting sensitive features under indirect questioning. We fervently hope these discussions provide readers with invaluable tools and practical examples to effectively apply data science methodologies in real-world scenarios.

As Guest Editors of this Special Issue, we extend our heartfelt gratitude to all the authors for their exceptional contributions, which have significantly enriched the content of this publication. We also express our sincere appreciation to the reviewers for their insightful comments and constructive feedback, which undoubtedly enhanced the quality and rigor of the submitted manuscripts. Additionally, we would like to acknowledge the invaluable support and assistance provided by the administrative staff of MDPI publications, whose dedication and professionalism have been instrumental in facilitating the completion of this project.

Special commendation is due to Ms. Caitlynn Tong, Section Managing Editor of this Special Issue, for her exemplary collaboration and unwavering commitment. Her exceptional guidance and expertise have played a pivotal role in steering this initiative towards fruition.

Niansheng Tang and Shen-Ming Lee
Editors

mathematics

MDPI

Article

Generalized Linear Models with Covariate Measurement Error and Zero-Inflated Surrogates

Ching-Yun Wang [1,*], Jean de Dieu Tapsoba [2], Catherine Duggan [1] and Anne McTiernan [1]

1 Division of Public Health Sciences, Fred Hutchinson Cancer Center, P.O. Box 19024, Seattle, WA 98109-1024, USA; cduggan@fredhutch.org (C.D.); amctiern@fredhutch.org (A.M.)
2 Vaccine and Infectious Disease Division, Fred Hutchinson Cancer Center, P.O. Box 19024, Seattle, WA 98109-1024, USA; jtapsoba@fredhutch.org
* Correspondence: cywang@fredhutch.org

Abstract: Epidemiological studies often encounter a challenge due to exposure measurement error when estimating an exposure–disease association. A surrogate variable may be available for the true unobserved exposure variable. However, zero-inflated data are encountered frequently in the surrogate variables. For example, many nutrient or physical activity measures may have a zero value (or a low detectable value) among a group of individuals. In this paper, we investigate regression analysis when the observed surrogates may have zero values among some individuals of the whole study cohort. A naive regression calibration without taking into account a probability mass of the surrogate variable at 0 (or a low detectable value) will be biased. We developed a regression calibration estimator which typically can have smaller biases than the naive regression calibration estimator. We propose an expected estimating equation estimator which is consistent under the zero-inflated surrogate regression model. Extensive simulations show that the proposed estimator performs well in terms of bias correction. These methods are applied to a physical activity intervention study.

Keywords: measurement error; surrogate; zero-inflated data

MSC: 62E20; 62F10; 62J12

Citation: Wang, C.-Y.; Tapsoba, J.d.D.; Duggan, C.; McTiernan, A. Generalized Linear Models with Covariate Measurement Error and Zero-Inflated Surrogates. *Mathematics* **2024**, *12*, 309. https://doi.org/10.3390/math12020309

Academic Editor: Chin-Shang Li

Received: 30 November 2023
Revised: 5 January 2024
Accepted: 15 January 2024
Published: 17 January 2024

1. Introduction

In biomedical research, regression analysis is an important tool to understand associations between disease outcomes and risk factors. In practice, however, a risk factor may not be measured precisely. This problem is often called covariate measurement error [1–3]. We consider an example when a biomarker is a risk factor for a disease outcome. In practice, the biomarker may have seasonal, daily, or even hourly variation, and a single measurement is prone to a covariate measurement error from instrumentation or human error. Hence, an average of an infinite number of the biomarker measurements during a specified period of time is, therefore, a more meaningful covariate variable than the average of a few observed measurements. However, in practice it is not feasible to make such measurements, and thus studies often rely on single measures at a specific time point with associated measurement error.

Physical activity and nutrient intake are important risk factors for disease incidence and mortality. However, physical activity and nutrient intake data may be measured with errors since they are generally self-report data. This issue is important since measurement error in diet or physical activity may have an attenuation effect on the regression coefficients of exposures in the range of approximately 20% to 50% [4–6]. That is, an odds ratio of 1.5 from diet or physical activity may be reduced to the range of 1.22 to 1.38 due to measurement errors in these measures. In addition, an important challenge in this research is that some physical activity or dietary data may have a zero value, such as 0 metabolic equivalent (MET) hours per week from moderate or vigorous physical activity or 0 alcohol intake. One MET is defined as the amount of oxygen consumed while at rest per kilogram of body weight [7]. A 3 MET activity expends three times the energy used by the body at rest. Hence, if a person does a 3 MET activity for 4 h in a week, he or she has done 12 MET hours of physical activity in a week. A naive method without taking into account measurement error may lead to biased effect estimation in regression analysis, and the bias is attenuation in most (but not all) cases [8]. A standard bias correction for measurement error without taking into account a subset of individuals with zero exposure value may be biased in the effect estimation.

One motivating example of our methodology research is covariate measurement error associated with the measurement of physical activity in the APPEAL study (A Program Promoting Exercise and Active Lifestyles; APPEAL: Clinicaltrials.gov NCT00668161) [9]. APPEAL was a year long randomized controlled trial of moderate-to-vigorous intensity exercise vs. control (no exercise) among 202 healthy, sedentary adults recruited between 2001 and 2004 primarily through physician practices, and randomized to an exercise program ($n = 100$) or a control group ($n = 102$). The trial was designed to test the effects of exercise on biomarkers of colon cancer and other physiologic and psychosocial outcomes. Numerous case-control and cohort studies have found an inverse association between physical activity and risk of colon cancer [10]. Physical activities are commonly quantified by determining the energy expenditure in kilocalories or by using the MET of the activity. A question of interest is whether there is an association between physical activity via MET-hours/week and c-reactive protein, a biomarker of inflammation, with elevated levels of CRP associated with risk of developing colon cancer. The true average of MET-hours/week is an unobserved variable that is the average of an infinite number of MET-hours/week scores. However, in practice it is not possible to obtain this measure and, thus, the true average of MET-hours/week scores cannot be observed.

In the motivating example given above, two methodology challenges are involved. The first challenge is regression analysis with covariate measurement error, which is due to physical activity (MET-hours/week). The observed error-prone variable is typically called a surrogate variable for the true but unobserved exposure. The second challenge is the zero-inflated surrogate model because some individuals may have zero MET-hours/week. The zero-inflated surrogate issue in some similar research examples is also called truncation of the observed surrogates. In our problem, the second challenge (zero-inflated surrogate modeling) is added to the first challenge (covariate measurement error). Methods for covariate measurement error have been well developed. For example, regression calibration (RC) for covariate measurement error is to replace an error-prone covariate by its conditional expectation given the observed covariates [11]. In linear regression, the RC estimator is a consistent estimator for regression coefficients (Buonaccorsi, 2010, Chapter 5) [12]. However, for logistic and Cox regression, it is known that it is not consistent (Carroll, et al., 2006, Chapter 4) [2]. There is further research on refinement of RC for logistic and Cox regression [13,14]. Another general approximation approach for covariate measurement error is the simulation extrapolation (SIMEX) approach [15,16]. An advantage of SIMEX is that it has the advantage of being easy to implement. There are methods to address the situation when the surrogate variables may be truncated (which is in general the same as zero-inflated surrogate modeling). Tooze et al. investigated a likelihood approach for repeated measures data with clumping at zero [17]. When the observed exposure variables are truncated by a lower limit, the estimation of the disease–exposure association due to measurement error and truncation may not always be attenuation [18].

As discussed above, there is relatively limited research that addresses the issue of measurement error when some individuals may have a zero value (or lower limit) in the observed surrogates. The main objective of the paper is to develop and apply methods to adjust for measurement error in generalized linear models when the observed surrogates may be truncated at a low value (such as 0) among some individuals. The paper is organized as follows: In Section 2, we describe the statistical models for the problem of interest, and discuss the bias issue when we apply a naive RC estimator without taking into account the zero-inflated surrogates. In Section 3, we study a regression calibration estimator for this problem. In Section 4, we propose a maximum likelihood estimator via expected estimating equations for this problem. In Section 5, the results from simulation studies are presented. In Section 6, we apply the methods to the APPEAL study data. We discuss the advantages and limitations of the proposed EEE estimator in Section 7. Concluding remarks are given in Section 8.

2. Statistical Models and Naive RC Estimator

We assume that the total sample size of the study cohort is n. The regression model of interest is the generalized linear model. Let Y_i be the response variable, X_i be the unobserved true covariate (dietary intake or physical activity) that cannot be precisely measured, and $\mathbf{Z}_i$ be the vector of covariates which is available for all individuals, i, $i = 1, \ldots, n$. For simplicity of presentation, the true unobserved exposure X is assumed to be a scalar throughout this paper. The main interest is to estimate the vector of regression coefficients $\boldsymbol{\beta} \equiv (\beta_0, \beta_1, \boldsymbol{\beta}_2')'$ in the followingregression model:

$$\mathrm{E}(Y_i|X_i, \mathbf{Z}_i) = g(\beta_0 + \beta_1 X_i + \boldsymbol{\beta}_2' \mathbf{Z}_i), \tag{1}$$

where $g(\cdot)$ is a specified function. Model (1) contains many important regression models. For example, $g(u) = u$ in linear regression, while $g(u) = (1 + e^{-u})^{-1}$ in logistic regression. The goal of the research is to develop valid estimation methods for the regression coefficients $\boldsymbol{\beta}$. For the true unobserved covariate X_i, we assume that there are k_i non–negative surrogate variables $W_{ij}, j = 1, \ldots, k_i$ such that $W_{ij} = \max(c, W_{ij}^*)$, where c is a detection limit, $W_{ij}^* = X_i + U_{ij}$, in which U_{ij} is an independent measurement error with $E(U_{ij}) = 0$. Let η_{ij} be the indicator function for a positive W_{ij} value, that is, $\eta_{ij} = I[W_{ij} > c]$. In a covariate measurement error problem when the surrogates are not truncated, replicates $W_{ij}, j = 1, \ldots, k_i$, are used to estimate the measurement error variance where k_i is the number of replicates. We use notation $\tilde{W}_i$ for $(W_{i1}, \ldots, W_{ik_i})$, $\tilde{W}_i^*$ for $(W_{i1}^*, \ldots, W_{ik_i}^*)$, and $\tilde{\eta}_i$ for $(\eta_{i1}, \ldots, \eta_{ik_i})$.

To understand the RC estimator, we consider a special linear regression case that $Y_i = \beta_0 + \beta_1 X_i + e_i$, where e_i is a mean-zero random residual term. Assume $W_{ij}^* = X_i + U_{ij}$, $j = 1, \ldots, k$, then it is easily seen that $\mathrm{E}(Y_i|\tilde{W}_i^*) = \beta_0 + \beta_1 \mathrm{E}(X_i|\tilde{W}_i)$. From this argument, it is seen that under the special linear regression case above, replacing an unobserved true X_i with $\mathrm{E}(X_i|\tilde{W}_i^*)$ will lead to a consistent estimator. This method is often called the RC estimator [2]. In this case, $\mathrm{E}(Y_i|\tilde{W}_i^*)$ is the calibration function. We may also use $\mathrm{E}(Y_i|\overline{W}_i^*)$, where $\overline{W}_i^* = \sum_{j=1}^k W_{ij}^*/k$, as the calibration function to replace the unobserved X_i. If replicates $W_{ij}^*, j = 1, \ldots, k_i$ are from a normal distribution, then $\mathrm{E}(Y_i|\overline{W}_i^*) = \mathrm{E}(Y_i|\tilde{W}_i^*)$ [14]. Let μ_x and σ_x denote the mean and standard deviation of any random variable X, respectively. Calculation of the conditional expectation of the unobserved exposure given the surrogates can be obtained based on a bivariate normal assumption such that

$$\mathrm{E}(X_i|\overline{W}_i^*) = \mu_x + \sigma_x^2 \left(\sigma_x^2 + \sigma_u^2/k\right)^{-1} \left(\overline{W}_i^* - \mu_x\right).$$

Therefore, $\mathrm{E}(Y_i|\overline{W}_i^*) = \beta_0 + \beta_1^* \, \overline{W}_i^*$, then $\beta_1^* = \{\sigma_x^2 \, (\sigma_x^2 + \sigma_u^2/k)^{-1}\}\beta_1$. From this calculation, a naive estimator using $\overline{W}_i^*$ as a replacement for X_i will have an attenuation effect. When $\mathbf{Z}$ is in the model, a standard RC estimator is to replace X_i with $\mathrm{E}(X_i|\overline{W}_i^*, \mathbf{Z}_i)$. This can be done by a multivariate-normal assumption with a conditional mean formula similar to the formula given above. However, a more practical approach is via a semiparametric RC approach by assuming a working regression model of $\mathrm{E}(W_{ij}^*|W_{ij'}^*, \mathbf{Z}_i) = \alpha_0 + \alpha_1 W_{ij'}^* + \boldsymbol{\alpha}_2' \mathbf{Z}_i$, where $j \neq j' = 1, \ldots, k$, and $(\alpha_0, \alpha_1, \boldsymbol{\alpha}_2')'$ is the vector of regression coefficients. This semi-parametric RC estimator does not assume a multivariate normality assumption of the observed surrogates and covariates [19,20].

However, in our problem, the observed W_{ij} is different from W_{ij}^* if $W_{ij}^* < c$. Using W_{ij} data will likely overestimate μ_x, but underestimate σ_x, and σ_u since $W_{ij} = c$ if $W_{ij}^* < c$. For linear regression with truncated surrogates, standard RC may be biased because $\mathrm{E}(X_i|\overline{W}_i)$ will be different from $\mathrm{E}(X_i|\overline{W}_i^*)$. One naive approach is to use the observed W_{ij} as W_{ij}^*, without taking into consideration the truncated surrogates, to calculate the RC estimator. We call this estimator a naive RC (NRC) estimator. As discussed above, the NRC estimator is biased even when the main regression model is linear. The asymptotic variance of the NRC estimator can be obtained by a sandwich variance estimator where the vector of the estimating equations is obtained by stacking the estimating equations for $\boldsymbol{\beta}$ and the nuisance parameters involved in the calculation of the calibration function $\mathrm{E}(X_i|\tilde{W}_i^*, \mathbf{Z}_i)$ (but noting that the NRC estimator assumes $\tilde{W}_i$ is the same as $\tilde{W}_i^*$). However, if there are many covariates in the modeling of the calibration function, then it will be computationally easier to use bootstrap variance estimation to obtain the standard errors.

3. Regression Calibration for Zero-Inflated Surrogates

The NRC estimator described in the previous section does not take into account zero values due to truncation. Now, we consider calibration based on truncate surrogates due to zero values. To understand the method, we first consider a linear regression model $Y_i = \beta_0 + \beta_1 X_i + \boldsymbol{\beta}_2' \mathbf{Z}_i + e_i$, where e_i has mean 0, and is independent of X_i and $\mathbf{Z}_i$. Then, $\mathrm{E}(Y_i|\tilde{W}_i, \mathbf{Z}_i) = \beta_0 + \beta_1 \mathrm{E}(X_i|\tilde{W}_i, \mathbf{Z}_i) + \boldsymbol{\beta}_2' \mathbf{Z}_i$. That is, replacing X_i with $\mathrm{E}(X_i|\tilde{W}_i, \mathbf{Z}_i)$ in the regression analysis may be a valid approach. Let $\widehat{X}_i \equiv \mathrm{E}(X|\tilde{W}, \mathbf{Z})$. The estimating equation for the RC estimator can be expressedas

$$\sum_{i=1}^{n} (1, \widehat{X}_i, \mathbf{Z}_i')' \{Y_i - (\beta_0 + \beta_1 \widehat{X}_i + \boldsymbol{\beta}_2' \mathbf{Z}_i)\} = \mathbf{0}. \tag{2}$$

Hence, when Y_i given $(X_i, \mathbf{Z}_i)$ is linear, we have the following result:

Proposition 1. *Assume the surrogate variables $W_{ij}^*, j = 1, \ldots, k_i$ may be truncated by a lower limit, and the truncation indicator $\tilde{\eta}_i$ is independent of Y_i given $(X_i, \mathbf{Z}_i)$. If $Y_i = \beta_0 + \beta_1 X_i + \boldsymbol{\beta}_2' \mathbf{Z}_i + e_i$, where e_i has mean 0, and is independent of X_i and $\mathbf{Z}_i$. Then the RC estimator solving (2) is a consistent estimator of $\boldsymbol{\beta}$.*

The proof of Proposition 1 is given in Appendix A. We note that because of the surrogate assumption, the measurement errors U_{ij} and e_i are independent, which is needed to ensure that estimating Equation (2) is unbiased. Hence, for linear regression with zero-inflated surrogates, the RC estimator is consistent. However, when the mean function of Y_i given $X_i, \mathbf{Z}_i$ is not linear, the RC estimator may be biased since the expectation of the estimating score will no longer be zero. For logistic regression, $\mathrm{pr}(Y_i = 1|X_i, \mathbf{Z}_i) = H(\beta_0 + \beta_1 X_i + \boldsymbol{\beta}_2' \mathbf{Z}_i)$, where $H(u) = \{1 + \exp(-u)\}^{-1}$ is the logistic function. Although the RC estimator is not consistent, the RC estimator can be considered as an improved estimator of the NRC estimator described in the last section. The calibration function can be calculated based on the likelihood function. We use notation $\mathcal{L}(X)$ to denote a likelihood function for any random variable X, and $\mathcal{L}(Y|X)$ to denote a conditional likelihood function of Y given X, for any two random variables X and Y. Generally, the conditional calibration function can be calculated by the following:

$$\mathrm{E}\{X_i|\tilde{W}_i, \mathbf{Z}_i\} = \frac{\int_x x \prod_j \{\mathcal{L}(W_{ij}|X_i = x, \mathbf{Z}_i)\}^{\eta_{ij}} \{\mathcal{L}(W_{ij} = c|X_i = x, \mathbf{Z}_i)\}^{1-\eta_{ij}} \mathcal{L}(\mathbf{Z}_i, X_i = x) dx}{\int_x \prod_j \{\mathcal{L}(W_{ij}|X_i = x, \mathbf{Z}_i)\}^{\eta_{ij}} \{\mathcal{L}(W_{ij} = c|X_i = x, \mathbf{Z}_i)\}^{1-\eta_{ij}} \mathcal{L}(\mathbf{Z}_i, X_i = x) dx}. \tag{3}$$

In (3), we note that $\mathcal{L}(W_{ij} = c|X_i = x, \mathbf{Z}_i) = \mathcal{L}(U_{ij} \leq c - x)$. From the argument given above, the RC estimator can be obtained by replacing an unobserved X_i by $\mathrm{E}\{X_i|\tilde{W}_i, \mathbf{Z}_i\}$ based on (3). The asymptotic variance of the RC estimator can be obtained by a stacked sandwich estimator that is similar to the one for the NRC estimator described in the last section, or by bootstrap variance estimation.

4. Expected Estimating Equation Estimator

We now develop another approach to this problem via the maximum likelihood (ML) estimation. We first take a different viewpoint linking the ML estimation and the conditional expectation of the *full data estimating equation*, namely, the estimating equation when there is no measurement error. The full data likelihood, $\mathcal{L}(Y_i|X_i, \mathbf{Z}_i)$, is the likelihood function of Y_i given $(X_i, \mathbf{Z}_i)$. The full data estimating equation for $\boldsymbol{\beta}$ can be expressed as $\sum_{i=1}^{n} \phi(Y_i, X_i, \mathbf{Z}_i, \boldsymbol{\beta}) = 0$, in which $\phi(Y_i, X_i, \mathbf{Z}_i, \boldsymbol{\beta})$ is the derivative of $\log\{\mathcal{L}(Y_i|X_i, \mathbf{Z}_i)\}$ with respect to $\boldsymbol{\beta}$. Because the true X_i is not observed, the full data estimating equation can not be directly applied to the data. With the observed data, the estimating score will be from the likelihood of Y_i given $\mathbf{Z}_i$ and W_i, denoted by $\mathcal{L}(Y_i|\mathbf{Z}_i, W_i)$. If the distribution of $(\tilde{W}_i, X_i, \mathbf{Z}_i)$ does not involve β, then

$$\frac{\partial}{\partial \boldsymbol{\beta}} \log \mathcal{L}(Y_i|\tilde{W}_i, \mathbf{Z}_i) = \frac{(\partial/\partial \boldsymbol{\beta}) \int_x \mathcal{L}(Y_i|X_i, \mathbf{Z}_i)\mathcal{L}(\tilde{W}_i|X_i = x, \mathbf{Z}_i)\mathcal{L}(X_i = x, \mathbf{Z}_i)dx}{\mathcal{L}(Y_i, \tilde{W}_i, \mathbf{Z}_i)}$$
$$= \mathrm{E}\{\frac{\partial}{\partial \boldsymbol{\beta}} \log \mathcal{L}(Y_i|X_i = x, \mathbf{Z}_i)|Y_i, \tilde{W}_i, \mathbf{Z}_i\}.$$

From the equations given above, the likelihood-based score of the observed data can be obtained by the conditional expectation of the likelihood-based score of the full data given the observed data. That is, the estimating score for an individual can be expressed as $\mathrm{E}\{\phi(Y_i, X_i, \mathbf{Z}_i, \boldsymbol{\beta})|Y_i, \tilde{W}_i, \mathbf{Z}_i\}$, which is the observed data estimating score. The ML estimator can be obtained from the idea of expected estimating equations [21]. Therefore, the ML estimator can be obtained by solving

$$\sum_{i=1}^{n} \mathrm{E}\{\phi(Y_i, X_i, \mathbf{Z}_i, \boldsymbol{\beta})|Y_i, \tilde{W}_i, \mathbf{Z}_i\} = 0. \tag{4}$$

In general, $\phi(Y_i, X_i, \mathbf{Z}_i, \boldsymbol{\beta})$ does not need to be the full data likelihood-based estimating score. It can be any estimating equation that satisfies $\mathrm{E}\{\phi(Y_i, X_i, \mathbf{Z}_i, \boldsymbol{\beta})\} = 0$. For example, it can be a weighted estimating equation of the ML estimator. The estimator solving (4) is the expected estimating equation (EEE) estimator for $\boldsymbol{\beta}$. Let Equation (4) be denoted by $S(\boldsymbol{\beta}, X, \mathbf{Z}) = 0$. Let the EEE estimator be denoted by $\widehat{\boldsymbol{\beta}}_{eee}$. The asymptotic distribution of $\widehat{\boldsymbol{\beta}}_{eee}$ can be presented as the following result:

Proposition 2. *Assume Y_i given $(X_i, \mathbf{Z}_i)$ follows (1), and the surrogate variables $W_{ij}^*, j = 1, \ldots, k_i$ may be truncated by a lower limit, and the truncation indicator $\tilde{\eta}_i$ is conditionally independent of Y_i given $(X_i, \mathbf{Z}_i)$. Assume $\phi(Y_i, X_i, \mathbf{Z}_i, \boldsymbol{\beta})$ is any estimating equation that satisfies $\mathrm{E}\{\phi(Y_i, X_i, \mathbf{Z}_i, \boldsymbol{\beta})\} = 0$. The EEE estimator solving (4) is consistent for $\boldsymbol{\beta}$. Furthermore, $n^{1/2}(\widehat{\boldsymbol{\beta}}_{eee} - \boldsymbol{\beta})$ is asymptotically normal with mean 0 and asymptotic variance given in Appendix A.*

The proof of Proposition 2 is given in Appendix A. The EEE in (4) can be calculated by the following:

$$\mathrm{E}\{\phi(Y_i, X_i, \mathbf{Z}_i, \boldsymbol{\beta})|Y_i, \tilde{W}_i, \mathbf{Z}_i\}$$
$$= \frac{\int_x \phi(Y_i, X_i, \mathbf{Z}_i)\mathcal{L}(Y_i|X_i = x, \mathbf{Z}_i)\{\prod_{j=1}^{k_i} \mathcal{L}(W_{ij}|X_i = x, \mathbf{Z}_i)\}\mathcal{L}(\mathbf{Z}_i, X_i = x)dx}{\int_x \mathcal{L}(Y_i|X_i = x, \mathbf{Z}_i)\{\prod_{j=1}^{k_i} \mathcal{L}(W_{ij}|X_i = x, \mathbf{Z}_i)\}\mathcal{L}(\mathbf{Z}_i, X_i = x)dx},$$

where $\mathcal{L}(W_{ij}|X_i = x, \mathbf{Z}_i) = \{\mathcal{L}(W_{ij}|X_i = x, \mathbf{Z}_i)\}^{\eta_{ij}}\{\mathcal{L}(W_{ij} = c|X_i = x, \mathbf{Z}_i)\}^{1-\eta_{ij}}$. The asymptotic variance of the EEE estimator solving (4) for $\boldsymbol{\beta}$ can be obtained by a sandwich variance estimator. The vector of the estimating equations is obtained by stacking two sets of estimating equations. The first set is the estimating equations for $\boldsymbol{\beta}$ and the second set is the nuisance parameters involved in the conditional distribution of Y_i given $(\mathbf{Z}_i, \tilde{W}_i)$. However, bootstrap variance estimation is another approach to obtain the standard errors of the EEE estimator.

5. Simulation Study

We conducted a simulation study to examine the finite sample performance of the NRC, RC, and EEE estimators with the naive estimator that used $\overline{W}_i$ for X_i. In Table 1, we illustrate the situation when the regression model is linear and the observed surrogates may have a zero value among some individuals. That is, the observed surrogates were truncated at $c = 0$ in the simulations. In this table, each individual's true covariate is X_i. We first generated $X_i, i = 1, \ldots, n$, from a normal distribution, where the sample size was $n = 500$, and $n = 1000$, respectively. We generated two replicates W_{i1}^* and W_{i2}^* for the unobserved X_i. With $\mu_x = 1.5, \sigma_x = 1$, and $\sigma_u = 0.707$. The percent of non–zero W_{ij} was $\overline{\eta} = 89\%$; 11% of W_{ij} was truncated at 0. We also considered the situation when $\sigma_u = 1, 1.5$, and $\sqrt{3}$, respectively, in which the percent of non-zero covariates were $\overline{\eta} = 86\%, 80\%$, and 77%, respectively. The outcomes were generated based on linear regression with coefficients $\beta_0 = 0.5$ and $\beta_1 = 1$, and the residuals were from a standard normal distribution. In Tables 1–4, "bias" was obtained from the average of the biases of the regression coefficients estimates of the 500 simulation replicates, "SD" was the sample standard deviation of the estimates, and "ASE" was the average of the estimated standard errors of the estimates. The 95% confidence interval coverage probabilities (CP) were also obtained. The standard errors of the estimates were obtained from sandwich variance estimation. From the result of Table 1, the NRC estimator was not much better than the naive estimator. The reason for limited improvement from the NRC over the naive estimator was because of truncated W values. The RC and EEE estimators were consistent with limited biases under this setting, and hence, they were better than the naive and NRC estimators. Under this setting, the RC and EEE were very comparable.

Table 1. Simulation study for linear regression with truncated surrogates.

		Naive	NRC	RC	EEE	Naive	NRC	RC	EEE
			$n = 500$				$n = 1000$		
	$\mu_x = 1.5, \sigma_x = 1, \sigma_u = 0.707, \overline{\eta} = 89\%$								
$\beta_0 = 0.5$	Bias	0.134	−0.230	−0.002	0.003	0.133	−0.228	−0.003	0.002
	SD	0.093	0.117	0.103	0.103	0.064	0.080	0.072	0.071
	ASE	0.093	0.117	0.106	0.106	0.066	0.083	0.075	0.074
	CP	0.684	0.486	0.972	0.962	0.460	0.180	0.954	0.966
$\beta_1 = 1$	Bias	−0.126	0.107	0.004	0.000	−0.127	0.103	0.001	−0.002
	SD	0.050	0.068	0.060	0.060	0.035	0.047	0.043	0.042
	ASE	0.049	0.068	0.061	0.061	0.035	0.048	0.043	0.043
	CP	0.270	0.658	0.958	0.954	0.056	0.446	0.956	0.960
	$\mu_x = 1.5, \sigma_x = 1, \sigma_u = 1, \overline{\eta} = 86\%$								
$\beta_0 = 0.5$	Bias	0.301	−0.349	−0.007	−0.006	0.299	−0.343	−0.005	−0.004
	SD	0.096	0.161	0.133	0.132	0.067	0.109	0.091	0.091
	ASE	0.095	0.162	0.136	0.136	0.068	0.113	0.095	0.095
	CP	0.122	0.404	0.960	0.952	0.002	0.106	0.966	0.962
$\beta_1 = 1$	Bias	−0.252	0.154	0.006	0.006	−0.252	0.147	0.003	0.002
	SD	0.050	0.096	0.080	0.079	0.035	0.066	0.056	0.056
	ASE	0.049	0.096	0.082	0.082	0.035	0.067	0.057	0.057
	CP	0.002	0.674	0.952	0.958	0.000	0.424	0.948	0.958

Table 1. *Cont.*

		Naive	NRC	RC	EEE	Naive	NRC	RC	EEE
		$n = 500$				$n = 1000$			
$\mu_X = 1.5, \sigma_X = 1, \sigma_u = 1.5, \overline{\eta} = 80\%$									
$\beta_0 = 0.5$	Bias	0.556	−0.652	−0.035	0.033	0.558	−0.616	−0.018	−0.019
	SD	0.101	0.341	0.244	0.241	0.070	0.217	0.156	0.157
	ASE	0.098	0.325	0.230	0.229	0.069	0.220	0.157	0.158
	CP	0.000	0.462	0.962	0.942	0.000	0.104	0.960	0.960
$\beta_1 = 1$	Bias	−0.445	0.263	0.023	0.022	−0.447	0.241	0.011	0.012
	SD	0.048	0.197	0.152	0.150	0.033	0.126	0.097	0.099
	ASE	0.047	0.188	0.144	0.144	0.033	0.128	0.099	0.099
	CP	0.000	0.846	0.960	0.942	0.000	0.558	0.952	0.954
$\mu_X = 1.5, \sigma_X = 1, \sigma_u = \sqrt{3}, \overline{\eta} = 77\%$									
$\beta_0 = 0.5$	Bias	0.655	−0.839	−0.057	−0.051	0.657	−0.769	−0.024	−0.025
	SD	0.101	0.609	0.323	0.307	0.070	0.302	0.197	0.198
	ASE	0.098	0.466	0.300	0.296	0.069	0.302	0.198	0.229
	CP	0.000	0.634	0.956	0.922	0.000	0.150	0.956	0.950
$\beta_1 = 1$	Bias	−0.519	0.327	0.038	0.034	−0.522	0.287	0.015	0.015
	SD	0.046	0.286	0.204	0.195	0.033	0.170	0.126	0.127
	ASE	0.045	0.263	0.191	0.189	0.032	0.170	0.126	0.148
	CP	0.000	0.972	0.956	0.918	0.000	0.716	0.948	0.930

NOTE: Naive is an estimator that uses the average of two replicates as the covariate, NRC is the naive RC estimator described in Section 2, RC is the RC estimator that uses $E(X|\tilde{W})$ as the covariate, and EEE is the expected estimating equation estimator described in Section 4.

Table 2. Simulation study for linear regression with truncated surrogates; misspecified distribution for covariate X or measurement error.

		Naive	NRC	RC	EEE	Naive	NRC	RC	EEE
		$n = 500$				$n = 1000$			
X is from a mixture of two normal distributions and the error is normal									
$\mu_X = 1.5, \sigma_X = 1, \sigma_u = 0.707, \overline{\eta} = 91\%$									
$\beta_0 = 0.5$	Bias	0.209	−0.096	0.041	0.036	0.204	−0.101	0.037	0.032
	SD	0.081	0.099	0.097	0.097	0.061	0.074	0.073	0.073
	ASE	0.084	0.105	0.103	0.103	0.060	0.074	0.072	0.073
	CP	0.300	0.878	0.940	0.946	0.074	0.720	0.900	0.916
$\beta_1 = 1$	Bias	−0.160	0.038	−0.020	−0.018	−0.158	0.041	−0.018	−0.016
	SD	0.045	0.058	0.057	0.057	0.033	0.043	0.042	0.042
	ASE	0.046	0.061	0.059	0.060	0.032	0.043	0.042	0.042
	CP	0.060	0.920	0.946	0.950	0.002	0.848	0.928	0.928
$\mu_X = 1.5, \sigma_X = 1, \sigma_u = 1, \overline{\eta} = 86\%$									
$\beta_0 = 0.5$	Bias	0.341	−0.199	0.051	0.036	0.336	−0.204	0.050	0.034
	SD	0.084	0.132	0.123	0.125	0.063	0.098	0.090	0.091
	ASE	0.086	0.139	0.130	0.131	0.061	0.098	0.091	0.092
	CP	0.024	0.734	0.928	0.946	0.000	0.460	0.902	0.920
$\beta_1 = 1$	Bias	−0.268	0.074	−0.024	−0.017	−0.265	0.076	−0.024	−0.017
	SD	0.045	0.078	0.075	0.076	0.033	0.058	0.054	0.055
	ASE	0.046	0.082	0.078	0.079	0.033	0.058	0.055	0.055
	CP	0.000	0.892	0.938	0.950	0.000	0.744	0.916	0.932

Table 2. *Cont.*

		Naive	NRC	RC	EEE	Naive	NRC	RC	EEE
			$n = 500$				$n = 1000$		
X is normal and the error is from a modified chi-square distribution									
$\mu_x = 1.5, \sigma_x = 1, \sigma_u = 1, \overline{\eta} = 87\%$									
$\beta_0 = 0.5$	Bias	0.384	−0.278	0.082	0.088	0.385	−0.275	0.085	0.091
	SD	0.095	0.169	0.134	0.134	0.067	0.118	0.094	0.094
	ASE	0.093	0.163	0.129	0.129	0.066	0.115	0.091	0.091
	CP	0.012	0.614	0.870	0.850	0.000	0.322	0.816	0.792
$\beta_1 = 1$	Bias	−0.295	0.125	−0.038	−0.040	−0.293	0.125	−0.038	−0.040
	SD	0.052	0.101	0.081	0.081	0.036	0.070	0.056	0.056
	ASE	0.050	0.097	0.078	0.078	0.036	0.069	0.055	0.055
	CP	0.000	0.764	0.898	0.890	0.000	0.594	0.880	0.882
X is normal and the error is from a mixture of two normal distribution									
$\mu_x = 1.5, \sigma_x = 1, \sigma_u = 1, \overline{\eta} = 84\%$									
$\beta_0 = 0.5$	Bias	0.376	−0.431	0.024	−0.024	0.380	−0.418	−0.018	−0.018
	SD	0.096	0.196	0.162	0.162	0.069	0.136	0.107	0.107
	ASE	0.096	0.198	0.160	0.161	0.068	0.139	0.112	0.112
	CP	0.030	0.402	0.954	0.958	0.000	0.114	0.954	0.958
$\beta_1 = 1$	Bias	−0.311	0.183	0.013	0.013	−0.314	0.175	0.009	0.009
	SD	0.048	0.116	0.098	0.098	0.033	0.080	0.066	0.066
	ASE	0.049	0.118	0.098	0.099	0.035	0.082	0.068	0.068
	CP	0.000	0.724	0.950	0.950	0.000	0.430	0.954	0.956

NOTE: See the footnote of Table 1 for notation.

We considered non-normal X in Table 2 to investigate if the estimators were sensitive to the normality assumption in the calculation. We also examined the sensitivity of the estimators to misspecification of the measurement error distribution. On the upper portion of Table 2, the unobserved X was generated from a mixture of two normal distributions; one with mean 2.5 and variance 1, and the other with mean 1 and variance 0.25, and the mixture percentages were (1/3, 2/3). The result from the upper portion of the table was similar to that of Table 1, except that there were small biases from the RC and EEE estimators. We found that the RC and EEE showed small biases when the unobserved exposure had a skewed distribution, but the bias was not too large in general. Nevertheless, the RC and EEE estimators were still better than the NRC and naive estimators under this situation. On the lower portion of Table 2, we considered the situation when X was normal but measurement error was from a location/scale-transformed chi-squared distribution and a mixture of two normal distributions, respectively. The specification of the mixture of two normal distributions was the same as the mixture of normal distributions given above. The location/scale-transformed chi-squared distribution has mean 0 and variance σ_u^2 after a chi-squared random variable was location/scale-transformed. From the sensitivity analysis, the RC and EEE estimators were not sensitive to mild violation due to a mixture of normal distributions since the biases were considered small. However, the biases may be sensitive to violation of the normality assumption while the true distribution was very skewed, as for chi-squared distributions. The biases were moderate, rather than small, when the errors were from chi-squared distributions.

Table 3. Simulation study for logistic regression with truncated surrogates.

		Naive	NRC	RC	EEE	Naive	NRC	RC	EEE
		$n = 500$				$n = 1000$			
$\mu_x = 1.5, \sigma_x = 1, \sigma_u = 0.707, \overline{\eta} = 89\%$									
$\beta_0 = 0$	Bias	0.065	−0.190	−0.010	−0.010	0.063	−0.190	−0.012	−0.012
	SD	0.191	0.234	0.203	0.208	0.136	0.169	0.147	0.150
	ASE	0.181	0.224	0.193	0.199	0.128	0.158	0.136	0.140
	CP	0.922	0.836	0.938	0.944	0.892	0.766	0.936	0.942
$\beta_1 = \ln(2)$	Bias	−0.080	0.083	−0.008	0.007	−0.079	0.083	−0.006	0.008
	SD	0.122	0.154	0.133	0.142	0.085	0.109	0.094	0.100
	ASE	0.115	0.147	0.126	0.134	0.082	0.104	0.089	0.095
	CP	0.868	0.914	0.928	0.930	0.788	0.874	0.936	0.944
$\beta_0 = 0$	Bias	0.069	−0.340	−0.014	−0.013	0.065	−0.341	−0.018	−0.016
	SD	0.207	0.266	0.219	0.232	0.148	0.189	0.159	0.169
	ASE	0.197	0.254	0.210	0.223	0.139	0.179	0.148	0.156
	CP	0.930	0.706	0.950	0.948	0.900	0.518	0.928	0.928
$\beta_1 = \ln(3)$	Bias	−0.116	0.146	−0.035	0.015	−0.114	0.145	−0.034	0.014
	SD	0.159	0.205	0.165	0.190	0.111	0.141	0.115	0.132
	ASE	0.149	0.191	0.155	0.178	0.106	0.135	0.109	0.125
	CP	0.848	0.884	0.920	0.940	0.766	0.836	0.920	0.942
$\mu_x = 1.5, \sigma_x^2 = 1, \sigma_u^2 = 1, \overline{\eta} = 86\%$									
$\beta_0 = 0$	Bias	0.175	−0.276	−0.014	−0.015	0.171	−0.277	−0.017	−0.016
	SD	0.186	0.277	0.222	0.230	0.135	0.203	0.166	0.172
	ASE	0.177	0.267	0.214	0.223	0.125	0.188	0.150	0.156
	CP	0.824	0.800	0.938	0.948	0.700	0.672	0.934	0.940
$\beta_1 = \ln(2)$	Bias	−0.173	0.108	−0.014	0.011	−0.171	0.109	−0.012	0.012
	SD	0.113	0.178	0.146	0.162	0.081	0.128	0.106	0.117
	ASE	0.108	0.171	0.140	0.155	0.076	0.121	0.098	0.109
	CP	0.610	0.914	0.948	0.946	0.404	0.856	0.926	0.940
$\beta_0 = 0$	Bias	0.232	−0.487	−0.028	−0.023	0.225	−0.487	−0.031	−0.023
	SD	0.204	0.333	0.249	0.269	0.146	0.236	0.183	0.199
	ASE	0.193	0.314	0.238	0.259	0.136	0.221	0.167	0.181
	CP	0.754	0.642	0.946	0.952	0.626	0.398	0.924	0.922
$\beta_1 = \ln(3)$	Bias	−0.273	0.175	−0.056	0.023	−0.270	0.174	−0.055	0.021
	SD	0.148	0.240	0.183	0.227	0.104	0.166	0.129	0.162
	ASE	0.138	0.222	0.171	0.213	0.098	0.156	0.120	0.148
	CP	0.488	0.892	0.900	0.946	0.230	0.824	0.902	0.940

NOTE: See the footnote of Table 1 for notation.

In Table 3, the data were generated similarly to those in Table 1 but the main model was logistic regression such that $\mathrm{pr}(Y_i = 1|X_i) = H(\beta_0 + \beta_1 X_i)$, where the regression coefficients were $\boldsymbol{\beta} = (0, \ln(2))$ and $\boldsymbol{\beta} = (0, \ln(3))$, respectively. The findings were similar to those from Table 1 for the situation when $\boldsymbol{\beta} = (0, \ln(2))$. The biases of the RC and EEE estimators were very small. Although RC is not consistent, it may have limited biases if the relative risk parameter is small to moderate, such as $\beta_1 = \ln(1.5)$ or $\beta_1 = \ln(2)$ when the exposure's standard deviation is about 1. However, when $\beta_1 = \ln(3)$, the biases of the RC estimator were larger than those of the EEE estimator. The reason is that the RC estimator's bias will increase if the relative risk parameter is large. The findings are typically similar to those for measurement error in longitudinal data and survival analysis with covariate measurement error [20,21].

In Table 4, we investigated the situation when both X and Z were included in a linear regression model. We first generated $X_i, i = 1, \ldots, n$ and two replicates W_{i1} and W_{i2} in the same way as those in Table 1. Covariate Z_i, $i = 1, \ldots, n$, were generated via $Z_i = \rho X_i/\sigma_x + \sqrt{1-\rho^2} V_i/\sigma_z$, where V_i were from $N(0, \sigma_z^2)$ and independent from X_i, $\sigma_z^2 = 1$ and $\rho = 0.2$. The outcomes were generated via $Y_i = \beta_0 + \beta_1 X_i + \beta_2 Z_i + e_i$, where $\beta_0 = 0.5$, $\beta_1 = 1$ and $\beta_2 = -1$, The residuals e_i, $i = 1, \ldots, n$, were generated from a standard normal random variable which was independent of X_i and Z_i. The findings were mostly similar to those from Table 1. That is, the naive and NRC estimators had large biases while the RC and EEE estimators were consistent with limited biases.

Table 4. Simulation study for linear regression model with truncated surrogates; covariates are X and Z.

		Naive	RC	CRC	EEE	Naive	RC	CRC	EEE
		$n = 500$				$n = 1000$			
	$\mu_x = 1.5, \sigma_x = 1, \sigma_u = 0.707, \overline{\eta} = 89\%$								
$\beta_0 = 0.5$	Bias	0.137	−0.225	−0.006	−0.001	0.134	−0.224	−0.001	0.005
	SD	0.095	0.122	0.109	0.110	0.065	0.082	0.074	0.073
	ASE	0.093	0.117	0.106	0.106	0.066	0.083	0.075	0.074
	CP	0.694	0.504	0.938	0.930	0.454	0.226	0.946	0.944
$\beta_1 = 1$	Bias	−0.137	0.094	0.004	0.001	−0.136	0.093	0.001	−0.003
	SD	0.051	0.071	0.071	0.065	0.033	0.048	0.044	0.043
	ASE	0.050	0.069	0.064	0.063	0.036	0.049	0.044	0.044
	CP	0.204	0.742	0.940	0.938	0.020	0.538	0.954	0.956
$\beta_2 = -1$	Bias	0.042	0.042	−0.004	−0.004	0.049	0.049	0.002	0.003
	SD	0.052	0.052	0.053	0.053	0.036	0.036	0.038	0.037
	ASE	0.050	0.050	0.050	0.050	0.035	0.035	0.036	0.036
	CP	0.852	0.852	0.938	0.938	0.704	0.704	0.942	0.942
	$\mu_x = 1.5, \sigma_x = 1, \sigma_u = 1, \overline{\eta} = 86\%$								
$\beta_0 = 0.5$	Bias	0.300	−0.347	−0.016	−0.016	0.298	−0.338	−0.005	−0.004
	SD	0.098	0.170	0.142	0.143	0.067	0.114	0.095	0.094
	ASE	0.095	0.162	0.136	0.136	0.067	0.113	0.095	0.094
	CP	0.110	0.406	0.944	0.944	0.006	0.132	0.956	0.954
$\beta_1 = 1$	Bias	−0.264	0.138	0.011	0.011	−0.264	0.132	0.004	0.002
	SD	0.051	0.099	0.087	0.087	0.033	0.068	0.060	0.059
	ASE	0.049	0.096	0.083	0.083	0.035	0.068	0.058	0.058
	CP	0.000	0.732	0.944	0.948	0.000	0.518	0.958	0.958
$\beta_2 = -1$	Bias	0.070	0.070	−0.005	−0.006	0.076	0.076	0.002	0.002
	SD	0.054	0.054	0.059	0.059	0.038	0.038	0.042	0.042
	ASE	0.052	0.052	0.053	0.054	0.037	0.037	0.038	0.038
	CP	0.736	0.736	0.934	0.938	0.464	0.464	0.922	0.920

NOTE: Naive is an estimator that uses the average of two replicates as the covariate, RC is the usual RC estimator that uses $E(X|\bar{W}, Z)$ as the covariate, CRC is a conditional RC estimator that uses $E(X|\bar{W}, Z, \eta)$ as the covariate, EEE is the expected estimating equation estimator described.

6. Analysis of APPEAL Data

The design of the APPEAL study was briefly reviewed in the Introduction. In this section, we are interested in investigating the association between physical activity measured via MET hours per week and CRP. The outcome variable of interest is the CRP value at baseline. In the APPEAL study, MET hours per week and other data including biomarkers were collected at both baseline and 12 months (end of study). In the control group who did not receive the exercise intervention, physical activity levels did not change significantly between baseline and 12 months. Hence, it seems reasonable to assume that the two MET-hours/week scores at baseline and 12 months in the control group (n = 102) can be treated as replicates. The MET-hours/week data for the exercise intervention group at 12 months were not included in the analysis as the MET-hours/week value changed significantly for study participants randomized to the exercise intervention between baseline and 12 months. As such, these values cannot be treated as replicates. The MET-hours/week scores at baseline and 12 months are surrogate variables (replicates, control arm only) for an unobserved true MET-hours/week score of an individual (unobserved underlying average of a period of time). The true unobserved average MET-hours/week variable is a variable to measure the actual physical activity which cannot be observed. In addition to MET-hours/week, age at baseline was another covariate in the regression analysis.

We first investigated an association between MET-hours/week and CRP at baseline. A scatterplot and a fitted kernel smoother of MET-hours/week and CRP at baseline are shown in the upper portion of Figure 1. The lower portion of Figure 1 is the scatterplot and a fitted kernel smoother of log(MET+1) and log(CRP) at baseline. We excluded 26 individuals with missing data and outliers (defined as values larger than median + 3× interquartile range) for CRP. Hence, a total of 176 individuals are included in the data analysis. The percentage of non-zero log(MET+1) at baseline is 67%, and 68% at 12 month. In our regression analysis, we used the log-transformed data since the transformed data were less skewed.

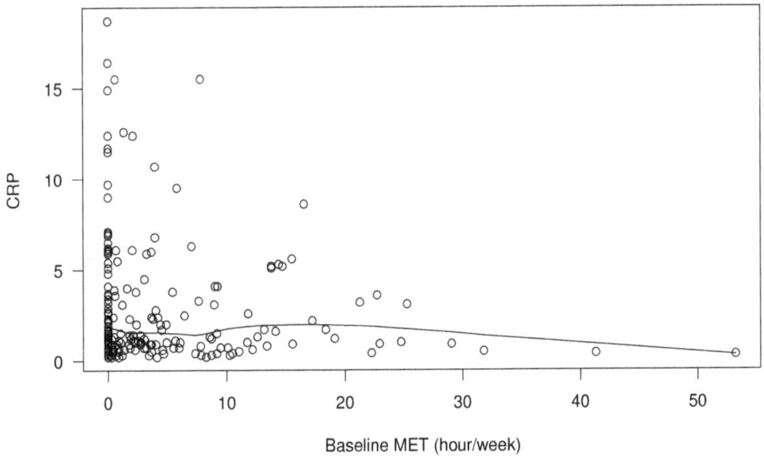

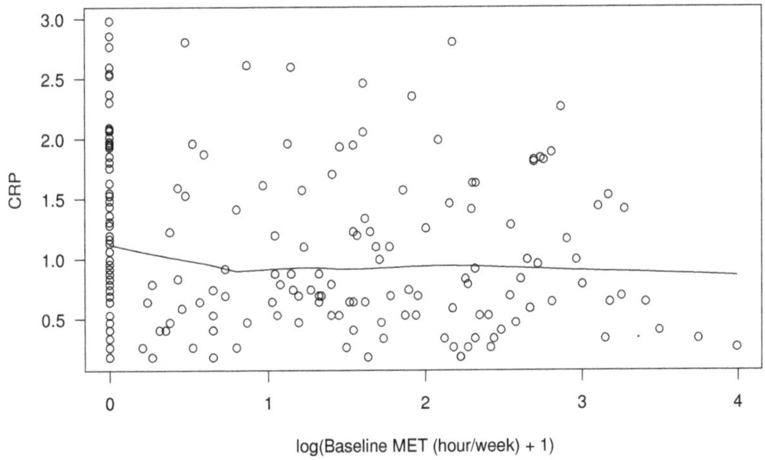

Figure 1. Upper: CRP versus MET; **Lower**: log(CRP) versus log(MET+1). The lines were obtained from fitting lowess smoothers.

In this section, the data analysis involved applying our methods to the regression association for the effects of physical activity (MET-hours/week) and age on CRP. The data application here is primarily for the purpose of a demonstration of our new methods. The regression coefficients were estimated based on the naive, RC, CRC, and EEE estimators. The results are given in Table 5. All the four estimators showed that MET was negatively associated with the inflammatory marker CRP; but not significant.

From the naive estimator, when the log(MET+1) score increased by 1 h/week, the CRP, on average, decreased by about 0.07 mg/L. From the NRC, RC, and EEE estimates, when the log(MET+1) score increased by 1 h/week, the CRP, on average, decreased by about 0.1 mg/L. It was observed that the standard errors from the NRC, RC, and EEE estimates were larger than those from the naive estimates. This was a general phenomenon of a bias–efficiency trade-off that has been reported in the measurement error literature, and is consistent with the findings from our simulations. Furthermore, all the four estimates demonstrated a significant effect of age on CRP. On average, an increase of 10 years in age was associated with an increase of approximately 0.15 mg/L in log(CRP).

Table 5. Analysis results of data from the APPEAL study.

		Naive	NRC	RC	EEE
Intercept	β_0	0.259	0.345	0.299	0.282
	SE	0.360	0.377	0.367	0.364
log(MET+1)	β_1	−0.067	−0.136	−0.107	−0.098
	SE	0.045	0.098	0.071	0.062
Age	β_2	0.015	0.015	0.014	0.015
	SE	0.006	0.006	0.007	0.007
		Nuisance parameters			
	μ_x		1.258	0.925	0.927
	SE		0.100	0.160	0.161
	σ_x^2		0.447	0.976	0.987
	SE		0.145	0.337	0.330
	σ_u^2		0.910	1.674	1.671
	SE		0.130	0.293	0.292

Note: See the footnote of Table 1 for notation. The percentages of non-zero log(1+MET) were 66.7% and 67.8% at baseline and 12 months among the participants in the control group, respectively. The total sample size in the analysis was 176.

7. Discussion

In the paper, we propose an EEE estimator for generalized linear models with covariate measurement error when the surrogate variables may have zero values among a subset of individuals. Our work is applicable to the situation for more applications when an exposure may be truncated. Our numerical studies show that RC is better than the naive estimator and NRC estimator in general, but it may be biased under some situations. Overall, the EEE estimator has smaller biases. There is a trade-off between bias and efficiency. The EEE has a larger SE due to this. One limitation of the proposed EEE estimator is that it may be biased if the likelihood function of the exposure variable is misspecified. Our simulation results demonstrate that the biases are moderate if the exposure distribution is not too skewed. Future research is needed to develop a non-parametric approach that does not require the exposure variable distribution [22].

In addition to physical activity or dietary data, biomarker measurements are important for the early detection and monitoring of disease progression. Our methods developed in this paper can be applied to biomarker data. When a biomarker is truncated due to a detection limit, decisions are required concerning how to handle values at or below the threshold in order to avoid biasing the parameter estimates. However, biomarkers are often measured with errors for many reasons, such as imperfect laboratory conditions, analytic variability of the assay, or temporal variability within individuals. The statistical modeling of zero-inflated surrogates in this paper can be applied to the situation when biomarker data are truncated due to a detection limit. Further research is needed if longitudinal biomarker, physical activity, or dietary data, are available over time [23–25].

8. Conclusions

We have developed an EEE approach for regression analysis with covariate measurement error when the surrogates may be truncated. One limitation of our proposed EEE estimator is that it is not consistent if the covariate distribution or the measurement error distribution is misspecified. In our simulations, the covariates and measurement errors are from normal distributions. Our simulation results demonstrate that if the misspecification is not too extreme, then the bias is typically small. Hence, if the covariates are skewed, then an appropriate (such as a logarithmic) transformation of the data may reduce the skewness of the data. Then the proposed EEE estimator may work well with likely minimal biases.

Author Contributions: Conceptualization, C.-Y.W. and A.M.; investigation, C.-Y.W. and J.d.D.T.; methodology, C.-Y.W. and J.d.D.T.; writing—original draft, C.-Y.W.; writing—review and editing, C.-Y.W., J.d.D.T., C.D. and A.M. All authors read and agreed to the published version of the manuscript.

Funding: This research was partially supported by US National Institute of Health grants CA235122 (Wang), HL130483 (Wang), CA77572 (McTiernan), CA239168 (Wang, Tapsoba, Duggan and McTiernan), a Breast Cancer Research Foundation award BCRF-23-107 (Wang, Tapsoba, Duggan and McTiernan), and a travel award from the Mathematics Research Promotion Center of the National Science Council of Taiwan (Wang).

Data Availability Statement: The data that support the findings of this study are not available for public access at this moment, but can be requested from the APPEAL study.

Conflicts of Interest: The authors declare no conflict of interest.

Appendix A. Proofs of Propositions 1 and 2

Proof of Proposition 1. Based on a standard surrogate assumption, the measurement errors U_{ij} and e_i are independent. Also, the truncation indicator $\tilde{\eta}_i$ is independent of e_i. Hence, $\mathrm{E}(e_i|\tilde{W}_i, \mathbf{Z}_i) = 0$. The unbiasedness of the estimating Equation (2) of the RC estimator can be obtained by calculating the expectation of the estimating score for individual i,

$$\begin{aligned} & \mathrm{E}\Big[(1, \widehat{X}_i, \mathbf{Z}_i')'\{Y_i - (\beta_0 + \beta_1 \widehat{X}_i + \boldsymbol{\beta}_2' \mathbf{Z}_i)\Big] \\ = \; & \mathrm{E}\Big((1, \widehat{X}_i, \mathbf{Z}_i')'\mathrm{E}\Big[\{Y_i - (\beta_0 + \beta_1 \widehat{X}_i + \boldsymbol{\beta}_2' \mathbf{Z}_i)\}|\tilde{W}_i, \mathbf{Z}_i\Big]\Big) \\ = \; & 0. \end{aligned}$$

Hence, for linear regression with zero-inflated surrogates, the RC estimator is consistent. □

Proof of Proposition 2. We note that $\boldsymbol{\phi}(Y_i, X_i, \mathbf{Z}_i, \boldsymbol{\beta})$ is an estimating score that satisfies $\mathrm{E}\{\boldsymbol{\phi}(Y_i, X_i, \mathbf{Z}_i, \boldsymbol{\beta})\} = 0$. We note that

$$\mathrm{E}\big[\mathrm{E}\{\boldsymbol{\phi}(Y_i, X_i, \mathbf{Z}_i, \boldsymbol{\beta})|Y_i, \tilde{W}_i, \mathbf{Z}_i\}\big] = E\{\phi(Y_i, X_i, \mathbf{Z}_i, \boldsymbol{\beta})\} = 0.$$

Hence, estimating Equation (4) for the EEE estimator is unbiased. We now develop the asymptotic distribution of the EEE estimator. Let the estimating score of the EEE estimator for the ith participant $\mathrm{E}\{\boldsymbol{\phi}(Y_i, X_i, \mathbf{Z}_i, \boldsymbol{\beta})|Y_i, \tilde{W}_i, \mathbf{Z}_i\}$ be denoted by $\psi(Y_i, \tilde{W}_i, \mathbf{Z}_i, \boldsymbol{\beta})$. Let $G(\boldsymbol{\beta}) = -\mathrm{E}\{\partial\boldsymbol{\psi}(Y, \tilde{W}, \mathbf{Z}, \boldsymbol{\beta})/\partial\boldsymbol{\beta}\}$. By a Taylor expansion of the estimating equation at the true $\boldsymbol{\beta}$, and under some regularity conditions, it can be shown that

$$n^{1/2}(\widehat{\boldsymbol{\beta}}_{eee} - \boldsymbol{\beta}) = G^{-1}(\boldsymbol{\beta}) n^{-1/2} \sum_{i=1}^{n} \boldsymbol{\psi}(Y_i, \tilde{W}_i, \mathbf{Z}_i, \boldsymbol{\beta}) + o_p(1),$$

Hence, it is seen that $n^{1/2}(\widehat{\boldsymbol{\beta}}_{eee} - \boldsymbol{\beta})$ is asymptotically normal with mean 0 and variance

$$\{G(\boldsymbol{\beta})\}^{-1} n^{-1} [\sum_{i=1}^{n} \boldsymbol{\psi}(Y_i, \tilde{W}_i, \mathbf{Z}_i, \boldsymbol{\beta}) \{\boldsymbol{\psi}(Y_i, \tilde{W}_i, \mathbf{Z}_i, \boldsymbol{\beta})\}'] \{G^{-1}(\boldsymbol{\beta})\}',$$

□

References

1. Fuller, W.A. *Measurement Error Models*; John Wiley & Sons: New York, NY, USA, 1987.
2. Carroll, R.J.; Ruppert, D.; Stefanski, L.A.; Crainiceanu, C.M. *Measurement Error in Nonlinear Models, A modern Perspective*, 2nd ed.; Chapman and Hall: London, UK, 2006.
3. Yi, G.Y. *Statistical Analysis with Measurement Error or Misclassification, Strategy, Methods and Application*; Springer: New York, NY, USA, 2017.
4. Freedman, L.S.; Carroll, R.J.; Wax, Y. Estimating the relationship between dietary intake obtained from a food frequency questionnaire and true average intake. *Am. J. Epidemiol.* **1991**, 134, 310–320. [CrossRef]
5. Kipnis, V.; Subar, A.F.; Midthune, D.; Freedman, L.S.; Ballard-Barbash, R.; Troiano, R.; Bingham, S.; Schoeller, D.A.; Schatzkin, A.; Carroll, R.J. The structure of dietary measurement error: Results of the OPEN biomarker study. *Am. J. Epidemiol.* **2003**, *158*, 14–21. [CrossRef]

6. Kipnis, V.; Midthune, D.; Buckman, D.W.; Dodd, K.W.; Guenther, P.M.; Krebs-Smith, S.M.; Subar, A.F.; Tooze, J.A.; Carroll, R.J.; Freedman, L.S. Modeling data with excess zeros and measurement error: Application to evaluating relationships between episodically consumed foods and health outcomes. *Biometrics* **2009**, 65, 1003–1010. [CrossRef]
7. Jette, M.; Sidney, K.; Blumchen, G. Metabolic equiva-lents (METS) in exercise testing, exercise prescription, and evaluation of functional capacity. *Clin Cardiol.* **1990**, *13*, 555–565. [CrossRef] [PubMed]
8. Carroll, R.J.; Galindo C.D. Measurement Error, Biases, and the Validation of Complex Models for Blood Lead Levels in Children. *Environ. Health Perspect.* **1998**, *106*, 1535–1539. [CrossRef] [PubMed]
9. McTiernan, A.; Yasui, Y.; Sorensen, B.; Irwin, M.L.; Morgan, A.; Rudolph, R.E.; Surawicz, C.; Lampe, J.W.; Ayub, K.; Potter, J.D.; Lampe, P.D. Effect of a 12-month exercise intervention on patterns of cellular proliferation in colonic crypts: A randomized controlled trial. *Cancer Epidemiol. Biomarkers Prev.* **2006**, *15*, 1588–1597. [CrossRef]
10. Slattery, M.L.; Potter, J.; Caan, B.; Edwards, S.; Coates, A.; Ma, K.N.; Berry, T.D. Energy balance and colon cancer—-beyond physical activity. *Cancer Res.* **1997**, *57*, 75–80. [PubMed]
11. Prentice, R.L. Covariate measurement errors and parameter estimation in a failure time regression model. *Biometrika* **1982**, *69*, 331–342. [CrossRef]
12. Buonaccorsi, J. *Measurement Error: Models, Methods, and Applications*; Hapman and Hall/CRC: Boca Raton, FL, USA, 2010.
13. Tsiatis, A.A.; DeGruttola, V.; Wulfsohn, M.S. Modeling the relationship of survival to longitudinal data measured with error. Applications to survival and CD4 count in patients with AIDS. *J. Am. Stat. Assoc.* **1995**, *90*, 27–37. [CrossRef]
14. Wang, C.Y.; Wang, N.; Wang, S. Regression analysis when covariates are regression parameters of a random effect model for observed longitudinal measurements. *Biometrics* **2000**, *56*, 487–495. [CrossRef]
15. Cook, J.; Stefanski, L.A. A simulation extrapolation method for parametric measurement error models. *J. Amer. Statist. Assoc.* **1994**, *89*, 1314–1328. [CrossRef]
16. Stefanski, L.A.; Cook, J.R. Simulation-Extrapolation: The Measurement Error Jackknife. *J. Am. Stat. Assoc.* **1995**, *90*, 1247–1256. [CrossRef]
17. Tooze, J.A.; Grunwald, G.K.; Jones, R.H. Analysis of repeated measures data with clumping at zero. *Stat. Methods Med. Res.* **2002**, *11*, 341–355. [CrossRef]
18. Richardson, D.B.; Ciampi, A. Effects of exposure measurement error when an exposure variable is constrained by a lower limit. *Am. J. Epidemiol.* **2003**, *15*, 355–363. [CrossRef]
19. Wang, C.Y.; Cullings, H.; Song, X.; Kopecky, K.J. Joint nonparametric correction estimation for excess relative risk regression in survival analysis. *J. Roy. Statist. Soc. Ser. B* **2017**, *79*, 1583–1599. [CrossRef]
20. Wang, C.Y.; Song, X. Semiparametric regression calibration for general hazard models in survival analysis with covariate measurement error; surprising performance under linear hazard. *Biometrics* **2021**, *77*, 561–572. [CrossRef]
21. Wang, C.Y.; Huang, Y.; Chao, E.C.; Jeffcoat M.K. Expected estimating equations for missing data, measurement error, and misclassification, with application to longitudinal nonignorably missing data. *Biometrics* **2008**, *64*, 85–95. [CrossRef] [PubMed]
22. Huang, Y.H.; Hwang, W.H.; Chen, F.Y. Differential measurement errors in zero-truncated regression models for count data. *Biometrics* **2011**, *67*, 1471–1480. [CrossRef] [PubMed]
23. Tsiatis, A.A.; Davidian, D. A semiparametric estimator for the proportional hazards model with longitudinal covariates measured with error. *Biometrika* **2001**, *88*, 447–458. [CrossRef]
24. Tsiatis, A.A.;Davidian, M. Joint modeling of longitudinal and time-to-event data: An overview. *Statistica Sinica* **2004**, *14*, 809–834.
25. Tooze, J.A.; Kipnis, V.; Buckman, D.W.; Carroll, R.J.; Freedman, L.S.; Guenther, P.M.; Krebs-Smith, S.M.; Subar, A.F.; Dodd, K.W. A mixed-effects model approach for estimating the distribution of usual intake of nutrients: The NCI method. *Stat. Med.* **2010**, *29*, 2857–2868. [CrossRef]

mathematics

Article

DINA Model with Entropy Penalization

Juntao Wang [1] and Yuan Li [2,*]

[1] School of Economics and Statistics, Guangzhou University, Guangzhou 510006, China; wangjt566@nenu.edu.cn
[2] Institute of Applied Mathematics, Shenzhen Polytechnic, Shenzhen 518000, China
* Correspondence: mathly@gzhu.edu.cn

Abstract: The cognitive diagnosis model (CDM) is an effective statistical tool for extracting the discrete attributes of individuals based on their responses to diagnostic tests. When dealing with cases that involve small sample sizes or highly correlated attributes, not all attribute profiles may be present. The standard method, which accounts for all attribute profiles, not only increases the complexity of the model but also complicates the calculation. Thus, it is important to identify the empty attribute profiles. This paper proposes an entropy-penalized likelihood method to eliminate the empty attribute profiles. In addition, the relation between attribute profiles and the parameter space of item parameters is discussed, and two modified expectation–maximization (EM) algorithms are designed to estimate the model parameters. Simulations are conducted to demonstrate the performance of the proposed method, and a real data application based on the fraction–subtraction data is presented to showcase the practical implications of the proposed method.

Keywords: cognitive diagnosis model; DINA model; penalized likelihood; Shannon entropy; EM algorithm

MSC: 62P25

Citation: Wang, J.; Li, Y. DINA Model with Entropy Penalization. *Mathematics* **2023**, *11*, 3993. http://doi.org/10.3390/math11183993

Academic Editors: Niansheng Tang and Shen-Ming Lee

Received: 22 August 2023
Revised: 15 September 2023
Accepted: 19 September 2023
Published: 20 September 2023

1. Introduction

CDMs are widely used in the field of educational and psychological assessments. These models are used to extract the examinees' latent binary random vectors, which can provide rich and comprehensive information about examinees. Different CDMs are proposed for different test scenarios. The popular CDMs include Deterministic Input, Noisy "And" gate (DINA) model [1], Deterministic Input, Noisy "Or" gate (DINO) model [2], Noisy Inputs, Deterministic "And" gate (NIDA) model [3], Noisy Inputs, Deterministic "Or" gate (NIDO) model [2], Reduced Reparameterized Unified Model (RRUM) [4,5] and Log-linear Cognitive Diagnosis Model (LCDM) [6]. The differences among the above-mentioned CDMs are the modeling methods of the positive response probabilities. CDMs can be summarized in more flexible frameworks such as the Generalized Noisy Inputs, Deterministic "And" gate (GDINA) model [7] and the General Diagnostic Model (GDM) [8]. The simplicity and interpretability of the DINA model have positioned it as one of the most popular CDMs.

The DINA model, also known as the latent classes model [9–13], is a mixture model, so it still suffers from the drawbacks of the mixture model. Too many latent classes may overfit the data, which means that data should have been characterized by a simpler model. Too few latent classes cannot characterize the true underlying data structure well and yield poor inference. In practical terms, identifying the empty latent classes will improve the model's interpretability and explain the data well. Chen [14] showed that the theoretical optimal convergence rate of the mixture model with the unknown number of classes is slower than the optimal convergence rate with the known number of classes. This means that the inference would strongly benefit from the known number of classes. Therefore, from both practical and theoretical views, eliminating the empty latent classes is a crucial issue in the DINA model.

Common reasons for empty attribute profiles include small sample sizes or highly correlated attributes. Let us explore a few examples to illustrate further. In a scenario where the sample size is smaller than the number of attribute profiles, it is inevitable that some attribute profiles will be empty. In another scenario with two attributes α_1 and α_2, the relation is assumed that $\alpha_2 = 1$ if and only if $\alpha_1 = 1$. Under the assumption of extremely correlated attributes, attribute profiles $(\alpha_1 = 1, \alpha_2 = 0)$ and $(\alpha_1 = 0, \alpha_2 = 1)$ do not appear. Situations with empty attribute profiles can occur in various scenarios [15].

The hierarchical diagnostic classification model [15,16] is a well-known method to eliminate empty attribute profiles. In the literature, directed acyclic graphs are employed to describe the relationships among the attributes, and the directions of edges impose strict constraints on attributes. If there is a directed edge from α_1 to α_2, the attribute profile (01) is forbidden. Gu and Xu [15] utilized penalized EM to select the true attribute profiles, avoid overfitting, and learn attribute hierarchies. Wang and Lu [17] compared two exploratory approaches of learning attribute hierarchies in the LCDM and DINA models. In essence, the attribute hierarchy can be regarded as a specific family of correlated attributes that can be effectively represented and described through a graph model.

The penalized methods have been widely researched in many statistical problems. In the regression model, the least absolute shrinkage and selection operator (LASSO) and its variants are analyzed by [18–20]. Fan and Li [21] proposed a nonconcave penalty smoothly clipped absolute deviation (SCAD) to reduce the bias of estimators. In the Gaussian mixture model, Ma and Wang, Huang et al. [22,23] proposed penalized likelihood methods to determine the number of components. In CDMs, Chen et al. [10] used SCAD to obtain the sparse item parameters and recovery Q matrix. Xu and Shang [11] applied a "L_0 norm" penalty to CDM and suggested a truncated "L_1 norm" penalty as the approximate calculation.

In the hierarchical diagnostic classification model, directed acyclic graphs of attributes often need to be specified in advance. A limitation of this model is that it is difficult to specify a graph in real scenarios. The penalty of the penalized EM proposed by Gu and Xu [15] involves two tuning parameters that complicate the implementation. Therefore, we hope to propose a method that does not require specifying a directed acyclic graph in advance and has a concise penalty term.

This paper makes two primary contributions. Firstly, it introduces an entropy-based penalty, and secondly, it develops the corresponding algorithms to utilize this penalty. This paper proposes a novel approach for estimating the DINA model, combining Shannon entropy and the penalized method. In information theory, "uncertainty" can be interpreted informally as the negative logarithm of probability, and Shannon entropy is the average effect of the "uncertainty". Shannon entropy can be used to characterize the distribution of attribute profiles. By utilizing the proposed method, the empty attribute profiles can be eliminated. We further develop the EM algorithm for the proposed method and conduct some simulations to verify the proposed method.

The rest of the paper is organized as follows. In Section 2, we give an overview of the DINA model and the estimation method. A definition of the feasible domain is defined to characterize the latent classes. Section 3 introduces the entropy penalized method, and the EM algorithm is employed to estimate the DINA model. The numerical studies of the entropy penalized method are shown in Section 4. Section 5 presents real data analysis based on the fractions–subtraction data. The summary of the paper and future research are given in Section 6. The details of the EM algorithm and proof are given in Appendices A–C.

2. DINA Model

2.1. Review of DINA Model

Firstly, some useful notations are introduced. For the examinee $i = 1, \dots, N$, the attribute profile $\boldsymbol{\alpha}_i$, also known as the latent class, is a K-dimensional binary vector

$\boldsymbol{\alpha}_i = (\alpha_{i1}, \alpha_{i2}, \ldots, \alpha_{iK})^\top$, and the corresponding response data to J items is a J-dimensional binary vector $\boldsymbol{y}_i = (y_{i1}, y_{i2}, \ldots, y_{iJ})^\top$, where "$\top$" is the transpose operation. Let $\boldsymbol{Y}$ and $\boldsymbol{\alpha}$ denote the collection of all $\boldsymbol{y}_i$ and $\boldsymbol{\alpha}_i$, respectively. The Q matrix is a $J \times K$ binary matrix, where if item j requires the attribute k, then the element q_{jk} is 1, otherwise, the element q_{jk} is 0. The j-th row vector is denoted by $\boldsymbol{q}_j^\top$. Given the fixed K, there are $C = 2^K$ latent classes. We use a multinomial distribution with the probability $\pi_{\boldsymbol{\Lambda}} \triangleq P(\boldsymbol{\alpha}_i = \boldsymbol{\Lambda})$ to describe the attribute profile $\boldsymbol{\Lambda} \in \{0,1\}^K$, where $\sum_{\boldsymbol{\Lambda} \in \{0,1\}^K} \pi_{\boldsymbol{\Lambda}} = 1$, and the population parameter $\boldsymbol{\pi}$ denotes the collection of probabilities for all attribute profiles.

The DINA model [1] supposes that, in an ideal scenario, the examinees with all required attributes will provide correct answers. For examinee i and item j, the ideal response is defined as $\eta_{j,\boldsymbol{\alpha}_i} = \prod_{k=1}^K \alpha_{ik}^{q_{jk}}$, where 0^0 is defined as 1. The slipping and guessing parameters are defined by conditional probabilities $s_j = P(y_{ij} = 0 | \eta_{j,\boldsymbol{\alpha}_i} = 1)$ and $g_j = P(y_{ij} = 1 | \eta_{j,\boldsymbol{\alpha}_i} = 0)$, respectively. The parameters $\boldsymbol{s}$ and $\boldsymbol{g}$ are the collections of all s_j and g_j, respectively.

In the DINA model, the positive response probability $\theta_{j,\boldsymbol{\alpha}_i}$ can be constructed as

$$\theta_{j,\boldsymbol{\alpha}_i} \triangleq P(y_{ij} = 1 | s_j, g_j, \boldsymbol{\alpha}_i; \boldsymbol{q}_j) = (1 - s_j)^{\eta_{j,\boldsymbol{\alpha}_i}} g_j^{1-\eta_{j,\boldsymbol{\alpha}_i}}. \quad (1)$$

If both $\boldsymbol{Y}$ and $\boldsymbol{\alpha}$ are observed, the likelihood function is

$$P(\boldsymbol{Y}, \boldsymbol{\alpha} | \boldsymbol{s}, \boldsymbol{g}) = \prod_{i=1}^N \pi_{\boldsymbol{\alpha}_i} \prod_{j=1}^J \left[(1 - s_j)^{\eta_{j,\boldsymbol{\alpha}_i}} g_j^{1-\eta_{j,\boldsymbol{\alpha}_i}} \right]^{y_{ij}} \left[s_j^{\eta_{j,\boldsymbol{\alpha}_i}} (1 - g_j)^{1-\eta_{j,\boldsymbol{\alpha}_i}} \right]^{1-y_{ij}}. \quad (2)$$

Given data $\boldsymbol{Y}$ and attribute profile $\boldsymbol{\alpha}$, the parameters $\boldsymbol{s}$ and $\boldsymbol{g}$ can be directly estimated by the maximum likelihood estimators:

$$\begin{aligned} \hat{s}_j &= \frac{\sum_{i=1}^N 1(\eta_{j,\boldsymbol{\alpha}_i} = 1 \ \& \ y_{ij} = 0)}{\sum_{i=1}^N 1(\eta_{j,\boldsymbol{\alpha}_i} = 1)}, \quad j = 1, \cdots, J, \\ \hat{g}_j &= \frac{\sum_{i=1}^N 1(\eta_{j,\boldsymbol{\alpha}_i} = 0 \ \& \ y_{ij} = 1)}{\sum_{i=1}^N 1(\eta_{j,\boldsymbol{\alpha}_i} = 0)}, \quad j = 1, \cdots, J, \end{aligned} \quad (3)$$

where $1(\cdot)$ is the indicator function. When $\boldsymbol{\alpha}$ is latent, by integrating out $\boldsymbol{\alpha}$, the marginal likelihood is

$$P(\boldsymbol{Y} | \boldsymbol{s}, \boldsymbol{g}, \boldsymbol{\pi}) = \prod_{i=1}^N \left[\sum_{\boldsymbol{\Lambda} \in \{0,1\}^K} \pi_{\boldsymbol{\Lambda}} \prod_{j=1}^J \left[(1 - s_j)^{\eta_{j,\boldsymbol{\Lambda}}} g_j^{1-\eta_{j,\boldsymbol{\Lambda}}} \right]^{y_{ij}} \left[s_j^{\eta_{j,\boldsymbol{\Lambda}}} (1 - g_j)^{1-\eta_{j,\boldsymbol{\Lambda}}} \right]^{1-y_{ij}} \right], \quad (4)$$

which is the primary focus of this paper.

2.2. Estimation Methods

EM and Markov chain Monte Carlo (MCMC) are two estimation methods for the DINA model. De la Torre [24] discussed the marginal maximum likelihood estimation for the DINA model, and the EM algorithm was employed where the objective function was Equation (4). Gu and Xu [15] proposed a penalized expectation–maximization (PEM) with the penalty

$$\lambda \sum_{\boldsymbol{\Lambda}} [1(\pi_{\boldsymbol{\Lambda}} > \rho_N) \log \pi_{\boldsymbol{\Lambda}} + 1(\pi_{\boldsymbol{\Lambda}} \leq \rho_N) \log \rho_N], \quad (5)$$

where $\lambda \in (-\infty, 0)$ controls the sparsity of $\boldsymbol{\pi}$ and ρ_N is a small threshold parameter the same order as N^{-d}, the constant $d \geq 1$. There are two tuning parameters λ and ρ_N in PEM. Additionally, a variational EM algorithm is proposed as an alternative approach.

Culpepper [25] proposed a Bayesian formulation for the DINA model and used Gibbs sampling to estimate parameters. The algorithm can be implemented by the R package "dina". The Gibbs sampling can be extended by a sequential method in the DINA and GDINA with many attributes [26], which provides an alternative approach to the traditional MCMC. As the focus of this paper does not revolve around the MCMC, we refrain from details.

2.3. The Property of DINA as Mixture Model

For a fixed K, the DINA model can be viewed as a mixture model comprising 2^K latent classes (i.e., components). In contrast to the Gaussian mixture model, where a change in the number of components will introduce or remove the mean and covariance parameters, the DINA model behaves differently. Specifically, a change in the number of latent classes does not necessarily affect the presence of item parameters. This means that there are two cases: (i) the latent classes have changed while the structure of the item parameters does not change, and (ii) the latent classes and the structure of the item parameters change simultaneously. To account for the two cases, a formal definition of the feasible domain of latent classes is introduced.

Definition 1. *Given $\mathbf{F} \subseteq \{0,1\}^K$ the subset of latent classes. If for any s_j or g_j, $j = 1, \ldots, J$, there exist some latent classes in $\mathbf{F}$, whose response function (i.e., the distribution of response data), is determined by s_j or g_j. We say that $\mathbf{F}$ is a feasible subset of latent classes and all feasible $\mathbf{F}$s make up the feasible domain $\mathcal{F}$.*

If all $\mathbf{\Lambda} \in \boldsymbol{F} \subseteq \{0,1\}^K$, the probability of $\mathbf{\Lambda} \notin \boldsymbol{F}$ is strictly 0. There exist some subsets $\boldsymbol{F}$ that will spoil the item parameter space. Let us see the following examples

$$Q \triangleq \begin{pmatrix} 1 & 0 & 0 \\ 0 & 1 & 0 \\ 0 & 0 & 1 \\ 1 & 1 & 0 \end{pmatrix}, F_1 \triangleq \begin{pmatrix} \mathbf{\Lambda}_{1,1} = 000 \\ \mathbf{\Lambda}_{1,2} = 111 \end{pmatrix}, F_2 \triangleq \begin{pmatrix} \mathbf{\Lambda}_{2,1} = 001 \\ \mathbf{\Lambda}_{2,2} = 110 \end{pmatrix}, F_3 \triangleq \begin{pmatrix} \mathbf{\Lambda}_{3,1} = 100 \\ \mathbf{\Lambda}_{3,2} = 010 \\ \mathbf{\Lambda}_{3,3} = 001 \end{pmatrix}. \tag{6}$$

Assume the response vector $\boldsymbol{y}_i = (y_{i1}, y_{i2}, y_{i3}, y_{i4})^\top$. If $\boldsymbol{\alpha}_i$ is from F_1, then for g_j, $j = 1,2,3,4$, we have

$$P(y_{ij}|\boldsymbol{\alpha}_i = \mathbf{\Lambda}_{1,1}) = g_j^{y_{ij}} 1 - g_j^{1-y_{ij}}, \tag{7}$$

which means that the $\mathbf{\Lambda}_{1,1}$'s response function is determined by g_j. For s_j, $j = 1,2,3,4$, we have

$$P(y_{ij}|\boldsymbol{\alpha}_i = \mathbf{\Lambda}_{1,2}) = s_j^{1-y_{ij}}(1-s_j)^{y_{ij}}, \tag{8}$$

which means that the $\mathbf{\Lambda}_{1,2}$'s response function is determined by s_j. The Equations (7) and (8) are obtained by calculating the ideal responses. To determine the response function of $\mathbf{\Lambda}_{1,1}$ and $\mathbf{\Lambda}_{1,2}$, all item parameters s_j and g_j are required. Based on similar discussions, $\mathbf{\Lambda}_{2,1}$'s response function is determined by g_1, g_2, s_3, g_4, and $\mathbf{\Lambda}_{2,2}$'s response function is determined by s_1, s_2, g_3, s_4. To determine the response function of $\mathbf{\Lambda}_{2,1}$ and $\mathbf{\Lambda}_{2,2}$, all item parameters s_j and g_j are required.

Then, a different case is presented. If $\boldsymbol{\alpha}_i$ is from F_3, $\mathbf{\Lambda}_{3,1}$'s response function is determined by s_1, g_2, g_3, g_4, $\mathbf{\Lambda}_{3,2}$'s response function is determined by g_1, s_2, g_3, g_4, and $\mathbf{\Lambda}_{3,3}$'s response function is determined by s_1, g_2, s_3, g_4. The item parameter s_4 cannot affect the response function of any attribute profile. Hence, s_4 is called a redundant parameter. Meanwhile, this indicates that there does not exist a slipping behavior for item 4, and we can let the redundant parameter $s_4 = 0$. If $\boldsymbol{\alpha}_i$ is from F_3, the item parameter space collapses from 8-dimensional to 7-dimensional. It is obvious that the subset $\mathbf{F} \in \mathcal{F}$ will not spoil item parameter space, and the feasible domain $\mathcal{F}$ depends on Q. However, a lemma can be given as follows. The proof is deferred to Appendix A.

Lemma 1. *If $\mathbf{F}$ contains $\mathbf{0}_K$ and $\mathbf{1}_K$, then $\mathbf{F}$ always lies in the feasible region $\mathcal{F}$, where $\mathbf{0}_K$ and $\mathbf{1}_K$ are K-dimensional vectors with all 0 and 1, respectively.*

3. Entropy Penalized Method

3.1. Entropy Penalty of DINA

Shannon entropy is $E(\boldsymbol{\pi}) = -\sum_{\Lambda} \pi_{\Lambda} \log \pi_{\Lambda}$, where the value of notation $0 \log 0$ is taken to be 0 according to $\lim_{x \to 0^+} x \log x = 0$ [27,28]. This section focuses on the case within the feasible domain, and the entropy penalized log-likelihood function with the constraint is

$$\mathcal{L}_{\lambda}(\boldsymbol{s}, \boldsymbol{g}, \boldsymbol{\pi}) = \log P(\boldsymbol{Y}|\boldsymbol{s}, \boldsymbol{g}, \boldsymbol{\pi}) - \lambda E(\boldsymbol{\pi}) \quad s.t. \ \boldsymbol{F} \in \mathcal{F}, \tag{9}$$

where the penalty parameter $\lambda \in (-\infty, 0)$ whose the interpretation coincides with [15]. Analogously, the penalty parameter λ still controls the sparsity of $\boldsymbol{\pi}$. The two penalties have different scales because π_{Λ} is not close to $\pi_{\Lambda} \log \pi_{\Lambda}$. If omitting the condition $\boldsymbol{F} \in \mathcal{F}$, the penalty λ going to the negative infinity implies that one latent class will be randomly selected (i.e., extremely sparse). The penalty λ going to zero implies all information comes from observed data. Compared with PEM, the proposed method only needs one tuning parameter.

The essential differences between the PEM and Entropy penalization methods are emphasized. PEM utilizes the term $1(\pi_{\Lambda} \leq \rho_N) \log \rho_N$ to handle the population probability $\pi_{\Lambda} = 0$, where ρ_N is pre-specified rather than determined by some fit indices. Hence, the selection of ρ_N will affect the performance of PEM. In the Entropy penalization method, $0 \log 0$ is well defined, and we do not need extra parameters. The performance of the Entropy penalization method is completely determined by the parameter λ.

Treating $\boldsymbol{\alpha}$ as the latent data, the expected log-likelihood function is

$$\mathbb{E}[\mathcal{L}_{\lambda}] = \mathbb{E}[\log P(\boldsymbol{Y}|\boldsymbol{s}, \boldsymbol{g}, \boldsymbol{\alpha}) P(\boldsymbol{\alpha}|\boldsymbol{\pi}) - \lambda E(\boldsymbol{\pi})] \quad s.t. \ \boldsymbol{F} \in \mathcal{F}, \tag{10}$$

where the expectation $\mathbb{E}$ is taken with respect to the distribution $P(\boldsymbol{\alpha}|\boldsymbol{Y}, \boldsymbol{s}, \boldsymbol{g}, \boldsymbol{\pi})$. Considering the constraint $\sum_{\Lambda} \pi_{\Lambda} = 1$, the Lagrange function can be defined as

$$\mathcal{L}_{\lambda}^{\mu} = \mathbb{E}[\mathcal{L}_{\lambda}] + \mu\Big(\sum_{\Lambda \in F} \pi_{\Lambda} - 1\Big) \quad s.t. \ \boldsymbol{F} \in \mathcal{F}. \tag{11}$$

Let the derivatives of $\frac{\partial \mathcal{L}_{\lambda}^{\mu}}{\partial \pi_{\Lambda}}$ and $\frac{\partial \mathcal{L}_{\lambda}^{\mu}}{\partial \mu}$ be 0, for any $\boldsymbol{\Lambda} \in \boldsymbol{F}$, we obtain

$$\begin{aligned} \sum_{i=1}^{N} \frac{h_{i,\Lambda}}{\pi_{\Lambda}} - \lambda(\log \pi_{\Lambda} + 1) + \mu = 0, \\ \sum_{\Lambda} \pi_{\Lambda} - 1 = 0, \end{aligned} \tag{12}$$

where $h_{i,\Lambda} = \frac{\pi_{\Lambda} P(y_i|s,g,\Lambda)}{\sum_{\Lambda \in F} \pi_{\Lambda} P(y_i|s,g,\Lambda)}$ is the posterior probability of the examinee i belonging to the latent class $\boldsymbol{\Lambda}$. The iterative formula of $\pi_{\Lambda}^{(t+1)}$ is proportional to $\max\{0, \sum_{i=1}^{N} h_{i,\Lambda}^{(t)} - \lambda \pi_{\Lambda}^{(t)} \log \pi_{\Lambda}^{(t)}\}$, where the superscript "(t)" indicates the values coming from the t-th iteration. Based on the iterative formula, a theorem is given to shrink the interval of λ.

Theorem 1. *For the DINA model with a fixed integer K, the penalty parameter λ of the penalized function Equation (9) should be in interval $(-\frac{N}{K \log 2}, 0)$.*

This theorem also indicates that λ and N have the same order, and $\frac{-1}{K \log 2}$ is the rate. This paper focuses on $\lambda \in \{-0.05N, -0.1N, \ldots, \frac{-N}{K \log 2}\}$. Algorithm 1 shows the schedules of EM for the DINA model within the feasible domain. When to implement algorithms, the algorithms of Gu and Xu [15] introduce an additional pre-specified constant c to update the population parameter $\pi_{\Lambda}^{(t+1)} \propto \max\{c, \sum_{i=1}^{N} h_{i,\Lambda}^{(t)} + \lambda\}$, where $c > 0$ is a small constant. Algorithm 1 does not rely on a pre-specified constant. In the method establishment and algorithm implementation, the algorithms of Gu and Xu [15] involve three parameters

λ, ρ_N, c, while Algorithm 1 only involves a parameter λ. We emphasize again that the parameter λ in the two methods has different scales. The calculation and proof are omitted, and more details are deferred to Appendix B.

Algorithm 1: EM of Entropy Penalized Method within the Feasible Domain.

Input: Observed data $\boldsymbol{Y}$, initial values $\boldsymbol{s}^{(0)}, \boldsymbol{g}^{(0)}, \boldsymbol{\pi}^{(0)}$, penalty parameter λ, initial feasible set $\boldsymbol{F}^{(0)}$ and maximum iterations T.
Output: The estimators $\hat{\boldsymbol{s}}, \hat{\boldsymbol{g}}, \hat{\boldsymbol{\pi}}$ and the final feasible set $\hat{\boldsymbol{F}}$.
while *$t < T$ and not converged* **do**
  for *$i \in 1, \cdots, N$ and $\boldsymbol{\Lambda} \in \boldsymbol{F}^{(t)}$* **do**
    $h_{i,\boldsymbol{\Lambda}} = \frac{\pi_{\boldsymbol{\Lambda}}^{(t)} P(\boldsymbol{y}_i | \boldsymbol{s}^{(t)}, \boldsymbol{g}^{(t)}, \boldsymbol{\Lambda})}{\sum_{\boldsymbol{\Lambda} \in \boldsymbol{F}^{(t)}} \pi_{\boldsymbol{\Lambda}}^{(t)} P(\boldsymbol{y}_i | \boldsymbol{s}^{(t)}, \boldsymbol{g}^{(t)}, \boldsymbol{\Lambda})}$
  end
  for $\boldsymbol{\Lambda} \in \boldsymbol{F}^{(t)}$ **do**
    $\pi_{\boldsymbol{\Lambda}}^{(t+1)} \propto \max\{0, \sum_{i=1}^N h_{i,\boldsymbol{\Lambda}}^{(t)} - \lambda \pi_{\boldsymbol{\Lambda}}^{(t)} \log \pi_{\boldsymbol{\Lambda}}^{(t)}\}$.
  end
  Remove the empty latent classes to obtain $\boldsymbol{F}^{(t+1)}$.
  if *$\boldsymbol{F}^{(t+1)}$ is feasible* **then**
    for *$i \in 1, \cdots, J$* **do**

$$s_j^{(t+1)} = \frac{\sum_{i=1}^N \sum_{\boldsymbol{\Lambda} \in \boldsymbol{F}^{(t+1)}} h_{i,\boldsymbol{\Lambda}} \cdot 1(\eta_{j,\boldsymbol{\Lambda}} = 1 \,\&\, y_{ij} = 0)}{\sum_{i=1}^N \sum_{\boldsymbol{\Lambda} \in \boldsymbol{F}^{(t+1)}} h_{i,\boldsymbol{\Lambda}} \cdot 1(\eta_{j,\boldsymbol{\Lambda}} = 1)}$$

$$g_j^{(t+1)} = \frac{\sum_{i=1}^N \sum_{\boldsymbol{\Lambda} \in \boldsymbol{F}^{(t+1)}} h_{i,\boldsymbol{\Lambda}} \cdot 1(\eta_{j,\boldsymbol{\Lambda}} = 0 \,\&\, y_{ij} = 1)}{\sum_{i=1}^N \sum_{\boldsymbol{\Lambda} \in \boldsymbol{F}^{(t+1)}} h_{i,\boldsymbol{\Lambda}} \cdot 1(\eta_{j,\boldsymbol{\Lambda}} = 0)}$$

    end
    Set $t = t + 1$
  end
  if *$\boldsymbol{F}^{(t+1)}$ is not feasible* **then**
    Stop the algorithm and export a warning "λ is too small".
  end
end
Output: $\hat{\boldsymbol{s}} = \boldsymbol{s}^{(t)}$, $\hat{\boldsymbol{g}} = \boldsymbol{g}^{(t)}$, $\hat{\boldsymbol{\pi}} = \boldsymbol{\pi}^{(t)}$ and $\hat{\boldsymbol{F}} = \boldsymbol{F}^{(t)}$.

Chen and Chen [29] proposed the extended Bayesian information criteria (EBIC) to conduct model selection from a large model space. The EBIC has the following form:

$$\text{EBIC} = -2\mathcal{L}_\lambda + (2J + ||\hat{\boldsymbol{F}}|| - 1)\log(N) + \log\binom{2^K}{||\hat{\boldsymbol{F}}||}, \tag{13}$$

where $||\hat{\boldsymbol{F}}||$ is the number of nonempty latent classes and $\binom{m}{n}$ indicates the binomial coefficient "m choose n". The smaller EBIC indicates a preferred model. In this paper, EBIC is used to select λ from the mentioned grid structure.

In the implementation of the EM algorithm, we assume that the initial $\boldsymbol{F}^{(0)}$ includes all latent classes to avoid missing important latent classes. The gaps between item parameters are used to check the convergence. If $\boldsymbol{F}^{(t+1)}$ are not feasible, it means that the penalty parameter λ is too small.

3.2. Modified EM

This section considers the case that $\boldsymbol{F}$ is not necessarily feasible. In this case, some g_j or s_j will disappear, which means that the observed data cannot provide any information about g_j or s_j. These redundant item parameters are set to zero. We focus on the Lagrange function without constraints as

$$\mathcal{L}^{\mu}_{\lambda} = \mathcal{L}_{\lambda}(\boldsymbol{s}, \boldsymbol{g}, \boldsymbol{\pi}) + \mu(\sum_{\boldsymbol{\alpha}} \pi_{\boldsymbol{\alpha}} - 1). \tag{14}$$

Because the space of item parameters may be collapsed, the dimension of item parameters needs to be recalculated. Meanwhile, EBIC will become

$$\text{EBIC} = -2\mathcal{L}_{\lambda} + (||\boldsymbol{s}|| + ||\boldsymbol{g}|| + ||\hat{\boldsymbol{F}}|| - 1)\log(N) + \log\binom{2^K}{||\hat{\boldsymbol{F}}||}, \tag{15}$$

where $||\boldsymbol{s}||$ and $||\boldsymbol{g}||$ indicate the numbers of nonzero slipping and guessing parameters, respectively. If all s and g exist, the summation of $||\boldsymbol{s}||$ and $||\boldsymbol{g}||$ is $2J$, which implies Equation (13).

The corresponding EM is shown in Algorithm 2, where the discussions of $\boldsymbol{F}^{(0)}$ and convergence are similar. However, this algorithm does not distinguish between feasible and not. To the best of our knowledge, no algorithms have handled the case without the feasible domain. More details are shown in Appendix B.

Algorithm 2: EM of Entropy Penalized Method without the Feasible Domain.

Input: Observed data $\boldsymbol{Y}$, initial values $\boldsymbol{s}^{(0)}, \boldsymbol{g}^{(0)}, \boldsymbol{\pi}^{(0)}$, penalty parameter λ, initial set $\boldsymbol{F}^{(0)}$ and maximum iterations T.
Output: The estimator $\hat{\boldsymbol{s}}, \hat{\boldsymbol{g}}, \hat{\boldsymbol{\pi}}$ and the final feasible set $\hat{\boldsymbol{F}}$.
while *$t < T$ and not converged* **do**
  for $i \in 1, \cdots, N$ *and* $\boldsymbol{\Lambda} \in \boldsymbol{F}^{(t)}$ **do**
    $$h_{i,\boldsymbol{\Lambda}} = \frac{\pi^{(t)}_{\boldsymbol{\Lambda}} P(y_j|\boldsymbol{s}^{(t)}, \boldsymbol{g}^{(t)}, \boldsymbol{\Lambda})}{\sum_{\boldsymbol{\Lambda} \in F^{(t)}} \pi^{(t)}_{\boldsymbol{\Lambda}} P(y_j|\boldsymbol{s}^{(t)}, \boldsymbol{g}^{(t)}, \boldsymbol{\Lambda})}$$
  end
  for $\boldsymbol{\Lambda} \in \boldsymbol{F}^{(t)}$ **do**
    $\pi^{(t+1)}_{\boldsymbol{\Lambda}} \propto \max\{0, \sum_{i=1}^{N} h^{(t)}_{i,\boldsymbol{\Lambda}} - \lambda \pi^{(t)}_{\boldsymbol{\Lambda}} \log \pi^{(t)}_{\boldsymbol{\Lambda}}\}.$
  end
  Remove the empty latent classes to obtain $\boldsymbol{F}^{(t+1)}$.
  for $i \in 1, \cdots, J$ **do**
    if $\sum_{i=1}^{N} \sum_{\boldsymbol{\Lambda} \in \boldsymbol{F}^{(t+1)}} h_{i,\boldsymbol{\Lambda}} \cdot 1(\eta_{j,\boldsymbol{\Lambda}} = 1) = 0$ **then**
      $$s^{(t+1)}_j = 0.$$
    end
    if $\sum_{i=1}^{N} \sum_{\boldsymbol{\Lambda} \in \boldsymbol{F}^{(t+1)}} h_{i,\boldsymbol{\Lambda}} \cdot 1(\eta_{j,\boldsymbol{\Lambda}} = 1) \neq 0$ **then**
      $$s^{(t+1)}_j = \frac{\sum_{i=1}^{N} \sum_{\boldsymbol{\Lambda} \in \boldsymbol{F}^{(t+1)}} h_{i,\boldsymbol{\Lambda}} \cdot 1(\eta_{j,\boldsymbol{\Lambda}} = 1 \,\&\, y_{ij} = 0)}{\sum_{i=1}^{N} \sum_{\boldsymbol{\Lambda} \in \boldsymbol{F}^{(t+1)}} h_{i,\boldsymbol{\Lambda}} \cdot 1(\eta_{j,\boldsymbol{\Lambda}} = 1)}$$
    end
    if $\sum_{i=1}^{N} \sum_{\boldsymbol{\Lambda} \in \boldsymbol{F}^{(t+1)}} h_{i,\boldsymbol{\Lambda}} \cdot 1(\eta_{j,\boldsymbol{\Lambda}} = 0) = 0$ **then**
      $$g^{(t+1)}_j = 0$$
    end
    if $\sum_{i=1}^{N} \sum_{\boldsymbol{\Lambda} \in \boldsymbol{F}^{(t+1)}} h_{i,\boldsymbol{\Lambda}} \cdot 1(\eta_{j,\boldsymbol{\Lambda}} = 0) \neq 0$ **then**
      $$g^{(t+1)}_j = \frac{\sum_{i=1}^{N} \sum_{\boldsymbol{\Lambda} \in \boldsymbol{F}^{(t+1)}} h_{i,\boldsymbol{\Lambda}} \cdot 1(\eta_{j,\boldsymbol{\Lambda}} = 0 \,\&\, y_{ij} = 1)}{\sum_{i=1}^{N} \sum_{\boldsymbol{\Lambda} \in \boldsymbol{F}^{(t+1)}} h_{i,\boldsymbol{\Lambda}} \cdot 1(\eta_{j,\boldsymbol{\Lambda}} = 0)}$$
    end
  end
  Set $t = t + 1$
end
Output: $\hat{\boldsymbol{s}} = \boldsymbol{s}^{(t)}$, $\hat{\boldsymbol{g}} = \boldsymbol{g}^{(t)}$, $\hat{\boldsymbol{\pi}} = \boldsymbol{\pi}^{(t)}$ and $\hat{\boldsymbol{F}} = \boldsymbol{F}^{(t)}$.

4. Simulation Studies

Three simulation studies are conducted to implement the standard EM accounting for all latent classes as a baseline for comparison to verify the selection validity of EBIC and the performance of the entropy penalized method, respectively. Each simulation study serves a specific purpose and contributes to the overall assessment of the proposed approach. For all simulation studies, we set $K = 5$, $J = 15$ and Q matrix has the following structure:

$$Q^\top \triangleq \begin{pmatrix} 1 & 0 & 0 & 0 & 0 & 1 & 0 & 0 & 0 & 0 & 1 & 0 & 0 & 0 & 1 \\ 0 & 1 & 0 & 0 & 0 & 0 & 1 & 0 & 0 & 0 & 1 & 1 & 0 & 0 & 0 \\ 0 & 0 & 1 & 0 & 0 & 0 & 0 & 1 & 0 & 0 & 0 & 1 & 1 & 0 & 0 \\ 0 & 0 & 0 & 1 & 0 & 0 & 0 & 0 & 1 & 0 & 0 & 0 & 1 & 1 & 0 \\ 0 & 0 & 0 & 0 & 1 & 0 & 0 & 0 & 0 & 1 & 0 & 0 & 0 & 1 & 1 \end{pmatrix}. \tag{16}$$

The Q matrix with two identity matrices satisfies the identifiable conditions [12,30,31]. All attributes are required by four items, and the design of the Q matrix is balanced.

4.1. Study I

In this study, the settings are $N = 150, 500, 1000$, and $s = g = 0.2$. The attribute profiles are generated from $\boldsymbol{F}$, and each attribute profile of $\boldsymbol{F}$ has a probability of $1/7$.

$$\boldsymbol{F}^\top \triangleq \begin{pmatrix} 0 & 1 & 0 & 0 & 0 & 0 & 1 \\ 0 & 0 & 1 & 0 & 0 & 0 & 1 \\ 0 & 0 & 0 & 1 & 0 & 0 & 1 \\ 0 & 0 & 0 & 0 & 1 & 0 & 1 \\ 0 & 0 & 0 & 0 & 0 & 1 & 1 \end{pmatrix}. \tag{17}$$

For the proposed EM, the penalty parameter $\lambda = -0.075N$. The method to explore λ will be discussed in the next simulation study. For each attribute α_{ik}, the classification accuracy is evaluated by the posterior marginal probability as

$$P(\alpha_{ik} = 1 | \boldsymbol{Y}, \hat{\boldsymbol{s}}, \hat{\boldsymbol{g}}, \hat{\boldsymbol{\pi}}) = \sum_{\{\boldsymbol{\alpha}_i | \alpha_{ik}=1\}} P(\boldsymbol{\alpha}_i | \boldsymbol{Y}, \hat{\boldsymbol{s}}, \hat{\boldsymbol{g}}, \hat{\boldsymbol{\pi}}), \tag{18}$$

where $P(\boldsymbol{\alpha}_i | \boldsymbol{Y}, \hat{\boldsymbol{s}}, \hat{\boldsymbol{g}}, \hat{\boldsymbol{\pi}})$ is the posterior probability of examinee i having attribute profile $\boldsymbol{\alpha}_i$. Given the posterior marginal probability, the logarithm of the posterior marginal likelihood as

$$\sum_{i=1}^{N} \sum_{j=1}^{J} \log[P(\alpha^*_{ik} = 1 | \boldsymbol{Y}, \hat{\boldsymbol{s}}, \hat{\boldsymbol{g}}, \hat{\boldsymbol{\pi}})^{\alpha^*_{ik}} P(\alpha^*_{ik} = 0 | \boldsymbol{Y}, \hat{\boldsymbol{s}}, \hat{\boldsymbol{g}}, \hat{\boldsymbol{\pi}})^{1-\alpha^*_{ik}}] \tag{19}$$

reflects the global classification accuracy, where α^*_{ik} denotes the true attribute during data generation.

This study focuses on the estimators of $\boldsymbol{\pi}$ and the classification accuracy. The results of $\boldsymbol{\pi}$ are shown in Figure 1. We observe that for both settings of N, the performance of standard EM is poor as it fails to eliminate any irrelevant attribute profiles. When the sample size is N, the probability $1/N$ can be treated as a threshold to distinguish irrelevant attribute profiles. This method can only eliminate the partially irrelevant attribute profiles. In fact, finding an appropriate threshold is challenging. In contrast, regardless of sample sizes, the proposed EM can find the true attribute profiles and set the probability of all irrelevant attribute profiles to zero. The logarithm of the posterior marginal likelihood for the six settings, namely $\{150, 500, 1000\} \otimes \{\text{proposed EM}, \text{standard EM}\}$, are -204.239, -453.163, -508.047, -514.681, -1046.273 and -1054.014 for settings $\{150, 500, 1000\} \otimes \{\text{proposed EM}, \text{standard EM}\}$, respectively. The likelihood of the proposed EM is consistently larger than that of the standard EM, indicating that the proposed EM enjoys higher classification accuracy. The results also show that the proposed method works well for the small sample size $N = 150$. Especially considering the posterior marginal likelihood, the proposed method has obvious advantages over the standard EM. Note that the discussion regarding the estimation of item parameters will be shown in the third simulation study.

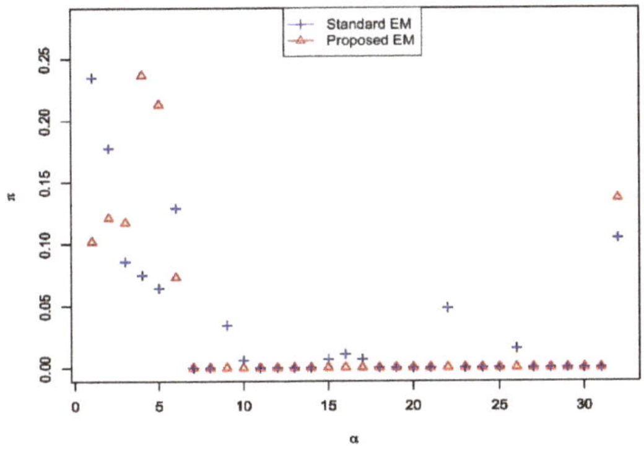

(**a**)

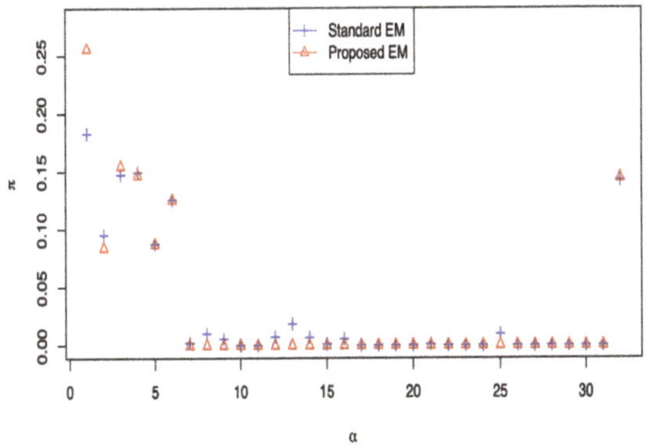

(**b**)

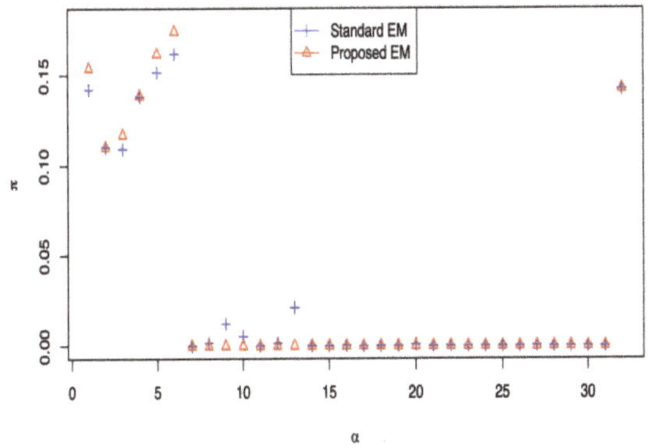

(**c**)

Figure 1. The results of estimated $\hat{\pi}$ for different sample sizes. The horizontal axis represents attribute profiles which can be concluded as $1 \triangleq (0,0,0,0,0)^{\top}, 2 \triangleq (1,0,0,0,0)^{\top}, 3 \triangleq (0,1,0,0,0)^{\top}, \ldots, 7 \triangleq (1,1,0,0,0)^{\top}, \ldots, 32 \triangleq (1,1,1,1,1)^{\top}$. The rules can also apply to different Ks. (**a**) The results of sample size $N = 150$. (**b**) The results of sample size $N = 500$. (**c**) The results of sample size $N = 1000$.

4.2. Study II

In this study, the solution paths of π versus λ are elaborated. The running settings of N, s, g and F are the same as the settings of Study I. The penalty parameter $\lambda \in \{-0.2N, -0.195N, \ldots, -0.01N\}$. Due to the similarity of results, only the results of the sample size $N = 500$ are presented. Figure 2 shows the solution paths of π, F and EBIC versus λ.

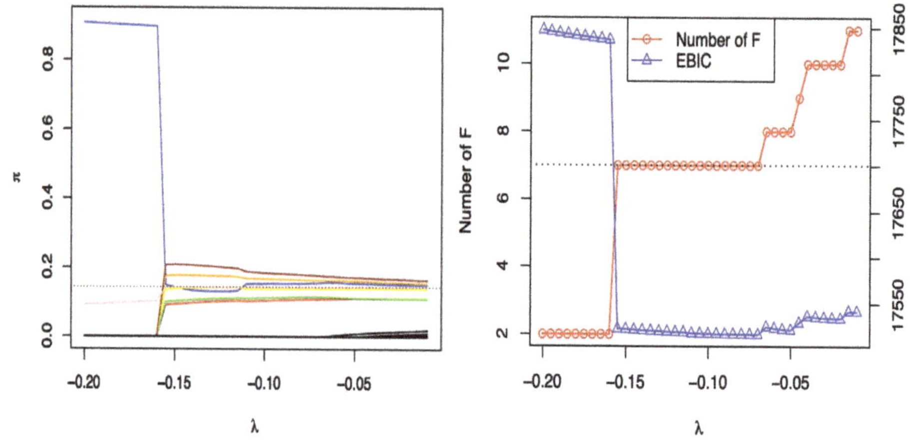

(a) (b)

Figure 2. Solution paths of the estimated π, the number of F and EBIC versus λ. (**a**) Solution paths of π. (**b**) Number of F and EBIC.

In Figure 2a, the colored lines indicate the true latent classes, while the black lines indicate the irrelevant latent classes. The dotted line represents the probability is $1/7$. Based on the figure, the interval $[-0.155N, -0.07N]$ can efficiently estimate the true π and eliminate the empty latent classes. For the large λ, the recovery of π does not appear to worsen much when estimating the probability of irrelevant latent classes. However, irrelevant latent classes cannot be strictly zero. In Figure 2b, the left and right vertical axes show results of the number of F and EBIC, respectively. The dotted line represents the true number of F. The Figure 2b shows that when the correct number of F is selected, the EBIC achieves the minimum. This study is an illustration of how to explore the values λ using EBIC.

4.3. Study III

In this study, the effects of sample sizes and item parameters are evaluated. We consider $N = 500, 1000$ and item parameters $s = g = 0.1, 0.2, 0.3$. The response data are generated with the more complex F, and each latent class of F has the probability $1/12$. In each setting, 200 independent data are generated.

$$F^\top \triangleq \begin{pmatrix} 0 & 1 & 0 & 0 & 0 & 0 & 1 & 0 & 0 & 0 & 1 & 1 \\ 0 & 0 & 1 & 0 & 0 & 0 & 1 & 1 & 0 & 0 & 0 & 1 \\ 0 & 0 & 0 & 1 & 0 & 0 & 0 & 1 & 1 & 0 & 0 & 1 \\ 0 & 0 & 0 & 0 & 1 & 0 & 0 & 0 & 1 & 1 & 0 & 1 \\ 0 & 0 & 0 & 0 & 0 & 1 & 0 & 0 & 0 & 1 & 1 & 1 \end{pmatrix}. \tag{20}$$

Firstly, the information criteria EBIC is used to select appropriate λ for each setting. The selection precision of the latent classes and Bias, RMSE of item parameters are used to evaluate the proposed method. The selection precision and Bias, RMSE of item parameters are listed in Table 1. The notation "ST/AT" denotes the ratio between selected true latent classes and all true latent classes. The notation "ST/AS" denotes the ratio between selected true latent classes and all selected latent classes. The subscript of Bias and RMSE indicates the type of item parameters. When the sample size N increases and $\boldsymbol{s}$, $\boldsymbol{g}$ decreases, both the selection precision and the performance of item parameters' estimators will be better. If $N = 1000$ and $\boldsymbol{s} = \boldsymbol{g} = 0.1$, the true $\boldsymbol{F}$ can be completely recovered. The RMSE and Bias of the guessing parameters are lower than the slipping parameters, which is due to the DINA model itself, as the guessing parameter is estimated from all latent groups that do not fully master the required attributes for an item. In contrast, the slipping parameter is estimated only for the latent group with complete mastery for that specific $\boldsymbol{q}_j$ vector.

Table 1. The selection precision of the latent classes and Bias, RMSE of item parameters. The results are based on 200 independent data.

s, g	N	ST/AT	ST/AS	Bias_s	RMSE_s	Bias_g	RMSE_g
0.1	500	1.0000	0.9950	0.0012	0.0315	−0.0003	0.0173
	1000	1.0000	1.0000	0.0001	0.0220	−0.0001	0.0123
0.2	500	0.9671	0.9291	0.0028	0.0553	−0.0012	0.0279
	1000	0.9933	0.9601	0.0035	0.0381	−0.0019	0.0197
0.3	500	0.7246	0.7040	0.0013	0.1138	−0.0149	0.0671
	1000	0.8483	0.8054	0.0021	0.0759	−0.0045	0.0388

5. Real Data Analysis

In this section, fraction–subtraction data are analyzed. For more about the data, please refer to the literature [7,32,33]. This data set contains responses of $N = 536$ middle school students to $J = 20$ items, where the responses are coded as 0 or 1. The test measures $K = 8$ attributes, so there are $2^8 = 256$ possible latent classes. The Q-matrix and item contents are shown in Table 2.

Table 2. The Q-matrix and contents of the fractions–subtraction data.

Item	α_1	α_2	α_3	α_4	α_5	α_6	α_7	α_8	Item	α_1	α_2	α_3	α_4	α_5	α_6	α_7	α_8
$\frac{5}{3}-\frac{3}{4}$	0	0	0	1	0	1	1	0	$4\frac{1}{3}-2\frac{4}{3}$	0	1	0	0	1	0	1	0
$\frac{3}{4}-\frac{3}{8}$	0	0	0	1	0	0	1	0	$\frac{11}{8}-\frac{1}{8}$	0	0	0	0	0	0	1	1
$\frac{5}{6}-\frac{1}{9}$	0	0	0	1	0	0	1	0	$3\frac{3}{8}-2\frac{6}{5}$	0	1	0	1	1	0	1	0
$3\frac{1}{2}-2\frac{3}{2}$	0	1	1	0	1	0	1	0	$3\frac{4}{5}-3\frac{2}{5}$	0	1	0	0	0	0	1	0
$4\frac{3}{5}-3\frac{4}{10}$	0	1	0	1	0	0	1	1	$2-\frac{1}{3}$	1	0	0	0	0	0	1	0
$\frac{6}{7}-\frac{4}{7}$	0	0	0	0	0	0	1	0	$4\frac{5}{7}-1\frac{4}{7}$	0	1	0	0	0	0	1	0
$3-2\frac{1}{5}$	1	1	0	0	0	0	1	0	$7\frac{3}{5}-2\frac{4}{5}$	0	1	0	0	1	0	1	0
$\frac{2}{3}-\frac{2}{3}$	0	0	0	0	0	0	1	0	$4\frac{1}{10}-2\frac{8}{10}$	0	1	0	0	1	1	1	0
$3\frac{7}{8}-2$	0	1	0	0	0	0	0	0	$4-1\frac{4}{3}$	1	1	1	0	1	0	1	0
$4\frac{4}{12}-2\frac{7}{12}$	0	1	0	0	1	0	1	1	$4\frac{1}{3}-1\frac{5}{3}$	0	1	1	0	1	0	1	0

Because the sample size $N = 536$ is not significantly larger than possible latent classes $2^K = 256$, we cannot ensure there are enough latent classes to guarantee that true $\boldsymbol{F}$ is feasible. Algorithm 2 is suggested for analyzing the real data. Firstly, EBIC is used to select the penalty parameter $\lambda \in \{-0.2N, -0.19N, \ldots, -0.01N\}$. The results around the optimal

EBIC are shown in Table 3, which is based on a stable interval of EBIC. We observe that when $\lambda = -0.17N$, the EBIC achieves the minimum. If $\lambda = -0.16N$, the number $||\hat{F}||$ changes from 76 to 20, and two guessing parameters disappear. For $\lambda = -0.16N$, if λ slightly increases, the model will be more complicated. Based on this fact, we discard the λs that are not less than $-0.16N$.

Table 3. EBIC and exploratory results about $||\hat{F}||$, $||\hat{g}||$, $||\hat{s}||$.

λ	$-0.19N$	$-0.18N$	$-0.17N$	$-0.16N$	$-0.15N$
EBIC	11,245.30	10,263.11	**9807.29**	10,342.25	10,173.47
$\|\|\hat{F}\|\|$	7	16	20	76	80
$\|\|\hat{g}\|\|$	14	15	18	20	20
$\|\|\hat{s}\|\|$	20	20	20	20	20

Next, the evaluation is based on Theorem 1 and estimators $\hat{s}$, $\hat{g}$, $\hat{F}$. We note that $-0.19 < \frac{-1}{8\log 2}$ does not satisfy Theorem 1, so the corresponding estimator eliminates many classes. Figure 3 presents the estimated $\hat{F}$ for different λ, and we can see that the results of Figure 3a are consistent with the conclusion of Theorem 1. The conclusion is that the λs no larger than $-0.19N$ are discarded. In addition, combined with Figure 3a–c, we know that attribute 7 is the most basic attribute. Figure 4a,b display the estimators of guessing and slipping parameters, respectively. According to the estimated $\hat{s}$, the results of $\lambda = -0.19N$ strongly shifted on items 2, 3, 5, 9, and 16. For different λs, the behavior of estimated $\hat{g}$ is too complex, and significant differences are found in items 8, 9, and 13.

Until now, the candidate penalties are $\lambda = -0.18N$ and $-0.17N$. The penalty $\lambda = -0.17N$ supports the criteria EBIC, and $\lambda = -0.18N$ prefers a simpler model. Furthermore, a denser grid between $[-0.18N, -0.16N]$ will give more detailed results.

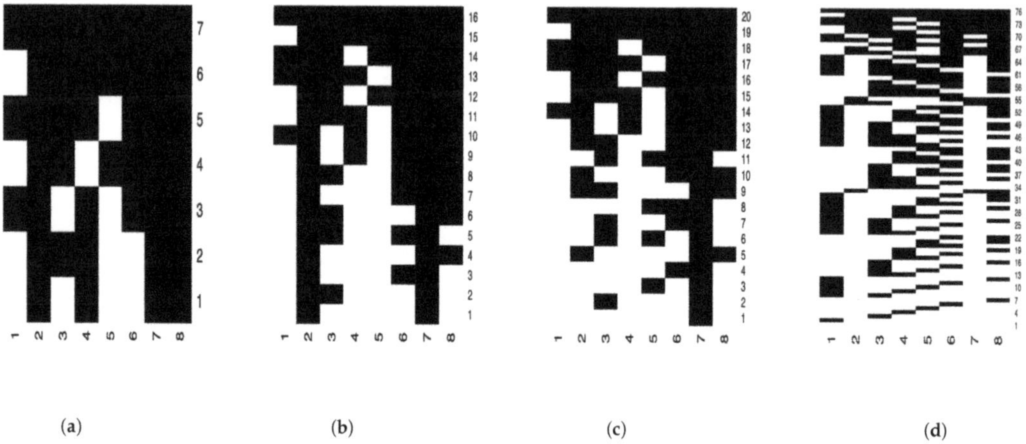

Figure 3. The estimators of item parameters s and g as the penalty parameter λ varies in the set $\{-0.19N, -0.18N, \cdots, -0.15N\}$. **(a)** $\lambda = -0.19N$. **(b)** $\lambda = -0.18N$. **(c)** $\lambda = -0.17N$. **(d)** $\lambda = -0.16N$.

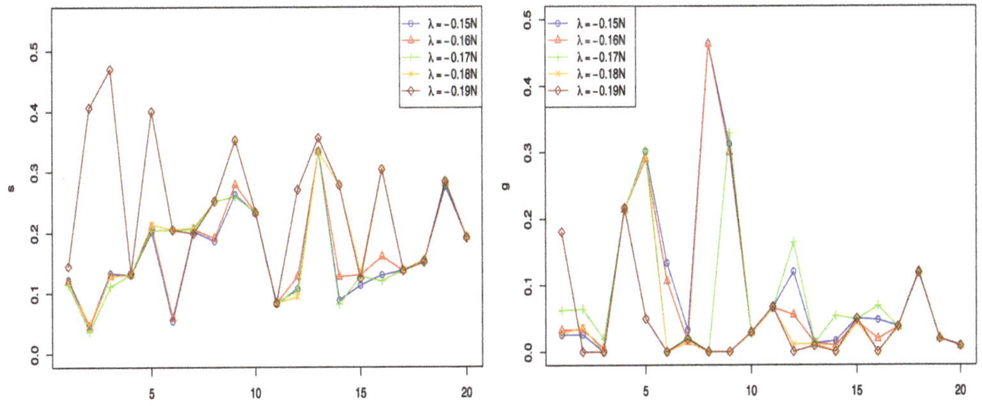

(**a**) (**b**)

Figure 4. The estimators of item parameters s and g as the penalty parameter λ varies in the set $\{-0.19N, -0.18N, \ldots, -0.15N\}$. (**a**) Slipping parameters. (**b**) Guessing parameters.

6. Discussion

In this paper, we study the penalized method for the DINA model. There are two contributions. Firstly, the entropy penalized method is proposed for the DINA model. The feasible domain is defined to describe the relation between latent classes and the parameter space of item parameters. This framework allows for distinguishing irrelevant attribute profiles. Second, based on the definition of the feasible domain, two modified EM algorithms are developed. In practice, it is recommended to perform exploratory analyses using Algorithm 2 before proceeding further, which can provide valuable insights and guidance to understand the data structure.

While this paper focuses on the DINA model, a natural extension would be the application of the entropy penalized method to other CDMs. Additionally, it is worth noting that this paper study involves situations with a maximum dimension of $K = 8$, which is relatively low. In high-dimensional cases of K, improving the power and performance of the entropy-penalized method is an interesting topic. A more challenging question is indicating how the specification of irrelevant latent classes may affect the classification accuracy and the estimation of the model. Those topics are left for future research.

Author Contributions: J.W. provided original idea and wrote the paper; Y.L. provided feedback on the manuscript and all authors contributed substantially to revisions. All authors have read and agreed to the published version of the manuscript.

Funding: This work was supported by the Humanities and Social Sciences Youth Foundation, Ministry of Education of China (No. 22YJC880073), the Guangdong Natural Science Foundation of China (2022A1515011899), and the National Natural Science Foundation of China (No. 11731015).

Data Availability Statement: The full data set used in the real data analysis is openly available as an example data set in the R package CDM on CRAN at https://CRAN.R-project.org/package=CDM (accessed on 25 August 2022).

Conflicts of Interest: The authors declare no conflict of interest.

Appendix A. Proof of Lemma 1

Proof. Assume the response vector $\boldsymbol{y}_i = (y_{i1}, \cdots, y_{iJ})^\top$. The vector $\boldsymbol{q}_j$ cannot be $\mathbf{0}_K$ because item j in the diagnostic test must measure some attribute. If $\boldsymbol{\alpha}_i = \mathbf{0}_K$ is from $\boldsymbol{F}$, then $\eta_{j,\mathbf{0}_K} = \prod_{k=1}^{K} 0^{q_{jk}} = 0$. For $g_j, j = 1, \cdots, J$, we have

$$P(y_{ij}|\boldsymbol{\alpha}_i = \mathbf{0}_K) = g_j^{y_{ij}} 1 - g_j^{1-y_{ij}}, \tag{A1}$$

which means that the $\mathbf{0}_K$'s response function is determined by g_j. If $\boldsymbol{\alpha}_i = \mathbf{1}_K$ is from $\boldsymbol{F}$, then $\eta_{j,\mathbf{1}_K} = \prod_{k=1}^{K} 1^{q_{jk}} = 1$. For $s_j, j = 1, \cdots, J$, we have

$$P(y_{ij}|\boldsymbol{\alpha}_i = \mathbf{1}_K) = s_j^{1-y_{ij}}(1 - s_j)^{y_{ij}}, \tag{A2}$$

which means that the $\mathbf{1}_K$'s response function is determined by s_j. Hence, we only need $\mathbf{0}_K$ and $\mathbf{1}_K$ to conclude that all item parameters g_j and s_j are required . □

Appendix B. The Details of EM Algorithm

For Algorithm 1, the Lagrange function becomes

$$\begin{aligned}
\mathcal{L}_\lambda^\mu &= \mathbb{E}[\mathcal{L}_\lambda] + \mu(\sum_{\boldsymbol{\Lambda}\in F} \pi_{\boldsymbol{\Lambda}} - 1) \\
&= \mathbb{E}[\log P(\mathbf{Y}|\boldsymbol{s}, \boldsymbol{g}, \boldsymbol{\alpha})P(\boldsymbol{\alpha}|\boldsymbol{\pi})] - \lambda E(\boldsymbol{\pi}) + \mu(\sum_{\boldsymbol{\Lambda}\in F} \pi_{\boldsymbol{\Lambda}} - 1) \\
&= \mathbb{E}\left\{\sum_{i=1}^{N}\sum_{\boldsymbol{\Lambda}\in F} 1(\boldsymbol{\alpha}_i = \boldsymbol{\Lambda})\left[\sum_{j=1}^{J} \log P(y_{ij}|s_j, g_j, \boldsymbol{\alpha}_i = \boldsymbol{\Lambda}) + \log P(\boldsymbol{\alpha}_i = \boldsymbol{\Lambda}|\boldsymbol{\pi})\right]\right\} \\
&\quad - \lambda E(\boldsymbol{\pi}) + \mu(\sum_{\boldsymbol{\Lambda}\in F} \pi_{\boldsymbol{\Lambda}} - 1) \\
&= \sum_{i=1}^{N}\sum_{\boldsymbol{\Lambda}\in F} \mathbb{E}1(\boldsymbol{\alpha}_i = \boldsymbol{\Lambda})\left[\sum_{j=1}^{J} \log P(y_{ij}|s_j, g_j, \boldsymbol{\alpha}_i = \boldsymbol{\Lambda}) + \log P(\boldsymbol{\alpha}_i = \boldsymbol{\Lambda}|\boldsymbol{\pi})\right] \\
&\quad - \lambda E(\boldsymbol{\pi}) + \mu(\sum_{\boldsymbol{\Lambda}\in F} \pi_{\boldsymbol{\Lambda}} - 1)
\end{aligned} \tag{A3}$$

where $\mathbb{E}1(\boldsymbol{\alpha}_i = \boldsymbol{\Lambda})$ is defined as $h_{i,\boldsymbol{\Lambda}}$. Given $\boldsymbol{s}$, $\boldsymbol{g}$ and $\boldsymbol{\pi}$, the expectation $\mathbb{E}$ is taken with respect to the distribution $P(\boldsymbol{\alpha}|\mathbf{Y}, \boldsymbol{s}, \boldsymbol{g}, \boldsymbol{\pi})$, and $h_{i,\boldsymbol{\Lambda}}$ is nothing but the posterior probability of examinee i belonging to the latent class $\boldsymbol{\Lambda}$. If $\pi_{\boldsymbol{\Lambda}} > 0$, Equation (12) can be strictly reduced to

$$\begin{aligned}
\sum_{i=1}^{N} h_{i,\boldsymbol{\Lambda}} - \lambda\pi_{\boldsymbol{\Lambda}}(\log \pi_{\boldsymbol{\Lambda}} + 1) + \mu\pi_{\boldsymbol{\Lambda}} &= 0, \\
\sum_{\boldsymbol{\Lambda}} \pi_{\boldsymbol{\Lambda}} - 1 &= 0.
\end{aligned} \tag{A4}$$

If $\pi_{\boldsymbol{\Lambda}} = 0$, the term $\sum_{i=1}^{N} h_{i,\boldsymbol{\Lambda}}$ will be positive and close to zero, the equation $\sum_{i=1}^{N} h_{i,\boldsymbol{\Lambda}} - \lambda\pi_{\boldsymbol{\Lambda}}(\log \pi_{\boldsymbol{\Lambda}} + 1) + \mu\pi_{\boldsymbol{\Lambda}} \approx 0$. Equation (A4) can be treated as the alternative of Equation (12). By taking summation over all $\boldsymbol{\Lambda}$, we could obtain,

$$\begin{aligned}
\sum_{i=1}^{N}\sum_{\boldsymbol{\Lambda}} h_{i,\boldsymbol{\Lambda}} - \lambda\sum_{\boldsymbol{\Lambda}} \pi_{\boldsymbol{\Lambda}}(\log \pi_{\boldsymbol{\Lambda}} + 1) + \mu &= 0 \\
N + \lambda E(\boldsymbol{\pi}) + \mu - \lambda &= 0 \\
N + \lambda E(\boldsymbol{\pi}) &= \lambda - \mu
\end{aligned} \tag{A5}$$

According to Equations (A4) and (A5), the iterative formula is

$$\pi_{\Lambda} = \begin{cases} 0 & \text{if } \sum_{i=1}^{N} h_{i,\Lambda} - \lambda\pi_{\Lambda}\log\pi_{\Lambda} < 0, \\ \dfrac{\sum_{i=1}^{N} h_{i,\Lambda} - \lambda\pi_{\Lambda}\log\pi_{\Lambda}}{N + \lambda E(\boldsymbol{\pi}) + \Delta} & \text{otherwise.} \end{cases} \tag{A6}$$

where $\Delta = \sum_{\Lambda}[(\sum_{i=1}^{N} h_{i,\Lambda} - \lambda\pi_{\Lambda}\log\pi_{\Lambda}) \cdot 1(\sum_{i=1}^{N} h_{i,\Lambda} - \lambda\pi_{\Lambda}\log\pi_{\Lambda} < 0)]$ is negative. It implies that $\boldsymbol{\pi}_{\Lambda}$ is proportional to $\max\{0, \sum_{i=1}^{N} h_{i,\Lambda}^{(t)} - \lambda\pi_{\Lambda}^{(t)}\log\pi_{\Lambda}^{(t)}\}$. Equation (A6) can also be used to explain why λ should be negative. We assume that λ is non-negative. For any $\boldsymbol{\Lambda} \in \{\boldsymbol{\Lambda}|\pi_{\Lambda}^{(t)} \neq 0\}$, the posterior probability $h_{i,\Lambda}^{(t)}$ is positive and the term $-\pi_{\Lambda}^{(t)}\log\pi_{\Lambda}^{(t)}$ with $0 < \pi_{\Lambda}^{(t)} < 1$ is positive. Due to the positive λ, we obtain that $\sum_{i=1}^{N} h_{i,\Lambda}^{(t)} - \lambda\pi_{\Lambda}^{(t)}\log\pi_{\Lambda}^{(t)}$ is positive, for all $\boldsymbol{\Lambda} \in \{\boldsymbol{\Lambda}|\pi_{\Lambda}^{(t)} \neq 0\}$. This result means that, from iteration t to iteration $t+1$, the positive λ cannot eliminate any attribute profiles. Hence, λ should be negative.

The derivatives of item parameters $\frac{\partial \mathcal{L}_{\lambda}^{\mu}}{\partial s_j}$ and $\frac{\partial \mathcal{L}_{\lambda}^{\mu}}{\partial g_j}$ are

$$\begin{aligned} \frac{\partial \mathcal{L}_{\lambda}^{\mu}}{\partial s_j} &= \sum_{i=1}^{N} h_{i,\Lambda} \sum_{\{\Lambda|\eta_{j,\Lambda}=1\}} \left[\frac{y_{ij}}{1-s_j} + \frac{1-y_{ij}}{s_j}\right], \\ \frac{\partial \mathcal{L}_{\lambda}^{\mu}}{\partial g_j} &= \sum_{i=1}^{N} h_{i,\Lambda} \sum_{\{\Lambda|\eta_{j,\Lambda}=0\}} \left[\frac{y_{ij}}{g_j} + \frac{1-y_{ij}}{1-g_j}\right]. \end{aligned} \tag{A7}$$

Therefore, the solutions of item parameters are

$$\begin{aligned} s_j &= \frac{\sum_{i=1}^{N} h_{i,\Lambda} \cdot 1(\eta_{j,\Lambda} = 1 \& y_{ij} = 0)}{\sum_{i=1}^{N} h_{i,\Lambda} \cdot 1(\eta_{j,\Lambda} = 1)}, \\ g_j &= \frac{\sum_{i=1}^{N} h_{i,\Lambda} \cdot 1(\eta_{j,\Lambda} = 0 \& y_{ij} = 1)}{\sum_{i=1}^{N} h_{i,\Lambda} \cdot 1(\eta_{j,\Lambda} = 0)}. \end{aligned} \tag{A8}$$

Equations (A6) and (A8) imply Algorithm 1.

For Algorithm 2, if some item parameters disappear, the derivatives $\frac{\partial \mathcal{L}_{\lambda}^{\mu}}{\partial s_j}$ and $\frac{\partial \mathcal{L}_{\lambda}^{\mu}}{\partial g_j}$ make no sense. The event is reflected in $h_{i,\Lambda}$ is that $\sum_{i=1}^{N} h_{i,\Lambda} \cdot 1(\eta_{j,\Lambda} = 1)$ or $\sum_{i=1}^{N} h_{i,\Lambda} \cdot 1(\eta_{j,\Lambda} = 1)$ takes the value 0. In Algorithm 2, we should find those items and set the corresponding item parameters to 0. This is the key difference between Algorithms 1 and 2.

Appendix C. Proof of Theorem 1

Proof of Theorem 1. The denominator of Equation (A6) must be positive, so $N + \lambda E(\boldsymbol{\pi}) + \Delta > 0$, for all $E(\boldsymbol{\pi})$. Due to $\Delta < 0$, then $N + \lambda E(\boldsymbol{\pi}) > 0$ must be positive. Noting the discrete Shannon entropy $E \in (0, K\log 2]$, the conclusion $\lambda > \max_{E(\boldsymbol{\pi})}\{\frac{-N}{E(\boldsymbol{\pi})}\} = \frac{-N}{K\log 2}$ can be obtained. □

References

1. Junker, B.W.; Sijtsma, K. Cognitive assessment models with few assumptions, and connections with nonparametric item response theory. *Appl. Psychol. Meas.* **2001**, *25*, 258–272. [CrossRef]
2. Templin, J.L.; Henson, R.A. Measurement of psychological disorders using cognitive diagnosis models. *Psychol. Methods* **2006**, *11*, 287–305. [CrossRef]
3. Maris, E. Estimating multiple classification latent class models. *Psychometrika* **1999**, *64*, 187–212. [CrossRef]
4. Hartz, S.M. A Bayesian Framework for the Unified Model for Assessing Cognitive Abilities: Blending Theory with Practicality. *Diss. Abstr. Int. B Sci. Eng.* **2002**, *63*, 864.

5. DiBello, L.V.; Stout, W.F.; Roussos, L.A. Unified cognitive/psychometric diagnostic assessment likelihood-based classification techniques. In *Cognitively Diagnostic Assessment*; Routledge: London, UK, 1995; pp. 361–389.
6. Henson, R.A.; Templin, J.L.; Willse, J.T. Defining a family of cognitive diagnosis models using log-linear models with latent variables. *Psychometrika* **2009**, *74*, 191–210. [CrossRef]
7. de la Torre, J. The generalized DINA model framework. *Psychometrika* **2011**, *76*, 179–199. [CrossRef]
8. von Davier, M. A general diagnostic model applied to language testing data. *ETS Res. Rep. Ser.* **2005**, *2005*, i-35. [CrossRef]
9. Liu, J.; Xu, G.; Ying, Z. Data-driven learning of Q-matrix. *Appl. Psychol. Meas.* **2012**, *36*, 548–564. [CrossRef]
10. Chen, Y.; Liu, J.; Xu, G.; Ying, Z. Statistical analysis of Q-matrix based diagnostic classification models. *J. Am. Stat. Assoc.* **2015**, *110*, 850–866. [CrossRef]
11. Xu, G.; Shang, Z. Identifying latent structures in restricted latent class models. *J. Am. Stat. Assoc.* **2018**, *113*, 1284–1295. [CrossRef]
12. Gu, Y.; Xu, G. Identification and Estimation of Hierarchical Latent Attribute Models. *arXiv* **2019**, arXiv:1906.07869.
13. Gu, Y.; Xu, G. Partial identifiability of restricted latent class models. *Ann. Stat.* **2020**, *48*, 2082–2107. [CrossRef]
14. Chen, J. Optimal rate of convergence for finite mixture models. *Ann. Stat.* **1995**, *23*, 221–233. [CrossRef]
15. Gu, Y.; Xu, G. Learning Attribute Patterns in High-Dimensional Structured Latent Attribute Models. *J. Mach. Learn. Res.* **2019**, *20*, 1–58.
16. Templin, J.; Bradshaw, L. Hierarchical diagnostic classification models: A family of models for estimating and testing attribute hierarchies. *Psychometrika* **2014**, *79*, 317–339. [CrossRef] [PubMed]
17. Wang, C.; Lu, J. Learning attribute hierarchies from data: Two exploratory approaches. *J. Educ. Behav. Stat.* **2021**, *46*, 58–84. [CrossRef]
18. Tibshirani, R. Regression shrinkage and selection via the lasso. *J. R. Stat. Soc. Ser. B (Methodol.)* **1996**, *58*, 267–288. [CrossRef]
19. Zou, H. The adaptive lasso and its oracle properties. *J. Am. Stat. Assoc.* **2006**, *101*, 1418–1429. [CrossRef]
20. Yuan, M.; Lin, Y. Model selection and estimation in regression with grouped variables. *J. R. Stat. Soc. Ser. B (Stat. Methodol.)* **2006**, *68*, 49–67. [CrossRef]
21. Fan, J.; Li, R. Variable selection via nonconcave penalized likelihood and its oracle properties. *J. Am. Stat. Assoc.* **2001**, *96*, 1348–1360. [CrossRef]
22. Ma, J.; Wang, T. Entropy penalized automated model selection on Gaussian mixture. *Int. J. Pattern Recognit. Artif. Intell.* **2004**, *18*, 1501–1512. [CrossRef]
23. Huang, T.; Peng, H.; Zhang, K. Model selection for Gaussian mixture models. *Stat. Sin.* **2017**, *27*, 147–169. [CrossRef]
24. de la Torre, J. DINA model and parameter estimation: A didactic. *J. Educ. Behav. Stat.* **2009**, *34*, 115–130. [CrossRef]
25. Culpepper, S.A. Bayesian estimation of the DINA model with Gibbs sampling. *J. Educ. Behav. Stat.* **2015**, *40*, 454–476. [CrossRef]
26. Wang, J.; Shi, N.; Zhang, X.; Xu, G. Sequential Gibbs Sampling Algorithm for Cognitive Diagnosis Models with Many Attributes. *Multivar. Behav. Res.* **2022**, *57*, 840–858. [CrossRef]
27. Shannon, C.E. A mathematical theory of communication. *Bell Syst. Tech. J.* **1948**, *27*, 379–423. [CrossRef]
28. Thomas, M.; Joy, A.T. *Elements of Information Theory*; Wiley-Interscience: Hoboken, NJ, USA, 2006.
29. Chen, J.; Chen, Z. Extended Bayesian information criteria for model selection with large model spaces. *Biometrika* **2008**, *95*, 759–771. [CrossRef]
30. Xu, G. Identifiability of restricted latent class models with binary responses. *Ann. Stat.* **2017**, *45*, 675–707. [CrossRef]
31. Xu, G.; Zhang, S. Identifiability of diagnostic classification models. *Psychometrika* **2016**, *81*, 625–649. [CrossRef]
32. Tatsuoka, C. Data analytic methods for latent partially ordered classification models. *J. R. Stat. Soc. Ser. C (Appl. Stat.)* **2002**, *51*, 337–350. [CrossRef]
33. de la Torre, J.; Douglas, J.A. Higher-order latent trait models for cognitive diagnosis. *Psychometrika* **2004**, *69*, 333–353. [CrossRef]

mathematics MDPI

Article

Ordinal Time Series Analysis with the R Package *otsfeatures*

Ángel López-Oriona * and José A. Vilar *

Research Group MODES, Research Center for Information and Communication Technologies (CITIC), University of A Coruña, 15071 A Coruña, Spain
* Correspondence: oriona38@hotmail.com or a.oriona@udc.es (Á.L.-O.); jose.vilarf@udc.es (J.A.V.)

Abstract: The 21st century has witnessed a growing interest in the analysis of time series data. While most of the literature on the topic deals with real-valued time series, ordinal time series have typically received much less attention. However, the development of specific analytical tools for the latter objects has substantially increased in recent years. The R package **otsfeatures** attempts to provide a set of simple functions for analyzing ordinal time series. In particular, several commands allowing the extraction of well-known statistical features and the execution of inferential tasks are available for the user. The output of several functions can be employed to perform traditional machine learning tasks including clustering, classification, or outlier detection. **otsfeatures** also incorporates two datasets of financial time series which were used in the literature for clustering purposes, as well as three interesting synthetic databases. The main properties of the package are described and its use is illustrated through several examples. Researchers from a broad variety of disciplines could benefit from the powerful tools provided by **otsfeatures**.

Keywords: **otsfeatures**; ordinal time series; feature extraction; cumulative probabilities; R package

MSC: 68N01; 62-07

1. Introduction

Time series data usually arise in a wide variety of disciplines as machine learning, biology, geology, finance and medicine, among many other fields. Typically, most of the works on the analysis of these objects have focused on real-valued time series, while the study of time series with alternative ranges has been given limited attention. However, the latter type of time series naturally appear in several fields when attempting to analyze several phenomena. For instance, weekly counts of new infections with a specific disease in a particular place are often modeled through integer-valued time series [1]. In some contexts, the time series under consideration do not even take numerical values (e.g., temporal records of EEG sleep states for an infant after birth [2]). A comprehensive introduction to the topic of time series with alternative ranges including classical models, recent advances, key references, and specific application areas is provided by [3].

Categorical time series (CTS) are characterized by taking values in a qualitative range consisting of a finite number of categories, which is called ordinal range (if the categories exhibit a natural ordering) or nominal range otherwise. In this paper, the specific case of an ordinal range is considered. Time series fulfilling this condition, frequently referred to as ordinal time series (OTS), pose several challenges to the statistical practitioner. Indeed, dealing with ordered qualitative outcomes implies that some classical analytic tools must be properly adapted. For instance, standard measures of location, dispersion and serial dependence cannot be defined in the same manner as in the real-valued case, but the underlying ordering existing in the series range still allows for a meaningful definition of the corresponding quantities in the ordinal setting. For instance, in [4], a unified approach based on expected distances is proposed to obtain well-interpretable statistical measures

Citation: López-Oriona, Á.; Vilar, J.A. Ordinal Time Series Analysis with the R Package *otsfeatures*. *Mathematics* **2023**, *11*, 2565. https://doi.org/10.3390/math11112565

Academic Editors: Niansheng Tang and Shen-Ming Lee

Received: 24 April 2023
Revised: 27 May 2023
Accepted: 30 May 2023
Published: 3 June 2023

for ordinal series. In addition, sample counterparts of the corresponding measures are introduced and their asymptotic properties are derived.

Ordinal series arise in multiple fields. Some interesting examples include credit ratings of different countries [4] or degree of cloud coverage in different regions [5]. In addition, OTS appear quite naturally in psychology, since temporal measurements in such discipline often originate from ordinal scales, such as Likert questionnaires. For instance, the so-called mood time series of the married couple [6,7] represents the daily mood of a married couple over a period of 144 days, which is recorded on Likert scales. Specifically, the mood measures arise from a questionnaire with 58 items such as *"Right now I feel good"*, being the momentary intensity of emotions rated with answers 1 = *definitely not*, 2 = *not*, 3 = *not really*, 4 = *a little*, 5 = *very much*, and 6 = *extremely*. Such types of time series are naturally considered as ordinal. On the contrary, in many situations, the series under consideration are actually real-valued, but they are treated as ordinal ones because this provides several advantages. For instance, in [8], the gross wage of different individuals is divided into six ordered categories according to the quintiles of the income distribution for each year. As stated by [8], one of the advantages of considering wage categories relies on the fact that no inflation adjustment has to be made. Another illustrative example involves the well-known air quality index (AQI), which presents the status of daily air quality and shows the degree of air pollution in a particular place [9]. The air quality is often classified into six different levels which are determined according to the concentrations of several air pollutants.

While the field of OTS data analysis is still in its early stages, there are already a few interesting works on the topic. In one of the first papers, ref. [10] proposed robust methods of time series analysis which use only comparisons of values and not their actual size. As previously stated, ref. [4] developed an interesting methodology for defining statistical features in the ordinal setting, which is based on expected distances. Later, ref. [11] proposed a family of signed dependence measures for analyzing the behavior of a given OTS. There are also some recent works involving machine learning tasks in the context of ordinal series. For instance, ref. [9] considered different models to forecast the air quality levels in 16 cities of Taiwan. Two novel distances between OTS were proposed in [12] and used to construct effective clustering algorithms. The approaches were applied to datasets of financial time series and interesting conclusions were reached. Previous references highlight the remarkable growth that OTS analysis has recently undergone.

In accordance with previous comments, it is clear that the construction of software tools specifically designed to deal with OTS is crucial. However there exist no software packages in well-known programming languages (e.g., R version 4.1.2 [13], Python version 3.11.1 [14], etc.) aimed at dealing with ordinal series. Moreover, there are only a few libraries focusing on the analysis of ordinal data without a temporal nature, which are mostly written in the R language, but too often restricted to specific statistical procedures. For instance, the package **ordinal** [15] implements cumulative link models for coping with ordinal response variables. Specific functions for generating multivariate ordinal data are provided through package **MultiOrd** [16]. In a purely machine learning context, an innovative computing tool named **ocapis** containing classification algorithms for ordinal data is described in [17]. In addition, the library includes two preprocessing techniques: an instance selector and a feature selector. Note that, although their usefulness is beyond doubt, none of the previously mentioned packages is suitable to execute simple exploratory analyses, a task which should be usually performed before moving on to more sophisticated procedures. In sum, there are currently no software tools allowing to compute classical features for ordinal series.

The goal of this manuscript is to present the R package **otsfeatures**, which includes several functions to compute well-known statistical features for ordinal series. As well as giving valuable information about the behavior of the time series, the corresponding features can be used as input for classical machine learning procedures, as clustering, classification, and outlier detection algorithms. In addition, **otsfeatures** also includes some commands allowing to perform traditional inferential tasks. The two databases of financial time series described in [12] are also available in the package, along with three synthetic datasets containing OTS which were generated from different underlying stochastic processes. These data collections allow the users to test the commands available in **otsfeatures**. It is worth mentioning that some functions of the package can also be employed to analyze ordinal data without a temporal character.

In summary, the package **otsfeatures** intends to integrate a set of simple but powerful functions for the statistical analysis of OTS into a single framework. The implementation of the package was performed by using the open-source R programming language due to the role of R as the most used programming language for statistical computing. **otsfeatures** is available from the Comprehensive R Archive Network (CRAN) at https://cran.r-project.org/web/packages/otsfeatures/index.html (accessed on 15 May 2023).

The rest of the paper is structured as follows. A summary of relevant features to analyze marginal properties and the serial dependence of ordinal series is presented in Section 2. Furthermore, some novel features measuring cross-dependence between ordinal and numerical processes are also introduced. The main functions implemented in **otsfeatures** and the available datasets are presented in Section 3 after providing some background on ordinal series. In Section 4, the functionality of the package is illustrated through several examples considering synthetic data and the financial databases included in **otsfeatures**. In addition, the process of using the output of some functions to carry out traditional data mining tasks is described. Some conclusions are given in Section 5.

2. Analyzing Marginal Properties and Serial Dependence of Ordinal Time Series

Let $\{X_t\}_{t\in\mathbb{Z}}$, $\mathbb{Z}=\{\ldots,-1,0,1,\ldots\}$, be a strictly stationary stochastic process having the ordered categorical range $\mathcal{S}=\{s_0,\ldots,s_n\}$ with $s_0 < s_1 < \ldots < s_n$. The process $\{X_t\}_{t\in\mathbb{Z}}$ is often referred to as an ordinal process, while the categories in $\mathcal{S}$ are frequently called the states. Let $\{C_t\}_{t\in\mathbb{Z}}$ be the count process with range $\{0,\ldots,n\}$ generating the ordinal process $\{X_t\}_{t\in\mathbb{Z}}$, i.e., $X_t = s_{C_t}$. It is well known that the distributional properties of $\{C_t\}_{t\in\mathbb{Z}}$ (e.g., stationarity) are properly inherited by $\{X_t\}_{t\in\mathbb{Z}}$ [3]. In particular, the marginal probabilities can be expressed as

$$p_i = P(X_t = s_i) = P(C_t = i),\ i = 0,\ldots,n, \tag{1}$$

while the lagged joint probabilities (for a lag $l \in \mathbb{Z}$) are given by

$$p_{ij}(l) = P(X_t = s_j, X_{t-l} = s_i) = P(C_t = j, C_{t-l} = i),\ i,j = 0,\ldots,n. \tag{2}$$

Note that both the marginal and the joint probabilities are still well defined in the general case of a stationary stochastic process with nominal range, i.e., when no underlying ordering exists in $\mathcal{S}$. By contrast, in an ordinal process, one can also consider the corresponding cumulative probabilities, which are defined as

$$\begin{aligned} f_i &= P(X_t \le s_i) = P(C_t \le i),\ i = 0,\ldots,n-1,\\ f_{ij}(l) &= P(X_t \le s_j, X_{t-l} \le s_i) = P(C_t \le j, C_{t-l} \le i),\\ &\qquad i,j = 0,\ldots,n-1,\ l \in \mathbb{Z}, \end{aligned} \tag{3}$$

for the marginal and the joint case, respectively.

In practice, the quantities p_i, $p_{ij}(l)$, f_i, and $f_{ij}(l)$ must be estimated from a T-length realization of the ordinal process, $\overline{X}_t = \{\overline{X}_1,\ldots,\overline{X}_T\}$, usually referred to as *ordinal time series* (OTS). Natural estimates of these probabilities are given by

$$\widehat{p}_i = \frac{\sum_{k=1}^{T} I(\overline{X}_k = s_i)}{T},\ \widehat{p}_{ij}(l) = \frac{\sum_{k=1}^{T-l} I(\overline{X}_k = s_i) I(\overline{X}_{k+l} = s_j)}{T-l}, \tag{4}$$

$$\widehat{f}_i = \frac{\sum_{k=1}^{T} I(\overline{X}_k \leq s_i)}{T}, \ \widehat{f}_{ij}(l) = \frac{\sum_{k=1}^{T-l} I(\overline{X}_k \leq s_i) I(\overline{X}_{k+l} \leq s_j)}{T-l}, \tag{5}$$

where $I(\cdot)$ denotes the indicator function.

Probabilities p_i, $p_{ij}(l)$, f_i, and $f_{ij}(l)$ can be used to represent the process $\{X_t\}_{t\in\mathbb{Z}}$ in terms of marginal and serial dependence patterns. An alternative way of describing a given ordinal process is by means of features measuring classical statistical properties (e.g., centrality, dispersion, etc.) in the ordinal setting. A practical approach to define these quantities consists of considering expected values of some distances between ordinal categories [4]. Specifically, a given distance measure d defined in $\mathcal{S} \times \mathcal{S}$ gives rise to specific ordinal features. Three of the most commonly used distances are the so-called Hamming, block, and Euclidean, which are defined as

$$d_{\mathrm{H}}(s_i, s_j) = 1 - \delta_{ij}, \ d_{o,1}(s_i, s_j) = |i-j| \text{ and } d_{o,2}(s_i, s_j) = (i-j)^2, \tag{6}$$

for a pair of states s_i and s_j, respectively, where δ_{ij} denotes the Kronecker delta. The first six quantities in Table 1 describe the marginal behavior of the process X_t for a given distance d. There, the notation DIVC stands for diversity coefficient, which is an approach for measuring dispersion proposed by [18], and X_t^1 and X_t^2 refer to independent copies of X_t. In addition, the notation X_t^r was used to define a reflected copy of X_t, that is, a stochastic process independent of X_t such that $P(X_t^r = s_i) = p_{n-i}, i = 0, \ldots, n$. Note that the considered location measures pertain to the ordinal set $\mathcal{S}$. For the remaining marginal features, some assumptions are needed to obtain the ranges provided in Table 1, where $d_0^n = d(s_0, s_n)$. Particularly, for these four measures, we assume that $d_0^n = \max_{x,y\in\mathcal{S}} d(x,y)$, a property which is usually referred to as maximization. In addition, for the asymmetry, we require that $(\boldsymbol{J} - \boldsymbol{I})\boldsymbol{D}$ is a positive semidefinite matrix, where $\boldsymbol{I}$ and $\boldsymbol{J}$ denote the identity and the counteridentity matrices of order $n+1$ and $\boldsymbol{D} = (d_{ij})_{1\leq i,j\leq n+1}$, where $d_{ij} = d(s_{i-1}, s_{j-1})$ is the corresponding pairwise distance matrix. Moreover, for both the asymmetry and the skewness to be reasonable measures, we assume that the distance d is centrosymmetric, that is, $d(s_i, s_j) = d(s_{n-i}, s_{n-j}), i, j = 0, \ldots, n$. Note that, for a symmetric process (that is, a process X_t such that X_t and X_t^r have the same marginal distribution), then both the asymmetry and the skewness are expected to be zero. It is worth highlighting that, under the required assumptions, the quantities $\mathrm{disp}_{\mathrm{loc},d}$, disp_d, asym_d and skew_d can be easily normalized to the interval $[0,1]$ (or $[-1,1]$ in the case of the skewness) by dividing them by d_0^n.

Estimates of the marginal features in Table 1, denoted by means of the notation $\widehat{(\cdot)}$, where $(\cdot)$ stands for the corresponding measure (e.g., disp_d), can be obtained by considering estimates of $E[d(X_t, s_i)]$ $(i = 0, \ldots, n)$, $E[d(X_t^1, X_t^2)]$ and $E[d(X_t, X_t^r)]$ given by

$$\begin{aligned} \widehat{E}[d(X_t, s_i)] &= \frac{1}{T}\sum_{t=1}^{T} d(\overline{X}_t, s_i), \\ \widehat{E}[d(X_t^1, X_t^2)] &= \sum_{i,j=0}^{n} d(s_i, s_j)\widehat{p}_i\widehat{p}_j, \\ \widehat{E}[d(X_t, X_t^r)] &= \sum_{i,j=0}^{n} d(s_i, s_j)\widehat{p}_i\widehat{p}_{n-j}, \end{aligned} \tag{7}$$

respectively. Table 1 also contains some features assessing the serial dependence in an ordinal process. In this context, one of the most common quantities is the so-called ordinal Cohen's κ, which measures the relative deviation of the dispersion for dependent and independent random variables at a given lag $l \in \mathbb{Z}$. This quantity can take either positive or negative values, with its upper bound being 1 and its lower bound being dependent on the underlying distance d. A sample version of $\kappa_d(l)$, denoted by $\widehat{\kappa}_d(l)$, is obtained by using $\widehat{\mathrm{disp}}_d$ and the standard estimate of $E[d(X_t, X_{t-l})]$ defined as

$$\widehat{E}[d(X_t, X_{t-l})] = \frac{1}{T-l} \sum_{t=l+1}^{T} d(\overline{X}_t, \overline{X}_{t-l}). \quad (8)$$

A detailed analysis of the marginal quantities in Table 1 plus the ordinal Cohen's κ is given in [4]. In particular, the asymptotic properties of the corresponding estimates are derived and their behavior is analyzed in some simulation experiments.

Table 1. Some features of an ordinal stochastic process (top) and measuring serial cross-dependence between an ordinal and a numerical process (bottom). DIVC stands for diversity coefficient. TCC stands for total cumulative correlation, TMCLC stands for total mixed cumulative linear correlation, and TMCQC stands for total mixed cumulative quantile correlation.

Ordinal Measure	**Definition**	**Range**	**Type**
Location (standard)	$x_{\text{loc},d} = \arg\min_{x\in\mathcal{S}} E[d(X_t, x)]$	$\mathcal{S}$	Marginal
Location (with respect to s_0)	$x^0_{\text{loc},d} = \arg\min_{x\in\mathcal{S}} \lvert E[d(X_t, s_0)] - d(x, s_0)\rvert$	$\mathcal{S}$	Marginal
Dispersion (standard)	$\text{disp}_{\text{loc},d} = E[d(X_t, x_{\text{loc},d})]$	$[0, d^n_0]$	Marginal
Dispersion (DIVC)	$\text{disp}_d = E[d(X^1_t, X^2_t)]$	$[0, d^n_0]$	Marginal
Asymmetry	$\text{asym}_d = E[d(X_t, X^r_t)] - \text{disp}_d$	$[0, d^n_0]$	Marginal
Skewness	$\text{skew}_d = E[d(X_t, s_n)] - E[d(X_t, s_0)]$	$[-d^n_0, d^n_0]$	Marginal
Ordinal Cohen's κ	$\kappa_d(l) = \frac{\text{disp}_d - E[d(X_t, X_{t-l})]}{\text{disp}_d}$	-	Serial
TCC	$\Psi^c(l) = \frac{1}{n^2}\sum_{i,j=0}^{n-1} \psi_{ij}(l)^2$	$[0,1]$	Serial
Ordinal and numerical measure	Definition	Range	Type
TMCLC	$\Psi^m_1(l) = \frac{1}{n}\sum_{i=0}^{n-1} \psi^*_i(l)^2$	$[0,1]$	Serial
TMCQC	$\Psi^m_2(l) = \frac{1}{n}\sum_{i=0}^{n-1} \int_0^1 \psi^\rho_i(l)^2 d\rho$	$[0,1]$	Serial

The serial dependence of an ordinal process can be evaluated by means of alternative quantities which do not pertain to the approach based on expected distances. First, let us define the cumulative binarization of the process X_t as the multivariate process $\{\boldsymbol{Y}_t = (Y_{t,0}, \ldots, Y_{t,n-1})^\top, t \in \mathbb{Z}\}$ such that $Y_{t,i} = 1$ if $X_t \leq s_i$, $i = 0, \ldots, n-1$. By considering pairwise correlations in the cumulative binarization and fixing a lag $l \in \mathbb{Z}$, we obtain the quantities

$$\psi_{ij}(l) = Corr(Y_{t,i}, Y_{t-l,j}) = \frac{f_{ij}(l) - f_i f_j}{\sqrt{f_i(1-f_i)f_j(1-f_j)}}. \quad (9)$$

$i, j = 0, \ldots, n-1$. The features in (9) are very convenient because they play a similar role than the autocorrelation function of a numerical stochastic process. A measure of dependence at lag l can be obtained by considering the sum of the squares of all features $\psi_{ij}(l)$. In this way, we define the total cumulative correlation (TCC) as

$$\Psi^c(l) = \frac{1}{n^2} \sum_{i,j=0}^{n-1} \psi_{ij}(l)^2. \quad (10)$$

An estimate of the previous quantity can be obtained by considering $\widehat{\Psi}^c(l) = \frac{1}{n^2}\sum_{i,j=0}^{n-1}\widehat{\psi}_{ij}(l)^2$, where $\widehat{\psi}_{ij}(l)$ is the natural estimate of $\psi_{ij}(l)$ obtained by replacing f_i, f_j and $f_{ij}(l)$ by $\widehat{f}_i$, $\widehat{f}_j$ and $\widehat{f}_{ij}(l)$ in (9) computed from the realization $\overline{X}_t$.

Another interesting phenomenon that can be analyzed when dealing with an ordinal process is to measure the degree of cross-dependence that the process displays with respect to a given real-valued process. To this aim, let $\{Z_t, t \in \mathbb{Z}\}$ be a strictly stationary real-valued process with variance σ^2 and consider the correlation

$$\psi_i^*(l) = Corr(Y_{t,i}, Z_{t-l}) = \frac{Cov(Y_{t,i}, Z_{t-l})}{\sqrt{f_i(1-f_i)\sigma^2}}, \tag{11}$$

$i = 0, \ldots, n-1$, which evaluates the level of linear dependence between state s_i of process X_t and the process Z_t at a given lag $l \in \mathbb{Z}$. A more complete measure assessing general types of dependence can be constructed by defining the quantity

$$\psi_i^\rho(l) = Corr(Y_{t,i}, I(Z_{t-l} \le q_{Z_t}(\rho))) = \frac{Cov(Y_{t,i}, I(Z_{t-l} \le q_{Z_t}(\rho))}{\sqrt{f_i(1-f_i)\rho(1-\rho)}}, \tag{12}$$

$i = 0, \ldots, n-1$, where $\rho \in (0,1)$ is a probability level, q_{Z_t} denotes the quantile function of process Z_t. Note that, by considering different values for ρ, dependence at different levels at lag l can be evaluated between processes X_t and Z_t.

The features of the form $\psi_i^*(l)$ can be combined in a proper way to obtain a suitable measure of the average linear correlation between an ordinal and a numerical process. In this way, we define the total mixed cumulative linear correlation (TMCLC) at lag l as

$$\Psi_1^m(l) = \frac{1}{n}\sum_{i=0}^{n-1}\psi_i^*(l)^2. \tag{13}$$

Analogously, a measure of the average quantile correlation between both processes, so-called the total mixed cumulative quantile correlation (TMCQC) at lag l, can be defined as

$$\Psi_2^m(l) = \frac{1}{n}\sum_{i=0}^{n-1}\int_0^1 \psi_i^\rho(l)^2 d\rho. \tag{14}$$

Note that both quantities $\Psi_1^m(l)$ and $\Psi_2^m(l)$ (see the lower part of Table 1) are naturally defined in the range $[0,1]$, with the value 0 being reached in the case of null cross-dependence between X_t and Z_t. On the contrary, larger values indicate a stronger degree of cross-dependence between both processes.

Natural estimates of $\Psi_1^m(l)$ and $\Psi_2^m(l)$, denoted by $\widehat{\Psi}_1^m(l)$ and $\widehat{\Psi}_2^m(l)$, respectively, can be obtained by considering standard estimates of $\psi_i^*(l)$ and $\psi_i^\rho(l)$, denoted by $\widehat{\psi}_i^*(l)$ and $\widehat{\psi}_i^\rho(l)$, respectively. To compute the latter estimates, a T-length realization of the bivariate process $\{(X_t, Z_t), t \in \mathbb{Z}\}$, that is $(\overline{X}_t, \overline{Z}_t) = \{(\overline{X}_1, \overline{Z}_1), \ldots, (\overline{X}_T, \overline{Z}_T)\}$, is needed. In this way, estimates $\widehat{\psi}_i^*(l)$ and $\widehat{\psi}_i^\rho(l)$ take the form

$$\begin{aligned} \widehat{\psi}_i^*(l) &= \frac{\widehat{Cov}(Y_{t,i}, Z_{t-l})}{\sqrt{\widehat{f}_i(1-\widehat{f}_i)\widehat{\sigma}^2}}, \\ \widehat{\psi}_i^\rho(l) &= \frac{\widehat{Cov}(Y_{t,i}, I(Z_{t-l} \le q_{Z_t}(\rho))}{\sqrt{\widehat{f}_i(1-\widehat{f}_i)\rho(1-\rho)}}, \end{aligned} \tag{15}$$

where $\widehat{Cov}(\cdot,\cdot)$ denotes the standard estimate of the covariance between two random variables, and $\widehat{\sigma}^2$ is the standard estimate of the variance of process Z_t computed from the realization $\overline{Z}_t$. Estimates in (15) give rise to the quantities $\widehat{\Psi}_1^m(l) = \frac{1}{n}\sum_{i=0}^{n-1}\widehat{\psi}_i^*(l)^2$ and $\widehat{\Psi}_2^m(l) = \frac{1}{n}\sum_{i=0}^{n-1}\int_0^1\widehat{\psi}_i^\rho(l)^2 d\rho$.

3. Main Functions in otsfeatures

This section is devoted to present the main content of package **otsfeatures**. First, the datasets available in the package are briefly described, and then the main functions of the package are introduced, including both graphical and analytical tools.

3.1. Available Datasets in otsfeatures

The package **otsfeatures** contains some OTS datasets which can be employed to compute ordinal features, evaluate different data mining algorithms, or simply for illustrative purposes. Specifically, **otsfeatures** includes two databases of financial time series that were introduced by [12]. In addition, three simulated data collections which were also used in [12] for the evaluation of clustering algorithms are provided. A description regarding the databases which are available in **otsfeatures** is provided below.

- **Financial datasets**. The first financial dataset contains credit ratings according to Standard & Poors (S&P) for the 27 countries of the European Union (EU) plus the United Kingdom [4,12]. Each country is described by means of a monthly time series with values ranging from "D" (worst rating) to "AAA" (best rating). Specifically, the whole range consists of the $n+1=23$ states $s_0, \ldots, s_{22}$, given by "D", "SD", "R", "CC", "CCC−", "CCC", "CCC+", "B−", "B", "B+", "BB−", "BB", "BB+", "BBB−", "BBB", "BBB+", "A−", "A", "A+", "AA−", "AA", "AA+", and "AAA", respectively. The sample period spans from January 2000 to December 2017, thus resulting serial realizations of length $T=216$. The second database consists of 9402 time series for Austrian men entering the labor market between 1975 and 1980 at an age of at most 25 years [8]. The time series represent gross wages categories in May of successive years, which are labeled with the integers from 0 to 5. The quintiles of the income distribution for a given year were used to define the wage categories. In this way, category 0 represents individuals with the lowest incomes, while category 5 represents individuals with the highest incomes. The series exhibit individual lengths ranging from 2 to 32 years with the median length being equal to 22. Note that, as a natural ordering exists in the set of wage categories, the corresponding time series can be naturally treated as OTS.
- **Synthetic datasets**. Each one of the synthetic datasets is associated with a particular ordinal model concerning the underlying count process of a given OTS, namely binomial AR(p) [19], binomial INARCH(p) [20], and ordinal logit AR(1) (see Examples 7.4.6 and 7.4.8 in [3]) models for the first, second, and third database, respectively. In all cases, the corresponding collection contains 80 series with $n+1=6$ categories and length $T=600$, which are split into 4 groups of 20 series each. All series in a given dataset were generated from the corresponding type of process but the coefficients of the generating model are different between groups. The specific coefficients were chosen by considering Scenarios 1, 2, and 3 in [12]. According to the structure of these data objects, the existence of 4 different classes can be assumed.

It is worth highlighting that the databases available in **otsfeatures** were already considered in the literature for several purposes. Specifically, the dataset of credit ratings was employed by [4] to perform data analysis of OTS, while the database of Austrian employees was used by [8] to carry out clustering of categorical time series. Additionally, in [12], both collections were considered for the application of clustering procedures specifically designed to deal with OTS. Thus, it is clearly beneficial for the user to have available the corresponding databases through **otsfeatures**. On the other hand, we should note that, in each one of the synthetic datasets, the different classes can be distinguished by means of both marginal distributions and serial dependence patterns. Hence, these data objects are suitable to evaluate the effectiveness of the features in Table 1 for several machine learning problems. In fact, the usefulness of these features to carry out clustering and classification tasks (among others) in these databases is illustrated in Section 4.3. Table 2 contains a summary of the 5 datasets included in **otsfeatures**. Specifically, the last column contains the number of classes existing in a given data collection according to a context of supervised classification. For instance, 4 different classes are assumed to exist in the synthetic databases due to the fact that the 80 time series in each one were generated from 4 different stochastic processes. It is worth highlighting that datasets **CreditRatings** and **AustrianWages** do not contain clearly defined classes, and thus the notation "-" was used in the last column for these databases.

Table 2. Summary of the datasets included in **otsfeatures**. The notation No. Series, T, $|\mathcal{S}|$, and No. Classes stands for the number of series, the length of the series, the number of categories in the range of the series and the number of classes existing in a given dataset.

Dataset	Object	No. Series	T	$\lvert\mathcal{S}\rvert$	No. Classes
Credit Ratings	*CreditRatings*	28	216	23	-
Austrian Wages	*AustrianWages*	9402	Variable	6	-
Synthetic I	*SyntheticData1*	80	600	6	4
Synthetic II	*SyntheticData2*	80	600	6	4
Synthetic III	*SyntheticData3*	80	600	6	4

3.2. *Functions for Inferential Tasks*

In this section, we present some of the tools available in **otsfeatures** to perform classical statistical tasks. In particular, we first describe one specific plot which can be used to analyze the serial dependence structure of a given ordinal series. Afterwards, we give an overview of some functions allowing to carry out hypothesis testing and the construction of confidence intervals for the quantities introduced in Section 2.

3.2.1. Serial Dependence Plot

When analyzing a real-valued processes, the autocorrelation function is a classical tool for describing the corresponding serial dependence structure. Note that, in the ordinal setting, this function can still be employed by considering the underlying count process C_t introduced in Section 2, which is indeed real-valued. However, using the autocorrelation function in this context has several drawbacks, since one is treating the ordinal process as a numerical process, thus ignoring the available information about the dissimilarity between the different ordinal categories. Therefore, an alternative, more suitable tool is required to examine the serial dependence patterns of an ordinal process. In this regard, one interesting possibility consists of considering the quantity $\kappa_d(l)$ in order to evaluate the degree of dependence exhibited by the process at a given lag $l \in \mathbb{Z}$. In fact, this quantity takes the value of 0 for an i.i.d. process, while positive or negative values are associated with different types of dependence structures. Clearly, in practice, one often works with the T-length realization $\overline{X}_t$ and computes the estimated Cohen's κ, $\widehat{\kappa}_d(l)$, which can be used to describe the serial dependence patterns of the underlying ordinal process.

It is worth highlighting that the asymptotic distribution of the previous estimate is well-known in the particular case of the distance d being the block distance. Specifically, according to Theorem 7.2.1 in [4], the distribution of the estimate $\widehat{\kappa}_{d_{o,1}}(l)$ can be approximated by a normal distribution with mean $-\frac{1}{T}$ and variance $\frac{4}{T\widehat{\text{disp}}^2_{d_{o,1}}}\sum_{k,l=0}^{n-1}\left(\widehat{f}_{\min\{k,l\}}-\widehat{f}_k\widehat{f}_l\right)^2$. The previous asymptotic result is rather useful in practice, since it can be used to test the null hypothesis of serial independence at lag l. In particular, critical values for a given significance level α can be computed, and these quantities do not depend on the specific lag. Thus, a serial dependence graph analogous to the ACF-based plot in the real-valued case can be constructed. Specifically, after setting a maximum lag of interest, L, the values of $\widehat{\kappa}_{d_{o,1}}(l)$ for lags ranging from 1 to L are simultaneously depicted in one graph. Next, the corresponding critical values are added to the plot by means of a horizontal lines.

According to the asymptotic approximation for $\widehat{\kappa}_{d_{o,1}}(l)$, the critical values for an arbitrary significance level α are given by

$$\pm\frac{2\sqrt{\sum_{k,l=0}^{n-1}\left(\widehat{f}_{\min\{k,l\}}-\widehat{f}_k\widehat{f}_l\right)^2}z_{1-\alpha/2}}{\sqrt{T}\widehat{\text{disp}}_{d_{o,1}}}-\frac{1}{T}, \tag{16}$$

where z_τ denotes the τ-quantile of the standard normal distribution. The corresponding graph allows one to easily identify the collection of significant lags for a given ordinal series. Similarly to the autocorrelation plot in the numerical setting, serial dependence plots for OTS can be used for several purposes, including model selection or identification of regular patterns in the series among others.

The right panel of Figure 1 shows the serial dependence plot based on $\widehat{\kappa}_{d_{o,1}}(l)$ for one of the time series in the dataset *AustrianWages*. A maximum lag $L = 10$ was considered. The function *plot_cohens_kappa()* was employed to construct the graph. It is worth remarking that, if the argument *plot = FALSE* is used in this function, then the output is not the serial dependence plot but a list containing the corresponding p-values and critical values.

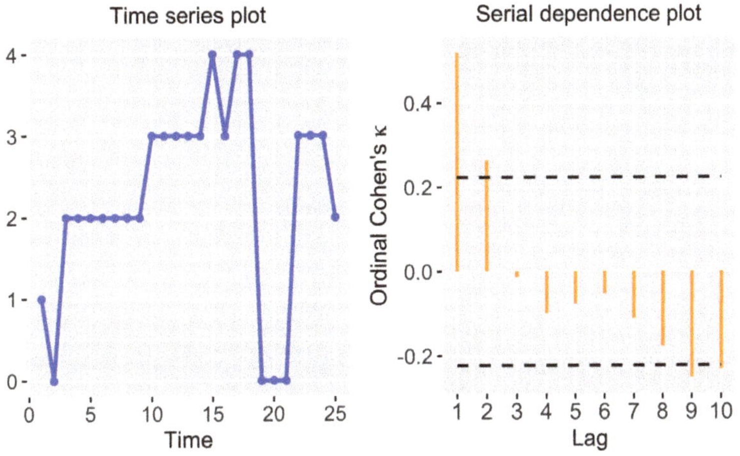

Figure 1. Time series plot (left panel) and serial dependence plot based on $\widehat{\kappa}_{d_{o,1}}(l)$ (right panel) for one of the series in dataset *AustrianWages*. The dashed lines indicate the critical values regarding the null hypothesis of the corresponding quantity being zero.

3.2.2. Hypothesis Testing and Confidence Intervals

The package **otsfeatures** allows us to perform hypothesis tests for alternative quantities in addition to $\kappa_{d_{o,1}}(l)$. In particular, there are some functions for testing that the quantities $\text{disp}_{d_{o,1}}$, $\text{asym}_{d_{o,1}}$ and $\text{skew}_{d_{o,1}}$ are equal to some specified values employing the corresponding estimates. In addition, confidence intervals for these quantities can be constructed through some commands available in the package. In both cases, the corresponding implementations rely on the asymptotic results provided in Theorem 7.1.1 in [4]. It is worth highlighting that these results are valid for the general case in which dependence between observations exist. However, when dealing with i.i.d. data, the corresponding expressions for the asymptotic means and variances are still valid but they are simplified. In this regard, package **otsfeatures** gives the user the possibility of performing hypothesis tests and constructing confidence intervals for i.i.d. data (see Theorem 4.1 in [4]). This is indicated to the corresponding functions by using the argument *temporal = FALSE*.

A summary of the main functions in **otsfeatures** allowing one to perform inferential tasks is given in Table 3.

Table 3. Some functions for inference tasks implemented in **otsfeatures**.

Output	Function in Otsfeatures
Serial dependence plot for $\widehat{\kappa}_{d_{o,1}}(l)$	*plot_ordinal_cohens_kappa()*
Test based on $\widehat{\kappa}_{d_{o,1}}(l)$	*plot_ordinal_cohens_kappa(plot = FALSE)*
Test based on $\widehat{\text{disp}}_{d_{o,1}}$	*test_ordinal_dispersion()*
Test based on $\widehat{\text{asym}}_{d_{o,1}}$	*test_ordinal_asymmetry()*
Test based on $\widehat{\text{skew}}_{d_{o,1}}$	*test_ordinal_skewness()*
Confidence interval for $\text{disp}_{d_{o,1}}$	*ci_ordinal_dispersion()*
Confidence interval for $\text{asym}_{d_{o,1}}$	*ci_ordinal_asymmetry()*
Confidence interval for $\text{skew}_{d_{o,1}}$	*ci_ordinal_skewness()*

3.3. *Functions for Feature Extraction in otsfeatures*

The package **otsfeatures** contains several functions allowing one to compute well-known statistical quantities for OTS measuring either marginal or serial properties. All commands of this type are based on the estimated features presented in Section 2. A summary of the corresponding functions is given in Table 4. In Section 4.3, the use of several functions for feature extraction available in **otsfeatures** is illustrated through several examples.

Table 4. Some functions for feature extraction implemented in **otsfeatures**.

Features	Function in Otsfeatures	Features	Function in Otsfeatures
$(\widehat{p}_0, \dots, \widehat{p}_n)$	*marginal_probabilities()*	$\widehat{\text{disp}}_d$	*ordinal_dispersion_2()*
$(\widehat{p}_{ij}(l))_{0 \leq i,j \leq n}$	*joint_probabilities()*	$\widehat{\text{asym}}_d$	*ordinal_asymmetry()*
$(\widehat{f}_0, \dots, \widehat{f}_{n-1})$	*c_marginal_probabilities()*	$\widehat{\text{skew}}_d$	*ordinal_skewness()*
$(\widehat{f}_{ij}(l))_{0 \leq i,j \leq n-1}$	*c_joint_probabilities()*	$\widehat{\kappa}_d(l)$	*ordinal_cohens_kappa()*
$\widehat{x}_{\text{loc},d}$	*ordinal_location_1()*	$\widehat{\Psi}^c(l)$	*total_c_cor()*
$\widehat{x}^0_{\text{loc},d}$	*ordinal_location_2()*	$\widehat{\Psi}^m_1(l)$	*total_mixed_c_cor()*
$\widehat{\text{disp}}_{\text{loc},d}$	*ordinal_dispersion_1()*	$\widehat{\Psi}^m_2(l)$	*total_mixed_c_qcor()*

4. Using the otsfeatures Package—AnIllustration

This section is devoted to illustrate the use of package **otsfeatures**. First we give some general considerations about the package and next, we provide some examples concerning the use of several functions for data analysis and feature extraction.

4.1. *Some Generalities about otsfeatures*

In **otsfeatures**, a T-length OTS with range $\mathcal{S} = \{s_0, s_1, \dots, s_n\}$, $\overline{X}_t = \{\overline{X}_1, \dots, \overline{X}_T\}$, is defined through a vector of length T whose possible values are the integer numbers from 0 to n. More precisely, the realization $\overline{X}_t$ is represented by using the associated realization of the generating count process C_t, that is, $\overline{C}_t = \{\overline{C}_1, \dots, \overline{C}_T\}$ such that $\overline{X}_j = s_{\overline{C}_j}, j = 1, \dots, T$. Note that the main advantage of this approach relies on the fact that only numerical vectors are needed for the representation of ordinal series.

The majority of functions in the package take as input a single OTS. For instance, functions in Table 4 return by default the corresponding estimate. Some of these functions admit the argument *features = TRUE*. In that case, the function returns a vector which contains the individual quantities which are considered to construct the corresponding estimate. For instance, the function *total_c_cor()* computes by default the estimate $\widehat{\Psi}^c(l)$. However, if we employ the argument *features = TRUE*, a matrix whose (i,j) entry contains the quantity $\widehat{\psi}_{ij}(l)$ is returned. In fact, the extraction of the individual components of some estimates can be very useful for several purposes. Functions *ots_plot()* and *plot_ordinal_cohens_kappa()* with the default settings produce the corresponding time series plot and serial dependence graph, respectively. On the contrary, the remaining functions and function *plot_ordinal_cohens_kappa()* with *plot = FALSE* return the results of the corresponding hypothesis tests, namely the test statistic, the critical value for a given significance level used as input, and the p-value. It is worth remarking that most commands in **otsfeatures** require the corresponding states to be specified in a vector of the form $(0, 1, \ldots, n)$. This is done by means of the argument *states*. In this way, several issues can be avoided. For instance, a particular realization may not include all the underlying ordinal values. Therefore, when analyzing such a series, one could ignore the existence of some states. This is properly solved by using the argument *states*.

The databases included in **otsfeatures** are defined by the means of a list named as indicated in the first column of Table 2. In the case of the synthetic databases, each list contains two elements, which are described below.

- The element called *data* is a list of vectors with the ordinal series of the corresponding collection.
- The element named *classes* includes a vector of class labels associated with the objects in *data*.

On the other hand, the lists associated with datasets *CreditRatings* and *AustrianWages* only include the element *data*, as there are no underlying class labels for these data collections.

Let us take a look at one time series in dataset *AustrianWages*, which represents a specific employee of the Austrian labor market.

```
> library(otsfeatures)
> AustrianWages$data[[10]]
[1] 3 3 3 3 3 0 0 3 2 0 4 0 0 3 3 3 4 5 4 4 4 5
```

In this series, the corresponding wage categories are identified with the integers from 0 to 5 as explained in Section 3.1 (category 0 represents the lowest incomes and category 5, the highest incomes). In this way, the previous sequence represents an individual who started with a moderate wage (category 3), then decreased his income level and finally ended up in the highest wage category. Note that this representation of the series by means of integer numbers provides a simple way of quickly examining the corresponding ordinal values.

4.2. Performing Inferential Tasks

The functions described in Section 3.2 allow the user to obtain valuable information from a given ordinal series. Let us start by analyzing one of the time series in the dataset *AustrianWages*. Before carrying out inferential tasks, we are going to visualize the corresponding time series as a preliminary step. To this aim, we can employ the function *ots_plot()*, which takes as input the time series we want to represent and a vector containing the different states.

```
ots_plot(AustrianWages$data[[100]], states = 0 : 5,
labels = 0 : 5)
```

We also employed the argument *labels = 0:5* to indicate that the states s_0 to s_5 are labeled with the integers from 0 to 5, since this is the labeling used in the original dataset (see Section 3.1). The corresponding graph is provided in the left panel of Figure 1. This series corresponds to an individual who belonged to all income levels except for the highest one (5). It is worth highlighting that, as the different states are located in the y-axis in increasing order, the plot is rather intuitive. In addition, note that, for the sake of simplicity, the different categories are treated as equidistant. Specifically, the graph is constructed by considering the block distance $d_{o,1}$ between states, which is not always suitable, since the true underlying distance often depends on the specific context. Therefore, the graph produced by function *ots_plot()* should not be treated as an accurate plot of the corresponding OTS, but as a rough representation thereof.

As stated in Section 3.2.1, function *plot_ordinal_cohens_kappa()* in **otsfeatures** allows to construct a serial dependence plot based on the estimate $\widehat{\kappa}_{d_{o,1}}(l)$. Let us represent such plot for the series in the left panel of Figure 1.

```
> sd_plot <- plot_ordinal_cohens_kappa(series = AustrianWages$data[[100]],
states = 0 : 5)
```

By default, the function considers lags from 1 to 10 (argument *max_lag*) and a significance level $\alpha = 0.05$ for the corresponding test (argument α). The resulting graph is given in the right panel of Figure 1. As the standard autocorrelation plot, the corresponding estimates are displayed in a sequential order, with dashed lines indicating the critical values for the associated test. In this case, the serial dependence plot indicates significant dependence at lags 1 and 2. Moreover, dependence at lags 9 and 10 could also be considered significant, but this may be due to chance, since multiple tests are simultaneously carried out. In addition to the dependence plot, function *plot_ordinal_cohens_kappa()* also produces numerical outputs. For instance, the corresponding p-values can be obtained by using the argument *plot = FALSE*.

```
> sd_plot <- plot_ordinal_cohens_kappa(series = AustrianWages$data[[100]],
states = 0 : 5, plot = FALSE)
> round(sd_plot$p_values, 2)
[1] 0.00 0.02 0.68 0.30 0.38 0.49 0.26 0.11 0.03 0.04
```

The p-values in the previous output corroborate that the quantity $\kappa_{d_{o,1}}(1)$ is significantly non-null, thus confirming the existence of serial dependence at the first lag. Note that the p-values associated with lags 2, 9 and 10 also indicate rejection of the null hypothesis at level $\alpha = 0.05$. However, the set of p-values should be properly adjusted to handle random rejections of the null hypothesis that can arise in a multiple testing context. For instance, the well-known Holm's method, which controls the family-wise error rate at a pre-specified α-level, could be applied to the p-values by executing the following command.

```
> p.adjust(round(sd_plot$p_values, 2), method = 'holm')
[1] 0.00 0.18 1.00 1.00 1.00 1.00 1.00 0.66 0.24 0.28
```

According to the corrected p-values, significant serial dependence still exists at lag 1, but the null hypothesis of serial independence at lags 2, 9 and 10 cannot be now rejected.

In additon to analyzing serial dependence, hypothesis tests and confidence intervals for classical ordinal quantities can be constructed by using **otsfeatures** (see Section 3.2.2). To illustrate these tasks, we consider again the previous OTS and start by testing the null hypothesis stating that the quantity $\text{skew}_{d_{o,1}}$ is equal to 0. To this aim, we employ the function *test_ordinal_skewness()*, whose main arguments are the corresponding ordinal series (argument *series*) and the assumed value for $\text{skew}_{d_{o,1}}$ (argument *true_skewness*), which is set to zero in this example.

```
> test_os <- test_ordinal_skewness(series = AustrianWages$data[[100]],
states = 0 : 5, true_skewness = 0)
> test_os$p_value
[1] 0.4239951
```

The p-value of the test resulted as 0.424. Therefore, the null hypothesis cannot be rejected at any reasonable significance level and we can assume that the series was generated from an ordinal process with 0 skewness. For illustrative purposes, let us repeat the previous test by setting *true_skewness = 2*.

```
> test_os <- test_ordinal_skewness(series = AustrianWages$data[[100]],
states = 0 : 5, true_skewness = 2)
> test_os$p_value
[1] 0.02287435
```

This time, the p-value indicates that the null hypothesis should be rejected at the standard significance level $\alpha = 0.05$; that is, we could assume that the true skewness is different from 2 at that level. However, this is no longer the case for stricter significance levels (e.g., $\alpha = 0.01$).

The construction of a confidence interval for the quantity $\text{skew}_{d_{o,1}}$ can be easily performed by using the function *ci_ordinal_skewness()*. By default, a confidence level of 0.95 is considered (argument *level*).

```
> ci_os <- ci_ordinal_skewness(series = AustrianWages$data[[100]],
states = 0 : 5)
> ci_os
Lower bound Upper bound
1  -0.7547583    1.794758
```

The lower and upper bounds of the confidence interval are given by −0.75 and 1.79, respectively. It is worth remarking that, as we are dealing with a rather short time series ($T = 25$), the interval is quite broad. In addition, note that 0 is included in the interval, which is coherent with the results of the first hypothesis test for $\text{skew}_{d_{o,1}}$ above. Let us now construct a confidence interval by considering a less strict confidence level, namely 0.90.

```
> ci_os <- ci_ordinal_skewness(series = AustrianWages$data[[100]],
states = 0 : 5, level = 0.90)
> ci_os
Lower bound Upper bound
1  -0.5498109    1.589811
```

As expected, the new interval has a shorter length than the previous one.

Inferential tasks for quantities $\text{disp}_{d_{o,1}}$, and $\text{asym}_{d_{o,1}}$ can be carried out in an analogous way by using the corresponding functions (see Table 3). Moreover, these commands can also be used when dealing with i.i.d. data by using the argument *temporal = FALSE*.

4.3. Performing Data Mining Tasks

Jointly used with external functions, **otsfeatures** becomes a versatile and helpful tool to carry out different data-mining tasks involving ordinal series. In this section, for illustrative purposes, we focus our attention on three important problems, namely classification, clustering, and outlier detection.

4.3.1. Performing OTS Classification

Firstly, we show how the output of the functions in Table 4 can be used to perform feature-based classification. We illustrate this approach by considering the data collection *SyntheticData1*, which contains 80 series generated from 4 different stochastic processes, each one of them giving rise to 20 OTS. The underlying processes are given by two binomial AR(1) and two binomial AR(2) models. Thus, each series in the dataset *SyntheticData1* has an associated class label determined by the corresponding generating process. Using the necessary functions, each series is replaced by a feature vector given by the quantities $\widehat{x}_{\text{loc},d_{o,1}}$, $\widehat{\text{disp}}_{d_{o,1}}$, $\widehat{\text{asym}}_{d_{o,1}}$, $\widehat{\text{skew}}_{d_{o,1}}$, $\widehat{\kappa}_{d_{o,1}}(1)$ and $\widehat{\kappa}_{d_{o,1}}(2)$. In all cases, the argument *distance = 'Block'* (default) is used to indicate that the block distance should be employed as the underlying block distance between states.

```
> features_1 <- unlist(lapply(SyntheticData1$data,
ordinal_location_1, states = 0 : 5, distance = 'Block'))
> features_2 <- unlist(lapply(SyntheticData1$data,
ordinal_dispersion_2, states = 0 : 5, distance = 'Block'))
> features_3 <- unlist(lapply(SyntheticData1$data,
ordinal_asymmetry, states = 0 : 5, distance = 'Block'))
> features_4 <- unlist(lapply(SyntheticData1$data,
ordinal_skewness, states = 0 : 5, distance = 'Block'))
```

```
> features_5 <- unlist(lapply(SyntheticData1$data,
ordinal_cohens_kappa, states = 0 : 5, distance = 'Block', lag = 1))
> features_6 <- unlist(lapply(SyntheticData1$data,
 ordinal_cohens_kappa, states = 0 : 5, distance = 'Block', lag = 2))
> feature_dataset <- cbind(features_1, features_2, features_3,
features_4, features_5, features_6)
```

Note that the ith row of the object *feature_dataset* contains estimated values characterizing the marginal and serial behavior of the ith OTS in the dataset. Therefore, several standard classification algorithms can be applied to these matrix by means of the R package **caret** [21]. Package **caret** requires the dataset of features to be an object of class *data.frame* whose last column must provide the class labels of the elements and be named *'Class'*. Thus, as a preliminary step, we create *df_feature_dataset,* a version of *feature_dataset* properly arranged to be used as input to **caret** functions, by means of the following chunk of code.

```
> df_feature_dataset <- data.frame(cbind(feature_dataset,
SyntheticData1$classes))
> colnames(df_feature_dataset)[7] <- 'Class'
> df_feature_dataset[,7] <- factor(df_feature_dataset[,7])
```

The function *train()* allows one to fit several classifiers to the corresponding dataset, while the selected algorithm can be evaluated, for instance, by leave-one-out cross-validation (LOOCV). A grid search in the hyperparameter space of the corresponding classifier is performed by default. First we consider a standard classifier based on k nearest neighbours (kNN) by using *method = 'knn'* as input parameter. By means of the command *trControl(),* we define LOOCV as evaluation protocol.

```
> library(caret)
> train_control <- trainControl(method = 'LOOCV')
> model_knn <- train(Class~., data = df_feature_dataset,
trControl = train_control, method = 'knn')
```

The object *model_kNN* contains the fitted model and the evaluation results, among others. The reached accuracy can be accessed as follows.

```
> max(model_knn$results$Accuracy)
[1] 0.95
```

The kNN classifier achieves an accuracy of 0.95 in the dataset *SyntheticData1*. Specifically, it produces only 4 misclassifications. Next, we study the performance of the random forest and the linear discriminant analysis. To this aim, we need to set *method = 'rf'* and *method = 'lda'*, respectively.

```
> model_rf <- train(Class~., data = df_feature_dataset,
trControl = train_control, method = 'rf')
> max(model_rf$results$Accuracy)
[1] 1

> model_lda <- train(Class~., data = df_feature_dataset,
trControl = train_control, method = 'lda')
> max(model_lda$results$Accuracy)
[1] 1
```

Both approaches reach a perfect accuracy of 1, thus improving the predictive effectiveness of the kNN classifier. For illustrative purposes, let us analyze the performance of the previous classifiers when the Hamming distance between ordinal categories is taken into account, which is indicated through the argument *distance = 'Hamming'*.

```
> features_1 <- unlist(lapply(SyntheticData1$data,
ordinal_location_1, states = 0 : 5, distance = 'Hamming'))
> features_2 <- unlist(lapply(SyntheticData1$data,
ordinal_dispersion_2, states = 0 : 5, distance = 'Hamming'))
> features_3 <- unlist(lapply(SyntheticData1$data,
ordinal_asymmetry, states = 0 : 5, distance = 'Hamming'))
> features_4 <- unlist(lapply(SyntheticData1$data,
ordinal_skewness, states = 0 : 5, distance = 'Hamming'))
> features_5 <- unlist(lapply(SyntheticData1$data,
ordinal_cohens_kappa, states = 0 : 5, distance = 'Hamming', lag = 1))
> features_6 <- unlist(lapply(SyntheticData1$data,
ordinal_cohens_kappa, states = 0 : 5, distance = 'Hamming', lag = 2))
> feature_dataset <- cbind(features_1, features_2, features_3,
features_4, features_5, features_6)

> df_feature_dataset <- data.frame(cbind(feature_dataset,
SyntheticData1$classes))
> colnames(df_feature_dataset)[7] <- 'Class'
> df_feature_dataset[,7] <- factor(df_feature_dataset[,7])

> model_knn <- train(Class~., data = df_feature_dataset,
trControl = train_control, method = 'knn')
> max(model_knn$results$Accuracy)
[1] 0.975

> model_rf <- train(Class~., data = df_feature_dataset,
trControl = train_control, method = 'rf')
> max(model_rf$results$Accuracy)
[1] 1

> model_lda <- train(Class~., data = df_feature_dataset,
trControl = train_control, method = 'lda')
> max(model_lda$results$Accuracy)
[1] 0.975
```

By considering the distance d_{H}, the kNN classifier slightly improves its performance while the linear discriminant analysis shows a small decrease in predictive effectiveness. The random forest still reaches perfect results. The classification ability of alternative sets of features, as well as the behavior of any other classifier, can be examined in an analogous way as above.

4.3.2. Performing OTS Clustering

The package **otsfeatures** also provides an excellent framework to carry out clustering of ordinal sequences. Let us consider now the dataset *SyntheticData2* and assume that the clustering structure is governed by the similarity between underlying models. In other terms, the ground truth is given by the 4 groups involving the 20 series from the same generating process (a specific binomial INARCH(p) process). We wish to perform clustering and, according to our criterion, the clustering effectiveness of each algorithm must be measured by comparing the experimental solution with the true partition defined by these four groups.

In cluster analysis, distances between data objects play an essential role. In our case, a suitable metric should take low values for pairs of series coming from the same stochastic process, and high values otherwise. A classical exploratory step to shed light on the quality of a particular metric consists of constructing a two-dimensional scaling (2DS) based on the corresponding pairwise distance matrix. In short, 2DS represents the pairwise distances in terms of Euclidean distances into a two-dimensional space preserving the original values as much as possible (by minimizing a loss function). For instance, we are going to construct the 2DS for dataset *SyntheticData2* by using two specific distances between CTS proposed by [12] and denoted by $\widehat{d}_1$ and $\widehat{d}_{PMF}$. More specifically, given two OTS $\overline{X}_t^{(1)}$ and $\overline{X}_t^{(2)}$, the metrics $\widehat{d}_1$ and $\widehat{d}_{PMF}$ are defined as follows:

$$\begin{aligned} \widehat{d}_1(\overline{X}_t^{(1)},\overline{X}_t^{(2)}) &= \sum_{i=0}^{n-1}\left(\widehat{f}_i^{(1)}-\widehat{f}_i^{(2)}\right)^2+\sum_{k=1}^{L}\sum_{i=0}^{n-1}\sum_{j=0}^{n-1}\left(\widehat{f}_{ij}^{(1)}(l_k)-\widehat{f}_{ij}^{(2)}(l_k)\right)^2, \\ \widehat{d}_{PMF}(\overline{X}_t^{(1)},\overline{X}_t^{(2)}) &= \sum_{i=0}^{n}\left(\widehat{p}_i^{(1)}-\widehat{p}_i^{(2)}\right)^2+\sum_{k=1}^{L}\sum_{i=0}^{n}\sum_{j=0}^{n}\left(\widehat{p}_{ij}^{(1)}(l_k)-\widehat{p}_{ij}^{(2)}(l_k)\right)^2, \end{aligned} \tag{17}$$

where $\mathcal{L} = \{l_1, \ldots, l_L\}$ is a set of L lags which must be determined in advance and the superscripts (1) and (2) indicate that the corresponding estimates are based on the realizations $\overline{X}_t^{(1)}$ and $\overline{X}_t^{(2)}$, respectively. Both dissimilarities assess discrepancies between the marginal distributions (first terms) and the serial dependence structures (last terms) of both series. Therefore, they seem appropriate to group the CTS of a given collection in terms of underlying stochastic processes. However, note that the distance $\widehat{d}_1$ is based on cumulative probabilities, thus taking into account the underlying ordering existing in the series range.

Let us first create the datasets *dataset_1* and *dataset_2* with the features required to compute $\widehat{d}_1$ and $\widehat{d}_{PMF}$, respectively. As the series in *SyntheticData2* were generated from binomial INARCH(1) and binomial INARCH(2) processes, we consider only the first two lags to construct the distance, i.e., we set $\mathcal{L} = \{1, 2\}$. We have to use the argument *features = TRUE* in the corresponding functions.

```
> list_marginal_1 <- lapply(SyntheticData2$data,
c_marginal_probabilities, states = 0 : 5)
> list_serial_1_1 <- lapply(SyntheticData2$data,
c_joint_probabilities, states = 0 : 5, lag = 1)
> list_serial_1_2 <- lapply(SyntheticData2$data,
c_joint_probabilities, states = 0 : 5, lag = 2)
> dataset_marginal_1 <- matrix(unlist(list_marginal_1),
nrow = 80, byrow = T)
> dataset_serial_1_1 <- matrix(unlist(list_serial_1_1),
nrow = 80, byrow = T)
> dataset_serial_1_2 <- matrix(unlist(list_serial_1_2),
nrow = 80, byrow = T)
> dataset_1 <- cbind(dataset_marginal_1, dataset_serial_1_1,
dataset_serial_1_2)

> list_marginal_2 <- lapply(SyntheticData2$data,
marginal_probabilities, states = 0 : 5)
> list_serial_2_1 <- lapply(SyntheticData2$data,
joint_probabilities, states = 0 : 5, lag = 1)
> list_serial_2_2 <- lapply(SyntheticData2$data,
joint_probabilities, states = 0 : 5, lag = 2)
> dataset_marginal_2 <- matrix(unlist(list_marginal_2),
nrow = 80, byrow = T)
> dataset_serial_2_1 <- matrix(unlist(list_serial_2_1),
nrow = 80, byrow = T)
> dataset_serial_2_2 <- matrix(unlist(list_serial_2_2),
nrow = 80, byrow = T)
> dataset_2 <- cbind(dataset_marginal_2, dataset_serial_2_1,
dataset_serial_2_2)
```

The 2DS planes can be built using the function *plot_2d_scaling()* of the R package **mlmts** [22], which takes as input a pairwise dissimilarity matrix.

```
> library(mlmts)
> distance_matrix_1 <- dist(dataset_1)
> plot_1 <- plot_2d_scaling(distance_matrix_1,
cluster_labels = otsfeatures::SyntheticData2$classes)$plot
> distance_matrix_2 <- dist(dataset_2)
> plot_2 <- plot_2d_scaling(distance_matrix_2,
cluster_labels = otsfeatures::SyntheticData2$classes)$plot
```

In the above code, the syntax *otsfeatures::* was employed because package **mlmts** includes a data collection which is also called *SyntheticData2*. The resulting plots are shown in Figure 2. In both cases, the points were colored according to the true partition defined by the generating models. For this, we had to include the argument *cluster_labels* in the function *plot_2d_scaling()*. This option is indeed useful to examine whether a specific metric is appropriate when the true class labels are known. The 2DS planes reveal that both metrics are able to identify the underlying structure rather accurately. However, there are two specific groups of OTS (the ones represented by red and purple points) exhibiting a certain degree of overlap in both plots, which suggests a high level of similarity between the corresponding generating processes.

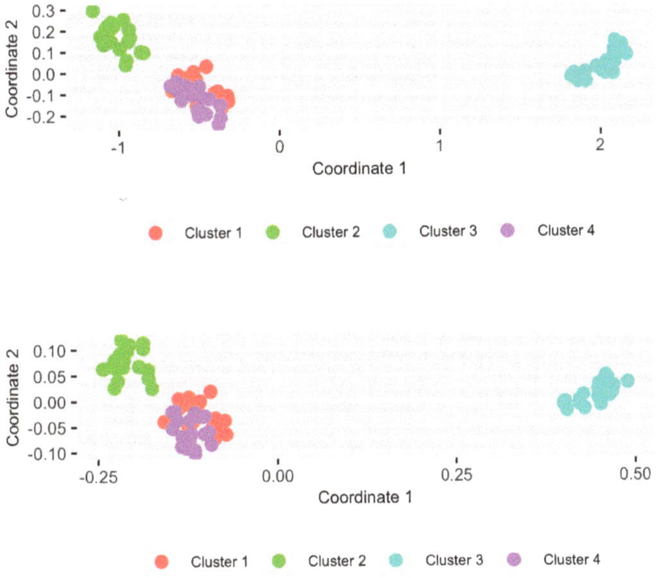

Figure 2. Two-dimensional scaling planes based on distances $\widehat{d}_1$ (top panel) and $\widehat{d}_{PMF}$ (bottom panel) for the 80 series in the dataset *SyntheticData2*.

To evaluate the clustering accuracy of both metrics, we consider the popular partitioning around medoids (PAM) algorithm, which is implemented in R through the function *pam()* of package **cluster** [23]. This function needs the pairwise distance matrix and the number of clusters. The latter argument is set to 4, since the series in dataset *SyntheticData2* were generated from 4 different stochastic processes.

```
> library(cluster)
> clustering_pam_1 <- pam(distance_matrix_1, k = 4)$clustering
> clustering_pam_2 <- pam(distance_matrix_2, k = 4)$clustering
```

The vectors *clustering_pam_1* and *clustering_pam_2* provide the respective clustering solutions based on both metrics. The evaluation of the quality of both partitions requires measuring their degree of agreement with the ground truth, which can be performed by using the Adjusted Rand Index (ARI) [24]. This index can be easily computed by means of the function *external_validation()* of package **ClusterR** [25].

```
> library(ClusterR)
> external_validation(clustering_pam_1,
otsfeatures::SyntheticData2$classes)
[1] 0.6545303
> external_validation(clustering_pam_2,
otsfeatures::SyntheticData2$classes)
[1] 0.6535088
```

The ARI index is bounded between −1 and 1 and admits a simple interpretation: the closer it is to 1, the better the agreement between the ground truth and the experimental solution is. Moreover, the value of 0 is associated with a clustering partition picked at random according to some simple hypotheses. Therefore, it can be concluded that both metrics $\widehat{d}_1$ and $\widehat{d}_{PMF}$, respectively attain moderate scores in this dataset when used with the PAM algorithm. In particular, both partitions are substantially similar. Note that a nonperfect value of ARI index was already expected from the 2DS plots in Figure 2 due to the overlapping character of Clusters 1 and 4.

The classical K-means clustering algorithm can be also executed by using **otsfeatures** utilities. In this case, we need to employ a dataset of features along with the *kmeans()* function of package stats [13].

```
set.seed(123)
clustering_kmeans_1 <- kmeans(dataset_1, c = 4)$cluster
external_validation(clustering_kmeans_1,
otsfeatures::SyntheticData2$classes)
[1] 0.6545303
> set.seed(123)
> clustering_kmeans_2 <- kmeans(dataset_2, c = 4)$cluster
> external_validation(clustering_kmeans_2,
otsfeatures::SyntheticData2$classes)
[1] 0.7237974
```

In the previous example, slightly better results are obtained when the $\widehat{d}_{PMF}$ is employed along with the K-means algorithm. Concerning $\widehat{d}_1$, its clustering accuracy is exactly the same as the one associated with the PAM algorithm. The performance of alternative dissimilarities or collections of features regarding a proper identification of the underlying clustering structure could be determined by following the same steps than in the previous experiments.

4.3.3. Performing Outlier Detection in OTS Datasets

The topic of outlier detection has received a lot of attention in the literature, either in the nontemporal setting (see, e.g., [26] for a review on outlier detection methods for univariate data) or in the context of time series data (see, e.g., [27] for a review on anomaly detection in time series data). Concerning the latter subject, it is worth noting that different notions of outlier are considered in this context (additive outliers, innovative outliers, and others). Here, we consider the outlying elements to be whole OTS objects. More specifically, an anomalous OTS is assumed to be a series generated from a stochastic process different from those generating the majority of the series in the database.

To illustrate how **otsfeatures** can be useful to carry out outlier identification, we create a dataset which includes two atypical elements. For it, we consider all the series in *SyntheticData3* along with the first two series in dataset *SyntheticData2*.

```
> data_outliers <- c(SyntheticData3$data, SyntheticData2$data[1:2])
```

The resulting data collection, *data_outliers*, contains 82 OTS. The first 80 OTS can be split into four homogeneous groups of 20 series, but those located into positions 81 and 82 are actually anomalous elements in the collection because they come from an ordinal logit AR(1) model (see Section 3.1).

A distance-based approach to perform anomaly detection consists of obtaining the pairwise distance matrix and proceeding in two steps as follows.

Step 1. For each element, compute the sum of its distances from the remaining objects in the dataset, which is expected to be large for anomalous elements.

Step 2. Sort the quantities computed in Step 1 in decreasing order and reorder the indexes according to this order. The first indexes in this new vector correspond to the most outlying elements, while the last ones to the least outlying elements.

We follow this approach to examine whether the outlying OTS in *data_outliers* can be identified by using the distance $\widehat{d}_1$ given in (17). First, we construct the pairwise dissimilarity matrix based on this metric for the new dataset.

```
> list_outl_1 <- lapply(data_outliers, c_marginal_probabilities,
states = 0 : 5)
> list_outl_2 <- lapply(data_outliers, c_joint_probabilities,
states = 0 : 5, lag = 1)
> list_outl_3 <- lapply(data_outliers, c_joint_probabilities,
states = 0 : 5, lag = 2)
> dataset_outl_1 <- matrix(unlist(list_outl_1), nrow = 82, byrow = T)
> dataset_outl_2 <- matrix(unlist(list_outl_2), nrow = 82, byrow = T)
> dataset_outl_3 <- matrix(unlist(list_outl_3),  nrow = 82, byrow = T)
> dataset_outl <- cbind(dataset_outl_1, dataset_outl_2, dataset_outl_3)
> distance_matrix_outl <- dist(dataset_outl)
```

Then, we apply the mentioned two-step procedure to matrix *distance_matrix_outl* by running

```
> order(colSums(as.matrix(distance_matrix_outl)), decreasing = T)[1:2]
[1] 81 82
```

The previous output corroborates that $\widehat{d}_1$ is able to properly identify the two series generated from anamalous stochastic processes. As an illustrative exercise, let us represent the corresponding 2DS plot for the dataset containing the two outlying OTS by using a different color for these elements.

```
> library(mlmts)
> labels <- c(otsfeatures::SyntheticData2$classes, 5, 5)
> plot_2d_scaling(distance_matrix_outl, cluster_labels = labels)$plot
```

The corresponding graph is shown in Figure 3. The 2DS configuration contains four groups of points which are rather well separated, plus two isolated elements representing the anomalous series appearing on the left part of the plot. Clearly, 2DS plots can be very useful for outlier identification purposes, since they provide a great deal of information on both the number of potential outliers and their location with respect to the remaining elements in the dataset.

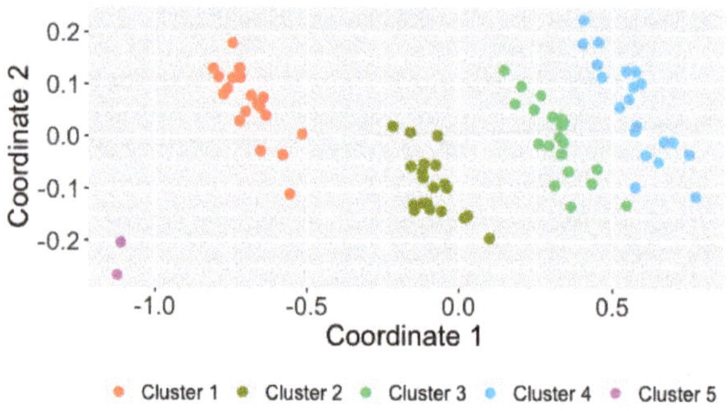

Figure 3. Two-dimensional scaling plane based on distance $\widehat{d}_1$ for the dataset containing 2 anomalous series.

In the previous example, the number of outliers was assumed to be known, which is not realistic in practice. In fact, when dealing with real OTS databases, one usually needs to determine whether the dataset at hand contains outliers. To that aim, it is often useful to define a measure indicating the outlying nature of each object (see, e.g., [28,29]), i.e., those elements with an extremely large scoring could be identified as outliers. In order to illustrate this approach, we consider the dataset *CreditRatings* and compute the pairwise distance matrix according to distance $\widehat{d}_{PMF}$.

```
> list_cr_1 <- lapply(CreditRatings$data,
marginal_probabilities, states = 0 : 22)
> list_cr_2 <- lapply(CreditRatings$data,
joint_probabilities, states = 0 : 22, lag = 1)
> list_cr_3 <- lapply(CreditRatings$data,
joint_probabilities, states = 0 : 22, lag = 2)
> dataset_cr_1 <- matrix(unlist(list_cr_1),
nrow = 28, byrow = T)
> dataset_cr_2 <- matrix(unlist(list_cr_2),
nrow = 28, byrow = T)
> dataset_cr_3 <- matrix(unlist(list_cr_3),
nrow = 28, byrow = T)
> dataset_cr <- cbind(dataset_cr_1, dataset_cr_2,
dataset_cr_3)
> distance_matrix_cr <- dist(dataset_cr)
```

As before, the sum of the distances between each series and the remaining ones is computed.

```
> outlier_score <- colSums(as.matrix(distance_matrix_cr))
```

The vector *outlier_score* contains the sum of the distances for each of the 28 countries. Since the ith element of this vector can be seen as a measure of the outlying character of the ith series, those countries associated with extremely large values in this vector are potential outliers. A simple way to detect these series consists of visualizing a boxplot based on the elements of *outlier_score* and checking whether there are points located into the upper part of the graph.

```
> boxplot(outlier_score, range = 1, col = 'blue')
```

The resulting boxplot is shown in Figure 4 and suggests the existence of one series with an abnormally high outlying score. Hence, this country could be considered to be anomalous and its individual properties be carefully investigated. Specifically, the uppermost point in Figure 4 corresponds to Belgium. Note that the prior empirical approach provides an automatic method to determine the number of outliers. Similar analyses could be carried out by considering alternative dissimilarity measures.

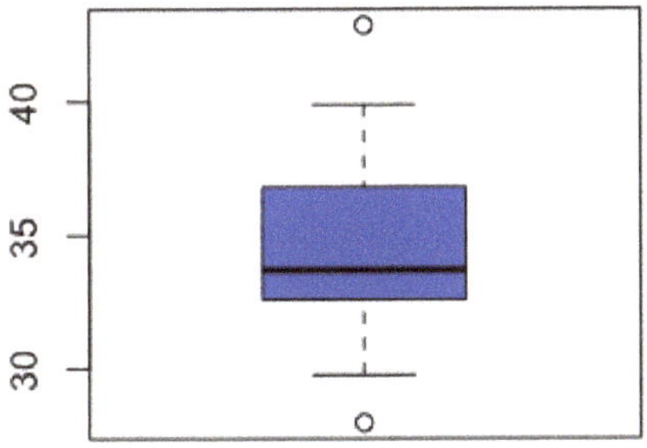

Figure 4. Boxplot of the outlying scores in dataset *CreditRatings* based on distance $\widehat{d}_{PMF}$.

5. Conclusions and Future Work

Statistical analysis of time series has experienced significant growth during the last 50 years. Although the majority of works focus on real-valued time series, ordinal time series have received a great deal of attention during the present century. The R package **otsfeatures** is fundamentally an attempt to provide different functions allowing the calculation of well-known statistical quantities for ordinal series. As well as providing an useful description about the behavior of the time series, the corresponding quantities can be used as input for traditional data mining procedures, as clustering, classification, and outlier detection algorithms. Additionally, **otsfeatures** includes some tools enabling the execution of classical inferential tasks, as hypothesis tests. It is worth highlighting that several functions of the package can also be used to analyze ordinal data without a temporal nature. The main motivation behind the package is that, to the best of our knowledge, no previous R packages are available for a general statistical analysis of ordinal datasets. In fact, the few software tools designed to deal with this class of databases focus on specific tasks (e.g., clustering or classification), application areas, or types of ordinal models. Package **otsfeatures** also incorporates two databases of financial time series and three synthetic datasets, which can be used for illustrative purposes. Although **otsfeatures** is rather simple, it provides the much-needed tools for the standard analyses which are usually performed before more complex tasks as modeling, inference, or forecasting.

A description of the functions available in **otsfeatures** is given in the first part of this manuscript to make clear the details behind the software and its scope. However, the readers particularly interested in specific tools are encouraged to check the corresponding key references, which are also provided in the paper. In the second part of the manuscript, the use of the package is illustrated by considering several examples involving synthetic and real data. This can be seen as a simple overview whose goal is to make the process of using **otsfeatures** as easy as possible for first-time users.

There are three main ways through which this work can be extended. First, as **otsfeatures** is under continuous development, we expect to perform frequent updates by incorporating functions for the computation of additional statistical features which are introduced in the future. Second, note that the statistical quantities available in **otsfeatures** are defined for univariate time series. However, multivariate time series [29,30] are becoming more and more common due to the advances in the storage capabilities of everyday devices. Thus, a software package allowing the computation of statistical features for multivariate ordinal series could be constructed in the future. Note that **otsfeatures** assumes that all the values of a given time series are known. Although this assumption is entirely reasonable, it can become too restrictive in practice, since some OTS can include missing values. In this regard, it would be interesting to implement some functions aimed at properly correcting these values so that the computation of ordinal features is not negatively affected.

Author Contributions: Conceptualization, Á.L.-O. and J.A.V.; Methodology, Á.L.-O.; Software, Á.L.-O.; Project administration, J.A.V. All authors have read and agreed to the published version of the manuscript.

Funding: This research has been supported by the Ministerio de Economía y Competitividad (MINECO) grants MTM2017-82724-R and PID2020-113578RB-100, the Xunta de Galicia (Grupos de Referencia Competitiva ED431C-2020-14), and the Centre for Information and Communications Technology Research (CITIC). CITIC is funded by the Xunta de Galicia through the collaboration agreement between the Consellería de Cultura, Educación, Formación Profesional e Universidades and the Galician universities for the support of research centers of the Sistema Universitario de Galicia (CIGUS). We would also like to acknowledge the support by the European Regional Development Fund (ERDF).

Data Availability Statement: The datasets used in this manuscript are provided in the package that the paper describes.

Acknowledgments: The authors thank the referees for their useful comments on an earlier draft of this article.

Conflicts of Interest: The authors declare no conflict of interest.

References

1. Weiß, C.H.; Pollett, P.K. Binomial autoregressive processes with density-dependent thinning. *J. Time Ser. Anal.* **2014**, *35*, 115–132. [CrossRef]
2. Stoffer, D.S.; Tyler, D.E.; Wendt, D.A. The spectral envelope and its applications. *Stat. Sci.* **2000**, *15*, 224–253. [CrossRef]
3. Weiß, C.H. *An Introduction to Discrete-Valued Time Series*; John Wiley & Sons: Hoboken, NJ, USA, 2018.
4. Weiß, C.H. Distance-based analysis of ordinal data and ordinal time series. *J. Am. Stat. Assoc.* **2020**, *115*, 1189–1200. [CrossRef]
5. Weiß, C.H. Regime-switching discrete ARMA models for categorical time series. *Entropy* **2020**, *22*, 458. [CrossRef]
6. Kupfer, J.; Brosig, B.; Brähler, E. A multivariate time-series approach to marital interaction. *GMS Psycho-Soc. Med.* **2005**, *2*, Doc08.
7. Stadnitski, T. Time series analyses with psychometric data. *PLoS ONE* **2020**, *15*, e0231785. [CrossRef] [PubMed]
8. Pamminger, C.; Frühwirth-Schnatter, S. Model-based clustering of categorical time series. *Bayes. Anal.* **2010**, *5*, 345–368.
9. Chen, C.W.; Chiu, L. Ordinal time series forecasting of the air quality index. *Entropy* **2021**, *23*, 1167. [CrossRef]
10. Bandt, C. Ordinal time series analysis. *Ecol. Model.* **2005**, *182*, 229–238. [CrossRef]
11. Weiß, C.H. Measuring Dispersion and Serial Dependence in Ordinal Time Series Based on the Cumulative Paired ϕ-Entropy. *Entropy* **2021**, *24*, 42. [CrossRef]
12. López-Oriona, Á.; Weiß, C.; Vilar, J.A. Fuzzy clustering of ordinal time series based on two novel distances with financial applications. *arXiv* **2023**, arXiv:2304.12249.
13. R Core Team. *R: A Language and Environment for Statistical Computing*; R Foundation for Statistical Computing: Vienna, Austria, 2021.
14. Van Rossum, G.; Drake, F.L. *Python 3 Reference Manual*; CreateSpace: Scotts Valley, CA, USA, 2009.
15. Christensen, R.H.B. Ordinal—Regression Models for Ordinal Data. R Package Version 2022.11-16. 2022. Available online: https://CRAN.R-project.org/package=ordinal (accessed on 15 May 2023).
16. Amatya, A.; Demirtas, H.; Gao, R. *MultiOrd: Generation of Multivariate Ordinal Variates*; R Package Version 2.4.3; R Foundation for Statistical Computing: Vienna, Austria, 2021.
17. Heredia-Gómez, M.C.; García, S.; Gutiérrez, P.A.; Herrera, F. Ocapis: R package for ordinal classification and preprocessing in scala. *Prog. Artif. Intell.* **2019**, *8*, 287–292. [CrossRef]
18. Rao, C.R. Diversity and dissimilarity coefficients: A unified approach. *Theor. Popul. Biol.* **1982**, *21*, 24–43. [CrossRef]
19. Weiß, C.H. A new class of autoregressive models for time series of binomial counts. *Commun. Stat.-Theory Methods* **2009**, *38*, 447–460. [CrossRef]
20. Ristić, M.M.; Weiß, C.H.; Janjić, A.D. A binomial integer-valued ARCH model. *Int. J. Biostat.* **2016**, *12*, 20150051. [CrossRef] [PubMed]
21. Kuhn, M. *Caret: Classification and Regression Training*; R Package Version 6.0-93; R Foundation for Statistical Computing: Vienna, Austria, 2022.
22. Lopez-Oriona, A.; Vilar, J.A. *mlmts: Machine Learning Algorithms for Multivariate Time Series*; R Package Version 1.1.1; R Foundation for Statistical Computing: Vienna, Austria, 2023.
23. Maechler, M.; Rousseeuw, P.; Struyf, A.; Hubert, M.; Hornik, K. *Cluster: Cluster Analysis Basics and Extensions*; R Package Version 2.1.2—For New Features, See the 'Changelog' File (in the Package Source); R Foundation for Statistical Computing: Vienna, Austria, 2021.

24. Campello, R.J. A fuzzy extension of the Rand index and other related indexes for clustering and classification assessment. *Pattern Recognit. Lett.* **2007**, *28*, 833–841. [CrossRef]
25. Mouselimis, L. *ClusterR: Gaussian Mixture Models, K-Means, Mini-Batch-Kmeans, K-Medoids and Affinity Propagation Clustering*; R Package Version 1.2.6; R Foundation for Statistical Computing: Vienna, Austria, 2023.
26. Shimizu, Y. Multiple Desirable Methods in Outlier Detection of Univariate Data with R Source Codes. *Front. Psychol.* **2022**, *12*, 6618. [CrossRef]
27. Blázquez-García, A.; Conde, A.; Mori, U.; Lozano, J.A. A review on outlier/anomaly detection in time series data. *ACM Comput. Surv. CSUR* **2021**, *54*, 1–33. [CrossRef]
28. Weng, X.; Shen, J. Detecting outlier samples in multivariate time series dataset. *Knowl.-Based Syst.* **2008**, *21*, 807–812. [CrossRef]
29. López-Oriona, Á.; Vilar, J.A. Outlier detection for multivariate time series: A functional data approach. *Knowl.-Based Syst.* **2021**, *233*, 107527. [CrossRef]
30. López-Oriona, Á.; Vilar, J.A. Quantile cross-spectral density: A novel and effective tool for clustering multivariate time series. *Expert Syst. Appl.* **2021**, *185*, 115677. [CrossRef]

mathematics

MDPI

Article

Optimal Model Averaging Estimation for the Varying-Coefficient Partially Linear Models with Missing Responses

Jie Zeng [1], Weihu Cheng [2] and Guozhi Hu [1,*]

[1] School of Mathematics and Statistics, Hefei Normal University, Hefei 230601, China; zengjie_zj@sohu.com
[2] Faculty of Science, Beijing University of Technology, Beijing 100124, China; chengweihu@bjut.edu.cn
* Correspondence: guozhihf@sohu.com

Abstract: In this paper, we propose a model averaging estimation for the varying-coefficient partially linear models with missing responses. Within this context, we construct a HRC$_p$ weight choice criterion that exhibits asymptotic optimality under certain assumptions. Our model averaging procedure can simultaneously address the uncertainty on which covariates to include and the uncertainty on whether a covariate should enter the linear or nonlinear component of the model. The simulation results in comparison with some related strategies strongly favor our proposal. A real dataset is analyzed to illustrate the practical application as well.

Keywords: model averaging; asymptotic optimality; HRC$_p$; varying-coefficient partially linear model; missing data

MSC: 62D10; 62G08; 62G20

Citation: Zeng, J.; Cheng, W.; Hu, G. Optimal Model Averaging Estimation for the Varying-Coefficient Partially Linear Models with Missing Responses. *Mathematics* **2023**, *11*, 1883. https://doi.org/10.3390/math11081883

Academic Editors: Niansheng Tang and Shen-Ming Lee

Received: 9 March 2023
Revised: 7 April 2023
Accepted: 12 April 2023
Published: 16 April 2023

1. Introduction

Model averaging, an alternative to model selection, addresses both model uncertainty and estimation uncertainty by appropriately compromising over the set of candidate models, instead of picking only one of them, and this generally leads to much smaller risk than that encountered in model selection. Over the past decade, various model averaging approaches, with optimal large sample properties have been actively proposed for complete data setting, such as the following: Mallows model averaging [1,2], optimal mean squared error averaging [3], jackknife model averaging [4–6], heteroscedasticity-robust C_p (HRC$_p$) model averaging [7], model averaging based on Kullback–Leibler distance [8], model averaging in a kernel regression setup [9], and model averaging based on K-fold cross-validation [10], among others.

In practice, many datasets in clinical trials, opinion polls and market research surveys often contain missing values. As far as we know, compared with the large body of research regarding model averaging for fully observed data, much less attention has been paid to performing optimal model averaging in the presence of missing data. Reference [11] studied a model averaging method applicable to situations in which covariates are missing completely at random, by adapting a Mallows criterion based on the data from complete cases. Reference [12] broadened the analysis in [11] to a fragmentary data and heteroscedasticity setup. By applying the HRC$_p$ approach in [7], Reference [13] developed an optimal model averaging method in the presence of responses missing at random (MAR). In the context of missing response data, Reference [14] constructed a model averaging method based on a delete-one cross-validation criterion. Reference [15] proposed a two-step model averaging procedure for high-dimensional regression with missing responses at random.

The aforementioned model averaging methods in a missing data setting are asymptotically optimal in the sense of minimizing the squared error loss in a large sample case, but they all concentrate mainly on the simple linear regression model. In the context of missing data, it would be interesting to study model averaging in the varying-coefficient partially linear model (VCPLM) introduced by [16], which allows interactions between a covariate and an unknown function through effect modifiers. Due to its flexible specification and explanatory power, this model has received extensive attention over the past decades. Different kinds of approaches have been raised to estimate the VCPLM, such as the following: estimation process based on the local polynomial fitting method [17], the general series method [18], and profile least squares estimation [19]. References [20–23] have developed various variable selection procedures in the VCPLM. As for model averaging in the VCPLM, only the following works have been conducted. In the measurement error model and the missing data model, References [24,25], respectively, established the limiting distribution of the resulting model averaging estimators of the unknown parameters of interest under the local misspecification framework. As pointed out by [26], this framework, which was suggested by [27], is a useful tool for asymptotic analysis, but its realism is subject to considerable criticism. Additionally, these two works studied existing model averaging strategies, based on the focused information criterion, but did not consider any new model averaging method with asymptotic optimality. When all data are available, References [26,28] developed two asymptotically optimal model averaging approaches for the VCPLM, based on a Mallows-type criterion and a jackknife criterion, respectively.

As far as we know, there remains no optimal model averaging approach developed for the VCPLM with missing responses. The main goal of the current paper was to fill this gap. To the best of our knowledge, this paper is the first to study the asymptotically optimal model averaging approach for the VCPLM in the presence of responses MAR without the local misspecification assumption. However, existing results are difficult to directly extend to our setup for the following two reasons. Firstly, existing optimal model averaging approaches in the VCPLM with complete data, such as the Mallows model averaging method proposed by [26], and the jackknife model averaging method advocated by [28], cannot be directly applied to our problem. Secondly, in contrast with the case in linear missing data models, studied by [13,14], our analysis is significantly complicated by two kinds of uncertainty in the VCPLM: the uncertainty on the selection of variables, and the uncertainty on whether a covariate should be allocated to the linear or nonlinear component of the model. These uncertainties have not been investigated much by the VCPLM literature. Motivated by these two challenges, we suggest a new model averaging approach for the VCPLM with responses MAR via the HRC_p criterion. This new approach was developed by introducing a synthetic response based on an inverse probability weighted (IPW) technique. Then, HRC_p model averaging could be conducted easily. Under certain assumptions, the weights selected by minimizing the HRC_p criterion are demonstrated to be asymptotically optimal. Furthermore, we numerically illustrate that our method is always superior to its rivals in several designs with different kinds of model uncertainty. The detailed research procedures and methods can be found in Figure 1.

The remainder of this article is organized as follows. We construct the model averaging estimator and establish its asymptotic optimality in Section 2. A simulation study is conducted in Section 3 to illustrate the finite sample performance of our strategy and a real data example is provided in Section 4. Section 5 contains some conclusions. Detailed proofs of the main results are relegated to the Appendix A.

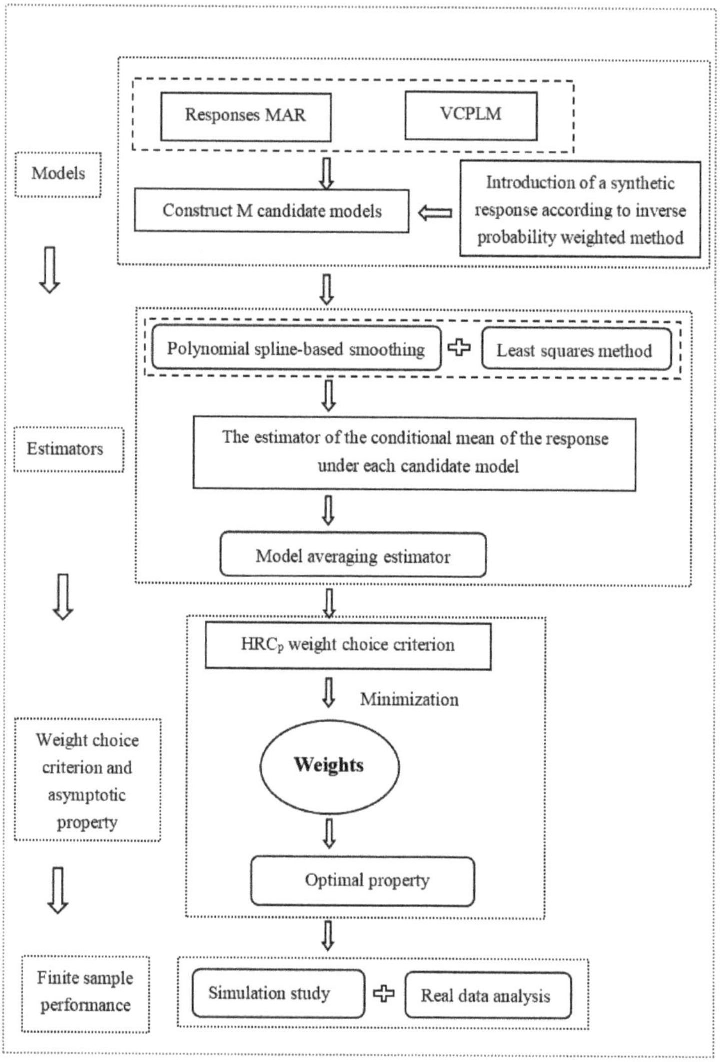

Figure 1. The flow chart of our research.

2. Model Averaging Estimation

2.1. Model and Estimators

We considered the following VCPLM:

$$y_i = \mu_i + \epsilon_i = X_i'\beta + Z_i'\alpha(u_i) + \epsilon_i = \sum_{p=1}^{\infty} x_{ip}\beta_p + \sum_{q=1}^{\infty} z_{iq}\alpha_q(u_i) + \epsilon_i, \qquad i = 1, \dots, n, \quad (1)$$

where y_i is a scalar response variable, (X_i, Z_i, u_i) are covariates with X_i and Z_i being countably infinite, β is an unknown coefficient vector associated with X_i, $\alpha(\cdot)$ is an unknown coefficient function vector associated with Z_i, ϵ_i is a random statistical error with $E(\epsilon_i|X_i, Z_i, u_i) = 0$ and $E(\epsilon_i^2|X_i, Z_i, u_i) = \sigma^2$. As in [26,29], we assume that the dimension of u_i is one. Model (1) is flexible enough to cover a variety of other existing models, such as the following: the linear model that was studied by [1,4], the partially linear model that was studied by [30] and the varying-coefficient model that was studied by [29]. For this model, we focus on the case where all covariates are always fully observed while some observations of the response variable may be missing. Specifically, we assume that y_i is MAR in the sense that:

$$P(\delta_i = 1 | y_i, X_i, Z_i, u_i) = P(\delta_i = 1 | X_i, Z_i, u_i) \equiv \pi(X_i, Z_i, u_i), \tag{2}$$

where $\delta_i = 1$ if y_i is completely observed, otherwise $\delta_i = 0$, and the selection probability function $\pi(X_i, Z_i, u_i)$ is bounded away from 0.

As in most literature on model averaging, we aimed to estimate the conditional mean of the response data $Y = (y_1, \ldots, y_n)'$, i.e., $\mu = (\mu_1, \ldots, \mu_n)'$, which is especially useful in prediction. However, owing to the presence of the missing data, none of the existing optimal model averaging estimations for complete data could be directly utilized in our setting. We addressed this problem by introducing a synthetic response $H_{\pi,i} = \delta_i y_i / \pi(X_i, Z_i, u_i)$. By the aforementioned MAR assumption and some simple calculations, it is easy to observe that $E(H_{\pi,i} | X_i, Z_i, u_i) = E(y_i | X_i, Z_i, u_i) = \mu_i$ and $\text{Var}(H_{\pi,i} | X_i, Z_i, u_i) = \sigma^2_{\pi,i}$, where $\sigma^2_{\pi,i} = [\{\pi(X_i, Z_i, u_i)\}^{-1} - 1]\mu_i^2 + \{\pi(X_i, Z_i, u_i)\}^{-1}\sigma^2$. Therefore, under Model (1) and the MAR assumption, we have:

$$H_{\pi,i} = \mu_i + \epsilon_{\pi,i}, \qquad i = 1, \ldots, n, \tag{3}$$

where $\epsilon_{\pi,i} = H_{\pi,i} - E(y_i | X_i, Z_i, u_i)$ satisfying $E(\epsilon_{\pi,i} | X_i, Z_i, u_i) = 0$ and $\text{Var}(\epsilon_{\pi,i} | X_i, Z_i, u_i) = \sigma^2_{\pi,i}$. As is apparent, in Model (3) the completely observed cases are weighted by their corresponding inverse selection probabilities, while the missing cases are weighted by zeros. Then, the analysis is conducted on the basis of the weighted data. By introducing the fully observed synthetic response $H_{\pi,i}$, we obtain a new Model (3) the conditional expectation of which is equivalent to that of Model (1). Thus, the HRC$_p$ model averaging estimation for μ_i, the conditional mean of Model (1), can be alternatively derived by studying the HRC$_p$ model averaging estimation for Model (3) with the synthetic data when $\pi(X_i, Z_i, u_i)$ is known.

Supposing that there are M candidate VCPLMs to approximate the true data generating process of y_i, which is given in (1), and the mth candidate VCPLM comprises p_m covariates in X_i and q_m covariates in Z_i. Accordingly, there are M candidate models to approximate Model (3), and the mth candidate model contains the same covariates as that of the mth candidate VCPLM for (1). Specifically, the mth candidate model is:

$$H_{\pi,i} = X'_{(m),i}\beta_{(m)} + Z'_{(m),i}\alpha_{(m)}(u_i) + e_{(m),i} + \epsilon_{\pi,i}, \qquad i = 1, \ldots, n, \tag{4}$$

where $X_{(m),i}$ is the p_m-dimensional sub-vector of X_i and $\beta_{(m)}$ is the corresponding unknown coefficient vector, $Z_{(m),i} = (z_{(m),i1}, \ldots, z_{(m),iq_m})'$ is the q_m-dimensional sub-vector of Z_i and $\alpha_{(m)}(u_i) = (\alpha_{(m),1}(u_i), \ldots, \alpha_{(m),q_m}(u_i))'$ is the corresponding unknown coefficient function, $e_{(m),i} = \mu_i - X'_{(m),i}\beta_{(m)} - Z'_{(m),i}\alpha_{(m)}(u_i)$ denotes the approximation error of the mth candidate model. Details of the model averaging estimation procedure in our setup are provided below.

We employed the polynomial spline-based smoothing strategy to estimate each coefficient function first. Without loss of generality, suppose that the covariate u is distributed on a compact interval $[0, 1]$. Denote the polynomial spline space of degree ϱ on interval $[0, 1]$ by Ψ. We introduce a sequence of knots on the interval $[0, 1]$: $k_{-\varrho} = \cdots = k_{-1} = k_0 = 0 < k_1 < \cdots < k_{J_n} < 1 = k_{J_n+1} = \cdots = k_{J_n+\varrho+1}$, where the number of interior knots J_n increases with sample size n. The spline basis functions are polynomials of degree ϱ on all sub-intervals $[k_j, k_{j+1}), j = 0, \ldots, J_n - 1$ and $[k_{J_n}, 1]$, and are $(\varrho - 1)$-times continuously differentiable on $[0, 1]$. Let $B(\cdot) = (B_{-\varrho}(\cdot), \ldots, B_{J_n}(\cdot))'$ be a vector of the B-spline basis function in space Ψ. According to B-spline theory, there exists a $B'(u)\theta_{(m),q}$ in Ψ for some $(J_n + \varrho + 1)$-dimensional spline coefficient vector $\theta_{(m),q} = (\theta_{(m),q,-\varrho}, \ldots, \theta_{(m),q,J_n})'$ such that $\max_{m,q} \sup_{u \in [0,1]} |\alpha_{(m),q}(u) - B'(u)\theta_{(m),q}| = O((J_n + \varrho + 1)^{-d})$, where $\alpha_{(m),q}(u)$ is the qth element of $\alpha_{(m)}(u)$. We would like to estimate $\beta_{(m)}$ and $\theta_{(m)} = (\theta'_{(m),1}, \ldots, \theta'_{(m),q_m})'$ by the least squares method based on the criterion:

$$\min_{\beta_{(m)},\theta_{(m)}} \sum_{i=1}^{n} \left\{ H_{\pi,i} - X'_{(m),i}\beta_{(m)} - \sum_{q=1}^{q_m} z_{(m),iq} B'(u_i)\theta_{(m),q} \right\}^2. \quad (5)$$

Let $G_{(m),i} = (z_{(m),i1}B'(u_i), \ldots, z_{(m),iq_m}B'(u_i))'$ be an $\{q_m(J_n + \varrho + 1)\}$-dimensional vector. Denote $H_\pi = (H_{\pi,1}, \ldots, H_{\pi,n})'$, $X_{(m)} = (X_{(m),1}, \ldots, X_{(m),n})'$ and $G_{(m)} = (G_{(m),1}, \ldots, G_{(m),n})'$. Here, we assume that the regressor matrix $\widetilde{X}_{(m)} = (X_{(m)}, G_{(m)})$ has full column rank $l_m = p_m + \{q_m(J_n + \varrho + 1)\}$. The solution to the minimization problem provided in (5) can be expressed as:

$$\hat{\beta}_{(m,\pi)} = \{X'_{(m)}(I - Q_{(m)})X_{(m)}\}^{-1}X'_{(m)}(I - Q_{(m)})H_\pi, \quad (6)$$

$$\hat{\theta}_{(m,\pi)} = (G'_{(m)}G_{(m)})^{-1}G'_{(m)}(H_\pi - X_{(m)}\hat{\beta}_{(m,\pi)}), \quad (7)$$

where $Q_{(m)} = G_{(m)}(G'_{(m)}G_{(m)})^{-1}G'_{(m)}$. Let $\Phi_{(m)} = (I - Q_{(m)})X_{(m)}$, then the estimator of μ under the mth candidate model follows:

$$\hat{\mu}_{(m,\pi)} = X_{(m)}\hat{\beta}_{(m,\pi)} + G_{(m)}\hat{\theta}_{(m,\pi)} = \{Q_{(m)} + \Phi_{(m)}(\Phi'_{(m)}\Phi_{(m)})^{-1}\Phi'_{(m)}\}H_\pi. \quad (8)$$

Denoting $P_{(m)} = Q_{(m)} + \Phi_{(m)}(\Phi'_{(m)}\Phi_{(m)})^{-1}\Phi'_{(m)}$, we obtain $\hat{\mu}_{(m,\pi)} = P_{(m)}H_\pi$.

To smooth estimators across all candidate models, we may define the model averaging estimator of μ as:

$$\hat{\mu}_\pi(w) = \sum_{m=1}^{M} w_m\hat{\mu}_{(m,\pi)} = \sum_{m=1}^{M} w_m P_{(m)}H_\pi \equiv P(w)H_\pi, \quad (9)$$

where $w = (w_1, \ldots, w_M)'$ is a weight vector in the set $\mathcal{W} = \{w \in [0,1]^M : \sum_{m=1}^{M} w_m = 1\}$.

2.2. Weight Choice Criterion and Asymptotically Optimal Property

Obviously, the weight vector w, which represents the contribution of each candidate model in the final estimation, plays a central role in (9). Our weight choice criterion was motivated by applying the HRC$_p$ method of [7], which is designed for the complete data setting, and is defined as follows:

$$C_\pi(w) = \|H_\pi - \hat{\mu}_\pi(w)\|^2 + 2\sum_{i=1}^{n} \hat{e}^2_{\pi,i}P_{ii}(w), \quad (10)$$

where $\hat{e}_{\pi,i}$ is the residual from a preliminary estimation, $P_{ii}(w)$ is the ith diagonal element of the matrix $P(w)$. As suggested by [7], $\hat{e}_{\pi,i}$ can be obtained by a model, indexed by M^*, which includes all the regressors in the candidate models. That is:

$$\hat{e}_\pi = \sqrt{n/(n - l_{M^*})}(I - P_{M^*})H_\pi, \quad (11)$$

where l_{M^*} is the rank of the regressor matrix in model M^*, $\hat{e}_\pi = (\hat{e}_{\pi,1}, \ldots, \hat{e}_{\pi,n})'$.

So far, we have assumed that the selection probability function is known. This is, of course, not the case in real-world data analysis, and the proposed criterion (10) is, hence, computationally infeasible. To obtain a feasible criterion in practice, we needed to estimate $\pi(X_i, Z_i, u_i)$ first. Following much of the missing data literature, and under the MAR assumption defined above, we assume that for an unknown parameter vector η and $T_i = (X'_i, Z'_i, u_i)'$ we have:

$$\pi(X_i, Z_i, u_i) = \pi(T_i, \eta), \quad (12)$$

for some function $\pi(\cdot, \eta)$, the form which is known to be a finite-dimensional parameter η. Let $\hat{\eta}$ be the maximum likelihood estimator (MLE) of η. Then the selection probability function can be estimated by $\pi(T_i, \hat{\eta})$. In what follows, the Greek letter indexed by $\hat{\pi}$ denotes that it is obtained by replacing $\pi(X_i, Z_i, u_i)$ in its equation with the estimator $\pi(T_i, \hat{\eta})$. A feasible form of the weight choice criterion based on HRC$_p$ method is, thus, given by:

$$C_{\hat{\pi}}(w) = \|H_{\hat{\pi}} - \hat{\mu}_{\hat{\pi}}(w)\|^2 + 2\sum_{i=1}^{n} \hat{e}^2_{\hat{\pi},i} P_{ii}(w), \tag{13}$$

and the weight vector can be obtained by:

$$\hat{w} = \arg\min_{w \in \mathcal{W}} C_{\hat{\pi}}(w). \tag{14}$$

Then, the corresponding model averaging estimator of μ can be expressed as $\hat{\mu}_{\hat{\pi}}(\hat{w})$, and its asymptotic optimality can be developed under some regularity conditions.

Some notations and definitions are required before we list these conditions. Write $l(\eta) = E[\delta \log \pi(T, \eta) + (1-\delta)\log\{1 - \pi(T, \eta)\}]$, $X = (X_1, \ldots, X_n)'$, $Z = (Z_1, \ldots, Z_n)'$, $U = (u_1, \ldots, u_n)'$. Define the squared error loss of $\hat{\mu}_\pi(w)$ and the corresponding risk as $L_\pi(w) = \|\hat{\mu}_\pi(w) - \mu\|^2$ and $R_\pi(w) = E(L_\pi(w)|X, Z, U)$. Let $\xi_\pi = \inf_{w \in \mathcal{W}} R_\pi(w)$, w^0_m be a $M \times 1$ vector with the mth element being 1 and the others being 0, and let Θ_η be the parameter space of η. Define r as a positive integer and $\tau \in (0, 1]$, such that $d = (r + \tau) > 0.5$. Let $\mathcal{S}$ be a collection of functions s on $[0, 1]$ whose rth derivative $s^{(r)}$ exists and satisfies the Lipschitz condition of order τ, i.e.,

$$|s^{(r)}(t^*) - s^{(r)}(t)| \le C_s |t^* - t|^\tau, \quad \text{for } 0 \le t^*, t \le 1,$$

where C_s is a positive constant. All limiting processes discussed throughout the paper are under $n \to \infty$. The conditions needed to derive asymptotic optimality are as follows:

- (Condition (C.1)) $l(\eta)$ has a unique maximum at η_0 in Θ_η, where η_0 is an inner point of Θ_η and Θ_η is compact. $\pi(T_i, \eta) \ge C_\pi > 0$, and $\pi(T_i, \eta)$ is twice continuously differentiable with respect to η, where C_π is a constant. $\max_{1 \le i \le n} \left\| \frac{\partial \pi(T_i, \eta)}{\partial \eta} \right\| = O_p(1)$ for all η's in a neighborhood of η_0.
- (Condition (C.2)) $\max_{1 \le i \le n} E(\epsilon_i^{4K} | X_i, Z_i, u_i) \le C_\epsilon < \infty$ for some integer $1 \le K < \infty$ and for some constant C_ϵ. There exists a constant C_μ, such that $\max_{1 \le i \le n} |\mu_i| \le C_\mu$.
- (Condition (C.3)) $M\xi_\pi^{-2K} \sum_{m=1}^{M} \{R_\pi(w^0_m)\}^K \to 0$, where K is given in Condition (C.2).
- (Condition (C.4)) Each coefficient function $\alpha_q(\cdot) \in \mathcal{S}$.
- (Condition (C.5)) The density function of u, say f, is bounded away from 0 and infinity on $[0, 1]$.
- (Condition (C.6)) $\max_{1 \le m \le M} \max_{1 \le i \le n} P_{(m),ii} = O(n^{-1/2})$, where $P_{(m),ii}$ denotes the ith diagonal element of $P_{(m)}$.
- (Condition (C.7)) $n^{1/2}/\xi_\pi \to 0$.
- (Condition (C.8)) $l_{M^*} = O(n^{1/2})$.

Condition (C.1) is from [31] and is similar to Condition (C1) of [13], which ensures the consistency and asymptotic normality of the MLE $\hat{\eta}$. The first part of Condition (C.2) is a commonly used assumption of the conditional moment of the random error term in model averaging literature; see, for example, [2,4,26]. The second part of Condition (C.2) is the same as the assumption (C.2) of [32] that bounds the conditional expectation μ_i. Condition (C.3) not only requires $\xi_\pi \to \infty$, but also requires that M and $\max_{1 \le m \le M} R_\pi(w^0_m)$ tend to infinity slowly enough. Such a condition can be viewed as an analogous version of Assumption 2.3 in [7], in which the authors proposed the HRC$_p$ model averaging method in a complete data setting. Conditions (C.4) and (C.5) are two general requirements that are necessary for studies of the B-spline basis, see [29,33]. Condition (C.6), an assumption that excludes peculiar models, is from [7]. A similar condition, which is frequently used in studies of optimal model averaging based on cross-validation, can be found in assumption (5.2) of [34] and (24) of [5]. Condition (C.7) states that ξ_π approaches infinity at a rate faster than $n^{1/2}$, and is the same as Condition (C.3) of [35] and implied by (A3) of [36]. Condition (C.8) limits the increasing rate of the number of covariates. A similar condition is used in other model averaging studies, such as (22) in [5]. In fact, (22) in [5] can be obtained by combining our Conditions (C.7) and (C.8).

The following theorem states the asymptotic optimality of the corresponding model averaging estimator based on the feasible HRC$_p$ criterion.

Theorem 1. *Suppose that Conditions (C.1)–(C.8) hold. Then, we have*

$$\frac{L_{\hat{\pi}}(\hat{w})}{\inf_{w\in\mathcal{W}} L_{\hat{\pi}}(w)} \to 1 \tag{15}$$

in probability as $n \to \infty$.

Theorem 1 reveals that when the selection probability function is estimated by $\pi(T_i, \hat{\eta})$ and the conditions listed are satisfied, $\hat{w}$, the weight vector selected by the feasible HRC$_p$ criterion leads to a squared error loss that is asymptotically identical to that of the infeasible best possible weight vector. This indicates the asymptotic optimality of the resulting model averaging estimator $\hat{\mu}_{\hat{\pi}}(\hat{w})$. The detailed proof of Theorem 1 is in Appendix A.

3. A Simulation Study

In this section, we conduct a simulation study with five designs to evaluate the performance of the proposed method, including selection of the interior knot number and a comparison of several model selection and model averaging procedures.

3.1. Data Generation Process

Our setup was based on the setting of [26], except that the response variable is subject to missingness. Specifically, we generated data from the following model:

$$y_i = \mu_i + \epsilon_i = \sum_{p=1}^{200} x_{ip}\beta_p + \sum_{q=1}^{200} z_{iq}\alpha_q(u_i) + \epsilon_i, \tag{16}$$

where $X_i = (x_{i1}, \ldots, x_{i200})'$ and $Z_i = (z_{i1}, \ldots, z_{i200})'$ are drawn from a multivariate normal distribution with mean 0 and covariance matrix $\Lambda = (\lambda_{ij})$ with $\lambda_{ij} = 0.5^{|i-j|}$, $u_i \sim \text{Uniform}(0,1)$, $\epsilon_i \sim N(0, \zeta^2(x_{i2}^2 + 0.01))$. We changed the value of ζ, so that the population $R^2 = \text{var}(\mu_i)/\text{var}(y_i)$ varied from 0.1 to 0.9, where var$(\cdot)$ was the sample variance. The coefficients of the linear part were set as $\beta_p = 1/p^2$, and the coefficient functions were determined by $\alpha_q(u_i) = \sin(2\pi q u_i)/q$. Under the MAR assumption, we generated the missingness indicator δ_i from the following two logistic regression models, respectively:

Case 1: $\text{logit}\{P(\delta_i = 1|X_i, Z_i, u_i)\} = 1.2 + 0.5u_i + 0.5x_{i1}$;
Case 2: $\text{logit}\{P(\delta_i = 1|X_i, Z_i, u_i)\} = 0.1 + 0.7u_i + 0.7x_{i1}$.

For the preceding two cases, the average missing rates (MR) were about 20% and 40%, respectively. In this simulation, we assumed the parametric function $\pi(T_i, \eta)$ applied in our proposed method was correctly specified in both cases.

To investigate the performance of the methods as comprehensively as possible, the sample sizes were taken to be $n = 100$ and $n = 200$, and five simulation designs, with different M and covariate settings, were considered. These five designs are displayed in Table 1, in which INT$(\cdot)$ returns the nearest integer from the corresponding element. So, in Design 1 and Design 3, $M = 14$ and 18 for the two sample sizes. We required every candidate model to contain at least one covariate in the linear part, leading to $2^5 - 1$ candidate models in Designs 2 and 4. In Design 5, each candidate model included at least one covariate of $\{x_{i1}, x_{i2}, x_{i3}, z_{i1}\}$ in the linear part and one covariate of $\{x_{i1}, x_{i2}, x_{i3}, z_{i1}\}$

in the nonparametric part, and each covariate could not exist in both parts. This led to $C_4^1(2^3-1)+C_4^2(2^2-1)+C_4^3=50$ candidate models. In summary, in the first four designs, Designs 1 and 3 for the nested case and Designs 2 and 4 for the non-nested case, there was, a priori knowledge of which covariates should enter the nonparametric part of the model, but the specification of the linear part was uncertain. The last design incorporated two types of uncertainty: uncertainty on the choice of variables and uncertainty on whether the variable should be in the linear or nonparametric part given that it is already included in the model.

Table 1. Summary of designs in simulation study.

Design	M	Covariate Setting
1	INT($3n^{1/3}$)	All candidate models shared a common nonparametric structure of $z_{i1}\alpha_1(u_i)$, and their parametric parts were a set of $\{x_{i1}, x_{i2}, \cdots, x_{iM}\}$, with the mth candidate model including the first m covariates. In other words, all of the candidate models were nested.
2	2^5-1	Identical to Design 1 except that all candidate models were non-nested, and their linear parts were constructed by varying combinations of $\{x_{i1}, x_{i2}, \cdots, x_{i5}\}$.
3	INT($3n^{1/3}$)	Identical to Design 1 except that all candidate models shared a common nonparametric structure of $z_{i1}\alpha_1(u_i)+z_{i2}\alpha_2(u_i)$.
4	2^5-1	Identical to Design 2 except that all candidate models shared a common nonparametric structure of $z_{i1}\alpha_1(u_i)+z_{i2}\alpha_2(u_i)$.
5	50	The covariate set included $\{x_{i1}, x_{i2}, x_{i3}, z_{i1}\}$. Each candidate model included at least one covariate in the linear part and one covariate in the nonparametric part, and each covariate could not exist in both parts.

3.2. *Estimation and Comparison*

3.2.1. Selection of the Knot Number

We used the cubic B-splines to approximate each nonparametric function, and the spline basis matrix was produced by the function "bs(·, df)" in the"splines" package of the R project, where the degree of freedom df = 4 + number of knots. We assessed the effect of the knot number on the performance of our proposal based on the following risk:

$$L_\mu = \frac{1}{1000}\sum_{r=1}^{1000} \|\hat{\mu}_{\hat{\pi}}(\hat{w})^{(r)} - \mu\|^2, \tag{17}$$

where 1000 was the number of simulation trials and $\hat{\mu}_{\hat{\pi}}(\hat{w})^{(r)}$ was the model averaging estimator of μ in the rth run.

We set $\zeta = 1$ and $n = 200$ to show the impact of the number of interior knots on the risk of our proposed procedure in the five designs. Since the simulated results produced were similar for Designs 1 and 2, and for Designs 3 and 4, we only report the results from Designs 1, 3 and 5, which are presented in Figure 2. This figure demonstrates the risk against df for a variety of combinations of designs and missing rates considered. From Figure 2, we note that, for almost all situations considered, generally the risk tended to increase with the number of knots. In other words, the larger number of knots yielded a more serious oversmoothing effect, and, hence, lower estimation accuracy. As suggested by this figure, for our proposed model averaging method, we specified df = 4, which corresponded to the smallest risk. Therefore, in this simulation, we adopted the suggestion of applying df = 4 for all five designs. In other words, the number of knots was set to be 0 in our analysis, which resulted in a basis for ordinary polynomial regression. The number of knots of the B-spline basis function was also set to be 0 in [29], which examined the influence of the knot number on the model averaging method for the varying-coefficient model when all data were available.

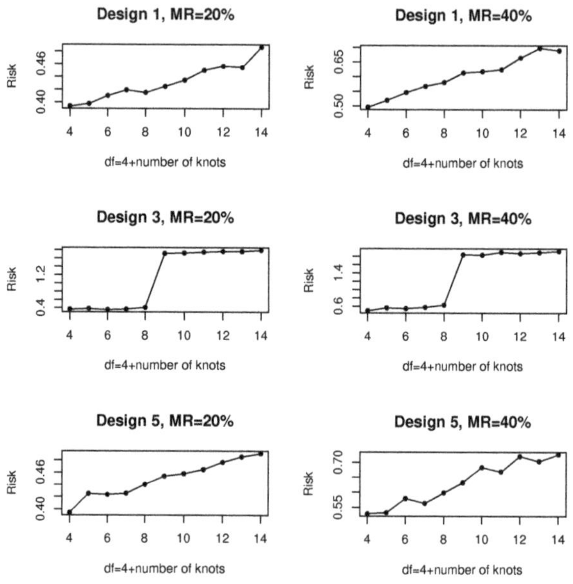

Figure 2. The curves of the risk with the number of knots over 1000 replications.

3.2.2. Alternative Methods

We conducted some simulation experiments to assess the finite sample performance of our proposed model averaging approach, called the HRC$_p$ approach, in VCPLM with missing data. We compared it with four alternatives, the missing data problems of which were addressed by the IPW method discussed in Section 2. The alternatives included two well-known model selection methods (AIC and BIC) and two widely-used model averaging methods (SAIC and SBIC). Along the lines of [32], we defined the AIC and BIC scores under the varying-coefficient partially linear missing data framework as:

$$AIC_m = \log(\hat{\sigma}^2_{(m,\hat{\pi})}) + 2n^{-1}tr(P_{(m)}), \tag{18}$$

and

$$BIC_m = \log(\hat{\sigma}^2_{(m,\hat{\pi})}) + n^{-1}tr(P_{(m)})\log(n), \tag{19}$$

where $\hat{\sigma}^2_{(m,\hat{\pi})} = n^{-1}\|H_{\hat{\pi}} - \hat{\mu}_{(m,\hat{\pi})}\|^2$. These two model selection methods select the model corresponding to the smallest score of the information criterion. The two model averaging methods, SAIC and SBIC, respectively, assign weights:

$$w_{AIC_m} = \exp(-AIC_m/2) \Big/ \sum_{m'=1}^{M} \exp(-AIC_{m'}/2) \tag{20}$$

and

$$w_{BIC_m} = \exp(-BIC_m/2) \Big/ \sum_{m'=1}^{M} \exp(-BIC_{m'}/2) \tag{21}$$

to the mth candidate model. As suggested by a referee, we also compared our proposal with the Mallows model averaging approach of [29] with a complete-case analysis, which just excluded the individuals with missingness (denoted as CC-MMA). We evaluated the performance of these six methods by computing their risks, and the corresponding results for Designs 1–5 are respectively displayed in Figures 3–7. For better comparison, all risks were normalized by the risk of the AIC model selection method.

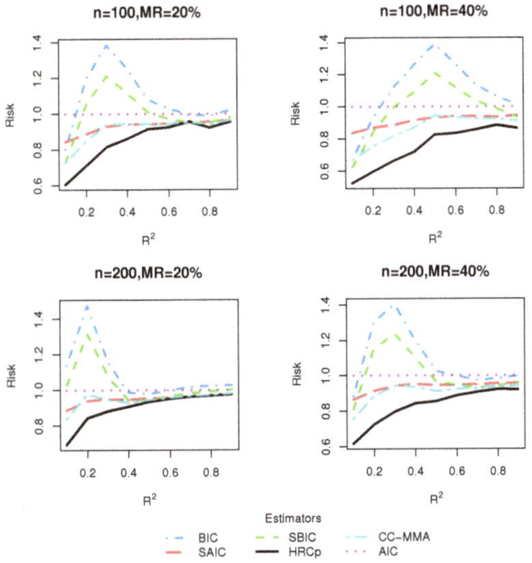

Figure 3. Risk comparisons for Design 1.

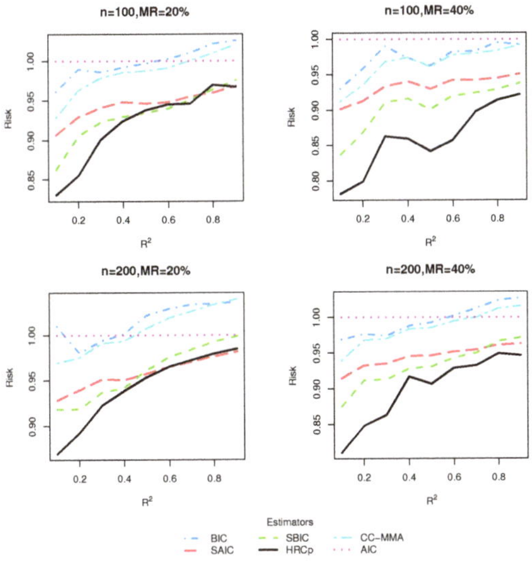

Figure 4. Risk comparisons for Design 2.

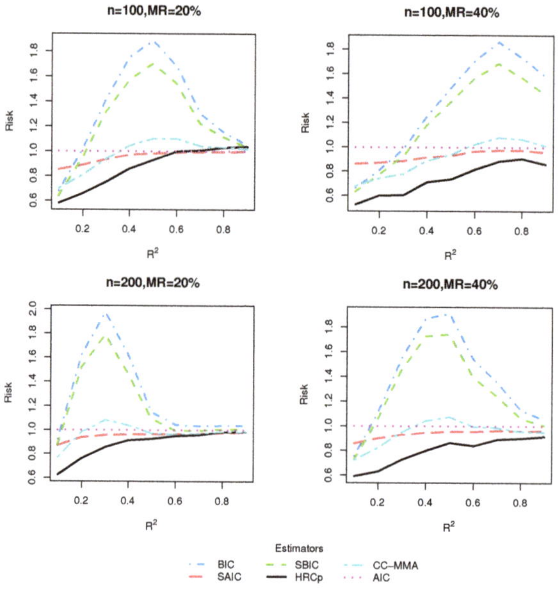

Figure 5. Risk comparisons for Design 3.

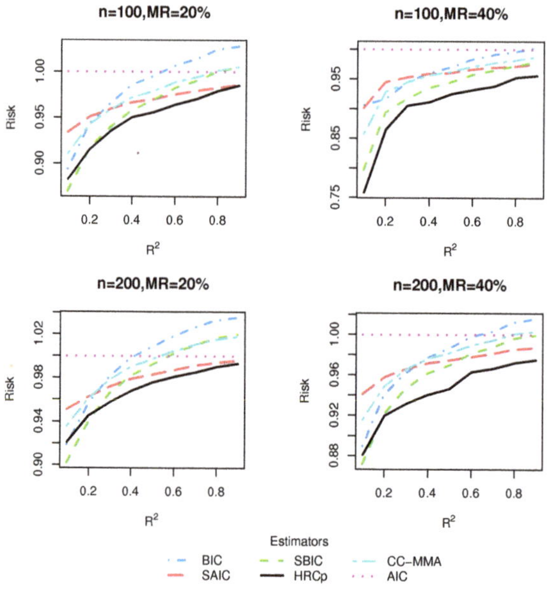

Figure 6. Risk comparisons for Design 4.

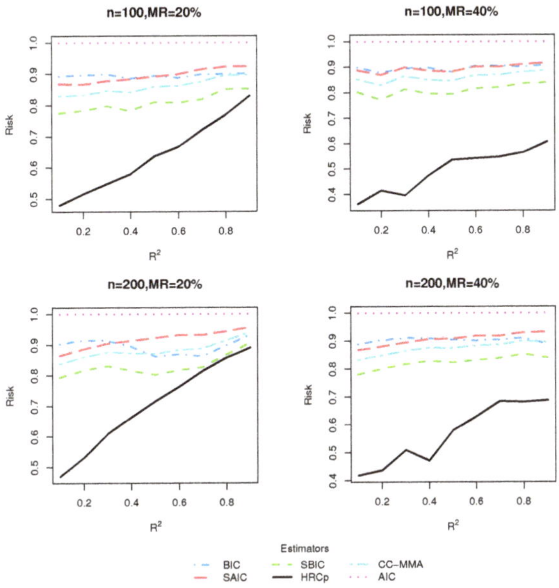

Figure 7. Risk comparisons for Design 5.

Besides, following an anonymous referee's suggestion, we make a comparison of computation time between different model selection and averaging methods. To be more specific, we examined the resulting computation time in seconds by, respectively, employing six methods for five designs when $n = 100$, $R^2 = 0.1$ and MR = 20%. The corresponding results are listed in Table 2.

Table 2. Averaged computation time in seconds over 3 runs, when $n = 100$, $R^2 = 0.1$ and MR = 20%.

Method	Design 1	Design 2	Design 3	Design 4	Design 5
AIC	0.213	0.223	0.220	0.223	0.248
BIC	0.220	0.229	0.219	0.218	0.247
SAIC	0.222	0.232	0.224	0.225	0.254
SBIC	0.224	0.229	0.222	0.222	0.249
CC-MMA	0.239	0.233	0.232	0.242	0.261
HRC_p	0.251	0.242	0.246	0.254	0.284

3.3. Simulation Results

3.3.1. Risk Comparison

From these five figures, we observe that, in general, model averaging approaches worked better than model selection approaches. As shown in most figures, the risk difference in favor of model averaging over model selection was more pronounced when R^2 was small or moderate than when R^2 was large. This is hardly surprising as it is hard to identify only one best model in the presence of much noise corresponding to a small R^2, while the model averaging method shields against selecting a very poor model by compromising across all possible models. On the other hand, when R^2 was large, model selection could sometimes be a better strategy than model averaging. A possible reason for this is that the small noise in the data allows the model selection strategy to select the right model with very high frequencies.

As for the comparison of HRC_p method with its rivals, we found that no matter whether the candidate models were nested or not, our proposed model averaging method yielded the smallest risk in almost all combinations of simulation designs, sample sizes and missing rates considered, although when R^2 was very high, the information criterion-based model averaging methods could sometimes be marginally preferable to ours. The superiority of our method was more marked in Design 5, which was subject to two kinds of uncertainty simultaneously, uncertainty in covariate inclusion and uncertainty in structure, than in Designs 1–4, which were only associated with uncertainty in the linear part specification. This finding provided evidence that our model averaging method was most effective when both the linear and nonlinear components of the model are uncertain, as in most real-world applications. The good performance of our method in finite samples can be partially explained by noting that the optimality of the HRC$_p$ estimator does not depend on the correct specification of candidate models. As expected, it was observed that information criterion-based model averaging methods invariably produced more accurate estimators than their model selection counterparts. The advantage of our approach became more noticeable as the missing rate increased.

To sum up, within the context of the VCPLM with missing responses, and when the missing data is handled by an IPW method, our proposed HRC$_p$ model averaging method performs better than information criterion-based model selection and averaging methods in terms of risk, especially when the model is characterized by much noise. By and large, our results are parallel to those of [26], which investigated model averaging in the VCPLM with complete data. Additionally, we found evidence of our proposed IPW technique-based model averaging method, HRC$_p$, enjoying significantly smaller risk than a model averaging method with complete-case analysis, CC-MMA.

3.3.2. Computation Time Comparison

According to Table 2, it was hardly surprising that model selection methods always needed less computation time than model averaging methods in all designs. Among all model averaging methods, two data-driven methods (CC-MMA and HRC$_p$) spent slightly more time than the two information criterion-based methods (SAIC and SBIC). As for the comparison between CC-MMA and HRC$_p$, it was expected that our method would perform slightly more slowly than CC-MMA because of the need to approximate the unknown propensity score function. In general, from the perspective of computation time, our method was slightly inferior to other methods, but it greatly dominated its competitors in terms of estimation accuracy. Thus, it is worthwhile to carry out the HRC$_p$ model averaging method to obtain a comparatively accurate estimator, even if a little computation time has to be sacrificed.

4. Real Data Analysis

In this section, we applied our model averaging method to analyze data including information about aged patients from 36 for-profit nursing homes in San Diego, California, provided in [37] and studied by [26,38]. The response variable, y, was the natural logarithm of the days in the nursing home. The five covariates were x_1, a binary variable indicating whether the patient was treated at a nursing home; x_2, a binary variable indicating whether the patient was male; x_3, a binary variable indicating whether the patient was married; x_4, a health status variable, with a smaller value indicating better health condition; $u = (\text{age} - 64)/(102 - 64)$, the normalized age of the patients was the effect modifier, with age ranging from 65 to 102.

We considered fitting the data by the VCPLM, but we were not sure which of x_1, x_2, x_3 and x_4 to include, and we were uncertain whether to assign a variable in the linear or nonparametric part. Therefore, we considered all possibilities, namely, a variable in the linear part or in the nonparametric part or not in the model. Similar to the simulation study, we required all candidate models to include no fewer than one linear and one nonparametric variable. This resulted in 50 possible models. In our analysis, we ignored 332 censored observations from the original data, and only focused on the remaining 1269 uncensored sample points. Further, we randomly selected n_0 observations from the 1269 uncensored observations as the training set and the remaining $n_1 = n - n_0$ observations were taken as test set, where $n_0 = 700, 800, 900, 1000$ and 1100. Since the data points we used could be fully observed, to illustrate the application of our method, we artificially created missing responses in the training data, according to the following missing data mechanism:

$$\text{logit}\{P(\delta_i = 1|X_i, Z_i, u_i)\} = 1 + 0.4u_i + 0.4x_{i1}. \tag{22}$$

Hence, the corresponding mean missing rate was about 20%.

We employed observations in the training set to obtain estimators of model parameters in each candidate model, and then performed four model averaging (HRC$_p$, CC-MMA, SAIC and SBIC) and two model selection (AIC and BIC) procedures. We fitted each candidate model by applying the estimation method introduced in Section 2. The cubic B-splines were adopted to approximate each coefficient function. Following the suggestion in the simulation study, we set the number of knots to be 0. We then evaluated the predictive performance of these six approaches by computing their mean squared prediction error (MSPE). As suggested by [4,26], the observations in the test set were utilized to compute the MSPE as follows:

$$\text{MSPE} = \frac{1}{n_1} \sum_{i=n_0+1}^{n} (y_i - \hat{\mu}_i)^2, \tag{23}$$

where $\hat{\mu}_i$ is the predicted value for the ith patient based on each approach. We repeated the above process 500 times and calculated the mean, median and standard deviation (SD) of the MSPEs of the six strategies across the replications. For comparison convenience, all MSPEs were normalized by dividing the MSPE of AIC, which was referred to as the relative MSPE (RMSPE). The results are summarized in Table 3.

Table 3. The mean, median and SD of RMSPE across 500 repetitions.

n_0	Method	BIC	SAIC	SBIC	CC-MMA	HRCp
700	mean	0.991	0.984	0.981	0.989	0.980
	median	0.997	0.989	0.988	0.993	0.985
	SD	0.624	0.660	0.573	0.622	0.619
800	mean	0.993	0.987	0.985	0.990	0.982
	median	0.997	0.990	0.988	0.994	0.985
	SD	0.882	0.909	0.866	0.881	0.884
900	mean	0.994	0.988	0.987	0.991	0.984
	median	0.995	0.989	0.988	0.992	0.986
	SD	0.827	0.861	0.792	0.847	0.836
1000	mean	0.995	0.989	0.988	0.991	0.985
	median	0.997	0.989	0.989	0.992	0.986
	SD	0.890	0.885	0.883	0.888	0.876
1100	mean	0.995	0.990	0.990	0.991	0.986
	median	0.998	0.993	0.991	0.992	0.990
	SD	0.968	0.968	0.957	0.966	0.939

The results in Table 3 show that in almost all situations, our proposed HRC$_p$ method had the best predictive efficiency among the six approaches considered. The superiority of our method was particularly obvious in terms of the mean and median, since the smallest mean and median were invariably produced by our method for all training sample sizes. The SBIC always yielded a mean and median that were second to the HRC$_p$ but the best among the remaining five methods. As for the comparison of SD, we found evidence that our method had an edge over other methods when n_0 was not less than 1000, while the SBIC frequently yielded the smallest SD when n_0 was less than 1000. This implied that our HRC$_p$ method outperformed the SBIC method when the size of the training set was large. We further noted that all numbers in this table were smaller than 1, which implied that the AIC was the worst method among those considered, irrespective of the performance yardstick.

We also provide the Diebold and Mariano test results for the differences in MSPE, which are displayed in Table 4. A positive/negative test statistic in this table denotes that the estimator in the numerator leads to a bigger/smaller MSPE than the estimator in the denominator. The test statistics and p-values listed in columns 3, 6, 7 and 9 provide evidence that the MSPE differences between our proposed HRC$_p$ estimator and the BIC, SAIC, AIC and CC-MMA estimators were statistically significant for all training set sizes. Considering the HRC$_p$ and SBIC estimators, column 8 demonstrates that the advantage of HRC$_p$ over SBIC was statistically significant in the case with $n_0 = 1000$ and 1100. However, the same cannot be reported about the differences in performance between the HRC$_p$ and SBIC estimators when n_0 was less than 1000, as presented in column 8. This result reinforced the intuition that the HRC$_p$ estimator was more reliable than the SBIC estimator when the training set size was large. The test results shown in columns 3–7 indicate that the MSPE differences between AIC estimator and the remaining five estimators were statistically significant in all situations. The test results given in columns 3, 8, 9 and 10 imply the same about the differences between the BIC and the other five estimators.

Table 4. Diebold–Mariano test results for the differences in MSPE.

n_0	Method	AIC/BIC	AIC/SAIC	AIC/SBIC	AIC/CC-MMA	AIC/HRCp	BIC/SAIC	BIC/SBIC	BIC/CC-MMA
700	DM	3.622	9.693	7.738	4.147	10.528	6.196	15.908	2.165
	p-value	0.000	0.000	0.000	0.000	0.000	0.000	0.000	0.030
800	DM	5.345	15.916	11.589	9.472	15.832	6.216	18.979	10.863
	p-value	0.000	0.000	0.000	0.000	0.000	0.000	0.000	0.000
900	DM	3.353	10.127	8.009	4.725	11.867	5.502	14.992	5.128
	p-value	0.001	0.000	0.000	0.000	0.000	0.000	0.000	0.000
1000	DM	2.930	9.012	7.165	4.192	12.665	7.697	17.102	3.214
	p-value	0.003	0.000	0.000	0.000	0.000	0.000	0.001	0.001
1100	DM	3.550	12.475	8.565	7.291	13.101	5.299	12.739	4.395
	p-value	0.000	0.000	0.000	0.000	0.000	0.000	0.000	0.000
n_0	Method	BIC/HRCp	SAIC/SBIC	SAIC/CC-MMA	SAIC/HRCp	SBIC/CC-MMA	SBIC/HRCp	CC-MMA/HRCp	
700	DM	9.173	3.452	−4.682	6.001	−7.245	0.942	11.426	
	p-value	0.000	0.001	0.000	0.000	0.000	0.346	0.000	
800	DM	12.102	3.276	−4.274	8.501	−6.835	1.827	12.183	
	p-value	0.000	0.001	0.000	0.000	0.000	0.068	0.000	
900	DM	8.740	2.935	−1.231	7.078	−5.352	1.301	10.278	
	p-value	0.000	0.000	0.218	0.000	0.000	0.193	0.000	
1000	DM	10.586	1.404	−2.053	8.353	−2.975	3.537	9.486	
	p-value	0.000	0.160	0.040	0.000	0.003	0.000	0.000	
1100	DM	9.937	1.154	−0.892	7.721	−1.626	4.149	11.254	
	p-value	0.006	0.249	0.372	0.000	0.104	0.000	0.000	

5. Conclusions

Considering model averaging estimation in the VCPLM with missing responses, we propose a HRC$_p$ weight choice criterion and its feasible form. Our model averaging process can jointly incorporate two layers of model uncertainty: the first concerns which covariates to include and the second further concerns whether a covariate should be in the linear or nonparametric component. The resultant model averaging estimator is shown to be asymptotically optimal in the sense of achieving the lowest possible squared error loss under certain regularity conditions. The simulation results demonstrated that, in several designs with different types of model uncertainty, our model averaging method always performed much better in comparison with existing methods. The real data analysis also reveals the superiority of the proposed strategy.

There are still many issues deserving future research. Firstly, we only considered model averaging for the VCPLM in the context of missing response data, so it would be worthwhile considering cases where some covariates are also subject to missingness, or missing data arise in a more general framework, such as the generalized VCPLM which permits a discrete response variable. Secondly, in our analysis the missing data mechanism was MAR. The development of a model averaging procedure in a more natural, but more complex, non-ignorable missing data case and the establishment of its asymptotic property is still challenging and warrants future studies. Thirdly, our procedure is applicable only when the dimension parameters p_m and q_m are less than the sample size n. The consideration of an asymptotically optimal model averaging method for high dimensional VCPLM with missing data is meaningful and, thus, merits future research.

Author Contributions: Conceptualization, W.C.; methodology, J.Z., W.C. and G.H.; software, J.Z. and G.H.; supervision, W.C. and G.H.; writing-original draft, J.Z.; writing—review and editing, G.H. All authors have read and agreed to the published version of the manuscript.

Funding: The work of Zeng is supported by the Important Natural Science Foundation of Colleges and Universities of Anhui Province (No.KJ2021A0929). The work of Hu is supported by the Important Natural Science Foundation of Colleges and Universities of Anhui Province (No.KJ2021A0930).

Institutional Review Board Statement: Not applicable.

Informed Consent Statement: Not applicable.

Data Availability Statement: The dataset used in real data analysis is available at: https://www.stats.ox.ac.uk/pub/datasets/csb/ (accessed on 27 January 2023).

Acknowledgments: The authors would like to thank the reviewers and editors for their careful reading and constructive comments.

Conflicts of Interest: The authors declare no conflict of interest.

Appendix A

Lemma A1. *If Conditions (C.1) and (C.2) hold, then there exists a positive constant C_{ϵ_π}, such that:*

$$\max_{1\le i\le n} E(\epsilon_{\pi,i}^{4K}|X_i, Z_i, u_i) \le C_{\epsilon_\pi},$$

where K is given in Condition (C.2).

Proof of Lemma A1. Note that:

$$\begin{aligned}|\epsilon_{\pi,i}| = |H_{\pi,i} - \mu_i| &= \left|\frac{\delta_i}{\pi(X_i, Z_i, u_i)} y_i - \mu_i\right| \le \frac{|\mu_i| + |\epsilon_i|}{\pi(X_i, Z_i, u_i)} + |\mu_i| \\ &\le \frac{|\mu_i| + |\epsilon_i|}{C_\pi} + |\mu_i| \le \frac{C_\mu}{C_\pi} + C_\mu + \frac{|\epsilon_i|}{C_\pi},\end{aligned}$$

where the second inequality is from Condition (C.1) and the third inequality from Condition (C.2). Let $C_1 = \frac{C_\mu}{C_\pi} + C_\mu$. By means of C_p inequality, we have:

$$|\epsilon_{\pi,i}|^{4K} \le 2^{4K-1}\left(C_1^{4K} + \left|\frac{1}{C_\pi}\right|^{4K} |\epsilon_i|^{4K}\right).$$

According to Condition (C.2), we obtain:

$$\max_{1\le i\le n} E(\epsilon_{\pi,i}^{4K}|X_i, Z_i, u_i) \le C_{\epsilon_\pi},$$

where $C_{\epsilon_\pi} = 2^{4K-1}\left(C_1^{4K} + \left|\frac{1}{C_\pi}\right|^{4K} C_\epsilon\right)$. □

Lemma A2. *Under Conditions (C.1) and (C.2), one has* $||H_\pi - H_{\hat{\pi}}||^2 = O_p(1)$.

Proof of Lemma A2. By Cauchy–Schwarz inequality and Taylor expansion, this lemma could be proved, based on some arguments used in the proof of Lemma 1 of [13]. So we omitted it here. □

Proof of Theorem 1. Let $\bar{\lambda}(\cdot)$ be the largest singular value of a matrix, $\widetilde{P}(w)$ be an $n \times n$ diagonal matrix whose ith diagonal element is $P_{ii}(w)$, Ω_π be an $n \times n$ diagonal matrix whose ith diagonal element is $\sigma^2_{\pi,i}$, $A(w) = I - P(w)$, $\epsilon_\pi = (\epsilon_{\pi,1}, \ldots, \epsilon_{\pi,n})'$. From Lemma 1, we obtain $\bar{\lambda}(\Omega_\pi) = O(1)$. After some simple calculations, we know $P_{(m)}$ is an idempotent matrix with $\bar{\lambda}(P_{(m)}) \le 1$, and, hence, $\bar{\lambda}(P(w)) \le \sum_{m=1}^{M} w_m \bar{\lambda}(P_{(m)}) \le 1$ for any $w \in \mathcal{W}$. Observe that:

$$\begin{aligned} C_{\hat{\pi}}(w) &= ||H_{\hat{\pi}} - \hat{\mu}_{\hat{\pi}}(w)||^2 + 2\hat{\epsilon}'_{\hat{\pi}}\widetilde{P}(w)\hat{\epsilon}_{\hat{\pi}} \\ &= ||H_{\hat{\pi}} - \mu||^2 + L_{\hat{\pi}}(w) + 2b_n(w) + 2d_n(w), \end{aligned}$$

where $b_n(w) = (H_{\hat{\pi}} - H_\pi)'\{\mu - \hat{\mu}_{\hat{\pi}}(w)\}$, $d_n(w) = \epsilon'_\pi\{\mu - \hat{\mu}_{\hat{\pi}}(w)\} + \hat{\epsilon}'_{\hat{\pi}}\widetilde{P}(w)\hat{\epsilon}_{\hat{\pi}}$. Since $||H_{\hat{\pi}} - \mu||^2$ is unrelated to w, minimizing $C_{\hat{\pi}}(w)$ is equivalent to minimizing $C_{\hat{\pi}}(w) - ||H_{\hat{\pi}} - \mu||^2$. Therefore, to prove Theorem 1, we only need to verify that:

$$\sup_{w\in\mathcal{W}} \left|\frac{L_{\hat{\pi}}(w)}{R_\pi(w)} - 1\right| = o_p(1), \tag{A1}$$

$$\sup_{w\in\mathcal{W}} \left|\frac{b_n(w)}{R_\pi(w)}\right| = o_p(1), \tag{A2}$$

$$\sup_{w\in\mathcal{W}} \left|\frac{d_n(w)}{R_\pi(w)}\right| = o_p(1). \tag{A3}$$

By the fact that

$$\begin{aligned} \left|\frac{L_{\hat{\pi}}(w)}{R_\pi(w)} - 1\right| &= \left|\frac{||\mu - \hat{\mu}_\pi(w) + \hat{\mu}_\pi(w) - \hat{\mu}_{\hat{\pi}}(w)||^2}{R_\pi(w)} - 1\right| \\ &\le \left|\frac{L_\pi(w)}{R_\pi(w)} - 1\right| + 2\left\{\frac{L_\pi(w)}{R_\pi(w)}\right\}^{1/2}\frac{||\hat{\mu}_\pi(w) - \hat{\mu}_{\hat{\pi}}(w)||}{\{R_\pi(w)\}^{1/2}} + \frac{||\hat{\mu}_\pi(w) - \hat{\mu}_{\hat{\pi}}(w)||^2}{R_\pi(w)}, \end{aligned}$$

and

$$\begin{aligned} ||\hat{\mu}_\pi(w) - \hat{\mu}_{\hat{\pi}}(w)||^2 &= ||P(w)H_\pi - P(w)H_{\hat{\pi}}||^2 \\ &\le \{\bar{\lambda}(P(w))\}^2||H_\pi - H_{\hat{\pi}}||^2 \le ||H_\pi - H_{\hat{\pi}}||^2, \end{aligned}$$

it is readily seen that the result of (A1) is valid if

$$\sup_{w\in\mathcal{W}} \left|\frac{L_\pi(w)}{R_\pi(w)} - 1\right| = o_p(1), \tag{A4}$$

and

$$\sup_{w\in\mathcal{W}} \frac{||H_\pi - H_{\hat{\pi}}||^2}{R_\pi(w)} = o_p(1). \tag{A5}$$

Note that: $L_\pi(w) - R_\pi(w) = ||P(w)\epsilon_\pi||^2 - 2\epsilon'_\pi P'(w)A(w)\mu - \text{trace}\{P'(w)P(w)\Omega_\pi\}$, so to prove (A4), it is sufficient to show that

$$\sup_{w\in\mathcal{W}} \left|\frac{||P(w)\epsilon_\pi||^2 - \text{trace}\{P'(w)P(w)\Omega_\pi\}}{R_\pi(w)}\right| = o_p(1), \tag{A6}$$

and

$$\sup_{\omega \in \mathcal{W}} \left| \frac{\epsilon_\pi' P'(w) A(w) \mu}{R_\pi(w)} \right| = o_p(1). \tag{A7}$$

We observe, for any $\nu > 0$, that:

$$\begin{aligned}
&\Pr\left\{ \sup_{w \in \mathcal{W}} \left| \frac{\|P(w)\epsilon_\pi\|^2 - \text{trace}\{P'(w)P(w)\Omega_\pi\}}{R_\pi(w)} \right| > \nu \middle| X, Z, U \right\} \\
\leq &\sum_{m=1}^{M} \sum_{m^*=1}^{M} \Pr\left\{ \left| \epsilon_\pi' P'(w_m^0) P(w_{m^*}^0) \epsilon_\pi - \text{trace}\{P'(w_m^0)P(w_{m^*}^0)\Omega_\pi\} \right| > \nu \xi_\pi \middle| X, Z, U \right\} \\
\leq &\nu^{-2K} \xi_\pi^{-2K} \sum_{m=1}^{M} \sum_{m^*=1}^{M} E\left[\left| \epsilon_\pi' P'(w_m^0) P(w_{m^*}^0) \epsilon_\pi - \text{trace}\{P'(w_m^0)P(w_{m^*}^0)\Omega_\pi\} \right|^{2K} \middle| X, Z, U \right] \\
\leq &C_2 \nu^{-2K} \xi_\pi^{-2K} \sum_{m=1}^{M} \sum_{m^*=1}^{M} \left| \text{trace}\left\{ P(w_m^0) P(w_{m^*}^0) \Omega_\pi P(w_{m^*}^0) P(w_m^0) \Omega_\pi \right\} \right|^{K} \\
\leq &C_2 \nu^{-2K} \xi_\pi^{-2K} \{\bar{\lambda}(\Omega_\pi)\}^K \{\bar{\lambda}(P(w_{m^*}^0))\}^{2K} M \sum_{m=1}^{M} \left| \text{trace}\left\{ P(w_m^0) P(w_m^0) \Omega_\pi \right\} \right|^{K} \\
\leq &C_2 \nu^{-2K} \xi_\pi^{-2K} \{\bar{\lambda}(\Omega_\pi)\}^K M \sum_{m=1}^{M} \{R_\pi(w_m^0)\}^K = o_p(1),
\end{aligned}$$

where C_2 is a constant, the second inequality is from Chebyshev's inequality, the third inequality is from Theorem 2 of [39], and the last inequality is because $\bar{\lambda}(P(w_{m^*}^0)) \leq 1$ and $\text{trace}\{P(w_m^0)P(w_m^0)\Omega_\pi\} \leq R_\pi(w_m^0)$, and the equality is ensured by Condition (C.3). Then (A6) holds because of the following fact:

$$\begin{aligned}
&\Pr\left\{ \sup_{w \in \mathcal{W}} \left| \frac{\|P(w)\epsilon_\pi\|^2 - \text{trace}\{P'(w)P(w)\Omega_\pi\}}{R_\pi(w)} \right| > \nu \right\} \\
&= E\left[\Pr\left\{ \sup_{w \in \mathcal{W}} \left| \frac{\|P(w)\epsilon_\pi\|^2 - \text{trace}\{P'(w)P(w)\Omega_\pi\}}{R_\pi(w)} \right| > \nu \middle| X, Z, U \right\} \right] = o_p(1).
\end{aligned}$$

By means of similar steps, we obtain

$$\begin{aligned}
&\Pr\left\{ \sup_{w \in \mathcal{W}} \left| \frac{\epsilon_\pi' P'(w) A(w) \mu}{R_\pi(w)} \right| > \nu \middle| X, Z, U \right\} \\
\leq &\sum_{m=1}^{M} \sum_{m^*=1}^{M} \Pr\left\{ \left| \epsilon_\pi' P'(w_m^0) A(w_{m^*}^0) \mu \right| > \nu \xi_\pi \middle| X, Z, U \right\} \\
\leq &\nu^{-2K} \xi_\pi^{-2K} \sum_{m=1}^{M} \sum_{m^*=1}^{M} E\left\{ \left| \epsilon_\pi' P'(w_m^0) A(w_{m^*}^0) \mu \right|^{2K} \middle| X, Z, U \right\} \\
\leq &C_3 \nu^{-2K} \xi_\pi^{-2K} \sum_{m=1}^{M} \sum_{m^*=1}^{M} \left\| \Omega_\pi^{1/2} P'(w_m^0) A(w_{m^*}^0) \mu \right\|^{2K} \\
\leq &C_3 \nu^{-2K} \xi_\pi^{-2K} \sum_{m=1}^{M} \sum_{m^*=1}^{M} \{\bar{\lambda}(P(w_m^0))\}^{2K} \{\bar{\lambda}(\Omega_\pi)\}^K \left\| A(w_{m^*}^0) \mu \right\|^{2K} \\
\leq &C_3 \nu^{-2K} \xi_\pi^{-2K} \{\bar{\lambda}(\Omega_\pi)\}^K M \sum_{m^*=1}^{M} \left\{ R_\pi(w_{m^*}^0) \right\}^K = o_p(1),
\end{aligned}$$

where C_3 is a constant, and the last inequality is due to $\bar{\lambda}(P(w_m^0)) \leq 1$ and $\|A(w_{m^*}^0)\mu\|^2 \leq R_\pi(w_{m^*}^0)$. Therefore, (A7) is satisfied by previous argument, which along with (A6), implies

(A4). On the other hand, (A5) can be easily obtained by Lemma A2 and Condition (C.7). So (A1) is correct.

From Cauchy–Schwarz inequality, (A1), Lemma A2 and Condition (C.7), one has:

$$\sup_{\omega \in \mathcal{W}} \left| \frac{b_n(w)}{R_\pi(w)} \right| \le \sup_{\omega \in \mathcal{W}} \left| \frac{\{\|H_{\hat{\pi}} - H_\pi\|^2 \|\mu - \hat{\mu}_{\hat{\pi}}(w)\|^2\}^{1/2}}{R_\pi(w)} \right|$$

$$\le \|H_{\hat{\pi}} - H_\pi\|^2 \sup_{\omega \in \mathcal{W}} \left\{ \frac{L_{\hat{\pi}}(w)}{R_\pi(w)} \right\}^{1/2} \sup_{\omega \in \mathcal{W}} \left\{ \frac{1}{R_\pi(w)} \right\}^{1/2} = o_p(1).$$

So, (A2) is true. In what follows, we provide the proof of (A3), which yields the desired result of Theorem 1.

By Cauchy–Schwarz inequality and some algebraic manipulations, we obtain:

$$\begin{aligned} |d_n(w)| &= \left| \epsilon'_\pi \{\mu - \hat{\mu}_{\hat{\pi}}(w)\} + \hat{\epsilon}'_{\hat{\pi}} \widetilde{P}(w) \hat{\epsilon}_{\hat{\pi}} \right| \\ &\le |\epsilon'_\pi A(w)\mu| + |\epsilon'_\pi P(w)\epsilon_\pi - \mathrm{trace}\{\Omega_\pi P(w)\}| + \|P(w)\epsilon_\pi\| \cdot \|H_\pi - H_{\hat{\pi}}\| \\ &+ \frac{n}{n - l_{M^*}} \bar{\lambda}(\widetilde{P}(w)) \|H_\pi - H_{\hat{\pi}}\|^2 + \frac{2n}{n - l_{M^*}} \bar{\lambda}(\widetilde{P}(w)) \|H_\pi - H_{\hat{\pi}}\| \cdot \|H_\pi\| \\ &+ \left| \hat{\epsilon}'_\pi \widetilde{P}(w) \hat{\epsilon}_\pi - \mathrm{trace}\{\Omega_\pi P(w)\} \right|. \end{aligned}$$

Therefore, (A3) is implied by:

$$\sup_{\omega \in \mathcal{W}} \left| \frac{\epsilon'_\pi A(w)\mu}{R_\pi(w)} \right| = o_p(1), \tag{A8}$$

$$\sup_{\omega \in \mathcal{W}} \left| \frac{\epsilon'_\pi P(w)\epsilon_\pi - \mathrm{trace}\{\Omega_\pi P(w)\}}{R_\pi(w)} \right| = o_p(1), \tag{A9}$$

$$\sup_{\omega \in \mathcal{W}} \left| \frac{\hat{\epsilon}'_\pi \widetilde{P}(w)\hat{\epsilon}_\pi - \mathrm{trace}\{\Omega_\pi P(w)\}}{R_\pi(w)} \right| = o_p(1), \tag{A10}$$

$$\sup_{\omega \in \mathcal{W}} \frac{\|P(w)\epsilon_\pi\|}{R_\pi(w)} = o_p(1), \tag{A11}$$

$$\sup_{\omega \in \mathcal{W}} \left| \frac{n}{n - l_{M^*}} \bar{\lambda}(\widetilde{P}(w)) \frac{\|H_\pi - H_{\hat{\pi}}\|^2}{R_\pi(w)} \right| = o_p(1), \tag{A12}$$

and

$$\sup_{\omega \in \mathcal{W}} \left| \frac{n}{n - l_{M^*}} \bar{\lambda}(\widetilde{P}(w)) \frac{\|H_\pi\|}{R_\pi(w)} \right| = o_p(1). \tag{A13}$$

Similar to the proof steps in (A7) and (A6), respectively, it is not difficult to obtain (A8) and (A9). As for (A10), it is readily seen that:

$$\begin{aligned} &\sup_{\omega \in \mathcal{W}} \left| \frac{\hat{\epsilon}'_\pi \widetilde{P}(w)\hat{\epsilon}_\pi - \mathrm{trace}\{\Omega_\pi P(w)\}}{R_\pi(w)} \right| \le \sup_{\omega \in \mathcal{W}} \left| \hat{\epsilon}'_\pi \widetilde{P}(w)\hat{\epsilon}_\pi - \mathrm{trace}\{\Omega_\pi \widetilde{P}(w)\} \right| \Big/ \xi_\pi \\ &\le \sup_{\omega \in \mathcal{W}} \left| \hat{\epsilon}'_\pi \widetilde{P}(w)\hat{\epsilon}_\pi - \epsilon'_\pi \widetilde{P}(w)\epsilon_\pi \right| \Big/ \xi_\pi + \sup_{\omega \in \mathcal{W}} \left| \epsilon'_\pi \widetilde{P}(w)\epsilon_\pi - \mathrm{trace}\{\Omega_\pi \widetilde{P}(w)\} \right| \Big/ \xi_\pi. \end{aligned} \tag{A14}$$

Following an argument similar to that used in [7], we know that both two terms in the second line of (A14) are equal to $o_p(1)$. So, (A10) is valid. We now prove (A11) and

(A12). From Lemma A1, we find that $E(\epsilon_{\pi,i}^4) = E\{E(\epsilon_{\pi,i}^4|X_i, Z_i, u_i)\} \leq C_{\epsilon_\pi}$, and, thus, $\|\epsilon_\pi\| = (\sum_{i=1}^n \epsilon_{\pi,i}^2)^{1/2} = O_p(n^{1/2})$. Consequently, based on Condition (C.7), we have:

$$\sup_{\omega \in \mathcal{W}} \frac{\|P(w)\epsilon_\pi\|}{R_\pi(w)} \leq \bar{\lambda}(P(w))\|\epsilon_\pi\| \Big/ \xi_\pi \leq O_p(n^{1/2}) \Big/ \xi_\pi = o_p(1).$$

So, we establish (A11). By Condition (C.6), it is easy to show that $\sup_{\omega \in \mathcal{W}} \bar{\lambda}(\widetilde{P}(w)) = O_p(n^{-1/2})$. This, together with Conditions (C.7) and (C.8), and Lemma A2, yields:

$$\begin{aligned} \sup_{\omega \in \mathcal{W}} \left| \frac{n}{n - l_{M^*}} \bar{\lambda}(\widetilde{P}(w)) \frac{\|H_\pi - H_{\hat{\pi}}\|^2}{R_\pi(w)} \right| &\leq \frac{n}{n - l_{M^*}} \sup_{\omega \in \mathcal{W}} \bar{\lambda}(\widetilde{P}(w)) \|H_\pi - H_{\hat{\pi}}\|^2 \xi_\pi^{-1} \\ &= O(1)O_p(n^{-1/2})O_p(1)o_p(n^{-1/2}) = o_p(1). \end{aligned}$$

So, (A12) is valid. From triangle inequality, Condition (C.2) and Lemma A1, we see that $\|H_\pi\| \leq \|\mu\| + \|\epsilon_\pi\| = O_p(n^{1/2})$. Hence, following the step of proving (A12), (A13) is valid. The proof of Theorem 1 is, thus, completed. □

References

1. Hansen, B.E. Least squares model averaging. *Econometrica* **2007**, *75*, 1175–1189. [CrossRef]
2. Wan, A.T.K.; Zhang, X.; Zou, G. Least squares model averaging by Mallows criterion. *J. Economet.* **2010**, *156*, 277–283. [CrossRef]
3. Liang, H.; Zou, G.; Wan, A.T.K.; Zhang, X. Optimal weight choice for frequentist model average estimators. *J. Am. Stat. Assoc.* **2011**, *106*, 1053–1066. [CrossRef]
4. Hansen, B.E.; Racine, J.S. Jackknife model averaging. *J. Economet.* **2012**, *167*, 38–46. [CrossRef]
5. Zhang, X.; Wan, A.T.K.; Zou, G. Model averaging by jackknife criterion in models with dependent data. *J. Economet.* **2013**, *174*, 82–94. [CrossRef]
6. Lu, X.; Su, L. Jackknife model averaging for quantile regressions. *J. Economet.* **2015**, *188*, 40–58. [CrossRef]
7. Liu, Q.; Okui, R. Heteroscedasticity-robust C_p model averaging. *Economet. J.* **2013**, *16*, 463–472. [CrossRef]
8. Zhang, X.; Zou, G.; Carroll, R.J. Model averaging based on Kullback-Leibler distance. *Stat. Sinica* **2015**, *25*, 1583–1598. [CrossRef] [PubMed]
9. Zhu, R.; Zhang, X.; Wan, A.T.K.; Zou, G. Kernel averaging estimators. *J. Bus. Econ. Stat.* **2022**, *41*, 157–169. [CrossRef]
10. Zhang, X.; Liu, C.A. Model averaging prediction by K-fold cross-validation. *J. Economet.* **2022**, *in press*.
11. Zhang, X. Model averaging with covariates that are missing completely at random. *Econ. Lett.* **2013**, *121*, 360–363. [CrossRef]
12. Fang, F.; Lan, W.; Tong, J.; Shao, J. Model averaging for prediction with fragmentary data. *J. Bus. Econ. Stat.* **2019**, *37*, 517–527. [CrossRef]
13. Wei, Y.; Wang, Q.; Liu, W. Model averaging for linear models with responses missing at random. *Ann. I. Stat. Math.* **2021**, *73*, 535–553. [CrossRef]
14. Wei, Y.; Wang, Q. Cross-validation-based model averaging in linear models with responses missing at random. *Stat. Probabil. Lett.* **2021**, *171*, 108990. [CrossRef]
15. Xie, J.; Yan, X.; Tang, N. A model-averaging method for high-dimensional regression with missing responses at random. *Stat. Sinica* **2021**, *31*, 1005–1026. [CrossRef]
16. Li, Q.; Huang, C.J.; Li, D.; Fu, T.T. Semiparametric smooth coefficient models. *J. Bus. Econ. Stat.* **2002**, *20*, 412–422. [CrossRef]
17. Zhang, W.; Lee, S.Y.; Song, X. Local polynomial fitting in semivarying coefficient model. *J. Multivariate Anal.* **2002**, *82*, 166–188. [CrossRef]
18. Ahmad, I.; Leelahanon, S.; Li, Q. Efficient estimation of a semiparametric partially linear varying coefficient model. *Ann. Stat.* **2005**, *33*, 258–283. [CrossRef]
19. Fan, J.; Huang, T. Profile likelihood inferences on semiparametric varying-coefficient partially linear models. *Bernoulli* **2005**, *11*, 1031–1057. [CrossRef]
20. Li, R.; Liang, H. Variable selection in semiparametric regression modeling. *Ann. Stat.* **2008**, *36*, 261–286. [CrossRef]
21. Zhao, P.; Xue, L. Variable selection for semiparametric varying coefficient partially linear models. *Stat. Probabil. Lett.* **2009**, *79*, 2148–2157. [CrossRef]
22. Zhao, P.; Xue, L. Variable selection for semiparametric varying coefficient partially linear errors-in-variables models. *J. Multivariate Anal.* **2010**, *101*, 1872–1883. [CrossRef]
23. Zhao, W.; Zhang, R.; Liu, J.; Lv, Y. Robust and efficient variable selection for semiparametric partially linear varying coefficient model based on modal regression. *Ann. I. Stat. Math.* **2014**, *66*, 165–191. [CrossRef]
24. Wang, H.; Zou, G.; Wan, A.T.K. Model averaging for varying-coefficient partially linear measurement error models. *Electron. J. Stat.* **2012**, *6*, 1017–1039. [CrossRef]

25. Zeng, J.; Cheng, W.; Hu, G.; Rong, Y. Model averaging procedure for varying-coefficient partially linear models with missing responses. *J. Korean Stat. Soc.* **2018**, *47*, 379–394. [CrossRef]
26. Zhu, R.; Wan, A.T.K.; Zhang, X.; Zou, G. A Mallows-type model averaging estimator for the varying-coefficient partially linear model. *J. Am. Stat. Assoc.* **2019**, *114*, 882–892. [CrossRef]
27. Hjort, N.L.; Claeskens, G. Frequentist model average estimators. *J. Am. Stat. Assoc.* **2003**, *98*, 879–899. [CrossRef]
28. Hu, G.; Cheng, W.; Zeng, J. Model averaging by jackknife criterion for varying-coefficient partially linear models. *Commun. Stat.-Theor. M.* **2020**, *49*, 2671–2689. [CrossRef]
29. Xia, X. Model averaging prediction for nonparametric varying-coefficient models with B-spline smoothing. *Stat. Pap.* **2021**, *62*, 2885–2905. [CrossRef]
30. Zhang, X.; Wang, W. Optimal model averaging estimation for partially linear models. *Stat. Sinica* **2019**, *29*, 693–718. [CrossRef]
31. White, J. Maximum likelihood estimation of misspecified models. *Econometrica* **1982**, *50*, 1–25. [CrossRef]
32. Liang, Z.; Chen, X.; Zhou, Y. Mallows model averaging estimation for linear regression model with right censored data. *Acta Math. Appl. Sin. E.* **2022**, *38*, 5–23. [CrossRef]
33. Zhang, X.; Liang, H. Focused information criterion and model averaging for generalized additive partial linear models. *Ann. Stat.* **2011**, *39*, 174–200. [CrossRef]
34. Li, K.C. Asymptotic optimality for C_p, C_L, cross-validation and generalized cross-validation: discrete index set. *Ann. Stat.* **1987**, *15*, 958–975. [CrossRef]
35. Zhang, X.; Yu, D.; Zou, G.; Liang, H. Optimal model averaging estimation for generalized linear models and generalized linear mixed-effects models. *J. Am. Stat. Assoc.* **2016**, *111*, 1775–1790. [CrossRef]
36. Ando, T.; Li, K.C. A weighted-relaxed model averaging approach for high-dimensional generalized linear models. *Ann. Stat.* **2017**, *45*, 2654–2679. [CrossRef]
37. Morris, C.N.; Norton, E.C.; Zhou, X.H. Parametric duration analysis of nursing home usage. In *Case Studies in Biometry*; Lang, N., Ryan, L., Billard, L., Brillinger, D., Conquest, L., Greenhouse, J., Eds.; Wiley: New York, NY, USA, 1994.
38. Fan, J.; Lin, H.; Zhou, Y. Local partial-likelihood estimation for lifetime data. *Ann. Stat.* **2006**, *34*, 290–325. [CrossRef]
39. Whittle, P. Bounds for the moments of linear and quadratic forms in independent variables. *Theor. Probab. Appl.* **1960**, *5*, 331–335. [CrossRef]

mathematics

MDPI

Article

Logistic Regression Based on Individual-Level Predictors and Aggregate-Level Responses

Zheng Xu

Department of Mathematics and Statistics, Wright State University, Dayton, OH 45435, USA;
zheng.xu@wright.edu; Tel.: +1-937-775-2103

Abstract: We propose estimation methods to conduct logistic regression based on individual-level predictors and aggregate-level responses. We derive the likelihood of logistic models in this situation and proposed estimators with different optimization methods. Simulation studies have been conducted to evaluate and compare the performance of the different estimators. A real data-based study has been conducted to illustrate the use of our estimators and compare the different estimators.

Keywords: Poisson binomial distribution; logistic regression; data aggregation; likelihood; numerical optimization

MSC: 62J12

1. Introduction

Data can be reported at different levels due to various considerations including economic, confidentiality, and data collection difficulty. For example, the US Census Bureau reports income at the household level. The aggregate-level data in this example are household income, which is a measure of the combined incomes of all people sharing a particular household or place of residence. The individual-level data in this example are individuals' incomes. The aggregate-level data are defined as data aggregated from individual-level data by groups. Although there are risks in estimating individual-level relationships based on aggregate-level data, such as unequal correlations between variables in aggregate-level data and between the same variables in individual-level data [1,2], researchers continue to use aggregate-level data because in many situations, individual-level data are not available and valid methods for estimating individual-level relationships based on aggregate-level data can be derived [1,3]. The terms "individual" and "aggregate" refer to the different levels and units of analysis [1].

This article intends to solve the problem of estimating models describing an individual-level relationship based on an aggregate-level response variable Y and individual-level predictors X. Examples of data situations include survey data, multivariate time series, social data, and biological data, collected and reported at different levels.

Our interest in developing methods to analyze aggregate data was motivated by real-life examples. One example is group testing of infectious diseases in bio-statistics. To reduce the costs, a two-stage sequential testing strategy is applied. In the first stage, group testing is conducted. Individuals showing positive in the first stage are called back for a follow-up individual test. With the first-stage group testing data available, analyses can be conducted. The second example is consumer demand studies in economics. The consumer's characteristics data are available at the individual level, whereas the consumer's purchase data are available only at the aggregate level. The third example is the analysis of multivariate time series. It is likely that different time series are reported at different frequencies. To study the relationships between multiple time series with different frequencies, researchers need to develop statistical methods.

Citation: Xu, Z. Logistic Regression Based on Individual-Level Predictors and Aggregate-Level Responses. *Mathematics* **2023**, *11*, 746. https://doi.org/10.3390/math11030746

Academic Editors: Niansheng Tang and Shen-Ming Lee

Received: 17 January 2023
Revised: 27 January 2023
Accepted: 30 January 2023
Published: 2 February 2023

Suppose there are n observations in the sample, $(X_i, Y_i), i = 1, 2, \ldots, n, X \in \mathcal{R}^p, Y \in \mathcal{R}$, aggregated into K groups, $G_1, G_2, \ldots, G_K$, with group sizes, respectively, of $n_1, n_2, \cdots, n_K$, $\sum n_g = n$. Denote the set of observations in Group g as $G_g = \{g1, g2, \ldots, gn_g\}$. Aggregate-level X and Y, i.e., $(X_g^*, Y_g^*), g = 1, 2, \ldots, K$ are

$$X_g^* = \sum_{i \in G_g} X_i = \sum_{i=1}^{n_g} X_{gi} \text{ and } Y_g^* = \sum_{i \in G_g} Y_i = \sum_{i=1}^{n_g} Y_{gi}. \quad (1)$$

Note that Y_g^* can be any summary statistic calculated from individual-level Y in Group g, and we study summation aggregation in this paper.

Researchers have solved this problem for linear models [4–6]. Suppose the linear model describing individual-level data (X_i, Y_i) is

$$Y_i = X_i^T \beta + \epsilon_i, i = 1, 2, \ldots, n.$$

Then, the corresponding model describing the aggregated data (X_g^*, Y_g^*) is

$$Y_g^* = (X_g^*)^T \beta + \epsilon_g^*, g = 1, 2, \ldots, K,$$

where $\epsilon_g^* = \sum_{i \in G_g} \epsilon_i$ is the aggregate-level error so that weighted least squares (WLS) can be applied when $\epsilon_i \sim i.i.d.\ N(0, \sigma^2)$ [4]. More estimators have been proposed for linear regression based on aggregate data or partially aggregate data including Palm and Nijman's MLE estimator [5] and Rawashdeh and Obeidat's Bayesian estimator [6].

Although the estimations of linear regression models in the above data situation have been well studied, more studies are needed for the estimations of other regression models. The aim of this article is to study the estimations of logistic models in the data situation of aggregate-level Y and individual-level X. We derive the likelihoods and our estimators with different optimization methods in Section 2, conduct simulation studies to evaluate and compare the performances of different estimators in Section 3, illustrate the use of different estimators in real data-based studies in Section 4, provide discussions in Section 5, and draw conclusions in Section 6.

2. Methods

Suppose n independent observations (X_i, Y_i) are modeled by a logistic model

$$\log(\frac{P(Y_i = 1)}{1 - P(Y_i = 1)}) = X_i^T \beta, i = 1, 2, \ldots, n. \quad (2)$$

Then, $Y_i \sim$ Bernoulli (π_i), where $\pi_i = P(Y_i = 1) = \frac{exp(X_i^T \beta)}{1 + exp(X_i^T \beta)}$. When individual-level X and Y are both available, the logistic model as a general linear model can be estimated using a range of methods including the Newton–Raphson method and Fisher's scoring method [7,8].

2.1. Likelihood of Aggregate-Level Y and Individual-Level X

When individual-level Y is not available, we can derive estimators based on aggregate-level Y and individual-level X. Suppose the n observations of (X_i, Y_i) are aggregated into K groups, as described in the introduction section, with the aggregated data (X_g^*, Y_g^*), $g = 1, \ldots, K$, defined in Equation (1).

Aggregate-level Y is obtained by summing all Y within each group. Thus, the distribution of the sum of multiple independent random variables is helpful for studying data aggregation. In our logistic regression scenario, we need to calculate the sum of multiple Bernoulli random variables. In statistics, the Poisson binomial distribution is the distribution of a sum of independent Bernoulli random variables, which do not necessarily have different success probabilities [9,10]. The term PoissonBinomial$(n, (\pi_1, \pi_2, \cdots, \pi_n))$

is used to refer to the distribution of the sum of n independent Bernoulli random variables with success probabilities $\pi_1, \pi_2, \cdots, \pi_n$ [9].

Because Y_g^* is the sum of n_g independent Bernoulli random variables,

$$Y_g^* \sim \text{PoissonBinomial}(n_g, (\pi_{g1}, \pi_{g2}, \cdots, \pi_{gn_g})), \tag{3}$$

where the success probability for the ith individual in Group g is

$$\pi_{gi} = P(Y_{gi} = 1) = \frac{exp(X_{gi}^T \beta)}{1 + exp(X_{gi}^T \beta)}. \tag{4}$$

Denote the individual likelihood for Y_g^* as $L_g(\beta) = P(Y_g^*; X_{g1}, \ldots, X_{gn_g}, \beta)$. Then, the aggregate likelihood $L(\beta) = \prod_{g=1}^K L_g(\beta)$.

2.2. Calculation and Maximization of Likelihood

Computing the likelihood function needs to calculate the probability mass function for $Y_g^* \sim \text{PoissonBinomial}(n_g, (\pi_{g1}, \pi_{g2}, \ldots, \pi_{gn_g}))$. The variable Y_g^* will reduce to $\text{Binomial}(n_g, \pi)$ when $\pi_{g1} = \pi_{g2} = \cdots = \pi_{gn_g}$. This case can happen when aggregation is based on the values of X and the individual-level predictors X_i are the same within each group. This specific aggregation has been well studied in the topic of logistic regression based on aggregate data [7,11]. We consider aggregation not based on X, i.e., allowing different values of X in a group, in this paper.

In general, for a variable $Y \sim \text{PoissonBinomial}(n, (\pi_1, \pi_2, \ldots, \pi_n))$, the probability mass function is $P(Y = y) = \sum_{A \in F_y} \prod_{i \in A} \pi_i \prod_{j \in A^c}(1 - \pi_j)$, where F_y is the set of all subsets of y integers that can be selected from $\{1, 2, 3, \ldots, n\}$ and A^c is the complement of A [9]. The set F_k contains $\binom{n}{k}$ elements so the sum over it is computationally intensive and even infeasible for large n. Instead, more efficient ways were proposed, including the use of a recursive formula to calculate $P(Y = y)$ based on $Pr(Y = k)$, $k = 0, \ldots, y - 1$, which is numerically unstable for large n [12], and the inverse Fourier transform method [13]. Hong [10] further developed it by proposing an algorithm that efficiently implements the exact formula with a closed expression for the Poisson binomial distribution. We adopted Hong's algorithm [10] and exact formula in calculating the likelihood function $L(\beta)$ since they are more precise and numerically stable.

Commonly used optimization methods were adopted to maximize the likelihood $L(\theta)$, including (1) Nelder and Mead's simplex method (NM) [14], (2) the Broyden–Fletcher–Goldfarb–Shanno (BFGS) method [15], and (3) the conjugate gradient (CG) method [16].

2.3. Large-Sample Properties of Estimators

As mentioned above, our proposed estimators are obtained by maximizing the aggregate likelihood $L(\beta)$ using different optimization methods (NM, BFGS, and CG). The MLE $\hat{\beta}_{MLE}$ is an estimator that maximizes the aggregate likelihood function, i.e., $\hat{\beta}_{MLE} = argmax_{\beta} L(\beta)$. If our three optimization methods can always obtain the maximizer of $L(\beta)$, the three estimators will be equal and exactly the same as the MLEs.

In practice, the three optimization methods may not obtain the same value as the MLE. We observed that as the sample size increases, the values obtained using the three optimizations become closer and nearly the same for a large sample size. In discussing large-sample properties, we refer to the scenario of an infinite number of observations and assume that the three optimization methods can always obtain MLEs under the scenario of large samples, i.e., the scenario of an infinite number of observations. Then, our three estimators are identical to the MLE and have the same large-sample properties as the MLE. We add a cautious note that if our estimators are still quite different from the MLE under the large-sample scenario, we cannot state that our estimators have the same large-sample properties as the MLE.

The large-sample properties of the MLE $\hat{\beta}_{MLE}$ [17] include (i) consistency, i.e., $\hat{\beta}_{MLE} \rightarrow \beta$ in probability, and (ii) asymptotic normality, i.e., $\hat{\beta}_{MLE} \sim N(\beta, I(\beta)^{-1})$, where $I(\beta)$ is the expected information matrix, defined as the negative expectation of the second derivative of the log-likelihood. The expected information matrix can be approximated using the observed information matrix, which is the negative of the second derivative (the Hessian matrix) of the log-likelihood function [17].

2.4. Software Implementation

All analyses in this paper were conducted using R software (version 4.2.0). Multiple R packages were used as follows:

- The *PoissonBiomial* package. This package implements multiple exact and approximate methods to calculate Poisson binomial distributions [10]. We used this package to calculate the Poisson binomial distributions and aggregate likelihood $L(\beta)$.
- The *stats* package. This package contains the $optim()$ function, which can conduct general-purpose optimization based on multiple optimization methods, including the Nelder–Mead, BFGS, and CG methods. We used this function to obtain our three estimators using three optimization methods.
- The glm package. This package can be used to fit generalized linear models including logistic regression. We used this package to conduct logistic regression.

2.5. Computational Burden

The computational burden of our method relies on three factors: (1) p, (2) aggregate-level data sample size K, and (3) group size n_g.

Our estimator for β is obtained by maximizing the aggregate likelihood $L(\beta) = \prod_{g=1}^{K} L_g(\beta), \beta \in \mathcal{R}^p$ using three optimization methods (NM, BFGS, and CG). The number of evaluations of the optimization function $L(\beta)$ and the derivatives will increase with respect to an increase in p. Large p will decrease the performance. Given a small fixed number p, the number of function evaluations is $O(1)$. Because $L(\beta) = \prod_{g=1}^{K} L_g(\beta)$, the computational amount for $L(\beta)$ is K times the computational amount for $L_g(\beta)$.

The computation of $L_g(\beta)$ includes two steps. In Step 1, the success probabilities are calculated using Equation (4). The computational burden of Step 1 is $O(n_g)$. In Step 2, the probability mass for a Poisson binomial random variable described in Equation (3) is calculated. This step adopts Hong's Algorithm A, which is an efficient implementation of the discrete Fourier transform of the characteristic function (DFT-CF) of the Poisson binomial distribution [10]. The computational burden of Step 2 is $O(n_g^2)$. In total, the computational burden of our estimation method is $O(1) \times K \times O(n_g^2) = O(Kn_g^2)$, given a small constant p.

3. Simulation Studies

We conducted simulation studies to evaluate the performance of the five estimators. The first estimator, named individual-LR, is the logistic regression estimator based on individual-level X and Y. This estimator is infeasible when only aggregate Y is available. Because aggregate-level Y contains less information compared to individual-level Y, we expect that this infeasible estimator can provide an upper bound for the performance of feasible estimators based on aggregate-level Y. The second estimator, named naive LR, is the logistic regression estimator based on the mean X in each group and the aggregate Y, i.e., $Y_g^* \sim Bin(n_g, X_g^*/n_g)$, $g = 1, 2, \ldots, K$. This estimator can provide a rough approximate estimation.

Estimators 3 to 5 are our estimators that maximize the aggregate likelihood $L(\beta)$ using the Nelder–Mead optimization, CG optimization, and BFGS optimization, named aggregate LR with NM, aggregate LR with CG, and aggregate LR based on BFGS, respectively.

The performances of the estimators were compared in three scenarios. In each scenario, simulations were conducted with sample sizes ($K = 300, 500, 1000$), equal group sizes ($n_g = 7, 30$), and different parameter values. Data were generated as follows:

- In Scenario 1, $X_{i1} \sim N(0,1)$, $X_i = (1, X_{i1})^T$, $Y_i \sim \text{Bernoulli}(e^{X_i^T\beta}/(1+e^{X_i^T\beta}))$, $\beta = (1,-2)^T$ (Scenario 1A) or $(1,3)^T$ (Scenario 1B).
- In Scenario 2, $X_{i1} \sim N(0,1)$, $X_{i2} \sim t(df = 5)$, $X_i = (1, X_{i1}, X_{i2})^T$, $Y_i \sim \text{Bernoulli}(e^{X_i^T\beta}/(1+e^{X_i^T\beta}))$, $\beta = (-1,1,2)^T$ (Scenario 2A) or $(0,-2,1)^T$ (Scenario 2B).
- In Scenario 3, $(X_{i1}, X_{i2}) \sim \text{BivariateNormal}(0,2,1,4,\rho = 0.5)$, $X_{i3} \sim \text{Cauchy}(0,1)$, $X_i = (1, X_{i1}, X_{i2}, X_{i3})^T$, $Y_i \sim \text{Bernoulli}(e^{X_i^T\beta}/(1+e^{X_i^T\beta}))$, $\beta = (-1,1,0,-1)^T$ (Scenario 3A) or $(0,-2,1,1)^T$ (Scenario 3B).

The bias, variance, mean square error (MSE), and mean absolute deviation (MAD) of each of the five estimators' (E1 to E5) model parameters $(\beta_0, \ldots, \beta_p)$ were calculated. Denote the bias, variance, MSE, and MAD of the q-th estimator of β_j as $Bias(\hat{\beta}_{j,E_q})$,$Var(\hat{\beta}_{j,E_q})$, $MSE(\hat{\beta}_{j,E_q})$, and$MAD(\hat{\beta}_{j,E_q})$. The average squared bias, variance, MSE, and MAD of the qth estimator were calculated as

$$\begin{aligned}
\overline{Bias^2}(E_q) &= [(Bias^2(\hat{\beta}_{0,E_q}) + \cdots + (Bias^2(\hat{\beta}_{p,E_q})]/(p+1), \\
\overline{Var}(E_q) &= [Var(\hat{\beta}_{0,E_q}) + \cdots + Var(\hat{\beta}_{p,E_q})]/(p+1), \\
\overline{MSE}(E_q) &= [MSE(\hat{\beta}_{0,E_q}) + \cdots + (MSE(\hat{\beta}_{p,E_q})]/(p+1), \\
\overline{MAD}(E_q) &= [MAD(\hat{\beta}_{0,E_q}) + \cdots + (MAD(\hat{\beta}_{p,E_q})]/(p+1).
\end{aligned}$$

Please note that we averaged over the squared bias instead of the bias because the positive bias and negative bias can cancel out when averaging the bias. The average across the parameters allows us to obtain the average performance in terms of the squared bias, variance, MSE, and MAD and still maintain the equality of the bias, variance, and MSE, i.e.,

$$\overline{MSE}(E_q) = \overline{Bias^2}(E_q) + \overline{Var}(E_q).$$

In Table 1, we report the average squared biases and variances for the five estimators (E1 to E5) under the different scenarios, sample sizes K, and aggregation sizes n_g. As we expected, there was a relatively large bias for the naive estimator E2, which used an approximate likelihood by conducting logistic regressions using the average X. Our estimators (E3 to E5) had relatively small biases because these estimators were working on the correct and exact likelihood functions. The first estimator E1 had the smallest bias by working on individual-level X and individual-level Y. This estimator is widely used when individual-level Y is available. However, under the scenario we intended to solve, only aggregate-level Y was available. Thus, the E1 estimator is infeasible. We still report the performance of E1 to provide some measurements of the possible upper bound of the performance. Because data aggregation will discard information, we expect that estimator E1 will generally perform better than the estimators based on aggregate Y.

Next, we check the variances of all five estimators. The variances of all five estimators were similar in the same magnitude level. There was no estimator that performed uniformly better or even generally better than the other estimators. The naive estimator E2 had similar performance or even slightly better performance in the average variance compared with the other estimators (E1, E3–E5). Our estimators (E3 to E5) were slightly worse in terms of variance. We think the slightly worse performance of our estimators (E3–E5) was likely due to the nonlinear optimization to find the MLE in our estimators. In comparison, the logistic regression estimators (E1 and E2) were calculated using iteratively re-weighted least squares (IRLS) (logistic regression ensures global concavity so that it is simpler to find the MLE), which was numerically more stable compared to the nonlinear optimization of a general likelihood function using (1) Nelder and Mead's simplex method [14], (2) the BFGS method [15], and (3) the conjugate gradient (CG) method [16].

Table 1. Average Squared Bias and Variance of Estimators E1 to E5 in Scenarios 1A to 3B. K is the sample size of the aggregate data. n_g is the group size in the aggregation.

			Average Squared Bias					Average Variance				
Scen.	**K**	n_g	**E1**	**E2**	**E3**	**E4**	**E5**	**E1**	**E2**	**E3**	**E4**	**E5**
1A	300	7	0.001	0.281	0.001	0.001	0.001	0.027	0.025	0.077	0.077	0.077
1A	300	30	0.000	0.344	0.001	0.001	0.001	0.006	0.018	0.071	0.071	0.071
1A	500	7	0.000	0.293	0.000	0.000	0.000	0.009	0.008	0.020	0.020	0.020
1A	500	30	0.000	0.358	0.000	0.000	0.000	0.002	0.005	0.017	0.017	0.017
1A	1000	7	0.000	0.288	0.000	0.000	0.000	0.005	0.005	0.011	0.011	0.011
1A	1000	30	0.000	0.351	0.000	0.000	0.000	0.001	0.003	0.012	0.012	0.012
1B	300	7	0.001	1.176	0.002	0.002	0.002	0.050	0.025	0.108	0.108	0.108
1B	300	30	0.000	1.367	0.000	0.000	0.000	0.012	0.014	0.099	0.098	0.099
1B	500	7	0.000	1.193	0.000	0.000	0.000	0.017	0.006	0.032	0.032	0.032
1B	500	30	0.000	1.369	0.000	0.000	0.000	0.004	0.004	0.032	0.030	0.033
1B	1000	7	0.000	1.181	0.000	0.000	0.000	0.009	0.004	0.018	0.018	0.018
1B	1000	30	0.000	1.388	0.000	0.000	0.000	0.002	0.003	0.019	0.019	0.019
2A	300	7	0.000	0.471	0.002	0.002	0.002	0.031	0.023	0.073	0.073	0.073
2A	300	30	0.000	0.523	0.004	0.004	0.004	0.007	0.016	0.071	0.071	0.071
2A	500	7	0.000	0.462	0.000	0.000	0.000	0.008	0.007	0.020	0.020	0.020
2A	500	30	0.000	0.538	0.000	0.000	0.000	0.002	0.006	0.019	0.019	0.019
2A	1000	7	0.000	0.464	0.000	0.000	0.000	0.005	0.004	0.012	0.012	0.012
2A	1000	30	0.000	0.532	0.000	0.000	0.000	0.001	0.003	0.013	0.013	0.013
2B	300	7	0.000	0.291	0.000	0.000	0.000	0.025	0.018	0.059	0.059	0.059
2B	300	30	0.000	0.336	0.003	0.003	0.003	0.006	0.016	0.066	0.066	0.066
2B	500	7	0.000	0.277	0.000	0.000	0.000	0.007	0.007	0.017	0.017	0.017
2B	500	30	0.000	0.340	0.000	0.000	0.000	0.002	0.005	0.017	0.017	0.017
2B	1000	7	0.000	0.282	0.000	0.000	0.000	0.005	0.004	0.012	0.012	0.012
2B	1000	30	0.000	0.340	0.000	0.000	0.000	0.001	0.003	0.012	0.012	0.012
3A	300	7	0.000	0.332	0.001	0.000	0.000	0.018	0.020	0.045	0.052	0.055
3A	300	30	0.000	0.345	0.003	0.002	0.001	0.004	0.019	0.045	0.049	0.055
3A	500	7	0.000	0.336	0.000	0.000	0.000	0.006	0.006	0.014	0.015	0.015
3A	500	30	0.000	0.344	0.000	0.000	0.000	0.001	0.006	0.013	0.016	0.017
3A	1000	7	0.000	0.340	0.000	0.000	0.000	0.003	0.004	0.008	0.009	0.009
3A	1000	30	0.000	0.346	0.000	0.000	0.000	0.001	0.004	0.008	0.008	0.010
3B	300	7	0.000	0.567	0.002	0.001	0.001	0.025	0.020	0.056	0.064	0.068
3B	300	30	0.000	0.603	0.005	0.004	0.003	0.006	0.014	0.063	0.069	0.077
3B	500	7	0.000	0.578	0.001	0.000	0.000	0.007	0.005	0.015	0.019	0.018
3B	500	30	0.000	0.614	0.000	0.000	0.000	0.002	0.005	0.018	0.025	0.022
3B	1000	7	0.000	0.587	0.000	0.000	0.000	0.005	0.003	0.010	0.010	0.010
3B	1000	30	0.000	0.608	0.000	0.000	0.000	0.001	0.003	0.010	0.012	0.012

We point out that although the naive estimator E2 worked on an incorrect (or approximate) likelihood function, which can lead to a large bias due to the incorrect likelihood function, the performance of the variance of E2 did not necessarily become worse. A similar phenomenon was the under-fitting in the data analysis. Suppose the true relationship is a quadratic function. If a linear function is used in model fitting, the estimator will have a large bias due to model mis-specification, whereas the variance may not increase. We note that the main disadvantage of estimator E2 was the use of an incorrect or approximate likelihood function, which can lead to a large bias. Using the correct exact likelihood, i.e., our estimators (E3 to E5), can solve the issue of bias due to the slight increase in variance from the switch in finding the MLE from iteratively reweighted least squares (IRLS) to nonlinear optimization using the Nelder and Mead's simplex, BFGS, and CG methods. We compared the decrease in bias and increase in variance and think the bias reduction will dominate the variance increase in our estimators. We calculated the overall performance in terms of the MSE and MAD to confirm it.

Our simulation results showed that the naive estimator had a large bias due to the use of an incorrect or approximate likelihood function, which can hurt the MSE. Thus, in Table 2, we report the average performance of the five estimators (E1 to E5) in terms of the MSE and MAD. Our simulation results indicated that our proposed estimators (E3 to E5) were better than the naive LR estimator (E2). As expected, the infeasible estimator (E1) based on individual-level Y performed better than the other four feasible estimators (E2 to E5) based on aggregate-level Y due to the loss of information in the data aggregation. Our estimator based on Nelder and Mead's simplex optimization (E3) performed slightly better than our estimator based on BFGS optimization (E4) and CG optimization (E5).

Table 2. Average MSE and MAD of Estimators E1 to E5 in Scenarios 1A to 3B. K is the sample size of the aggregate data. n_g is the group size in the aggregation.

			Average MSE					Average MAD				
Scen.	**K**	n_g	**E1**	**E2**	**E3**	**E4**	**E5**	**E1**	**E2**	**E3**	**E4**	**E5**
1A	300	7	0.027	0.307	0.078	0.078	0.078	0.129	0.504	0.198	0.198	0.198
1A	300	30	0.006	0.362	0.072	0.072	0.072	0.062	0.558	0.192	0.192	0.192
1A	500	7	0.009	0.302	0.020	0.020	0.020	0.075	0.515	0.109	0.109	0.109
1A	500	30	0.002	0.363	0.017	0.017	0.017	0.036	0.568	0.093	0.093	0.093
1A	1000	7	0.005	0.293	0.011	0.011	0.011	0.057	0.509	0.080	0.080	0.080
1A	1000	30	0.001	0.354	0.012	0.012	0.012	0.028	0.563	0.078	0.078	0.078
1B	300	7	0.051	1.200	0.109	0.109	0.109	0.173	0.970	0.235	0.235	0.235
1B	300	30	0.012	1.380	0.099	0.098	0.099	0.084	1.046	0.222	0.221	0.222
1B	500	7	0.017	1.200	0.032	0.032	0.032	0.098	0.977	0.130	0.130	0.130
1B	500	30	0.004	1.373	0.033	0.031	0.033	0.048	1.048	0.129	0.125	0.129
1B	1000	7	0.009	1.185	0.018	0.018	0.018	0.072	0.973	0.100	0.100	0.100
1B	1000	30	0.002	1.390	0.019	0.019	0.019	0.038	1.054	0.098	0.098	0.098
2A	300	7	0.031	0.494	0.075	0.075	0.075	0.138	0.627	0.204	0.204	0.204
2A	300	30	0.007	0.539	0.075	0.075	0.075	0.065	0.661	0.200	0.200	0.200
2A	500	7	0.008	0.469	0.021	0.021	0.021	0.070	0.622	0.111	0.111	0.111
2A	500	30	0.002	0.543	0.020	0.020	0.020	0.036	0.669	0.106	0.106	0.106
2A	1000	7	0.005	0.468	0.012	0.012	0.012	0.057	0.620	0.084	0.084	0.084
2A	1000	30	0.001	0.535	0.013	0.013	0.013	0.030	0.667	0.085	0.085	0.085
2B	300	7	0.025	0.309	0.059	0.059	0.059	0.124	0.445	0.182	0.182	0.182
2B	300	30	0.006	0.352	0.068	0.068	0.068	0.060	0.464	0.180	0.180	0.180
2B	500	7	0.007	0.284	0.017	0.017	0.017	0.065	0.424	0.099	0.099	0.099

Table 2. *Cont.*

Scen.	K	n_g	Average MSE E1	E2	E3	E4	E5	Average MAD E1	E2	E3	E4	E5
2B	500	30	0.002	0.344	0.018	0.018	0.018	0.034	0.463	0.093	0.093	0.093
2B	1000	7	0.005	0.286	0.012	0.012	0.012	0.054	0.425	0.081	0.081	0.081
2B	1000	30	0.001	0.343	0.012	0.012	0.012	0.024	0.461	0.075	0.075	0.075
3A	300	7	0.018	0.352	0.046	0.052	0.055	0.104	0.486	0.162	0.168	0.170
3A	300	30	0.004	0.364	0.047	0.051	0.056	0.049	0.495	0.161	0.165	0.170
3A	500	7	0.006	0.342	0.014	0.015	0.015	0.058	0.474	0.090	0.091	0.091
3A	500	30	0.001	0.350	0.014	0.016	0.017	0.028	0.481	0.088	0.090	0.091
3A	1000	7	0.003	0.344	0.008	0.009	0.009	0.043	0.475	0.066	0.067	0.067
3A	1000	30	0.001	0.350	0.008	0.008	0.009	0.022	0.480	0.069	0.069	0.070
3B	300	7	0.025	0.587	0.058	0.065	0.069	0.119	0.645	0.178	0.184	0.188
3B	300	30	0.006	0.617	0.068	0.073	0.079	0.057	0.656	0.180	0.184	0.190
3B	500	7	0.007	0.584	0.015	0.019	0.018	0.066	0.644	0.092	0.095	0.095
3B	500	30	0.002	0.619	0.019	0.025	0.022	0.033	0.659	0.096	0.102	0.099
3B	1000	7	0.005	0.590	0.010	0.010	0.010	0.055	0.647	0.075	0.075	0.075
3B	1000	30	0.001	0.611	0.011	0.012	0.012	0.026	0.655	0.072	0.074	0.074

We found the performances of our estimators (E3, E4, E5) were slightly worse when the group size $n_g = 30$ compared with the performances of our estimators when the group size $n_g = 7$. We expect that the performance of our estimators may decrease for a large group size n_g due to rounding errors in computation.

4. Real Data-Based Studies

We used real data to illustrate the use of our estimators and compare the different estimators. The dataset used was the "Social-Network-Ads" dataset from the Kaggle Machine Learning Forum (https://www.kaggle.com, accessed on 12 January 2023).

The dataset has been used by statisticians and data scientists to illustrate the use of logistic regression in categorical data analysis. We used the dataset to illustrate the use of our method to conduct logistic regression in the presence of data aggregation.

The Social-Network-Ads dataset in Kaggle is a categorical dataset for determining whether a user purchased a particular product. The dataset (https://www.kaggle.com/datasets, accessed on 12 January 2023) contains 400 people/observations. The information about the person's purchase action (purchased with a binary variable of 1 denotes purchased and 0 denotes not purchased), as well as the person's age and estimated salary, is provided. Logistic regression has been recommended in Kaggle to model the person's purchase action based on the person's age and estimated salary. We intend to apply our method to this dataset in the presence of data aggregation.

The original dataset is at the individual level, which allows us to conduct logistic regression based on individual-level Y and X. We standardized X by $X^* = (X - mean(X))/sd(X)$ in data pre-processing. Standardization of X allows for better estimation and interpretation. Standardized coefficients β^* are obtained by logistics regression of Y on standardized data X^*. The original slope coefficients in β can be calculated by the formula $\hat{\beta} = \hat{\beta}^* \times sd(X)$ and then the intercept coefficient can be calculated.

We imposed data aggregation on this dataset with an aggregation size $n_g = 3, 5, 7$. We randomly divided the persons into groups of size n_g and calculated the group aggregate of the purchase actions Y. Due to confidentiality and the cost of collecting individual-level data, businesses and organizations can choose to post data information at an aggregate level. We mimicked the data aggregation process by random grouping and calculated the aggregate-level Y based on the individual-level Y. We repeated the data aggregation 300 times. In this way, we generated 300 datasets, with the individual-level X and aggregate-level Y calculated.

For each dataset, we conducted logistic regression based on individual-level X and Y and obtained our estimator E1. Since data aggregation discards information, we evaluated the other estimators by checking whether they were close to estimator E1. Because the true values of the coefficients in individual-level logistic regression models are not known in real data-based studies, we used estimator E1 as a gold-standard estimator. We compared the other estimators based on aggregate-level Y to determine which estimator was closer to our gold-standard estimator E1. Note that E1 is an infeasible estimator when individual-level X is not available.

The estimator E1 was calculated based on individual-level X and individual-level Y. The estimated value of estimator E1 remained the same in our 300 generated datasets and E1 was treated as the gold-standard estimator; thus, we denote it as $(\beta_0, \beta_1, \beta_2)$.

Denote the estimated value of β_i for the j-th estimator in the k-th dataset by $\hat{\beta}_{i,Ej}(D_k)$. The bias, variance, MSE, and MAD of estimators E2 to E5 for β_0,β_1, and β_2 were calculated by the formulae

$$\begin{aligned}
\overline{\hat{\beta}_{i,Ej}} &= \sum_{k=1}^{300} \hat{\beta}_{i,Ej}(D_k)/300 \\
Bias(\hat{\beta}_{i,Ej}) &= \overline{\hat{\beta}_{i,Ej}} - \beta_i \\
Var(\hat{\beta}_{i,Ej}) &= \sum_{k=1}^{300} \{\hat{\beta}_{i,Ej}(D_k) - \overline{\hat{\beta}_{i,Ej}}\}^2/300 \\
MSE(\hat{\beta}_{i,Ej}) &= \sum_{k=1}^{300} \{\hat{\beta}_{i,Ej}(D_k) - \beta_i\}^2/300 \\
MAD(\hat{\beta}_{i,Ej}) &= \sum_{k=1}^{300} |\hat{\beta}_{i,Ej}(D_k) - \beta_i|/300
\end{aligned}$$

For the four estimators based on aggregate-level Y and individual-level X, i.e., E2 to E5, we report the biases and variances in Table 3. We can see that in most cases, there are large biases in estimating β_0 and β_2 and relatively smaller biases in estimating β_1 using the naive estimator E2. Our proposed estimators (E3 to E5) always achieved smaller biases compared to the naive estimator E2. This is because the naive estimator E2 used an approximate likelihood instead of an exact likelihood, which our proposed estimators are based on. In terms of variance, the naive estimator had a relatively smaller variance compared with our estimators E3 to E5. We point out that the calculation algorithm used in E2, i.e., iteratively reweighted least squares (IRLS), was more numerically stable compared with the nonlinear optimization algorithms adopted by our estimators, i.e., Nelder and Mead's simplex method, the BFGS method, and the conjugate gradient method.

We then checked the overall performance of the different estimators and report the MSE and MAD in Table 4. We found that our estimators (E3 to E5) had better performance than the naive estimator (E2) in terms of the MSE and MAD in all situations based on the Social-Network-Ads dataset.

Table 3. Biases and Variances of Estimators E2 to E5 based on Aggregate-Level Y and Individual-Level X. n_g is the group size in the aggregation.

		Bias				Variance			
Coef.	n_g	**E2**	**E3**	**E4**	**E5**	**E2**	**E3**	**E4**	**E5**
β_0	3	1.580	−0.018	0.620	−0.017	0.094	0.160	0.125	0.160
β_0	5	1.721	−0.054	0.877	−0.054	0.115	0.383	0.218	0.383
β_0	7	1.769	−0.156	1.019	−0.156	0.194	0.721	0.319	0.721
β_1	3	−0.163	0.001	−0.073	0.001	0.002	0.003	0.002	0.003
β_1	5	−0.176	0.005	−0.108	0.005	0.002	0.006	0.004	0.006
β_1	7	−0.180	0.016	−0.127	0.016	0.004	0.012	0.006	0.012
β_2	3	−1.007	0.039	−0.195	0.039	0.025	0.062	0.026	0.062
β_2	5	−1.123	0.075	−0.258	0.075	0.043	0.174	0.053	0.174
β_2	7	−1.141	0.150	−0.266	0.150	0.053	0.260	0.087	0.260

Table 4. MSE and MAD of Estimators E2 to E5 based on Aggregate-Level Y and Individual-Level X. n_g is the group size in the aggregation.

		MSE				MAD			
Coef.	n_g	**E2**	**E3**	**E4**	**E5**	**E2**	**E3**	**E4**	**E5**
β_0	3	2.591	0.160	0.509	0.160	1.580	0.317	0.644	0.317
β_0	5	3.076	0.385	0.986	0.385	1.721	0.480	0.909	0.480
β_0	7	3.322	0.743	1.356	0.742	1.769	0.651	1.036	0.650
β_1	3	0.028	0.003	0.008	0.003	0.163	0.041	0.077	0.041
β_1	5	0.033	0.006	0.016	0.006	0.176	0.060	0.112	0.060
β_1	7	0.036	0.012	0.023	0.012	0.181	0.085	0.130	0.085
β_2	3	1.039	0.063	0.064	0.063	1.007	0.186	0.222	0.186
β_2	5	1.304	0.179	0.120	0.179	1.123	0.325	0.297	0.325
β_2	7	1.356	0.282	0.157	0.282	1.141	0.409	0.331	0.409

5. Discussion

Our estimators are obtained by maximizing the nonlinear likelihood function $L(\beta)$, $\beta \in \mathcal{R}^p$. Different optimization methods can influence the performance of our estimators. Further studies can be conducted on other optimization methods such as the genetic algorithm or using multiple starting values. The performance of optimization is expected to decrease when p increases.

We only consider independent individual-level data, i.e., $(X_i, Y_i), i = 1, 2, \cdots, n$. The n observations are randomly divided into groups of size n_g and the aggregate-level Y is calculated after grouping. In this paper, we only consider the situation of "grouping completely at random", which means that the grouping mechanism is completely random. The values of X and Y do not influence the grouping. Further studies can be conducted beyond this type of grouping mechanism.

Our aggregation scheme is based on independent individual-level data. There are more aggregations schemes. For example, temporal aggregation can aggregate dependent data, which can generate aggregated low-frequency time series based on high-frequency time series by summing every m consecutive time points. For example, we can aggregate daily time series into weekly time series by summing every $m = 7$ consecutive daily observations. Temporal aggregation is often based on a time series model such as an integer-valued generalized autoregressive conditional heteroskedasticity (INGARCH) [18].

We note that the proposed methods also allow for other link functions in addition to the logit link. For example, when a probit link function is used, we can estimate individual-level probit models based on aggregate-level Y and individual-level X. In addition, we only consider binary responses in this paper. A follow-up study to extend our methods to handle responses with more than two levels are under development.

6. Conclusions

We proposed methods to estimate logistic models based on individual-level predictors and aggregate-level responses. We conducted simulation studies to evaluate the performance of the estimators and show the advantage of our estimators. We then used the Social-Network-Ads dataset to illustrate the use of our estimators in the presence of data aggregation and compared the different estimators. Both the simulation studies and real data-based studies have shown the advantage of our estimators in estimating logistics models describing individual-level behaviors based on aggregate-level Y and individual-level X, i.e., when there is data aggregation in the response variable.

Funding: This research received no external funding.

Data Availability Statement: All data used in the study are publicly available.

Conflicts of Interest: The author declares no conflict of interest.

Abbreviations

The following abbreviations are used in this manuscript:

BFGS	Broyden–Fletcher–Goldfarb–Shanno method
CF	Characteristic function
CG	Conjugate gradient
DFT	Discrete Fourier transform
IRLS	Iteratively re-weighted least squares
LR	Logistics regression
MAD	Mean Absolute Deviation
MSE	Mean Square Error
NM	Nelder-Mead method

References

1. Firebaugh, G. A rule for inferring individual-level relationships from aggregate data. *Am. Sociol. Rev.* **1978**, *43*, 557–572. [CrossRef]
2. Robinson, W.S. Ecological correlations and the behavior of individuals. *Int. J. Epidemiol.* **2009**, *38*, 337–341. [CrossRef]
3. Hammond, J.L. Two sources of error in ecological correlations. *Am. Sociol. Rev.* **1973**, *38*, 764–777. [CrossRef]
4. Hsiao, C. Linear regression using both temporally aggregated and temporally disaggregated data. *J. Econom.* **1979**, *10*, 243–252. [CrossRef]
5. Palm, F.C.; Nijman, T.E. Linear regression using both temporally aggregated and temporally disaggregated data. *J. Econom.* **1982**, *19*, 333–343. [CrossRef]
6. Rawashdeh, A.; Obeidat, M. A Bayesian Approach to Estimate a Linear Regression Model with Aggregate Data. *Austrian J. Stat.* **2019**, *48*, 90–100. [CrossRef]
7. Agresti, A. *Categorical Data Analysis*; Wiley Series in Probability and Statistics; Wiley: Hoboken, NJ, USA, 2013.
8. Givens, G.; Hoeting, J. *Computational Statistics*; Wiley Series in Probability and Statistics; Wiley: Hoboken, NJ, USA, 2012.
9. Wang, Y.H. On the number of successes in independent trials. *Stat. Sin.* **1993**, *3*, 295–312.
10. Hong, Y. On computing the distribution function for the Poisson binomial distribution. *Comput. Stat. Data Anal.* **2013**, *59*, 41–51. [CrossRef]
11. Bilder, C.; Loughin, T. *Analysis of Categorical Data with R*; Chapman & Hall/CRC Texts in Statistical Science; CRC Press: Boca Raton, FL, USA, 2014.
12. Chen, X.H.; Dempster, A.P.; Liu, J.S. Weighted finite population sampling to maximize entropy. *Biometrika* **1994**, *81*, 457–469. [CrossRef]
13. Fernández, M.; Williams, S. Closed-form expression for the poisson-binomial probability density function. *IEEE Trans. Aerosp. Electron. Syst.* **2010**, *46*, 803–817. [CrossRef]
14. Nelder, J.A.; Mead, R. A simplex method for function minimization. *Comput. J.* **1965**, *7*, 308–313. [CrossRef]

15. Fletcher, R. A new approach to variable metric algorithms. *Comput. J.* **1970**, *13*, 317–322. [CrossRef]
16. Flecher, R.; Reeves, C. Function minimization by conjugate gradient. *Comput. J.* **1964**, *7*, 149–154. [CrossRef]
17. Shao, J. *Mathematical statistics*; Springer Science & Business Media: Berlin/Heidelberg, Germany, 2003.
18. Su, B.; Zhu, F. Temporal aggregation and systematic sampling for INGARCH processes. *J. Stat. Plan. Inference* **2022**, *219*, 120–133. [CrossRef]

mathematics

Article

A Flexible Method for Diagnostic Accuracy with Biomarker Measurement Error

Ching-Yun Wang * and Ziding Feng

Division of Public Health Sciences, Fred Hutchinson Cancer Research Center, P.O. Box 19024, Seattle, WA 98109-1024, USA
* Correspondence: cywang@fredhutch.org

Abstract: Diagnostic biomarkers are often measured with errors due to imperfect lab conditions or analytic variability of the assay. The ability of a diagnostic biomarker to discriminate between cases and controls is often measured by the area under the receiver operating characteristic curve (AUC), sensitivity, specificity, among others. Ignoring measurement error can cause biased estimation of a diagnostic accuracy measure, which results in misleading interpretation of the efficacy of a diagnostic biomarker. Existing assays available are either research grade or clinical grade. Research assays are cost effective, often multiplex, but they may be associated with moderate measurement errors leading to poorer diagnostic performance. In comparison, clinical assays may provide better diagnostic ability, but with higher cost since they are usually developed by industry. Correction for attenuation methods are often valid when biomarkers are from a normal distribution, but may be biased with skewed biomarkers. In this paper, we develop a flexible method based on skew–normal biomarker distributions to correct for bias in estimating diagnostic performance measures including AUC, sensitivity, and specificity. Finite sample performance of the proposed method is examined via extensive simulation studies. The methods are applied to a pancreatic cancer biomarker study.

Keywords: biomarkers; correction for attenuation; measurement error

MSC: 62F10; 62H30; 62J20

Citation: Wang, C.-Y.; Feng, Z. A Flexible Method for Diagnostic Accuracy with Biomarker Measurement Error. *Mathematics* **2023**, *11*, 549. https://doi.org/10.3390/math11030549

Academic Editors: Manuel Franco and Christophe Chesneau

Received: 29 November 2022
Revised: 13 January 2023
Accepted: 17 January 2023
Published: 19 January 2023

1. Introduction

Most biomarkers are measured with research assays that may have poorer analytical reproducibility as compared to clinical grade assays. However clinical assay development is expensive, and there is no resource or incentive for academic labs to develop it. Diagnostic companies, on the other hand, would first evaluate if a biomarker may have good performance, before they decide whether to invest in it to develop clinical assays. Therefore, some potentially useful biomarkers are dropped from the pipeline due to inadequate performance, while their performance could be adequate if they were evaluated using clinical grade assays. An important question is whether we could quantify the potential improvement in performance between research assays and clinical assays. This will help in making a decision regarding the development of clinical grade biomarkers. Another motivation is that clinical assays are usually in an ELISA format which requires a larger volume as compared to some multiplex research assay platforms such as antibody arrays. At the discovery and triage stage, a lot of candidates are evaluated and it is not possible to use clinical grade assays due to blood volume constraint. Therefore, it is desirable to have a fair appraisal of these candidates under these constraints.

A motivating example for our study is biomarker development for pancreatic cancer. Research in Early Detection Research Network (EDRN) laboratories and elsewhere has produced several candidate biomarkers for the detection of early-stage pancreatic ductal adenocarcinoma (PDAC) [1]. The goal is to find biomarkers that could improve upon the performance of the current best marker, CA19-9 for early detection of PDAC. A study aim of an EDRN pancreatic cancer bake-off study is to compare the performance of several candidate biomarkers for discriminating resectable PDAC from benign pancreatic disease, both alone and in combination with CA19-9. Resectable PDAC and benign pancreatic disease are determined either by biopsy or by adequate follow up. The study's goal is to find biomarkers that can distinguish them without the need for surgery biopsy or long term follow up. Malignant lesions will progress during follow-up, and hence the clinical need is to be able to make a decision sooner. However, most biomarkers are measured using research assays that have poorer analytical reproducibility as compared to clinical grade assays. Figure 1 shows the association between a clinical assay and research assay measures. Variability due to measurement error can attenuate diagnostic efficacy. To help decision making during the biomarker development process, we aim to estimate the loss of diagnostic efficacy of a biomarker due to analytic variability from measurement errors.

Standard diagnostic measures to evaluate the performance of biomarkers include sensitivity, specificity, the receiver operating characteristic (ROC) curve, area under the ROC curve (AUC), among others. There are several criteria for the determination of the most appropriate cutoff value in a diagnostic test with continuous values. The Youden's index (sensitivity + specificity − 1) would be the point to maximize the summation of sensitivity and specificity [2]. A second common criterion to choose the cutoff point of a biomarker is the point on the ROC curve with minimum distance from the left-upper corner of the unit square [3]. In the presence of biomarker measurement error, Coffin and Sukhatme developed a bias correction method for estimation of AUC using non-parametric kernel smoothers [4]. Faraggi derived an exact relationship between the observed AUC and the true AUC under the assumption that the biomarker is from a normal distribution among the controls and cases, respectively, and the measurement errors are also normal [5]. Under most situations, ignoring measurement error can typically attenuate AUC and hence under-estimate the efficacy of a diagnostic biomarker. In the presence of internal reliability data, White and Xie developed bias-corrected estimators for sensitivity, specificity, and other diagnostic measures [6]. Rosner et al. developed an approximation method to correct for measurement error in the biomarkers, but without the normality assumption [7]. Their approximation is based on a probit–shift model, which assumes that the distributions of cases and controls satisfy a location-shift property. When a validation subset is available, inverse probability weighting can be applied to adjust for bias from biomarker measurement error [8].

The methods reviewed above, in general, assume a normal distribution for the true unobserved biomarkers and measurement errors. One challenge in the methods for biomarker measurement error is that the existing methods often rely on a normal or symmetric distribution of the biomarkers. However, in practice biomarker data are often skewed in the distribution. For log normal distributions, the data will have a normal distribution after taking a log transformation. Hence, applying the existing correction for the attenuation method to the transformed data will be a fine approach. However, for general skewed biomarkers, there may not be a suitable transformation so that the transformed data are normal. This is also an important reason for the development of the new method in the paper. An important strength of our method development is that our new method is valid for both symmetric and skewed biomarkers. In addition, in the development of the methods, we do not need to assume availability of either a validation subset or a reliability subset with replicates.

In this paper, we propose a flexible method based on skew-normal distributions under general measurement error models to adjust for estimation of AUC, sensitivity, and specificity due to measurement errors in biomarkers. The paper is organized as follows. In Section 2, we describe the statistical models for the problem of interest. We review a few important corrections for attenuation methods when a reliability or validation subset is available. In Section 3, we develop statistical methods to address our research problem of biomarker measurement error when two different assay measurements of a biomarker are available. To avoid a normality assumption for the biomarker distribution, in Section 4 we propose a more general class of distributions for biomarkers than the normal distribution. In Section 5, results from simulation studies are presented. We demonstrate that the proposed skew-normal biomarker correction estimator works well when the biomarkers are from a normal distribution, and it works better than a correction for attenuation estimator when the biomarkers are skewed. In Section 6, we illustrate the proposed method with the pancreatic cancer biomarker study described above. In Section 7, we discuss the strengths and limitations of the methods, and potential future developments in this research. Some concluding remarks are given in Section 8.

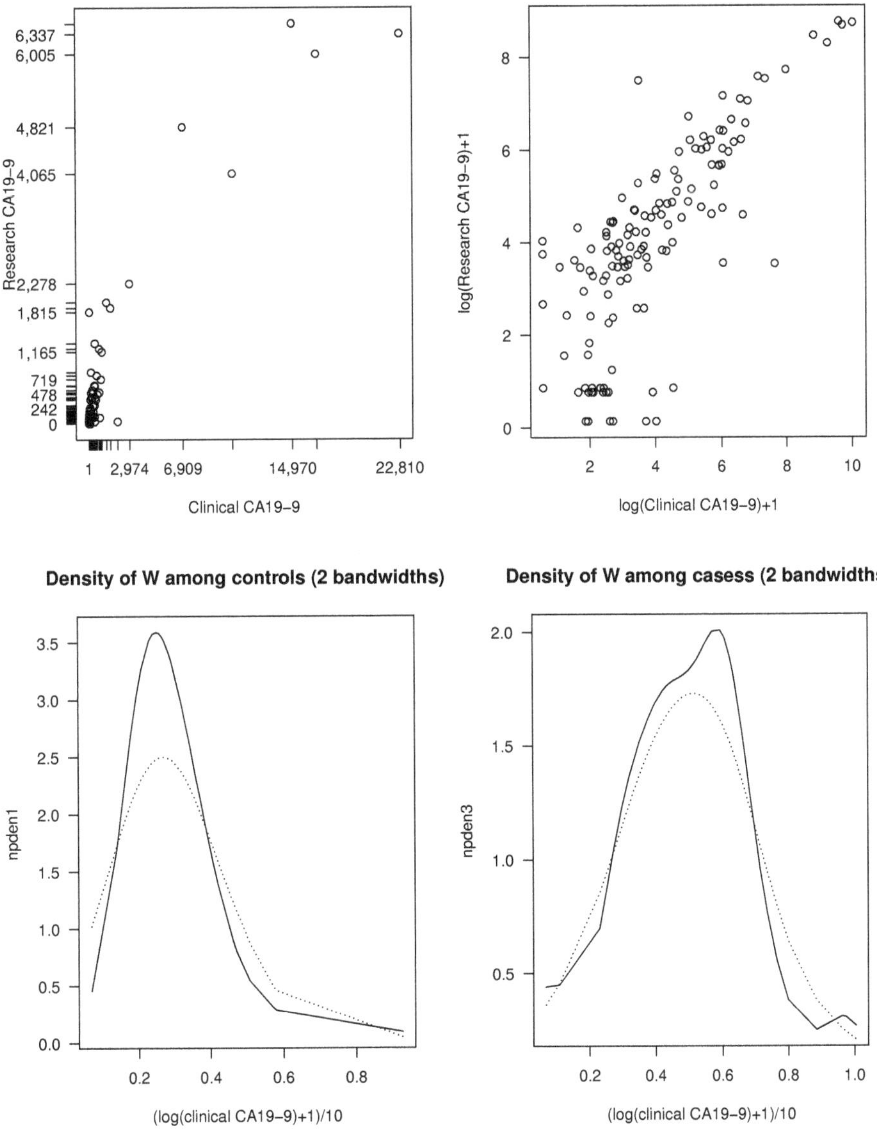

Figure 1. **Upper**: clinical assay versus research assay; **lower**: density estimation of log(clinical CA19-9 + 1)/10 based on two bandwidths (dotted curves from wider bandwidth) .

2. Statistical Models and Correction for Attenuation

The statistical models in the following will be general enough to include not only the situation when replicates of a biomarker are available, but also the situation with two different test measures of the same biomarker, such as research assays and clinical assays for CA19–9. Under this situation, the methodology development will help in understanding the degree of improvement of a clinical assay over a research assay. In addition, the models may be applied to the situation when two different test measures of the same biomarker may be linearly associated. Assume the total sample size is n. Let the disease status be denoted by Y_i for individual i, $i = 1, \ldots, n$, in which $Y_i = 0$ or controls and $Y_i = 1$ for cases. Let W_i be a biomarker assay measure from individual i, and X_i be the true underlying biomarker. Let M_i be another assay measure of the same biomarker. We assume the following models:

$$\begin{aligned} W_i &= X_i + U_i, \quad \mathrm{E}(U_i|X_i) = 0, \\ M_i &= \alpha_0 + \alpha_1 X_i + V_i, \quad \mathrm{E}(V_i|X_i) = 0, \end{aligned} \tag{1}$$

where U_i is the measurement error from biomarker assay W_i, V_i is the measurement error from biomarker assay M_i, and U_i and V_i are independent. Let μ_x and σ_x be the mean and standard deviation of any random variable X, respectively. The first application of model (1) is for the situation when replicates are available, in which $(\alpha_0, \alpha_1) = (0, 1)$ and $\sigma_u = \sigma_v$, where σ_u is the standard deviation of U. The second application of model (1) is for the situation when clinical assay measure and research assay measure are available for a specific biomarker in which $(\alpha_0, \alpha_1) = (0, 1)$ but σ_u and σ_v are different. If we let W_i be the clinical assay measure from individual i and M_i be the research assay measure, then usually σ_u is smaller than σ_v. The third application of model (1) is when W_i is an *unbiased* measure of one biomarker (i.e., true X plus an error), but M_i is a *biased* measure of the same biomarker such that M_i is a linear function of X_i. The third application is common since many research assays use a different technology (e.g., mass spectrometry) from that used for a clinical assay (e.g., ELISA).

We first study the effect of bias when using the observed error-prone biomarker data W_i $(i = 1, \ldots, n)$ on diagnostic performance. Let $\mu_{x,0}$ and $\mu_{x,1}$ denote $\mathrm{E}(X|Y = 0)$ and $\mathrm{E}(X|Y = 1)$, respectively. By convention, we assume larger values of a biomarker are associated with disease, that is, $\mu_{x,1} \geq \mu_{x,0}$. For a potential cutoff point c of the continuous biomarker, an individual is classified as diseased if $X_i \geq c$ or classified as non-diseased if $X_i < c$. Sensitivity of biomarker X is the true positive rate, and specificity is the true negative rate. When biomarkers are measured with errors, the cutoff point c will likely be different from the cutoff point when the true X is available. In this paper, for simplicity, we assume a fixed cutoff point c that has been determined in advance. Assume there are n_0 controls and n_1 cases ($\sum_{i=1}^{n} Y_i = n_1$). Let $X_{(0),i}$, $i = 1, \ldots, n_0$ be the ith X biomarker in the controls ($Y = 0$), and $X_{(1),i}$, $i = 1, \ldots, n_1$ be the ith X biomarker in the cases ($Y = 1$), $U_{(0),i}$ and $U_{(1),i}$ be the measurement errors in both groups, respectively. Bamber showed that the AUC of X is known to be the same as $\mathrm{pr}(X_{(1)} > X_{(0)})$ [9]; hence it is a general measure of how well the biomarker distinguishes between cases and controls. Let $\mathcal{A}_x$ denote the AUC when X is the true biomarker, $\sigma^2_{x_0}$ and $\sigma^2_{x_1}$ be the variances of X among controls and cases, respectively, $\sigma^2_{u,0}$ and $\sigma^2_{u,1}$ be the variances of U among controls and cases, respectively. We assume that X and U are independent, which is reasonable in general applications. If $\sigma^2_{x,0} = \sigma^2_{x,1} = \sigma^2_x$, $\sigma^2_{u,0} = \sigma^2_{u,1} = \sigma^2_u$, then $\lambda^2 \equiv \sigma^2_u / \sigma^2_x$ is the intra versus inter-individual variance ratio which provides a standardized measure of the size of measurement error. Under this situation, if X is normally distributed among the controls and among the cases, then the AUC based on X and the AUC based on W can be expressed as

$$\mathcal{A}_x = \mathrm{pr}(X_{(1)} > X_{(0)}) = \Phi\left(\frac{\mu_{x,1} - \mu_{x,0}}{\sqrt{2}\sigma_x}\right), \mathcal{A}_w = \mathrm{pr}(W_{(1)} > W_{(0)}) = \Phi\left(\frac{\mu_{x,1} - \mu_{x,0}}{\sqrt{2}\sigma_x\sqrt{1+\lambda^2)}}\right),$$

where $\Phi(\cdot)$ is the cumulative distribution function of the standard normal distribution [5]. Based on the calculation given above, Faraggi (2000) showed that the AUC with the true X can be represented as a function of the AUC with the error-prone W and the intra versus inter-individual variance ratio

$$\mathcal{A}_x = \Phi\{\Phi^{-1}(\mathcal{A}_w)\sqrt{1+\lambda^2}\}. \tag{2}$$

The correction method via (2) provides a simple adjustment for AUC estimation if the measurement error variance is known. For example, if the AUC estimate of an error-prone biomarker is 0.75 and if $\sigma_u = \sigma_x$, then the AUC from the true assay without measurement error will be 0.83. If a clinical grade is available and if it has very small measurement error then the expected AUC will likely be about 0.83; an improvement from the AUC of 0.75 of the research assay.

There could be situations when the biomarker variances among the controls and cases are different. When $\sigma_{x,0}$ may be different from $\sigma_{x,1}$, and $\sigma_{u,0}$ may be different from $\sigma_{u,1}$, the AUC based on X and the AUC based on W can be expressed as

$$\mathcal{A}_x = \Phi\left(\frac{\mu_{x,1}-\mu_{x,0}}{\sqrt{\sigma^2_{x,0}+\sigma^2_{x,1}}}\right), \qquad \mathcal{A}_w = \Phi\left(\frac{\mu_{x,1}-\mu_{x,0}}{\sqrt{\sigma^2_{x,0}+\sigma^2_{x,1}}\sqrt{1+\lambda^2_*)}}\right),$$

where $\lambda^2_* = (\sigma^2_{u,0}+\sigma^2_{u,1})/(\sigma^2_{x,0}+\sigma^2_{x,1})$. Based on the calculation given above, Reiser showed that under this situation, the correction has the same form as (2), but the λ^2 should be replaced with λ^2_* [10]. The correction for attenuation (CFA) method via (2) can be also called a *de-attenuation* method.

Let Se_x and Se_w denote the sensitivity of X and W, Sp_x and Sp_w denote the specificity of X and W, respectively. If X and U among the cases ($Y = 1$) are normally distributed, then the sensitivity for X and the sensitivity for W can be expressed as

$$Se_x = 1-\Phi\left(\frac{c-\mu_{x,1}}{\sigma_{x,1}}\right), \qquad Se_w = 1-\Phi\left(\frac{c-\mu_{x,1}}{\sigma_{x,1}\sqrt{1+(\sigma^2_{u,1}/\sigma^2_{x,1})}}\right).$$

If X and U among the controls ($Y = 0$) are normally distributed, then the specificity for X and the specificity for W can be expressed as

$$Sp_x = \Phi\left(\frac{c-\mu_{x,0}}{\sigma_{x,0}}\right), \qquad Sp_w = \Phi\left(\frac{c-\mu_{x,0}}{\sigma_{x,0}\sqrt{1+(\sigma^2_{u,0}/\sigma^2_{x,0})}}\right).$$

Based on the calculation given above, White and Xie showed that approximately

$$Se_x \approx 1-\Phi\{\Phi^{-1}(1-Se_w)\sqrt{1+\lambda_1^2}\},\ Sp_x \approx \Phi\{\Phi^{-1}(Sp_w)\sqrt{1+\lambda_0^2}\}, \tag{3}$$

in which $\lambda_1^2 = \sigma^2_{u,1}/\sigma^2_{x,1}$, and $\lambda_0^2 = \sigma^2_{u,0}/\sigma^2_{x,0}$ [6]. The approximation in (3) is equal if the sample size increases to infinity. Hence, under the normality assumption given above, sensitivity and specificity of a biomarker will be attenuated if the biomarker measurement is measured with errors. Approximation (3) provides CFA estimation for sensitivity and specification that may work well for symmetric biomarker data.

We will investigate this in a more general measurement error model (1) that will include the situation with two different test measures of the same biomarker, which will address the issue of how much improvement clinical assays may obtain over research assays. Model (1) will also include the situation when test measure W is unbiased with an error, while test measure M is biased but linearly associated with the true biomarker.

Hence, further developments of the methods will be needed to address practical problems that we described in the introduction.

3. Correction for Attenuation with Two Biomarker Measures

In this section, we will apply the existing CFA methods for the situation when two assay measures of a biomarker are available. For example, when there are two research grade assays for the same biomarker, we develop a CFA method to make use of the two different research assays to achieve the best AUC estimation. The composite CFA estimator can correct for the bias of a naive estimator which does not take into account measurement error in the estimation of sensitivity, specificity, and AUC. We assume that the available data are based on the measurement error model (1). First, we consider the situation when the two test measures W and M are unbiased for the same biomarker (but with random errors), and they satisfy a special case of (1) such that

$$\begin{aligned} W_i &= X_i + U_i, \quad \mathrm{E}(U_i|X_i) = 0, \\ M_i &= X_i + V_i, \quad \mathrm{E}(V_i|X_i) = 0, \end{aligned} \tag{4}$$

in which σ_u may be different from σ_v. A special case of model (4) is the design with biomarker replicates, in which $\sigma_u = \sigma_v$. Under this design with replicates, estimations of σ_u and σ_x can be obtained similarly to the standard calculation of within and between individual variations [11,12]. An important application of (4) is when W_i is the clinical grade assay from individual i, and M_i is a corresponding research grade assay for the same biomarker of interest, and under this situation, σ_u in general would be smaller than σ_v. Estimation of the parameters associated with (4) can be obtained from the following result:

Proposition 1. *In model (4), let X be a random variable with mean $\mu_X < \infty$ and variance $\sigma_x^2 < \infty$, U be a random error with mean 0 and variance $\sigma_u^2 < \infty$, V be a random error with mean 0 and variance $\sigma_v^2 < \infty$. Assume that X, U and V are mutually independent. Then*

$$n^{-1}\sum_{i=1}^{n}(W_i + M_i)/2 \to \mu_x, \qquad n^{-1}\sum_{i=1}^{n} W_i M_i \to \sigma_x^2 + \mu_x^2,$$

$$n^{-1}\sum_{i=1}^{n}(W_i - \mu_x)^2 \to \sigma_x^2 + \sigma_u^2, \qquad n^{-1}\sum_{i=1}^{n}(M_i - \mu_x)^2 \to \sigma_x^2 + \sigma_v^2,$$

where $\to$ denotes convergence in probability.

Proposition 1 can be shown by first noting that $\mathrm{E}\{(W + M)/2\} = \mu_x$ given that $\mathrm{E}(U) = 0$ and $\mathrm{E}(V) = 0$. Because X, U and V are mutually independent, $\mathrm{E}(WM) = \sigma_x^2 + \mu_x^2$. Similarly, by direct calculation, $\mathrm{var}(W) = \sigma_x^2 + \sigma_u^2$, and $\mathrm{var}(M) = \sigma_x^2 + \sigma_v^2$. Hence, by the law of large numbers, Proposition 1 has been shown. The calculations given above in Proposition 1 are based on the assumption that the measurement error variances for the controls ($Y = 0$) and for the cases ($Y = 1$) are the same. If $\sigma_{u,0}$ is different from $\sigma_{u,1}$, then the calculations above for the variance components can be obtained within the control group and case group, respectively. With the correction method (2), the corrected AUC using W can be obtained, and the corrected AUC using M can be obtained as well. Likewise, sensitivity and specificity estimations can be obtained by the correction method (3).

If W_i is a clinical grade assay from individual i and M_i is a corresponding research grade assay for the same biomarker of interest, then in practice W_i will be the biomarker assay to be used for the diagnosis of the specific disease outcome. If in case the measurement error variance for W is not too small (compared with that for M, or vice versa), then it will be more efficient to use the best combination of M and W. That is, in addition to adjusting for measurement error using biomarker measures W and M, respectively, we are interested in the best combination of them. We consider a linear combination of W and M, $\gamma W + (1 - \gamma)M$ where γ is between 0 and 1. Under this situation, we aim for an optimal γ such that the variance of $\gamma W + (1-\gamma)M$ is minimized. Under (4), this is the same as minimizing the variance of $\gamma U + (1-\gamma)V$. By simple calculation, the best γ is $\sigma_v^2/(\sigma_u^2+\sigma_v^2)$.

Now, we investigate the situation when W is unbiased for X (although with a random error), but M is linearly associated with X, which is the biomarker of interest to distinguish disease outcomes (Y for disease indicator). For a more general model (1), $M_i = \alpha_0 + \alpha_1 X_i + V_i$, the parameters in the model, cannot be identified based on the moments of W and M only. Under this situation, the parameters in (1) can be identified by using the moments of Y, W, M. However, with the more general model for M, it is necessary to assume that the measurement error variances are the same for the controls and cases. That is $\sigma_{u,0}^2 = \sigma_{u,1}^2$ and $\sigma_{v,0}^2 = \sigma_{v,1}^2$. Then γ_0 and γ_1 can be estimated by noting that $\alpha_1 = \text{cov}(Y, M)/\text{cov}(Y, W), \gamma_0 = \text{E}(M - \alpha_1 W)$. Then, we may rewrite $M_i = \alpha_0 + \alpha_1 X_i + V_i$ as $M_i^* = X_i + V_i^*$, where $M_i^* = \{(M_i - \alpha_0)/\alpha_1\}$ and $V_i^* = V_i/\alpha_1$. As a result, M_i^* is also unbiased for X_i, but with error V_i^*. Therefore, W_i and M_i^* will follow the special case (4) discussed above. The intra versus inter-individual variance ratio λ^2 can be calculated within the controls ($Y = 0$) and the cases ($Y = 1$), respectively. The correction for attenuation (2) for AUC, and (3) for sensitivity and specificity can be obtained as well.

In general, when research grade assays and clinical assays are available for either the study cohort or a subset, model (4) could be reasonable for the analysis to adjust for measurement errors in both types of measures if they have the same measurement scale. However, if two types of different assays are from different labs, then they may have different measurement scales. Under this situation, model (1) will be more appropriate when the two biomarker assays are linearly associated. There is no need to assume a validation set for the biomarker of interest. Of course, if there is a validation subset available for the biomarker of interest, then the methods given above can be further modified. To be focused, we will not investigate the situation with a validation subset in this paper.

4. Skew-Normal Biomarker Correction Estimator

The correction for attenuation estimator described in the last section is based on the assumption that the true biomarker data and measurement errors are both normally distributed. From our simulations, they may still work with limited bias for symmetric data even though there is a small violation of normality. However, the bias could be moderate or large if the data are very skewed. From our data example, biomarkers are often skewed. Hence, it is important to correct biomarker measurement errors without the normality assumptions. Methods to estimate the density function of the unobserved biomarker based on error-prone measures can be obtained by via deconvolution [13]. However, this approach is generally technical and very challenging in data applications. Therefore, a more practical approach is to consider a class of distributions that contain both symmetric and skewed distributions.

Our approach to correct for estimation of sensitivity, specificity, and AUC due to measurement error is to consider a flexible class of distributions for the unobserved biomarkers. Although there are various classes of distributions for this purpose, we propose to construct bias correction based on a class of skew-normal distributions. The skew-normal (SN) distribution was introduced by Azzalini, which includes normal distributions [14]. One main difference between the SN distribution and the normal distribution is that the SN contains a skewness parameter. Azzalini defined the SN distribution for a random variable Z that has the following density

$$g(z, \alpha) = 2\phi(z)\mathbf{\Phi}(\alpha z), \qquad (-\infty < z < \infty),$$

where $\lambda \in R$ is the skewness parameter, $\phi(\cdot)$ and $\mathbf{\Phi}$ denotes the standard normal density and distribution functions, respectively. Azzalini derived the following moment generating function:

$$M_Z(t) = 2e^{t^2/2}\mathbf{\Phi}(\frac{\alpha t}{\sqrt{1+\alpha^2}}).$$

By using the moment-generating function, we can obtain $E(Z) = \sqrt{2/\pi}\delta$, where $\delta = \alpha/\sqrt{1+\alpha^2}$, $\mathrm{var}(Z) = 1-(2/\pi)\delta^2$, and the skewness $\{(4-\pi)/2\}\{\delta\sqrt{2/\pi}\}^3/\{\mathrm{var(Z)}\}^{3/2}$.

Let $X = \xi + \omega Z$, which is an SN distribution with parameters (ξ, ω, α). The density of X can be written as

$$f(x, \xi, \omega, \alpha) = \frac{2}{\omega}\phi(\frac{x-\xi}{\omega})\Phi(\alpha\frac{x-\xi}{\omega}),$$

where ξ and ω are the location and scale parameters, respectively, and α is the skewness parameter. When $\alpha = 0$, the specific SN distribution is a normal distribution. A logarithmic transformation for skewed data may reduce the skewness, but the transformed data may still be skewed. Hence, the skew-normal distribution will be more flexible in fitting the data.

If X values were available, then ξ, ω, and α could be estimated via the maximum likelihood estimator or the method of moments. There could be more than one root for the parameter estimation, especially when α is close to 0, i.e., normal densityHowever, from our numerical experience, different roots by the method of moments will still lead to the same SN distribution. Hence, when X is observed, estimation of sensitivity, specificity, and AUC will be valid if X is from an SN distribution. Let γ_3 be the third central moment of X. We note that $\mu_x = \xi + \omega\delta\sqrt{2/\pi}$, where $\delta = \alpha/\sqrt{1+\alpha^2}$, $\sigma_x^2 = \omega^2\{1-2(\delta^2/\pi)\}$, and $\gamma_3 = \{(4-\pi)/2\}\{\delta\sqrt{2/\pi}\}^3/\{1-2(\delta^2/\pi)\}^{3/2}$. Because biomarker measurements are associated with errors, additional calculations will be needed to identify the parameters involved in the observed data. If X is SN and U is from a symmetric distribution, then we note that $E(W) = E(X)$, $\mathrm{var}(W) = \sigma_x^2 + \sigma_u^2$, and $E(W-\mu_x)^3 = E(X-\mu_x)^3$. Under this situation, the parameters of the SN distribution can be identified as long as σ_u^2 can be consistently estimated. The sensitivity of X at a point c can be estimated by calculating $\mathrm{pr}(X \geq c|Y=1)$, in which σ_u may be different from σ_v.

A special case of model (4) is the design with biomarker replicates in which $\sigma_u = \sigma_v$. Under this design with replicates, estimations of σ_u and σ_x can be obtained similarly to the standard calculation of within and between individual variations [10, 11]. An important application of (4) is when W_i is the clinical grade assay from individual i and M_i is a corresponding research grade assay for the same biomarker of interest, and under this situation, σ_u in general would be smaller than σ_v. The estimation of $\sigma_{u,1}^2$ can follow the procedure that we discussed in Section 3, which would need to use both the W and M data. Then, we will estimate the parameters of the SN distribution of $X_{(1)}$ using data $W_{(1),1}, \ldots, W_{(1),n_1}$ among the W data from the n_1 cases. Based on the first three moments of $W_{(1)}$ given above, the (ξ, ω, α) parameters for $X_{(1)}$ can be estimated by the following estimating equations:

$$\sum_{i=1}^{n_1}\{W_{(1),i} - \xi - \omega\delta\sqrt{2/\pi}\} = 0;$$

$$\sum_{i=1}^{n_1}\{W_{(1),i} - \xi - \omega\delta\sqrt{2/\pi}\}^2 - \omega^2\{1-2(\delta^2/\pi)\} - \sigma_{u,1}^2 = 0;$$

$$\sum_{i=1}^{n_1}\frac{\{W_{(1),i} - \xi - \omega\delta\sqrt{2/\pi}\}^3}{\{\omega^2\{1-2(\delta^2/\pi)\}\}^{3/2}} - \frac{\{(4-\pi)/2\}\{\delta\sqrt{2/\pi}\}^3}{\{1-2(\delta^2/\pi)\}^{3/2}} = 0.$$

Hence, using the estimated (ξ, ω, α) from the calculations given above, the cumulative distribution of the SN distribution at point c, $\mathrm{pr}(X \leq c|Y=1)$, is obtained. Then, the sensitivity of X at c, $\mathrm{pr}(X \geq c|Y=1)$ is obtained by using W data from the cases. Similarly, the specificity of X at a point c can be estimated by calculating $\mathrm{pr}(X \leq c|Y=0)$. We can apply the estimating procedure for (ξ, ω, α) given above to estimate the SN distribution of $X_{(0)}$ using data $W_{(0),1}, \ldots, W_{(0),n_0}$ among the W data from the n_0 cases. Then, the specificity of X at c, $\mathrm{pr}(X \leq c|Y=0)$ is obtained by using W data from the contrin in which σ_u may be different from σ_v. A special case of model (4) is the design with biomarker replicates in which $\sigma_u = \sigma_v$. Under this design with replicates, estimation of σ_u and σ_x can be obtained similarly to the standard calculation of within and between individual variations [10, 11]. An important application of (4) is when W_i is the clinical grade assay from individual i and M_i is a corresponding research grade assay for the same biomarker of interest, and under this situation, σ_u in general would be smaller than σ_v.ols.

Thereafter, as described above, the sensitivity and specificity can be estimated based on the SN distributions by calculating the conditional distributions for cases and controls, respectively. The ROC curve can then be obtained by calculating the sensitivity and specificity values at a sequence of cutoff points (c). After the ROC curve is obtained, the AUC can then be obtained. The method described above is the SN biomarker correction estimator, which is new in the literature.

5. Simulation Study

We conducted a simulation study to examine finite sample performance of our proposed skew-normal biomarker correction estimator, and the correction for attenuation methods when diagnostic biomarkers may be measured with errors. In Table 1, we investigate the situation when the true biomarkers X for controls and cases are either from a normal, skew-normal, or log normal distribution, respectively. We first generated $X_{(0)}$ from a normal distribution with mean 3 and standard deviation 1 for the controls. Then, we generated the biomarkers for the cases from the same distribution, except that $\mathrm{E}(X|Y=1) = \mathrm{E}(X|Y=0) + \ln(3.2)$. The sample size was $n = 300$, and the disease rate was 50%. We also generated skew-normal biomarkers based on the same process. When we generated skew-normal biomarkers for the controls, we first generated the data with the parameters being $\xi = 0$, $\omega = 1$, and $\alpha = 6$ and then we standardized the variables so that the variables had mean 3 and standard deviation 1. For the situation with log normal variables, the distribution of the logarithm of the controls had a normal distribution with mean 1 and standard deviation 0.3, and the distribution of the logarithm of the cases had a normal distribution with mean 1.5 and standard deviation 0.3. The true AUC was about 0.795 if the true X measures were normal biomarkers, and was about 0.806 if they were skew-normal biomarkers, and was about 0.811 if they were log normal biomarkers. To evaluate estimation of the sensitivity and specificity, the cutoff point of the biomarker was chosen as the point on the ROC curve which has the minimum distance from the left upper corner of the unit square (which was the point that a perfect test would pass through) [3]. The sensitivity and specificity values are given in the tables. We generated error-prone measures W and M based on model (4), $W_i = X_i + U_i$ and $M_i = X_i + V_i$, in which U and V are normal with $\sigma_u = 1$ and $\sigma_v = 1$. Under this model, the observed measures W and M are like research grade biomarker replicates for the unobserved X. We calculated a naive estimator based on M measures only (Naive–M), a CFA estimator based on W measures (CFA–W), a CFA estimator based on M measures (CFA–M), a CFA estimator based on both W and M measures (CFA–WM), and the proposed SN correction estimator based on both W and M measures (SN–WM). In the tables, "bias" was calculated by taking the average of the biases of AUC estimates from the 500 simulation replicates; "SD" denoted the sample standard deviation of the estimates; "ASE" denoted the average of the estimated standard errors of the estimates. We also calculated the 95% confidence interval coverage probabilities (CP). The standard errors of the estimates were obtained from bootstrap. When the biomarkers were from a normal distribution, all the three CFA methods were unbiased for AUC, sensitivity, and specificity estimation, and the CFA method based on the best linear combination of W and M was the most efficient among the three correction estimators. The SN correction estimator had slightly bigger biases than the CFA-WM estimates when the biomarkers were from a normal distribution, but it was still valid since the biases were relatively less than the SE. When the biomarkers were from a skew-normal distribution, some of the three CFA estimates may have been biased. When the biomarkers were from a SN distribution, the SN correction estimators were better than the CFA estimators in terms of bias and efficiency in most cases. The bias of the SN correction estimate for sensitivity was not smaller than the CFA estimates; this was due to finite sample performance, since the bias disappeared when we increased the sample size. When the biomarkers were from a log normal distribution, the CFA estimators and SN correction estimator had small to moderate biases. The SN correction estimator was better than the CFA estimator for AUC estimation.

We made the choice of the parameters $\mu_x = 3$ and $\sigma_x = 1$ in Table 1 in the controls, since assay data are positive in general. The result will not change if we replace $\mu_x = 3$ with another value. However, the result will be different if we change the variance of X or the variance of the measurement errors. In the Appendix A, we consider the situation similar to Table 1 but with $\sigma_u = \sigma_v = 0.71$ (Table A1). The biases in Table A1 were smaller than those from Table 1 in general. In Table A2, we consider the situation similar to Table 1 but with $\sigma_u = \sigma_v = 1.22$. The biases in Table A2 were typically larger than those from Table 1 due to larger measurement errors.

In Table 2, we also investigated a scenario similar to Table 1, but the measurement error variances for W and M are $\sigma_u = 0.2$ and $\sigma_v = 1$. The scenario in this table can be considered as the case when W_i was a clinical grade measure and M_i was a research grade measure, if they had the same measurement scale. The result from Table 2 was slightly different from that from Table 1. When the biomarkers were from a normal distribution, the three CFA estimators and the SN correction estimator were unbiased. There was a very minor difference between the CFA estimator using W data and the CFA estimator using the best linear combination of W and M. This was reasonable since if W had a much smaller measurement error variance than that of M, then the additional contribution of M would be very limited. Hence, when clinical grade biomarker measures are available and if they have very minimal measurement errors, then research grade measures in general would not provide additional efficiency gain in AUC, sensitivity, or specificity estimation. When the true biomarkers were from a skew-normal distribution, the CFA–M estimator was biased due to skewed biomarkers. The biases from the CFA estimator using W or using both W and M were small. The reason was likely because the measurement error in W was very small (σ_u is much smaller than σ_x). Similar to Table 1, the SN correction estimator had slightly bigger biases than the CFA-WM estimates when the biomarkers were from a normal distribution, but it was still valid since the biases were relatively less than the SE. With log normal biomarkers, the CFA estimators using W or the best linear combination of W and M and SN correction estimator had small biases because the error from W was very small. The SN correction estimator was better than the CFA estimator using M only for AUC estimation under this scenario.

In Table 3, same as Table 1, we generated the biomarkers for the cases and controls with the same distribution based on $\mathrm{E}(X|Y=1) = \mathrm{E}(X|Y=0) + \ln(3.2)$. The sample size and disease rate are the same as those in Table 1. We investigated the situation when W is unbiased for X (although with a random error) but M is linearly associated with X such that $W_i = X_i + U_i$ and $M_i = 0.2 + 0.8X_i + V_i$, in which $\sigma_u = 1$ and $\sigma_v = 1$. The AUC values in this table are the same as those in Table 1. Similar to Tables 1 and 2, the naive estimates were biased while the three CFA estimators were unbiased when the biomarkers were from a normal distribution. For the CFA, de-attenuation methods were unbiased when X was normal, but could be biased when X was skewed. The main findings from Table 3 were mostly similar to those from Tables 1 and 2. The proposed SN correction estimator, in general, performed better than the CFA estimators when the underlying biomarkers were from a skew-normal distribution. When the biomarkers were from a log normal distribution, the CFA estimators and SN correction estimator had small to moderate biases.

Table 1. Simulation study when $\sigma_u = \sigma_v = 1$ (replicates).

		Naive–M	**CFA–W**	**CFA–M**	**CFA–WM**	**SN–WM**
		Normal biomarkers				
AUC	Bias	−0.075	−0.001	0.000	−0.000	0.003
(0.795)	SD	0.029	0.034	0.036	0.030	0.030
	ASE	0.029	0.037	0.037	0.033	0.032
	CP	0.246	0.970	0.936	0.952	0.952
Sensitivity	Bias	−0.058	0.000	0.002	0.001	−0.010
(0.719)	SD	0.040	0.049	0.053	0.043	0.039
	ASE	0.038	0.053	0.052	0.048	0.045
	CP	0.696	0.952	0.940	0.968	0.970
Specificity	Bias	−0.062	−0.001	−0.000	0.000	0.011
(0.720)	SD	0.038	0.049	0.052	0.047	0.035
	ASE	0.038	0.053	0.052	0.048	0.036
	CP	0.652	0.964	0.948	0.954	0.932
		Skew-normal biomarkers				
AUC	Bias	−0.083	−0.007	−0.006	−0.005	0.001
(0.806)	SD	0.028	0.037	0.035	0.032	0.032
	ASE	0.029	0.037	0.036	0.033	0.032
	CP	0.136	0.938	0.956	0.946	0.938
Sensitivity	Bias	−0.066	0.007	0.009	0.008	0.011
(0.771)	SD	0.037	0.048	0.047	0.041	0.045
	ASE	0.037	0.046	0.045	0.043	0.044
	CP	0.586	0.918	0.916	0.948	0.932
Specificity	Bias	−0.065	−0.019	−0.019	−0.011	−0.007
(0.775)	SD	0.035	0.055	0.051	0.046	0.037
	ASE	0.039	0.056	0.056	0.050	0.039
	CP	0.642	0.936	0.956	0.950	0.954
		Log normal biomarkers				
AUC	Bias	−0.080	−0.014	−0.013	−0.010	0.004
(0.856)	SD	0.026	0.028	0.029	0.025	0.026
	ASE	0.027	0.030	0.030	0.027	0.028
	CP	0.112	0.954	0.936	0.952	0.942
Sensitivity	Bias	−0.048	−0.003	−0.003	−0.003	−0.011
(0.772)	SD	0.037	0.040	0.041	0.038	0.039
	ASE	0.036	0.042	0.042	0.040	0.039
	CP	0.782	0.960	0.942	0.954	0.950
Specificity	Bias	−0.096	−0.012	−0.012	−0.007	−0.011
(0.775)	SD	0.038	0.053	0.056	0.049	0.036
	ASE	0.038	0.056	0.055	0.050	0.039
	CP	0.292	0.966	0.922	0.940	0.946

NOTE: Naive–M is the AUC estimator using M measures directly, CFA–W is a CFA AUC estimator based on W measures, CFA–M is a CFA AUC estimator based on M measures, CFA–WM is a CFA AUC estimator based on both W and M measures, and SN–WM is the SN correction estimator assuming X is skew-normal using both W and M measures.

Table 2. Simulation study when $\sigma_u = 0.2$ (clinical assay), $\sigma_v = 1$ (research assay).

		Naive–M	**CFA–W**	**CFA–M**	**CFA–WM**	**SN–WM**
		Normal biomarkers				
AUC	Bias	−0.075	0.002	0.000	0.002	0.002
(0.795)	SD	0.029	0.025	0.035	0.025	0.025
	ASE	0.029	0.027	0.035	0.027	0.026
	CP	0.246	0.954	0.924	0.950	0.956

Table 2. *Cont.*

		Naive–M	CFA–W	CFA–M	CFA–WM	SN–WM
Sensitivity	Bias	−0.058	0.005	0.001	0.005	−0.001
(0.719)	SD	0.040	0.036	0.052	0.036	0.032
	ASE	0.038	0.038	0.050	0.039	0.034
	CP	0.696	0.952	0.932	0.956	0.956
Specificity	Bias	−0.062	0.000	−0.002	0.000	0.007
(0.720)	SD	0.038	0.036	0.051	0.037	0.030
	ASE	0.038	0.038	0.050	0.039	0.030
	CP	0.652	0.960	0.942	0.960	0.940
	Skew-normal biomarkers					
AUC	Bias	−0.083	0.003	−0.007	0.003	−0.002
(0.806)	SD	0.028	0.026	0.034	0.026	0.027
	ASE	0.029	0.026	0.035	0.026	0.028
	CP	0.136	0.922	0.952	0.922	0.942
Sensitivity	Bias	−0.066	0.005	0.008	0.007	0.011
(0.781)	SD	0.037	0.035	0.045	0.036	0.034
	ASE	0.037	0.035	0.043	0.036	0.033
	CP	0.586	0.942	0.910	0.940	0.914
Specificity	Bias	−0.065	0.002	−0.019	0.002	−0.001
(0.679)	SD	0.035	0.039	0.049	0.038	0.031
	ASE	0.039	0.039	0.055	0.040	0.032
	CP	0.642	0.946	0.960	0.950	0.952
	Log normal biomarkers					
AUC	Bias	−0.080	0.001	−0.013	0.001	−0.003
(0.856)	SD	0.026	0.021	0.028	0.021	0.022
	ASE	0.027	0.022	0.029	0.022	0.024
	CP	0.112	0.954	0.934	0.952	0.960
Sensitivity	Bias	−0.048	0.003	−0.003	0.004	−0.009
(0.772)	SD	0.037	0.033	0.041	0.034	0.035
	ASE	0.036	0.035	0.041	0.036	0.033
	CP	0.782	0.950	0.940	0.950	0.914
Specificity	Bias	−0.096	0.000	−0.014	−0.001	−0.010
(0.775)	SD	0.038	0.035	0.053	0.035	0.029
	ASE	0.038	0.037	0.052	0.037	0.030
	CP	0.292	0.954	0.920	0.948	0.944

NOTE: See the footnote of Table 1 for notation. The sample size $n = 300$. The results were from 500 simulation replicates.

Table 3. Simulation when $W_i = X_i + U_1$, $M_i = 0.2 + 0.8X_i + V_i$, in which $\sigma_u = 1$ and $\sigma_v = 1$.

		Naive–M	CFA–W	CFA–M	CFA–WM	B
	Normal biomarkers					
AUC	Bias	−0.099	−0.001	−0.001	−0.001	0.003
(0.795)	SD	0.030	0.032	0.033	0.032	0.032
	ASE	0.030	0.035	0.035	0.035	0.034
	CP	0.086	0.956	0.944	0.952	0.938
Sensitivity	Bias	−0.075	0.000	0.003	0.001	−0.011
(0.780)	SD	0.038	0.049	0.053	0.048	0.044
	ASE	0.039	0.053	0.056	0.052	0.049
	CP	0.500	0.956	0.942	0.958	0.954
Specificity	Bias	−0.080	−0.001	−0.002	−0.003	0.011
(0.720)	SD	0.038	0.049	0.053	0.049	0.039
	ASE	0.039	0.053	0.056	0.053	0.040
	CP	0.482	0.956	0.946	0.960	0.946

Table 3. *Cont.*

		Naive–M	CFA–W	CFA–M	CFA–WM	B
	Skew-normal biomarkers					
AUC	Bias	−0.107	−0.007	−0.008	−0.006	−0.001
(0.806)	SD	0.029	0.035	0.034	0.034	0.034
	ASE	0.030	0.035	0.035	0.035	0.034
	CP	0.036	0.946	0.950	0.946	0.944
Sensitivity	Bias	−0.088	0.007	0.009	0.008	0.013
(0.780)	SD	0.041	0.048	0.050	0.046	0.052
	ASE	0.037	0.047	0.051	0.048	0.050
	CP	0.368	0.922	0.932	0.950	0.918
Specificity	Bias	−0.082	−0.020	−0.025	0.016	−0.010
(0.720)	SD	0.038	0.054	0.054	0.050	0.043
	ASE	0.040	0.056	0.061	0.056	0.044
	CP	0.442	0.934	0.948	0.956	0.942
	Log normal biomarkers					
AUC	Bias	−0.106	−0.014	−0.015	−0.012	−0.005
(0.856)	SD	0.028	0.026	0.027	0.027	0.028
	ASE	0.028	0.029	0.029	0.029	0.030
	CP	0.016	0.942	0.936	0.946	0.940
Sensitivity	Bias	−0.063	−0.003	−0.002	−0.002	−0.010
(0.772)	SD	0.038	0.041	0.041	0.041	0.041
	ASE	0.037	0.041	0.044	0.042	0.041
	CP	0.622	0.958	0.950	0.950	0.946
Specificity	Bias	−0.122	−0.012	−0.019	−0.007	−0.013
(0.775)	SD	0.036	0.053	0.057	0.053	0.039
	ASE	0.039	0.057	0.061	0.056	0.043
	CP	0.076	0.954	0.942	0.946	0.954

NOTE: See the footnote of Table 1 for notation. The sample size $n = 300$. The results were from 500 simulation replicates.

6. Analysis of PDAC Data

The PDAC study has been briefly described in the introduction section. The primary aim is to develop biomarkers for the detection of early-stage PDAC. In this section, our purpose is to demonstrate our methods to estimate diagnostic efficacy of CA19-9 when the assays are measured with errors. In our analysis, CA19-9 research assays from a lab and clinical grade assays are available. Clinical grade assays, in general, still may be measured with errors, even though the magnitude of errors is typically smaller than that from research grade assays. There are 68 early-stage PDAC cases and 67 controls in the analysis.

From the top portion of Figure 1, we observe the association between measures from a clinical assay and a research assay. We note that the distributions of the two assay measures are skewed and there are some very large values. The association between the clinical and research assays is approximately linear after taking a log transform. The lower portion of Figure 1 shows density estimation of the clinical assays (logarithm transform of (CA19-9 + 1) then divided by 10), with two different bandwidths for kernel density estimation. The two bandwidths in the controls are $2\sigma_{w,0}n_0^{-1/3}$ and $4\sigma_{w,0}n_0^{-1/3}$, in which $\sigma_{w,0}$ is the standard deviation of W among the controls. From the simulation result of Wang and Hsu, both bandwidths work well, but the first selection is slightly better [15]. The two bandwidths in the cases are chosen similarly to the controls. The density estimation is for the purpose to demonstrate that the density of logarithm transform of CA19-9 (plus 1, then divided by 10) is still skewed. The density estimation is not for the unobserved true CA19-9, which would involve deconvolution in nonparametric estimation. Deconvolution for density estimation is rather technical, which is not the focus of this research.

The clinical assays and research assays are from different techniques, and they have different measurement scales. Hence, the models in the analysis are $W_i = X_i + U_i$ and $M_i = \alpha_0 + \alpha_1 X_i + V_i$. The analysis results are given in Table 4. We present the naive estimates using the research assay, the CFA estimates and SN estimates using both types of assays. For sensitivity and specificity estimation, the cutoff point of the biomarker is first chosen as the point on the ROC curve of the clinical assay which has the minimum distance from the left upper corner of the unit square. We also consider the cutoff point of the biomarker with the best specificity, such that the sensitivity using the clinical assay is at least 75%. Because the distribution of CA19–9 is likely skewed (Figure 1), it is possible that the three CFA estimators may be biased. The SN correction estimator may be more suitable for this analysis. From these estimates, based on the CFA and SN estimates, the AUC of the true unobserved CA19–9 is at least 0.8. In addition, based on the two cutoff points chosen, the sensitivity and specificity estimates are close to 0.75. Nevertheless, the data analysis based on the small sample size is only for demonstration; future research with a larger sample size is warranted.

Table 4. Pancreatic ductal adenocarcinoma Data Analysis.

	Naive–M	CFA–W	CFA–M	CFA–WM	SN–WM
cutoff point: minimum distance from the left upper corner					
AUC	0.749	0.849	0.801	0.822	0.812
SE	0.037	0.039	0.045	0.040	0.036
Sensitivity	0.735	0.789	0.770	0.723	0.751
SE	0.054	0.065	0.061	0.058	0.042
Specificity	0.537	0.826	0.553	0.811	0.734
SE	0.063	0.055	0.088	0.063	0.045
cutoff point: sensitivity using W is at least 75%					
AUC	0.749	0.838	0.815	0.815	0.809
SE	0.042	0.038	0.042	0.042	0.035
Sensitivity	0.735	0.776	0.716	0.690	0.733
SE	0.048	0.047	0.055	0.059	0.043
Specificity	0.537	0.821	0.600	0.821	0.756
SE	0.058	0.049	0.096	0.048	0.048

NOTE: We assume that $W = X + U$ and $M = \alpha_0 + \alpha_1 X + V$, where W is a clinical assay measure, M is a research assay measure. Naive–M is the AUC estimator using M measures directly, CFA–W is a corrected AUC estimator based on W measures, CFA–M is a corrected AUC estimator based on M measures, CFA–WM is a corrected AUC estimator based on both W and M measures, and SN–WM is the method of moments estimator, assuming X is skew-normal based on both W and M measures.

7. Discussion

In this paper, we mainly address the issue of adjusting for measurement error in the biomarkers in the estimation of diagnostic accuracy. Estimation of sensitivity and specificity with measurement error is to address the issue of estimating conditional probabilities for a cutoff point. The estimation of AUC with measurement error means addressing the issue of calculating $\mathrm{pr}(X_1 > X_0)$ when X is not observed. Nonparametric estimation for this problem would involve the challenging research problem of deconvolution in the density estimation with measurement error [13]. Hence, our proposed SN correction estimator provides a flexible approach to address this issue. Attwood et al. proposed using the skew exponential power (SEP) distribution to model the ROC curve and related metrics in the presence of non-normal data [16]. The SN distribution is a particular case of the SEP distribution. It will be a future research aim to extend the SEP distribution for diagnostic accuracy when biomarkers are measured with errors.

From this research, we note that it is very challenging to develop nonparametric methods for AUC, sensitivity, or specificity when biomarkers are measured with errors. The proposed SN distribution for biomarkers to adjust for measurement error is from the view point of a class of skewed distributions. For example, SN distributions will be more flexible than an exponential distribution or a normal distribution. If the true biomarker distribution is zero-inflated, then the bias in estimating AUC, sensitivity, and specificity will likely depend on the probability mass at 0. It will be interesting in future research to develop a more flexible approach to correct for measurement error when the true biomarker distribution may be skewed or zero-inflated.

Another general approximation approach that could be applied to this problem is the simulation extrapolation (SIMEX) approach. Cook and Stefanski studied this approach for covariate measurement error problems [17]. An advantage of SIMEX is that it has the advantage of being easy to implement. The use of SIMEX for AUC may have limited bias [18]. However, bias from SIMEX for estimation of sensitivity and specificity could be large. It remains a research problem to develop a valid SIMEX estimator for this problem, especially when the biomarkers are skewed in the distribution.

8. Conclusions

We have developed a flexible modeling approach for measurement error in the biomarkers in the estimation of diagnostic accuracy. One limitation of our proposed SN correction estimator is that it is not consistent for the class of all distributions. Nevertheless, with the consideration that biomarkers are often skewed in the distribution, our proposed estimator is expected to be valid in many general applications.

Author Contributions: Conceptualization, Z.F.; investigation, C.-Y.W. and Z.F.; methodology, C.-Y.W. and Z.F.; writing—original draft, C.-Y.W.; writing—review and editing, C.-Y.W. and Z.F. All authors read and agreed to the published version of the manuscript.

Funding: This research was partially supported by the US National Institutes of Health grants CA189532, CA235122, CA239168 (Wang), and CA086368 (Wang and Feng), and a travel award from the Mathematics Research Promotion Center of the National Science and Technology Council of Taiwan (Wang).

Data Availability Statement: The data that support the findings of this study are not available for public access at this moment, but can be requested from EDRN.

Conflicts of Interest: The authors did not have any conflicts of interest.

Appendix A. Additional Simulations

We consider the situation similar to Table 1 but with $\sigma_u = \sigma_v = 0.71$ (Table A1). Because σ_u and σ_v are smaller than those in Table 1, the biases in Table A1 were smaller than those from Table 1 in general. In Table A2, we consider the situation similar to Table 1 but with $\sigma_u = \sigma_v = 1.22$. The biases in Table A2 were larger than those from Table 1 in general. In summary, the results of Tables A1 and A2 were similar to the findings from Table 1 except the magnitude of biases were slightly different because of the differences in measurement error variances.

Table A1. Simulation study when $\sigma_u = \sigma_v = 0.71$ (replicates).

		Naive–M	CFA–W	CFA–M	CFA–WM	SN–WM
		Normal biomarkers				
AUC	Bias	−0.046	0.000	0.000	−0.001	0.002
(0.795)	SD	0.027	0.029	0.030	0.027	0.027
	ASE	0.028	0.032	0.031	0.029	0.029
	CP	0.632	0.962	0.932	0.960	0.948

Table A1. *Cont.*

		Naive–M	CFA–W	CFA–M	CFA–WM	SN–WM
Sensitivity	Bias	−0.036	0.000	0.001	0.001	−0.006
(0.719)	SD	0.039	0.043	0.046	0.040	0.034
	ASE	0.038	0.045	0.045	0.042	0.038
	CP	0.858	0.958	0.940	0.952	0.970
Specificity	Bias	−0.039	−0.001	−0.001	−0.001	0.008
(0.720)	SD	0.037	0.042	0.044	0.041	0.032
	ASE	0.038	0.045	0.045	0.043	0.032
	CP	0.840	0.970	0.946	0.958	0.938
	Skew-normal biomarkers					
AUC	Bias	−0.051	−0.005	−0.004	−0.002	0.000
(0.806)	SD	0.027	0.032	0.030	0.029	0.028
	ASE	0.028	0.031	0.031	0.029	0.028
	CP	0.552	0.936	0.956	0.948	0.940
Sensitivity	Bias	−0.037	0.006	0.009	0.007	0.009
(0.771)	SD	0.036	0.040	0.041	0.037	0.038
	ASE	0.035	0.040	0.039	0.039	0.037
	CP	0.828	0.936	0.918	0.944	0.924
Specificity	Bias	−0.040	−0.009	−0.009	−0.004	−0.005
(0.775)	SD	0.035	0.047	0.044	0.040	0.034
	ASE	0.039	0.048	0.048	0.045	0.035
	CP	0.828	0.936	0.918	0.944	0.952
	Log normal biomarkers					
AUC	Bias	−0.049	−0.010	−0.010	−0.007	−0.004
(0.856)	SD	0.024	0.024	0.024	0.022	0.023
	ASE	0.025	0.026	0.026	0.024	0.025
	CP	0.490	0.962	0.942	0.954	0.948
Sensitivity	Bias	−0.027	−0.002	−0.001	−0.001	−0.012
(0.772)	SD	0.036	0.038	0.037	0.034	0.036
	ASE	0.035	0.038	0.038	0.038	0.035
	CP	0.888	0.950	0.950	0.962	0.930
Specificity	Bias	−0.062	−0.008	−0.007	−0.004	−0.012
(0.775)	SD	0.036	0.042	0.046	0.042	0.032
	ASE	0.036	0.046	0.045	0.042	0.033
	CP	0.622	0.968	0.926	0.940	0.946

NOTE: See the footnote of Table 1 for notation. The sample size $n = 300$. The results were from 500 simulation replicates.

Table A2. Simulation study when $\sigma_u = \sigma_v = 1.22$ (replicates).

		Naive–M	CFA–W	CFA–M	CFA–WM	SN–WM
	Normal biomarkers					
AUC	Bias	−0.060	−0.001	0.000	0.000	0.005
(0.795)	SD	0.030	0.039	0.041	0.034	0.034
	ASE	0.030	0.042	0.041	0.037	0.036
	CP	0.092	0.964	0.934	0.956	0.948
Sensitivity	Bias	−0.074	0.000	0.002	0.000	−0.013
(0.719)	SD	0.040	0.057	0.060	0.048	0.045
	ASE	0.039	0.060	0.059	0.053	0.052
	CP	0.530	0.960	0.928	0.972	0.964

Table A2. *Cont.*

		Naive–M	CFA–W	CFA–M	CFA–WM	SN–WM
Specificity (0.720)	Bias	−0.077	0.001	0.000	0.000	0.015
	SD	0.039	0.055	0.060	0.052	0.039
	ASE	0.039	0.060	0.059	0.053	0.040
	CP	0.520	0.962	0.934	0.962	0.942
	Skew-normal biomarkers					
AUC (0.806)	Bias	−0.104	−0.008	−0.007	−0.006	0.001
	SD	0.029	0.042	0.040	0.036	0.035
	ASE	0.030	0.042	0.041	0.036	0.035
	CP	0.050	0.936	0.948	0.942	0.942
Sensitivity (0.771)	Bias	−0.085	0.009	0.012	0.009	0.014
	SD	0.037	0.054	0.053	0.046	0.053
	ASE	0.037	0.053	0.052	0.048	0.052
	CP	0.398	0.922	0.926	0.944	0.930
Specificity (0.775)	Bias	−0.080	−0.026	−0.024	−0.015	−0.008
	SD	0.037	0.063	0.059	0.050	0.041
	ASE	0.040	0.064	0.064	0.056	0.043
	CP	0.462	0.922	0.948	0.948	0.956
	Log normal biomarkers					
AUC (0.856)	Bias	−0.103	−0.016	−0.015	−0.012	−0.004
	SD	0.027	0.031	0.032	0.028	0.029
	ASE	0.028	0.034	0.033	0.030	0.031
	CP	0.022	0.950	0.934	0.954	0.944
Sensitivity (0.772)	Bias	−0.064	−0.005	−0.004	−0.004	−0.011
	SD	0.038	0.044	0.045	0.041	0.042
	ASE	0.037	0.046	0.045	0.043	0.042
	CP	0.628	0.948	0.954	0.952	0.950
Specificity (0.775)	Bias	−0.118	−0.016	−0.015	−0.008	−0.011
	SD	0.040	0.062	0.066	0.056	0.041
	ASE	0.038	0.066	0.065	0.057	0.045
	CP	0.118	0.950	0.920	0.952	0.952

NOTE: See the footnote of Table 1 for notation. The sample size $n = 300$. The results were from 500 simulation replicates.

References

1. Liu, Y.; Kaur S.; Huang, Y.; Fahrmann, J.F.; Rinaudo, J.A.; Hanash, S.M.; Batra, S.K.; Singhi, A.D.; Brand, R.E.; Maitra, A.; et al. Biomarkers and Strategy to Detect Preinvasive and Early Pancreatic Cancer: State of the Field and the Impact of the EDRN. *Cancer Epidemiol. Biomarkers Prev.* **2020**, *29*, 2513–2523. [CrossRef] [PubMed]
2. Youden, W.J. Index for rating diagnostic tests. *Cancer* **1950**, *3*, 32–35. [CrossRef] [PubMed]
3. Perkins, N.J.; Schisterman, E.F. The inconsistency of "optimal" cutpoints obtained using two criteria based on the receiver operating characteristic curve. *Am. J. Epidemiol.* **2006**, *163*, 670–675. [CrossRef] [PubMed]
4. Coffin, M.; Sukhatme, S. Receiver operating characteristic studies and measurement errors. *Biometrics* **1997**, *53*, 823–837. [CrossRef] [PubMed]
5. Faraggi, D. The effect of random measurement error on receiver operating characteristic (ROC) curves. *Stat. Med.* **2000**, *19*, 61–70. [CrossRef]
6. White, M.T.; Xie, S.X. Adjustment for measurement error in evaluating diagnostic biomarkers by using an internal reliability sample. *Stat. Med.* **2013**, *32*, 4709–4725. [CrossRef] [PubMed]
7. Rosner, B.; Tworoger, S.; Qiu, W. Correcting AUC for Measurement Error. *J. Biom. Biostat.* **2015**, *6*. [CrossRef] [PubMed]
8. He, H.; Lyness, J.M.; McDermott, M.P. Direct estimation of the area under the receiver operating characteristic curve in the presence of verification bias. *Stat. Med.* **2009**, *28*, 361–376. [CrossRef] [PubMed]
9. Bamber, D. The area above the ordinal dominance graph and the area below the receiver operating characteristic graph. *J. Math. Psychol.* **1975**, *12*, 387– 415. [CrossRef]
10. Reiser, B. Measuring the effectiveness of diagnostic markers in the presence of measurement error through the use of ROC curves. *Stat. Med.* **2000**, *19*, 2115–2129. [CrossRef] [PubMed]
11. Buonaccorsi, J. *Measurement Error: Models, Methods, and Applications*; Hapman and Hall/CRC: Boca Raton, FL, USA, 2010.

12. Carroll, R.J.; Ruppert, D.; Stefanski, L.A.; Crainiceanu, C.M. *Measurement Error in Nonlinear Models, a Modern Perspective*, 2nd ed.; Chapman and Hall: London, UK, 2006.
13. Stefanski, L.; Carroll, R.J. Deconvolving kernel density estimators. *Statistics* **1990**, *2*, 169–184. [CrossRef]
14. Azzalini, A. A class of distributions which includes the normal ones. *Scand. J. Stat.* **1986**, *12*, 171–178.
15. Wang, C.Y.; Hsu, L. Multinomial logistic regression with missing outcome data. *Stat. Med.* **2020**, *39*, 3299–3312. [CrossRef] [PubMed]
16. Attwood, K.; Hou, S.; Hutson, A. Application of the skew exponential power distribution to ROC curves. *J. Appl. Stat.* **2022**, 1–16. [CrossRef]
17. Cook, J.; Stefanski, L.A. A simulation extrapolation method for parametric measurement error models. *J. Am. Statist. Assoc.* **1995**, *89*, 1314–1328. [CrossRef]
18. Kim, J. Gleser, L.J. Simex approaches to measurement error in roc studies. *Commun. Stat. Theory Methods* **2000**, *29*, 2473–2491. [CrossRef]

mathematics MDPI

Article

A Proposed Simulation Technique for Population Stability Testing in Credit Risk Scorecards

Johan du Pisanie, James Samuel Allison and Jaco Visagie *

School of Mathematical and Statistical Sciences, North-West University, Potchefstroom 2531, South Africa
* Correspondence: jaco.visagie@nwu.ac.za

Abstract: Credit risk scorecards are logistic regression models, fitted to large and complex data sets, employed by the financial industry to model the probability of default of potential customers. In order to ensure that a scorecard remains a representative model of the population, one tests the hypothesis of population stability; specifying that the distribution of customers' attributes remains constant over time. Simulating realistic data sets for this purpose is nontrivial, as these data sets are multivariate and contain intricate dependencies. The simulation of these data sets are of practical interest for both practitioners and for researchers; practitioners may wish to consider the effect that a specified change in the properties of the data has on the scorecard and its usefulness from a business perspective, while researchers may wish to test a newly developed technique in credit scoring. We propose a simulation technique based on the specification of bad ratios, this is explained below. Practitioners can generally not be expected to provide realistic parameter values for a scorecard; these models are simply too complex and contain too many parameters to make such a specification viable. However, practitioners can often confidently specify the bad ratio associated with two different levels of a specific attribute. That is, practitioners are often comfortable with making statements such as "on average a new customer is 1.5 times as likely to default as an existing customer with similar attributes". We propose a method which can be used to obtain parameter values for a scorecard based on specified bad ratios. The proposed technique is demonstrated using a realistic example, and we show that the simulated data sets adhere closely to the specified bad ratios. The paper provides a link to a Github project with the R code used to generate the results.

Keywords: credit risk scorecards; hypothesis testing; population stability; simulation

MSC: 62D99; 62P20

Citation: du Pisanie, J.; Allison, J.S.; Visagie, J. A Proposed Simulation Technique for Population Stability Testing in Credit Risk Scorecards. *Mathematics* **2023**, *11*, 492. https://doi.org/10.3390/math11020492

Academic Editors: Niansheng Tang and Shen-Ming Lee

Received: 30 November 2022
Revised: 10 January 2023
Accepted: 12 January 2023
Published: 16 January 2023

1. Introduction and Motivation

Credit scoring is an important technique used in many financial institutions in order to model the probability of default, or some other event of interest, of a potential client. For example, a bank typically has access to data sets containing information pertinent to credit risk, which may be used in order to assess the credit worthiness of potential clients. The characteristics or covariates recorded in such a data set are referred to as attributes throughout; these include information such as income, the total amount of outstanding debt held and the number of recent credit enquiries. A bank may use logistic regression to model an applicant's probability of default as a function of their recorded attributes; these logistic regression models are referred to as credit risk scorecards. In addition to informing the decision as to whether or not a potential borrower is provided with credit, the scorecard is typically used to determine the quoted interest rate. For a detailed treatment of scorecards, see [1] as well as [2].

The development of credit risk scorecards are expensive and time consuming. As a result, once properly trained and validated, a bank may wish to keep a scorecard in use for an extended period, provided that the model continues to be a realistic representation of the attributes of the applicants in the population. One way to determine whether or not a scorecard remains a representative model is to test the hypothesis of population stability. This hypothesis states that the distribution of the attributes remains unchanged over time (i.e., that the distribution of the attributes at present is the same as the distribution observed when the scorecard was developed). When the distribution of the attributes changes, it provides the business with an early indication that the scorecard may no longer be a useful model. Further explanations and examples regarding population stability testing can be found in [3,4] as well as [5].

In the context of testing for population stability, performing scenario testing requires the ability to simulate realistic data sets. To this end, this paper proposes a simple technique for the simulation of such data sets. This enables practitioners to consider scenarios with predefined deviations from specified distributions for the attributes, which allows them to gauge the effects that changes in the distribution of one or more attributes have on the predictions made using the model. Furthermore, the business may also wish to consider the effects of a certain strategy before said strategy is implemented. As a concrete example, consider the case where a bank markets more aggressively to younger people. In this case, they may wish to test the effect of a shift in the distribution of the age of their clients.

The concept of population stability can be further illustrated by means of a simple example. Consider a model that predicts whether someone is wealthy based on a single attribute; the value of the property owned. If this attribute exceeds a specified value, the model predicts that a person is wealthy. Due to house price inflation, the overall prices of houses rise over time. Thus, after a substantial amount of time has passed, the data can no longer be interpreted in the same way as before, and the hypothesis of population stability is rejected, meaning that a new model (or perhaps just a new cut off point) is required.

Population stability metrics measure the magnitude of the change in the distribution of the attributes over time. A number of techniques have been described in the literature, whereby population stability may be tested; see [6,7] as well as [8]. For practical implementations of techniques for credit risk scorecards, see [9] in the statistical software R as well as [10] in Statistical Analysis Software (SAS). The mentioned papers typically provide one or more numerical examples illustrating the use of the proposed techniques. The data sets upon which these techniques are used are typically protected by regulations, meaning that including examples based on the observed data is problematic. As a result, authors often use simulated data. However, the settings wherein these examples are to be found are often oversimplified, stylized and not entirely realistic. This can, at least in part, be ascribed to the difficulties associated with the simulation of realistic data sets. These difficulties arise as a result of the complexity of the nature of the relationship between the attributes and the response.

The data sets typically used for scorecard development have a number of features in common. They are usually relatively large; typical ranges for the number of observations range from one thousand observations to one hundred thousand, while a sample size of one million observations is not unheard of. The data used are multivariate; the number of attributes used varies according to the type of scorecard, what the scorecard will be used for and other factors, but scorecards based on five to fifteen attributes are common. The inclusion of attributes in a scorecard depends on the predictive power of the attribute as well as more practical considerations. These can include the ability to obtain the required data in the future (for example, changing legislation may, in the future, prohibit the inclusion of certain attributes such as gender into the model) as well as the stability of the attribute over the expected lifetime of the scorecard. Care is usually taken to include only attributes with a low level of association with each other so as to avoid the problems associated with multicolinearity.

This paper proposes a simple simulation technique, which may be used for the construction of realistic data sets for use in credit risk scorecards. These data sets contain the attributes of hypothetical customers as well as the associated outcomes. The constructed data sets can be used to perform empirical investigations into the effects of changes in the distribution of the attributes as well as changes in the relationship between these attributes and the outcome. In summary, the advantages of the newly proposed simulation technique are:

1. It is a simple technique.
2. It allows the generation of realistic data sets.
3. These data sets can be used to perform scenario testing.

It should be noted at the outset that the proposed technique is not restricted to the context of credit scoring, or even to the case of logistic regression, but rather has a large number of other modeling applications. However, we restrict our attention to this important special case for the remainder of the paper.

The idea underlying the proposed simulation technique can be summarized as follows. When building a scorecard, practitioners cannot be expected to specify realistic values for the parameters in the model which will ultimately be used. The large number of parameters in the model coupled with the complex relationships between these parameters conspire to make this task almost impossible. However, practitioners can readily be called on to have intuition regarding the bad ratios associated with different states of an attribute. That is, practitioners are often comfortable making statements such as "on average new customers are 1.5 times as likely to default as existing customers with similar attributes". It should be noted that techniques such as the so-called Delphi method can be used in order to make statement such as these; for a recent reference, see [11].

This paper proposes a technique that can be used to choose parameter values that mimic these specified bad ratios. The inputs required for the proposed technique are the overall bad rate, the specified bad ratios and the marginal distributions of the attributes. It should be noted that the proposed technique can be used to generate data without reference to an existing data set. As such, it is not a data augmentation technique. However, in the event that a reference data set is available, these techniques can be implemented in order to achieve similar goals. An example of a data augmentation technique that can be implemented in this context is so-called generalised adversarial networks, see [12]. Another useful reference on data augmentation is [13]. We emphasize that the newly proposed method can be used in cases where classical data augmentation techniques are not appropriate as the new technique does not require the availability of a data set in order to perform a simulation. As a result, classical data augmentation techniques are not considered further in this paper.

A final noteworthy advantage of the newly proposed technique is its simplicity. Since not all users of scorecards are trained in statistics, the simple nature of the proposed simulation technique (i.e., specifying bad ratios and choosing parameters accordingly) is advantageous.

The remainder of the paper is structured as follows. Section 2 shows several examples of settings in which logistic regression is used in order to model the likelihood of an outcome based on attributes. Here, we demonstrate the need for the proposed simulation procedure. A realistic setting is specified in this section which is used throughout the paper. Section 3 proposes a method that may be used to translate specified bad ratios into model parameters emulating these bad ratios using simulation, followed by parameter estimation. We discuss the numerical results obtained using the proposed simulation technique in Section 4. Section 5 provides some conclusions as well as directions for future research.

2. Motivating Examples

This section outlines several examples. We begin by considering a simple model and we show that the parameters corresponding to a single specified bad ratio can be calculated explicitly, negating the need for the proposed simulation technique. Thereafter, we consider slightly more complicated settings and demonstrate that, in general, no solution exists for a specified set of bad ratios. We also highlight the difficulties encountered when attempting to find the required parameters, should a solution exist. Finally, we consider a realistic model, similar to what one would use in practice.

It should be noted that we consider both discrete and continuous attributes below. There does not seem to be general consensus between practitioners on whether or not continuous attributes should be included in the model, as these attributes are often discretized during the modeling process (some practitioners may argue that we only need consider discrete attributes while others argue against this discretization); for a discussion, see pages 45 to 56 of [1]. Since the number of attributes considered simultaneously using the proposed simulation technique is arbitrary, we may simply chose to replace any continuous attribute by its discretized counterpart. As a result, the techniques described below are applicable in either setting mentioned above.

2.1. A Simple Example

Let X_j be a single attribute, associated with the jth applicant, with two levels, 0 and 1. Denote the respective frequencies with which these values occur by p and $1-p$, respectively;

$$X_j = \begin{cases} 1, \text{ with probability } p, \\ 0, \text{ with probability } 1-p, \end{cases}$$

for $j \in \{1, \ldots, n\}$. Let Y_j be the indicator of default for the jth applicant. Denote the overall bad rate by d; meaning that the unconditional probability of default is $d := P(Y=1)$. Let γ be the bad ratio of $X_j = 1$ relative to $X_j = 0$. That is, γ is the ratio of the conditional probabilities that $Y_j = 1$ given $X_j = 1$ and $X_j = 0$, respectively; $\gamma := P(Y_j = 1|X_j = 1)/P(Y_j = 1|X_j = 0)$. We may call upon a practitioner to specify appropriate values for d and γ.

Using the information above, we are able to calculate the conditional default rates $d_0 := P(Y_j = 1|X_j = 0)$ and $d_1 := P(Y_j = 1|X_j = 1)$. Simple calculations yield

$$d_0 = \frac{d}{p\gamma + 1 - p}, \quad d_1 = \frac{d\gamma}{p\gamma + 1 - p}.$$

In this setting, building a scorecard requires that the following logistic regression model be fitted:

$$\log\left(\frac{d_j}{1-d_j}\right) = \beta_0 + j\beta_1, \quad j \in \{0,1\}. \tag{1}$$

Calculating the parameters of the model that give rise to the specified bad ratio requires solving the two equations in (1) in two unknowns. The required solution is calculated to be

$$\beta_0 = \log\left(\frac{d_0}{1-d_0}\right), \quad \beta_1 = \log\left(\frac{d_1}{1-d_1}\right) - \beta_0.$$

As a result, given the values of p, d and γ, we can find a model that perfectly mimics the specified overall probability of default as well as the bad ratio. However, the above example is clearly unrealistically simple.

2.2. Slightly More Complicated Settings

Consider the case where we have three discrete attributes, each with five nominal levels. In this case, the practitioner in question would be required to specify bad ratios for each level of each attribute. This would translate into fifteen equations in fifteen unknowns (since the model would require fifteen parameters in this setting). Solving such a system of equations is already a taxing task, but two points should be emphasized. First, the models used in practice typically have substantially more parameters than fifteen, making the proposition of finding an analytical solution very difficult. Second, there is no guarantee that a solution will exist in this case.

Next, consider the case where a single continuous attribute, say income, is used in the model. When the scorecard is developed, it is common practice to discretize continuous variables such as income into a number of so-called buckets. As a result, the practitioner may suggest, for example, that the population be split into four categories and they may specify a bad ratio for each of these buckets. However, the "true" model underlying the data generates income from a continuous distribution and assigns a single parameter to this attribute in the model. Therefore, this example results in a model with a single parameter which needs to be chosen to satisfy four different constraints (in the form of specified bad ratios). Algebraically, this results in an over specified system in which the number of equations exceed the number of unknowns. In general, an over-specified system of equations cannot be solved.

The two examples above illustrate that, even in unrealistically simple cases, we may not be able to obtain parameters that result in the specified bad ratios.

2.3. A Realistic Setting

We now turn our attention to a realistic setting. Consider the case where ten attributes are used; some of which are continuous while others are discrete. For the discrete case, we distinguish between attributes measured on a nominal scale and attributes measured on a ratio scale. An example of an attribute measured on a nominal scale is the application method used by the applicant as the numerical value assigned to this attribute does not allow direct interpretation. On the other hand, the number of credit cards that an applicant has with other credit providers is measured on an ratio scale, and the numerical value of this attribute allows direct interpretation. In the model used, we treat discrete attributes measured on a ratio scale in the same way as continuous variables; that is, each of these attributes are associated with a single parameter in the model.

As mentioned above, we consider a model containing ten attributes. However, since several discrete attributes are measured on a nominal scale, the number of parameters in the model exceeds the number of attributes. To be precise, let l denote the number of parameters in the model and let m denote the number of attributes measured. Note that $l \geq m$, with equality holding only if no discrete attributes measured on a nominal scale are present. Let $\mathbf{Z}_j = \{Z_{j,1}, \ldots, Z_{j,l}\}$ be the set of attributes associated with the jth applicant. This vector contains the values of observed continuous and discrete, ratio scaled, and attributes. Additionally, $\mathbf{Z}_j$ includes dummy variables capturing the information contained in the discrete, nominal scaled, attributes. Define $\pi_j = E[Y_j|\mathbf{Z}_j]$; the conditional probability of default associated with the jth applicant. The model used can be expressed as

$$\log\left(\frac{\pi_j}{1-\pi_j}\right) = \mathbf{Z}_j^\top \boldsymbol{\beta}, \tag{2}$$

where $\boldsymbol{\beta} = (\beta_1, \ldots, \beta_l)^\top$ is a vector of l parameters.

The names of the attributes included in the model, as well as the scales on which these attributes are measured can be found in Table 1. Care has been taken to use attributes which are often included in credit risk scorecards so as to provide a realistic example. For a discussion of the selection of attributes, see pages 60 to 63 of [1]. Additionally, Table 1 reports the information value of each attribute; this value measures the ability of a specified attribute to predict the value of the default indicator (higher information values indicate higher levels of predictive ability). Consider a discrete attribute with k levels. Let D be the number of defaults in the data set, let D_j be the number of defaults associated with the jth level of this attribute and let n_j be the total number of observations associated with the jth level of this attribute. In this case, the information value of the variable in question is

$$\mathrm{IV} = \sum_{j=1}^{k}\left(\frac{n_j - D_j}{n-D} - \frac{D_j}{D}\right)\log\left(\frac{D(n_j - D_j)}{D_j(n-D)}\right).$$

All calculations below are performed in the statistical software R; see [14].

Table 1. The name, measurement scale and information value of the attributes included in the model.

Name	Scale	Information Value
Gender	Ordinal	0.499
Existing customer	Ordinal	0.441
Number of enquiries	Ratio	0.394
Credit cards with other providers	Ratio	0.515
Province of residence	Ordinal	0.284
Application method	Ordinal	0.222
Age	Ratio	0.164
Total amount outstanding	Ratio	0.083
Income	Ratio	0.182
Balance of recent defaults	Ratio	0.192

For the sake of brevity, we only discuss four of the attributes in detail in the main text of the paper. However, the details of the remaining six attributes, including the numerical results obtained, can be found in Appendix A.

We specify the distribution of the attributes below. For each attribute, we also specify the levels used as well as the bad ratio associated with each of these levels. Care has been taken to use realistic distributions and bad ratios in this example. Admittedly, the process of specifying bad rates is subjective, but we base these values on many years of practical experience in credit scoring, and we believe that most risk practitioners will consider the chosen values plausible. However, it should be stressed that the modeler is not bound to the specific example used here; the proposed technique is general, and the number and distributions of attributes are easily changed. The attributes are treated separately below.

2.4. Existing Customer

Existing customers are usually assumed to be associated with lower levels of risk than is the case for applicants who are not existing customers. This can be due to the fact that existing customers have already shown their ability to repay credit extended to them in the past, or are more likely to pay the company where they have other products. We specify that 80% of applicants are exiting customers and that the bad ratio is 2.7, meaning that the probability of default for a new customer is, on average, 2.7 times higher than the probability of default of an existing customer with the same remaining attributes.

2.5. Credit Cards with Other Providers

This attribute is an indication of the clients exposure to potential credit. A client could, for example, have a low outstanding balance, but through multiple credit cards have access to a large amount of credit. Depending on the type of product being assessed, this could signal higher risk. Table 2 shows the assumed distribution of this attribute together with the specified bad ratios.

Table 2. Credit cards with other providers.

Group	Description	Proportion	Bad Ratio
0	No credit cards at another provider	50%	1.0
1	Credit card at another provider	30%	1.2
2	Credit cards at another provider	15%	1.7
3	Three or more credit cards at another provider	5%	2.5

2.6. Application Method

The method of application is often found to be a very predictive indicator in credit scorecards. A customer actively seeking credit, especially in the unsecured credit space, is often found to be of a higher risk than customers opting in for credit through an outbound method like a marketing call. We distinguish four different application methods:

- Branch—Applications done in the branch.
- Online—Application done through an online application channel.
- Phone—Applications done through a non-direct channel.
- Marketing call—Application done after being prompted by the credit provider.

Table 3 specifies the distribution of this attribute as well as the associated bad ratios.

Table 3. Application method.

Group	Description	Proportion	Bad Ratio
0	Branch	30%	1.0
1	Online	40%	0.5
2	Phone	15%	1.5
3	Marketing Call	15%	0.4

2.7. Age

Younger applicants tend to be higher risk, with risk decreasing as the applicants become older. We assume that the ages of applicants are uniformly distributed between 18 and 75 years. We divide these ages into seven groups, see Table 4.

Table 4. Age.

Group	Proportion	Bad Ratio
18–21	5%	1.00
22–25	7%	0.85
26–30	9%	0.78
31–45	26%	0.66
46–57	21%	0.50
58–63	11%	0.43
64–75	21%	0.31

As was mentioned above, the remaining attributes are discussed in Appendix A. In the next section, we turn our attention to the proposed simulation technique.

3. Proposed Simulation Technique

Having described the details of the attributes included in the model, we turn our attention to finding a model that results in bad ratios approximately equal to those specified. This is done by simulating a large data set, containing attributes as well as default indicators. Thereafter, the parameters of the scorecard are estimated by fitting a logistic regression model to the simulated data. We demonstrate in Section 4 that the resulting parameters constitute a model that closely corresponds to the specified bad ratios and other characteristics. The steps used to arrive at the parameters for the model as well as, ultimately, a simulated data set are as follows:

1. Specify the global parameters.
2. Simulate each attribute separately.
3. Combine the simulated attributes.
4. Fit a logistic regression model.
5. Simulate the final default indicators.

It should be noted that the procedure detailed below assumes independence between the attributes. We opt to incorporate this assumption because it is often made in credit scoring in practice. However, augmenting the procedure below to incorporate dependence between attributes is a simple matter. For example, we can drop the assumption of independent attributes by simulating a group of attributes from a specified copula. Although we do not pursue the use of copulas further below, the reader is referred to [15] for more details.

3.1. Specify the Global Parameters

We specify a fixed, large sample size. It is important that the initial simulated data set be large even in the case where the final simulated sample may be of more modest size, as this will reduce the effect of sample variability. We also specify the overall bad rate. It should be noted that overly small bad rates will tend to decrease the information value of the attributes included in the model (for fixed sets of bad ratios). This is due to the difficulty associated with predicting extremely rare events. We use a sample size of 50,000 and an overall bad rate of 10% to obtain the numerical results shown in the next section.

3.2. Simulate Each Attribute Separately

The next step entails specifying the marginal distribution as well as the bad ratio associated with each attribute. In the case of discrete attributes, a bad ratio is specified for each of the levels of the attribute. In the case of continuous attributes, the attributes are required to be discretized and a bad ratio is specified for each level of the resulting discrete attribute. Given the marginal distribution and the bad ratios of an attribute, we explicitly calculate the bad rate for each level of the attribute. Consider an attribute with k levels and let δ_j be the average bad rate associated with the jth level of the attribute for $j \in \{1, \ldots, k\}$. In this case,

$$\delta_j = \frac{\mu_j d}{\sum_{l=1}^{k} \mu_l p_l}, \text{ where } \mu_j = \frac{\gamma_j p_j}{\sum_{l=1}^{k} \gamma_l}.$$

We now simulate a sample of attributes from the specified marginal distribution. Given the values of these attributes, we simulate default indicators from the conditional distribution of these indicators. That is, given that the jth level of the specific attribute is observed, simulate a 1 for the default indicator with probability δ_j.

3.3. Combine the Simulated Attributes

Upon completion of the previous step, we have a realized sample for each of the attributes with a corresponding default indicator. Denoting the sample size by n, the expected number of defaults for each attribute is nd. However, due to sample variation, the number of defaults simulated for the various attributes will differ, which complicates the process of combining the attributes to form a set of simulated attributes for a (simulated) applicant. In order to overcome this problem, we need to ensure that the number of defaults per attribute are equal.

For each attribute, the number of defaults follows a binomial distribution with parameters n and d. As a result, the number of defaults have an expected value nd and variance $nd(1-d)$. Therefore, for large values of n, the ratio of the expected and simulated number of defaults converges to 1 in probability. To illustrate the effect of sample variation, consider the following example. If a sample size of $n = 10^6$ is used and the overall default rate is set to 5%, then the expected number of defaults is 50,000 for each attribute. Due to sample variation, the number of defaults will vary. However, this variation is small when compared to the expected number of defaults; in fact, a 95% confidence interval for the number of defaults is given by $[49\,572; 50\,428]$. Stated differently, the probability that the simulated number of defaults will be within 1% of the expected number is approximately 97.8% in this case, while the probability that the realized number of defaults differ from the expected number by more than 2% is less than 1 in 200,000.

The examples above indicate that the simulated number of defaults will generally be close to nd, and we may assume that changing the simulated number of defaults to exactly nd will not have a large effect on the relationships between the values of the attribute and the default indicator. As a result, we proceed as follows. If the number of defaults exceed nd, we arbitrarily replace 1s with 0s in the default indicator in order to reduce the simulated number of defaults to nd. Similarly, if the number of defaults is less than nd, we replace 0s with 1s.

Following the previous step, the number of defaults per attribute are equal, and we simply combine these attributes according to the default indicator. That is, in order to arrive at the details of a simulated applicant who defaults, we arbitrarily choose one realization of each attributed that resulted in default. The same procedure is used to combine the attributes of applicants who do not default.

3.4. Fit a Logistic Regression Model

We now have a (large) data set containing all of the required attributes as well as the simulated default indicators. We fit a logistic regression model to this data in order to find a parameter set that mimics the specified bad ratios. That is, we estimate the set of regression coefficients in (2). The required estimation is standard, and the majority of statistical analysis packages includes a function to perform the required estimation; the results shown below are obtained using the *glm* function in the *Stats* package of R.

3.5. Simulate the Final Default Indicators

When considering the data set constructed up to this point, the simulated values for the individual attributes are realized from the marginal distribution specified for that attribute. As a result, we need only concern ourselves with the distribution of the default indicator. We now replace the initial default indicator by an indicator simulated from the conditional distribution given the attributes (which is a simple matter since the required parameter estimates are now available). The simulated values of the attributes together with this default indicator constitute the final data set.

The following link contains the R code used for the simulation of a data set using the proposed method; https://bit.ly/3FFLSpp. We emphasize that the user is not bound by the specifications chosen in this paper, as the code is easily amended in order to change the distributions of attributes, to specify other bad ratios and to add or remove attributes from the data set.

4. Performance of the Fitted Model

In order to illustrate the techniques advocated for above, we use the proposed technique to simulate a number of data sets using the specifications in Section 3. Below, we report the means (denoted "Observed bad rate") and standard deviations (denoted "Std dev of obs bad rate") of the observed bad ratios obtained when generating 10,000 data sets, each of size 50,000.

In Tables 5–8, we consider each of the four attributes discussed in the previous section in the main text, while the results associated with the remaining attributes are considered in Appendix B. Tables 5–8 indicate that the average observed bad ratios are remarkably close to the nominally specified bad ratios. Furthermore, the standard deviations of the observed bad ratios are also shown to be quite small, indicating that the proposed method results in data sets in which the specifications provided in Section 3 are closely adhered to.

Table 5. Existing customers.

Group	Description	Specified Bad Rate	Observed Bad Rate	Std Dev of Obs Bad Rate
0	Yes	7.46%	7.48%	0.14%
1	No	20.15%	20.09%	0.46%

Table 6. Credit cards with other providers.

Group	Description	Specified Bad Rate	Observed Bad Rate	Std Dev of Obs Bad Rate
0	No Credit Cards	4.00%	4.70%	0.16%
1	One Credit Card	12.00%	10.43%	0.24%
2	Two Credit Cards	20.00%	19.49%	0.46%
3	Three or more Credit Cards	28.00%	31.90%	1.01%

Table 7. Application method.

Group	Description	Specified Bad Rate	Observed Bad Rate	Std Dev of Obs Bad Rate
0	Branch	12.74%	12.73%	0.32%
1	Online	6.37%	6.39%	0.21%
2	Phone	19.11%	19.05%	0.55%
3	Marketing Call	5.10%	5.12%	0.34%

Table 8. Age.

Group	Description	Specified Bad Rate	Observed Bad Rate	Std Dev of Obs Bad Rate
0	18–21	17.54%	16.82%	0.77%
1	22–25	14.91%	15.19%	0.63%
2	26–30	13.68%	13.89%	0.53%
3	31–45	11.58%	11.46%	0.27%
4	46–57	8.77%	8.66%	0.28%
5	58–63	7.54%	7.28%	0.37%
6	64–75	5.44%	5.82%	0.26%

The marginal distributions of the attributes are not reported in the tables since the average observed proportions coincide with the specified proportions up to 0.01% in all cases. This result is not unexpected, when taking the large sample sizes used into account.

Although less common in practice, smaller sample sizes occur from time to time. This is usually due to constraints placed on the sampling itself; for example, a high cost associated with sampling or regulatory restrictions. When considering smaller sample sizes, the proposed method can still be used. However, in this case the standard deviations of the observed bad rates are increased.

5. Practical Application

The method described above provides a way to arrive at a parametric model, which can be used for simulation purposes, via specification of bad ratios for each attribute considered. One interesting application of this procedure is to specify a deviation from the distribution of the attributes and default indicator and to simulate a second data set. This deviation may, for instance, be in the form of specifying a change in the marginal distribution associated with one or more attributes. The newly simulated data set can then be analyzed in order to gauge the effect of the change to, for example, the overall credit risk of the population.

In practice, a common metric used to measure the level of population stability is the aptly named population stability index (PSI). The PSI quantifies the discrepancy between the observed proportions per level of a given attribute in two samples. Typically, the first data set is observed when the scorecard is developed (we refer to this data set as the *base* data set) and the second is a more recent sample (referred to as the *test* data set). Letting k be the number of levels of the attributes, the PSI is calculated as follows:

$$PSI = \sum_{j=1}^{k}(T_j - B_j)\log\left(\frac{T_j}{B_j}\right), \quad (3)$$

where T_j and B_j, respectively, represent the proportion of the jth level of the attribute in question in the test and base data sets. The following rule-of-thumb for the interpretation of PSI values is suggested in [1]; a value of less than 0.1 indicates that the population shows no substantial changes, a PSI between 0.1 and 0.25 indicates a small change and a PSI of more than 0.25 indicates a substantial change.

It should be noted that the PSI is closely related to the Kullback–Leibler divergence. Let $\mathbf{B} = (B_1, \ldots, B_k)$ and $\mathbf{T} = (T_1, \ldots, T_k)$. The Kullback–Leibler divergence between the base and test populations is defined to be

$$D(\mathbf{B}, \mathbf{T}) = \sum_{j=1}^{k} B_j \log\left(\frac{B_j}{T_j}\right) = -\sum_{j=1}^{k} B_j \log\left(\frac{T_j}{B_j}\right),$$

see [16] as well as [17]. Note that the Kullback–Leibler divergence is an asymmetric discrepancy measure, meaning that the discrepancy between the base and test populations, $D(\mathbf{B}, \mathbf{T})$, need not equal the discrepancy between the test and base populations, $D(\mathbf{T}, \mathbf{B})$. In order to arrive at a symmetric discrepancy measure, one may simply add $D(\mathbf{T}, \mathbf{B})$ to $D(\mathbf{B}, \mathbf{T})$;

$$\begin{aligned} D(\mathbf{B}, \mathbf{T}) + D(\mathbf{B}, \mathbf{T}) &= -\sum_{j=1}^{k} B_j \log\left(\frac{T_j}{B_j}\right) + \sum_{j=1}^{k} T_j \log\left(\frac{B_j}{T_j}\right) \\ &= \sum_{j=1}^{k} (T_j - B_j) \log\left(\frac{T_j}{B_j}\right), \end{aligned}$$

which equals the PSI between the base and test populations. A further discussion of the Kullback–Leibler divergence can be found in [18].

In order to illustrate the use of the PSI, consider the following setup. A single realization of the base data set is simulated using the marginal distributions and the bad ratios specified in Section 2 and Appendix A. We also simulate a test data set using the same specifications, with only the following changes:

- The proportion of existing customers is changed from 80% to 57%. The new distribution is chosen such as to have a PSI value that is approximately 0.25.
- The distribution for the number of enquiries is changed from (30%, 25%, 20%, 15%, 5%, 5%) to (10%, 10%, 20%, 50%, 5%, 5%).

Following these changes, a test data sets is simulated from the distribution specified above and the resulting PSI is calculated for each attribute. This process is repeated 1000 times in order to arrive at 1000 PSI values for each attribute.

In addition to considering the magnitude in the change of the distribution of the attributes, we are interested in measuring the change in the overall credit risk of the population. In order to achieve this, it is standard practice to divide the applicants into various so-called risk buckets based on their probability of default as calculated by the scorecard. In the example used here, we proceed as follows; at the time when the data for the base data set is collected, the applicants may be segmented into ten risk buckets, each containing 10% of the applicants. That is, the $10\%, 20\%, \ldots, 90\%$ quantiles of the probabilities of default of the base data set are calculated. Then, given the test data set, we calculate the proportions of applicants for whom the calculated probability of default is between the $10(j-1)\%$ and $10j\%$ quantiles of the base data set, for $j \in \{1, 2, \ldots, 10\}$. These proportions are then compared to those of the base data set (which are clearly 10% for each risk bucket) in the same way as the proportions associated with the various levels of the attributes are compared. Table 9 contains the average and standard deviations of the PSI calculated for each of the attributes as well as for the risk buckets.

Table 9. Population stability index.

Attribute	Average PSI	Standard Dev of PSI
Gender	0.0001	0.0002
Existing customer	0.2557	0.0102
Number of enquiries	0.7988	0.0178
Credit cards with other providers	0.0005	0.0004
Province of residence	0.0012	0.0005
Application method	0.0005	0.0004
Age	0.0008	0.0004
Total amount outstanding	0.0011	0.0006
Income	0.0008	0.0004
Balance of recent defaults	0.0005	0.0003
Risk buckets	0.0926	0.0061

When considering the results in Table 9, three observations are in order. First, the PSI values calculated for the risk buckets are less than 0.1, indicating that no substantial change in the distribution of the data is observed. Second, the PSI values for the attribute "existing customer" are, on average, 0.2557. Based on the average PSI, the analyst would typically conclude that the variable is unstable as the calculated average PSI value exceeds the cut-off of 0.25. However, in 27.5% of the simulated test data sets, the PSI was calculated to be less than 0.25. This demonstrates that the proposed simulation technique enables us to perform sensitivity analysis in cases where a change in the distribution of the attributes results in PSI values close to the cut-off value of 0.25. When considering the attribute "Number of enquiries", the PSI indicates that a substantial change has occurred. The PSI values calculated for this attribute has an average of 0.7988 and a standard deviation of 0.0178.

6. Conclusions

We propose a simulation technique that can be used in order to generate data sets for use with credit scoring, and we specifically demonstrated the usefulness of this technique for testing population stability. The proposed technique is based on the simple idea of specifying bad ratios and finding parameters that approximately adhere to the specified bad ratios. Using a realistic example, we demonstrate that the proposed technique is able to mimic the specified bad ratios with a high degree of accuracy.

The proposed simulation method enables one to study the properties of population stability metrics in a systematic manner. This allows for the direct comparison of the various measures commonly used in practice in order to identify the strengths and weaknesses of each; research into this topic is currently underway. The proposed method also simplifies the study of newly proposed tests for population stability. Furthermore, another direction for future research is to generalize the proposed simulation technique to the multivariate case; for instance, in the context of multinomial regression. Finally, future research may include extending the proposed methodology to include dependent attributes using copula models. An example of the use of copulas in the context of credit risk can be found in [19].

Author Contributions: Conceptualization, J.d.P., J.S.A. and J.V.; Methodology, J.d.P., J.S.A. and J.V.; Writing—original draft, J.d.P., J.S.A. and J.V.; Writing—review & editing, J.d.P., J.S.A. and J.V. All authors have read and agreed to the published version of the manuscript.

Funding: This research received no external funding.

Acknowledgments: The work of J.S. Allison and I.J.H. Visagie are based on research supported by the National Research Foundation (NRF). Any opinion, finding and conclusion or recommendation expressed in this material is that of the authors and the NRF does not accept any liability in this regard.

Conflicts of Interest: The authors declare no conflict of interest.

Appendix A

Below, we specify the marginal distributions and the specified bad ratios for the characteristics not discussed in detail in the main text of Section 2. Again, we treat each attribute separately.

Appendix A.1. Gender

We assume that 60% of applicants are female and 40% are male, and we specify the bad ratio of males to females to be 3.

Appendix A.2. Number of Enquiries

The number of enquiries is a measure of the client's appetite for credit. A client with a large credit appetite will apply for a number of loans. The number of enquiries provides a view of both the client's successful and unsuccessful applications. Higher numbers of enquiries are often associated with increased levels of risk. Table A1 specifies the distribution associated with various levels of this attribute.

Table A1. Number of enquiries.

Group	Description	Proportion	Bad Ratio
0	No enquiries	30%	1.0
1	One enquiry	25%	1.3
2	Two enquiries	20%	1.8
3	Three enquiries	15%	1.9
4	Four enquiries	5%	2.1
5	Five or more enquiries	5%	2.7

Appendix A.3. Province of Residence

Some provinces are greater economic hubs, which may result in inhabitants with lower levels of credit risk. Table A2 shows the marginal distribution as well as bad ratios assumed for the 9 provinces of South Africa.

Table A2. Province of residence.

Group	Description	Proportion	Bad Ratio
0	Gauteng	40%	1.0
1	Western Cape	30%	0.7
2	KwaZulu Natal	7%	1.8
3	Mpumalanga	5%	1.5
4	North West	5%	3.0
5	Limpopo	4%	2.5
6	Eastern Cape	4%	2.0
7	Northern Cape	3%	4.0
8	Free State	2%	1.2

Appendix A.4. Total Amount Outstanding

An applicant's total amount outstanding is an indication of the current indebtedness and provides a view of the client's previous commitments. Excessively low or high levels of this variable may be associated with higher levels of risk; i.e., a customer with no outstanding amount could be a result of not being able to obtain credit while very high levels of this attribute may indicate difficulty in paying current commitments. The marginal distribution specified for this attribute is standard lognormal, rescaled by a factor of 10,000. The lognormal distribution is chosen since its shape is reminiscent of the empirical distribution typically observed in practice, while the scaling factor is incorporated in order to ensure that the numbers used are of a realistic magnitude. The resulting proportions and bad ratios can be found in Table A3.

Table A3. Total amount outstanding.

Group	Grouping	Proportion	Bad Ratio
0	0–5000	24.4%	1.0
1	5000–10,000	25.6%	1.2
2	10,000–25,000	32.0%	2.0
3	25,000–100,000	16.9%	2.1
4	more than 100,000	1.1%	0.8

Appendix A.5. Income

Income is a strong indicator of the ability to repay debt and it is often used directly or indirectly in the scoring process. Direct use occurs through inclusion into the scoring model as an attribute, while indirect use can be accomplished through using income as an entry criteria for the application. The distribution used for income is a mixture with several local models. The associated proportions and bad ratios can be found in Table A4.

Table A4. Income.

Group	Grouping	Proportion	Bad Ratio
0	0–5000	3.2%	3.0
1	5000–11,000	15.6%	2.5
2	11,000–20,000	20.4%	2.0
3	20,000–30,000	21.8%	1.4
4	30,000–70,000	24.0%	1.2
5	more than 70,000	15.0%	1.0

Balance of Recent Defaults

Recent defaults are an indication that a customer is no longer able to pay their debts. This attribute specifically speaks to customers that have recently defaulted, as all customers without defaults are grouped at zero. Table A5 specifies a distribution in which the majority of applicants have recent defaults with a value of less than 1000 units, indicating that the majority of applicants have not defaulted recently.

Table A5. Balance of recent defaults.

Group	Grouping	Proportion	Bad Ratio
0	0–1000	60.0%	1.0
1	1000–3000	1.1%	1.1
2	3000–5000	2.1%	2.0
3	5000–30,000	18.9%	2.5
4	30,000–1,000,000	18.0%	3.0
5	more than 1,000,000	0.0%	3.3

Appendix B

Tables A6–A11 report the specified bad rate, the average observed bad rate as well as the standard deviation of this bad rate for each of the attributes not treated in the main text of Section 4.

Table A6. Gender.

Group	Description	Specified Bad Rate	Observed Bad Rate	Std Dev of Obs Bad Rate
0	Female	5.56%	5.58%	0.16%
1	Male	16.67%	16.62%	0.27%

Table A7. Number of enquiries.

Group	Description	Specified Bad Rate	Observed Bad Rate	Std Dev of Obs Bad Rate
0	No Enquiries	6.62%	6.97%	0.23%
1	One Enquiry	8.61%	8.62%	0.25%
2	Two Enquiries	11.92%	10.89%	0.30%
3	Three Enquiries	12.58%	12.74%	0.39%
4	Four Enquiries	13.91%	14.96%	0.73%
5	Five or more Enquiries	17.88%	18.28%	0.84%

Table A8. Province of residence.

Group	Description	Specified Bad Rate	Observed Bad Rate	Std Dev of Obs Bad Rate
0	Gauteng	7.78%	7.79%	0.22%
1	Western Cape	5.45%	5.47%	0.24%
2	KwaZulu Natal	14.01%	14.00%	0.74%
3	Mpumalanga	11.67%	11.67%	0.83%
4	North West	23.35%	23.27%	1.05%
5	Limpopo	19.46%	19.40%	1.11%
6	Eastern Cape	15.56%	15.51%	1.05%
7	Northern Cape	31.13%	30.98%	1.50%
8	Free State	9.34%	9.32%	1.22%

Table A9. Amount outstanding.

Group	Description	Specified Bad Rate	Observed Bad Rate	Std Dev of Obs Bad Rate
0	0–5000	6.43%	8.52%	0.26%
1	5000–10,000	7.72%	9.01%	0.25%
2	10,000–25,000	12.86%	10.78%	0.23%
3	25,000–100,000	13.51%	11.93%	0.36%
4	more than 100,000	5.15%	12.17%	2.98%

Table A10. Income.

Group	Description	Specified Bad Rate	Observed Bad Rate	Std Dev of Obs Bad Rate
0	0–5000	19.07%	14.51%	0.95%
1	5000–11,000	15.89%	12.65%	0.44%
2	11,000–20,000	12.71%	11.66%	0.34%
3	20,000–30,000	8.90%	10.28%	0.29%
4	30,000–70,000	7.63%	9.70%	0.30%
5	more than 70,000	6.36%	4.08%	0.44%

Table A11. Balance of recent defaults.

Group	Description	Specified Bad Rate	Observed Bad Rate	Std Dev of Obs Bad Rate
0	1000–3000	6.11%	8.41%	0.18%
1	3000–5000	6.72%	4.51%	0.91%
2	5000–30,000	12.22%	5.78%	0.75%
3	30,000–1,000,000	15.28%	8.21%	0.32%
4	more than 1,000,000	18.33%	17.99%	0.45%

References

1. Siddiqi, N. *Credit Risk Scorecards*; John Wiley and Sons, Inc.: Hoboken, NJ, USA, 2006.
2. Siddiqi, N. *Intelligent Credit Scoring: Building and Implementing Better Credit Risk Scorecards*; John Wiley and Sons, Inc.: Hoboken, NJ, USA, 2016.

3. Anderson, R. *The Credit Scoring Toolkit: Theory and Practice for Retail Credit Risk Management and Decision Automation;* Oxford University Press: Oxford, UK, 2007.
4. Karakoulas, G. Empirical Validation of Retail Credit-Scoring Models. *RMA J.* **2004**, *87*, 56–60.
5. Lewis, E.M. *An Introduction to Credit Scoring;* Athena Press: London, UK, 1994.
6. Taplin, R.; Hunt, C. The Population Accuracy Index: A New Measure of Population Stability for Model Monitoring. *Risks* **2019**, *7*, 53. [CrossRef]
7. Yurdakul, B.; Naranjo, J. Statistical properties of the population stability index. *J. Risk Model Valid.* **2019**, *14*. [CrossRef]
8. Du Pisanie, J.; Visagie, I.J.H. On testing the hypothesis of population stability for credit risk scorecards. *ORiON J.* **2020**, *36*, 19–34. [CrossRef]
9. Fan, D. creditmodel: Toolkit for Credit Modelling; R Package Version 1.1.9. 2020. Available online: https://cran.r-project.org/web/packages/creditmodel/index.html (accessed on 1 November 2022).
10. Pruitt, R. The Applied Use of Population Stability Index (PSI) in SAS Enterprise Miner Posters. *SAS Global Forum.* 2010. Available online: http://support.sas.com/resources/papers/proceedings10/288-2010.pdf (accessed on 1 November 2022).
11. Markmann, C.; Spickermann, A.; von der Gracht, H.A.; Brem, A. Improving the question formulation in Delphi-like survey: Analysis of the effects of abstract language and amount of information on response behavior. *Futur. Foresight Sci.* **2020**, *3*, e56. [CrossRef]
12. Goodfellow, I.; Pouget-Abadie, J.; Mirza, M.; Xu, B.; Warde-Farley, D.; Ozair, S.; Courville, A.; Bengio, Y. Generative Adversarial Networks. *Adv. Neural Inf. Process. Syst.* **2014**, *3*. [CrossRef]
13. Bedrick, E.J.; Christensen, R.; Johnson, W. A new perspective on priors for generalized linear models. *J. Am. Stat. Assoc.* **1996**, *91*, 1450–1460. [CrossRef]
14. R Core Team. *R: A Language and Environment for Statistical Computing;* R Foundation for Statistical Computing: Vienna, Austria, 2019.
15. Nelson, R.G. *An Introduction to Copulas;* Springer: New York, NY, USA, 2006.
16. Kullback, S.; Leibler, R.A. On information and sufficiency. *Ann. Math. Stat.* **1951**, *22*, 79–86. [CrossRef]
17. Kullback, S. *Information Theory and Statistics;* John Wiley and Sons, Inc.: London, UK, 1959.
18. Wu, D.; Olson, D. Enterprise risk management: Coping with model risk in a large bank. *J. Oper. Res. Soc.* **2010**, *61*, 179–190. [CrossRef]
19. Lu, M.J.; Chen, C.Y.H.; H ardle, W.K. Copula-based factor model for credit risk analysis. *Rev. Quant. Financ. Account.* **2017**, *49*, 949–971. [CrossRef]

mathematics

Article

Prediction of a Sensitive Feature under Indirect Questioning via Warner's Randomized Response Technique and Latent Class Model

Shen-Ming Lee [1], Phuoc-Loc Tran [2], Truong-Nhat Le [3] and Chin-Shang Li [4,*]

1 Department of Statistics, Feng Chia University, Taichung 40724, Taiwan
2 Department of Mathematics, College of Natural Science, Can Tho University, Can Tho, Vietnam
3 Faculty of Mathematics and Statistics, Ton Duc Thang University, Ho Chi Minh City, Vietnam
4 School of Nursing, The State University of New York, University at Buffalo, Buffalo, NY 14214, USA
* Correspondence: csli2003@gmail.com or chinshan@buffalo.edu

Abstract: We investigate the association of a sensitive characteristic or latent variable with observed binary random variables by the randomized response (RR) technique of Warner in his publication (Warner, S.L. *J. Am. Stat. Assoc.* **1965**, *60*, 63–69) and a latent class model. First, an expectation-maximization (EM) algorithm is provided to easily estimate the parameters of the null and alternative/full models for the association between a sensitive characteristic and an observed categorical random variable under the RR design of Warner's paper above. The likelihood ratio test (LRT) is utilized to identify observed categorical random variables that are significantly related to the sensitive trait. Another EM algorithm is then presented to estimate the parameters of a latent class model constructed through the sensitive attribute and the observed binary random variables that are obtained from dichotomizing observed categorical random variables selected from the above LRT. Finally, two classification criteria are conducted to predict an individual in the sensitive or non-sensitive group. The practicality of the proposed methodology is illustrated with an actual data set from a survey study of the sexuality of first-year students, except international students, at Feng Chia University in Taiwan in 2016.

Keywords: bootstrap; expectation-maximization (EM) algorithm; latent class; likelihood ratio test; maximum likelihood; randomized response; sensitive attribute

MSC: 62F03; 62F40; 62F86

Citation: Lee, S.-M.; Tran, P.-L.; Le, T.-N.; Li, C.-S. Prediction of a Sensitive Feature under Indirect Questioning via Warner's Randomized Response Technique and Latent Class Model. *Mathematics* **2023**, *11*, 345. https://doi.org/10.3390/math11020345

Academic Editor: Manuel Franco

Received: 3 December 2022
Revised: 30 December 2022
Accepted: 5 January 2023
Published: 9 January 2023

1. Introduction

Questionnaire surveys have been widely used to gather data for studies in various research fields, including behavioral science, education, sociology, economics, psychology, bio-medicine, etc., via Google form, email, phone call, or face-to-face interview. The information gathered from these surveys is utilized to estimate, compare, and forecast unknown population proportions of sensitive characteristics of interest. However, it will be likely to misreport the proportion of individuals who self-report some sensitive characteristic, such as political opinions, domestic violence, discrimination, abortion, drug use, gender identity, sexual behavior, anti-social behavior, exam fraud, plagiarism, illegal income, tax evasion, and gambling, or to refuse to answer when asked directly a sensitive question. This can lead to errors in analysis results and mistakes in statistical inferences. For example, in a study conducted by [1] that involved direct interviews with unemployment benefit recipients, 75% of the survey participants who had engaged in welfare or unemployment benefits deception denied doing so. In addition, according to [2], if respondents were forced to answer directly sensitive questions, the percentage of non-heterosexual participants in a community is typically underestimated. Therefore, various indirect questioning techniques, such as randomized response (RR), unmatched count, and crosswise model techniques, have been proposed to lessen potential bias due to non-response and social desirability response and, as a result, improve the reliability of data obtained from responses to sensitive topics to estimate better the population proportion of people bearing a sensitive attribute. See, e.g., [3–6] for more details.

The RR technique (RRT), initially introduced by Warner [3], is one of the most famous indirect questioning techniques and has been widely used to collect sensitive data. The main idea of this technique is to safeguard respondents' privacy by concealing their answers or without disclosing their actual status by using a random device, such as spinners, a deck of cards, dice, or random number generators. Specifically, Warner [3] suggested the related-question RRT via a sensitive question of interest and its complement. Respondents can feel more comfortable choosing which question to honestly answer "yes" or "no" based on the results of running a random device because the interviewer does not know precisely their responses. However, Warner's RRT still has limitations, such as not working when the probability that the sensitive question is selected to answer is 0.5. Therefore, various extensions of Warner's RRT have been suggested to overcome its limitations and enhance computing effectiveness. For example, Horvitz et al. [7] and Greenberg et al. [8] proposed an unrelated-question RR design in which the first one is a sensitive question, as in Warner's design, and the second one is innocuous and independent of the sensitive question. Mangat and Singh [9] proposed a two-stage RR design that used two random devices in the procedure. Christofides [10] suggested a generalized RRT. Huang [11] applied the two-stage RRT to enhance the performance of Warner's RRT. Tian and Tang [12] provided another classification for the RRTs. The related literature can also be found in [2,5,13–21].

Data of some auxiliary variables are also gathered under direct questions when collecting sensitive trait or behavior data. The effects of these auxiliary variables on the population proportion of a sensitive characteristic are also quite essential and mentioned in many studies. For instance, by using the RRT of [3], Maddala [22] estimated the effects of the auxiliary variables, e.g., sex, age, and place of residence, on drug use by utilizing a logistic regression model. Scheers and Dayton [23] obtained sensitive information through the RR designs of [3,8], respectively. They proposed using the logistic regression model to establish the influence model of the accompanying variables on the sensitive feature and to provide a method for estimating the regression parameters. Hsieh et al. [14,24] proposed semiparametric methods of estimating the parameters of a logistic regression model when values of some of the covariates on some subjects are missing at random to gather information about sensitive characteristics based on the RR design of [8]. Chang et al. [17] developed a covariate extension of the two-stage RR design of [11] by employing logistic regression to investigate the effects of two covariates of interest on the sensitive attribute and the truthful response to the directly asked sensitive question in the first stage for a sensitive trait respondent to estimate the probability of a sensitive feature respondent's honest response in the first stage and the probability of a respondent with the sensitive feature based on the logistic regression parameter estimates. Furthermore, in some practical applications, in addition to using an RR design to collect data on sensitive characteristics or behaviors, the related scale data are also frequently gathered to use as auxiliary variables. For example, Lee et al. [19] studied students' attitudes toward love, gender identity, and online dating experience through the survey study of the sexuality of first-year students, except international students, at Feng Chia University in Taiwan in 2016. They used the sum of scores of responses to six internet dating experience statements (statements 40–45) as the auxiliary variable for the sensitive issue, question 67: "Have you ever had a one-night stand through a dating site or mobile app?" in which response data were gathered by the generalized RRT of Christofides [10]. They utilized the proposed Bayesian estimation methods to estimate the parameters of the normal independent and dependent models for the association of the response to question 67 with the sum of scores of responses to the six internet dating experiences. Two Bayesian model selection criteria were proposed to choose one of the two models as an appropriate model to describe this association.

In another approach to sample survey research, several latent variable models, which are statistical models and relate a set of observed variables (so-called indicators/manifest variables) to a latent variable, have been widely used in various sciences, such as the social, economic, behavioral, and health sciences. The main types of latent variable models can be classified based on whether the manifest and latent variables are categorical or continuous as in (Table 7.1 [25], p. 178). See, e.g., [13,25,26] for more details. Some other extensions of latent variable models, where the manifest variables are treated as ordinal categorical variables, count variables, or other metrics, can be found in [27,28].

Because both the latent and indicators/manifest/observed variables are categorical, the latent class (LC) analysis (LCA) is recommended for applications. Lazarsfeld [29] first introduced the conceptual foundation of LCA, which was used as a tool for building typologies based on observed dichotomous variables, in research about the ethnocentrism of American soldiers during World War II [28,30]. Lazarsfeld and Henry [31] provided a thorough and in-depth conceptual and mathematical treatment of the LCA, but there was a lack of reliable parameter estimation methods. Since then, the LC model (LCM) has been improved and applied in various science fields. For example, Goodman [32,33] provided a relatively simple method, which was later shown to be closely related to the expectation-maximization (EM) algorithm [34], to obtain the maximum likelihood (ML) estimates of LCM parameters and goodness-of-fit methods for the model for fitting the observed data. Haberman [35] demonstrated the connection between LCMs and log-linear models for frequency tables with missing (unknown) cell counts. Dayton and Macready [36] proposed a new development by incorporating covariates into an LCM. Muthén and Shedden [37] improved the models that identified latent growth trajectory class membership in longitudinal data based on individual growth trajectories and were estimated by the EM algorithm. Stern et al. [38] applied LCA in studying the two main temperamental types of children: inhibited and uninhibited. LCMs have been used to investigate the initiation of substance use habits throughout adolescence, such as alcohol, caffeine, and tobacco [39]. Vermunt [40] provided an overview of applications of LCMs in social science research and an extension of the LCM to deal with nested data structures. Collins and Lanza [26] presented the methodology and applications of LCA for social, behavioral, and health sciences data. Nasiopoulou et al. [41] applied LCA to investigate the professional profiles of Swedish preschool teachers. LCA was used to determine the cause of occupational fatalities in the study of [42]. Wu et al. [43] used LCA to stratify the risk of incident diabetes in Chinese adults. For other studies about LCA and its applications, see, e.g., [26,44–48].

However, to the best of our knowledge, there has not been any research about applying the combination of the RRT and LCM to estimate the proportion of a sensitive or latent characteristic based on observed variables. Therefore, we are strongly motivated by the issue to introduce the proposed models, estimation methods, likelihood ratio test (LRT), and reality applications. This study first presents an EM algorithm for estimating the parameters of the null and alternative/full model for the association between the sensitive attribute and an observed categorical random variable in which the RRT of Warner [3] is used. Note that our approaches are different from those of Lee et al. [19] in which they used a Markov chain Monte Carlo estimation method and generalized RRT of [10]. The LRT is then applied to assess whether there is a difference in the distribution of the observed categorical random variable (i.e., auxiliary variable) between the sensitive and non-sensitive groups. Finally, a combination of the RRT of [3] and LCA is introduced in which the indicators/manifest/observed variables are binary. After collecting questions/statements significantly related to the sensitive characteristic from the results of the LRTs, an LCM is used to classify an individual in the sensitive or non-sensitive group.

Section 2.1 reviews the RR design of [3]. In Section 2.2, we introduce a model for the association between a sensitive variable and an observed categorical random variable, which is presented in [19], by using the RRT of [3]. The EM algorithm, called EM algorithm 1, is applied to estimate the parameters of this model, and the LRT is used to evaluate whether the observed categorical random variable is significantly associated with the sensitivity characteristic variable. Section 2.3 provides an LCM to relate observed dichotomous random variables, obtained from dichotomizing the significant observed categorical random variables, to a latent variable that is the sensitive attribute from the RR design of [3]. Another EM algorithm, called EM algorithm 2, is proposed to estimate the parameters of the LCM. A classification criterion is conducted to predict an individual in a sensitive or non-sensitive group in this section. In Section 3, data from the survey of the sexuality of freshmen, except international students, at Feng Chia University in Taiwan in 2016 are used to demonstrate practical applications of the proposed methodology. Another classification criterion is proposed to forecast students in the sensitive or non-sensitive group. Conclusions and some remarks are given in Section 4.

2. Models and Methods

2.1. Warner's RR Design

The fundamental idea of the related-question RR design of [3] is to protect respondents' privacy by concealing their responses via a random device, e.g., spinners and dice, a deck of cards, etc. For example, assume that each respondent receives randomly a deck of cards marked with question A or $\overline{A}$ as follows:

A : Have you ever had a one-night stand through a dating site or mobile app?

$\overline{A}$: Have you never had a one-night stand through a dating site or mobile app?

Respondents report a truthful "yes" or "no" response to the question they receive without showing the interviewer which question has been selected. The actual status of the respondents regarding whether or not they have ever had a one-night stand through a dating site or mobile app remains undisclosed, and, therefore, their privacy is protected because neither the interviewer nor the researcher is even aware of the question to which the released answer refers.

Let θ be the population proportion of persons bearing the sensitive trait *having ever had a one-night stand through a dating site or mobile app*, p the probability of cards marked with the question A, and $1-p$ the probability of cards marked with the question $\overline{A}$. Assume that p is known. The probability of answering "yes" is then

$$\begin{aligned} P(\text{yes}) &= p(A)P(\text{yes}|A) + P(\overline{A})P(\text{yes}|\overline{A}) \\ &= \theta p + (1-\theta)(1-p) \\ &= \theta(2p-1) + 1 - p. \end{aligned}$$

Let $\widehat{\lambda}$ be the proportion of respondents who answer "yes". Because $2p-1 \neq 0$, the estimate of θ can be obtained as follows:

$$\widehat{\theta}_w = \frac{\widehat{\lambda} - (1-p)}{2p-1}.$$

However, using random devices may make a respondent report different answers when repeating the survey twice. Yu et al. [5] pointed out that this is a repetitive phenomenon and, hence, provided another design in which a respondent chooses question A or $\overline{A}$ to answer according to her/his characteristic. For example, if a respondent were born between August 11 and December 31, she/he chooses question $\overline{A}$ to answer and chooses question A to answer otherwise. Therefore, if the respondent repeated the survey twice, the results are the same. In addition, it can prevent respondents from rejecting interviews and providing false answers and, hence, improve estimation efficiency through this random birthday design to obtain data of responses to sensitive questions. In this study, for simplicity, we use the birthday design of [5] for the RR design of [3] by using the data in the study of [19] as reality analysis. By this approach, it is only necessary that specific explanations are written in the questionnaire, and students can then answer questions by themselves without using a random device. The details of specific explanations are given in Section 3.

2.2. Model for the Association between Sensitive Attribute and Categorical Variable

2.2.1. Model

Let Y_i, $i = 1, 2, \ldots, n$, denote whether the ith sample respondent has the sensitive attribute A in which $Y_i = 1$ if yes and $Y_i = 0$ otherwise. Assume that Z_i denotes the ith respondent's response to a direct inquiry, which is a categorical random variable with values $1, 2, \ldots, B$ or a quantitative variable.

The model for the association between Y_i and Z_i is considered as follows:

$$\begin{aligned} &P(Y_i = y) = \theta^y(1-\theta)^{1-y}, \\ &P(Z_i = z|Y_i = y) = \pi_{yz},\ z = 1, 2, \ldots, B,\ y = 0, 1. \end{aligned} \tag{1}$$

From the above model, one can then obtain

$$P(Z_i = z, Y_i = y) = \theta^y(1-\theta)^{1-y}\pi_{yz},\ z = 1, 2, \ldots, B,\ y = 0, 1. \tag{2}$$

Let Y_i^0 be the result of using this non-random answering design as given in Table 10 of [17]. Let $Y_i^0 = 1$ denote the answer of "A" to a sensitive question and $Y_i^0 = 0$ the answer of "B" to the sensitive question. Assume that p is the probability of respondents' birthday between January 1 and August 10. $P(Z_i = z, Y_i^0 = y^0)$ can then be expressed as follows:

$$\begin{aligned} P(Z_i = z, Y_i^0 = 1) &= P(Z_i = z, Y_i^0 = 1, Y_i = 1) + P(Z_i = z, Y_i^0 = 1, Y_i = 0) \\ &= P(Z_i = z, Y_i^0 = 1|Y_i = 1)P(Y_i = 1) + P(Z_i = z, Y_i^0 = 1|Y_i = 0)P(Y_i = 0) \\ &= \pi_{1z}p\theta + \pi_{0z}(1-p)(1-\theta). \end{aligned}$$

and

$$\begin{aligned} P(Z_i = z, Y_i^0 = 0) &= P(Z_i = z, Y_i^0 = 0, Y_i = 1) + P(Z_i = z, Y_i^0 = 0, Y_i = 0) \\ &= P(Z_i = z, Y_i^0 = 0|Y_i = 1)P(Y_i = 1) + P(Z_i = z, Y_i^0 = 0|Y_i = 0)P(Y_i = 0) \\ &= \pi_{1z}(1-p)\theta + \pi_{0z}p(1-\theta). \end{aligned}$$

Let $\boldsymbol{y}^0 = (y_1^0, y_2^0, \ldots, y_n^0)$, $\boldsymbol{z} = (z_1, z_2, \ldots, z_n)$, $\boldsymbol{\pi}_y = (\pi_{y1}, \pi_{y2}, \ldots, \pi_{yB})$, $y = 0, 1$, and $\boldsymbol{\Theta} = (\theta, \boldsymbol{\pi}_0, \boldsymbol{\pi}_1)$. Because only (Y_i^0, Z_i), $i = 1, 2, \ldots, n$, can be observed, the observed-data likelihood function of $\boldsymbol{\Theta}$ can then be written as

$$\begin{aligned} &L_{obs}(\boldsymbol{\Theta}|\boldsymbol{y}^0, \boldsymbol{z}) \\ &= \prod_{i=1}^{n}\Big\{\big[p\theta\pi_{1z_i} + (1-p)(1-\theta)\pi_{0z_i}\big]^{I(y_i^0=1)}\big[p(1-\theta)\pi_{0z_i} + (1-p)\theta\pi_{1z_i}\big]^{I(y_i^0=0)}\Big\} \\ &= \prod_{i=1}^{n}\prod_{j=1}^{B}\Big\{\big[p\theta\pi_{1j} + (1-p)(1-\theta)\pi_{0j}\big]^{I(y_i^0=1)}\big[p(1-\theta)\pi_{0j} + (1-p)\theta\pi_{1j}\big]^{I(y_i^0=0)}\Big\}^{I(z_i=j)} \\ &= \prod_{j=1}^{B}\Big\{\big[p\theta\pi_{1j} + (1-p)(1-\theta)\pi_{0j}\big]^{\sum_{i=1}^{n} I(y_i^0=1, z_i=j)}\big[p(1-\theta)\pi_{0j} + (1-p)\theta\pi_{1j}\big]^{\sum_{i=1}^{n} I(y_i^0=0, z_i=j)}\Big\}. \end{aligned}$$

Given an initial value for $\boldsymbol{\Theta}$, the R function *optim* or *nlminb* can then be used to obtain the ML estimate of $\boldsymbol{\Theta}$. However, in practice, when using the R function *optim* or *nlminb* to find the ML estimate of $\boldsymbol{\Theta}$ for the RR design of [3], it may lead to encountering the problem of non-convergence, or the estimate is not in the parameter space of $\boldsymbol{\Theta}$. Therefore, an EM algorithm is proposed to overcome this problem in the next section.

2.2.2. EM Algorithm 1

The EM algorithm developed by Dempster et al. [34] has been the most widely used iterative technique for computing ML estimates from incomplete data. The EM algorithm consists of two steps: the expectation (E)-step and maximization (M)-step. In the E-step, the latent or unobserved data are estimated by their expectation given the observed data and current parameter estimates. The M-step is used to maximize the expectation in the E-step to update estimates of unknown parameters.

Let $\boldsymbol{y} = (y_1, y_2, \ldots, y_n)$. The complete-data likelihood function of $\boldsymbol{\Theta}$ given $(\boldsymbol{y}, \boldsymbol{y}^0, \boldsymbol{z})$ is written as follows:

$$\begin{aligned} L_c(\boldsymbol{\Theta}|\boldsymbol{y}, \boldsymbol{y}^0, \boldsymbol{z}) &= \prod_{i=1}^{n} \Big\{ \big[p\theta\pi_{1z_i}\big]^{I(y_i^0=1, y_i=1)} \big[(1-p)\theta\pi_{1z_i}\big]^{I(y_i^0=0, y_i=1)} \\ &\quad \times \big[(1-p)(1-\theta)\pi_{0z_i}\big]^{I(y_i^0=1, y_i=0)} \big[p(1-\theta)\pi_{0z_i}\big]^{I(y_i^0=0, y_i=0)} \Big\} \\ &= \prod_{i=1}^{n}\prod_{j=1}^{B} \Big\{ \big[p\theta\pi_{1j}\big]^{y_i^0 y_i} \big[(1-p)\theta\pi_{1j}\big]^{(1-y_i^0)y_i} \\ &\quad \times \big[(1-p)(1-\theta)\pi_{0j}\big]^{y_i^0(1-y_i)} \big[p(1-\theta)\pi_{0j}\big]^{(1-y_i^0)(1-y_i)} \Big\}^{I(z_i=j)}. \end{aligned}$$

The complete-data log-likelihood function of $\boldsymbol{\Theta}$ given $(\boldsymbol{y}, \boldsymbol{y}^0, \boldsymbol{z})$ can then be expressed as follows:

$$\begin{aligned} \ell_c(\boldsymbol{\Theta}|\boldsymbol{y}, \boldsymbol{y}^0, \boldsymbol{z}) = \sum_{j=1}^{B}\sum_{i=1}^{n} \Big\{ & y_i^0 y_i I(z_i=j) \ln(p\theta\pi_{1j}) + (1-y_i^0) y_i I(z_i=j) \ln[(1-p)\theta\pi_{1j}] \\ & + y_i^0(1-y_i) I(z_i=j) \ln[(1-p)(1-\theta)\theta\pi_{0j}] \\ & + (1-y_i^0)(1-y_i) I(z_i=j) \ln[p(1-\theta)\pi_{0j}] \Big\}. \end{aligned} \quad (3)$$

Note that although Y is a latent or unobserved variable, one can obtain $P(Y_i = y|Z_i = j, Y_i^0 = y^0), y = 0, 1, y^0 = 0, 1, j = 1, 2, \ldots, B$, as follows:

$$\begin{aligned} P(Y_i = 1|Z_i = j, Y_i^0 = 1) &= \frac{p\theta\pi_{1j}}{p\theta\pi_{1j} + (1-p)(1-\theta)\pi_{0j}}, \\ P(Y_i = 1|Z_i = j, Y_i^0 = 0) &= \frac{(1-p)\theta\pi_{1j}}{(1-p)\theta\pi_{1j} + p(1-\theta)\pi_{0j}}, \\ P(Y_i = 0|Z_i = j, Y_i^0 = 1) &= \frac{(1-p)(1-\theta)\pi_{0j}}{p\theta\pi_{1j} + (1-p)(1-\theta)\pi_{0j}}, \\ P(Y_i = 0|Z_i = j, Y_i^0 = 0) &= \frac{p(1-\theta)\pi_{0j}}{(1-p)\theta\pi_{1j} + p(1-\theta)\pi_{0j}}. \end{aligned}$$

Therefore, it can yield the following results:

$$\begin{aligned} E\Big(Y_i|Z_i = j, Y_i^0 = 1\Big) &= P(Y_i = 1|Z_i = j, Y_i^0 = 1) \\ &= \frac{p\theta\pi_{1j}}{p\theta\pi_{1j} + (1-p)(1-\theta)\pi_{0j}}, \end{aligned}$$

$$\begin{aligned} E\Big(Y_i|Z_i = j, Y_i^0 = 0\Big) &= P(Y_i = 1|Z_i = j, Y_i^0 = 0) \\ &= \frac{(1-p)\theta\pi_{1j}}{(1-p)\theta\pi_{1j} + p(1-\theta)\pi_{0j}}, \end{aligned}$$

$$E\Big((1-Y_i)|Z_i=j,Y_i^0=1\Big)=P(Y_i=0|Z_i=j,Y_i^0=1)$$
$$=\frac{(1-p)(1-\theta)\pi_{0j}}{p\theta\pi_{1j}+(1-p)(1-\theta)\pi_{0j}},$$

$$E\Big((1-Y_i)|Z_i=j,Y_i^0=0\Big)=P(Y_i=0|Z_i=j,Y_i^0=0)$$
$$=\frac{p(1-\theta)\pi_{0j}}{(1-p)\theta\pi_{1j}+p(1-\theta)\pi_{0j}}.$$

E-step: E-step is to take the expectation of $\ell_c(\boldsymbol{\Theta}|\boldsymbol{y},\boldsymbol{y}^0,\boldsymbol{z})$ in (3) with respect to the conditional distributions of the unobserved variables Y_is given the current estimate of $\boldsymbol{\Theta}$ and the observed data $(\boldsymbol{y}^0,\boldsymbol{z})$. Let $\widehat{\boldsymbol{\Theta}}^{(m)}=(\widehat{\theta}^{(m)},\widehat{\boldsymbol{\pi}}_0^{(m)},\widehat{\boldsymbol{\pi}}_1^{(m)})$ be an estimate of $\boldsymbol{\Theta}$ at the mth iteration, where $\widehat{\boldsymbol{\pi}}_y^{(m)}=(\widehat{\pi}_{y1}^{(m)},\widehat{\pi}_{y2}^{(m)},\ldots,\widehat{\pi}_{yB}^{(m)}),y=0,1$. $\widehat{\theta}^{(0)}=\max\{0.001,[\overline{y}^0-(1-p)]/(2p-1)\}$, where $\overline{y}^0=n^{-1}\sum_{i=1}^n y_i^0$, and $\widehat{\pi}_{1j}^{(0)}=\widehat{\pi}_{0j}^{(0)}=n^{-1}\sum_{i=1}^n I(z_i=j)$ are initial values. Given the observed data $(\boldsymbol{y}^0,\boldsymbol{z})$ and $\widehat{\boldsymbol{\Theta}}^{(m)}$, by taking the expectation of $\ell_c(\boldsymbol{\Theta}|\boldsymbol{Y},\boldsymbol{Y}^0,\boldsymbol{Z})$ in (3), where $\boldsymbol{Y}^0=(Y_1^0,Y_2^0,\ldots,Y_n^0)$, $\boldsymbol{Y}=(Y_1,Y_2,\ldots,Y_n)$, and $\boldsymbol{Z}=(Z_1,Z_2,\ldots,Z_n)$, the Q-function can be given as follows:

$$\begin{aligned}
Q\Big(\boldsymbol{\Theta}|\widehat{\boldsymbol{\Theta}}^{(m)}\Big)&=E\Big[\ell_c(\boldsymbol{\Theta}|\boldsymbol{Y},\boldsymbol{Y}^0,\boldsymbol{Z})|\boldsymbol{y}^0,\boldsymbol{z},\widehat{\boldsymbol{\Theta}}^{(m)}\Big]\\
&=\sum_{j=1}^B\left\{\left[\sum_{i=1}^n y_i^0 I(z_i=j)E\Big(Y_i|\boldsymbol{y}^0,\boldsymbol{z},\widehat{\boldsymbol{\Theta}}^{(m)}\Big)\right]\ln(p\theta\pi_{1j})\right\}\\
&+\sum_{j=1}^B\left\{\left[\sum_{i=1}^n (1-y_i^0) I(z_i=j)E\Big(Y_i|\boldsymbol{y}^0,\boldsymbol{z},\widehat{\boldsymbol{\Theta}}^{(m)}\Big)\right]\ln[(1-p)\theta\pi_{1j}]\right\}\\
&+\sum_{j=1}^B\left\{\left[\sum_{i=1}^n y_i^0 I(z_i=j)E\Big(1-Y_i|\boldsymbol{y}^0,\boldsymbol{z},\widehat{\boldsymbol{\Theta}}^{(m)}\Big)\right]\ln[(1-p)(1-\theta)\pi_{0j}]\right\}\\
&+\sum_{j=1}^B\left\{\left[\sum_{i=1}^n (1-y_i^0) I(z_i=j)E\Big(1-Y_i|\boldsymbol{y}^0,\boldsymbol{z},\widehat{\boldsymbol{\Theta}}^{(m)}\Big)\right]\ln[p(1-\theta)\pi_{0j}]\right\}.
\end{aligned}\tag{4}$$

Let $\widehat{\mathcal{A}}_y^{(m)}=\sum_{j=1}^B\widehat{\mathcal{A}}_{yj}^{(m)}$, $y=0,1$, where

$$\begin{aligned}
\widehat{\mathcal{A}}_{1j}^{(m)}&=\sum_{i=1}^n E\Big\{Y_iY_i^0I(Z_i=j)|Z_i=j,Y_i^0=1,\widehat{\boldsymbol{\Theta}}^{(m)}\Big\}\\
&=\sum_{i=1}^n\left[y_i^0I(z_i=j)\left\{\frac{p\widehat{\theta}^{(m)}\widehat{\pi}_{1j}^{(m)}}{p\widehat{\theta}^{(m)}\widehat{\pi}_{1j}^{(m)}+(1-p)(1-\widehat{\theta}^{(m)})\widehat{\pi}_{0j}^{(m)}}\right\}\right],\\
\widehat{\mathcal{A}}_{0j}^{(m)}&=\sum_{i=1}^n E\Big\{Y_i(1-Y_i^0)I(Z_i=j)|Z_i=j,Y_i^0=0,\widehat{\boldsymbol{\Theta}}^{(m)}\Big\}\\
&=\sum_{i=1}^n\left[(1-y_i^0)I(z_i=j)\left\{\frac{(1-p)\widehat{\theta}^{(m)}\widehat{\pi}_{1j}^{(m)}}{(1-p)\widehat{\theta}^{(m)}\widehat{\pi}_{1j}^{(m)}+p(1-\widehat{\theta}^{(m)})\widehat{\pi}_{0j}^{(m)}}\right\}\right].
\end{aligned}$$

Let

$$\widehat{\mathcal{K}}_{1j}^{(m)} = \sum_{i=1}^{n} E\left\{(1-Y_i)Y_i^0 I(Z_i=j)|Z_i=j, Y_i^0=1, \widehat{\mathbf{\Theta}}^{(m)}\right\}$$
$$= \sum_{i=1}^{n}\left[y_i^0 I(z_i=j)\left\{\frac{(1-p)(1-\widehat{\theta}^{(m)})\widehat{\pi}_{0j}^{(m)}}{p\widehat{\theta}^{(m)}\widehat{\pi}_{1j}^{(m)}+(1-p)(1-\widehat{\theta}^{(m)})\widehat{\pi}_{0j}^{(m)}}\right\}\right],$$
$$\widehat{\mathcal{K}}_{0j}^{(m)} = \sum_{i=1}^{n} E\left\{(1-Y_i)(1-Y_i^0) I(Z_i=j)|Z_i=j, Y_i^0=0, \widehat{\mathbf{\Theta}}^{(m)}\right\}$$
$$= \sum_{i=1}^{n}\left[(1-y_i^0) I(z_i=j)\left\{\frac{p(1-\widehat{\theta}^{(m)})\widehat{\pi}_{0j}^{(m)}}{(1-p)\widehat{\theta}^{(m)}\widehat{\pi}_{1j}^{(m)}+p(1-\widehat{\theta}^{(m)})\widehat{\pi}_{0j}^{(m)}}\right\}\right].$$

Note that $\widehat{\mathcal{K}}_{1j}^{(m)}+\widehat{\mathcal{A}}_{1j}^{(m)}=\sum_{i=1}^{n} y_i^0 I(z_i=j)$ and $\widehat{\mathcal{K}}_{0j}^{(m)}+\widehat{\mathcal{A}}_{0j}^{(m)}=\sum_{i=1}^{n}(1-y_i^0)I(z_i=j)$. These imply $\sum_{j=1}^{B}(\widehat{\mathcal{K}}_{1j}^{(m)}+\widehat{\mathcal{A}}_{1j}^{(m)})=\sum_{i=1}^{n} y_i^0$ and $\sum_{j=1}^{B}(\widehat{\mathcal{K}}_{0j}^{(m)}+\widehat{\mathcal{A}}_{0j}^{(m)})=\sum_{i=1}^{n}(1-y_i^0)$. Hence, $\sum_{j=1}^{B}\widehat{\mathcal{K}}_{1j}^{(m)}=\sum_{i=1}^{n} y_i^0-\widehat{\mathcal{A}}_{1}^{(m)}$ and $\sum_{j=1}^{B}\widehat{\mathcal{K}}_{0j}^{(m)}=n-\sum_{i=1}^{n} y_i^0-\widehat{\mathcal{A}}_{0}^{(m)}$. Based on these results, the Q-function in (4) can be re-written as follows:

$$\begin{aligned}
Q\left(\mathbf{\Theta}|\widehat{\mathbf{\Theta}}^{(m)}\right) &= \sum_{j=1}^{B}\Big\{\widehat{\mathcal{A}}_{1j}^{(m)}\ln(p\theta\pi_{1j})+\widehat{\mathcal{A}}_{0j}^{(m)}\ln[(1-p)\theta\pi_{1j}] \\
&\quad+\widehat{\mathcal{K}}_{1j}^{(m)}\ln[(1-p)(1-\theta)\theta\pi_{0j}]+\widehat{\mathcal{K}}_{0j}^{(m)}\ln[p(1-\theta)\pi_{0j}]\Big\} \\
&= \sum_{j=1}^{B}\Big\{\widehat{\mathcal{A}}_{1j}^{(m)}[\ln p+\ln\theta+\ln\pi_{1j}]+\widehat{\mathcal{A}}_{0j}^{(m)}[\ln(1-p)+\ln\theta+\ln\pi_{1j}] \\
&\quad+\widehat{\mathcal{K}}_{1j}^{(m)}[\ln(1-p)+\ln(1-\theta)+\ln\pi_{0j}]+\widehat{\mathcal{K}}_{0j}^{(m)}[\ln p+\ln(1-\theta)+\ln\pi_{0j}]\Big\} \\
&= \sum_{j=1}^{B}\Big\{(\widehat{\mathcal{A}}_{1j}^{(m)}+\widehat{\mathcal{K}}_{0j}^{(m)})\ln p+(\widehat{\mathcal{A}}_{0j}^{(m)}+\widehat{\mathcal{K}}_{1j}^{(m)})\ln(1-p)\Big\} \\
&\quad+\sum_{j=1}^{B}\Big\{(\widehat{\mathcal{A}}_{1j}^{(m)}+\widehat{\mathcal{A}}_{0j}^{(m)})\ln\theta+(\widehat{\mathcal{K}}_{1j}^{(m)}+\widehat{\mathcal{K}}_{0j}^{(m)})\ln(1-\theta)\Big\} \\
&\quad+\sum_{j=1}^{B}\Big\{(\widehat{\mathcal{A}}_{1j}^{(m)}+\widehat{\mathcal{A}}_{0j}^{(m)})\ln\pi_{1j}+(\widehat{\mathcal{K}}_{1j}^{(m)}+\widehat{\mathcal{K}}_{0j}^{(m)})\ln\pi_{0j}\Big\} \\
&= \sum_{j=1}^{B}\Big\{(\widehat{\mathcal{A}}_{1j}^{(m)}+\widehat{\mathcal{K}}_{0j}^{(m)})\ln p+(\widehat{\mathcal{A}}_{0j}^{(m)}+\widehat{\mathcal{K}}_{1j}^{(m)})\ln(1-p)\Big\} \\
&\quad+\Big\{(\widehat{\mathcal{A}}_{1}^{(m)}+\widehat{\mathcal{A}}_{0}^{(m)})\ln\theta+(n-\widehat{\mathcal{A}}_{1}^{(m)}+\widehat{\mathcal{A}}_{0}^{(m)})\ln(1-\theta)\Big\} \\
&\quad+\sum_{j=1}^{B-1}\Big\{(\widehat{\mathcal{A}}_{1j}^{(m)}+\widehat{\mathcal{A}}_{0j}^{(m)})\ln\pi_{1j}+(\widehat{\mathcal{K}}_{1j}^{(m)}+\widehat{\mathcal{K}}_{0j}^{(m)})\ln\pi_{0j}\Big\} \\
&\quad+(\widehat{\mathcal{A}}_{1B}^{(m)}+\widehat{\mathcal{A}}_{0B}^{(m)})\ln\left(1-\sum_{j=1}^{B-1}\pi_{1j}\right)+(\widehat{\mathcal{K}}_{1B}^{(m)}+\widehat{\mathcal{K}}_{0B}^{(m)})\ln\left(1-\sum_{j=1}^{B-1}\pi_{0j}\right).
\end{aligned} \tag{5}$$

M-step: The M-step is to maximize $Q(\boldsymbol{\Theta}|\widehat{\boldsymbol{\Theta}}^{(m)})$ in (5) with respect to $\boldsymbol{\Theta}$ given $\widehat{\boldsymbol{\Theta}}^{(m)}$ to update the estimate of $\boldsymbol{\Theta}$ denoted by $\widehat{\boldsymbol{\Theta}}^{(m+1)} = (\widehat{\theta}^{(m+1)}, \widehat{\boldsymbol{\pi}}_0^{(m+1)}, \widehat{\boldsymbol{\pi}}_1^{(m+1)})$ by solving the equations $\partial Q(\boldsymbol{\Theta}|\widehat{\boldsymbol{\Theta}}^{(m)})/\partial\boldsymbol{\Theta} = \mathbf{0}$, which are expressed as follows:

$$\widehat{\theta}^{(m+1)} = \frac{\widehat{\mathcal{A}}_1^{(m)} + \widehat{\mathcal{A}}_0^{(m)}}{n}, \quad \widehat{\pi}_{1j}^{(m+1)} = \frac{\widehat{\mathcal{A}}_{1j}^{(m)} + \widehat{\mathcal{A}}_{0j}^{(m)}}{\widehat{\mathcal{A}}_1^{(m)} + \widehat{\mathcal{A}}_0^{(m)}}, \quad \widehat{\pi}_{0j}^{(m+1)} = \frac{\widehat{\mathcal{K}}_{1j}^{(m)} + \widehat{\mathcal{K}}_{0j}^{(m)}}{n - (\widehat{\mathcal{A}}_1^{(m)} + \widehat{\mathcal{A}}_0^{(m)})}.$$

Iterate the E-step and M-step until $\left|\widehat{\boldsymbol{\Theta}}^{(m+1)} - \widehat{\boldsymbol{\Theta}}^{(m)}\right| < \varepsilon = 5 \times 10^{-5}$ in this study.

Under the null hypothesis $H_0 : \pi_{1z} = \pi_{0z} = \pi_{\cdot z}, z = 1, 2, \ldots, B$, the model in (1), called an alternative/full model, is reduced to the following null model:

$$\begin{aligned} &P(Y_i = y) = \theta^y (1-\theta)^{1-y}, \\ &P(Z_i = z|Y_i = y) = \pi_{\cdot z}, \ z = 1, 2, \ldots, B, \ y = 0, 1. \end{aligned} \tag{6}$$

Based on the above null model, $P(Z_i = z, Y_i = y)$ can then be expressed as

$$P(Z_i = z, Y_i = y) = \theta^y (1-\theta)^{1-y} \pi_{\cdot z}, \ z = 1, 2, \ldots, B, \ y = 0, 1. \tag{7}$$

$P(Y_i = 1|Z_i = j, Y_i^0 = y^0)$ can be given by

$$\begin{aligned} P(Y_i = 1|Z_i = j, Y_i^0 = 1) &= \frac{p\theta}{p\theta + (1-p)(1-\theta)}, \\ P(Y_i = 1|Z_i = j, Y_i^0 = 0) &= \frac{(1-p)\theta}{(1-p)\theta + p(1-\theta)}, \\ P(Y_i = 0|Z_i = j, Y_i^0 = 1) &= \frac{(1-p)(1-\theta)}{p\theta + (1-p)(1-\theta)}, \\ P(Y_i = 0|Z_i = j, Y_i^0 = 0) &= \frac{p(1-\theta)}{(1-p)\theta + p(1-\theta)}. \end{aligned}$$

Based on the arguments similar to those in EM algorithm 1, one can obtain an estimate of θ at the $(m+1)$th iteration of the EM algorithm as follows:

$$\widetilde{\theta}^{(m+1)} = \frac{\widetilde{A}_1^{(m)} + \widetilde{A}_0^{(m)}}{n},$$

where

$$\begin{aligned} \widetilde{A}_1^{(m)} &= \sum_{i=1}^{n} \left[I(y_i^0 = 1) \left\{ \frac{p\widetilde{\theta}^{(m)}}{p\widetilde{\theta}^{(m)} + (1-p)(1-\widetilde{\theta}^{(m)})} \right\} \right], \\ \widetilde{A}_0^{(m)} &= \sum_{i=1}^{n} \left[I(y_i^0 = 0) \left\{ \frac{(1-p)\widetilde{\theta}^{(m)}}{(1-p)\widetilde{\theta}^{(m)} + p(1-\widetilde{\theta}^{(m)})} \right\} \right]. \end{aligned}$$

Note that the ML estimate of $\pi_{\cdot z}$ in (6) and (7) is $\sum_{i=1}^{n} I(z_i = z)/n, z = 1, 2, \ldots, B$.

2.2.3. Likelihood Ratio Test (LRT)

The LRT of Neyman and Pearson [49] is utilized to determine which model is appropriate for the association of the sensitive feature with an observed categorical random variable by testing the following hypotheses:

$$\begin{aligned} &H_0 : \pi_{1j} = \pi_{0j} = \pi_{\cdot j}, \text{ for all } j = 1, 2, \ldots, B, \\ &H_1 : \pi_{1j} \neq \pi_{0j}, \text{ for some } j = 1, 2, \ldots, B. \end{aligned} \tag{8}$$

Let $\boldsymbol{\pi}_{\cdot} = (\pi_{\cdot 1}, \pi_{\cdot 2}, \ldots, \pi_{\cdot B})$. Under H_0, the observed-data likelihood function of $(\theta, \boldsymbol{\pi}_{\cdot})$ is given by

$$
\begin{aligned}
&L_{obs}(\theta, \boldsymbol{\pi}_{\cdot}|\boldsymbol{y}_0, \boldsymbol{z}) \\
=&\prod_{i=1}^{n}\left\{[p\theta\pi_{\cdot z_i} + (1-p)(1-\theta)\pi_{\cdot z_i}]^{I(y_i^0=1)}[p(1-\theta)\pi_{\cdot z_i} + (1-p)\theta\pi_{\cdot z_i}]^{I(y_i^0=0)}\right\} \\
=&\prod_{i=1}^{n}\prod_{j=1}^{B}\left\{[p\theta\pi_{\cdot j} + (1-p)(1-\theta)\pi_{\cdot j}]^{I(y_i^0=1)}[p(1-\theta)\pi_{\cdot j} + (1-p)\theta\pi_{\cdot j}]^{I(y_i^0=0)}\right\}^{I(z_i=j)} \\
=&\left\{\prod_{i=1}^{n}[p\theta + (1-p)(1-\theta)]^{I(y_i^0=1)}[p(1-\theta) + (1-p)\theta]^{I(y_i^0=0)}\right\}\left\{\prod_{i=1}^{n}\prod_{j=1}^{B}[\pi_{\cdot j}]^{I(z_i=j)}\right\} \\
=&[p\theta + (1-p)(1-\theta)]^{\sum_{i=1}^{n} I(y_i^0=1)}[p(1-\theta) + (1-p)\theta]^{\sum_{i=1}^{n} I(y_i^0=0)}\prod_{j=1}^{B}[\pi_{\cdot j}]^{\sum_{i=1}^{n} I(z_i=j)}.
\end{aligned}
$$

Therefore, one can use the following LRT statistic

$$
\Lambda = -2\log\left\{\frac{\sup_{\theta,\boldsymbol{\pi}_{\cdot}} L_{obs}(\theta, \boldsymbol{\pi}_{\cdot}|\boldsymbol{y}_0, \boldsymbol{z})}{\sup_{\theta,\boldsymbol{\pi}_0,\boldsymbol{\pi}_1} L_{obs}(\theta, \boldsymbol{\pi}_0, \boldsymbol{\pi}_1|\boldsymbol{y}_0, \boldsymbol{z})}\right\} \xrightarrow{d} \chi^2_{B-1} \tag{9}
$$

to determine whether to reject H_0 in (8).

2.3. *A Latent Class Model Incorporating Warner's RRT*

2.3.1. Model

Let $\{\widetilde{Z}_{si}\}_{s=1}^{k}$ be k observed ordinal categorical random variables each with values $1, 2, \ldots, B$ for respondent i, where $\widetilde{Z}_{si}$ denotes the respondent's response to the sth selected question or statement by the LRT, which is significantly associated with the sensitive attribute at a significance level α. Define $\widetilde{K}_{si} = 1$ if $\widetilde{Z}_{si} \in \{1, 2, \ldots, q^*\}$ and $\widetilde{K}_{si} = 0$ if $\widetilde{Z}_{si} \in \{q^*+1, q^*+2, \ldots, B\}$, where q^* is smaller than B. That is, $\widetilde{Z}_{si}$ is dichotomized based on the criterion $\widetilde{Z}_{si} \leq q^*$. Based on a latent variable model, it is assumed that under the group to which an individual is known to belong, the corresponding observed/manifest variables are independent. Therefore, assume that $\widetilde{K}_{1i}, \widetilde{K}_{2i}, \ldots, \widetilde{K}_{ki}$ given Y_i, $i = 1, 2, \ldots, n$, are independent. The aims are to estimate the parameters of the following LCM

$$
P(Y_i = y|Y_i^0, \widetilde{K}_{1i}, \widetilde{K}_{2i}, \ldots, \widetilde{K}_{ki}),\ y = 0, 1, \tag{10}
$$

via an EM algorithm and to predict an individual in a sensitive group or not.

Define $P(\widetilde{K}_{si} = 1|Y_i = y) = \alpha_{ys}$, $y = 0, 1$, $s = 1, 2, \ldots, k$. Under the assumption that $\widetilde{K}_{1i}, \widetilde{K}_{2i}, \ldots, \widetilde{K}_{ki}$ given Y_i are independent, one can obtain the following results:

$$
\begin{aligned}
&P(Y_i^0 = 1, \widetilde{K}_{1i} = \tilde{k}_{1i}, \widetilde{K}_{2i} = \tilde{k}_{2i}, \ldots, \widetilde{K}_{ki} = \tilde{k}_{ki}) \\
&= P(Y_i^0 = 1, \widetilde{K}_{1i} = \tilde{k}_{1i}, \widetilde{K}_{2i} = \tilde{k}_{2i}, \ldots, \widetilde{K}_{ki} = \tilde{k}_{ki}|Y_i = 1)P(Y_i = 1) \\
&\quad + P(Y_i^0 = 1, \widetilde{K}_{1i} = \tilde{k}_{1i}, \widetilde{K}_{2i} = \tilde{k}_{2i}, \ldots, \widetilde{K}_{ki} = \tilde{k}_{ki}|Y_i = 0)P(Y_i = 0) \\
&= p\theta\prod_{s=1}^{k}\alpha_{1s}^{\tilde{k}_{si}}(1-\alpha_{1s})^{1-\tilde{k}_{si}} + (1-p)(1-\theta)\prod_{s=1}^{k}\alpha_{0s}^{\tilde{k}_{si}}(1-\alpha_{0s})^{1-\tilde{k}_{si}}
\end{aligned} \tag{11}
$$

and

$$\begin{aligned}
&P(Y_i^0=0,\widetilde{K}_{1i}=\tilde{k}_{1i},\widetilde{K}_{2i}=\tilde{k}_{2i},\ldots,\widetilde{K}_{ki}=\tilde{k}_{ki})\\
&=P(Y_i^0=0,\widetilde{K}_{1i}=k_{1i},\widetilde{K}_{2i}=\tilde{k}_{2i},\ldots,\widetilde{K}_{ki}=\tilde{k}_{ki}|Y_i=1)P(Y_i=1)\\
&\quad+P(Y_i^0=0,\widetilde{K}_{1i}=\tilde{k}_{1i},\widetilde{K}_{2i}=\tilde{k}_{2i},\ldots,\widetilde{K}_{ki}=\tilde{k}_{ki}|Y_i=0)P(Y_i=0)\\
&=(1-p)\theta\prod_{s=1}^{k}\alpha_{1s}^{\tilde{k}_{si}}(1-\alpha_{1s})^{1-\tilde{k}_{si}}+p(1-\theta)\prod_{s=1}^{k}\alpha_{0s}^{\tilde{k}_{si}}(1-\alpha_{0s})^{1-\tilde{k}_{si}}.
\end{aligned}\tag{12}$$

Let $\widetilde{\boldsymbol{\Theta}}=(\theta,\boldsymbol{\alpha}_0,\boldsymbol{\alpha}_1)$, where $\boldsymbol{\alpha}_y=(\alpha_{y1},\alpha_{y2},\ldots,\alpha_{yk})$, $y=0,1$. The observed data likelihood function of $\widetilde{\boldsymbol{\Theta}}$ given $(\boldsymbol{Y}^0,\widetilde{\boldsymbol{K}}_1,\widetilde{\boldsymbol{K}}_2,\ldots,\widetilde{\boldsymbol{K}}_k)$ is

$$\begin{aligned}
&L_{obs}(\widetilde{\boldsymbol{\Theta}}|\boldsymbol{Y}^0,\widetilde{\boldsymbol{K}}_1,\widetilde{\boldsymbol{K}}_2,\ldots,\widetilde{\boldsymbol{K}}_k)\\
&=\prod_{i=1}^{n}\left\{p\theta\prod_{s=1}^{k}\alpha_{1s}^{\widetilde{K}_{si}}(1-\alpha_{1s})^{1-\widetilde{K}_{si}}+(1-p)(1-\theta)\prod_{s=1}^{k}\alpha_{0s}^{\widetilde{K}_{si}}(1-\alpha_{0s})^{1-\widetilde{K}_{si}}\right\}^{Y_i^0}\\
&\quad\times\left\{(1-p)\theta\prod_{s=1}^{k}\alpha_{1s}^{\widetilde{K}_{si}}(1-\alpha_{1s})^{1-\widetilde{K}_{si}}+p(1-\theta)\prod_{s=1}^{k}\alpha_{0s}^{\widetilde{K}_{si}}(1-\alpha_{0s})^{1-\widetilde{K}_{si}}\right\}^{1-Y_i^0},
\end{aligned}\tag{13}$$

where $\boldsymbol{Y}^0=(Y_1^0,Y_2^0,\ldots,Y_n^0)$ and $\widetilde{\boldsymbol{K}}_s=(\widetilde{K}_{s1},\widetilde{K}_{s2},\ldots,\widetilde{K}_{sn})$, $s=1,2,\ldots,k$. The R function *optim* or *nlminb* can be used to obtain the ML estimate of $\widetilde{\boldsymbol{\Theta}}$ in (13), but to avoid encountering the problem of divergence, we provide an EM algorithm in the following section to solve this problem.

2.3.2. EM Algorithm 2

Suppose that $(Y_i,Y_i^0,\widetilde{K}_{1i},\widetilde{K}_{2i},\ldots,\widetilde{K}_{ki})$, $i=1,2,\ldots,n$, are observable. One can then express $P(Y_i=y,Y_i^0=y^0,\widetilde{K}_{1i}=\tilde{k}_{1i},\widetilde{K}_{2i}=\tilde{k}_{2i},\ldots,\widetilde{K}_{ki}=\tilde{k}_{ki})$, $y=0,1$, $y^0=0,1$, as follows:

$$P(Y_i=1,Y_i^0=1,\widetilde{K}_{1i}=\tilde{k}_{1i},\widetilde{K}_{2i}=\tilde{k}_{2i},\ldots,\widetilde{K}_{ki}=\tilde{k}_{ki})=p\theta\prod_{s=1}^{k}\alpha_{1s}^{\tilde{k}_{si}}(1-\alpha_{1s})^{1-\tilde{k}_{si}},$$

$$P(Y_i=0,Y_i^0=1,\widetilde{K}_{1i}=\tilde{k}_{1i},\widetilde{K}_{2i}=\tilde{k}_{2i},\ldots,\widetilde{K}_{ki}=\tilde{k}_{ki})=(1-p)(1-\theta)\prod_{s=1}^{k}\alpha_{0s}^{\tilde{k}_{si}}(1-\alpha_{0s})^{1-\tilde{k}_{si}},$$

$$P(Y_i=1,Y_i^0=0,\widetilde{K}_{1i}=\tilde{k}_{1i},\widetilde{K}_{2i}=\tilde{k}_{2i},\ldots,\widetilde{K}_{ki}=\tilde{k}_{ki})=(1-p)\theta\prod_{s=1}^{k}\alpha_{1s}^{\tilde{k}_{si}}(1-\alpha_{1s})^{1-\tilde{k}_{si}},$$

$$P(Y_i=0,Y_i^0=0,\widetilde{K}_{1i}=\tilde{k}_{1i},\widetilde{K}_{2i}=\tilde{k}_{2i},\ldots,\widetilde{K}_{ki}=\tilde{k}_{ki})=p(1-\theta)\prod_{s=1}^{k}\alpha_{0s}^{\tilde{k}_{si}}(1-\alpha_{0s})^{1-\tilde{k}_{si}}.$$

The complete-data likelihood function of $\widetilde{\boldsymbol{\Theta}}$ given $(\boldsymbol{Y},\boldsymbol{Y}^0,\widetilde{\boldsymbol{K}}_1,\widetilde{\boldsymbol{K}}_2,\ldots,\widetilde{\boldsymbol{K}}_k)$ can be written as

$$\begin{aligned}
&L_c(\widetilde{\boldsymbol{\Theta}}|\boldsymbol{Y},\boldsymbol{Y}^0,\widetilde{\boldsymbol{K}}_1,\widetilde{\boldsymbol{K}}_2,\ldots,\widetilde{\boldsymbol{K}}_k)\\
&=\prod_{i=1}^{n}\left\{p\theta\prod_{s=1}^{k}\alpha_{1s}^{\widetilde{K}_{si}}(1-\alpha_{1s})^{1-\widetilde{K}_{si}}\right\}^{Y_i^0Y_i}\left\{(1-p)(1-\theta)\prod_{s=1}^{k}\alpha_{0s}^{\widetilde{K}_{si}}(1-\alpha_{0s})^{1-\widetilde{K}_{si}}\right\}^{Y_i^0(1-Y_i)}\\
&\quad\times\left\{(1-p)\theta\prod_{s=1}^{k}\alpha_{1s}^{\widetilde{K}_{si}}(1-\alpha_{1s})^{1-\widetilde{K}_{si}}\right\}^{(1-Y_i^0)Y_i}\left\{p(1-\theta)\prod_{s=1}^{k}\alpha_{0s}^{\widetilde{K}_{si}}(1-\alpha_{0s})^{1-\widetilde{K}_{si}}\right\}^{(1-Y_i^0)(1-Y_i)}.
\end{aligned}$$

With a bit of algebra, $L_c(\widetilde{\boldsymbol{\Theta}}|\boldsymbol{Y},\boldsymbol{Y}^0,\widetilde{\boldsymbol{K}}_1,\widetilde{\boldsymbol{K}}_2,\ldots,\widetilde{\boldsymbol{K}}_k)$ can be re-expressed as

$$
\begin{aligned}
&L_c(\widetilde{\boldsymbol{\Theta}}|\boldsymbol{Y},\boldsymbol{Y}^0,\widetilde{\boldsymbol{K}}_1,\widetilde{\boldsymbol{K}}_2,\ldots,\widetilde{\boldsymbol{K}}_k) \\
&= p^{\sum_{i=1}^n [Y_i^0 Y_i+(1-Y_i^0)(1-Y_i)]}(1-p)^{\sum_{i=1}^n [Y_i^0(1-Y_i)+(1-Y_i^0)Y_i]}\theta^{\sum_{i=1}^n Y_i}(1-\theta)^{\sum_{i=1}^n (1-Y_i)} \\
&\times \prod_{s=1}^k \alpha_{1s}^{\sum_{i=1}^n Y_i\widetilde{K}_{si}}(1-\alpha_{1s})^{\sum_{i=1}^n Y_i(1-\widetilde{K}_{si})}\prod_{s=1}^k \alpha_{0s}^{\sum_{i=1}^n (1-Y_i)\widetilde{K}_{si}}(1-\alpha_{0s})^{\sum_{i=1}^n (1-Y_i)(1-\widetilde{K}_{si})}.
\end{aligned}
$$

The complete-data log-likelihood of $\widetilde{\boldsymbol{\Theta}}$ given $(\boldsymbol{Y},\boldsymbol{Y}^0,\widetilde{\boldsymbol{K}}_1,\widetilde{\boldsymbol{K}}_2,\ldots,\widetilde{\boldsymbol{K}}_k)$ can then be expressed as

$$
\begin{aligned}
&\ell_c(\widetilde{\boldsymbol{\Theta}}|\boldsymbol{Y},\boldsymbol{Y}_0,\widetilde{\boldsymbol{K}}_1,\widetilde{\boldsymbol{K}}_2,\ldots,\widetilde{\boldsymbol{K}}_k) \\
&= \sum_{i=1}^n \Big\{[Y_i^0 Y_i + (1-Y_i^0)(1-Y_i)]\ln p + [Y_i^0(1-Y_i) + (1-Y_i^0)Y_i]\ln(1-p)\Big\} \\
&\quad + \sum_{i=1}^n \{Y_i \ln\theta + (1-Y_i)\ln(1-\theta)\} \\
&\quad + \sum_{s=1}^k\sum_{i=1}^n \Big\{Y_i\widetilde{K}_{si}\ln\alpha_{1s} + Y_i(1-\widetilde{K}_{si})\ln(1-\alpha_{1s}) + (1-Y_i)\widetilde{K}_{si}\ln\alpha_{0s} \\
&\qquad\qquad + (1-Y_i)(1-\widetilde{K}_{si})\ln(1-\alpha_{0s})\Big\}.
\end{aligned}
\tag{14}
$$

Y_i is a latent or unobserved variable, but one can obtain $P(Y_i = y|Y_i^0 = y^0, \widetilde{K}_{1i} = \tilde{k}_{1i}, \widetilde{K}_{2i} = \tilde{k}_{2i}, \ldots, \widetilde{K}_{ki} = \tilde{k}_{ki})$, $y = 0,1$, $y^0 = 0,1$, as follows:

$$
\begin{aligned}
&P(Y_i = 1|Y_i^0 = 1, \widetilde{K}_{1i} = \tilde{k}_{1i}, \widetilde{K}_{2i} = \tilde{k}_{2i}, \ldots, \widetilde{K}_{ki} = \tilde{k}_{ki}) \\
&= \frac{p\theta\prod_{s=1}^k \alpha_{1s}^{\tilde{k}_{si}}(1-\alpha_{1s})^{1-\tilde{k}_{si}}}{p\theta\prod_{s=1}^k \alpha_{1s}^{\tilde{k}_{si}}(1-\alpha_{1s})^{1-\tilde{k}_{si}} + (1-p)(1-\theta)\prod_{s=1}^k \alpha_{0s}^{\tilde{k}_{si}}(1-\alpha_{0s})^{1-\tilde{k}_{si}}},
\end{aligned}
$$

$$
\begin{aligned}
&P(Y_i = 0|Y_i^0 = 1, \widetilde{K}_{1i} = \tilde{k}_{1i}, \widetilde{K}_{2i} = \tilde{k}_{2i}, \ldots, \widetilde{K}_{ki} = \tilde{k}_{ki}) \\
&= \frac{(1-p)(1-\theta)\prod_{s=1}^k \alpha_{0s}^{\tilde{k}_{si}}(1-\alpha_{0s})^{1-\tilde{k}_{si}}}{p\theta\prod_{s=1}^k \alpha_{1s}^{\tilde{k}_{si}}(1-\alpha_{1s})^{1-\tilde{k}_{si}} + (1-p)(1-\theta)\prod_{s=1}^k \alpha_{0s}^{\tilde{k}_{si}}(1-\alpha_{0s})^{1-\tilde{k}_{si}}},
\end{aligned}
$$

$$
\begin{aligned}
&P(Y_i = 1|Y_i^0 = 0, \widetilde{K}_{1i} = \tilde{k}_{1i}, \widetilde{K}_{2i} = \tilde{k}_{2i}, \ldots, \widetilde{K}_{ki} = \tilde{k}_{ki}) \\
&= \frac{(1-p)\theta\prod_{s=1}^k \alpha_{1s}^{\tilde{k}_{si}}(1-\alpha_{1s})^{1-\tilde{k}_{si}}}{(1-p)\theta\prod_{s=1}^k \alpha_{1s}^{\tilde{k}_{si}}(1-\alpha_{1s})^{1-\tilde{k}_{si}} + p(1-\theta)\prod_{s=1}^k \alpha_{0s}^{\tilde{k}_{si}}(1-\alpha_{0s})^{1-\tilde{k}_{si}}},
\end{aligned}
$$

$$P(Y_i = 0|Y_i^0 = 0, \widetilde{K}_{1i} = k_{1i}, \widetilde{K}_{2i} = \tilde{k}_{2i}, \ldots, \widetilde{K}_{ki} = \tilde{k}_{ki})$$
$$= \frac{p(1-\theta)\prod_{s=1}^{k} \alpha_{0s}^{\tilde{k}_{si}}(1-\alpha_{0s})^{1-\tilde{k}_{si}}}{(1-p)\theta\prod_{s=1}^{k} \alpha_{1s}^{\tilde{k}_{si}}(1-\alpha_{1s})^{1-\tilde{k}_{si}} + p(1-\theta)\prod_{s=1}^{k} \alpha_{0s}^{\tilde{k}_{si}}(1-\alpha_{0s})^{1-\tilde{k}_{si}}}.$$

E-step: Let $\widehat{\widetilde{\boldsymbol{\Theta}}}^{(m)} = (\widehat{\theta}^{(m)}, \widehat{\boldsymbol{\alpha}}_0^{(m)}, \widehat{\boldsymbol{\alpha}}_1^{(m)})$ be an estimate of $\widetilde{\boldsymbol{\Theta}}$ at the mth iteration, where $\widehat{\boldsymbol{\alpha}}_y^{(m)} = (\hat{\alpha}_{y1}^{(m)}, \hat{\alpha}_{y2}^{(m)}, \ldots, \hat{\alpha}_{yk}^{(m)})$, $y = 0, 1$. Let $\hat{\theta}^{(0)} = \max\{0.001, [\overline{y}^0 - (1-p)]/(2p-1)\}$, where $\overline{y}^0 = n^{-1}\sum_{i=1}^{n} y_i^0$, and $\widehat{\alpha}_{0s}^{(0)} = \widehat{\alpha}_{1s}^{(0)} = n^{-1}\sum_{i=1}^{n} \tilde{k}_{si}$ be initial values. Given observed data $(\boldsymbol{y}^0, \tilde{\boldsymbol{k}}_1, \tilde{\boldsymbol{k}}_2, \ldots, \tilde{\boldsymbol{k}}_k)$, by taking the expectation of $\ell_c(\widetilde{\boldsymbol{\Theta}}|\boldsymbol{Y}, \boldsymbol{Y}^0, \widetilde{\boldsymbol{K}}_1, \widetilde{\boldsymbol{K}}_2, \ldots, \widetilde{\boldsymbol{K}}_k)$ in (14) given $(\boldsymbol{y}^0, \tilde{\boldsymbol{k}}_1, \tilde{\boldsymbol{k}}_2, \ldots, \tilde{\boldsymbol{k}}_k, \widehat{\widetilde{\boldsymbol{\Theta}}}^{(m)})$, the Q-function can be given as follows:

$$Q\left(\boldsymbol{\Theta}|\widehat{\widetilde{\boldsymbol{\Theta}}}^{(m)}\right) = E\left[\ell_c(\widetilde{\boldsymbol{\Theta}}|\boldsymbol{Y}, \boldsymbol{Y}^0, \widetilde{\boldsymbol{K}}_1, \widetilde{\boldsymbol{K}}_2, \ldots, \widetilde{\boldsymbol{K}}_k)|\boldsymbol{y}^0, \tilde{\boldsymbol{k}}_1, \tilde{\boldsymbol{k}}_2, \ldots, \tilde{\boldsymbol{k}}_k, \widehat{\widetilde{\boldsymbol{\Theta}}}^{(m)}\right]. \quad (15)$$

Define $\widetilde{\widetilde{\mathcal{B}}}_{1i}^{(m)}$ and $\widetilde{\widetilde{\mathcal{B}}}_{0i}^{(m)}$ as follows:

$$\widetilde{\widetilde{\mathcal{B}}}_{1i}^{(m)} = E\left\{Y_i\middle|Y_i^0 = 1, \widetilde{K}_{1i} = \tilde{k}_{1i}, \widetilde{K}_{2i} = \tilde{k}_{2i}, \ldots, \widetilde{K}_{ki} = \tilde{k}_{ki}, \widehat{\widetilde{\boldsymbol{\Theta}}}^{(m)}\right\}$$
$$= \frac{I(Y_i^0 = 1)p\widehat{\theta}^{(m)}\prod_{r=1}^{k}[\widehat{\alpha}_{1r}^{(m)}]^{\tilde{k}_{ri}}[1-\widehat{\alpha}_{1r}^{(m)}]^{1-\tilde{k}_{ri}}}{p\widehat{\theta}^{(m)}\prod_{r=1}^{k}[\widehat{\alpha}_{1r}^{(m)}]^{\tilde{k}_{ri}}[1-\widehat{\alpha}_{1r}^{(m)}]^{1-\tilde{k}_{ri}} + (1-p)(1-\widehat{\theta}^{(m)})\prod_{r=1}^{k}[\widehat{\alpha}_{0r}^{(m)}]^{\tilde{k}_{ri}}[1-\widehat{\alpha}_{0r}^{(m)}]^{1-\tilde{k}_{ri}}},$$

$$\widetilde{\widetilde{\mathcal{B}}}_{0i}^{(m)} = E\left\{Y_i\middle|Y_i^0 = 0, \widetilde{K}_{1i} = \tilde{k}_{1i}, \widetilde{K}_{2i} = \tilde{k}_{2i}, \ldots, \widetilde{K}_{ki} = \tilde{k}_{ki}, \widehat{\widetilde{\boldsymbol{\Theta}}}^{(m)}\right\}$$
$$= \frac{I(Y_i^0 = 0)(1-p)\widehat{\theta}^{(m)}\prod_{r=1}^{k}[\widehat{\alpha}_{1r}^{(m)}]^{\tilde{k}_{ri}}(1-\widehat{\alpha}_{1r}^{(m)})^{1-\tilde{k}_{ri}}}{(1-p)\widehat{\theta}^{(m)}\prod_{r=1}^{k}[\widehat{\alpha}_{1r}^{(m)}]^{\tilde{k}_{ri}}(1-\widehat{\alpha}_{1r}^{(m)})^{1-\tilde{k}_{ri}} + p(1-\widehat{\theta}^{(m)})\prod_{r=1}^{k}[\widehat{\alpha}_{0r}^{(m)}]^{\tilde{k}_{ri}}(1-\widehat{\alpha}_{0r}^{(m)})^{1-\tilde{k}_{ri}}}.$$

Let $\widetilde{\widetilde{\mathcal{A}}}_1^{(m)} = \sum_{i=1}^{n} \widetilde{\widetilde{\mathcal{B}}}_{1i}^{(m)}$ and $\widetilde{\widetilde{\mathcal{A}}}_0^{(m)} = \sum_{i=1}^{n} \widetilde{\widetilde{\mathcal{B}}}_{0i}^{(m)}$. Hence, one can obtain

$$
\begin{aligned}
&Q\left(\Theta\middle|\widehat{\widehat{\Theta}}^{(m)}\right)\\
&=E\left[\ell_c\left(\widetilde{\Theta}|\boldsymbol{Y},\boldsymbol{Y}^0,\widetilde{\boldsymbol{K}}_1,\widetilde{\boldsymbol{K}}_2,\ldots,\widetilde{\boldsymbol{K}}_k\middle|\boldsymbol{y}^0,\tilde{\boldsymbol{k}}_1,\tilde{\boldsymbol{k}}_2,\ldots,\tilde{\boldsymbol{k}}_k,\widehat{\widehat{\Theta}}^{(m)}\right)\right]\\
&=\sum_{i=1}^{n}\left\{\left(Y_i^0\widetilde{\widetilde{\mathcal{B}}}_{1i}^{(m)}+(1-Y_{i0})\left(1-\widetilde{\widetilde{\mathcal{B}}}_{0i}^{(m)}\right)\right)\ln p+\left(Y_i^0\left(1-\widetilde{\widetilde{\mathcal{B}}}_{1i}^{(m)}\right)+(1-Y_i^0)\widetilde{\widetilde{\mathcal{B}}}_{0i}^{(m)}\right)\ln(1-p)\right\}\\
&\quad+\sum_{i=1}^{n}\left\{\left(\widetilde{\widetilde{\mathcal{B}}}_{1i}^{(m)}+\widetilde{\widetilde{\mathcal{B}}}_{1i}^{(m)}\right)\ln\theta+\left[1-\left(\widetilde{\widetilde{\mathcal{B}}}_{1i}^{(m)}+\widetilde{\widetilde{\mathcal{B}}}_{0i}^{(m)}\right)\right]\ln(1-\theta)\right\}\\
&\quad+\sum_{s=1}^{k}\sum_{i=1}^{n}\left\{\left(\widetilde{\widetilde{\mathcal{B}}}_{1i}^{(m)}+\widetilde{\widetilde{\mathcal{B}}}_{0i}^{(m)}\right)\tilde{k}_{si}\ln\alpha_{1s}+\left(\widetilde{\widetilde{\mathcal{B}}}_{1i}^{(m)}+\widetilde{\widetilde{\mathcal{B}}}_{0i}^{(m)}\right)(1-\tilde{k}_{si})\ln(1-\alpha_{1s})\right\}\\
&\quad+\sum_{s=1}^{k}\sum_{i=1}^{n}\left\{\left[1-\left(\widetilde{\widetilde{\mathcal{B}}}_{1i}^{(m)}+\widetilde{\widetilde{\mathcal{B}}}_{0i}^{(m)}\right)\right]\tilde{k}_{si}\ln\alpha_{0s}+\left[1-\left(\widetilde{\widetilde{\mathcal{B}}}_{1i}^{(m)}+\widetilde{\widetilde{\mathcal{B}}}_{0i}^{(m)}\right)\right](1-\tilde{k}_{si})\ln(1-\alpha_{0s})\right\}\\
&=\left(\widetilde{\widetilde{\mathcal{A}}}_1^{(m)}+\sum_{i=1}^{n}(1-Y_{i0})-\widetilde{\widetilde{\mathcal{A}}}_0^{(m)}\right)\ln p+\left(\sum_{i=1}^{n}Y_i^0-\widetilde{\widetilde{\mathcal{A}}}_1^{(m)}+\widetilde{\widetilde{\mathcal{A}}}_0^{(m)}\right)\ln(1-p)\\
&\quad+\left(\widetilde{\widetilde{\mathcal{A}}}_1^{(m)}+\widetilde{\widetilde{\mathcal{A}}}_0^{(m)}\right)\ln\theta+\left(n-\widetilde{\widetilde{\mathcal{A}}}_1^{(m)}-\widetilde{\widetilde{\mathcal{A}}}_0^{(m)}\right)\ln(1-\theta)\\
&\quad+\sum_{s=1}^{k}\sum_{i=1}^{n}\left\{\left(\widetilde{\widetilde{\mathcal{B}}}_{1i}^{(m)}+\widetilde{\widetilde{\mathcal{B}}}_{0i}^{(m)}\right)\tilde{k}_{si}\ln\alpha_{1s}+\left(\widetilde{\widetilde{\mathcal{B}}}_{1i}^{(m)}+\widetilde{\widetilde{\mathcal{B}}}_{0i}^{(m)}\right)(1-\tilde{k}_{si})\ln(1-\alpha_{1s})\right\}\\
&\quad+\sum_{s=1}^{k}\sum_{i=1}^{n}\left\{\left[1-\left(\widetilde{\widetilde{\mathcal{B}}}_{1i}^{(m)}+\widetilde{\widetilde{\mathcal{B}}}_{0i}^{(m)}\right)\right]\tilde{k}_{si}\ln\alpha_{0s}\right.\\
&\qquad\qquad\left.+\left[1-\left(\widetilde{\widetilde{\mathcal{B}}}_{1i}^{(m)}+\widetilde{\widetilde{\mathcal{B}}}_{0i}^{(m)}\right)\right](1-\tilde{k}_{si})\ln(1-\alpha_{0s})\right\}.
\end{aligned}
\tag{16}
$$

M-step: Update the estimate of Θ, denoted by $\widehat{\widehat{\Theta}}^{(m+1)}$ by maximizing (15), given as follows:

$$
\widehat{\theta}^{(m+1)}=\frac{\widetilde{\widetilde{\mathcal{A}}}_1^{(m)}+\widetilde{\widetilde{\mathcal{A}}}_0^{(m)}}{n},
$$

$$
\widehat{\alpha}_{1s}^{(m+1)}=\frac{\sum_{i=1}^{n}\left(\widetilde{\widetilde{\mathcal{B}}}_{1i}^{(m)}+\widetilde{\widetilde{\mathcal{B}}}_{0i}^{(m)}\right)\tilde{k}_{si}}{\sum_{i=1}^{n}\left(\widetilde{\widetilde{\mathcal{B}}}_{1i}^{(m)}+\widetilde{\widetilde{\mathcal{B}}}_{0i}^{(m)}\right)},\quad \widehat{\alpha}_{0s}^{(m+1)}=\frac{\sum_{i=1}^{n}\left[1-\left(\widetilde{\widetilde{\mathcal{B}}}_{1i}^{(m)}+\widetilde{\widetilde{\mathcal{B}}}_{0i}^{(m)}\right)\right]\tilde{k}_{si}}{\sum_{i=1}^{n}\left[1-\left(\widetilde{\widetilde{\mathcal{B}}}_{1i}^{(m)}+\widetilde{\widetilde{\mathcal{B}}}_{0i}^{(m)}\right)\right]},\ s=1,2,\ldots,k.
$$

The E-step and M-step are iterated until $\left|\widehat{\widehat{\Theta}}^{(m+1)}-\widehat{\widehat{\Theta}}^{(m)}\right|<\varepsilon=5\times10^{-5}$ in this study.

Based on the estimate $\widehat{\widehat{\Theta}}=(\widehat{\theta},\widehat{\boldsymbol{\alpha}}_0,\widehat{\boldsymbol{\alpha}}_1)$ of $\widetilde{\Theta}=(\theta,\boldsymbol{\alpha}_0,\boldsymbol{\alpha}_1)$, we propose the first criterion of classifying whether or not the ith individual belongs to the sensitive group, which is described below. If the ith individual were with $(Y_i^0=1,\widetilde{K}_{1i}=\tilde{k}_{1i},\widetilde{K}_{2i}=\tilde{k}_{2i},\ldots,\widetilde{K}_{ki}=\tilde{k}_{ki})$ and

$$
\begin{aligned}
&\widehat{P}(Y_i=1|Y_i^0=1,\widetilde{K}_{1i}=\tilde{k}_{1i},\widetilde{K}_{2i}=\tilde{k}_{2i},\ldots,\widetilde{K}_{ki}=\tilde{k}_{ki})\\
&=\frac{p\widehat{\theta}\prod_{s=1}^{k}\widehat{\alpha}_{1s}^{\tilde{k}_{si}}(1-\widehat{\alpha}_{1s})^{1-\tilde{k}_{si}}}{p\widehat{\theta}\prod_{s=1}^{k}\widehat{\alpha}_{1s}^{\tilde{k}_{si}}(1-\widehat{\alpha}_{1s})^{1-\tilde{k}_{si}}+(1-p)(1-\widehat{\theta})\prod_{s=1}^{k}\widehat{\alpha}_{0s}^{\tilde{k}_{si}}(1-\widehat{\alpha}_{0s})^{1-\tilde{k}_{si}}}\geq 0.5,
\end{aligned}
\tag{17}
$$

then she/he is predicted to belong to the sensitive group. If she/he were with $(Y_i^0 = 0, \widetilde{K}_{1i} = \tilde{k}_{1i}, \widetilde{K}_{2i} = \tilde{k}_{2i}, \ldots, \widetilde{K}_{ki} = \tilde{k}_{ki})$ and

$$\widehat{P}(Y_i = 1 | Y_i^0 = 0, \widetilde{K}_{1i} = \tilde{k}_{1i}, \widetilde{K}_{2i} = \tilde{k}_{2i}, \ldots, \widetilde{K}_{ki} = \tilde{k}_{ki})$$

$$= \frac{(1-p)\widehat{\theta} \prod_{s=1}^{k} \widehat{\alpha}_{1s}^{\tilde{k}_{si}} (1-\widehat{\alpha}_{1s})^{1-\tilde{k}_{si}}}{(1-p)\widehat{\theta} \prod_{s=1}^{k} \widehat{\alpha}_{1s}^{\tilde{k}_{si}} (1-\widehat{\alpha}_{1s})^{1-\tilde{k}_{si}} + p(1-\widehat{\theta}) \prod_{s=1}^{k} \widehat{\alpha}_{0s}^{\tilde{k}_{si}} (1-\widehat{\alpha}_{0s})^{1-\tilde{k}_{si}}} \geq 0.5. \quad (18)$$

then she/he is classified to be in the sensitive group.

3. Real Data Application

The proposed methodology is employed to demonstrate its practical applications by using the survey study data of the sexuality of 3027 freshmen (1193 females, 1792 males, 29 non-binary, 13 no response), not including international students, enrolled based on convenience sampling at Feng Chia University in Taiwan in 2016. Because 262 (8.7%) respondents had missing data, 2765 respondents are used for the purpose. Through this face-to-face survey, respondents answered a questionnaire of 67 statements or questions, including three parts: demographic questions, attitude to love, and online dating experience. This questionnaire did not collect personal information such as respondents' name and age. In addition, data of responses to the sensitive question, question 37: "What is your sexual orientation?", were collected by using the multichotomous RR design of Groenitz [50,51]. We collected data of responses to the two sensitive questions, question 38: "Have you ever had sex?" and question 39: "Have you ever had a one-night stand through a dating site or mobile app?", via the design of [3] and birthday interval as a non-random device. The generalized RR design of [10] was employed to collect data of responses to the sensitive question, question 67: "Have you ever had a one-night stand through a dating site or mobile app?", which is the same question as question 39. Therefore, the privacy of respondents was protected.

There were 27 statements in the third part about online dating experience for respondents to answer. In addition, question 39: "Have you ever had a one-night stand through a dating site or mobile app?" was designed to collect data on the sexual behavior. Because people in eastern cultures are often shy about referring to sexual behavior or reluctant to provide correct answers, the indirect question technique of [3] was used in this study. Expressly, two birthday intervals, January 1 to August 30 and August 11 to December 31, were set up as a non-random device so that interviewees based on their birthday could answer "yes" or "no" to question 39. The design detail of question 39 is as given in Table 10 of [17]. More specifically, if a respondent whose birthday was between January 1 and August 10 had ever had a one-night stand through a dating site or mobile app, answer "A" denoted "yes" to the question, and answer "B" denoted "no". If a respondent whose birthday was between August 11 and December 31 had ever had a one-night stand through a dating site or mobile app, answer "B" denoted "yes" to the question, and answer "A" denoted "no". In addition, statements 40–66 are direct ones about interviewees' thoughts and evaluation on making friends on the internet, finding a lover or sex partner, and attitude toward online dating. Each statement had five response options, i.e., 1 = "very consistent", 2 = "almost consistent", 3 = "fairly consistent", 4 = "a bit consistent", and 5 = "very inconsistent".

As in Section 2.2, the binary variable Y_i denotes whether respondent i has ever had a one-night stand through a dating site or mobile app in which $Y_i = 1$ indicates yes, and $Y_i = 0$ otherwise. $P(Y_i = 1) = \theta$ is the population proportion of the sensitive attribute, *having ever had a one-night stand through a dating site or mobile app*. $p = 0.6082$ is the probability of people whose birthday is between January 1 and August 10 by assuming that birthdays are uniformly distributed. The LRT statistic in (9) is utilized to identify which statements from statements 40–66 are significantly related to question 39 based on data of responses to these 27 statements and question 39 at $\alpha = 0.1$. Table 1 displays the analysis results, including estimates of the parameters of the alternative/full model in (1) and null model in (6) for the association of this sensitive attribute with response to each of these 27 statements under H_0 and H_1 in (8) and corresponding p-values of the LRTs. As seen from these results, the p-values of the LRTs corresponding to statements 43, 45, 55, and 61 are 0.0187, 0.0836, 0.0259, and 0.0757, respectively, which imply that question 39 was significantly associated with response to each of these four statements at $\alpha = 0.1$. The selected four statements are listed below.

Q43. Finding friends on the internet can improve your social circle.

Q45. You can find people with similar interests online.

Q55. I am a homebody, so I want to make friends online.

Q61. I want to find my partner through online dating.

Let $\{\widetilde{Z}_{si}\}_{s=1}^{4}$ denote the ith respondent's response to the aforementioned four statements selected by the LRTs at $\alpha = 0.1$ with full probability model $P(\widetilde{Z}_{si} = z|Y_i = y) = \pi_{yz}^{(s)}$, $s = 1,2,3,4$, $z = 1,2,3,4,5$, $y = 0,1$. Table 2 presents estimates of $\theta^{(s)}$, $\pi_{0z}^{(s)}$, and $\pi_{1z}^{(s)}$ with their estimated standard errors (SEs) for the alternative/full model for the association between the sensitive feature and each of $\{\widetilde{Z}_{si}\}_{s=1}^{4}$, respectively. Note that the estimated SEs are obtained by the bootstrap method with 200 replications. It can be seen from Table 2 that the estimated SEs of $\widehat{\theta}^{(s)}$ are around 0.04, and the estimated SEs of $\widehat{\pi}_{0z}^{(s)}$ are, respectively, smaller than those of $\widehat{\pi}_{1z}^{(s)}$ mainly because there is more sample information to estimate $\pi_{0z}^{(s)}$.

Based on $\widehat{\theta}^{(s)}$, $\widehat{\pi}_{0z}^{(s)}$, and $\widehat{\pi}_{1z}^{(s)}$, one can estimate $P(Y_i = 1|\widetilde{Z}_{si} = z, Y_i^0 = y^0)$ as follows:

$$\widehat{P}(Y_i = 1|\widetilde{Z}_{si} = z, Y_i^0 = y^0) = \begin{cases} \dfrac{p\widehat{\theta}^{(s)}\widehat{\pi}_{1z}^{(s)}}{p\widehat{\theta}^{(s)}\widehat{\pi}_{1z}^{(s)} + (1-p)(1-\widehat{\theta}^{(s)})\widehat{\pi}_{0z}^{(s)}} & \text{as } y^0 = 1, \\ \dfrac{(1-p)\widehat{\theta}^{(s)}\widehat{\pi}_{1z}^{(s)}}{(1-p)\widehat{\theta}^{(s)}\widehat{\pi}_{1z}^{(s)} + p(1-\widehat{\theta}^{(s)})\widehat{\pi}_{0z}^{(s)}} & \text{as } y^0 = 0. \end{cases}$$

According to the estimated posterior probability of $Y_i = 1$ given $\widetilde{Z}_{si} = z$ and $Y_i^0 = y^0$, define C_{si}

$$C_{si} = \begin{cases} 1 & \text{when } \widehat{P}(Y_i = 1|\widetilde{Z}_{si} = z, Y_i^0 = y^0) \geq 0.5, \\ 0 & \text{when } \widehat{P}(Y_i = 1|\widetilde{Z}_{si} = z, Y_i^0 = y^0) < 0.5, \end{cases} \tag{19}$$

as a conditional classifier to identify whether the ith respondent has the sensitive attribute. As a second classification criterion, the proposed classification criterion is to predict the ith respondent in the sensitive group, i.e., she/he has ever had a one-night stand through a dating website or mobile app, if any of the C_{si}, $s = 1,2,3,4$, is 1, i.e., if

$$\sum_{s=1}^{4} C_{si} \geq 1. \tag{20}$$

By applying the proposed methodology in Section 2.3 to the real data set, we define $\widetilde{K}_{si} = 1$ if $\widetilde{Z}_{si} \in \{1,2\}$ and $\widetilde{K}_{si} = 0$ if $\widetilde{Z}_{si} \in \{3,4,5\}$. $\{\widetilde{K}_{si}\}_{s=1}^{4}$ and Y_i are observed binary and latent variables in the LCM, respectively. Then, $P(\widetilde{K}_{si} = 1|Y_i = 0) = \alpha_{0s}$ and $P(\widetilde{K}_{si} = 1|Y_i = 1) = \alpha_{1s}$, $s = 1,2,3,4$.

Table 3 displays the estimates of θ, α_{0s}, and α_{1s} in the proposed LCM incorporating the RRT of [3] with their estimated SEs. The SEs are estimated by using the bootstrap method with 200 replications. The estimate of θ is 0.2201, and its estimated SE is 0.0127. This estimate of θ is reasonable because this estimate is still within each of the 95% confidence intervals (CIs) of $\widehat{\theta}^{(s)}$, $(\widehat{\theta}^{(s)} - 1.96\widehat{\text{SE}}_{\widehat{\theta}^{(s)}}, \widehat{\theta}^{(s)} + 1.96\widehat{\text{SE}}_{\widehat{\theta}^{(s)}})$, for the selected statements 43, 45,

55, and 61, which are $(0.1412, 0.2862)$, $(0.1343, 0.2863)$, $(0.1261, 0.2935)$, and $(0.1332, 0.2896)$, respectively, where $\widehat{\theta}^{(s)}$ and $\widehat{\text{SE}}_{\widehat{\theta}^{(s)}}$, $s = 1, 2, 3, 4$, are given in Table 2. On the other hand, if using the estimate of θ, 0.2201, and its estimated SE, 0.0127, to construct a 95% CI, the 95% CI $(0.1952, 0.2450)$ also contains each of these four estimates of θ, $0.2137, 0.2103, 0.2098$, and 0.2201, in Table 2.

Table 4 shows the classifications of 2765 respondents based on the two proposed classification criteria in (17), (18) and (20), respectively. Based on classification criterion 1, the estimated proportion of respondents who *"have ever had a one-night stand through a dating site or mobile app"* is 0.2 (553/2765), which is quite close to the estimates of θ, 0.2201, given in Table 3, obtained from fitting the LCM in (10). By applying the second classification criterion, 246 respondents (with estimated proportion $0.089 = 246/2765$) are predicted to have the sensitive attribute, *"having ever had a one-night stand through a dating site or mobile app"*, while the estimates of θ given in Table 2 are around 0.21, which are obtained from fitting the alternative/full model for the association of this sensitive attribute with each of the four observed ordinal categorical variables for online dating experience corresponding to selected statements 43, 45, 55, and 61, respectively, by the LRT at $\alpha = 0.1$.

Table 1. Results of the likelihood ratio test and the null and alternative/full models for the association between the sensitive characteristic variable from question 39: "Have you ever had a one-night stand through a dating site or mobile app?", and each of the 27 observed ordinal categorical random variables for online dating experience corresponding to statements 40 to 66.

Parameter	θ	π_{01}	π_{02}	π_{03}	π_{04}	π_{05}	π_{11}	π_{12}	π_{13}	π_{14}	π_{15}	p-Value
Q_{40} H_1	0.2106	0.1083	0.1775	0.2702	0.2445	0.1995	0.1538	0.1814	0.2236	0.1275	0.3136	0.6644
H_0	0.2084	0.1180	0.1780	0.2600	0.2200	0.2240						
Q_{41} H_1	0.2144	0.0401	0.0989	0.2833	0.3089	0.2689	0.0691	0.1438	0.0433	0.3829	0.3609	0.1905
H_0	0.2084	0.0460	0.1080	0.2320	0.3250	0.2890						
Q_{42} H_1	0.2105	0.0226	0.1326	0.2437	0.3439	0.2571	0.1007	0.0626	0.3316	0.2168	0.2883	0.3650
H_0	0.2084	0.0390	0.1180	0.2620	0.3170	0.2640						
Q_{43} H_1	0.2137	0.0347	0.1494	0.3448	0.3156	0.1555	0.1822	0.2913	0.3848	0.0590	0.0827	**0.0187**
H_0	0.2084	0.0660	0.1800	0.3530	0.2610	0.1400						
Q_{44} H_1	0.2098	0.0335	0.1344	0.2532	0.3433	0.2356	0.0636	0.0730	0.3340	0.3290	0.2004	0.8481
H_0	0.2084	0.0400	0.1220	0.2700	0.3400	0.2280						
Q_{45} H_1	0.2103	0.0704	0.2526	0.3725	0.2018	0.1028	0.1606	0.1282	0.3657	0.2467	0.0989	**0.0836**
H_0	0.2084	0.0890	0.2260	0.3710	0.2110	0.1020						
Q_{46} H_1	0.2108	0.0753	0.2644	0.3688	0.1905	0.1009	0.1625	0.2111	0.3143	0.2114	0.1008	0.8095
H_0	0.2084	0.0940	0.2530	0.3570	0.1950	0.1010						
Q_{47} H_1	0.2095	0.0805	0.2249	0.3769	0.2054	0.1123	0.1002	0.2614	0.3092	0.2297	0.0995	1.0000
H_0	0.2084	0.0850	0.2330	0.3630	0.2100	0.1100						
Q_{48} H_1	0.2107	0.1024	0.2693	0.3614	0.1716	0.0954	0.2465	0.2786	0.2871	0.1073	0.0805	0.5409
H_0	0.2084	0.1330	0.2710	0.3460	0.1580	0.0920						
Q_{49} H_1	0.2101	0.0297	0.1155	0.2440	0.3280	0.2828	0.0502	0.0547	0.2857	0.3041	0.3054	1.0000
H_0	0.2084	0.0340	0.1030	0.2530	0.3230	0.2880						
Q_{50} H_1	0.2095	0.0368	0.1083	0.2961	0.3547	0.2040	0.0838	0.1558	0.2878	0.2394	0.2331	0.7806
H_0	0.2084	0.0470	0.1180	0.2940	0.3310	0.2100						
Q_{51} H_1	0.2097	0.0353	0.1485	0.3369	0.2945	0.1847	0.1015	0.1302	0.3531	0.2042	0.2111	0.7475
H_0	0.2084	0.0490	0.1450	0.3400	0.2760	0.1900						
Q_{52} H_1	0.2237	0.0230	0.1126	0.2543	0.3377	0.2724	0.0656	0.0038	0.3335	0.3315	0.2656	0.1262
H_0	0.2084	0.0330	0.0880	0.2720	0.3360	0.2710						
Q_{53} H_1	0.2104	0.0356	0.1396	0.2733	0.3128	0.2386	0.0555	0.0484	0.2411	0.3369	0.3181	0.7395
H_0	0.2084	0.0400	0.1200	0.2670	0.3180	0.2550						

Table 1. *Cont.*

Parameter	θ	π_{01}	π_{02}	π_{03}	π_{04}	π_{05}	π_{11}	π_{12}	π_{13}	π_{14}	π_{15}	p-Value
Q_{54} H_1	0.2099	0.0269	0.0940	0.2819	0.3636	0.2336	0.0540	0.1373	0.3190	0.2182	0.2715	1.0000
H_0	0.2084	0.0330	0.1030	0.2900	0.3330	0.2420						
Q_{55} H_1	0.2098	0.0062	0.0234	0.1420	0.3001	0.5282	0.0782	0.0704	0.0960	0.1953	0.5600	**0.0259**
H_0	0.2084	0.0210	0.0330	0.1320	0.2780	0.5350						
Q_{56} H_1	0.2101	0.0104	0.0236	0.0960	0.2575	0.6124	0.0315	0.0333	0.0383	0.1681	0.7288	1.0000
H_0	0.2084	0.0150	0.0260	0.0840	0.2390	0.6370						
Q_{57} H_1	0.2113	0.0758	0.2109	0.3783	0.1956	0.1393	0.2031	0.2552	0.2960	0.1993	0.0464	0.3833
H_0	0.2084	0.1030	0.2200	0.3610	0.1960	0.1200						
Q_{58} H_1	0.2093	0.0328	0.0998	0.2735	0.3070	0.2870	0.0316	0.1121	0.2024	0.4333	0.2205	0.8481
H_0	0.2084	0.0330	0.1020	0.2590	0.3330	0.2730						
Q_{59} H_1	0.2111	0.0355	0.0856	0.2273	0.2875	0.3641	0.0044	0.0671	0.2078	0.4214	0.2993	0.6802
H_0	0.2084	0.0290	0.0820	0.2230	0.3160	0.3500						
Q_{60} H_1	0.2088	0.0278	0.0812	0.2478	0.3212	0.3220	0.0435	0.1029	0.1609	0.3263	0.3664	0.9284
H_0	0.2084	0.0310	0.0860	0.2300	0.3220	0.3310						
Q_{61} H_1	0.2114	0.0002	0.0260	0.1039	0.2794	0.5904	0.0624	0.0005	0.1599	0.2253	0.5519	**0.0757**
H_0	0.2084	0.0130	0.0210	0.1160	0.2680	0.5820						
Q_{62} H_1	0.2052	0.0000	0.0279	0.0977	0.2705	0.6039	0.0687	0.0170	0.1611	0.2390	0.5143	0.3277
H_0	0.2084	0.0140	0.0260	0.1110	0.2640	0.5860						
Q_{63} H_1	0.2078	0.0001	0.0239	0.0794	0.2823	0.6143	0.0745	0.0132	0.2108	0.1630	0.5384	0.9950
H_0	0.2084	0.0160	0.0220	0.1070	0.2580	0.5990						
Q_{64} H_1	0.2099	0.0030	0.0297	0.0819	0.1839	0.7015	0.0939	0.0241	0.0432	0.0953	0.7434	0.1355
H_0	0.2084	0.0220	0.0290	0.0740	0.1650	0.7100						
Q_{65} H_1	0.2108	0.0035	0.0139	0.0738	0.1903	0.7184	0.0674	0.0594	0.0926	0.0733	0.7074	0.9131
H_0	0.2084	0.0170	0.0240	0.0780	0.1660	0.7160						
Q_{66} H_1	0.2097	0.0048	0.0304	0.0624	0.1278	0.7747	0.0976	0.0287	0.0632	0.0859	0.7245	0.1985
H_0	0.2084	0.0240	0.0300	0.0630	0.1190	0.7640						

Table 2. (Results extracted from Table 1) Summary of significant results of the alternative/full model for the association between the sensitive characteristic variable from question 39: "Have you ever had a one-night stand through a dating site or mobile app?", and each of the four observed ordinal categorical random variables for online dating experience corresponding to selected statements 43, 45, 55, and 61, respectively, by the likelihood ratio test at $\alpha = 0.1$.

Parameter	θ	π_{01}	π_{02}	π_{03}	π_{04}	π_{05}	π_{11}	π_{12}	π_{13}	π_{14}	π_{15}
Q_{43} Estimate	0.2137	0.0347	0.1494	0.3448	0.3156	0.1555	0.1822	0.2913	0.3848	0.0590	0.0827
SE	0.0370	0.0142	0.0217	0.0225	0.0197	0.0173	0.0604	0.0721	0.0737	0.0556	0.0464
Q_{45} Estimate	0.2103	0.0704	0.2526	0.3725	0.2018	0.1028	0.1606	0.1282	0.3657	0.2467	0.0989
SE	0.0388	0.0176	0.0213	0.0320	0.0266	0.0170	0.0679	0.0642	0.1134	0.0992	0.0646
Q_{55} Estimate	0.2098	0.0062	0.0234	0.1420	0.3001	0.5282	0.0782	0.0704	0.0960	0.1953	0.5600
SE	0.0427	0.0064	0.0076	0.0174	0.0260	0.0233	0.0314	0.0299	0.0570	0.0943	0.0778
Q_{61} Estimate	0.2114	0.0002	0.0260	0.1039	0.2794	0.5904	0.0624	0.0005	0.1599	0.2253	0.5519
SE	0.0399	0.0019	0.0043	0.0156	0.0268	0.0269	0.0173	0.0058	0.0723	0.0841	0.0995

Table 3. Estimates of parameters of the latent class model for the association between the sensitive characteristic variable from question 39: "Have you ever had a one-night stand through a dating site or mobile app?", and the four observed dichotomized random variables for online dating experience corresponding to selected statements 43, 45, 55, and 61 by the likelihood ratio test at $\alpha = 0.1$.

	θ	α_{01}	α_{02}	α_{03}	α_{04}	α_{11}	α_{12}	α_{13}	α_{14}
Estimate	0.2201	0.0594	0.1602	0.0145	0.0052	0.9068	0.8668	0.1966	0.1361
SE	0.0127	0.0097	0.0095	0.0033	0.0019	0.0262	0.0257	0.0166	0.0142

Table 4. Comparison of results of predicting respondents to have ever had a one-night stand through a dating site or mobile app based on classification criterion 1 in (17) and (18) and criterion 2 in (20).

Classification Criterion 2	Classification Criterion 1		Total
	Having Ever Had a One-Night Stand through a Dating Site or Mobile App	Having Never Had a One-Night Stand through a Dating Site or Mobile App	
Having ever had a one-night stand through a dating site or mobile app	212	34	246
Having never had a one-night stand through a dating site or mobile app	341	2178	2519
Total	553	2212	2765

4. Conclusions

A combination of the RRT of [3] and an LCM has been proposed to investigate the association between a sensitive character or latent variable and the observed binary random variables, which were obtained from dichotomizing the observed ordinal categorical variables selected by the LRT. The concept of the relationship between a sensitive attribute variable and auxiliary random variables in [19] has been extended by applying the RR design of [3] to collect sensitive characteristic information. The EM algorithm, called EM algorithm 1, has been provided to easily estimate the parameters of the null and alternative models for the association of the sensitive attribute variable with each of the auxiliary ordinal categorical random variables. The LRT has been utilized to select ordinal categorical random variables that are significantly associated with the sensitive attribute variable.

An LCM has been proposed to relate observed binary random variables to a sensitive characteristic or latent variable under the RRT of [3]. The EM algorithm, called EM algorithm 2, has been proposed to easily estimate its parameters and the population proportion of the sensitive characteristic. Two classification criteria have been conducted to predict the presence of the sensitive attribute in an individual. Practical applications of the proposed methodology have been demonstrated with the survey data from the study of the sexuality of freshmen, except international students, at Feng Chia University in Taiwan in 2016. Finally, the proposed methodology can be generalized to other RRTs to make inferences for a sensitive characteristic variable. This issue can also be solved by using the Bayesian approach.

Author Contributions: Conceptualization, S.-M.L. and C.-S.L.; methodology, S.-M.L. and C.-S.L.; investigation, S.-M.L.; writing—original draft preparation, P.-L.T. and T.-N.L.; writing—review and editing, S.-M.L. and C.-S.L.; visualization, S.-M.L. and C.-S.L.; software, S.-M.L.; supervision, S.-M.L. and C.-S.L. All authors have read and agreed to the published version of the manuscript.

Funding: Lee's research was supported by Ministry of Science and Technology (MOST) Grant of Taiwan, ROC, MOST-109-2118-M-035-002-MY3.

Data Availability Statement: Data sharing is not applicable to this article.

Conflicts of Interest: The authors declare no conflict of interest.

References

1. van der Heijden, P.G.M.; van Gils, G.; Bouts, J.A.N.; Hox, J.J. A comparison of randomized response, computer-assisted self-interview, and face-to-face direct questioning: Eliciting sensitive information in the context of welfare and unemployment benefit. *Sociol. Methods Res.* **2000**, *28*, 505–537. [CrossRef]
2. Hsieh, S.H.; Perri, P.F. Estimating the proportion of non-heterosexuals in Taiwan using Christofides' randomized response model: A comparison of different estimation methods. *Soc. Sci. Res.* **2021**, *93*, 102475. [CrossRef] [PubMed]
3. Warner, S.L. Randomized response: A survey technique for eliminating evasive answer bias. *J. Am. Stat. Assoc.* **1965**, *60*, 63–69. [CrossRef] [PubMed]
4. Dalton, D.R.; James, C.W.; Catherine, M.D. Using the unmatched count technique (UCT) to estimate base rates for sensitive behavior. *Pers. Psychol.* **1994**, *47*, 817–827. [CrossRef]
5. Yu, J.W.; Tian, G.L.; Tang, M.L. Two new models for survey sampling with sensitive characteristic: Design and analysis. *Metrika* **2008**, *67*, 251–263. [CrossRef]
6. Groenitz, H. Logistic regression analyses for indirect data. *Commun. Stat.-Theory Methods* **2018**, *47*, 3838–3856. [CrossRef]
7. Horvitz, D.G.; Shah, B.V.; Simmons, W.R. The unrelated question randomized response model. *Proc. Soc. Stat. Sect. Am. Stat. Assoc.* **1967**, *62*, 65–72.
8. Greenberg, B.G.; Abul-Ela, A.L.A.; Simmons, W.R.; Horvitz, D.G. The unrelated question randomized response model: Theoretical framework. *J. Am. Stat. Assoc.* **1969**, *64*, 520–539. [CrossRef]
9. Mangat, N.S.; Singh, R. An alternative randomized response procedure. *Biometrika* **1990**, *77*, 439–442. [CrossRef]
10. Christofides, T.C. A generalized randomized response technique. *Metrika* **2003**, *57*, 195–200. [CrossRef]
11. Huang, K.C. A Survey technique for estimating the proportion and sensitivity in a dichotomous finite population. *Stat. Neerl.* **2004**, *58*, 75–82. [CrossRef]
12. Tian, G.L.; Tang, M.L. *Incomplete Categorical Data Design: Non-Randomized Response Techniques for Sensitive Questions in Surveys*; Chapman & Hall/CRC: Boca Raton, FL, USA, 2013.
13. Bhargava, M.; Singh, R. A modified randomization device for Warner's model. *Statistica* **2000**, *60*, 315–322.
14. Hsieh, S.H.; Lee, S.M.; Shen, P.S. Semiparametric analysis of randomized response data with missing covariates in logistic regression. *Comput. Stat. Data Anal.* **2009**, *53*, 2673–2692. [CrossRef]
15. Blair, G.; Imai, K.; Zhou, Y.Y. Design and analysis of the randomized response technique. *J. Am. Stat. Assoc.* **2015**, *110*, 1304–1319. [CrossRef]
16. Hsieh, S.H.; Lee, S.M.; Tu, S.H. Randomized response techniques for a multi-level attribute using a single sensitive question. *Stat. Pap.* **2018**, *59*, 291–306. [CrossRef]
17. Chang, P.C.; Pho, K.H.; Lee, S.M.; Li, C.S. Estimation of parameters of logistic regression for two-stage randomized response technique. *Comput. Stat.* **2021**, *36*, 2111–2133. [CrossRef]
18. Hsieh, S.H.; Lee, S.M.; Li, C.S. A two-stage multilevel randomized response technique with proportional odds models and missing covariates. *Sociol. Methods Res.* **2022**, *51*, 439–467. [CrossRef]
19. Lee, S.M.; Le, T.N.; Tran, P.L.; Li, C.S. Investigating the association of a sensitive attribute with a random variable using the Christofides generalised randomised response design and Bayesian methods. *J. R. Stat. Soc. Ser. C* **2022**, *71*, 1471–1502. [CrossRef]
20. Tang, M.L.; Tian, G.L.; Tang, N.S.; Liu, Z. A new non-randomized multi-category response model for surveys with a single sensitive question: Design and analysis. *J. Korean Stat. Soc.* **2009**, *38*, 339–349. [CrossRef]
21. Tang, M.L.; Wu, Q.; Tian, G.L.; Guo, J.H. Two-sample non randomized response techniques for sensitive questions. *Commun. Stat.-Theory Methods* **2014**, *43*, 408–425. [CrossRef]
22. Maddala, G.S. *Limited-Dependent and Qualitative Variables in Econometrics;* Cambridge University Press: Cambridge, MA, USA, 1983.
23. Scheers, N.J.; Dayton, C.M. Covariate randomized response models. *J. Am. Stat. Assoc.* **1988**, *83*, 969–974. [CrossRef]
24. Hsieh, S.H.; Lee S.M.; Shen, P.S. Logistic regression analysis of randomized response data with missing covariates. *J. Stat. Plan. Inference* **2010**, *140*, 927–940. [CrossRef]
25. Bartholomew, D.J.; Steele, F.; Moustaki, I.; Galbraith, J.I. *Analysis of Multivariate Social Science Data,* 2nd ed.; Chapman & Hall/CRC: Boca Raton, FL, USA, 2011.
26. Collins, L.M.; Lanza, S.T. *Latent Class and Latent Transition Analysis: With Applications in the Social, Behavioral, and Health Sciences;* John Wiley & Sons: New York, NY, USA, 2009.
27. Böckenholt, U. Mixed-effects analyses of rank-ordered data. *Psychometrika* **2001**, *66*, 45–62. [CrossRef]
28. Vermunt, J.K.; Magidson, J. Latent class cluster analysis. In *Applied Latent Class Analysis;* Hagenaars, J.A., McCutcheon, A.L., Eds., Cambridge University Press: Cambridge, MA, USA, 2002; pp. 89–106.
29. Lazarsfeld, P.F. The logical and mathematical foundation of latent structure analysis. In *Studies in Social Psychology in World War II Vol. IV: Measurement and Prediction;* Princeton University Press: Princeton, NJ, USA, 1950; pp. 362–412.
30. Andersen, E.B. Latent structure analysis: A survey. *Scand. J. Stat.* **1982**, *9*, 1–12.
31. Lazarsfeld, P.F.; Henry, N.W. *Latent Structure Analysis;* Houghton Mifflin: Boston, MA, USA, 1968.

32. Goodman, L.A. The analysis of systems of qualitative variables when some of the variables are unobservable. Part IA modified latent structure approach. *Am. J. Sociol.* **1974**, *79*, 1179–1259. [CrossRef]
33. Goodman, L.A. Exploratory latent structure analysis using both identifiable and unidentifiable models. *Biometrika* **1974**, *61*, 215–231. [CrossRef]
34. Dempster, A.P.; Laird, N.M.; Rubin, D.B. Maximum likelihood from incomplete data via the EM algorithm. *J. R. Stat. Soc. Ser. B* **1977**, *39*, 1–22.
35. Haberman, S.J. *Analysis of Qualitative Data, Vol 2: New Developments;* Academic Press: New York, NY, USA, 1979.
36. Dayton, C.M.; Macready, G.B. Concomitant-variable latent-class models. *J. Am. Stat. Assoc.* **1988**, *83*, 173–178. [CrossRef]
37. Muthén, B.; Shedden, K. Finite mixture modeling with mixture outcomes using the EM algorithm. *Biometrics* **1999**, *55*, 463–469. [CrossRef]
38. Stern, H.S.; Arcus, D.; Kagan, J.; Rubin, D.B.; Snidman, N. Using mixture models in temperament research. *Int. J. Behav. Dev.* **1995**, *18*, 407–423. [CrossRef]
39. Collins, L.M.; Graham, J.W.; Rousculp, S.S.; Hansen, W.B. Heavy caffeine use and the beginning of the substance use onset process: An illustration of latent transition analysis. In *The Science of Prevention: Methodological Advances from Alcohol and Substance Abuse Research*; Bryant, K.J., Windle, M., Eds.; American Psychological Association: Washington, DC, USA, 1997.
40. Vermunt, J.K. Applications of latent class analysis in social science research. In *European Conference on Symbolic and Quantitative Approaches to Reasoning and Uncertainty;* Springer: Berlin/Heidelberg, Germany, 2003.
41. Nasiopoulou, P.; Williams, P.; Sheridan, S.; Hansen, K.Y. Exploring preschool teachers' professional profiles in Swedish preschool: A latent class analysis. *Early Child Dev. Care* **2019**, *189*, 1306–1324. [CrossRef]
42. Farina, E.; Bianco, S.; Bena, A.; Pasqualini, O. Finding causation in occupational fatalities: A latent class analysis. *Am. J. Ind. Med.* **2019**, *62*, 123–130. [CrossRef] [PubMed]
43. Wu, Y.; Hu, H.; Cai, J.; Chen, R.; Zuo, X.; Cheng, H.; Yan, D. Applying latent class analysis to risk stratification of incident diabetes among Chinese adults. *Diabetes Res. Clin. Pract.* **2021**, *174*, 108742. [CrossRef] [PubMed]
44. Hagenaars, J.A.; McCutcheon, A.L. (Eds.) *Applied Latent Class Analysis;* Cambridge University Press: Cambridge, MA, USA, 2002.
45. Lanza, S.T.; Cooper, B.R. Latent class analysis for developmental research. *Child Dev. Perspect.* **2016**, *10*, 59–64. [CrossRef]
46. Nagin, D.S. *Group-Based Modeling of Development*; Harvard University Press: Cambridge, MA, USA, 2005.
47. Petersen, K.J.; Qualter, P.; Humphrey, N. The application of latent class analysis for investigating population child mental health: A systematic review. *Front. Psychol.* **2019**, *10*, 1214. [CrossRef]
48. Aflaki, K.; Vigod, S.; Ray, J.G. Part II: A step-by-step guide to latent class analysis. *J. Clin. Epidemiol.* **2022**, *148*, 170–173. [CrossRef]
49. Neyman, J.; Pearson, E.S. On the use and interpretation of certain test criteria for purposes of statistical inference: Part I. *Biometrika* **1928**, *20A*, 175–240.
50. Groenitz, H. A new privacy-protecting survey design for multichotomous sensitive variables. *Metrika* **2014**, *77*, 211–224. [CrossRef]
51. Groenitz, H. Using prior information in privacy-protecting survey designs for categorical sensitive variables. *Stat. Pap.* **2015**, *56*, 167–189. [CrossRef]

mathematics

Article

Non-Parametric Non-Inferiority Assessment in a Three-Arm Trial with Non-Ignorable Missing Data

Wei Li, Yunqi Zhang and Niansheng Tang *

Yunnan Key Laboratory of Statistical Modeling and Data Analysis, Yunnan University, Kunming 650091, China
* Correspondence: nstang@ynu.edu.cn; Tel.: +86-871-65032416

Abstract: A three-arm non-inferiority trial including a placebo is usually utilized to assess the non-inferiority of an experimental treatment to a reference treatment. Existing methods for assessing non-inferiority mainly focus on the fully observed endpoints. However, in some clinical trials, treatment endpoints may be subject to missingness for various reasons, such as the refusal of subjects or their migration. To address this issue, this paper aims to develop a non-parametric approach to assess the non-inferiority of an experimental treatment to a reference treatment in a three-arm trial with non-ignorable missing endpoints. A logistic regression is adopted to specify a non-ignorable missingness data mechanism. A semi-parametric imputation method is proposed to estimate parameters in the considered logistic regression. Inverse probability weighting, augmented inverse probability weighting and non-parametric methods are developed to estimate treatment efficacy for known and unknown parameters in the considered logistic regression. Under some regularity conditions, we show asymptotic normality of the constructed estimators for treatment efficacy. A bootstrap resampling method is presented to estimate asymptotic variances of the estimated treatment efficacy. Three Wald-type statistics are constructed to test the non-inferiority based on the asymptotic properties of the estimated treatment efficacy. Empirical studies show that the proposed Wald-type test procedure is robust to the misspecified missingness data mechanism, and behaves better than the complete-case method in the sense that the type I error rates for the former are closer to the pre-given significance level than those for the latter.

Keywords: bootstrap resampling; imputation; non-inferiority assessment; non-ignorable missing data; three-arm trial

MSC: 62G05; 62D10

Citation: Li, W.; Zhang, Y.; Tang, N. Non-Parametric Non-Inferiority Assessment in a Three-Arm Trial with Non-Ignorable Missing Data. *Mathematics* **2023**, *11*, 246. https://doi.org/10.3390/math11010246

Academic Editor: Leonid V. Bogachev

Received: 25 October 2022
Revised: 27 December 2022
Accepted: 28 December 2022
Published: 3 January 2023

1. Introduction

Non-inferiority (NI) trials are often performed to verify that the efficacy of an experimental treatment with low toxicity or small side-effects is non-inferior to that of a reference treatment by more than a pre-given small margin [1,2]. Many methods have been presented to assess the NI of an experimental treatment to a reference treatment via the efficacy in a two-arm NI trial. For example, see Tang et al. [3] for a score test via relative risk in a matched-pair NI trial; Tang et al. [4] for exact and approximate unconditional confidence intervals for rate difference based on a score test statistic in a small-sample paired NI trial; Wellek [5] for frequentist and Bayesian approaches to testing NI in a matched-pair design with binary endpoints; Freitag et al. [6] for a non-parametric approach to testing NI with censored data; Arboretti et al. [7] and Pesarin et al. [8] for a permutation test in a non-inferiority trial, and Gamalo et al. [9] for a Bayesian method for testing NI with normally distributed endpoints. However, it is widely recognized that there are two key problems for two-arm NI trials [10]. The first issue is the selection of the NI margin (i.e., the clinically acceptable amount or a combination of statistical reasoning and clinical judgement), and the second is the evaluation of assay sensitivity (i.e., the ability of a trial to distinguish an effective treatment from a less effective or ineffective treatment). To solve the aforementioned problems, if ethically acceptable and practically feasible, a three-arm trial including a placebo, which is called a three-arm NI trial, is usually conducted to assess the NI of an experimental treatment to the active reference treatment [11].

Many methods have been developed to draw statistical inferences based on a three-arm NI trial over the past years. For example, Pigeot et al. [12] studied an NI assessment problem via mean difference in a three-arm trial with normally distributed endpoints; Tang and Tang [10] proposed two asymptotic approaches to testing NI via a rate difference for binary outcomes; Mielke and Munk [13] considered the NI testing problem for Poisson-distributed endpoints; Lui and Chang [14] discussed the NI testing problem via a generalized odds ratio for ordinal data; Brannath et al. [15] considered an NI adaptive testing and sample size determination problem in a three-arm trial with normally distributed endpoints; Tang et al. [16] developed exact and approximate unconditional, and bootstrap-resampling-based approaches to testing NI for binary outcomes; Tang and Yu [17] presented a hybrid approach to constructing simultaneous confidence intervals for simultaneously assessing NI and assay sensitivity for binary endpoints; Tang and Yu [18] utilized two Bayesian approaches (i.e., posterior variance and Bayes factor approaches) to determine the sample size required in a three-arm NI trial with binary endpoints; Paul et al. [19] presented both frequentist and Bayesian procedures for testing NI via the risk difference in a three-arm trial with binary endpoints; Homma and Diamon [20] investigated the assay sensitivity hypothesis and the sample size calculation problem for gold-standard NI trials with two fixed margins and negative binomial endpoints; Ghosh et al. [21] presented a new method to test NI for Poisson-distributed endpoints; Ghosh et al. [22] considered a hierarchical testing procedure with two stages in three-arm NI trials; Scharpenberg and Brannath [23] discussed simultaneous confidence intervals of risk differences in three-arm non-inferiority trials; and Tang and Liang [24] constructed two simultaneous confidence intervals for assessing NI and assay sensitivity in a three-arm trial. However, when misspecifying the distributions of treatment endpoints, statistical inference obtained with the aforementioned methods may be misleading or unreasonable. To this end, a number of non-parametric methods were proposed to make statistical inference on three-arm NI trials under an unknown distribution assumption of endpoints. For example, see Munzel [25] for a rank-based NI test and Tseng and Hsu [26] for binomially distributed outcomes. The aforementioned methods were developed for the fully observed endpoints in a three-arm trial.

However, in some clinical trials, treatment endpoints may be subject to missingness occurring for various reasons, such as unwillingness of some respondents to answer sensitivity questions, loss of information caused by uncontrollable factors, or drop-out from the study in clinical trials [27]. For example, for a clinical trial associated with HIV patients in the AIDS Clinical Trial Group (ACTG) Study 193A, the primary endpoint was the CD4 cell count, which was scheduled to be observed at baseline and eight-week intervals during the follow-up period, potentially subject to missingness due to skipped visits and dropouts. In this study, 1309 patients were randomly assigned to one of the following four daily regimens: zidovudine alternating monthly with 400 mg didanosine (regarded as "Treatment 1"), zidovudine plus 2.25 mg of zalcitabine (regarded as "Treatment 2"), zidovudine plus 400 mg of didanosine (regarded as "Treatment 3"), zidovudine plus 400 mg of didanosine plus 400 mg of nevirapine (regarded as "Treatment 4"). As an illustration, we here take "Treatment 1", "Treatment 2" and "Treatment 4" as the placebo, reference and experiment, respectively, let the log-transformed CD4 cell counts (i.e., log(1 + CD4 cell counts at time interval (4,12])) be the treatment endpoints, and regard log(baseline measurement + 1) as an instrument variable for skipped visits or dropouts. Because the baseline measurements were considered before the treatments were assigned, it was reasonable to assume that the dropouts were missing not at random (MNAR) or due to non-ignorable missing. The average missing proportions of endpoints for the placebo, reference and experiment treatments were 29.74%, 30.99% and 28.65%, respectively. Our main purpose is to test the NI of treatment 4 to treatment 2 in terms of the assay sensitivity and the internal validity of treatment 4 in a three-arm trial with unknown distributed endpoints in the presence of non-ignorable missing endpoints.

For the above described example, the simplest and most intuitive method for handling missing data is the well-known complete-case ('CC') method, i.e., deleting subjects with missing data. But the CC method may lead to a biased estimator of treatment efficacy when the missingness data mechanism does not involve missing completely at random. To this end, several alternative methods have been proposed to make statistical inferences in two-arm trials with missing endpoints. For example, Choi and Stablein [28] considered the problem of testing the equality of two treatments in a paired two-arm trial with missing at random (MAR) endpoints based on large sample theory, while Tang and Tang [29] developed unconditional exact procedures for testing the equality of two treatments in a paired two-arm trial with MAR endpoints. In addition, some permutation tests were proposed for endpoints with missing data in two-arm trials, for example, see Maritz [30], Yu et al. [31], Pesarin [32], and Pesarin et al. [33]. However, the aforementioned studies mainly focused on equivalence assessment in two-arm trials with a MAR assumption based on two independent binomial distributions for endpoints with non-ignorable missing and a multinomial distribution for the fully observed endpoints. Moreover, to our knowledge, there has been little work undertaken on NI assessment in three-arm trials with unknown distributed endpoints and non-ignorable missing data. Hence, this paper aims to develop a non-parametric approach to testing NI in a three-arm trial with a mixed unknown distribution of endpoints and an MNAR assumption of missing endpoints.

There are many approaches to handling non-ignorable missing data. For example, see Robins et al. [34] for an inverse probability weighting (IPW) method, Lee and Tang [35] and Wang and Tang [36] for Bayesian approaches combining the Gibbs sampler and Metropolis–Hastings algorithm, Kim and Yu [37] for a semi-parametric approach to estimating mean functions in the presence of non-ignorable missing responses, and Tang et al. [38] for an empirical likelihood method for generalized estimating equations with non-ignorable missing data due to certain merits of empirical likelihood, such as feasibly incorporating auxiliary information to improve the efficiency of parameter estimation [39]. Choi and Stablein [40] and Li et al. [41] investigated the equivalence test problem in a paired two-arm trial with non-ignorable missing endpoints under some known distribution assumptions for treatment endpoints. However, the aforementioned approaches cannot be directly used to test NI in a three-arm trial with non-ignorable missing endpoints due to the complexity of the considered test problem, including the imputation of missing endpoints, the estimation problem of treatment efficacy under unknown distribution assumptions of treatment endpoints, and the critical value determination of test statistics at some pre-given significance level.

The main contributions of this paper include: (i) presentation of a logistic regression to specify the propensity score function associated with respondent endpoints; (ii) proposal of IPW, augmented IPW (AIPW) and non-parametric imputation methods to estimate treatment efficacy in the presence of non-ignorable missing endpoints; (iii) development of a semi-parametric imputation method to estimate unknown parameters in the considered logistic regression by imputing mean score functions rather than missing endpoints using a kernel non-parametric regression method; (iv) establishment of some asymptotic properties of the estimated treatment efficacy; (v) refinement of a bootstrap-resampling method to consistently estimate asymptotic variances of the estimated treatment efficacy; (vi) construction of three Wald-type statistics to test the NI of an experimental treatment to a reference treatment in a three-arm trial with unknown distributed and non-ignorable missing endpoints.

The rest of this paper is organized as follows: Section 2 describes a three-arm NI trial with MNAR endpoints. Section 3 discusses the estimation problem of treatment efficacy and propensity score function. The asymptotic properties of the estimated treatment efficacy and the resultant Wald-type statistics for testing NI are given in Section 4. The simulation studies investigating the finite sample performance of the proposed test statistics are described in Section 5. A real example taken from the ACTG study is illustrated using the proposed method in Section 6. Some concluding remarks are given in Section 7. Technical details are presented in Appendix A.

2. A Three-Arm NI Trail with MNAR Endpoints

2.1. A Three-Arm NI Trial

For a three-arm randomized clinical trial with experimental (E), reference (R) and placebo (P) treatments, we assume that their corresponding clinical endpoints Y_E, Y_R and Y_P independently follow unknown distributions $f_E(y_E|\mu_E)$, $f_R(y_R|\mu_R)$ and $f_P(y_P|\mu_P)$, respectively, where μ_E, μ_R and μ_P are their corresponding treatment efficacies, respectively. Generally, we assume that a larger value of treatment efficacy indicates a more favorable treatment.

Following Hida and Tango [42], to test the NI of the experimental treatment to the reference treatment in terms of assay sensitivity in a three-arm trial, we need to simultaneously demonstrate (i) the superiority of the experimental treatment to placebo, (ii) the NI of the experimental treatment to the reference treatment for a pre-specified maximal clinically irrelevant or NI margin $\delta > 0$, and (iii) the superiority of the reference treatment to placebo by more than δ. That is, μ_E, μ_R and μ_P must satisfy the following inequalities: $\mu_P < \mu_R - \delta < \mu_E$, which leads to consideration of the following hypothesis-testing problem:

$$\begin{array}{ll} H_0 : \mu_E \leq \mu_R - \delta \ \text{ versus } \ H_1 : \mu_E > \mu_R - \delta, \\ K_0 : \mu_R \leq \mu_P + \delta \ \text{ versus } \ K_1 : \mu_R > \mu_P + \delta. \end{array} \tag{1}$$

Clearly, simultaneously rejecting H_0 and K_0 at some pre-given significance level yields the above desirable inequalities: $\mu_P < \mu_R - \delta < \mu_E$ indicating the NI of the experimental treatment to the reference treatment and assay sensitivity. Generally, the selection of the NI margin δ should combine statistical reasoning and clinical judgement [17]. In a similar way to many three-arm trial studies, the fraction margin approach can be used to specify δ.

Following Kieser and Friede [43], δ can be mathematically expressed as a positive fraction f of the unknown efficacy difference between the reference treatment and placebo, i.e., $\delta = g(\mu_R - \mu_P)$, where g lies in the interval $[0,1]$. The NI margin δ defined above indicates that the condition of assay sensitivity holds, i.e., $\mu_R - \mu_P > 0$. Following the argument of Ghosh et al. [44], one can take $g = 1/2$ or $1/3$. To explain the hypotheses considered above, we set $a = 1 - g \in (0,1)$, whose different values have different statistical meanings [12]. Under the above assumption, we only need to test H_0 rather than hypothesis (1). That is, for the NI margin δ defined above, we only need to test the following hypothesis:

$$H_0 : \mu_E - a\mu_R - (1-a)\mu_P \leq 0 \ \text{ versus } \ H_1 : \mu_E - a\mu_R - (1-a)\mu_P > 0. \tag{2}$$

Rejecting H_0 at some pre-given significance level indicates the NI of the experimental treatment to the reference treatment under the condition of assay sensitivity. For simplicity, we denote $\psi(\mu) = \mu_E - a\mu_R - (1-a)\mu_P$, where $\mu = \{\mu_E, \mu_R, \mu_P\}$. In this case, the hypothesis (2) can re-expressed as

$$\tilde{H}_0 : \psi(\mu) \leq 0 \ \text{ versus } \ \tilde{H}_1 : \psi(\mu) > 0. \tag{3}$$

2.2. Missingness Data Mechanism

Let $\{Y_{\ell i} : i = 1, \ldots, n_\ell\}$ be the clinical observations of Y_ℓ for n_ℓ subjects randomly assigned to treatment ℓ for $\ell = E, R, P$. Here, we assume that $Y_{\ell i}$'s may be subject to missingness, let $D_{\ell i}$ be the indicator of non-missing observation $Y_{\ell i}$, i.e., $D_{\ell i} = 1$ if $Y_{\ell i}$ is observed, and $D_{\ell i} = 0$ if $Y_{\ell i}$ is missing, and define $\mathbf{X}_{\ell i}$ as a vector of covariates for $\ell = E, R, P$ and $i = 1, \ldots, n_\ell$. It is also assumed that $\mathbf{X}_{\ell i}$'s are fully observed, $D_{\ell i_1}$ is independent of $D_{\ell i_2}$ for $i_1 \neq i_2 \in \{1, \ldots, n_\ell\}$, and $D_{\ell i}$ depends on the observed covariates $\mathbf{X}_{\ell i}$ and missing observation $Y_{\ell i}$, which indicates that the considered non-missingness data mechanism is non-ignorable. Under the above assumption, we consider the following non-missingness data mechanism model:

$$\pi_{\ell i}(\boldsymbol{\eta}_\ell; \mathbf{X}_{\ell i}, Y_{\ell i}) = \Pr(D_{\ell i} = 1 | \mathbf{X}_{\ell i}, Y_{\ell i}; \boldsymbol{\eta}_\ell), \ \ell = E, R, P, \ \ i = 1, \ldots, n_\ell,$$

where $\boldsymbol{\eta}_\ell$ is a vector of unknown parameters to be estimated, and $\pi_{\ell i}(\boldsymbol{\eta}_\ell; \mathbf{X}_{\ell i}, Y_{\ell i})$ is usually called the propensity score function in the missing data literature.

Many methods can be employed to specify the propensity score function $\pi_{\ell i}(\boldsymbol{\eta}_\ell; \mathbf{X}_{\ell i}, Y_{\ell i})$. For example, see Lee and Tang [35] for a logistic regression, Kim and Yu [37] and Tang et al. [38] for an exponential tilting model, and Wang and Tang [36] for a probit regression model. Here, similarly to Lee and Tang [35], we consider the following logistic regression model for $\pi_{\ell i}(\boldsymbol{\eta}_\ell; \mathbf{X}_{\ell i}, Y_{\ell i})$:

$$\text{logit}\{\pi_{\ell i}(\boldsymbol{\eta}_\ell; \mathbf{X}_{\ell i}, Y_{\ell i})\} = \alpha_{\ell 0} + \boldsymbol{\alpha}_{\ell 1}^\top \mathbf{X}_{\ell i} + \gamma_\ell Y_{\ell i}, \ \ell = E, R, P, i = 1, \ldots, n_\ell,$$

where $\text{logit}(c) = \log\{c/(1-c)\}$, and $\boldsymbol{\eta}_\ell = (\alpha_{\ell 0}, \boldsymbol{\alpha}_{\ell 1}^\top, \gamma_\ell)^\top$. It is well-known that, when γ_ℓ is unknown, the above specified logistic regression model is unidentifiable. To address this issue, we decompose $\mathbf{X}_{\ell i}$ as $\mathbf{X}_{\ell i} = (\mathbf{Z}_{\ell i}^\top, \boldsymbol{U}_{\ell i}^\top)^\top$, where $\mathbf{Z}_{\ell i}$ may be associated with the propensity score function, and $\boldsymbol{U}_{\ell i}$ is a vector of instrumental variables that is not directly associated with the propensity score function but related to observations $Y_{\ell i}$. In this case, we can consider the following propensity score function

$$\text{logit}\{\pi_{\ell i}(\boldsymbol{\eta}_\ell; \mathbf{Z}_{\ell i}, Y_{\ell i})\} = \alpha_{\ell 0} + \boldsymbol{\alpha}_{\ell 1}^\top \mathbf{Z}_{\ell i} + \gamma_\ell Y_{\ell i}, \ \ell = E, R, P, i = 1, \ldots, n_\ell. \tag{4}$$

Clearly, when $\gamma_\ell = 0$, the above defined missingness data mechanism reduces to MAR.

3. Estimation of Treatment Efficacy

3.1. Estimating Treatment Efficacy

When the endpoints are completely observed, treatment efficacy μ_ℓ can be consistently estimated by its corresponding sample mean, i.e., $\hat{\mu}_\ell = n_\ell^{-1} \sum_{i=1}^{n_\ell} Y_{\ell i}$ for $\ell = E, R, P$.

When $Y_{\ell i}$'s are subject to missingness and the true propensity score function $\pi_{\ell i}(\boldsymbol{\eta}_\ell; \mathbf{Z}_{\ell i}, Y_{\ell i})$ is known, the IPW method can be employed to estimate μ_ℓ for $\ell = E, R, P$. That is, μ_ℓ can be estimated by

$$\hat{\mu}_\ell^{HT} = \frac{1}{n_\ell} \sum_{i=1}^{n_\ell} \frac{D_{\ell i}}{\pi_{\ell i}(\boldsymbol{\eta}_\ell; \mathbf{Z}_{\ell i}, Y_{\ell i})} Y_{\ell i}, \ \ell = E, R, P. \tag{5}$$

Note that the above defined estimator $\hat{\mu}_\ell^{HT}$ may be sensitive to the misspecification of the propensity score function. To address this issue, an imputation technique is adopted to construct a consistent estimator of μ_ℓ in the presence of MNAR. That is, let $m_{\ell i}^0(\gamma_\ell; \mathbf{Z}_{\ell i}) = E(Y_{\ell i} | \mathbf{Z}_{\ell i}, D_{\ell i} = 0)$, an imputation-based estimator of μ_ℓ has the form

$$\hat{\mu}_\ell^{RI} = \frac{1}{n_\ell} \sum_{i=1}^{n_\ell} \left\{ D_{\ell i} Y_{\ell i} + (1 - D_{\ell i}) m_{\ell i}^0(\gamma_\ell; \mathbf{Z}_{\ell i}) \right\}, \ \ell = E, R, P. \tag{6}$$

The AIPW approach can also be utilized to estimate μ_ℓ in the presence of MNAR. That is, an AIPW-based estimator of μ_ℓ can be expressed as

$$\hat{\mu}_\ell^{AI} = \frac{1}{n_\ell} \sum_{i=1}^{n_\ell} \left\{ \frac{D_{\ell i}}{\pi_{\ell i}(\boldsymbol{\eta}_\ell; \mathbf{Z}_{\ell i}, Y_{\ell i})} Y_{\ell i} + \left(1 - \frac{D_{\ell i}}{\pi_{\ell i}(\boldsymbol{\eta}_\ell; \mathbf{Z}_{\ell i}, Y_{\ell i})}\right) m_{\ell i}^0(\gamma_\ell; \mathbf{Z}_{\ell i}) \right\}, \ \ell = E, R, P. \tag{7}$$

In many clinical trials, the cumulative distribution functions of $Y_{\ell i}$'s are usually unknown; thus, $m_{\ell i}^0(\gamma_\ell; \mathbf{Z}_{\ell i})$'s are also unknown. On the other hand, $\pi_{\ell i}(\boldsymbol{\eta}_\ell; \mathbf{Z}_{\ell i}, Y_{\ell i})$ is also unknown in the presence of MNAR. Hence, it is impossible to directly evaluate $\hat{\mu}_\ell^{HT}$, $\hat{\mu}_\ell^{RI}$

and $\hat{\mu}_\ell^{AI}$ using the above defined forms. In what follows, we consider the estimation problem of $m_{\ell i}^0(\gamma_\ell; \mathbf{Z}_{\ell i})$ and $\pi_{\ell i}(\boldsymbol{\eta}_\ell; \mathbf{Z}_{\ell i}, Y_{\ell i})$.

3.2. Estimation of Conditional Mean $m_{\ell i}^0(\gamma_\ell; \mathbf{Z}_{\ell i})$

Here a non-parametric method given in Tang et al. [38] is adopted to estimate $m_{\ell i}^0(\gamma_\ell; \mathbf{Z}_{\ell i})$ in the presence of MNAR.

Let $f_{0\ell}(y_{\ell i})$ and $f_{1\ell}(y_{\ell i})$ be the conditional probability densities of $Y_{\ell i}$ given $D_{\ell i} = 0$ and $D_{\ell i} = 1$, respectively. Following the argument of Tang et al. [38], we have

$$f_{0\ell}(y_{\ell i}) = f_{1\ell}(y_{\ell i}) \times \frac{O(\boldsymbol{\eta}_\ell; \mathbf{Z}_{\ell i}, Y_{\ell i})}{E\{O(\boldsymbol{\eta}_\ell; \mathbf{Z}_{\ell i}, y_{\ell i}) | \mathbf{Z}_{\ell i}, D_{\ell i} = 1\}}, \quad \ell = E, R, P, \tag{8}$$

where $O(\boldsymbol{\eta}_\ell; \mathbf{Z}_{\ell i}, y_{\ell i}) = \{1 - \pi_{\ell i}(\boldsymbol{\eta}_\ell; \mathbf{Z}_{\ell i}, Y_{\ell i})\} / \pi_{\ell i}(\boldsymbol{\eta}_\ell; \mathbf{Z}_{\ell i}, Y_{\ell i})$. Substituting $\pi_{\ell i}(\boldsymbol{\eta}_\ell; \mathbf{Z}_{\ell i}, Y_{\ell i})$ defined in Equation (4) into (8) leads to

$$f_{0\ell}(y_{\ell i}) = f_{1\ell}(y_{\ell i}) \times \frac{\exp(-\gamma_\ell Y_{\ell i})}{E\{\exp(-\gamma_\ell Y_{\ell i}) | \mathbf{Z}_{\ell i}, D_{\ell i} = 1\}}, \quad \ell = E, R, P, \tag{9}$$

which shows that we can utilize the conditional distribution $f_{1\ell}(y_{\ell i})$ of the observed endpoints rather than that of missing endpoints (i.e., $f_{0\ell}(y_{\ell i})$) to make statistical inferences, where $E(\cdot)$ represents the expectation taken with respect to $f_{1\ell}(y_{\ell i})$. Clearly, when $\gamma_\ell = 0$, we obtain $f_{0\ell}(y_{\ell i}) = f_{1\ell}(y_{\ell i})$.

Following the argument of Tang et al. [38], it follows from Equation (9) that

$$m_{\ell i}^0(\gamma_\ell; \mathbf{Z}_{\ell i}) = \frac{E\{D_{\ell i} Y_{\ell i} \exp(-\gamma_\ell Y_{\ell i}) | \mathbf{Z}_{\ell i}\}}{E\{D_{\ell i} \exp(-\gamma_\ell Y_{\ell i}) | \mathbf{Z}_{\ell i}\}},$$

which implies that a non-parametric regression estimator of $m_{\ell i}^0(\gamma_\ell; \mathbf{Z}_{\ell i})$ can be expressed as

$$\hat{m}_{\ell i}^0(\gamma_\ell; \mathbf{Z}_{\ell i}) = \sum_{k=1}^{n_\ell} \omega_{\ell k 0}^i(\gamma_\ell; \mathbf{Z}_{\ell i}) Y_{\ell k}, \tag{10}$$

where $\omega_{\ell k 0}^i(\gamma_\ell; \mathbf{Z}_{\ell i})$'s are the weights assigned to $Y_{\ell k}$, and have the form

$$\omega_{\ell k 0}^i(\gamma_\ell; \mathbf{Z}_{\ell i}) = \frac{D_{\ell k} \exp(-\gamma_\ell Y_{\ell k}) K_{h_\ell}(\mathbf{Z}_{\ell i} - \mathbf{Z}_{\ell k})}{\sum_{j=1}^{n_\ell} D_{\ell j} \exp(-\gamma_\ell Y_{\ell j}) K_{h_\ell}(\mathbf{Z}_{\ell i} - \mathbf{Z}_{\ell j})}$$

in which $K_{h_\ell}(v) = h_\ell^{-1} K(v/h_\ell)$, $K(\cdot)$ is the multi-dimensional kernel function, and $h_\ell = h_{n_\ell}$ is the bandwidth.

3.3. Estimation of Propensity Score Function

Note that the above considered propensity score function has a parametric form indexed by the parameter vector $\boldsymbol{\eta}_\ell$, which indicates that, if we can obtain the estimation of $\boldsymbol{\eta}_\ell$ (denoted as $\hat{\boldsymbol{\eta}}_\ell$), the estimation of the propensity score function is easily evaluated by $\hat{\pi}_{\ell i}(\hat{\boldsymbol{\eta}}_\ell; \mathbf{Z}_{\ell i}, Y_{\ell i})$. In the following, we discuss the estimation problem of $\boldsymbol{\eta}_\ell$.

The mean score approach of Morikawa et al. [45] is employed here to estimate $\boldsymbol{\eta}_\ell$ based on the observed data $\mathcal{D}_\ell = \{(\mathbf{X}_{\ell i}, Y_{\ell i}, D_{\ell i}) : i = 1, \ldots, n_\ell\}$ for $\ell = E, R, P$. For simplicity, we denote $\mathcal{D}_{\text{obs}}^\ell = \{\mathbf{X}_\ell, Y_{\text{obs}}^\ell, D_\ell\}$, where $\mathbf{X}_\ell = \{\mathbf{X}_{\ell i} : i = 1, \ldots, n_\ell\}$, $D_\ell = \{D_{\ell i} : i = 1, \ldots, n_\ell\}$ and Y_{obs}^ℓ is the observed dataset of $Y_{\ell i}$'s.

When the density function $f_\ell(Y_{\ell i} | \mu_\ell; \mathbf{X}_{\ell i})$ of $Y_{\ell i}$ is known, the maximum likelihood estimator (MLE) of $\boldsymbol{\eta}_\ell$ can be obtained by maximizing the following likelihood of the observed data $\mathcal{D}_{\text{obs}}^\ell$:

$$\mathcal{L}_{\text{obs}}(\eta_\ell|\mathcal{D}^\ell_{\text{obs}}) = \prod_{i=1}^{n_\ell}\left[\pi_{\ell i}(\eta_\ell;\mathbf{Z}_{\ell i},Y_{\ell i})f_\ell(Y_{\ell i}|\mu_\ell;\mathbf{X}_{\ell i})\right]^{D_{\ell i}} \times\left[\int\{1-\pi_{\ell i}(\eta_\ell;\mathbf{Z}_{\ell i},Y_{\ell i})\}f_\ell(Y_{\ell i}|\mu_\ell;\mathbf{X}_{\ell i})dY_{\ell i}\right]^{1-D_{\ell i}}.$$

It follows from Morikawa et al. [45] and the mean score theorem that the MLE of η_ℓ can be obtained by solving the following "mean score equation":

$$\frac{1}{n}\sum_{i=1}^{n_\ell}[D_{\ell i}s(\eta_\ell;D_{\ell i},\mathbf{Z}_{\ell i},y_{\ell i})+(1-D_{\ell i})E\{s(\eta_\ell;D_{\ell i},\mathbf{Z}_{\ell i},Y_{\ell i})|\mathbf{Z}_{\ell i},D_{\ell i}=0\}]=0,$$

where $s(\eta_\ell;D_{\ell i},\mathbf{Z}_{\ell i},Y_{\ell i})$ has the form

$$\begin{aligned} s(\eta_\ell;D_{\ell i},\mathbf{Z}_{\ell i},Y_{\ell i}) &= \frac{\partial}{\partial\eta}\log\left[\pi_{\ell i}(\eta_\ell;\mathbf{Z}_{\ell i},Y_{\ell i})^{D_{\ell i}}\{1-\pi_{\ell i}(\eta_\ell;\mathbf{Z}_{\ell i},Y_{\ell i})\}^{1-D_{\ell i}}\right] \\ &= \frac{D_{\ell i}-\pi_{\ell i}(\eta_\ell;\mathbf{Z}_{\ell i},Y_{\ell i})}{\pi_{\ell i}(\eta_\ell;\mathbf{Z}_{\ell i},Y_{\ell i})\{1-\pi_{\ell i}(\eta_\ell;\mathbf{Z}_{\ell i},Y_{\ell i})\}}\dot{\pi}_{\ell i}(\eta_\ell;\mathbf{Z}_{\ell i},Y_{\ell i}), \end{aligned}$$

and $\dot{\pi}_{\ell i}(\eta_\ell;\mathbf{Z}_{\ell i},Y_{\ell i})=\partial\pi_{\ell i}(\eta_\ell;\mathbf{Z}_{\ell i},Y_{\ell i})/\partial\eta_\ell$.

Denote $s_{\ell 0}(\eta_\ell) = E\{s(\eta_\ell;D_{\ell i},\mathbf{Z}_{\ell i},Y_{\ell i})|\mathbf{Z}_{\ell i},D_{\ell i} = 0\}$. Again, it follows from Tang et al. [38] and Equation (9) that a non-parametric estimator of $s_{\ell 0}(\eta_\ell)$ is given as

$$\hat{s}_{\ell 0}(\eta_\ell;D_{\ell i},\mathbf{Z}_{\ell i},Y_{\ell i})=\sum_{k=1}^{n_\ell}\omega^i_{\ell k0}(\gamma_\ell;\mathbf{Z}_{\ell i})s(\eta_\ell;D_{\ell k},\mathbf{Z}_{\ell k},Y_{\ell k}),$$

where $\omega^i_{\ell k0}(\gamma_\ell;\mathbf{Z}_{\ell i})$ is defined in Equation (10). Thus, the estimated "mean score equation" can be written as

$$\frac{1}{n}\sum_{i=1}^{n_\ell}\{D_{\ell i}s(\eta_\ell;D_{\ell i},\mathbf{Z}_{\ell i},y_{\ell i})+(1-D_{\ell i})\hat{s}_{\ell 0}(\eta_\ell;D_{\ell i},\mathbf{Z}_{\ell i},Y_{\ell i})\}=0, \tag{11}$$

which shows that the MLE $\hat{\eta}_\ell$ of η_ℓ can be obtained by solving the non-linear equation (11) with respect to η.

Once we obtain MLE $\hat{\eta}_\ell$ of η_ℓ, substituting $\hat{\eta}_\ell$ into Equations (4) and (10) leads to the estimated propensity score function $\hat{\pi}_{\ell i}(\hat{\eta}_\ell;\mathbf{Z}_{\ell i},Y_{\ell i})$ and the estimated mean functions $\hat{m}^0_{\ell i}(\hat{\gamma}_\ell,\mathbf{Z}_{\ell i})$. Thus, substituting $\hat{\pi}_{\ell i}(\hat{\eta}_\ell;\mathbf{Z}_{\ell i},Y_{\ell i})$ and $\hat{m}^0_{\ell i}(\hat{\gamma},\mathbf{Z}_{\ell i})$ into Equations (5)–(7) yields non-parametric estimators of treatment efficacy μ_ℓ for $\ell=E,R,P$.

3.4. Dimension Reduction

In some clinical trials, the number of covariates $\mathbf{Z}_\ell\in\mathcal{R}^{d_\ell}$ may be large. In this case, the kernel-based estimators of $s(\eta_\ell;D_{\ell i},\mathbf{Z}_{\ell i},Y_{\ell i})$ and $m^0_{\ell i}(\gamma_\ell,\mathbf{Z}_{\ell i})$ may suffer from the well-known curse of dimensionality. The dimension reduction technique of Tang et al. [38] is used to solve this problem.

Let $\mathcal{G}_\ell:\mathcal{R}^{d_\ell}\to\mathcal{R}$ be a mapping function such that $\mathcal{G}_{\ell i}=\mathcal{G}_\ell(\mathbf{Z}_{\ell i})$ is univariate. In particular, we assume that $E\{s(\eta_\ell;D_{\ell i},\mathbf{Z}_{\ell i},Y_{\ell i})|\mathcal{G}_{\ell i},D_{\ell i}=0\}$ and $E(Y_{\ell i}|\mathcal{G}_{\ell i},D_{\ell i}=0)$ have the same structures as $s_{\ell 0}(\eta_\ell) = E\{s(\eta_\ell;D_{\ell i},\mathbf{Z}_{\ell i},Y_{\ell i})|\mathbf{Z}_{\ell i},D_{\ell i} = 0\}$ and $m^0_{\ell i}(\gamma_\ell;\mathbf{Z}_{\ell i}) = E(Y_{\ell i}|\mathbf{Z}_{\ell i},D_{\ell i} = 0)$, except that $\mathbf{Z}_{\ell i}$ is replaced by $\mathcal{G}_{\ell i}$. Given the MLE $\hat{\eta}_\ell$ of η_ℓ obtained with the above introduced approach, we can obtain non-parametric dimension reduction estimators of treatment efficacy μ_ℓ for $\ell=E,R,P$.

4. Asymptotic Properties and Test Statistics

4.1. Asymptotic Properties

In the following, we investigate the consistency and asymptotic normality of the proposed estimators $\hat{\mu}^{HT}_\ell,\hat{\mu}^{RI}_\ell,\hat{\mu}^{AI}_\ell$ with the known and estimated values of parameters η_ℓ.

The notation $\xrightarrow{\mathcal{L}}$ represents convergence in distribution and $\mathcal{N}(\cdot,\cdot)$ denotes the normal distribution.

From Morikawa et al. [45], we obtain the following proposition.

Proposition 1. *Suppose that Assumptions A1–A3 given in the Appendix A hold. The MLE $\hat{\eta}_\ell$ of η_ℓ satisfies*

$$\sqrt{n_\ell}\left(\hat{\eta}_\ell - \eta_\ell^0\right) \xrightarrow{\mathcal{L}} \mathcal{N}(\mathbf{0}, \mathbf{\Sigma}_{\eta\ell}) \text{ as } n_\ell \to \infty,$$

where η_ℓ^0 is the true value of η_ℓ, $\mathbf{\Sigma}_{\eta\ell} = \mathcal{I}_{22\ell}^{-1} E\{\exp(-\gamma_\ell^0 Y_{\ell i}) s_{\ell 0}(\eta_\ell^0) s_{\ell 0}(\eta_\ell^0)^\top\} \mathcal{I}_{22\ell}^{-\top}$, $s_{\ell 0}(\eta_\ell^0)$ represents $s_{\ell 0}(\eta_\ell)$ evaluated at $\eta_\ell = \eta_\ell^0$, $\mathcal{I}_{22\ell} = -E\{s_{\ell 0}(\eta_\ell^0)\dot{\pi}_{\ell i}^\top(\eta_\ell^0)/\pi_{\ell i}(\eta_\ell^0)\}$, and $\dot{\pi}_{\ell i}(\eta_\ell) = \dot{\pi}_{\ell i}(\eta_\ell; \mathbf{Z}_{\ell i}, Y_{\ell i})$ and $\pi_{\ell i}(\eta_\ell^0) = \pi_{\ell i}(\eta_\ell^0; \mathbf{Z}_{\ell i}, Y_{\ell i}))$ for $\ell = E, R, P$.

Proof of Proposition 1 can be found in Morikawa et al. [45]. To save space, we omit it. Proposition 1 shows that the MLE $\hat{\eta}_\ell$ of η_ℓ is consistent and asymptotically distributed as the multivariate normal distribution.

Theorem 1. *Suppose that Assumptions A1–A3 given in the Appendix A hold. For a known value η_ℓ^0 of η_ℓ, given the true value μ_ℓ^0 of μ_ℓ, the proposed estimators $\hat{\mu}_\ell^{HT}$, $\hat{\mu}_\ell^{RI}$ and $\hat{\mu}_\ell^{AI}$ satisfy*

$$\sqrt{n_\ell}(\hat{\mu}_\ell^h - \mu_\ell^0) \xrightarrow{\mathcal{L}} \mathcal{N}(0, \sigma_\ell^2) \text{ as } n_\ell \to \infty$$

for $h = HT, RI, AI$ and $\ell = E, R, P$, where $\sigma_\ell^2 = \text{var}(\tau_{\ell i})$ with $\tau_{\ell i} = m_{\ell i}^0(\gamma_\ell; \mathbf{Z}_{\ell i}) + D_{\ell i}\pi_{\ell i}^{-1}(\eta_\ell^0)\{Y_{\ell i} - m_{\ell i}^0(\gamma_\ell; \mathbf{Z}_{\ell i})\}$. In addition, σ_ℓ^2 can be rewritten as $\sigma_\ell^2 = \text{var}(Y_{\ell i}) + E\{[\pi_{\ell i}^{-1}(\eta_\ell^0) - 1][Y_{\ell i} - m_{\ell i}^0(\gamma_\ell; \mathbf{Z}_{\ell i})]^2\}$.

Theorem 1 shows that the proposed estimators of μ_ℓ are consistent and asymptotically distributed as the normal distribution with zero mean and the same variance.

Following the argument of Kim and Yu [37], σ_ℓ^2 can be consistently estimated by

$$\hat{\sigma}_\ell^2 = \frac{1}{n_\ell}\sum_{i=1}^{n_\ell} \hat{\tau}_{\ell i}^2 - \left(\frac{1}{n_\ell}\sum_{i=1}^{n_\ell} \hat{\tau}_{\ell i}\right)^2,$$

where $\hat{\tau}_{\ell i} = \hat{m}_{\ell i}^0(\gamma_\ell^0; \mathbf{Z}_{\ell i}) + D_{\ell i}\hat{\pi}_{\ell i}^{-1}(\eta_\ell^0)\{Y_{\ell i} - \hat{m}_{\ell i}^0(\gamma_\ell^0; \mathbf{Z}_{\ell i})\}$.

When η_ℓ is unknown, we replace η_ℓ or γ_ℓ in Equations (5)–(7) by their corresponding consistent estimators $\hat{\eta}_\ell$ or $\hat{\gamma}_\ell$, respectively. Thus, we can obtain their corresponding plug-in estimators (denoted as $\hat{\mu}_\ell^{SHT}$, $\hat{\mu}_\ell^{SRI}$ and $\hat{\mu}_\ell^{SAI}$, respectively) of μ_ℓ.

Theorem 2. *Suppose that Assumptions A1–A3 given in the Appendix A hold, the propensity score function (4) is correctly specified, and Proposition 1 holds. The plug-in estimators $\hat{\mu}_\ell^{SHT}$, $\hat{\mu}_\ell^{SRI}$ and $\hat{\mu}_\ell^{SAI}$ of μ_ℓ satisfy*

$$\sqrt{n_\ell}\left(\hat{\mu}_\ell^h - \mu_\ell^0\right) \xrightarrow{\mathcal{L}} \mathcal{N}(0, \sigma_{\ell,h}^2) \text{ as } n_\ell \to \infty,\ h = SHT, SRI, SAI,\ \ell = E, R, P,$$

where $\sigma_{\ell,h}^2 = \text{var}(e_{\ell,hi})$ with $e_{\ell,hi} = \{D_{\ell i}\pi_{\ell i}^{-1}(\eta_\ell)\{Y_{\ell i} - m_{\ell i}^0(\gamma_\ell; \mathbf{Z}_{\ell i})\} + m_{\ell i}^0(\gamma_\ell; \mathbf{Z}_{\ell i}) - \mu_\ell^0 + \mathcal{I}_{22\ell}^{-1} s_{\ell i}(\eta_\ell) H_{\ell,h}\}$, $s_{\ell i}(\eta_\ell)$ is the ith term in Equation (11), $H_{\ell,SHT} = E\{(\pi_{\ell i}(\eta_\ell) - 1)Y_{\ell i}(1, \mathbf{Z}_{\ell i}^\top, Y_\ell)^\top\}$, $H_{\ell,SRI} = E\{(1 - D_{\ell i})(0, \mathbf{0}_{p_\ell - 1}^\top, (Y_{\ell i} - m_{\ell i}^0(\gamma_\ell; \mathbf{Z}_{\ell i}))^2)^\top\}$, $H_{\ell,SAI} = H_{\ell,SHT} + M_{\ell,SAI}$, $M_{\ell,SAI} = E\{(1 - \pi_{\ell i}(\eta_\ell))m_{\ell i}^0(\gamma_\ell; \mathbf{Z}_{\ell i})(1, \mathbf{Z}_{\ell i}^\top, Y_{\ell i})^\top\}$, $\mathbf{0}_{p_\ell - 1}$ is a $(p_\ell - 1) \times 1$ zero vector and p_ℓ is the number of covariate vector $\mathbf{Z}_{\ell i}$.

Note that the asymptotic variance $\sigma_{\ell,h}^2$ has a complicated form; thus, it is rather difficult to compute the estimate of $\sigma_{\ell,h}^2$. To overcome this difficulty, we utilize a bootstrap-resampling method or empirical jack-knife method to evaluate the estimated asymptotic variances.

4.2. Wald-Type Statistics for Testing $\tilde{H}_0$

In what follows, we construct three Wald-type statistics for testing hypothesis $H_0: \psi(\boldsymbol{\mu}) \leq 0$ based on the asymptotic properties of three different estimators given in Theorem 2.

Based on the properties of estimator $\hat{\boldsymbol{\mu}}^h = (\hat{\mu}_E^h, \hat{\mu}_R^h, \hat{\mu}_P^h)^\top$ for $\boldsymbol{\mu} = (\mu_E, \mu_R, \mu_P)^\top$, we obtain that (i) $\hat{\psi}(\hat{\boldsymbol{\mu}}^h) = \hat{\mu}_E^h - a\hat{\mu}_R^h - (1-a)\hat{\mu}_P^h$ is a consistent estimator of $\psi(\boldsymbol{\mu})$, (ii) variance of $\hat{\psi}(\hat{\boldsymbol{\mu}}^h)$ is $\text{var}\{\hat{\psi}(\hat{\boldsymbol{\mu}}^h)\} = \text{var}(\hat{\mu}_E^h) + a^2\text{var}(\hat{\mu}_R^h) + (1-a)^2\text{var}(\hat{\mu}_P^h)$, which can consistently be estimated by $\widehat{\text{var}}\{\hat{\psi}(\hat{\boldsymbol{\mu}}^h)\} = \tilde{\sigma}_{E,h}^2/n_E + a^2\tilde{\sigma}_{R,h}^2/n_R + (1-a)^2\tilde{\sigma}_{P,h}^2/n_P$, where $\tilde{\sigma}_{E,h}^2$, $\tilde{\sigma}_{R,h}^2$ and $\tilde{\sigma}_{P,h}^2$ defined in Theorem 2 are the consistent estimators of $\sigma_{E,h}^2$, $\sigma_{R,h}^2$ and $\sigma_{P,h}^2$, respectively, for $h = SHT, SRI, SAI$; (iii) $(\hat{\psi}(\hat{\boldsymbol{\mu}}^h) - \psi(\boldsymbol{\mu}))/\sqrt{\widehat{\text{var}}\{\hat{\psi}(\hat{\boldsymbol{\mu}}^h)\}} \xrightarrow{\mathcal{L}} \mathcal{N}(0,1)$ as $\min\{n_E, n_R, n_P\} \to \infty$. Thus, the Wald-type statistic for testing $\tilde{H}_0: \psi(\boldsymbol{\mu}) \leq 0$ can be expressed as

$$T_W^h = \frac{\hat{\psi}(\hat{\boldsymbol{\mu}}^h)}{\sqrt{\widehat{\text{var}}\{\hat{\psi}(\hat{\boldsymbol{\mu}}^h)\}}} = \frac{\hat{\mu}_E^h - a\hat{\mu}_R^h - (1-a)\hat{\mu}_P^h}{\sqrt{\tilde{\sigma}_{E,h}^2/n_E + a^2\tilde{\sigma}_{R,h}^2/n_R + (1-a)^2\tilde{\sigma}_{P,h}^2/n_P}}$$

for $h = SHT, SRI, SAI$, which are asymptotically distributed as the standard normal distribution under $\tilde{H}_0$ as $\min\{n_E, n_R, n_P\} \to \infty$.

Note that the asymptotic properties of the parameter estimators and test statistics presented above only hold as $n_\ell \to \infty$ ($\ell = E, R, P$). However, for the finite samples, before using asymptotic normality of the estimators $\hat{\boldsymbol{\mu}}_\ell^h$ ($\ell = E, R, P$) and test statistics T_W^h ($h = SHT, SRI, SAI$), one should utilize the concept of goodness-of-fit tests [46,47] to check the plausibility of their normality assumption.

5. Simulation Study

In this section, simulation studies were conducted to assess the finite sample performance of the proposed test procedures in terms of empirical type I error rates and empirical powers under four missingness data mechanisms.

For $\ell = E, R, P$, the data $\{\mathbf{X}_{\ell i} : i = 1, \cdots, n_\ell\}$ were independently generated from the multivariate normal distribution, i.e., $\mathbf{X}_{\ell i} = (Z_{\ell i}, U_{\ell i}) \overset{\text{i.i.d}}{\sim} \mathcal{N}(\boldsymbol{\xi}, \boldsymbol{\Sigma})$, and the data $\{Y_{\ell i} : i = 1, \cdots, n_\ell\}$ were independently generated by $Y_{\ell i} = \mathbf{X}_{\ell i}^\top \boldsymbol{\beta}_\ell + \varepsilon_{\ell i}$, where $\varepsilon_{\ell i}$'s were independently sampled from the following normal distributions (denoted as 'scenario (A)'): $\varepsilon_{Ei} \sim \mathcal{N}(a\mu_R + (1-a)\mu_P, 0.34)$, $\varepsilon_{Ri} \sim \mathcal{N}(\mu_R, 0.37)$ and $\varepsilon_{Pi} \sim \mathcal{N}(\mu_P, 0.2)$ with $a = 0.8$, which was the three-arm "gold threshold" recommended in the considered literature [18]. The true values of $\boldsymbol{\xi}$, $\boldsymbol{\Sigma}$, $\boldsymbol{\beta}_E$, $\boldsymbol{\beta}_R$, $\boldsymbol{\beta}_P$, μ_R and μ_P were taken as $\boldsymbol{\xi} = (0.0, 0.0)^\top$, $\boldsymbol{\Sigma} = \text{diag}(0.25, 0.25)$, $\boldsymbol{\beta}_E = (1.0, 1.0)^\top$, $\boldsymbol{\beta}_R = (1.0, 1.1)^\top$, $\boldsymbol{\beta}_P = (0.5, 0.5)^\top$, $\mu_R = 1.1$ and $\mu_P = 0.6$, respectively, which were only chosen as an illustration of the proposed methodologies. For comparison with the cases used widely or always justified, we considered the following two scenarios: (B) $\varepsilon_{Ei} \sim \mathcal{N}(a\mu_R + (1-a)\mu_P, 0.8)$, $\varepsilon_{Ri} \sim \mathcal{N}(\mu_R, 0.8)$ and $\varepsilon_{Pi} \sim \mathcal{N}(\mu_P, 0.5)$; (C) $\varepsilon_{Ei} \sim \mathcal{N}(a\mu_R + (1-a)\mu_P, 1.0)$, $\varepsilon_{Ri} \sim \mathcal{N}(\mu_R, 1.0)$ and $\varepsilon_{Pi} \sim \mathcal{N}(\mu_P, 0.5)$. Under the above specified setting, we have $\psi(\boldsymbol{\mu}) = 0$, where $\boldsymbol{\mu} = \{\mu_E, \mu_R, \mu_P\}$. That is, the data $\{(\mathbf{X}_{\ell i}, Y_{\ell i}) : \ell = E, R, P, i = 1, \cdots, n_\ell\}$ were independently generated from the null hypothesis $\tilde{H}_0$, and were used to compute empirical type I error rates. To compute empirical powers, the data $\{(\mathbf{X}_{\ell i}, Y_{\ell i}) : \ell = E, R, P, i = 1, \cdots, n_\ell\}$ were independently generated with the above presented settings, except for $a = (\mu_E - \mu_P)/(\mu_R - \mu_P) > 0.8$, which implied that the data $\{(\mathbf{X}_{\ell i}, Y_{\ell i}) : \ell = E, R, P, i = 1, \cdots, n_\ell\}$ were sampled from the alternative hypothesis $\tilde{H}_1 : \psi(\mu) > 0$.

To create missing data for $Y_{\ell i}$, we assumed that the missing indicators $D_{\ell i}$'s were independently generated from the Bernoulli distribution with the respondent probability $\pi_{\ell i}$ for $\ell = E, R, P$. Here, we considered the following respondent probabilities for the reference treatment and placebo:

$$\text{logit}(\pi_{Ri}) = 1.6 + 0.2Z_{Ri} - 0.15Y_{Ri}, \quad \text{logit}(\pi_{Pi}) = 1.5 + 0.15Z_{Pi} - 0.18Y_{Pi},$$

which indicated that missingness data mechanisms were non-ignorable, and the following four respondent probabilities for experimental treatment:

Case E1: $\text{logit}(\pi_{Ei}) = \alpha_{E0} + \alpha_{E1} Z_{Ei}$, which led to a MAR missingness data mechanism, where the true values of α_{E0} and α_{E1} were taken to be 1.3 and 0.1, respectively.

Case E2: $\text{logit}(\pi_{Ei}) = \alpha_{E0} + \alpha_{E1} Z_{Ei} + \gamma_E Y_{Ei}$, which resulted in a non-ignorable missingness data mechanism, where the true values of α_{E0}, α_{E1} and γ_E were taken as 1.3, 0.1 and -0.1, respectively.

Case E3: $\text{logit}(\pi_{Ei}) = \alpha_{E0} + \alpha_{E1}\sin(Z_{Ei}) + \gamma_E Y_{Ei}$, which yielded a non-linear non-ignorable missingness data mechanism with respect to Z_{Ei}, where the true values of α_{E0}, α_{E1} and γ_E were set to be 1.3, 0.1 and 0.12, respectively.

Case E4: $\text{logit}(\pi_{Ei}) = \alpha_{E0} + \alpha_{E1} Z_{Ei} + \gamma_E Z_{Ei} Y_{Ei}$, which implied a non-linear non-ignorable missingness data mechanism with an interaction of Z_{Ei} and Y_{Ei}, where the true values of α_{E0}, α_{E1} and γ_E were set as 1.3, 0.1 and -0.1, respectively.

The titling parameters γ_ℓ corresponding to $Y_{\ell i}$ ($\ell = E, R, P$) were set to be roughly -0.2 for showing a moderately negative effect on the probability of the data observed, and $\alpha_{\ell 0}$ and $\alpha_{\ell 1}$ were chosen so that the average missing rates were roughly 25%. Case E1 was MAR, which was a special case of the considered missingness data mechanism model (4) with $\gamma_E = 0$ and was used to show that the proposed method can still capture missingness data characteristics even if the true missingness data mechanism was MAR; the other three missingness data mechanisms were non-ignorable and Case E2 satisfied the assumption of model (4), but Cases E3 and E4, which did not satisfy the assumed non-ignorable missingness data mechanism model (4), were used to show that the proposed test procedure was not sensitive to the assumed missingness data mechanism model (4). Here, we consider three balanced designs, i.e., $n_E = n_R = n_P = n$ with $n = 50, 100, 150$ for three scenarios, and the following unbalanced designs with the allocation ratios taken as 2:2:1, 3:3:1, 4:4:1, 2:1:1, 3:2:1, 4:3:1, 4:2:1, 3:1:1, 4:1:1 for Scenario (A) and 2:1:1, 2:2:1, 3:2:1 for Scenarios (B) and (C). The total sample sizes $N = n_E + n_R + n_P$ were set as 200 and 500 for Scenario (A) and 200, 300 and 400 for Scenarios (B) and (C), with a significance level $\alpha = 5\%$ for the three scenarios.

The average missing rates for the experimental, reference and placebo treatments among the 1000 replications were roughly 23.15%, 19.23% and 21.08%, respectively.

For each of the settings described above, we generated 1000 Monte Carlo samples. To evaluate the accuracy of the mean function estimates $\hat{m}^0_{\ell i}(\gamma_\ell; z_{\ell i})$ and the propensity score function estimates $\hat{\pi}_\ell(\boldsymbol{\eta}_\ell; z_{\ell i}, y_{\ell i})$, we took the Gaussian kernel function with $K(Z_\ell) = (2\pi)^{-1/2}\exp(-Z_\ell^2/2)$ and set the bandwidths h_ℓ as $\hat{\sigma}_{Z_\ell} n_\ell^{-1/3}$, where $\hat{\sigma}_{Z_\ell}$ was the standard deviation of observations $\{Z_{\ell i} : i = 1, \ldots, n_\ell\}$ for $\ell = E, R, P$. To compute the estimated asymptotic variances of $\hat{\mu}^k_\ell$, we conducted 100 bootstrap replications.

Empirical type I error rates for 1000 replications in Scenario (A) are given in Table 1 for balanced designs with the above considered four missingness data mechanisms and Table 2 for unbalanced designs with only the missingness data mechanism E2. To save space, we moved the corresponding results in Scenarios (B) and (C) to Tables A1 and A2 in the Appendix A. Examination of Tables 1, 2, A1 and A2 showed that (i) the proposed three statistics for testing $\tilde{H}_0$ have similar performance because their type I error rates are quite close to the pre-given significance level for all the considered cases, which is consistent with the theoretical properties presented in Theorems 1 and 2; (ii) the proposed three statistics for testing $\tilde{H}_0$ performed better than the CC method regardless of the sample sizes, missingness data mechanisms, balanced and unbalanced designs, and the variances of the treatment effects in that the type I error rates of the former were closer to the pre-given significance level than those for the latter; (iii) the type I error rate increased as the sample size increased for the CC method, which was consistent with the observations of Cook and Zea [48]; (iv) empirical type I error rates were not sensitive to the balanced or unbalanced designs.

Table 1. Empirical type I error rates for balanced designs in the first simulation study.

	n = 50				n = 100				n = 150			
Case	SHT	SRI	SAI	CC	SHT	SRI	SAI	CC	SHT	SRI	SAI	CC
E1	0.048	0.051	0.053	0.057	0.048	0.050	0.052	**0.074**	0.050	0.051	0.050	**0.083**
E2	0.053	0.055	0.055	0.052	0.048	0.049	0.050	0.055	0.054	0.055	0.055	**0.092**
E3	0.049	0.055	0.054	**0.070**	0.053	0.053	0.058	**0.095**	0.052	0.054	0.054	**0.117**
E4	0.051	0.053	0.052	**0.061**	0.048	0.050	0.053	**0.086**	0.047	0.051	0.049	**0.088**

Note: SHT, SRI, SAI and CC denote Wald-type test approaches based on IPW, regression imputation, AIPW and CC, respectively.

Table 2. Empirical type I error rates for unbalanced designs in the first simulation study.

	N = 200			N = 500		
n_E:n_R:n_P	SHT	SRI	SAI	SHT	SRI	SAI
2:2:1	0.046	0.048	0.048	0.049	0.050	0.051
3:3:1	0.053	0.053	0.051	0.045	0.046	0.046
4:4:1	0.053	0.054	0.058	0.045	0.047	0.050
2:1:1	0.048	0.051	0.050	0.045	0.044	0.045
3:2:1	0.055	0.059	0.060	0.047	0.049	0.046
4:3:1	0.038	0.044	0.047	0.054	0.055	0.055
4:2:1	0.048	0.051	0.053	0.063	0.064	0.059
3:1:1	0.055	0.056	0.057	0.052	0.055	0.056
4:1:1	0.050	0.057	0.058	0.051	0.052	0.054

We computed empirical powers against $a = (\mu_E - \mu_P)/(\mu_R - \mu_P)$, the sample sizes, the treatment effects, and the alpha and gamma parameters for missingness data mechanism models E1–E4 when the null hypothesis was not true. To save space, we only present empirical powers against the sample size in Figure 1 for balanced design and Figure 2 for unbalanced design (i.e., n_E:n_R:n_P = 2:1:1) under the considered four missingness data mechanism models. Other results are given in Figures A1–A8 in the Appendix A. Inspection of these figures showed that (i) empirical power increases as a or the sample size n increases, regardless of the missingness data mechanisms and balanced/unbalanced designs and the considered four tests; (ii) empirical power slightly increased as α_{E1} increased regardless of the missingness data mechanisms and balanced/unbalanced designs and the considered SHT, SRI and SAI tests, while the empirical power for the CC method showed an increasing tendency as α_{E1} increased for missingness data mechanisms E3 and E4, which might be explained by non-linear non-ignorable missing data; (iii) the empirical powers with the proposed three test statistics were larger than those with the CC method for non-ignorable missing data (i.e., E2–E4), regardless of the sample sizes, a, treatment effects, α_{E1} and γ; (iv) the observation that the CC method had a slightly larger empirical power than the three tests considered might be explained by its inflated type I error.

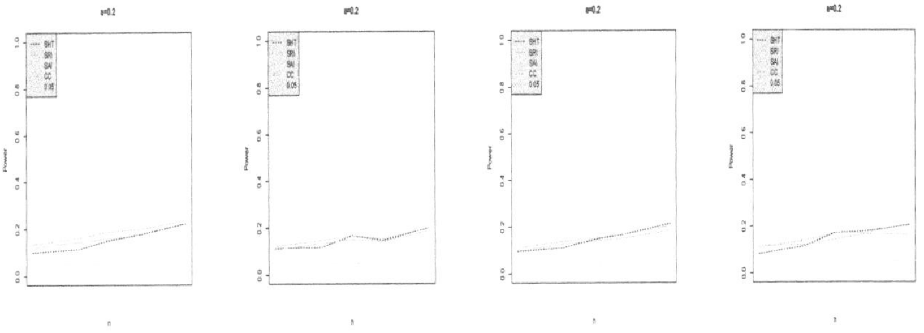

Figure 1. SHT, SRI, SAI and CC represent empirical powers evaluated from IPW, regression imputation, AIPW and CC methods against the sample size n under balanced design with missingness data mechanism models E1 (**left panel**), E2 (**left second panel**), E3 (**right second panel**) and E4 (**right panel**) for $a = 0.2$.

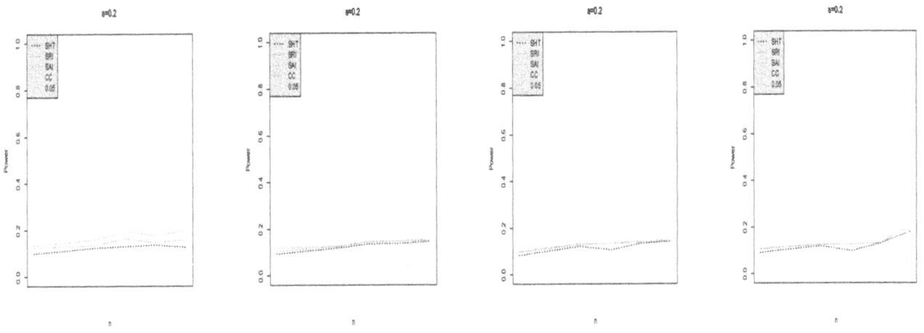

Figure 2. SHT, SRI, SAI and CC represent empirical powers evaluated from IPW, regression imputation, AIPW and CC methods against the sample size n under unbalanced design (i.e., n_E:n_R:n_P = 2:1:1), with missingness data mechanism models E1 (**left panel**), E2 (**left second panel**), E3 (**right second panel**) and E4 (**right panel**) for $a = 0.2$.

To investigate the effect of the amount of departure from the MAR mechanism (i.e., the change in γ_E) on type I error rates under the missingness data mechanism model E2, with the same values of α_{E0} and α_{E1} (i.e., $\alpha_{E0} = 1.3$ and $\alpha_{E1} = 0.1$) as those given in the first simulation study, we conducted a second simulation study. In this simulation study, 1000 Monte Carlo datasets $\{(\mathbf{X}_{\ell i}, Y_{\ell i}, D_{\ell i}) : i = 1, \cdots, n_\ell\}$ were independently generated, as in the first simulation study, with $\gamma_E = -0.2, -0.1, -0.05, 0, 0.05, 0.1$. Empirical type I error rates for the balanced design with the sample sizes $n = 50$ and 150 are given in Table 3. Inspection of Table 3 yielded that (i) statistics with the IPW, regression imputation and AIPW methods behaved better than those with the CC method because the type I error rates for the former were closer to the pre-given significance level than those for the latter, regardless of the values of γ_E and the sample sizes; and (ii) statistics with the IPW, regression imputation and AIPW methods were not sensitive to γ_E.

Table 3. Sensitivity analysis of the proposed test statistics in the second simulation study.

	$n = 50$				$n = 150$			
γ_E	SHT	SRI	SAI	CC	SHT	SRI	SAI	CC
−0.2	0.038	0.046	0.044	0.033	0.051	0.050	0.051	0.033
−0.1	0.053	0.055	0.055	0.052	0.054	0.055	0.055	**0.092**
−0.05	0.041	0.045	0.046	**0.066**	0.045	0.048	0.047	**0.061**
0.0	0.048	0.051	0.053	0.057	0.050	0.051	0.050	**0.083**
0.05	0.050	0.051	0.052	**0.065**	0.054	0.055	0.055	**0.092**
0.1	0.047	0.051	0.056	**0.087**	0.053	0.056	0.055	**0.111**

6. An Example

In this section, a real example described in the Introduction is used to illustrate the proposed methodologies. In this dataset, we regarded zidovudine plus 400 mg of didanosine plus 400 mg of nevirapine as the experimental treatment with 330 patients, zidovudine plus 2.25 mg of zalcitabine as the reference treatment with 324 patients, and zidovudine alternating monthly with 400 mg didanosine as the placebo with 325 patients, respectively. CD4 counts were scheduled to be collected at baseline and eight-week intervals during the follow-up. Due to mistimed measurements, CD4 count data were subject to missingness, which led to unbalanced designs. There were 94 patient dropouts at the interval (4,12] among the 330 patients, 97 patient dropouts at the interval (4,12] and two patient dropouts at baseline among the 324 patients, and 95 patient dropouts at the interval (4,12] and five patient dropouts at baseline among the 325 patients. As an illustration, we took log(CD4 count at baseline + 1) as the dropout instrument variable Z, and only considered the data at the interval (4,12], i.e., treatment endpoints were CD4 counts at the interval (4,12], which led to $n_E = 328$, $n_R = 313$ and $n_P = 316$, whose average missing rates were 29.74%, 30.99%, and 28.65%, respectively. The dataset was obtained from the R package "ALA". Our main purpose was to test the NI of the experimental treatment to the reference treatment in the considered three-arm design. To this end, we took the fraction margin as $\delta = g(\mu_R - \mu_P)$ with $g = 0.2$, which led to $a = 0.8$, i.e., the experimental treatment achieved more than 80 percent of the reference treatment compared with the placebo to be claimed as NI.

To compute $\hat{m}^0_{\ell i}(\hat{\gamma}_\ell; Z_{\ell i})$ and $\hat{\pi}_\ell(\hat{\eta}_\ell; Z_{\ell i}, Y_{\ell i})$, we took the Gaussian kernel function as $K(x_\ell) = (2\pi)^{-1/2}\exp(-x_\ell^2/2)$ and set the bandwidth h_ℓ to be $\hat{\sigma}_{X_\ell} n_\ell^{-1/3}$, where $\hat{\sigma}_{X_\ell}$ was the standard deviation of $X_{\ell i}$'s. The p-values for testing $\tilde{H}_0$ were 0.0037, 0.0035, 0.0033 and 0.0136 for the Wald-type statistics with the IPW, regression imputation, AIPW and CC methods, respectively, which indicated the NI of the experimental treatment to the reference treatment was at the 5% significance level.

7. Conclusions

This paper considers the non-inferiority assessment problem of an experimental treatment to a reference treatment in a three-arm trial with non-ignorable missing data. A logistic regression was employed to specify the non-ignorable missing endpoint mechanism. Three methods, including the IPW, imputation regression and AIPW methods, were proposed to estimate the treatment efficacy for the known and unknown propensity score functions. The asymptotic properties of estimators for treatment efficacy were established under some regularity conditions. Based on these asymptotic properties, three Wald-type statistics for testing the NI of the experimental treatment to the reference treatment were constructed. Simulation studies indicated that the proposed test procedures behaved better than those with complete-case data in terms of type I error rates and powers, i.e., the type I error rates for the former were closer to the pre-given significance level than those for the latter and the powers for the former were larger than those for the latter; the proposed test procedures were not sensitive to misspecified missingness data mechanisms.

Author Contributions: W.L. carried out the simulation studies, the statistical analysis and drafted the manuscript; Y.Z. drafted the manuscript and conducted the statistical analysis; N.T. conceived the research questions and idea, developed the methods and revised the manuscript. All authors have read and agreed to the published version of the manuscript.

Funding: The authors are very grateful to the Editor, the Associate Editor and the three anonymous referees for their valuable comments that significantly improved this work. This work was supported by grants from the National Natural Science Foundation of China (No. 12271472), the National Key R&D Program of China (No. 2022YFA1003701), and the China Postdoctoral Science Foundation (No. 2021M702778).

Data Availability Statement: The datasets generated and analysed during the current study are available from the corresponding author on reasonable request.

Conflicts of Interest: The authors declare no competing interest.

Appendix A

Appendix A.1. Regularity Conditions

To obtain asymptotic properties of $\hat{\mu}_\ell$ for $\ell = E, R, P$, we need the following regularity conditions.

Assumption A1. *The true respondent model given in Equation (4) satisfies (i) that there exists a true value $\boldsymbol{\eta}_\ell^0$ of $\boldsymbol{\eta}_\ell$ such that $E\{s(\boldsymbol{\eta}_\ell^0; \mathbf{Z}_\ell, Y_\ell)\} = 0$; (ii) for $\boldsymbol{\eta}_\ell$, in a neighborhood of $\boldsymbol{\eta}_\ell^0$, $E\{||s(\boldsymbol{\eta}_\ell^0; \mathbf{Z}_\ell, Y_\ell)||^2\} < \infty$ and $E\{\partial s(\boldsymbol{\eta}_\ell^0; \mathbf{Z}_\ell, Y_\ell)/\partial \eta_\ell^T\}$ exists and is nonsingular.*

Assumption A2. *(i) The marginal probability density function $f(z)$ of the random variable z is bounded away from ∞ in the support of z, and the second derivative of $f(z)$ in z is continuous and bounded; (ii) The respondent probabilities $\pi_{\ell i}(\boldsymbol{\eta}_\ell; \mathbf{Z}_{\ell i}, Y_{\ell i})$ satisfy $\min_{1\le i\le n_\ell} \pi_{\ell i}(\boldsymbol{\eta}_\ell; \mathbf{Z}_{\ell i}, Y_{\ell i}) \ge c_0$ a.s. for some positive constant c_0.*

Assumption A3. *The kernel function $K_\ell(\cdot)$ satisfies (i) it is bounded and has compact support; (ii) it is symmetric with $\int \omega^2 K_\ell(\omega)d\omega < \infty$; (iii) $K_\ell(\cdot) \ge D_\ell$ for $D_\ell > 0$ in some closed interval centered at zero; (iv) $n_\ell h_\ell \to \infty$ and $n_\ell h_\ell^4 \to 0$ as $n_\ell \to \infty$.*

Remark A1. *Assumption A1 is used to establish asymptotic normality of $\hat{\boldsymbol{\eta}}_\ell$. Assumption A2 is commonly adopted in the missing data literature. Assumption A3 is a standard assumption for the kernel regression method.*

Proof of Theorem 1. By the definition of $\hat{\mu}_\ell^{HT}$, we have the following decomposition

$$\begin{aligned}\sqrt{n_\ell}(\hat{\mu}_\ell^{HT} - \mu_\ell^0) =& n_\ell^{-1/2}\sum_{i=1}^{n_\ell}\left\{\frac{D_{\ell i}Y_{\ell i}}{\pi_{\ell i}(\boldsymbol{\eta}_\ell; \mathbf{Z}_{\ell i}, Y_{\ell i})} - \mu_\ell^0\right\} \\ =& n_\ell^{-1/2}\sum_{i=1}^{n_\ell}\frac{D_{\ell i}\{Y_{\ell i} - m_{\ell i}^0(\gamma_\ell; \mathbf{Z}_{\ell i})\}}{\pi_{\ell i}(\boldsymbol{\eta}_\ell; \mathbf{Z}_{\ell i}, Y_{\ell i})} + n_\ell^{-1/2}\sum_{i=1}^{n_\ell}\left\{m_{\ell i}^0(\gamma_\ell; \mathbf{Z}_{\ell i}) - \mu_\ell^0\right\} \\ &+ n_\ell^{-1/2}\sum_{i=1}^{n_\ell}\left\{\frac{D_{\ell i}}{\pi_{\ell i}(\boldsymbol{\eta}_\ell; \mathbf{Z}_{\ell i}, Y_{\ell i})} - 1\right\}m_{\ell i}^0(\gamma_\ell; \mathbf{Z}_{\ell i}) \triangleq H_{1n_\ell} + H_{2n_\ell} + H_{3n_\ell}.\end{aligned}$$

By the law of large numbers, it is easily shown that $H_{3n_\ell} = o_p(1)$. Thus, combining the above results leads to

$$\sqrt{n_\ell}(\hat{\mu}_\ell^{HT} - \mu_\ell^0) = n_\ell^{-1/2}\sum_{i=1}^{n_\ell}\frac{D_{\ell i}\{Y_{\ell i} - m_{\ell i}^0(\gamma_\ell; \mathbf{Z}_{\ell i})\}}{\pi_{\ell i}(\boldsymbol{\eta}_\ell; \mathbf{Z}_{\ell i}, Y_{\ell i})} + n_\ell^{-1/2}\sum_{i=1}^{n_\ell}\left\{m_{\ell i}^0(\gamma_\ell; \mathbf{Z}_{\ell i}) - \mu_\ell^0\right\} + o_p(1).$$

Let $\tau_{\ell i} = m_{\ell i}^0(\gamma_\ell; \mathbf{Z}_{\ell i}) + D_{\ell i}\pi_{\ell i}^{-1}(\eta_\ell^0)\{y_{\ell i} - m_{\ell i}^0(\gamma_\ell; \mathbf{Z}_{\ell i})\}$. Then, we have

$$\sqrt{n_\ell}\left(\hat{\mu}_\ell^{HT} - \mu_\ell^0\right) \xrightarrow{\mathcal{L}} N\left(0, \sigma_\ell^2\right) \quad as \quad n_\ell \to \infty, \text{ for } \ell = E, R, P,$$

where $\sigma_\ell^2 = \text{var}(\tau_{\ell i})$. It is easily shown that $E\left\{D_{\ell i}\pi_{\ell i}(\eta_\ell; \mathbf{Z}_{\ell i}, Y_{\ell i})^{-1}\{Y_{\ell i} - m_{\ell i}^0(\gamma_\ell; \mathbf{Z}_{\ell i})\}\right\} = 0$, and $E\{m_{\ell i}^0(\gamma_\ell; \mathbf{Z}_{\ell i}) - \mu_\ell^0\} = 0$. Since $m_{\ell i}^0(\gamma_\ell; \mathbf{Z}_{\ell i})$ is independent of $Y_{\ell i} - m_{\ell i}^0(\gamma_\ell; \mathbf{Z}_{\ell i})$, we have $\sigma_\ell^2 = E\{\pi_{\ell i}(Z_{\ell i}, Y_{\ell i}; \eta_\ell^0)^{-1}[Y_{\ell i} - m_{\ell i}^0(\gamma_\ell; \mathbf{Z}_{\ell i}]^2\} + E\left[m_{\ell i}^0(\gamma_\ell; \mathbf{Z}_{\ell i})\right]^2$.

Next, we show the asymptotic property of $\hat{\mu}_\ell^{RI}$. By the definition of $\hat{\mu}_\ell^{RI}$, we obtain

$$\begin{aligned}
\sqrt{n_\ell}(\hat{\mu}_\ell^{RI} - \mu_\ell^0) &= n_\ell^{-1/2}\sum_{i=1}^{n_\ell}\left\{D_{\ell i}Y_{\ell i} + (1 - D_{\ell i})\hat{m}_{\ell i}^0(\gamma_\ell; \mathbf{Z}_{\ell i}) - \mu_\ell^0\right\} \\
&= n_\ell^{-1/2}\sum_{i=1}^{n_\ell} D_{\ell i}\left\{Y_{\ell i} - m_{\ell i}^0(\gamma_\ell; \mathbf{Z}_{\ell i})\right\} + n_\ell^{-1/2}\sum_{i=1}^{n_\ell}(1 - D_{\ell i})\left\{\hat{m}_{\ell i}^0(\gamma_\ell; \mathbf{Z}_{\ell i}) - m_{\ell i}^0(\gamma_\ell; \mathbf{Z}_{\ell i})\right\} \\
&+ n_\ell^{-1/2}\sum_{i=1}^{n_\ell}\left\{m_{\ell i}^0(\gamma_\ell; \mathbf{Z}_{\ell i}) - \mu_\ell^0\right\} \triangleq R_{1n_\ell} + R_{2n_\ell} + H_{2n_\ell}.
\end{aligned}$$

Using the similar arguments as given in Tang et al. [38], it is easily shown that

$$R_{2n_\ell} = n_\ell^{-1/2}\sum_{i=1}^{n_\ell} D_{\ell i}[1 - \pi_{\ell i}(\eta_\ell^0; \mathbf{Z}_{\ell i}, Y_{\ell i})]\{Y_{\ell i} - m_{\ell i}^0(\gamma_\ell; \mathbf{Z}_{\ell i})\}/\pi_{\ell i}(\eta_\ell^0; \mathbf{Z}_{\ell i}, Y_{\ell i}) + o_p(1).$$

Thus, we have

$$\sqrt{n_\ell}(\hat{\mu}_\ell^{RI} - \mu_\ell^0) = H_{1n_\ell} + H_{2n_\ell} + o_p(1) = \sqrt{n_\ell}(\hat{\mu}_\ell^{HT} - \mu_\ell^0) + o_p(1).$$

By the Slutsky Theorem and the asymptotic property of $\hat{\mu}_\ell^{HT}$, we obtain

$$\sqrt{n_\ell}\left(\hat{\mu}_\ell^{RI} - \mu_\ell^0\right) \xrightarrow{\mathcal{L}} N\left(0, \sigma_\ell^2\right) \quad as \quad n_\ell \to \infty, \text{ for } \ell = E, R, P,$$

where σ_ℓ^2 is defined in the proof of the asymptotic properties of $\hat{\mu}_\ell^{HT}$.

Now, we prove the asymptotic properties of the estimator $\hat{\mu}_\ell^{AI}$. By the definition of the $\hat{\mu}_\ell^{AI}$, we obtain

$$\begin{aligned}
\sqrt{n_\ell}(\hat{\mu}_\ell^{AI} - \mu_\ell^0) &= n_\ell^{-1/2}\sum_{i=1}^{n_\ell}\left\{\frac{D_{\ell i}Y_{\ell i}}{\pi_{\ell i}(\eta_\ell; \mathbf{Z}_{\ell i}, Y_{\ell i})} + \left(1 - \frac{D_{\ell i}}{\pi_{\ell i}(\eta_\ell; \mathbf{Z}_{\ell i}, Y_{\ell i})}\right)\hat{m}_{\ell i}^0(\gamma_\ell; \mathbf{Z}_{\ell i}) - \mu_\ell^0\right\} \\
&= n_\ell^{-1/2}\sum_{i=1}^{n_\ell}\frac{D_{\ell i}}{\pi_{\ell i}(\eta_\ell; \mathbf{Z}_{\ell i}, Y_{\ell i})}\left\{Y_{\ell i} - m_{\ell i}^0(\gamma_\ell; \mathbf{Z}_{\ell i})\right\} + n_\ell^{-1/2}\sum_{i=1}^{n_\ell}\left\{m_{\ell i}^0(\gamma_\ell; \mathbf{Z}_{\ell i}) - \mu_\ell^0\right\} \\
&+ n_\ell^{-1/2}\sum_{i=1}^{n_\ell}\left(1 - \frac{D_{\ell i}}{\pi_{\ell i}(\eta_\ell; \mathbf{Z}_{\ell i}, Y_{\ell i})}\right)\left\{\hat{m}_{\ell i}^0(\gamma_\ell; \mathbf{Z}_{\ell i}) - m_{\ell i}^0(\gamma_\ell; \mathbf{Z}_{\ell i})\right\} \triangleq H_{1n_\ell} + H_{2n_\ell} + A_{n_\ell}.
\end{aligned}$$

Following a similar argument as given in the proof of Theorem 4 in Zhao et al. [49], we have $A_{n_\ell} = o_p(1)$. Combining the above results yields

$$\sqrt{n_\ell}(\hat{\mu}_\ell^{AI} - \mu_\ell^0) = H_{1n_\ell} + H_{2n_\ell} + o_p(1) = \sqrt{n_\ell}(\hat{\mu}_\ell^{HT} - \mu_\ell^0) + o_p(1).$$

Using the same arguments as given in the proof of the asymptotic properties for $\hat{\mu}_\ell^{RI}$, we obtain

$$\sqrt{n_\ell}\left(\hat{\mu}_\ell^{AI} - \mu_\ell^0\right) \xrightarrow{\mathcal{L}} N\left(0, \sigma_\ell^2\right) \quad as \quad n_\ell \to \infty, \text{ for } \ell = E, R, P,$$

where σ_ℓ^2 is defined in the proof of the asymptotic properties of $\hat{\mu}_\ell^{HT}$. □

Proof of Theorem 2. We first consider the asymptotic properties of $\hat{\mu}_\ell^{SHT}$ based on the following form:

$$\sqrt{n_\ell}(\hat{\mu}_\ell^{SHT} - \mu_\ell^0) = n_\ell^{-1/2}\sum_{i=1}^{n_\ell}\Big\{\frac{D_{\ell i}Y_{\ell i}}{\pi_{\ell i}(\hat{\boldsymbol{\eta}}_\ell; \mathbf{Z}_{\ell i}, Y_{\ell i})} - \mu_\ell^0\Big\}.$$

Taking the Taylor expansion of $\pi_{\ell i}(\hat{\boldsymbol{\eta}}_\ell; \mathbf{Z}_{\ell i}, Y_{\ell i})$ at $\boldsymbol{\eta}_\ell$ yields

$$\begin{aligned} n_\ell^{-1/2}\sum_{i=1}^{n_\ell}\frac{D_{\ell i}Y_{\ell i}}{\pi_{\ell i}(\hat{\boldsymbol{\eta}}_\ell; \mathbf{Z}_{\ell i}, Y_{\ell i})} &= n_\ell^{-1/2}\sum_{i=1}^{n_\ell}\frac{D_{\ell i}Y_{\ell i}}{\pi_{\ell i}(\boldsymbol{\eta}_\ell; \mathbf{Z}_{\ell i}, Y_{\ell i})} \\ &+ n_\ell^{1/2}(\hat{\boldsymbol{\eta}}_\ell - \boldsymbol{\eta}_\ell)^\top \frac{1}{n_\ell}\sum_{i=1}^{n_\ell} D_{\ell i}Y_{\ell i}\frac{\partial}{\partial \boldsymbol{\eta}_\ell}\pi_{\ell i}^{-1}(\boldsymbol{\eta}_\ell; \mathbf{Z}_{\ell i}, Y_{\ell i})\big|_{\boldsymbol{\eta}_\ell = \tilde{\boldsymbol{\eta}}_\ell} + o_p(1) \end{aligned}$$

where $\tilde{\boldsymbol{\eta}}_\ell$ lies in the line segment between $\hat{\boldsymbol{\eta}}_\ell$ and $\boldsymbol{\eta}_\ell$, $\partial\pi_{\ell i}^{-1}(\boldsymbol{\eta}_\ell; \mathbf{Z}_{\ell i}, Y_{\ell i})/\partial\boldsymbol{\eta}_\ell\big|_{\boldsymbol{\eta}_\ell = \tilde{\boldsymbol{\eta}}_\ell} = \{1 - \pi_{\ell i}^{-1}(\boldsymbol{\eta}_\ell; \mathbf{Z}_{\ell i}, Y_{\ell i})\}(1, \mathbf{Z}_{\ell i}^\top, Y_{\ell i})^\top$. Following the arguments of the proof of Theorem 1, we get

$$\begin{aligned} n_\ell^{-1/2}\sum_{i=1}^{n_\ell}\Big\{\frac{D_{\ell i}Y_{\ell i}}{\pi_{\ell i}(\boldsymbol{\eta}_\ell; \mathbf{Z}_{\ell i}, Y_{\ell i})} - \mu_\ell^0\Big\} &= n_\ell^{-1/2}\sum_{i=1}^{n_\ell}\frac{D_{\ell i}\{Y_{\ell i} - m_{\ell i}^0(\gamma_\ell; \mathbf{Z}_{\ell i})\}}{\pi_{\ell i}(\boldsymbol{\eta}_\ell; \mathbf{Z}_{\ell i}, Y_{\ell i})} \\ &\quad + n_\ell^{-1/2}\sum_{i=1}^{n_\ell}\{m_{\ell i}^0(\gamma_\ell; \mathbf{Z}_{\ell i}) - \mu_\ell^0\} + o_p(1). \end{aligned}$$

Combining the above results yields

$$\begin{aligned} \sqrt{n_\ell}(\hat{\mu}_\ell^{SHT} - \mu_\ell^0) =& n_\ell^{-1/2}\sum_{i=1}^{n_\ell}\frac{D_{\ell i}\{Y_{\ell i} - m_{\ell i}^0(\gamma_\ell; \mathbf{Z}_{\ell i})\}}{\pi_{\ell i}(\boldsymbol{\eta}_\ell; \mathbf{Z}_{\ell i}, Y_{\ell i})} + n_\ell^{-1/2}\sum_{i=1}^{n_\ell}\{m_{\ell i}^0(\gamma_\ell; \mathbf{Z}_{\ell i}) - \mu_\ell^0\} \\ &+ n_\ell^{1/2}(\hat{\boldsymbol{\eta}}_\ell - \boldsymbol{\eta}_\ell)^\top\frac{1}{n_\ell}\sum_{i=1}^{n_\ell} D_{\ell i}Y_{\ell i}\Big(1 - \frac{1}{\pi_{\ell i}(\tilde{\boldsymbol{\eta}}_\ell; \mathbf{Z}_{\ell i}, Y_{\ell i})}\Big)(1, \mathbf{Z}_{\ell i}^\top, Y_{\ell i})^\top + o_p(1) \\ =& n_\ell^{-1/2}\sum_{i=1}^{n_\ell}\left\{\frac{D_{\ell i}\{Y_{\ell i} - m_{\ell i}^0(\gamma_\ell; \mathbf{Z}_{\ell i})\}}{\pi_{\ell i}(\boldsymbol{\eta}_\ell; \mathbf{Z}_{\ell i}, Y_{\ell i})} + \Big\{m_{\ell i}^0(\gamma_\ell; \mathbf{Z}_{\ell i}) - \mu_\ell^0\Big\}\right\} \\ &+ n_\ell^{1/2}(\hat{\boldsymbol{\eta}}_\ell - \boldsymbol{\eta}_\ell)^\top H_{\ell,SHT} + o_p(1) \\ =& n_\ell^{-1/2}\sum_{i=1}^{n_\ell} e_{\ell,SHTi} + o_p(1), \end{aligned}$$

where

$$e_{\ell,SHTi} = \{D_{\ell i}\pi_{\ell i}^{-1}(\boldsymbol{\eta}_\ell; \mathbf{Z}_{\ell i}, Y_{\ell i})\{Y_{\ell i} - m_{\ell i}^0(\gamma_\ell; \mathbf{Z}_{\ell i})\} + m_{\ell i}^0(\gamma_\ell; \mathbf{Z}_{\ell i}) - \mu_\ell^0 + \mathcal{I}_{22\ell}^{-1}s_{\ell i}(\boldsymbol{\eta}_\ell)H_{\ell,SHT}\},$$

$s_{\ell i}(\boldsymbol{\eta}_\ell)$ is the ith term in Equation (11), $H_{\ell,SHT} = E[\{\pi_\ell(\boldsymbol{\eta}_\ell; \mathbf{Z}_\ell, Y_\ell) - 1\}Y_\ell(1, \mathbf{Z}_\ell^\top, Y_\ell)^\top]$. By the Slutsky Theorem and the asymptotic property of $\hat{\mu}_\ell^{HT}$, it is easily shown that

$$\sqrt{n_\ell}\left(\hat{\mu}_\ell^{SHT} - \mu_\ell^0\right) \xrightarrow{\mathcal{L}} N\left(0, \sigma_{\ell,SHT}^2\right) \quad as \quad n_\ell \to \infty, \text{ for } \ell = E, R, P,$$

where $\sigma_{\ell,SHT}^2 = \mathrm{Var}(e_{\ell,SHTi})$.

Now, we show the asymptotic property of $\hat{\mu}_\ell^{SRI}$ for unknown $\boldsymbol{\eta}_\ell$. By the definition of $\hat{\mu}_\ell^{SRI}$, we have the following form:

$$\sqrt{n_\ell}(\hat{\mu}_\ell^{SRI} - \mu_\ell^0) = n_\ell^{-1/2}\sum_{i=1}^{n_\ell}\Big\{D_{\ell i}Y_{\ell i} + (1 - D_{\ell i})\hat{m}_{\ell i}^0(\hat{\gamma}_\ell; \mathbf{Z}_{\ell i}) - \mu_\ell^0\Big\}.$$

Taking the Taylor expansion of $\hat{m}_{\ell i}^0(\hat{\gamma}_\ell; \mathbf{Z}_{\ell i})$ at $\boldsymbol{\eta}_\ell$ yields

$$\sum_{i=1}^{n_\ell}(1-D_{\ell i})\hat{m}^0_{\ell i}(\hat{\gamma}_\ell;\mathbf{Z}_{\ell i}) = \sum_{i=1}^{n_\ell}(1-D_{\ell i})\hat{m}^0_{\ell i}(\gamma_\ell;\mathbf{Z}_{\ell i}) + n_\ell^{1/2}(\hat{\boldsymbol{\eta}}_\ell-\boldsymbol{\eta}_\ell)^\top\frac{1}{n_\ell}\sum_{i=1}^{n_\ell}(1-D_{\ell i})\frac{\partial}{\partial\boldsymbol{\eta}_\ell}m^0_{\ell i}(\gamma_\ell;\mathbf{Z}_{\ell i})\Big|_{\boldsymbol{\eta}_\ell=\tilde{\boldsymbol{\eta}}_\ell}+o_p(1).$$

Using the conclusion given in the proof of Theorem 1, we can easily get $\sqrt{n_\ell}(\hat{\mu}_\ell^{RI}-\mu_\ell^0)=\sqrt{n_\ell}(\hat{\mu}_\ell^{HT}-\mu_\ell^0)+o_p(1)$. Combining the above results yields

$$\begin{aligned}\sqrt{n_\ell}(\hat{\mu}_\ell^{SRI}-\mu_\ell^0) =& n_\ell^{-1/2}\sum_{i=1}^{n_\ell}\Big\{D_{\ell i}Y_{\ell i}+(1-D_{\ell i})\hat{m}^0_{\ell i}(\gamma_\ell;\mathbf{Z}_{\ell i})-\mu_\ell^0\Big\}\\ &+n_\ell^{1/2}(\hat{\boldsymbol{\eta}}_\ell-\boldsymbol{\eta}_\ell)^\top\frac{1}{n_\ell}\sum_{i=1}^{n_\ell}(1-D_{\ell i})Y_{\ell i}\frac{\partial}{\partial\boldsymbol{\eta}_\ell}\hat{m}^0_{\ell i}(\gamma_\ell;\mathbf{Z}_{\ell i})\Big|_{\boldsymbol{\eta}_\ell=\tilde{\boldsymbol{\eta}}_\ell}\\ =& n_\ell^{-1/2}\sum_{i=1}^{n_\ell}\frac{D_{\ell i}\{Y_{\ell i}-m^0_{\ell i}(\gamma_\ell;\mathbf{Z}_{\ell i})\}}{\pi_{\ell i}(\boldsymbol{\eta}_\ell;\mathbf{Z}_{\ell i},Y_{\ell i})}+n_\ell^{-1/2}\sum_{i=1}^{n_\ell}\Big\{m^0_{\ell i}(\gamma_\ell;\mathbf{Z}_{\ell i})-\mu_\ell^0\Big\}\\ &+n_\ell^{1/2}(\hat{\boldsymbol{\eta}}_\ell-\boldsymbol{\eta}_\ell)^\top\mathcal{I}_{22\ell}^{-1}s_{\ell i}(\boldsymbol{\eta}_\ell)H_{\ell,SRI}+o_p(1)\\ =& n_\ell^{-1/2}\sum_{i=1}^{n_\ell}e_{\ell,SRIi}+o_p(1),\end{aligned}$$

where $\tilde{\boldsymbol{\eta}}_\ell$ lies in the line segment between $\hat{\boldsymbol{\eta}}_\ell$ and $\boldsymbol{\eta}_\ell$, $e_{\ell,SRIi}=D_{\ell i}\pi_{\ell i}^{-1}(\boldsymbol{\eta}_\ell;\mathbf{Z}_{\ell i},Y_{\ell i})\{Y_{\ell i}-m^0_{\ell i}(\gamma_\ell;\mathbf{Z}_{\ell i})\}+m^0_{\ell i}(\gamma_\ell;\mathbf{Z}_{\ell i})-\mu_\ell^0+\mathcal{I}_{22\ell}^{-1}s_{\ell i}(\boldsymbol{\eta}_\ell)H_{\ell,SRI}$, $H_{\ell,SRI}=E\{(1-D_{\ell i})(0,\mathbf{0}_{p_\ell-1}^\top,(Y_{\ell i}-m^0_{\ell i}(\gamma_\ell;\mathbf{Z}_{\ell i}))^2)^\top\}$ and $\mathbf{0}_{p_\ell-1}$ is a $(p_\ell-1)\times 1$ zero vector and p_ℓ is the dimension of covariate $\mathbf{Z}_{\ell i}$. By the Slutsky Theorem and the asymptotic property of $\hat{\mu}_\ell^{SHT}$, it is easily shown that

$$\sqrt{n_\ell}\Big(\hat{\mu}_\ell^{SRI}-\mu_\ell^0\Big)\xrightarrow{\mathcal{L}}N\Big(0,\sigma^2_{\ell,SRI}\Big)\quad as\quad n_\ell\to\infty,\quad \text{for } \ell=E,R,P,$$

where $\sigma^2_{\ell,SRI}=\mathrm{Var}(e_{\ell,SRIi})$.

Now, we prove the asymptotic properties of $\hat{\mu}_\ell^{SAI}$ for unknown $\boldsymbol{\eta}_\ell$. Combining the above results and taking the Taylor expansion of $\hat{\mu}_\ell^{SAI}$ at $\boldsymbol{\eta}_\ell$, we obtain

$$\begin{aligned}\sqrt{n_\ell}(\hat{\mu}_\ell^{SAI}-\mu_\ell^0) =& n_\ell^{-1/2}\sum_{i=1}^{n_\ell}\Big\{\frac{D_{\ell i}Y_{\ell i}}{\pi_{\ell i}(\boldsymbol{\eta}_\ell;\mathbf{Z}_{\ell i},Y_{\ell i})}+\Big(1-\frac{D_{\ell i}}{\pi_{\ell i}(\boldsymbol{\eta}_\ell;\mathbf{Z}_{\ell i},Y_{\ell i})}\Big)\hat{m}^0_{\ell i}(\gamma_\ell;\mathbf{Z}_{\ell i})-\mu_\ell^0\Big\}\\ &+n_\ell^{1/2}(\hat{\boldsymbol{\eta}}_\ell-\boldsymbol{\eta}_\ell)^\top\frac{1}{n_\ell}\sum_{i=1}^{n_\ell}D_{\ell i}Y_{\ell i}\frac{\partial}{\partial\boldsymbol{\eta}_\ell}\pi_{\ell i}^{-1}(\boldsymbol{\eta}_\ell;\mathbf{Z}_{\ell i},Y_{\ell i})|_{\boldsymbol{\eta}_\ell=\tilde{\boldsymbol{\eta}}_\ell}\\ &+n_\ell^{1/2}(\hat{\boldsymbol{\eta}}_\ell-\boldsymbol{\eta}_\ell)^\top\frac{1}{n_\ell}\sum_{i=1}^{n_\ell}\hat{m}^0_{\ell i}(\gamma_\ell;\mathbf{Z}_{\ell i})\frac{\partial}{\partial\boldsymbol{\eta}_\ell}\Big(1-\frac{D_{\ell i}}{\pi_{\ell i}(\boldsymbol{\eta}_\ell;\mathbf{Z}_{\ell i},Y_{\ell i})}\Big)\Big|_{\boldsymbol{\eta}_\ell=\tilde{\boldsymbol{\eta}}_\ell}\\ &+n_\ell^{1/2}(\hat{\boldsymbol{\eta}}_\ell-\boldsymbol{\eta}_\ell)^\top\frac{1}{n_\ell}\sum_{i=1}^{n_\ell}\Big(1-\frac{D_{\ell i}}{\pi_{\ell i}(\boldsymbol{\eta}_\ell;\mathbf{Z}_{\ell i},Y_{\ell i})}\Big)\frac{\partial}{\partial\boldsymbol{\eta}_\ell}\hat{m}^0_{\ell i}(\gamma_\ell;\mathbf{Z}_{\ell i})\Big|_{\boldsymbol{\eta}_\ell=\tilde{\boldsymbol{\eta}}_\ell}\end{aligned}$$

where $\tilde{\boldsymbol{\eta}}_\ell$ lies in the line segment between $\hat{\boldsymbol{\eta}}_\ell$ and $\boldsymbol{\eta}_\ell$. Using the conclusion given in the proof of Theorem 1, we have

$$\sqrt{n_\ell}(\hat{\mu}_\ell^{AI}-\mu_\ell^0)=\sqrt{n_\ell}(\hat{\mu}_\ell^{HT}-\mu_\ell^0)+o_p(1),$$

$$\frac{1}{n_\ell}\sum_{i=1}^{n_\ell}\Big(1-\frac{D_{\ell i}}{\pi_{\ell i}(\boldsymbol{\eta}_\ell;\mathbf{Z}_{\ell i},Y_{\ell i})}\Big)\frac{\partial}{\partial\boldsymbol{\eta}_\ell}\hat{m}^0_{\ell i}(\gamma_\ell;\mathbf{Z}_{\ell i})|_{\boldsymbol{\eta}_\ell=\tilde{\boldsymbol{\eta}}_\ell}=o_p(1),$$

$$\frac{1}{n_\ell}\sum_{i=1}^{n_\ell}\hat{m}^0_{\ell i}(\gamma_\ell;\mathbf{Z}_{\ell i})\frac{\partial}{\partial\boldsymbol{\eta}_\ell}\Big(1-\frac{D_{\ell i}}{\pi_{\ell i}(\boldsymbol{\eta}_\ell;\mathbf{Z}_{\ell i},Y_{\ell i})}\Big)|_{\boldsymbol{\eta}_\ell=\tilde{\boldsymbol{\eta}}_\ell}=M_{\ell SAI}+o_p(1),$$

where $M_{\ell,SAI} = E\{(1-\pi_{\ell i}(\boldsymbol{\eta}_\ell;\mathbf{Z}_{\ell i},Y_{\ell i}))m^0_{\ell i}(\gamma_\ell;\mathbf{Z}_{\ell i})(1,\mathbf{Z}^\top_{\ell i},Y_{\ell i})^\top\}$. Combining the above results leads to

$$\begin{aligned}\sqrt{n_\ell}(\hat{\mu}^{SAI}_\ell-\mu^0_\ell) =& n_\ell^{-1/2}\sum_{i=1}^{n_\ell}\left[\frac{D_{\ell i}\{Y_{\ell i}-m^0_{\ell i}(\gamma_\ell;\mathbf{Z}_{\ell i})\}}{\pi_{\ell i}(\boldsymbol{\eta}_\ell;\mathbf{Z}_{\ell i},Y_{\ell i})}+\left\{m^0_{\ell i}(\gamma_\ell;\mathbf{Z}_{\ell i})-\mu^0_\ell\right\}\right] \\ &+n_\ell^{1/2}(\hat{\boldsymbol{\eta}}_\ell-\boldsymbol{\eta}_\ell)^\top\mathcal{I}^{-1}_{22\ell}s_{\ell i}(\boldsymbol{\eta}_\ell)(H_{\ell,SHT}+M_{\ell,SAI})+o_p(1) \\ =& n_\ell^{-1/2}\sum_{i=1}^{n_\ell}e_{\ell,SAIi}+o_p(1),\end{aligned}$$

where $e_{\ell,SAIi} = D_{\ell i}\pi^{-1}_{\ell i}(\boldsymbol{\eta}_\ell;\mathbf{Z}_{\ell i},Y_{\ell i})\{Y_{\ell i}-m^0_{\ell i}(\gamma_\ell;\mathbf{Z}_{\ell i})\}+m^0_{\ell i}(\gamma_\ell;\mathbf{Z}_{\ell i})-\mu^0_\ell+\mathcal{I}^{-1}_{22\ell}s_{\ell i}(\boldsymbol{\eta}_\ell)$ $H_{\ell,SRI}$, $H_{\ell,SAI} = H_{\ell,SHT}+M_{\ell,SAI}$. By the Slutsky Theorem and the asymptotic property of $\hat{\mu}^{SHT}_\ell$, it is easily shown that

$$\sqrt{n_\ell}\left(\hat{\mu}^{SRI}_\ell-\mu^0_\ell\right)\xrightarrow{\mathcal{L}}N\left(0,\sigma^2_{\ell,SAI}\right)\quad as\quad n_\ell\to\infty,\ \text{ for } \ell=E,R,P,$$

where $\sigma^2_{\ell,SRI} = \mathrm{Var}(e_{\ell,SAIi})$. □

Appendix A.2. Tables: Empirical Type I Error Rates for Scenarios (B) and (C) with Balanced and Unbalanced Designs

Table A1. Empirical Type I error rates for Scenarios (B) and (C) with balanced designs.

		n = 50				n = 100				n = 150			
Scenario	**Case**	**SHT**	**SRI**	**SAI**	**CC**	**SHT**	**SRI**	**SAI**	**CC**	**SHT**	**SRI**	**SAI**	**CC**
(B)	E1	0.041	0.055	0.055	0.068	0.042	0.053	0.059	0.082	0.048	0.058	0.062	0.090
	E2	0.046	0.049	0.050	0.052	0.045	0.051	0.052	0.060	0.042	0.054	0.054	0.066
	E3	0.045	0.045	0.044	0.051	0.037	0.053	0.054	0.060	0.046	0.056	0.058	0.060
	E4	0.050	0.048	0.047	0.052	0.032	0.055	0.058	0.060	0.046	0.052	0.054	0.056
(C)	E1	0.040	0.065	0.064	0.081	0.031	0.052	0.056	0.082	0.046	0.062	0.064	0.082
	E2	0.030	0.052	0.043	0.057	0.046	0.053	0.052	0.063	0.044	0.050	0.056	0.068
	E3	0.034	0.058	0.055	0.060	0.034	0.050	0.053	0.060	0.036	0.048	0.054	0.060
	E4	0.031	0.044	0.043	0.042	0.041	0.052	0.056	0.082	0.048	0.054	0.054	0.075

Note: SHT, SRI, SAI and CC denote Wald-type test approaches based on IPW, regression imputation, AIPW and CC, respectively.

Table A2. Empirical Type I error rates for Scenarios (B) and (C) with unbalanced designs.

			N = 200				N = 300				N = 400			
Scen.	n_E:n_R:n_P	**Case**	**SHT**	**SRI**	**SAI**	**CC**	**SHT**	**SRI**	**SAI**	**CC**	**SHT**	**SRI**	**SAI**	**CC**
(B)	2:1:1	E1	0.035	0.058	0.058	0.068	0.034	0.053	0.059	0.082	0.036	0.062	0.060	0.078
		E2	0.042	0.052	0.046	0.062	0.042	0.053	0.050	0.064	0.046	0.052	0.050	0.070
		E3	0.041	0.066	0.061	0.056	0.038	0.062	0.058	0.042	0.034	0.051	0.049	0.048
		E4	0.033	0.054	0.051	0.050	0.037	0.056	0.051	0.049	0.046	0.052	0.051	0.068
	2:2:1	E1	0.026	0.052	0.050	0.079	0.049	0.068	0.066	0.083	0.030	0.040	0.042	0.080
		E2	0.031	0.051	0.049	0.037	0.041	0.059	0.057	0.047	0.046	0.058	0.056	0.062
		E3	0.026	0.046	0.045	0.040	0.040	0.058	0.052	0.048	0.049	0.056	0.052	0.060
		E4	0.029	0.044	0.042	0.042	0.031	0.046	0.045	0.035	0.030	0.044	0.038	0.044
	3:2:1	E1	0.041	0.060	0.063	0.072	0.037	0.050	0.046	0.069	0.040	0.046	0.046	0.078
		E2	0.032	0.055	0.057	0.054	0.035	0.046	0.043	0.049	0.034	0.044	0.042	0.042
		E3	0.032	0.051	0.045	0.055	0.038	0.056	0.052	0.050	0.032	0.049	0.045	0.046
		E4	0.033	0.047	0.053	0.050	0.032	0.059	0.057	0.052	0.038	0.050	0.048	0.038

Table A2. *Cont.*

			N = 200				N = 300				N = 400			
Scen.	n_E:n_R:n_P	Case	SHT	SRI	SAI	CC	SHT	SRI	SAI	CC	SHT	SRI	SAI	CC
(C)	2:1:1	E1	0.033	0.067	0.064	0.077	0.029	0.054	0.050	0.069	0.032	0.062	0.054	0.082
		E2	0.043	0.059	0.056	0.051	0.048	0.047	0.047	0.066	0.050	0.058	0.052	0.064
		E3	0.027	0.050	0.049	0.050	0.042	0.062	0.060	0.042	0.028	0.050	0.051	0.059
		E4	0.028	0.051	0.051	0.043	0.026	0.044	0.042	0.042	0.026	0.046	0.045	0.050
	2:2:1	E1	0.021	0.049	0.047	0.081	0.044	0.068	0.067	0.082	0.030	0.042	0.044	0.090
		E2	0.026	0.047	0.043	0.037	0.039	0.058	0.056	0.060	0.024	0.040	0.042	0.054
		E3	0.026	0.046	0.045	0.040	0.058	0.052	0.048	0.049	0.049	0.056	0.052	0.060
		E4	0.029	0.044	0.042	0.042	0.031	0.046	0.045	0.035	0.030	0.044	0.038	0.044
	3:2:1	E1	0.039	0.069	0.069	0.082	0.036	0.051	0.048	0.074	0.034	0.046	0.044	0.082
		E2	0.039	0.058	0.055	0.065	0.037	0.045	0.047	0.052	0.034	0.044	0.042	0.042
		E3	0.031	0.051	0.050	0.046	0.030	0.056	0.054	0.050	0.029	0.050	0.047	0.050
		E4	0.029	0.050	0.052	0.048	0.036	0.058	0.060	0.058	0.031	0.044	0.044	0.045

Note: SHT, SRI, SAI and CC denote Wald-type test approaches based on IPW, terline regression imputation, AIPW and CC, respectively.

Appendix A.3. Figures: Powers for Scenario (A) with a, n, Treatment Effects, Parameters α and γ

Figure A1 presents empirical powers against $a = (\mu_E - \mu_P)/(\mu_R - \mu_P)$ for missingness data mechanism models E1–E4 under the balanced designs, with n = 50, 100 and 150. Figure A2 presents empirical powers against $a = (\mu_E - \mu_P)/(\mu_R - \mu_P)$ for missingness data mechanism models E1–E4 under the unbalanced designs with n_E:n_R:n_P = 2:1:1.

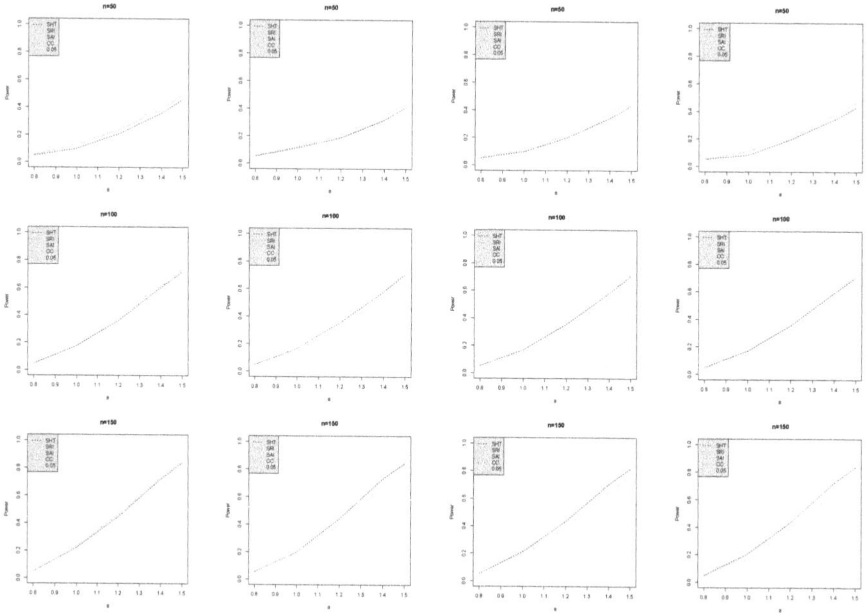

Figure A1. SHT, SRI, SAI and CC represent empirical powers evaluated from IPW, regression imputation, AIPW and CC methods against a for missingness data mechanism model E1 (left panel), E2 (left second panel), E3 (right second panel) and E4 (right panel) for n = 50 (the first row), 100 (middle row) and 150 (the last row) under the balanced designs.

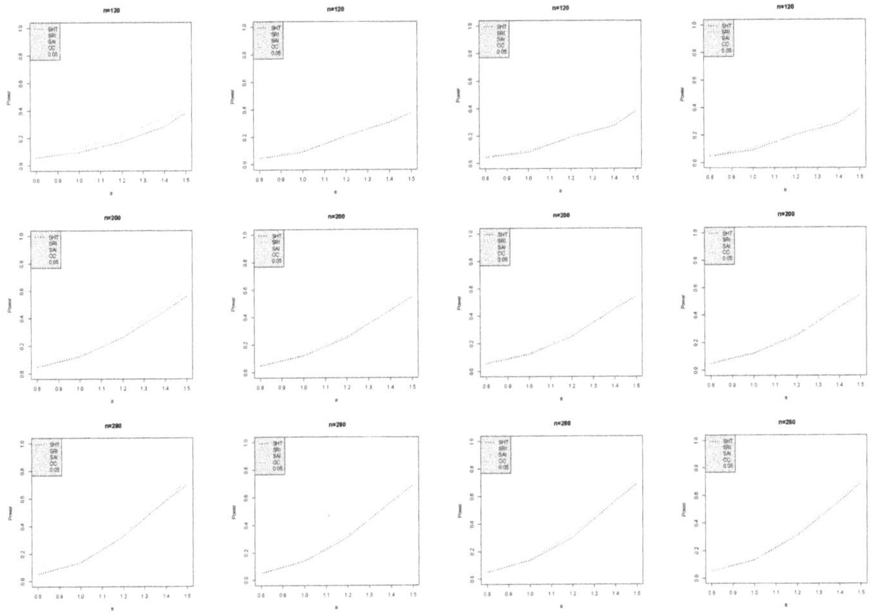

Figure A2. SHT, SRI, SAI and CC represent empirical powers evaluated from IPW, regression imputation, AIPW and CC methods against a for missingness data mechanism models E1 (left panel), E2 (left second panel), E3 (right second panel) and E4 (right panel) for N = 120 (the first row), 200 (middle row) and 280 (the last row) under the unbalanced designs with n_E:n_R:n_P = 2:1:1.

Figure A3 presents empirical powers against the sample size n for missingness data mechanism models E1–E4 under balanced design for $a = 0.4$ and 0.6. Figure A4 presents empirical powers against the sample size n for missingness data mechanism models E1–E4 under unbalanced design with n_E:n_R:n_P = 2:1:1.

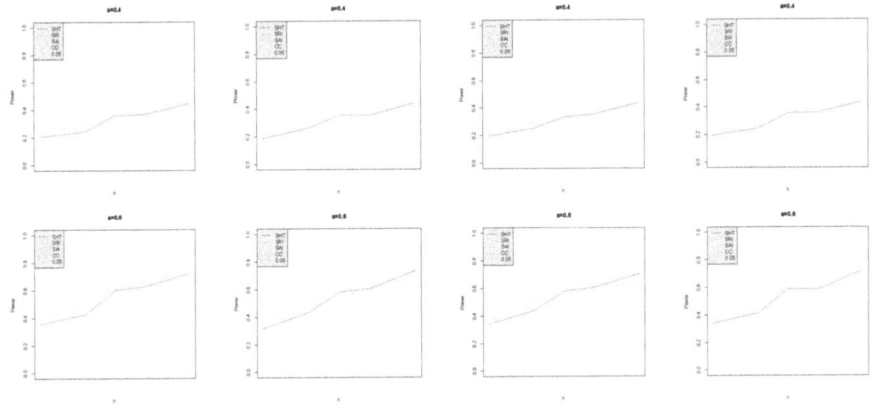

Figure A3. SHT, SRI, SAI and CC represent empirical powers evaluated from IPW, regression imputation, AIPW and CC methods against the sample size n for missingness data mechanism models E1 (left panel), E2 (left second panel), E3 (right second panel) and E4 (right panel) for $a = 0.4$ (upper row) and 0.6 (lower row) under balanced design.

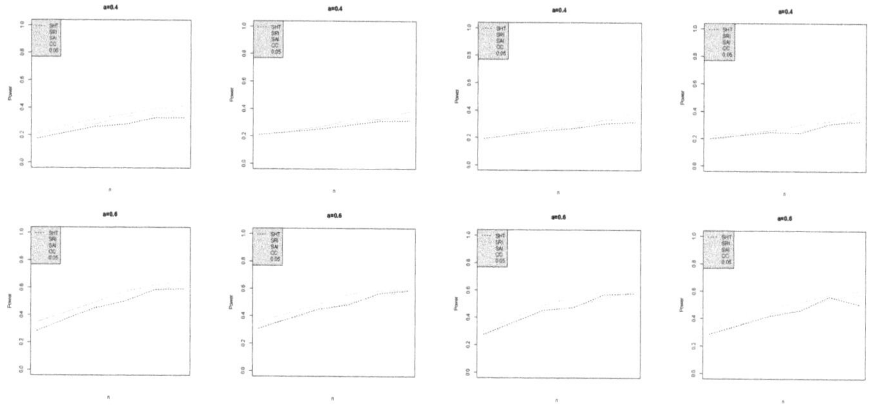

Figure A4. SHT, SRI, SAI and CC represent empirical powers evaluated from IPW, regression imputation, AIPW and CC methods against the sample size n for missingness data mechanism models E1 (left panel), E2 (left second panel), E3 (right second panel) and E4 (right panel) for $a = 0.4$ (upper row) and 0.6 (lower row) under unbalanced design (n_E:n_R:n_P = 2:1:1).

Figure A5 presents empirical powers against treatment effect α_{E1} for four missingness data mechanism models E1–E4 under balanced design. Figure A6 presents empirical powers against treatment effects α_{E1} for four missingness data mechanism models E1–E4 under unbalanced design with n_E:n_R:n_P = 2:1:1.

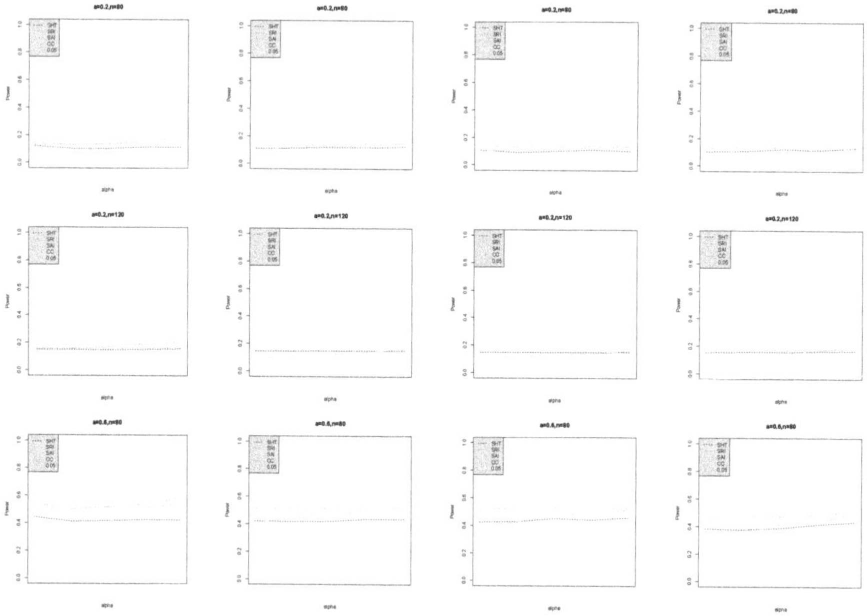

Figure A5. *Cont.*

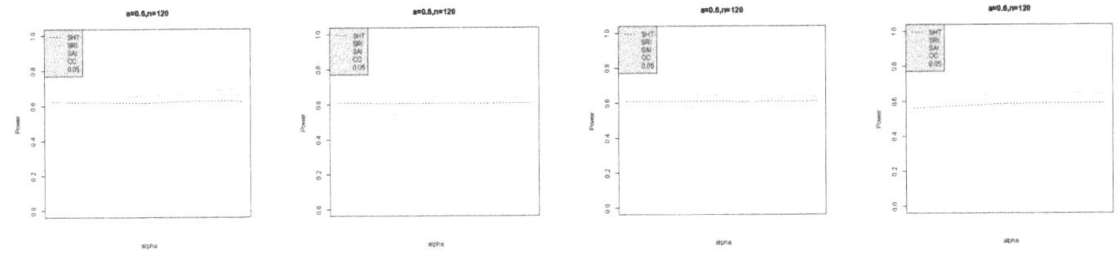

Figure A5. SHT, SRI, SAI and CC represent empirical powers evaluated from IPW, regression imputation, AIPW and CC methods against treatment effect α_{E1} for missingness data mechanism models E1 (left panel), E2 (left second panel), E3 (right second panel) and E4 (right panel) for (a, n) = (0.2,80) (the first row), (0.2,120) (the second row), (0.6,80) (the third row) and (0.6,120) (the last row) under the balanced designs.

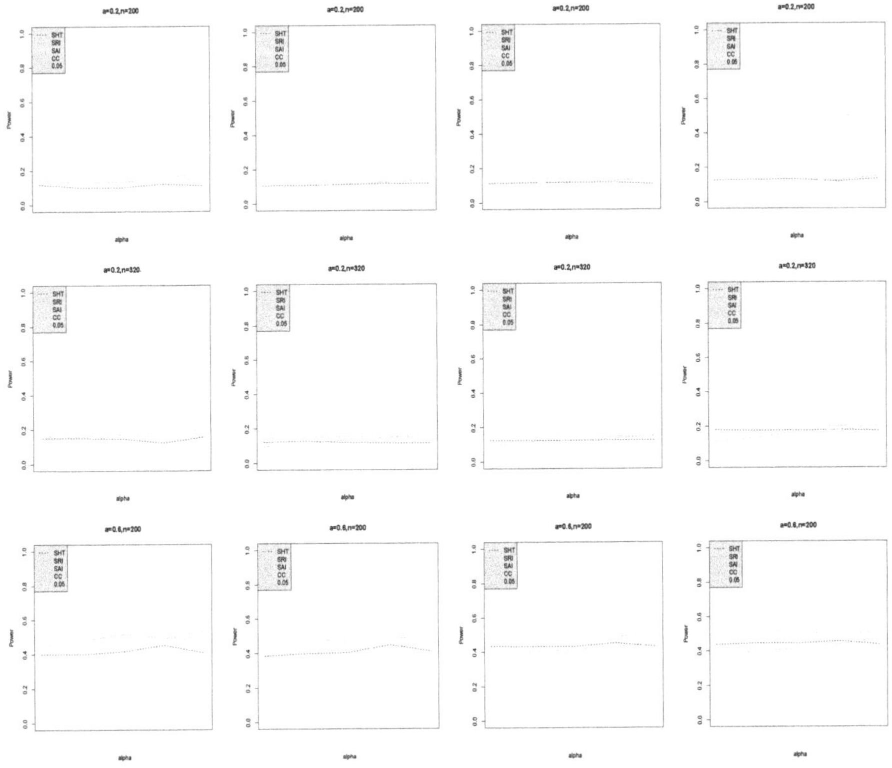

Figure A6. *Cont.*

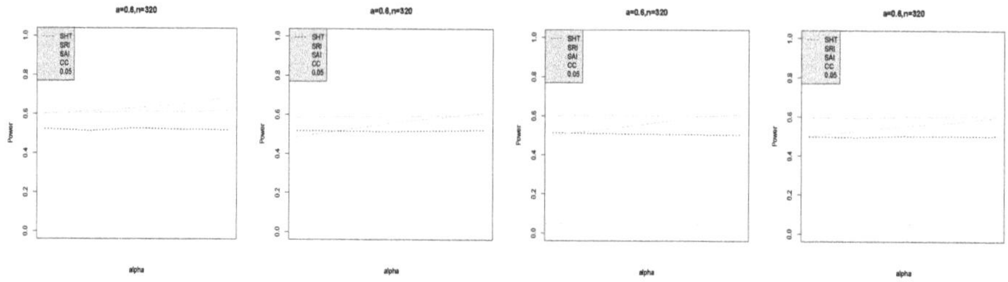

Figure A6. SHT, SRI, SAI and CC represent empirical powers evaluated from IPW, regression imputation, AIPW and CC methods against treatment effect α_{E1} for missingness data mechanism models E1 (left panel), E2 (left second panel), E3 (right second panel) and E4 (right panel) for (a, n) = (0.2,200) (the first row), (0.2,320) (the second row), (0.6,200) (the third row), and (0.6,320) (the last row) under the unbalanced designs with n_E:n_R:n_P = 2:1:1.

Figure A7 presents empirical powers against the tilting parameter γ for three missingness data mechanism models E2–E4 under balanced design. Figure A8 presents empirical powers against the tilting parameter γ for three missingness data mechanism models E2–E4 under unbalanced design with n_E:n_R:n_P = 2:1:1.

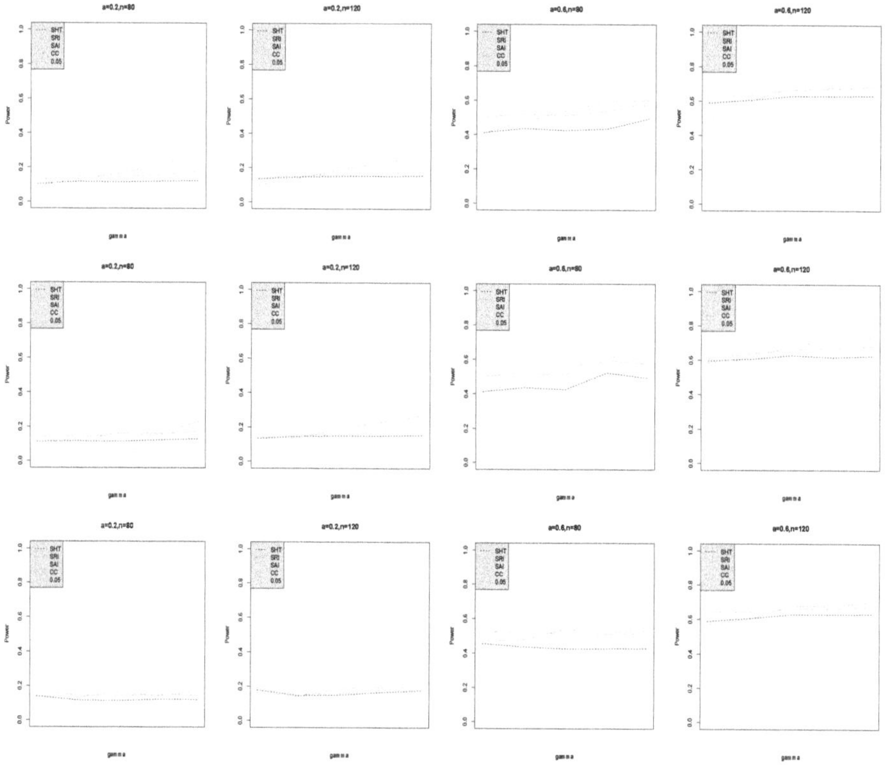

Figure A7. SHT, SRI, SAI and CC represent empirical powers evaluated from IPW, regression imputation, AIPW and CC methods against γ for missingness data mechanism models E2 (the first row), E3 (the middle row) and E4 (the last row) together with (a, n) = (0.2,80), (0.2,120), (0.6,80) and (0.6,120), respectively, under the balanced designs.

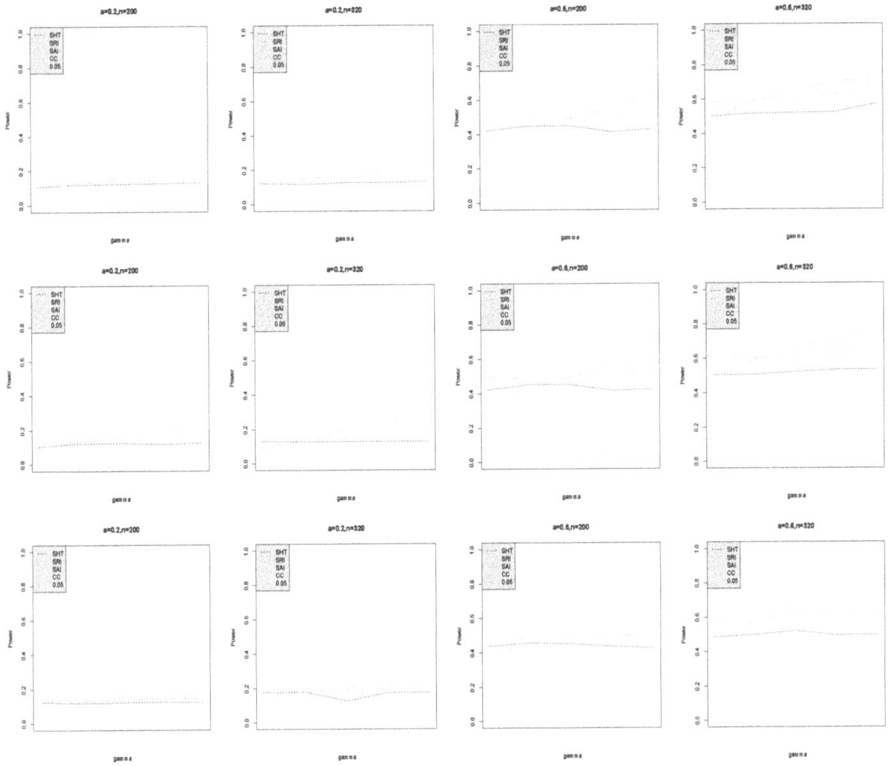

Figure A8. SHT, SRI, SAI and CC represent empirical powers evaluated from IPW, regression imputation, AIPW and CC methods against γ for missingness data mechanism models E2 (the first row), E3 (the middle row) and E4 (the last row) together with (a, n) = (0.2,200), (0.2,320), (0.6,200) and (0.6,320), respectively, under the unbalanced designs with $n_E{:}n_R{:}n_P$ = 2:1:1.

References

1. Rothmann, M.D.; Wiens, B.L.; Chan, I.S.F. *Design and Analysis of Non-Inferiority Trials*; (Chapman & Hall/CRC Biostatistics Series, 43); Chapman & Hall/CRC Press: New York, NY, USA, 2011; pp. 149–166.
2. Tang, M.L.; Tang, N.S.; Chan, I.S.; Chan, B.P. Sample size determination for establishing equivalence/noninferiority via ratio of two proportions in matched-pair design. *Biometrics* **2002**, *58*, 957–963. [CrossRef] [PubMed]
3. Tang, N.S.; Tang, M.L.; Chan, S.F. On tests of equivalence via non-unity relative risk for matached-pair design. *Stat. Med.* **2003**, *22*, 1217–1233. [CrossRef] [PubMed]
4. Tang, N.S.; Tang, M.L.; Chan, S.F. Confidence interval construction for proportion difference in small-sample paired studies. *Stat. Med.* **2010**, *24*, 3565–3579. [CrossRef]
5. Wellek, S. Statistical methods for the analysis of two-arm non-inferiority trials with binary outcomes. *Biom. J.* **2005**, *47*, 48–61. [CrossRef] [PubMed]
6. Freitag, G.; Lange, S.; Munk, A. Non-parametric assessment of non-inferiority with censored data. *Stat. Med.* **2006**, *25*, 1201–1217. [CrossRef] [PubMed]
7. Arboretti, G.R.; Bonnini, S.; Solmi, F. Non-parametric two-stage active control testing method for non-inferiority tests. *Quad. Stat.* **2008**, *10*, 73–98.
8. Pesarin, F.; Salmaso, L.; Carrozzo, E.; Arboretti, R. Union-intersection permutation solution for two-sample equivalence testing. *Stat. Comput.* **2016**, *26*, 693–701. [CrossRef]
9. Gamalo, M.A.; Wu, R.; Tiwari, R.C. Bayesian approach to non-inferiority trials for normal means. *Stat. Methods Med. Res.* **2016**, *25*, 221–240. [CrossRef]
10. Tang, M.L.; Tang, N.S. Tests of noninferiority via rate difference for three-arm clinical trials with placebo. *J. Biopharm. Stat.* **2004**, *14*, 337–347. [CrossRef]

11. Koch, G.G.; Röhmel, J. Hypothesis testing in the gold standard design for proving the efficacy of an experimental treatment relative to placebo and a reference. *J. Biopharm. Stat.* **2004**, *14*, 315–325. [CrossRef]
12. Pigeot, I.; Schafer, J.; Rohmel, J.; Hauschke, D. Assessing non-inferiority of a new treatment in a three-arm clinical trial including a placebo. *Stat. Med.* **2003**, *22*, 883–899. [CrossRef] [PubMed]
13. Mielke, M.; Munk, A. The assessment and planning of non-inferiority trials for retention of effect hypotheses-towards a general approach. *arXiv* **2009**, arXiv:0912.4169.
14. Lui, K.; Chang, K. Notes on testing noninferiority in ordinal data under the parallel groups design. *J. Biopharm. Stat.* **2013**, *3*, 1294–1307. [CrossRef] [PubMed]
15. Brannath, W.; Scharpenberg, M.; Schmidt, S. Single-stage, three-arm, adaptive test strategies for non-inferiority trials with an unstable reference. *Stat. Med.* **2022**, *41*, 5033–5045. [CrossRef]
16. Tang, N.S.; Yu, B.; Tang, M.L. Testing non-inferiority of a new treatment in three-arm clinical trials with binary endpoints. *BMC Med. Res. Methodol.* **2014**, *14*, 134. [CrossRef] [PubMed]
17. Tang, N.S.; Yu, B. Simultaneous confidence interval for assessing non-inferiority with assay sensitivity in a three-arm trial with binary endpoints. *Pharm. Stat.* **2020**, *19*, 518–531. [CrossRef] [PubMed]
18. Tang, N.S.; Yu, B. Bayesian sample size determination in a three-arm non-inferiority trial with binary endpoints. *J. Biopharm. Stat.* **2022**, *32*, 768–788. [CrossRef]
19. Paul, E.; Tiwari, R.C.; Chowdhury, S.; Ghosh, S. A more powerful test for three-arm non-inferiority via risk difference: Frequentist and Bayesian approaches. *J. Appl. Stat.* **2022**, *12*, 1–23. [CrossRef]
20. Homma, G.; Diamon, T. Sample size calculation for "gold-standard" noninferiority trials with fixed margins and negative binomial endpoints. *Stat. Biopharm. Res.* **2021**, *13*, 435–447. [CrossRef]
21. Ghosh, S.; Paul, E.; Chowdhury, S.; Tiwari, R.C. New approaches for testing non-inferiority for three-arm trials with Poisson distributed outcomes. *Biostatistics* **2022**, *23*, 136–156. [CrossRef]
22. Ghosh, S.; Guo, W.; Ghosh, S. A hierarchical testing procedure for three arm non-inferiority trials. *Comput. Stat. Data Anal.* **2022**, *174*, 107521. [CrossRef]
23. Scharpenberg, M.; Brannath, W. Simultaneous confidence intervals for an extended Koch-Röhmel design in three-arm non-inferiority trials. *arXiv* **2022**, arXiv:2210.08931.
24. Tang, N.S.; Liang, F. Confidence intervals for assessing non-inferiority with assay sensitivity in a three-arm trial with normally distributed endpoints. *Mathematics* **2022**, *10*, 167. [CrossRef]
25. Munzel, U. Nonparametric non-inferiority analyses in the three-arm design with active control and placebo. *Stat. Med.* **2009**, *28*, 3643–3656. [CrossRef] [PubMed]
26. Tseng, Y.K.; Hsu, K.N. Study design for a three-arm equivalence clinical trial with binomially distributed outcomes. *J. Biopharm. Stat.* **2021**, *31*, 736–744. [CrossRef] [PubMed]
27. Little, R.J.A.; Rubin, D.B. *Statistical Analysis with Missing Data*, 3rd ed.; (Wiley Series in Probability and Statistics); John Wiley & Sons: Hoboken, NJ, USA, 2020; pp. 45–87.
28. Choi, S.C.; Stablein, D.M. Practical tests for comparing two proportions with incomplete data. *J. R. Stat. Soc. Ser. C* **1982**, *31*, 256–262. [CrossRef]
29. Tang, M.L.; Tang, N.S. Exact tests for comparing two paired proportions with incomplete data. *Biom. J.* **2004**, *14*, 72–82. [CrossRef]
30. Maritz, J.S. A permutation paired test allowing for missing values. *Aust. N. Z. J. Stat.* **1995**, *37*, 153–159. [CrossRef]
31. Yu, D.; Lim, J.; Liang, F.; Kim, K.; Kim, B.S.; Jang, W. Permutation test for incomplete paired data with application to cDNA microarray data. *Comput. Stat. Data Anal.* **2013**, *56*, 510–521. [CrossRef]
32. Pesarin, F. *Multivariate Permutation Tests: With Applications in Biostatistics*; (Wiley Series in Probability and Statistics); John Wiley & Sons: Chichester, UK, 2001; pp. 279–303.
33. Pesarin, F.; Celant, G.; Salmaso, L. Two sample permutation tests for repeated measures with missing values. *J. Appl. Stat. Sci.* **2000**, *9*, 291–304.
34. Robins, J.; Rotnitzky, A.; Zhao, L.P. Estimation of regression coefficients when some regressors are not always observed. *J. Am. Stat. Assoc.* **1994**, *89*, 846–866. [CrossRef]
35. Lee, S.Y.; Tang, N.S. Bayesian analysis of nonlinear structural equation models with nonignorable missing data. *Psychometrika* **2006**, *71*, 541–564. [CrossRef]
36. Wang, Z.Q.; Tang, N.S. Bayesian quantile regression with mixed discrete and nonignorable missing covariates. *Bayesian Anal.* **2020**, **15**, 579–604. [CrossRef]
37. Kim, J.K.; Yu, C.L. A semiparametric estimation of mean functionals with nonignorable missing data. *J. Am. Stat. Assoc.* **2011**, *106*, 157–165. [CrossRef]
38. Tang, N.S.; Zhao, P.Y.; Zhu, H.T. Empirical likelihood for estimating equations with nonignorable missing data. *Stat. Sin.* **2014**, *24*, 723–747. [PubMed]
39. Qin, J.; Lawless, J. Empirical likelihood and general estimating equations. *Ann. Stat.* **1994**, *22*, 300–325. [CrossRef]
40. Choi, S.C.; Stablein, D.M. Comparing incomplete paired binomial data under non-random mechanisms. *Stat. Med.* **1988**, *7*, 929–939. [CrossRef]
41. Li, H.Q.; Tian, G.L.; Tang, N.S.; Cao, H.Y. Assessing non-inferiority for incomplete paired-data under non-ignorable missing mechanism. *Comput. Stat. Data Anal.* **2018**, *127*, 69–81. [CrossRef]

42. Hida, E.; Tango, T. On the three-arm non-inferiority trial including a placebo with a prespecified margin. *Stat. Med.* **2011**, *30*, 224–231. [CrossRef]
43. Kieser, M.; Friede, T. Planning and analysis of three-arm non-inferiority trials with binary endpoints. *Stat. Med.* **2007**, *26*, 253–273. [CrossRef]
44. Ghosh, P.; Nathoo, F.; Gönen, M.; Tiwari, R.C. Assessing non-inferiority in a three-arm trial using the Bayesian approach. *Stat. Med.* **2011**, *30*, 1795–1808. [CrossRef] [PubMed]
45. Morikawa, K.; Kim, J.K.; Kano, Y. Semiparametric maximum likelihood estimation with data missing not at random. *Can. J. Stat.* **2017**, *45*, 393–409. [CrossRef]
46. Arnastauskaite, J.; Ruzgas, T.; Brazenas, M. A new goodness of fit test for multivariate normality and comparative simulation study. *Mathematics* **2021**, *9*, 3003. [CrossRef]
47. Elbouch, S.E.; Michel, O.J.; Comon, P. A normality test for multivariate dependent samples. *Signal Process.* **2022**, *201*, 108705. [CrossRef]
48. Cook, T.; Zea, R. Missing data and sensitivity analysis for binary data with implications for sample size and power of randomized clinical trials. *Stat. Med.* **2019**, *39*, 192–204. [CrossRef] [PubMed]
49. Zhao, P.Y.; Tang, M.L.; Tang, N.S. Robust estimation of distribution functions and quantiles with non-ignorable missing data. *Can. J. Stat.* **2013**, *129*, 193–205. [CrossRef]

mathematics

MDPI

Article

Estimation Curve of Mixed Spline Truncated and Fourier Series Estimator for Geographically Weighted Nonparametric Regression

Lilis Laome [1,2], I Nyoman Budiantara [1,*] and Vita Ratnasari [1]

1 Department of Statistics, Institut Teknologi Sepuluh Nopember, Surabaya 60111, Indonesia
2 Department of Statistics, Faculty of Mathematics and Natural Sciences, Universitas Halu Oleo, Kendari 93132, Indonesia
* Correspondence: i_nyoman_b@statistika.its.ac.id

Abstract: Geographically Weighted Regression (GWR) is the development of multiple linear regression models used in spatial data. The assumption of spatial heterogeneity results in each location having different characteristics and allows the relationships between the response variable and each predictor variable to be unknown, hence nonparametric regression becomes one of the alternatives that can be used. In addition, regression functions are not always the same between predictor variables. This study aims to use the Geographically Weighted Nonparametric Regression (GWNR) model with a mixed estimator of truncated spline and Fourier series. Both estimators are expected to overcome unknown data patterns in spatial data. The mixed GWNR model estimator is then determined using the Weighted Maximum Likelihood Estimator (WMLE) technique. The estimator's characteristics are then determined. The results of the study found that the estimator of the mixed GWNR model is an estimator that is not biased and linear to the response variable y.

Keywords: GWNR; linear estimator; mixed estimator; spatial data; unbiased

MSC: 62J05; 62J10; 62J12; 62J20

Citation: Laome, L.; Budiantara, I.N.; Ratnasari, V. Estimation Curve of Mixed Spline Truncated and Fourier Series Estimator for Geographically Weighted Nonparametric Regression. *Mathematics* **2023**, *11*, 152. https://doi.org/10.3390/math11010152

Academic Editors: Niansheng Tang and Shen-Ming Lee

Received: 29 November 2022
Revised: 18 December 2022
Accepted: 23 December 2022
Published: 28 December 2022

1. Introduction

Regression analysis is a statistical method used to determine the relationship between response variables and one or more predictor variables [1]. Regression is divided into three types: parametric regression, nonparametric regression, and semiparametric regression. Parametric regression is used when the shape of the regression curve is known, whether linear, quadratic, cubic or otherwise. Whereas, nonparametric regression is used when the shape of the regression curve is unknown. As for semiparametric regression, it is a combination of parametric and nonparametric regression.

Nonparametric regression is a method used to model regression curves of unknown shape [2]. This method is a more flexible approach because the data is expected to look for the estimation form of the regression curve itself without being influenced by the researcher's subjectivity factor [3]. Some of the estimators used in nonparametric regression include spline estimators, Fourier series, kernels, and local polynomials. Each estimator has its characteristics to approach unknown regression functions. Research on nonparametric regression has been widely conducted by single estimators [4,5] and mixed estimators [6,7]. However, its application is still limited to nonspatial data. In fact, there are many problems related to spatial data. Spatial data is data that contains size and location information [8]. Methods used in spatial data analysis include Spatial Autocorrelation, Spatial Error Model, Geographically weighted regression, and others.

According to [8], Geographically Weighted Regression (GWR) is a statistical method that can analyze spatial heterogeneity. Spatial heterogeneity is one of the same predictor variables exerting unequal influences on different locations within a study site. The GWR model generates an estimator of model parameters that are local to each point or location where the data is observed. Research on GWR by [9,10] shows that the GWR model is better than the global model that can overcome spatial heterogeneity. It was further developed on a nonparametric GWR with a single estimator [11–13]. In addition, the relationship between response variables and some predictor variables can vary [14]. Therefore, a nonparametric GWR model with mixed truncated spline and Fourier series would be developed. The truncated spline estimator in GWR is expected to overcome the changing curve pattern at certain sub intervals [11]. In contrast, the Fourier series estimator is expected to model the repeating data pattern [6]. This study aims to create a Geographically Weighted Nonparametric Regression (GWNR) model with a mixed truncated spline and Fourier series estimator, to determine the parameter estimate of the GWNR model with the Weighted Maximum Likelihood Estimator method, and evaluate the properties the mixed GWNR model.

The following discussion in this paper is divided into three main topics. Section 2 discusses the GWNR Model and method estimation of WMLE. Section 3 presents the estimation parameter model GWNR; unbiased and linear estimator properties; and data application. Section 4 is the conclusions.

2. Materials and Methods

2.1. Geographically Weighted Nonparametric Regression (GWNR)

The GWNR model is a development of GWR in nonparametric regression. Provided paired data $(x_{1i},\ldots,x_{Pi},z_{1i},\ldots,z_{Qi},y_i)$ and assumed relationships between predictor variables $(x_{1i},\ldots,x_{Pi},z_{1i},\ldots,z_{Qi})$ with response variables (y_i) following a multivariable regression model [11] are as follows:

$$y_i = \mu(x_{1i},\ldots,x_{Pi},z_{1i},\ldots,z_{Qi}) + \varepsilon_i,\ i = 1,2,\ldots,n \quad (1)$$

where, y_i is a response variable, $\mu(x_{1i},\ldots,x_{Pi},z_{1i},\ldots,z_{Qi})$ is a regression curve of unknown shape, P is the predictor variables with a truncated spline function, Q is the predictor variables approached with Fourier series functions, and n is a number of observations and is assumed to be additive. If the function $\mu(x_{1i},\ldots,x_{Pi},z_{1i},\ldots,z_{Qi})$ is approached with truncated spline functions and Fourier series, then Equation (1) can be written:

$$y_i = \mu(x_{1i},\ldots,x_{Pi},z_{1i},\ldots,z_{Qi}) + \varepsilon_i$$

$$y_i = \sum_{p=1}^{P} f_p(x_{pi}) + \sum_{q=1}^{Q} g_q(z_{qi}) + \varepsilon_i,\ i = 1,2,\ldots,n$$

where,

$$\begin{aligned}\sum_{p=1}^{P} f_p(x_{pi}) &= f_1(x_{1i}) + \ldots + f_P(x_{Pi}) \\ &= \mathbf{X}_1\boldsymbol{\beta}_1(u_i,v_i) + \ldots + \mathbf{X}_P\boldsymbol{\beta}_P(u_i,v_i) \\ &= \begin{bmatrix} \mathbf{X}_1 & \ldots & \mathbf{X}_P \end{bmatrix}\begin{bmatrix} \boldsymbol{\beta}_1(u_i,v_i) \\ \vdots \\ \boldsymbol{\beta}_P(u_i,v_i) \end{bmatrix} \\ &= \mathbf{X}\boldsymbol{\beta}(u_i,v_i)\end{aligned}$$

is a truncated spline component with P predictor variables and

$$\begin{aligned}\sum_{q=1}^{Q} g_q(z_{qi}) &= g_1(z_{1i}) + \ldots + g_Q(z_{Qi}) \\ &= \mathbf{Z}_1\mathbf{a}_1(u_i, v_i) + \ldots + \mathbf{Z}_Q\mathbf{a}_Q(u_i, v_i) \\ &= \begin{bmatrix} \mathbf{Z}_1 & \cdots & \mathbf{Z}_Q \end{bmatrix} \begin{bmatrix} \mathbf{a}_1(u_i, v_i) \\ \vdots \\ \mathbf{a}_Q(u_i, v_i) \end{bmatrix} \\ &= \mathbf{Za}(u_i, v_i)\end{aligned}$$

is a Fourier series component with Q other predictor variables. By matrix notation, it can be written with:

$$\mathbf{y} = \mathbf{X}\boldsymbol{\beta}(u_i, v_i) + \mathbf{Za}(u_i, v_i) + \boldsymbol{\varepsilon} \quad (2)$$

where:

$$\mathbf{y} = \begin{bmatrix} y_1 \\ \vdots \\ y_n \end{bmatrix}, \ \boldsymbol{\varepsilon} = \begin{bmatrix} \varepsilon_1 \\ \vdots \\ \varepsilon_n \end{bmatrix}$$

$$\mathbf{X} = \begin{bmatrix} \mathbf{X}_1 & \vdots & \cdots & \vdots & \mathbf{X}_P \end{bmatrix}$$

$$\mathbf{Z} = \begin{bmatrix} \mathbf{Z}_1 & \vdots & \cdots & \vdots & \mathbf{Z}_Q \end{bmatrix}$$

$$\boldsymbol{\beta}(u_i, v_i) = \begin{bmatrix} \boldsymbol{\beta}_1{}^T(u_i, v_i) & \vdots & \cdots & \vdots & \boldsymbol{\beta}_P{}^T(u_i, v_i) \end{bmatrix}^T$$

$$\mathbf{a}(u_i, v_i) = \begin{bmatrix} \mathbf{a}_1{}^T(u_i, v_i) & \vdots & \cdots & \vdots & \mathbf{a}_Q{}^T(u_i, v_i) \end{bmatrix}^T$$

$$(u_i, v_i) = (\text{longitude, latitude}), \ i = 1, 2, \ldots, n$$

2.2. *Weighted Maximum Likelihood Estimator (WMLE)*

Maximum likelihood estimation from the parameters μ and σ^2 with a distributed *n-sized* sample $y_i \sim N(\mu, \sigma^2)$, $i = 1, 2, \ldots, n$ can be written with:

$$f(y_1, y_2, \ldots, y_n) = \prod_{i=1}^{n} \frac{1}{\sqrt{2\pi\sigma^2}} \exp\left(-\frac{1}{2}\left(\frac{y_i - \mu}{\sigma}\right)\right)^2$$

so that the likelihood function for $y_i, i = 1, 2, \ldots, n$ is

$$L\left(\mu, \sigma^2 | y_i\right) = (2\pi)^{-\frac{n}{2}} \left(\sigma^2\right)^{-\frac{n}{2}} \exp\left(-\frac{1}{2\sigma^2} \sum_{i=1}^{n} (y_i - \mu)^2\right) \quad (3)$$

Next, by multiplying by the weighting matrix $\mathbf{W} = diag(w_{1i^*}, w_{2i^*}, \ldots, w_{ni^*})$, the log likelihood function is obtained in terms of weighted function w_{ii*} as [15]:

$$\ln L^*\left(\mu, \sigma^2(u_{i*}, v_{i*}) | y_i\right) = \sum_{i=1}^{n} w_{ii*} \ln\left(\frac{1}{\sqrt{2\pi\sigma^2(u_{i*}, v_{i*})}} \exp\left(-\frac{1}{2}\left(\frac{y_i - \mu}{\sigma(u_{i*}, v_{i*})}\right)^2\right)\right), \ i = 1, 2, \ldots, n \quad (4)$$

The role of weights in the GWNR model is very important because the weighting values will represent the location of observational data from one another. One method that can be used is the Gaussian Kernel function [8]. Equation (4) estimates the GWNR parameter with the WMLE method.

Furthermore, steps are given in estimating the parameters of a mixed GWNR model with the WMLE Method as follows:

1. Defining a mixed GWNR model
2. Assuming distribution ε
3. Determining the distribution of **y**
4. Forming a likelihood function
5. Forming a weighted likelihood function
6. Specifying the first partial derivative of the likelihood function against the mixed GWNR model parameter
7. Getting an estimate of mixed GWNR model parameters.

3. Results

3.1. Parameter Estimation

Estimation of parameters on GWNR models with mixed estimators uses Weighted Maximum Likelihood Estimator (WMLE). The WMLE method is obtained by knowing the distribution of the response variable $y_i, i = 1, 2, \ldots, n$ in advance. Then, it is determined by the weighting matrix for each location to i, $i = 1, 2, \ldots, n$. The weighting used is a Fixed Gaussian Kernel function. Next, it is given the form of a distribution of the GWNR model that is presented on Lemma 1.

Lemma 1. *Given the GWNR model in Equation (2), with $\varepsilon_i, i = 1, 2, \ldots, n$ is normally distributed with mean equal to zero and variance $\sigma^2(u_i, v_i)$, hence $y_i, i = 1, 2, \ldots, n$ is normally distributed with mean*

$$\beta_0(u_i, v_i) + \sum_{p=1}^{P}\sum_{m=1}^{M} \beta_{mp}(u_i, v_i) x_{pi}^m + \sum_{p=1}^{P}\sum_{r=1}^{R} \beta_{(r+M)p}(u_i, v_i)(x_{pi} - t_{pp})_+^m$$
$$+ \sum_{q=1}^{Q}\left(\gamma_q(u_i, v_i) z_{qi} + \frac{1}{2}\theta_{0q}(u_i, v_i) + \sum_{h=1}^{H} \theta_{hq}(u_i, v_i)\cos(h z_{qi})\right)$$

and variance, $\sigma^2(u_i, v_i)$.

where:

P: number of spline components
M: polynomial degree of spline
R: number of knot points
Q: number of Fourier components
H: number of oscillation parameters.

Lemma 1 has been proven in Appendix A.

Theorem 1. *If given a model on Equation (2) with $\varepsilon_i, i = 1, 2, \ldots, n$ normally distributed with mean zero and variance $\sigma^2(u_i, v_i)$ and the weighted likelihood function given to (4), by the MLE method, an estimator is obtained $\hat{\boldsymbol{\beta}}(u_i, v_i)$ and $\hat{\mathbf{a}}(u_i, v_i)$ as follows:*

$$\hat{\boldsymbol{\beta}}(u_i, v_i) = \mathbf{A}(t, h)\mathbf{y}$$
$$\hat{\mathbf{a}}(u_i, v_i) = \mathbf{B}(t, h)\mathbf{y}$$

where:

$$\mathbf{A}(t,h) = \mathbf{R}\left(\mathbf{X}^T\mathbf{W}(u_i,v_i)\mathbf{X}\right)^{-1}\left[\mathbf{X}^T\mathbf{W}(u_i,v_i) - \mathbf{X}^T\mathbf{W}(u_i,v_i)\mathbf{Z}\left(\mathbf{Z}^T\mathbf{W}(u_i,v_i)\mathbf{Z}\right)^{-1}\mathbf{Z}^T\mathbf{W}(u_i,v_i)\right]$$
$$\mathbf{B}(t,h) = \mathbf{S}\left(\mathbf{Z}^T\mathbf{W}(u_i,v_i)\mathbf{Z}\right)^{-1}\left[\mathbf{Z}^T\mathbf{W}(u_i,v_i) - \mathbf{Z}^T\mathbf{W}(u_i,v_i)\mathbf{X}\left(\mathbf{X}^T\mathbf{W}(u_i,v_i)\mathbf{X}\right)^{-1}\mathbf{X}^T\mathbf{W}(u_i,v_i)\right]$$

t = knot point for spline component
h = oscillation parameter component.

Proof of Theorem 1. Is given to Appendix B. □

3.2. Unbiased and Linear Estimator Properties

Lemma 2. *If $\hat{\boldsymbol{\beta}}(u_i, v_i)$ is a truncated spline component parameter estimator of the GWNR model with a mixed estimator approach that follows Equation (4), so $\hat{\boldsymbol{\beta}}(u_i, v_i)$ is an unbiased estimator and belongs to the class of linear estimators in observation y.*

Furthermore, it can be seen in Appendix C which is the proof of Lemma 2.

Lemma 3. *If $\hat{\mathbf{a}}(u_i, v_i)$ is a Fourier series component parameter estimator of the GWNR model with a mixed estimator approach that follows Equation (4), so $\hat{\mathbf{a}}(u_i, v_i)$ is an unbiased estimator and belongs to the class of linear estimators in observation y.*

Lemma 3 is the last proven lemma and is described in Appendix D.

Lemma 4. *If $\hat{\boldsymbol{\beta}}(u_i, v_i)$ and $\hat{\mathbf{a}}(u_i, v_i)$ are given by Theorem 1, hence the estimator for $\hat{\mathbf{f}}$, $\hat{\mathbf{g}}$ and $\hat{\boldsymbol{\mu}}$ is hence given by:*

$$\hat{\mathbf{f}} = \mathbf{X}\hat{\boldsymbol{\beta}}(u_i, v_i)$$

$$\hat{\mathbf{g}} = \mathbf{Z}\hat{\mathbf{a}}(u_i, v_i)$$

so that the following is obtained:

$$\hat{\boldsymbol{\mu}} = \mathbf{X}\hat{\boldsymbol{\beta}}(u_i, v_i) + \mathbf{Z}\hat{\mathbf{a}}(u_i, v_i) = \mathbf{C}(t, h)\mathbf{y}$$

Proof. Next, to determine the function estimator $\hat{\mathbf{f}}$, $\hat{\mathbf{g}}$ and $\hat{\boldsymbol{\mu}}(u_i, v_i)$ are described as follows. Based on Theorem 1, it can be substituted $\hat{\boldsymbol{\beta}}(u_i, v_i)$ and $\hat{\mathbf{a}}(u_i, v_i)$ so that it is obtained:

$$\begin{aligned}\hat{\mathbf{f}} &= \mathbf{X}\hat{\boldsymbol{\beta}}(u_i, v_i)\\ &= \mathbf{X}\mathbf{A}(t, h)\mathbf{y}\end{aligned}$$

and

$$\begin{aligned}\hat{\mathbf{g}} &= \mathbf{Z}\hat{\mathbf{a}}(u_i, v_i)\\ &= \mathbf{Z}\mathbf{B}(t, h)\mathbf{y}\end{aligned}$$

As a result, obtained estimator $\hat{\boldsymbol{\mu}}$ be

$$\begin{aligned}\hat{\boldsymbol{\mu}} &= \hat{\mathbf{f}} + \hat{\mathbf{g}}\\ &= \mathbf{X}\hat{\beta}(u_i, v_i) + \mathbf{Z}\mathbf{a}(u_i, v_i)\\ &= \mathbf{X}\mathbf{A}(t, h)\mathbf{y} + \mathbf{Z}\mathbf{B}(t, h)\mathbf{y}\\ &= \mathbf{C}(t, h)\mathbf{y}\end{aligned}$$

where $\mathbf{C}(t, h) = \mathbf{X}\mathbf{A}(t, h) + \mathbf{Z}\mathbf{B}(t, h)$ is a hat matrix containing knot points t and the parameter of the h oscillation on the mixed GWNR model with the approach of truncated spline and Fourier series estimator. □

3.3. Data Application

The data used are secondary data from [16–21] with research variables, percentage of the poor population (y), CPI (x_1), TPT (x_2), longitude and latitude coordinates (u_i, v_i), and as many as 81 districts/cities on Sulawesi Island.

The following steps for applying the estimated parameters of the GWNR model to poverty data on Sulawesi Island in 2020 are as follows:

1. Making a scatter plot between the variables x_1 and y, as well as x_2 and y

2. Defining the initial model
3. Selecting optimum knots and oscillation parameters
4. Estimating parameters of global model with the OLS method based on the initial model formed
5. Testing assumptions of spatial heterogeneity on residual values on global models
6. Determining the weighting matrix
7. Estimating parameters of the GWNR model with the WMLE method
8. Choosing the best model based on MSE and R^2
9. Making conclusions

Based on the above step, the variable x_1 as a component of the Fourier series and the variable x_2 as the spline component are obtained based on the scatter plot shown. Furthermore, the test of spatial assumptions is obtained that the assumption of spatial heterogeneity is met, so the global model is less suitable for use because the residual properties are not homogeneous. One alternative model that can be used is the GWNR model. Use of this GWNR model is expected to overcome heteroskedasticity by generating a local model for each location. Here are some local models generated:

$$\hat{y}_{ken} = 47.59 - 0.5x_1 - 0.17x_2 + 0.43\cos(x_1) + 0.22(x_2 - 8.55) \tag{5}$$

$$\hat{y}_{mks} = 49.9 - 0.58x_1 - 0.07x_2 + 0.08\cos(x_1) + 0.47(x_2 - 8.55) \tag{6}$$

$$\hat{y}_{man} = 44.19 - 0.46x_1 - 0.15x_2 + 0.11\cos(x_1) + 0.19(x_2 - 8.55) \tag{7}$$

$$\hat{y}_{pal} = 40.79 - 0.47x_1 + 0.3x_2 - 0.48\cos(x_1) - 0.27(x_2 - 8.55) \tag{8}$$

$$\hat{y}_{gor} = 44.12 - 0.3x_1 - 2.25x_2 - 0.05\cos(x_1) + 2.38(x_2 - 8.55) \tag{9}$$

$$\hat{y}_{maj} = 39.88 - 0.43x_1 + 0.04x_2 + 0.02\cos(x_1) + 0.22(x_2 - 8.55) \tag{10}$$

where:

y_{ken} = estimated poverty percentage for Kendari City
y_{mks} = estimated poverty percentage for Makassar City
y_{man} = estimated poverty percentage for Manado City
y_{pal} = estimated poverty percentage for Palu City
y_{gor} = estimated poverty percentage for Gorontalo City
y_{maj} = estimated poverty percentage for Mamuju City.

GWNR mixed with oscillation parameters k =1 and linear spline t =1 resulted in MSE and R^2 values of 3.65 and 74.65 per cent, respectively. Based on several local models above, it shows that poverty in Sulawesi Island is influenced by HDI and TPT, where the increasing HDI will result in a decrease in the percentage of poverty. Conversely, an increase in TPT will increase the percentage of poverty.

4. Conclusions

Estimation of GWNR using the truncated spline and Fourier series was successfully formulated. It was found that:

1. The GWNR model using a mixed estimator of truncated spline and Fourier series is $\mathbf{y} = \mathbf{X}\boldsymbol{\beta}(u_i, v_i) + \mathbf{Z}\mathbf{a}(u_i, v_i) + \boldsymbol{\varepsilon}$
   Where $\mathbf{f} = \mathbf{X}\boldsymbol{\beta}(u_i, v_i)$ is a truncated spline component, $\mathbf{g} = \mathbf{Z}\mathbf{a}(u_i, v_i)$ is a component of a Fourier series, and $\boldsymbol{\varepsilon}$ is a residual component.
2. Estimators of GWNR are $\hat{\boldsymbol{\beta}}(u_i, v_i) = \mathbf{A}(t, h)\mathbf{y}$, $\hat{\mathbf{a}}(u_i, v_i) = \mathbf{B}(t, h)\mathbf{y}$, and $\hat{\boldsymbol{\mu}} = \mathbf{C}(t, h)\mathbf{y}$. The estimator is an unbiased and linear estimator to observe the response variable.

Author Contributions: Conceptualization: L.L., I.N.B. and V.R.; methodology, L.L. and I.N.B.; writing-original draft preparation, L.L.; writing—review and editing, L.L., I.N.B. and V.R. All authors have read and agreed to the published version of the manuscript.

Funding: This research was funded by Deputi Bidang Penguatan Riset dan Pengembangan, Ministry of Research and Technology/National Research and Innovation Agency (Kemenristek), the Republic of Indonesia, via grant Penelitian Disertasi Doktor (PDD) in 2022.

Data Availability Statement: Not applicable.

Conflicts of Interest: The authors declare no conflict of interest.

Appendix A

From the Equation (2), it is assumed that $\varepsilon_i \sim N(0, \sigma^2(u_i, v_i))$ so that the probability function $\varepsilon_1, \varepsilon_2, \ldots, \varepsilon_n$ written with

$$f(\varepsilon_1, \varepsilon_2, \ldots, \varepsilon_n) = \prod_{i=1}^{n} \left\{ \frac{1}{2\pi\sigma^2(u_i, v_i)} \exp\left(-\frac{1}{2\sigma^2(u_i, v_i)} \varepsilon_i^2 \right) \right\}$$

Therefore, the likelihood function for $\varepsilon_i, i = 1, 2, \ldots, n$ is as follows:

$$\begin{aligned} &L(\boldsymbol{\beta}(u_i, v_i), \mathbf{a}(u_i, v_i), \sigma^2(u_i, v_i) \mid \boldsymbol{\varepsilon}) = \prod_{i=1}^{n} \Bigg[\tfrac{1}{2\pi\sigma^2(u_i,v_i)} \exp\Bigg[-\tfrac{1}{2\sigma^2(u_i,v_i)} \\ &\Bigg[y_i - \Bigg(\beta_0(u_i, v_i) + \sum_{p=1}^{P} \sum_{m=1}^{M} \beta_{mp}(u_i, v_i) x_{pi}^m \\ &\sum_{p=1}^{P} \sum_{r=1}^{R} \beta_{(r+M)p}(u_i, v_i) (x_{pi} - t_{rp})_+^M + \sum_{q=1}^{Q} \Bigg(\gamma_q(u_i, v_i) z_{qi} + \tfrac{1}{2}\theta_{0q}(u_i, v_i) + \\ &\sum_{h=1}^{H} \theta_{hq}(u_i, v_i) \cos(hz_i) \Bigg) \Bigg) \Bigg]^2 \Bigg] \Bigg] \end{aligned}$$

Due to the fact that $\varepsilon_i \sim N(0, \sigma^2(u_i, v_i))$, therefore

$$\begin{aligned} E(\mathbf{y}) = E\Bigg(&\beta_0(u_i, v_i) + \sum_{p=1}^{P} \sum_{m=1}^{M} \beta_{mp}(u_i, v_i) x_{pi}^m + \sum_{p=1}^{P} \sum_{r=1}^{R} \beta_{(r+M)p}(u_i, v_i) (x_{pi} - t_{pp})_+^M \\ &+ \sum_{q=1}^{Q} \Bigg(\gamma_q(u_i, v_i) z_{qi} + \tfrac{1}{2}\theta_{0q}(u_i, v_i) + \sum_{h=1}^{H} \theta_{hq}(u_i, v_i) \cos(hz_i) \Bigg) + \varepsilon_i \Bigg) \\ = E\Bigg(&\beta_0(u_i, v_i) + \sum_{p=1}^{P} \sum_{m=1}^{M} \beta_{mp}(u_i, v_i) x_{pi}^m + \sum_{p=1}^{P} \sum_{r=1}^{R} \beta_{(r+M)p}(u_i, v_i) (x_{pi} - t_{rp})_+^M \\ &+ \sum_{q=1}^{Q} \Bigg(\gamma_q(u_i, v_i) z_{qi} + \tfrac{1}{2}\theta_{0q}(u_i, v_i) + \sum_{h=1}^{H} \theta_{hq}(u_i, v_i) \cos(hz_i) \Bigg) \Bigg) + E(\varepsilon_i) \\ = &\beta_0(u_i, v_i) + \sum_{p=1}^{P} \sum_{m=1}^{M} \beta_{mp}(u_i, v_i) x_{pi}^m + \sum_{p=1}^{P} \sum_{r=1}^{R} \beta_{(r+M)p}(u_i, v_i) (x_{pi} - t_{rp})_+^M \\ &+ \sum_{q=1}^{Q} \Bigg(\gamma_q(u_i, v_i) z_{qi} + \tfrac{1}{2}\theta_{0q}(u_i, v_i) + \sum_{h=1}^{H} \theta_{hq}(u_i, v_i) \cos(hz_i) \Bigg) \end{aligned}$$

and

$$\begin{aligned} \mathrm{var}(\mathbf{y}) = \mathrm{var}\Bigg(&\beta_0(u_i, v_i) + \sum_{p=1}^{P} \sum_{m=1}^{M} \beta_{mp}(u_i, v_i) x_{pi}^m + \sum_{p=1}^{P} \sum_{r=1}^{R} \beta_{(r+M)p}(u_i, v_i) (x_{pi} - t_{rp})_+^M \\ &+ \sum_{q=1}^{Q} \Bigg(\gamma_q(u_i, v_i) z_{qi} + \tfrac{1}{2}\theta_{0q}(u_i, v_i) + \sum_{h=1}^{H} \theta_{hq}(u_i, v_i) \cos(hz_i) \Bigg) \Bigg) + \mathrm{var}(\varepsilon_i) \\ &= \sigma^2(u_i, v_i) \end{aligned}$$

Consequently,

$$y_i \sim N\left(\beta_0(u_i,v_i) + \sum_{p=1}^{P}\sum_{m=1}^{M}\beta_{mp}(u_i,v_i)x_{pi}^m + \sum_{p=1}^{P}\sum_{r=1}^{R}\beta_{(r+M)p}(u_i,v_i)(x_{pi}-t_{rp})_+^M + \sum_{q=1}^{Q}\left(\gamma_q(u_i,v_i)z_{qi} + \tfrac{1}{2}\theta_{0q}(u_i,v_i) + \sum_{h=1}^{H}\theta_{hq}(u_i,v_i)\cos(hz_i)\right), \sigma^2(u_i,v_i)\right) \quad (A1)$$

Appendix B

Equation (A1) obtained the likelihood function of y_i, $i=1,2,\ldots,n$ and at its location is

$$L\left(\boldsymbol{\beta}(u_i,v_i),\mathbf{a}(u_i,v_i),\sigma^2(u_i,v_i)\mid \varepsilon\right) = \prod_{i=1}^{n} f\left(y_i\mid \boldsymbol{\beta}(u_i,v_i),\mathbf{a}(u_i,v_i),\sigma^2(u_i,v_i)\right)$$

$$= \prod_{i=1}^{n}\left[\frac{1}{2\pi\sigma^2(u_i,v_i)}\exp\left[-\frac{1}{2\sigma^2(u_i,v_i)}\left[y_i - \left(\beta_0(u_i,v_i) + \sum_{p=1}^{P}\sum_{m=1}^{M}\beta_{mp}(u_i,v_i)x_{pi}^m + \sum_{p=1}^{P}\sum_{r=1}^{R}\beta_{(r+M)p}(u_i,v_i)(x_{pi}-t_{rp})_+^M + \sum_{q=1}^{Q}\left(\gamma_q(u_i,v_i)z_{qi} + \tfrac{1}{2}\theta_{0q}(u_i,v_i) + \sum_{h=1}^{H}\theta_{hq}(u_i,v_i)\cos(hz_i)\right)\right)\right]^2\right]\right]$$

$$= (2\pi)^{-\frac{n}{2}}\left(\sigma^2(u_i,v_i)\right)^{-\frac{n}{2}}\exp\left[-\frac{1}{2\sigma^2(u_i,v_i)}\left[y_i - \left(\beta_0(u_i,v_i) + \sum_{p=1}^{P}\sum_{m=1}^{M}\beta_{mp}(u_i,v_i)x_{pi}^m + \sum_{p=1}^{P}\sum_{r=1}^{R}\beta_{(r+M)p}(u_i,v_i)(x_{pi}-t_{pp})_+^M + \sum_{q=1}^{Q}\left(\gamma_q(u_i,v_i)z_{qi} + \tfrac{1}{2}\theta_{0q}(u_i,v_i) + \sum_{h=1}^{H}\theta_{hq}(u_i,v_i)\cos(hz_i)\right)\right)\right]^2\right] \quad (A2)$$

The geographical location factor is the weighting factor in the GWR model, so Equation (A2) is given a weighting $w_{i(j)}$ to obtain the local model of GWNR, then a natural logarithm operation is performed as follows:

$$L^*\left(\boldsymbol{\beta}(u_i,v_i),\mathbf{a}(u_i,v_i),\sigma^2(u_i,v_i)\mid \mathbf{y}\right) = \prod_{i=1}^{n}\left(f\left(y_i\mid \boldsymbol{\beta}(u_i,v_i),\mathbf{a}(u_i,v_i),\sigma^2(u_i,v_i)\right)\right)^{w_i(\lambda)}$$

$$= \prod_{i=1}^{n}\left[\frac{1}{2\pi\sigma^2(u_i,v_i)}\exp\left[-\frac{1}{2\sigma^2(u_i,v_i)}\left[y_i - \left(\beta_0(u_i,v_i) + \sum_{p=1}^{P}\sum_{m=1}^{M}\beta_{mp}(u_i,v_i)x_{pi}^m + \sum_{p=1}^{P}\sum_{r=1}^{R}\beta_{(r+M)p}(u_i,v_i)(x_{pi}-t_{pp})_+^M + \sum_{q=1}^{Q}\left(\gamma_q(u_i,v_i)z_{qi} + \tfrac{1}{2}\theta_{0q}(u_i,v_i) + \sum_{h=1}^{H}\theta_{hq}(u_i,v_i)\cos(hz_i)\right)\right)\right]^2\right]\right]^{w_{i(j)}} \quad (A3)$$

$$\begin{aligned}
&\ln\left(L^*\left(\boldsymbol{\beta}(u_i,v_i),\mathbf{a}(u_i,v_i),\sigma^2(u_i,v_i)\mid\mathbf{y}\right)\right) = \\
&= \sum_{i=1}^{n} w_{ij}\ln\left(\frac{1}{2\pi\sigma^2(u_i,v_i)}\exp\left[-\frac{1}{2\sigma^2(u_i,v_i)}\left[y_i - (\beta_0(u_i,v_i) + \right.\right.\right. \\
&\sum_{p=1}^{P}\sum_{m=1}^{M}\beta_{mp}(u_i,v_i)x_{pi}^{m} + \sum_{p=1}^{P}\sum_{r=1}^{R}\beta_{(r+M)p}(u_i,v_i)(x_{pi}-t_{pp})_{+}^{M} \\
&\left.\left.\left.+\sum_{q=1}^{Q}\left(\gamma_q(u_i,v_i)z_{qi} + \tfrac{1}{2}\theta_{0q}(u_i,v_i) + \sum_{h=1}^{H}\theta_{hq}(u_i,v_i)\cos(hz_i)\right)\right)\right]^2\right]\right) \\
&= \sum_{i=1}^{n} w_{i(j)}\left(-\tfrac{1}{2}\right)\ln(2\pi) - \sum_{i=1}^{n} w_{i(j)}\left(\tfrac{1}{2}\right)\ln(\sigma^2(u_i,v_i)) - \frac{1}{2\sigma^2(u_i,v_i)}\sum_{i=1}^{n} w_{i(j)} \\
&\left(y_i - \left(\beta_0(u_i,v_i) + \sum_{p=1}^{P}\sum_{m=1}^{M}\beta_{mp}(u_i,v_i)x_{pi}^{m} + \sum_{p=1}^{P}\sum_{r=1}^{R}\beta_{(r+M)p}(u_i,v_i)(x_{pi}-t_{rp})_{+}^{M}\right.\right. \\
&\left.\left.+\sum_{q=1}^{Q}\left(\gamma_q(u_i,v_i)z_{qi} + \tfrac{1}{2}\theta_{0q}(u_i,v_i) + \sum_{h=1}^{H}\theta_{hq}(u_i,v_i)\cos(hz_i)\right)\right)\right)^2 \\
&= \sum_{i=1}^{n} w_{i(j)}\left(-\tfrac{1}{2}\right)\ln(2\pi) - \sum_{i=1}^{n} w_{i(j)}\left(\tfrac{1}{2}\right)\ln(\sigma^2(u_i,v_i)) - \frac{1}{2\sigma^2(u_i,v_i)}T^*
\end{aligned} \tag{A4}$$

where:

$$\begin{aligned}
T^* &= \sum_{i=1}^{n} w_{i(j)}\left(y_i - \left(\beta_0(u_i,v_i) + \sum_{p=1}^{P}\sum_{m=1}^{M}\beta_{mp}(u_i,v_i)x_{pi}^{m} + \sum_{p=1}^{P}\sum_{r=1}^{R}\beta_{(r+M)p}(u_i,v_i)(x_{pi}-t_{rp})_{+}^{M}\right.\right. \\
&\left.\left.+\sum_{q=1}^{Q}\left(\gamma_q(u_i,v_i)z_{qi} + \tfrac{1}{2}\theta_{0q}(u_i,v_i) + \sum_{h=1}^{H}\theta_{hq}(u_i,v_i)\cos(hz_i)\right)\right)\right)^2 \\
&= (\mathbf{y}-\mathbf{X}\boldsymbol{\beta}(u_i,v_i)-\mathbf{Z}\mathbf{a}(u_i,v_i))^T\mathbf{W}(u_i,v_i)(\mathbf{y}-\mathbf{X}\boldsymbol{\beta}(u_i,v_i)-\mathbf{Z}\mathbf{a}(u_i,v_i))
\end{aligned}$$

Parameter estimations of $\hat{\boldsymbol{\beta}}(u_i,v_i)$ and $\hat{\mathbf{a}}(u_i,v_i)$ are obtained by maximizing $\ln L^*$ on Equation (A3). Estimator $\hat{\boldsymbol{\beta}}(u_i,v_i)$ is obtained by deriving the Equation (A4) against $\hat{\boldsymbol{\beta}}(u_i,v_i)$, which then equates to zero so that it is obtained:

$$\begin{aligned}
\frac{\partial\ln L^*}{\partial\boldsymbol{\beta}(u_i,v_i)} &= \frac{\partial\left(\sum_{i=1}^{n} w_{i(j)}\left(-\frac{1}{2}\right)\ln(2\pi) - \sum_{i=1}^{n} w_{i(j)}\left(\frac{1}{2}\right)\ln(\sigma^2(u_i,v_i)) - \frac{1}{2\sigma^2(u_i,v_i)}T^*\right)}{\partial\boldsymbol{\beta}(u_i,v_i)} \\
0 &= \frac{\partial(\mathbf{y}-\mathbf{X}\boldsymbol{\beta}(u_i,v_i)-\mathbf{Z}\mathbf{a}(u_i,v_i))^T\mathbf{W}(u_i,v_i)(\mathbf{y}-\mathbf{X}\boldsymbol{\beta}(u_i,v_i)-\mathbf{Z}\mathbf{a}(u_i,v_i))}{\partial\boldsymbol{\beta}(u_i,v_i)} \\
0 &= -2\mathbf{X}^T\mathbf{W}(u_i,v_i)\mathbf{y} + 2\mathbf{X}^T\mathbf{W}(u_i,v_i)\mathbf{Z}\mathbf{a}(u_i,v_i) + 2\mathbf{X}^T\mathbf{W}(u_i,v_i)\mathbf{X}\boldsymbol{\beta}(u_i,v_i) \\
\hat{\boldsymbol{\beta}}(u_i,v_i) &= (\mathbf{X}^T\mathbf{W}(u_i,v_i)\mathbf{X})^{-1}(\mathbf{X}^T\mathbf{W}(u_i,v_i)\mathbf{y} - \mathbf{X}^T\mathbf{W}(u_i,v_i)\mathbf{Z}\mathbf{a}(u_i,v_i))
\end{aligned}$$

Therefore, the estimation of the parameters $\boldsymbol{\beta}(u_i,v_i)$ is

$$\hat{\boldsymbol{\beta}}(u_i,v_i) = \left(\mathbf{X}^T\mathbf{W}(u_i,v_i)\mathbf{X}\right)^{-1}\left(\mathbf{X}^T\mathbf{W}(u_i,v_i)\mathbf{y} - \mathbf{X}^T\mathbf{W}(u_i,v_i)\mathbf{Z}\hat{\mathbf{a}}(u_i,v_i)\right) \tag{A5}$$

Furthermore, parameter estimation is carried out for $\mathbf{a}(u_i,v_i)$. To obtain an estimator $\hat{\mathbf{a}}(u_i,v_i)$ and then derive Equation (A4) against $\mathbf{a}(u_i,v_i)$ which then equates to zero, is the following is thus obtained:

$$\begin{aligned}
\frac{\partial\ln L^*}{\partial\mathbf{a}(u_i,v_i)} &= \frac{\partial(\mathbf{y}-\mathbf{X}\boldsymbol{\beta}(u_i,v_i)-\mathbf{Z}\mathbf{a}(u_i,v_i))^T\mathbf{W}(u_i,v_i)(\mathbf{y}-\mathbf{X}\boldsymbol{\beta}(u_i,v_i)-\mathbf{Z}\mathbf{a}(u_i,v_i))}{\partial\mathbf{a}(u_i,v_i)} \\
0 &= -2\mathbf{Z}^T\mathbf{W}(u_i,v_i)\mathbf{y} + 2\mathbf{Z}^T\mathbf{W}(u_i,v_i)\mathbf{X}\boldsymbol{\beta}(u_i,v_i) + 2\mathbf{Z}^T\mathbf{W}(u_i,v_i)\mathbf{Z}\mathbf{a}(u_i,v_i) \\
\hat{\mathbf{a}}(u_i,v_i) &= (\mathbf{Z}^T\mathbf{W}(u_i,v_i)\mathbf{Z})^{-1}(\mathbf{Z}^T\mathbf{W}(u_i,v_i)\mathbf{y} - \mathbf{Z}^T\mathbf{W}(u_i,v_i)\mathbf{X}\boldsymbol{\beta}(u_i,v_i))
\end{aligned}$$

Therefore, the estimation of the parameters $\mathbf{a}(u_i,v_i)$ is

$$\hat{\mathbf{a}}(u_i,v_i) = \left(\mathbf{Z}^T\mathbf{W}(u_i,v_i)\mathbf{Z}\right)^{-1}\left(\mathbf{Z}^T\mathbf{W}(u_i,v_i)\mathbf{y} - \mathbf{Z}^T\mathbf{W}(u_i,v_i)\mathbf{X}\hat{\boldsymbol{\beta}}(u_i,v_i)\right) \tag{A6}$$

Estimator $\hat{\boldsymbol{\beta}}(u_i, v_i)$ in Equation (A5) still contains an estimator $\hat{\mathbf{a}}(u_i, v_i)$. Like wise, estimators $\hat{\mathbf{a}}(u_i, v_i)$ in Equation (A6) still contain an estimator $\hat{\boldsymbol{\beta}}(u_i, v_i)$. In order to obtain a free form of an estimator, it is necessary to make a substitution. To obtain an estimator $\hat{\boldsymbol{\beta}}(u_i, v_i)$, which is free from $\hat{\mathbf{a}}(u_i, v_i)$, it is then substituted Equation (A6) into Equation (A5) as follows:

$$\begin{aligned}
&\hat{\boldsymbol{\beta}}(u_i, v_i) = \left(\mathbf{X}^T\mathbf{W}(u_i, v_i)\mathbf{X}\right)^{-1}\left(\mathbf{X}^T\mathbf{W}(u_i, v_i)\mathbf{y} - \mathbf{X}^T\mathbf{W}(u_i, v_i)\mathbf{Z}\hat{\mathbf{a}}(u_i, v_i)\right)\\
&= \left(\mathbf{X}^T\mathbf{W}(u_i, v_i)\mathbf{X}\right)^{-1}\left(\mathbf{X}^T\mathbf{W}(u_i, v_i)\mathbf{y} - \mathbf{X}^T\mathbf{W}(u_i, v_i)\mathbf{Z}\right.\\
&\left.\left(\mathbf{Z}^T\mathbf{W}(u_i, v_i)\mathbf{Z}\right)^{-1}\left(\mathbf{Z}^T\mathbf{W}(u_i, v_i)\mathbf{y} - \mathbf{Z}^T\mathbf{W}(u_i, v_i)\mathbf{X}\hat{\beta}(u_i, v_i)\right)\right)\\
&= \left(\mathbf{X}^T\mathbf{W}(u_i, v_i)\mathbf{X}\right)^{-1}\mathbf{X}^T\mathbf{W}(u_i, v_i)\mathbf{y} -\\
&\left(\mathbf{X}^T\mathbf{W}(u_i, v_i)\mathbf{X}\right)^{-1}\mathbf{X}^T\mathbf{W}(u_i, v_i)\mathbf{Z}\left(\mathbf{Z}^T\mathbf{W}(u_i, v_i)\mathbf{Z}\right)^{-1}\mathbf{Z}^T\mathbf{W}(u_i, v_i)\mathbf{y} +\\
&\left(\mathbf{X}^T\mathbf{W}(u_i, v_i)\mathbf{X}\right)^{-1}\mathbf{X}^T\mathbf{W}(u_i, v_i)\mathbf{Z}\left(\mathbf{Z}^T\mathbf{W}(u_i, v_i)\mathbf{Z}\right)^{-1}\mathbf{Z}^T\mathbf{W}(u_i, v_i)\mathbf{X}\hat{\beta}(u_i, v_i)\Big)
\end{aligned}$$

Then, they are merged in the same field containing $\hat{\boldsymbol{\beta}}(u_i, v_i)$, so that the following is obtained:

$$\begin{aligned}
&\hat{\boldsymbol{\beta}}(u_i, v_i) - \left(\mathbf{X}^T\mathbf{W}(u_i, v_i)\mathbf{X}\right)^{-1}\mathbf{X}^T\mathbf{W}(u_i, v_i)\mathbf{Z}\left(\mathbf{Z}^T\mathbf{W}(u_i, v_i)\mathbf{Z}\right)^{-1}\mathbf{Z}^T\mathbf{W}(u_i, v_i)\mathbf{X}\hat{\boldsymbol{\beta}}(u_i\\
&= \left(\mathbf{X}^T\mathbf{W}(u_i, v_i)\mathbf{X}\right)^{-1}\mathbf{X}^T\mathbf{W}(u_i, v_i)\mathbf{y} - \left(\mathbf{X}^T\mathbf{W}(u_i, v_i)\mathbf{X}\right)^{-1}\mathbf{X}^T\mathbf{W}(u_i, v_i)\mathbf{Z}\\
&\left(\mathbf{Z}^T\mathbf{W}(u_i, v_i)\mathbf{Z}\right)^{-1}\mathbf{Z}^T\mathbf{W}(u_i, v_i)\mathbf{y}\\
&\hat{\boldsymbol{\beta}}(u_i, v_i) = \mathbf{R}\Big[\left(\mathbf{X}^T\mathbf{W}(u_i, v_i)\mathbf{X}\right)^{-1}\mathbf{X}^T\mathbf{W}(u_i, v_i)\\
&-\left(\mathbf{X}^T\mathbf{W}(u_i, v_i)\mathbf{X}\right)^{-1}\mathbf{X}^T\mathbf{W}(u_i, v_i)\mathbf{Z}\left(\mathbf{Z}^T\mathbf{W}(u_i, v_i)\mathbf{Z}\right)^{-1}\mathbf{Z}^T\mathbf{W}(u_i, v_i)\Big]\mathbf{y}
\end{aligned}$$

where:

$$\mathbf{R} = \left[\mathbf{I} - \left(\mathbf{X}^T\mathbf{W}(u_i, v_i)\mathbf{X}\right)^{-1}\mathbf{X}^T\mathbf{W}(u_i, v_i)\mathbf{Z}\left(\mathbf{Z}^T\mathbf{W}(u_i, v_i)\mathbf{Z}\right)^{-1}\mathbf{Z}^T\mathbf{W}(u_i, v_i)\mathbf{X}\hat{\boldsymbol{\beta}}(u_i, v_i)\right)\right]^{-1}$$

Therefore, the following is obtained:

$$\hat{\boldsymbol{\beta}}(u_i, v_i) = \mathbf{A}(t, h)\mathbf{y} \tag{A7}$$

with

$$\begin{aligned}
&\mathbf{A}(t, h) = \mathbf{R}\Big[\left(\mathbf{X}^T\mathbf{W}(u_i, v_i)\mathbf{X}\right)^{-1}\mathbf{X}^T\mathbf{W}(u_i, v_i) - \left(\mathbf{X}^T\mathbf{W}(u_i, v_i)\mathbf{X}\right)^{-1}\mathbf{X}^T\mathbf{W}(u_i, v_i)\mathbf{Z}\\
&\left(\mathbf{Z}^T\mathbf{W}(u_i, v_i)\mathbf{Z}\right)^{-1}\mathbf{Z}^T\mathbf{W}(u_i, v_i)\Big]
\end{aligned}$$

To obtain an estimator $\hat{\mathbf{a}}(u_i, v_i)$ which is free from $\hat{\boldsymbol{\beta}}(u_i, v_i)$, it is substituted Equation (A5) to Equation (A6) as follows:

$$\begin{aligned}
&\hat{\mathbf{a}}(u_i, v_i) = \left(\mathbf{Z}^T\mathbf{W}(u_i, v_i)\mathbf{Z}\right)^{-1}\left(\mathbf{Z}^T\mathbf{W}(u_i, v_i)\mathbf{y} - \mathbf{Z}^T\mathbf{W}(u_i, v_i)\mathbf{X}\hat{\beta}(u_i, v_i)\right)\\
&= \left(\mathbf{Z}^T\mathbf{W}(u_i, v_i)\mathbf{Z}\right)^{-1}\left(\mathbf{X}^T\mathbf{W}(u_i, v_i)\mathbf{y} - \mathbf{Z}^T\mathbf{W}(u_i, v_i)\mathbf{X}\right.\\
&\left.\left(\mathbf{X}^T\mathbf{W}(u_i, v_i)\mathbf{X}\right)^{-1}\left(\mathbf{X}^T\mathbf{W}(u_i, v_i)\mathbf{y} - \mathbf{X}^T\mathbf{W}(u_i, v_i)\mathbf{Z}\hat{\mathbf{a}}(u_i, v_i)\right)\right)\\
&= \left(\mathbf{Z}^T\mathbf{W}(u_i, v_i)\mathbf{Z}\right)^{-1}\mathbf{Z}^T\mathbf{W}(u_i, v_i)\mathbf{y} -\\
&\left(\mathbf{Z}^T\mathbf{W}(u_i, v_i)\mathbf{Z}\right)^{-1}\mathbf{Z}^T\mathbf{W}(u_i, v_i)\mathbf{X}\left(\mathbf{X}^T\mathbf{W}(u_i, v_i)\mathbf{X}\right)^{-1}\mathbf{X}^T\mathbf{W}(u_i, v_i)\mathbf{y} +\\
&\left(\mathbf{Z}^T\mathbf{W}(u_i, v_i)\mathbf{Z}\right)^{-1}\mathbf{Z}^T\mathbf{W}(u_i, v_i)\mathbf{X}\left(\mathbf{X}^T\mathbf{W}(u_i, v_i)\mathbf{X}\right)^{-1}\mathbf{X}^T\mathbf{W}(u_i, v_i)\mathbf{Z}\hat{\mathbf{a}}(u_i, v_i)\Big)
\end{aligned}$$

Then, it is merged in the same field containing $\hat{\mathbf{a}}(u_i, v_i)$, so that the following is obtained:

$$\hat{\mathbf{a}}(u_i, v_i) - (\mathbf{Z}^T\mathbf{W}(u_i, v_i)\mathbf{Z})^{-1}\mathbf{Z}^T\mathbf{W}(u_i, v_i)\mathbf{X}(\mathbf{X}^T\mathbf{W}(u_i, v_i)\mathbf{X})^{-1}\mathbf{x}^T\mathbf{W}(u_i, v_i)\mathbf{Z}\hat{\mathbf{a}}(u_i, v_i)\Big)$$
$$= (\mathbf{Z}^T\mathbf{W}(u_i, v_i)\mathbf{Z})^{-1}\mathbf{z}^T\mathbf{W}(u_i, v_i)\mathbf{y} - (\mathbf{z}^T\mathbf{W}(u_i, v_i)\mathbf{Z})^{-1}\mathbf{Z}^T\mathbf{W}(u_i, v_i)\mathbf{X}$$
$$(\mathbf{X}^T\mathbf{W}(u_i, v_i)\mathbf{X})^{-1}\mathbf{x}^T\mathbf{W}(u_i, v_i)\mathbf{y}$$
$$\hat{\mathbf{a}}(u_i, v_i) = \mathbf{S}\Big[(\mathbf{Z}^T\mathbf{W}(u_i, v_i)\mathbf{Z})^{-1}\mathbf{Z}^T\mathbf{W}(u_i, v_i)$$
$$-(\mathbf{Z}^T\mathbf{W}(u_i, v_i)\mathbf{Z})^{-1}\mathbf{Z}^T\mathbf{W}(u_i, v_i)\mathbf{X}(\mathbf{X}^T\mathbf{W}(u_i, v_i)\mathbf{X})^{-1}\mathbf{X}^T\mathbf{W}(u_i, v_i)\Big]\mathbf{y}$$

where:

$$\mathbf{S} = \left[\mathbf{I} - \left(\mathbf{Z}^T\mathbf{W}(u_i, v_i)\mathbf{Z}\right)^{-1}\mathbf{Z}^T\mathbf{W}(u_i, v_i)\mathbf{X}\left(\mathbf{X}^T\mathbf{W}(u_i, v_i)\mathbf{X}\right)^{-1}\mathbf{X}^T\mathbf{W}(u_i, v_i)\mathbf{Z}\hat{\mathbf{a}}(u_i, v_i)\Big)\right]^{-1}$$

Therefore, the following is obtained:

$$\hat{\mathbf{a}}(u_i, v_i) = \mathbf{B}(t, h)\mathbf{y} \tag{A8}$$

with

$$\mathbf{B}(t, h) = \mathbf{S}\Big[(\mathbf{Z}^T\mathbf{W}(u_i, v_i)\mathbf{Z})^{-1}\mathbf{Z}^T\mathbf{W}(u_i, v_i) - (\mathbf{Z}^T\mathbf{W}(u_i, v_i)\mathbf{Z})^{-1}\mathbf{Z}^T\mathbf{W}(u_i, v_i)\mathbf{X}$$
$$(\mathbf{X}^T\mathbf{W}(u_i, v_i)\mathbf{X})^{-1}\mathbf{X}^T\mathbf{W}(u_i, v_i)\Big]$$

Appendix C

The unbiased nature of the parameter $\hat{\boldsymbol{\beta}}(u_i, v_i)$ can be indicated by:

$$E\left(\hat{\boldsymbol{\beta}}(u_i, v_l)\right) = E(\mathbf{A}(t, h)\mathbf{y})$$
$$= E\Big(\mathbf{R}\Big[(\mathbf{X}^T\mathbf{W}(u_i, v_l)\mathbf{X})^{-1}\mathbf{X}^\tau\mathbf{W}(u_i, v_l) - (\mathbf{X}^T\mathbf{W}(u_l, v_l)\mathbf{X})^{-1}$$
$$\mathbf{X}^\tau\mathbf{W}(u_i, v_l)\mathbf{Z}(\mathbf{Z}^\tau\mathbf{W}(u_i, v_l)\mathbf{Z})^{-1}\mathbf{Z}^\tau\mathbf{W}(u_i, v_l)\Big]\mathbf{y}\Big)$$
$$= \Big(\mathbf{R}\Big[(\mathbf{X}^\tau\mathbf{W}(u_i, v_i)\mathbf{X})^{-1}\mathbf{X}^\tau\mathbf{W}(u_i, v_i) - (\mathbf{X}^\tau\mathbf{W}(u_i, v_i)\mathbf{X})^{-1}$$
$$\mathbf{X}^\tau\mathbf{W}(u_i, v_i)\mathbf{Z}(\mathbf{Z}^\tau\mathbf{W}(u_i, v_i)\mathbf{Z})^{-1}\mathbf{Z}^\tau\mathbf{W}(u_i, v_l)\Big]\Big)E(\mathbf{y})$$
$$= \Big(\mathbf{R}\Big[(\mathbf{X}^\tau\mathbf{W}(u_i, v_i)\mathbf{X})^{-1}\mathbf{X}^\tau\mathbf{W}(u_i, v_l) - (\mathbf{X}^\tau\mathbf{W}(u_i, v_l)\mathbf{X})^{-1}$$
$$\mathbf{X}^\tau\mathbf{W}(u_i, v_i)\mathbf{Z}(\mathbf{Z}^\tau\mathbf{W}(u_i, v_i)\mathbf{Z})^{-1}\mathbf{Z}^\tau\mathbf{W}(u_i, v_l)\Big]\Big)(\mathbf{X}\boldsymbol{\beta}(u_l, v_i) + \mathbf{Za}(u_i, v_i))$$
$$= \mathbf{R}(\mathbf{X}^T\mathbf{W}(u_i, v_i)\mathbf{X})^{-1}\mathbf{X}^T\mathbf{W}(u_i, v_i)\mathbf{X}\boldsymbol{\beta}(u_i, v_i) +$$
$$\mathbf{R}(\mathbf{X}^\tau\mathbf{W}(u_i, v_l)\mathbf{X})^{-1}\mathbf{X}^\tau\mathbf{W}(u_i, v_l)\mathbf{Za}(u_i, v_i) -$$
$$\mathbf{R}(\mathbf{X}^\tau\mathbf{W}(u_i, v_i)\mathbf{X})^{-1}\mathbf{X}^\tau\mathbf{W}(u_i, v_i)\mathbf{Z}(\mathbf{Z}^\tau\mathbf{W}(u_i, v_l)\mathbf{Z})^{-1}\mathbf{Z}^\tau\mathbf{W}(u_i, v_l)\mathbf{X}\boldsymbol{\beta}(u_i, v_l)$$
$$-\mathbf{R}(\mathbf{X}^\tau\mathbf{W}(u_i, v_i)\mathbf{X})^{-1}\mathbf{X}^\tau\mathbf{W}(u_i, v_i)\mathbf{Z}(\mathbf{Z}^\tau\mathbf{W}(u_i, v_i)\mathbf{Z})^{-1}\mathbf{Z}^\tau\mathbf{W}(u_i, v_l)\mathbf{Za}(u_i, v_i)$$
$$= \mathbf{R}\boldsymbol{\beta}(u_i, v_i) - \mathbf{R}(\mathbf{X}^\tau\mathbf{W}(u_i, v_i)\mathbf{X})^{-1}\mathbf{X}^\tau\mathbf{W}(u_i, v_i)\mathbf{Z}(\mathbf{Z}^\tau\mathbf{W}(u_i, v_i)\mathbf{Z})^{-1}$$
$$\mathbf{Z}^\tau\mathbf{W}(u_i, v_i)\mathbf{X}\boldsymbol{\beta}(u_i, v_i)$$
$$= \Big[\mathbf{I} - (\mathbf{X}^\tau\mathbf{W}(u_i, v_l)\mathbf{X})^{-1}\mathbf{X}^\tau\mathbf{W}(u_i, v_l)\mathbf{Z}(\mathbf{Z}^\tau\mathbf{W}(u_i, v_l)\mathbf{Z})^{-1}\mathbf{Z}^\tau\mathbf{W}(u_i, v_l)\mathbf{X}\Big]$$
$$\mathbf{R}\boldsymbol{\beta}(u_i, v_i)$$
$$= \Big[\mathbf{I} - (\mathbf{X}^\tau\mathbf{W}(u_i, v_l)\mathbf{X})^{-1}\mathbf{X}^\tau\mathbf{W}(u_i, v_l)\mathbf{Z}(\mathbf{Z}^\tau\mathbf{W}(u_i, v_l)\mathbf{Z})^{-1}\mathbf{Z}^\tau\mathbf{W}(u_l, v_l)\mathbf{X}\Big]$$
$$\Big[\mathbf{I} - (\mathbf{x}^T\mathbf{W}(u_i, v_i)\mathbf{X})^{-1}\mathbf{x}^T\mathbf{W}(u_i, v_i)\mathbf{Z}(\mathbf{Z}^T\mathbf{W}(u_i, v_i)\mathbf{Z})^{-1}\mathbf{Z}^T\mathbf{W}(u_i, v_i)\mathbf{X}\Big]^{-1}$$
$$\boldsymbol{\beta}(u_i, v_i)$$
$$= \boldsymbol{\beta}(u_i, v_i)$$

Since $E(\hat{\boldsymbol{\beta}}(u_i, v_i)) = \boldsymbol{\beta}(u_i, v_i)$, it can be said that $\hat{\boldsymbol{\beta}}(u_i, v_i)$ is an unbiased estimator for $\boldsymbol{\beta}(u_i, v_i)$. Next, it can be written that $\hat{\boldsymbol{\beta}}(u_i, v_i) = \mathbf{A}(t, h)\mathbf{y}$, and it is clearly seen that the estimator $\hat{\boldsymbol{\beta}}(u_i, v_i)$ is a linear estimator in observation $\mathbf{y}$.

Appendix D

The unbiased nature of the parameter $\hat{\mathbf{a}}(u_i, v_i)$ can be indicated by:

$$
\begin{aligned}
&E(\hat{\mathbf{a}}(u_i,v_i)) = E(\mathbf{B}(t,h)\mathbf{y}) \\
&= E\Big(\mathbf{S}\Big[\left(\mathbf{Z}^T\mathbf{W}(u_i,v_i)\mathbf{Z}\right)^{-1}\mathbf{Z}^T\mathbf{W}(u_i,v_i) - \left(\mathbf{Z}^T\mathbf{W}(u_i,v_i)\mathbf{Z}\right)^{-1} \\
&\mathbf{Z}^T\mathbf{W}(u_i,v_i)\mathbf{X}\left(\mathbf{X}^T\mathbf{W}(u_i,v_i)\mathbf{X}\right)^{-1}\mathbf{X}^T\mathbf{W}(u_i,v_i)\Big]\mathbf{y}\Big) \\
&= \Big(\mathbf{S}\Big[\left(\mathbf{Z}^T\mathbf{W}(u_i,v_i)\mathbf{Z}\right)^{-1}\mathbf{Z}^T\mathbf{W}(u_i,v_i) - \left(\mathbf{Z}^T\mathbf{W}(u_i,v_i)\mathbf{Z}\right)^{-1} \\
&\mathbf{Z}^T\mathbf{W}(u_i,v_i)\mathbf{X}\left(\mathbf{X}^T\mathbf{W}(u_i,v_i)\mathbf{X}\right)^{-1}\mathbf{X}^T\mathbf{W}(u_i,v_i)\Big]\Big)E(\mathbf{y}) \\
&= \Big(\mathbf{S}\Big[\left(\mathbf{Z}^T\mathbf{W}(u_i,v_i)\mathbf{Z}\right)^{-1}\mathbf{Z}^T\mathbf{W}(u_i,v_i) - \left(\mathbf{Z}^T\mathbf{W}(u_i,v_i)\mathbf{Z}\right)^{-1} \\
&\mathbf{Z}^T\mathbf{W}(u_i,v_i)\mathbf{X}\left(\mathbf{X}^T\mathbf{W}(u_i,v_i)\mathbf{X}\right)^{-1}\mathbf{X}^T\mathbf{W}(u_i,v_i)\Big]\Big)(\mathbf{X}\boldsymbol{\beta}(u_i,v_i) + \mathbf{Z}\mathbf{a}(u_i,v_i)) \\
&= \mathbf{S}\left(\mathbf{Z}^T\mathbf{W}(u_i,v_i)\mathbf{Z}\right)^{-1}\mathbf{Z}^T\mathbf{W}(u_i,v_i)\mathbf{X}\boldsymbol{\beta}(u_i,v_i) + \\
&\mathbf{S}\left(\mathbf{Z}^T\mathbf{W}(u_i,v_i)\mathbf{Z}\right)^{-1}\mathbf{Z}^T\mathbf{W}(u_i,v_i)\mathbf{Z}\mathbf{a}(u_i,v_i) - \\
&\mathbf{S}\left(\mathbf{Z}^T\mathbf{W}(u_i,v_i)\mathbf{Z}\right)^{-1}\mathbf{Z}^T\mathbf{W}(u_i,v_i)\mathbf{X}\left(\mathbf{X}^T\mathbf{W}(u_i,v_i)\mathbf{X}\right)^{-1}\mathbf{X}^T\mathbf{W}(u_i,v_i)\mathbf{X}\boldsymbol{\beta}(u_i,v_i) \\
&-\mathbf{S}\left(\mathbf{Z}^T\mathbf{W}(u_i,v_i)\mathbf{Z}\right)^{-1}\mathbf{Z}^T\mathbf{W}(u_i,v_i)\mathbf{X}\left(\mathbf{X}^T\mathbf{W}(u_i,v_i)\mathbf{X}\right)^{-1}\mathbf{X}^T\mathbf{W}(u_i,v_i)\mathbf{Z}\mathbf{a}(u_i,v_i) \\
&= \mathbf{S}\mathbf{a}(u_i,v_i) - \mathbf{S}\left(\mathbf{Z}^T\mathbf{W}(u_i,v_i)\mathbf{Z}\right)^{-1}\mathbf{Z}^T\mathbf{W}(u_i,v_i)\mathbf{X}\left(\mathbf{X}^T\mathbf{W}(u_i,v_i)\mathbf{X}\right)^{-1} \\
&\mathbf{X}^T\mathbf{W}(u_i,v_i)\mathbf{Z}\mathbf{a}(u_i,v_i) \\
&= \Big[\mathbf{I} - \left(\mathbf{Z}^T\mathbf{W}(u_i,v_i)\mathbf{Z}\right)^{-1}\mathbf{Z}^T\mathbf{W}(u_i,v_i)\mathbf{X}\left(\mathbf{X}^T\mathbf{W}(u_i,v_i)\mathbf{X}\right)^{-1}\mathbf{X}^T\mathbf{W}(u_i,v_i)\mathbf{Z}\Big] \\
&\mathbf{S}\mathbf{a}(u_i,v_i) \\
&= \Big[\mathbf{I} - \left(\mathbf{Z}^T\mathbf{W}(u_i,v_i)\mathbf{Z}\right)^{-1}\mathbf{Z}^T\mathbf{W}(u_i,v_i)\mathbf{X}\left(\mathbf{X}^T\mathbf{W}(u_i,v_i)\mathbf{X}\right)^{-1}\mathbf{X}^T\mathbf{W}(u_i,v_i)\mathbf{Z}\Big] \\
&= \Big[\mathbf{I} - \left(\mathbf{Z}^T\mathbf{W}(u_i,v_i)\mathbf{Z}\right)^{-1}\mathbf{Z}^T\mathbf{W}(u_i,v_i)\mathbf{X}\left(\mathbf{X}^T\mathbf{W}(u_i,v_i)\mathbf{X}\right)^{-1}\mathbf{X}^T\mathbf{W}(u_i,v_i)\mathbf{Z}\Big]^{-1} \\
&\mathbf{a}(u_i,v_i) \\
&= \mathbf{a}(u_i,v_i)
\end{aligned}
$$

Due to the fact that $E(\hat{\mathbf{a}}(u_i,v_i)) = \mathbf{a}(u_i,v_i)$, then it can be said that $\hat{\mathbf{a}}(u_i,v_i)$ is an unbiased estimator for $\mathbf{a}(u_i,v_i)$. Next, it can be written that $\hat{\mathbf{a}}(u_i,v_i) = \mathbf{B}(t,h)\mathbf{y}$ and hence it is clearly seen that the estimator $\hat{\mathbf{a}}(u_i,v_i)$ is linear in observation $\mathbf{y}$.

References

1. Draper, N.R.; Smith, H. *Applied Regression Analysis*, 3rd ed.; John Wiley & Sons Inc.: Hoboken, NJ, USA, 2014; pp. 1–716. [CrossRef]
2. Budiantara, I.N. The combination of spline and kernel estimator for nonparametric regression and its properties. *Appl. Math. Sci.* **2015**, *9*, 6083–6094. [CrossRef]
3. Cheng, M.; Paige, R.L.; Sun, S.; Yan, K. Variance reduction for kernel estimators in clustered/longitudinal data analysis. *J. Stat. Plan. Inference* **2010**, *140*, 1389–1397. [CrossRef]
4. Octavanny, M.A.D.; Budiantara, I.N.; Ratnasari, V. Pemodelan faktor-faktor yang memengaruhi provinsi jawa timur menggunakan pendekatan regresi semiparametrik spline. *J. Sains Seni ITS* **2017**, *6*, 1–7.
5. Hidayat, M.F.; Achmad, R.F.A.; Solimun. Estimation of truncated spline function in non-parametric path analysis based on weighted least square (WLS). *IOP Conf. Ser. Mater. Sci. Eng.* **2019**, *546*, 5–10. [CrossRef]
6. Sudiarsa, W.; Budiantara, I.N.; Suhartono, S.; Purnami, S.W. Combined estimator fourier series and spline truncated in multivariable nonparametric regression. *Appl. Math. Sci.* **2015**, *9*, 4997–5010. [CrossRef]
7. Mariati, N.P.A.M.; Budiantara, I.N.; Ratnasari, V. Combination estimation of smoothing spline and fourier series in nonparametric regression. *J. Math.* **2020**, *2020*, 4712531. [CrossRef]
8. Fotheringham, A.S.; Brundson, C.; Charlton, M. *Geographically Weighted Regression, the Analysis of Spatially Varying Relationships*; John Wiley & Sons Ltd.: Chichester, UK, 2002.
9. Tang, J.; Gao, F.; Liu, F.; Zhang, W.; Qi, Y. Understanding spatio-temporal characteristics of urban travel demand based on the combination of GWR and GLM. *Sustainabily* **2019**, *11*, 5525. [CrossRef]
10. Dziauddin, M.F. Estimating land value uplift around light rail transit stations in Greater Kuala Lumpur: An empirical study based on geographically weighted regression (GWR). *Res. Transp. Econ.* **2019**, *74*, 10–20. [CrossRef]
11. Sifriyani; Kartiko, S.H.; Budiantara, I.N.; Gunardi. Development of nonparametric geographically weighted regression using truncated spline approach. *Songklanakarin J. Sci. Technol.* **2018**, *40*, 909–920.
12. Fitri, N.; Sifriyani, S.; Yuniarti, D. Nonparametric geographically weighted regression dengan pendekatan spline truncated. *Pros. Semin. Nas. Mat. Dan Stat.* **2019**, 98–105.

13. Sifriyani, S. Simultaneous hypothesis testing of multivariable nonparametric spline regression in the GWR model. *Int. J. Stat. Probab.* **2019**, *8*, 32. [CrossRef]
14. Nurcahayani, H.; Budiantara, I.N.; Zain, I. The curve estimation of combined truncated spline and fourier series estimator for multiresponse nonparametric regression. *Mathematics* **2021**, *9*, 1141. [CrossRef]
15. Akbarov, A.; Wu, S. Waranty claim forecasting based on weighted maximum likelihood estimator. *Qual. Reliab. Eng. Int.* **2012**, *28*, 663–669. [CrossRef]
16. BPS. *Provinsi Sulawesi Tenggara dalam Angka 2021*; UD. Resky Bersama: Kendari, Indonesia, 2021.
17. BPS. *Provinsi Sulawesi Selatan dalam Angka 2021*; BPS Press: Makassar, Indonesia, 2021.
18. BPS. *Provinsi Sulawesi Utara dalam Angka 2021*; Perum Percetakan NRI: Manado, Indonesia, 2021.
19. BPS. *Provinsi Sulawesi Tengah dalam Angka 2021*; UD. Rio: Palu, Indonesia, 2021.
20. BPS. *Provinsi Sulawesi Barat dalam Angka 2021*; Erlangga: Mamuju, Indonesia, 2021.
21. BPS. *Provinsi Gorontalo dalam Angka 2021*; CV. Rifaldi: Gorontalo, Indonesia, 2021.

mathematics

MDPI

Article

Application of an Empirical Best Linear Unbiased Prediction Fay–Herriot (EBLUP-FH) Multivariate Method with Cluster Information to Estimate Average Household Expenditure

Armalia Desiyanti [1,*], Irlandia Ginanjar [2] and Toni Toharudin [2]

[1] Post-Graduate Program in Applied Statistics, Faculty of Mathematics and Natural Sciences, Padjadjaran University, Bandung 45363, Indonesia
[2] Department of Statistics, Faculty of Mathematics and Natural Sciences, Padjadjaran University, Bandung 45363, Indonesia
* Correspondence: armalia21001@mail.unpad.ac.id

Abstract: Data at a smaller regional level has now become a necessity for local governments. The average data on household expenditure on food and non-food is designed for provincial and district/city estimation levels. Subdistrict-level statistics are not currently available. Small area estimation (SAE) is one method to address the problem. The Empirical Best Linear Unbiased Prediction (EBLUP)—Fay Herriot Multivariate method estimates the average household expenditure on food and non-food at the sub-district level in Central Java Province in 2020. Meanwhile, for the sub-districts that are not sampled, the estimation of average household expenditure is done by adding cluster information to the EBLUP Multivariate modeling. The K-Medoids Cluster method is used to classify sub-districts based on their characteristics. Small area estimation using the EBLUP-FH Multivariate method can enhance the parameter estimations obtained using the direct estimation method because it results in a lower level of variation (RSE). For sub-districts that are not sampled, the Residual Standard Error (RSE) value from the estimated results using the EBLUP-FH Multivariate method with cluster information is lower than 25%, indicating that the estimate is accurate.

Keywords: clustering; correlation; REML; multivariate linear mixed models

MSC: 62F10

Citation: Desiyanti, A.; Ginanjar, I.; Toharudin, T. Application of an Empirical Best Linear Unbiased Prediction Fay–Herriot (EBLUP-FH) Multivariate Method with Cluster Information to Estimate Average Household Expenditure. *Mathematics* **2023**, *11*, 135. https://doi.org/10.3390/math11010135

Academic Editors: Niansheng Tang and Shen-Ming Lee

Received: 29 November 2022
Revised: 23 December 2022
Accepted: 24 December 2022
Published: 27 December 2022

1. Introduction

Unquestionably, the current era of economic disruption has a negative side that is particularly felt by middle- to low-income individuals. Disruptions to the economy can eliminate the economic growth momentum generated by demographic bonuses. Numerous jobs previously performed by humans are being replaced by technological innovation and various forms of artificial intelligence. It will lead to new inequality issues as a result of labour reduction, ultimately affecting the welfare of the community. In order to prevent economic disruption from aggravating existing welfare issues in Indonesia, particularly for vulnerable communities and households, the government must implement optimal policies.

The welfare of the population in an area can be described through several indicators, one of which is household consumption expenditure (Sekhampu and Niyimbanira [1]; Irawan et al. [2]). The presentation of household consumption expenditure data produced by the Central Bureau of Statistics (BPS) via the National Socio-Economic Survey (Susenas) must be expanded in order to estimate population parameters at the national, provincial, and district/city levels. It is not designed to estimate population parameters in smaller areas, such as sub-districts or villages, because the sample size is insufficient. The government now requires data presented at a more detailed and accurate regional level in order to conduct development planning and evaluation as well as address population welfare and inequality issues in a targeted and effective manner. Due to a lack of information at the subregional level, policymaking and implementation by local governments are less optimized.

In addition, the sustainable development goals (SDGs) targeted by the United Nations (UN) must be provided by each member country, including Indonesia. Obviously, the fulfillment of the SDGs target requires an estimation level at smaller geographical areas such as districts/cities, sub-districts, and even at the village level. However, the limited number of samples in surveys conducted by BPS will result in inadequate precision for estimation values or parameter estimation in small areas due to the large variance of the resulting estimates. The provision of more budget to increase the number of samples and the number of survey officers is one effort that can be made so that the existing survey design is able to provide a direct estimation of statistical output in small areas with adequate precision, one of which is for the estimation of average household expenditure.

This data is one of the key components required in calculating the poverty rate of a region. The estimation of average household expenditure data up to the sub-district level can later be used as an indicator in grouping sub-districts in a region based on expenditure groups. In addition, the estimated data can be used as an indicator to rank regions to obtain regions that will be the target of poverty alleviation programs or community welfare improvement programs by the regional government. The importance of the need for information down to the small-area level and the limitations of existing resources make it necessary for BPS to apply a statistical method capable of handling these problems. According to Notodiputro and Kurnia [3], one possible solution is the indirect estimator, known as small area estimation (SAE).

Rao and Molina [4] explained that the application of SAE is conducted by borrowing strength from the information of auxiliary variables associated with the response variable or the estimated variable. This condition allows SAE to be employed to improve the effectiveness of survey sample collection at BPS. Several estimation methods can be conducted in SAE, including Best Linear Unbiased Prediction (BLUP), Empirical Best Linear Unbiased Prediction (EBLUP), Hierarchical Bayes (HB), and Empirical Bayes (EB). In general, the selection criteria for these estimation methods are determined based on the type of data on the response variable. EB and HB methods are generally used on response variables that are binary or enumerated, while BLUP and EBLUP methods are more appropriate for continuous response variables (Rao and Molina [4]). The EBLUP method is a form of General Linear Mix Model (GLMM) when the parameter variance is unknown and is considered to have several advantages over other models (Ghosh and Rao [5]). Fay and Herriot [6] initiated using the EBLUP estimation method in area-level SAE to estimate the logarithm of the per capita income of the United States population. Therefore, this model is known as the Fay–Herriot model.

Many research variables, including variables generated from BPS surveys, have strong correlations. One example is the correlation between average household food expenditure and average household non-food expenditure (Nurizza [7]). These strongly correlated variables can be estimated together using the Multivariate EBLUP SAE method and are expected to have a more efficient estimation value than Univariate EBLUP SAE (Datta, Fay, and Ghosh, [8]). The Multivariate Fay–Herriot or Multivariate EBLUP model was then developed by Benavent and Morales [9] by presenting four different estimation models based on the structure of the covariance matrix.

Based on the condition of the March 2020 National Socio-Economic Survey (Susenas) data for Central Java Province, out of a total of 576 sub-districts, 573 sub-districts were included as samples. There were three sub-districts that were not selected as Susenas samples (BPS [10]). Because not all sub-districts were selected as Susenas samples, the problem is how to estimate the parameters for unsampled sub-districts. In estimating EBLUP for unsampled areas, a global synthetic model is usually used. Rao [11] stated that a synthetic estimator is an unbiased estimator in a large area that is used to obtain an indirect estimator in a small area, assuming that the small area has the same characteristics as the large area. The synthetic estimator model will ignore the random area effect since the random area effect information does not exist in the unsampled area (Saei and Chambers [12]), so that the estimation in unsampled subdistricts may be biased.

Some studies with the EBLUP method utilize the addition of cluster information in estimating unsampled areas. Ginanjar [13] researched some of them, who estimated per capita expenditure at the sub-district level in Jambi Province in unsampled sub-districts using the univariate EBLUP method with the addition of cluster information. With the same method, Anisa et al. [14] also added the mean value of the random area effect estimator in each cluster to the prediction model to estimate the unsampled area. Meanwhile, with the Fay–Herriot Multivariate model, Nuryadin [15] applied cluster information to predict the average per capita expenditure per village for food and non-food in unsampled villages. These studies conclude that models that are first clustered turn out to provide better predictions than models without clustering. There has been no research on the EBLUP-FH Multivariate method with K-Medoids Cluster information for actual data compared with the direct estimation method.

The clustering technique commonly used by researchers is K-Means Cluster. However, K-Means Cluster is highly sensitive to large data containing outliers, so the K-Medoids Cluster technique is a better alternative in this condition because it is more robust to outliers (Patel and Singh [16]; Sangga [17]). Based on this explanation, this study compares the direct estimation method and the EBLUP-FH Multivariate method in estimating the average household expenditure on food and non-food at the sub-district level in Central Java Province. In addition, this research also estimates the average household expenditure on food and non-food in non-sampled areas (sub-districts) using the EBLUP-FH Multivariate method by applying K-Medoids Cluster information. The K-Medoids cluster technique is based on considering a large amount of data and the presence of outliers in the auxiliary variables used.

2. Materials and Methods

Table 1 below presents a summary of the materials and methods used in this research. The detailed explanation will be presented in the following subsections.

2.1. Average of Household Expenditures

BPS [10] defines average household expenditure as the monthly costs incurred for all household members' consumption, divided by the number of households. Household consumption can be divided into food and non-food consumption and is restricted to spending on household necessities only, without consideration of sources. The forms of consumption expenditures include purchases, gifts, and items generated by the household (excluding expenditures used for business purposes or those given to other parties).

The calculation of average household expenditure in the i-th area can be mathematically formulated as follows:

$$y_i = \frac{Expend_i}{n_{RT}} \quad , \ i = 1, 2, \ldots, m$$

where:

y_i: average monthly household expenditure in the i-th area (rupiah)
$Expend_i$: total household expenditure in a month in the i-th area (rupiah)
n_{RT}: number of households

Table 1. Summary of Research Materials and Methods.

No	Material	Method	Description
(1)	(2)	(3)	(4)
1	Estimation of Average Household Expenditure on food and non-food for the sampled sub-districts		
	Average of Household expenditures on food (Y1) and on non-food (Y2)	1. Direct Estimation Method (based on the sampling design of March 2020 Susenas) 2. Indirect Estimation Method (EBLUP-FH Multivariate Method)	This study compares the direct estimation and EBLUP-FH Multivariate methods based on the RSE value.
	Selection of auxiliary variables for Y1 Selection of auxiliary variables for Y2	Stepwise Selection Method	1. The auxiliary variables used in SAE must be related to the response variable. 2. Selection of auxiliary variables in this study used the stepwise selection method.
2	Estimation of Average Household Expenditure on food and non-food for the non-sampled sub-districts		
	Average of household Expenditures on food (Y1) and on non-food (Y2)	EBLUP-FH Multivariate Method with K-Medoids Cluster Information	1. The sampled and non-sampled sub-districts will be grouped based on the auxiliary variables so that the cluster for each sub-district can be identified. 2. In the sampled area, the known random area effects components are averaged in each cluster. 3. The average of the random area effect per cluster will be entered into the prediction model as the estimator of the random area effect. 4. The average random effect area is used as additional information in areas with no samples in the corresponding cluster using the EBLUP-FH Multivariate method.
	Clustering of the auxiliary variables for Y1 Clustering of the auxiliary variables for Y2	K-Medoids Cluster	1. The auxiliary variables used are selected variables that have met the assumptions of sample adequacy (KMO value) and non-multicollinearity (VIF value) first. 2. Standardization is first carried out using the Z-Score method for each auxiliary variable used in clustering.

2.2. Related Research on Determining Auxiliary Variables

Rao [18] states that in conducting indirect estimation, the choice of auxiliary variables is very significant in determining the accuracy of the resulting estimates. Estimation of per capita expenditure variables using small area estimation, or SAE, has been done quite a lot in Indonesia. Desiyanti et al. [19] use the EBLUP Univariate method to estimate average per capita expenditure at the sub-district level in West Sumatra. However, estimation of unsampled sub-districts still uses synthetic estimators. Auxiliary variables used in indirect estimation are the number of non-electricity user families, the number of non-PLN electricity user families, the number of polyclinics/medical centers, the number of minimarkets/supermarkets, the number of SD/MI, and the number of doctor's practices.

In Amaliana and Lestari's research [20] on the application of the EBLUP Univariate method to the Fay–Herriot SAE model, the auxiliary variables used including the percentage of agricultural households, the number of Insurance for the Indigence recipients, State Electricity Company (PLN) electricity users, the number of Elementary School (SD)-Junior High School (SMP)-High School (SMA)- University (PT), the number of families living in slums, the number of Certificate of Indigence (SKTM) owners, the number of educational institutions and skills, and the number of Indonesian migrant workers (TKI) have a significant effect in indirectly estimating per capita expenditure in the Jember District.

Furthermore, Nurizza and Ubaidillah [21] used the SAE multivariate approach in estimating food and non-food per capita expenditure in Indonesia. Their results shows that in estimating indirect per capita food expenditure, the variables of the number of non-PLN electricity users, the number of riverbank settlements, the number of migrant workers, elementary schools, vocational schools, universities, auxiliary health centers, polyclinics, doctor's offices, village maternity clinics, integrated health posts, medium and small industries (IMK), restaurants and inns had a significant effect. Meanwhile, for the indirect estimation of non-food per capita expenditure in Indonesia, the variables that have a significant effect are the number of PLN electricity users, non-PLN users, migrant workers, elementary schools, midwife practice sites, doctor practice sites, village maternity clinics, integrated health posts, community health centers without inpatient care, auxiliary community health centers, polyclinics, pharmacies, and restaurants.

Small-area estimation of per capita expenditure at the subdistrict level was also conducted by Ginanjar [13] using the EBLUP method in Jambi Province. In this study, there were eight auxiliary variables or predictor variables that significantly influenced per capita expenditure at the subdistrict level in Jambi Province, namely population, number of universities, the ratio of school facilities, number of polyclinics/health centers, coverage of doctors, coverage of health workers, coverage of people with disabilities, and the ratio of midwives.

2.3. Small Area Estimation

An area is considered large if the sample drawn from it is large enough to yield a direct estimate with sufficient precision. Conversely, an area or domain is considered small if the domain-specific sample is not large enough to support direct estimation with sufficient precision or accuracy (Rao and Molina [4]). Small area estimation (SAE) is an indirect estimation technique in small areas that is conducted by borrowing strengths from related areas and/or periods to increase the effectiveness of the sample size and decrease the standard error, allowing the estimation results to have sufficient precision (Rao and Molina [4]).

The main problems in SAE are how to produce reasonably good parameter estimates in an area with a relatively small sample size and how to estimate the mean square error (MSE) of the resulting parameter estimates (Pfeffermann [22]). Both of these main points can be generated by borrowing additional information from within the area, outside the area, or outside the survey (auxiliary variables), which can usually be obtained from census or administrative data.

Based on the availability of auxiliary variables, SAE can be classified into two types (Rao dan Molina [4]).

2.3.1. Basic Unit-Level Model

The unit-based small area estimation model is an SAE model with available auxiliary variables corresponding to response variables observed up to the unit level. Assumed auxiliary variables are available for every j-th element in the i-th area. $\boldsymbol{x}_{ij} = \left(x_{ij1}, x_{ij2}, \ldots, x_{ijp}\right)^T$ available for each j-th element in the i-th area. The variables of interest are y_{ij} assumed to have a relationship with x_{ij} through the following equation:

$$y_{ij} = \boldsymbol{x}_{ij}{}^T\boldsymbol{\beta} + v_i + e_{ij} \; ; \; j = 1, 2, \ldots, n_i \; ; \; i = 1, 2, \ldots, m$$

Area random effects are denoted by v_i, a random variable that is assumed to be independent and identically distributed. While for $e_{ij} = k_{ij}\widetilde{e}_{ij}$ with k_{ij} a known constant and $\widetilde{e}_{ij}$ are random variables that are mutually independent and identically distributed with respect to v_i. In other words, v_i and $\widetilde{e}_{ij}$ are generally assumed to have a normal probability distribution.

2.3.2. Area-Level Model (Basic Area-Level)

The area-based SAE model introduced by Fay and Herriot in 1979 is part of the General Linear Mixed Model (GLMM). This GLMM model is built based on the availability of predictor variables and direct estimation at a certain area level. Suppose there are a number of small areas as many as m $(i = 1, \ldots, m)$ with auxiliary variable data available for each i-th small area being $x_i = (x_{1i}, x_{2i,\ldots,} x_{pi,})^T$, with the parameters to be estimated being θ_i. The θ_i is assumed to be linearly related to x_i through the following equation (Ubaidillah [23]):

$$\theta_i = x_i^T \beta + b_i u_i \,,\; i = 1, \ldots, m \tag{1}$$

By:

$\beta = (\beta_1, \beta_2, \ldots, \beta_p)^T$ is a vector of regression coefficients of size p × 1
b_i: known positive constant
u_i: small area random effects, with u_i assumed to be independent and identically distributed (iid) with $E(u_i) = 0$ and $V(u_i) = \sigma_u^2$.

If assumed $\hat{y}_i$ is an unbiased direct estimator for θ_i, where the estimator θ_i contains the error of the sample draw, namely e_i, then the sampling model can be formulated as follows:

$$\hat{\theta}_i = g(\hat{y}_i) = \theta_i + e_i \rightarrow , \qquad i = 1, \ldots, m \tag{2}$$

where e_i is a sampling error that is assumed to be independent of each other with its variance assumed to be known (ψ_i) or $E(e_i) = 0$ and $V(e_i) = \psi_i$.

Combining Equations (1) and (2) will result in a General Linear Mixed Model of area-based small area estimation known as the Fay–Herriot model, namely:

$$\hat{\theta}_i = x_i^T \beta + b_i u_i + e_i \,, \qquad i = 1, \ldots, m \tag{3}$$

In the model Equation (3) above, the variation of the response variable in a small area is assumed to be explained by the relationship between the response variable and the auxiliary variables, which is called the fixed effect model. In addition, this model also contains a small area random effect component, which is a small area-specific variation component that cannot be explained by the auxiliary variables. The combination of these two assumptions (the fixed effect model and the random effect model) forms a linear mixed model.

2.4. *Multivariate Fay–Herriot Models*

The Multivariate Fay–Herriot model is a development of the Univariate Fay–Herriot model that can be used for more than one response variable (Ubaidillah [23]). Suppose the population is partitioned into m area. Let $\mu_d = (\mu_{1d}, \ldots, \mu_{md})^T$ be a vector of the d-th variable of interest, with $d = 1, \ldots, D$. Meanwhile, the vector of d-th direct estimators of μ_d is denoted by $y_d = (y_{1d}, \ldots, y_{mD})^T$. As for μ_d, it is assumed to be related to p_d area-specific auxiliary variables $\mathbf{X}_d = (\mathbf{X}_1, \ldots, \mathbf{X}_D)^T$ through a linear model (Ubaidillah, 2017):

$$\mu_d = \mathbf{X}_d\, \beta_d + u_d \,,\; u_d \sim iid\; N(0, V_{u_d}) \,,\; d = 1, \ldots, D \tag{4}$$

where:

$u_d = (u_{1d}, \ldots, u_{mD})^T$: vector of area random effects
$V_{u_d} = diag_{1 \le d \le D}\left(\sigma_{u_d}^2\right)$: covariance matrix of area random effects of size $D \times D$
$\mathbf{X}_d = (\mathbf{X}_1, \ldots, \mathbf{X}_D)^T$: d-th matrix of area-specific auxiliary variables of size $m \times p_d$ with $p = \sum_{d=1}^{D} p_d$
$\beta = (\beta_1^T, \ldots, \beta_d^T)^T{}_{p \times 1}$: vector of regression coefficients, with $\beta_d = \left(\beta_{d1}, \ldots, \beta_{dp_d}\right)_{p_d \times 1}$

The sampling model can be formulated as follows:

$$y_d = \mu_d + e_d \,, \qquad e_d \sim iid\; N(0,\, V_{e_d}), \qquad d = 1, \ldots, D \tag{5}$$

where e_d is the vector of sampling errors and V_{e_d} is a known covariance matrix of size $m \times m$. By combining Equations (4) and (5), the Multivariate Fay–Herriot model is generated as follows:

$$y_d = X_d \beta_d + u_d + e_d, \quad d = 1, \ldots, D \tag{6}$$

where u_d and e_d are independent.

The model in Equation (6) can be written in matrix form as follows (Benavent and Morales, 2016):

$$\mathbf{y} = \mathbf{X\beta} + \mathbf{Zu} + \mathbf{e}\ ,\ \mathbf{u} \sim N(0, G)\ ,\ \mathbf{e} \sim \mathrm{N}(0, \mathbf{R}) \tag{7}$$

where $\mathbf{u} = col_{1 \le d \le D}(\mathbf{u}_\mathrm{d})$ and $\mathbf{e} = col_{1 \le d \le D}(\mathbf{e}_\mathrm{d})$ are mutually independent. $\mathbf{Z}$ is a matrix of random effect constants that are assumed to be known. The matrix $\mathbf{X} = diag_{1 \le d \le D}(\mathbf{X}_\mathrm{d})$ with $\mathbf{X}_\mathrm{d} = col_{1 \le i \le m}(\mathbf{x}_\mathrm{id})$ is a matrix of auxiliary variables with $\mathbf{x}_\mathrm{id} = \left(\mathrm{x}_{\mathrm{i}1}, \ldots, \mathrm{x}_{\mathrm{i}p_d}\right)^T$. The vector $\mathbf{y} = col_{1 \le d \le D}(\mathbf{y}_\mathrm{d})$ is the $Dm \times 1$ vector of variables of interest with $\mathbf{y}_\mathrm{d} = \left(\mathrm{y}_{1\mathrm{d}}, \ldots, \mathrm{y}_{\mathrm{md}}\right)^T$. The col operator means stacking matrix by column. The matrix $\boldsymbol{G} = \boldsymbol{V}_u \otimes \boldsymbol{I}_m$ is the covariance matrix of the random effects area where $\boldsymbol{I}_m$ is the identity matrix of size $m \times m$, and $\otimes$ denotes a Kronecker product. While $\mathbf{R}$ is a sampling covariance matrix of size $Dm \times Dm$ which is assumed to be known and obtained from sampling error in the survey.

Empirical Best Linear Unbiased Prediction (EBLUP) Multivariate

Under the model in Equation (7), it holds that $E(y) = \mathbf{X\beta}$ and $\mathrm{var}(y) = \mathbf{ZGZ}^\mathrm{T} + \mathbf{R} = \mathbf{\Omega}$. The best linear unbiased prediction (BLUP) of $\boldsymbol{\mu} = col_{1 \le d \le D}(\boldsymbol{\mu}_\mathrm{d})$ where $\boldsymbol{\mu}_\mathrm{d} = \left(\mu_{1\mathrm{d}}, \ldots, \mu_{\mathrm{md}}\right)^T$ is:

$$\widetilde{\mu} = X\widetilde{\beta} + ZGZ^T\Omega^{-1}(y - X\widetilde{\beta}) \tag{8}$$

where $\widetilde{\beta} = \left(\mathbf{X}^\mathrm{T}\mathbf{\Omega}^{-1}\mathbf{X}\right)^{-1}\mathbf{X}^\mathrm{T}\mathbf{\Omega}^{-1}y$ is the best linear unbiased estimator (BLUE) of β.

Since the value of the random effect variance component, δ, is unknown, it must be determined from empirical data when modeling parameters using the EBLUP-Fay–Herriot approach. There are several estimation methods that can be performed on the random effect variance component, such as the Maximum Likelihood (ML) and Restricted Maximum Likelihood (REML) methods based on normal likelihood (Patterson and Thompson [24]).

As stated earlier, the multivariate BLUP estimator (8) depends on the variance parameter δ of $\boldsymbol{G}(\delta)$ where $\delta = \left(\delta_{u1}^2, \ldots, \delta_{uq}^2\right)$. The variance parameter, δ, cannot be known and is estimated using the REML approach. Restricted log-likelihood of the joint probability density of y^* which is expressed as a function of δ is given as follows (Benavent and Morales [9]):

$$l_R(\delta) = -\frac{Dm - p}{2}\log(2\pi) + \frac{1}{2}\log\left|\mathbf{X}^\mathrm{T}\mathbf{X}\right| - \frac{1}{2}\log|\mathbf{\Omega}| - \frac{1}{2}\log\left|\mathbf{X}^\mathrm{T}\mathbf{\Omega}\mathbf{X}\right| - \frac{1}{2}y^\mathrm{T}\mathbf{P}\mathbf{y} \tag{9}$$

where $\mathbf{P} = \mathbf{\Omega}^{-1} - \mathbf{\Omega}^{-1}\mathbf{X}\left(\mathbf{X}^T\mathbf{\Omega}^{-1}\mathbf{X}\right)^{-1}\mathbf{X}\mathbf{\Omega}^{-1}$. By taking the partial derivative of Equation (9) with respect to δ with k-th element, where $k = 1, \ldots, q$, then the score vector is obtained $\mathbf{s}(\delta) = \left(s_1(\delta), \ldots, s_q(\delta)\right)$ where:

$$s_k(\delta) = \frac{\partial l_R(\delta)}{\partial \delta_k} = -\frac{1}{2}\mathrm{tr}\left(\mathbf{P}\mathbf{\Omega}_{(k)}\right) + \frac{1}{2}y^\mathrm{T}\mathbf{P}\mathbf{\Omega}_{(k)}\mathbf{P}\mathbf{y},\ k = 1, \ldots, q$$

where $\mathbf{\Omega}_{(\mathrm{k})} = \partial\mathbf{\Omega}/\partial\delta_\mathrm{k}$ is the partial derivative of $\mathbf{\Omega}$ with respect to k-th element of $\boldsymbol{\delta}$. By taking the second order partial derivative of Equation (9) with respect to $\boldsymbol{\delta}$ with kl-th element, changing sign and taking expectations, then the Fisher Information matrix is obtained as follows:

$$\mathfrak{I}_{kl}(\delta) = \frac{1}{2}\mathrm{tr}\left(\mathbf{P}\mathbf{\Omega}_{(l)}\mathbf{P}\mathbf{\Omega}_{(k)}\right),\ k, l = 1, \ldots, q$$

The iterative a of Fisher-scoring algorithm for REML estimation of δ is:

$$\hat{\delta}^{(a+1)} = \hat{\delta}^{(a)} + \mathfrak{I}_{kl}^{-1}\left(\hat{\delta}^{(a)}\right) \mathbf{s}\left(\hat{\delta}^{(a)}\right) \quad (10)$$

Furthermore, the Empirical Best Linear Unbiased Prediction (EBLUP) estimator for the Multivariate Fay–Herriot model is obtained by plugging $\hat{\delta}$ in $\mathbf{G}$ and $\boldsymbol{\Omega}$ of Equation (8) as follows:

$$\hat{\boldsymbol{\mu}} = \mathbf{X}\hat{\boldsymbol{\beta}} + \mathbf{Z}\hat{\mathbf{G}}\mathbf{Z}^{\mathrm{T}}\hat{\boldsymbol{\Omega}}^{-1}\left(y - \mathbf{X}\hat{\boldsymbol{\beta}}\right) \quad (11)$$

where $\hat{\boldsymbol{\beta}} = (\mathbf{X}^{\mathrm{T}}\hat{\boldsymbol{\Omega}}^{-1}\mathbf{X})^{-1}\mathbf{X}^{\mathrm{T}}\hat{\boldsymbol{\Omega}}^{-1}y$ is the Best Linear Unbiased Estimator (BLUE) for $\boldsymbol{\beta}$ with covariance matrix $\mathrm{cov}(\hat{\boldsymbol{\beta}}) = (\mathbf{X}^{\mathrm{T}}\hat{\boldsymbol{\Omega}}^{-1}\mathbf{X})^{-1}$.

2.5. Direct Estimation

Estimation of population parameters in a region based only on sample data from that region is said to be direct estimation (Rao and Molina [4]). This direct estimation method is design-based or depends on the sampling design used. The March 2020 National Socio-Economic Survey (Susenas) results were used in this study to directly estimate the response variable on average household expenditure on food and non-food.

2.6. Selection of Auxiliary Variables

The auxiliary variables used in SAE must be related to the response variable. The auxiliary variables used in this study were taken from the variables used in related studies and then grouped into variable groups with the following details:

a. Population
b. Education
c. Health
d. Economy (industry)
e. Economy (other than industry)
f. Economy (financial inclusiveness)

There are methods we can use to select auxiliary variables, including forward, backward, and stepwise methods. The stepwise selection method combines the forward and backward selection methods. The stepwise method modifies the forward selection method. When a new variable is added, all candidate variables in the model are checked again to see if they are still significant. If there is a variable that becomes insignificant based on the specified significance level, then the variable is removed (backward). In this stepwise method, there are two levels of significance: adding variables and removing variables from the model.

2.7. Multivariate EBLUP Method with Added Cluster Information

The EBLUP method is generally used to estimate an area that contains a sample. Unsampled areas can usually be estimated using a synthetic model. The problem with the synthetic model is that it does not consider the random effect area because it does not have enough information about the area that was not sampled. It can lead to an estimated value with a large bias (. Therefore, adding cluster information to the EBLUP method should improve estimates for unsampled areas. Clustering is conducted based on auxiliary variables so that all areas will be included in certain clusters, both with and without samples.

The addition of cluster information is based on the assumption that an area has a pattern of close relationships with other areas. The random area effect has a similarity pattern between areas, allowing it to be analyzed using cluster techniques from the auxiliary variables in each small area. In estimating an unsampled area, the random area effect is often ignored due to the absence of such information. The EBLUP estimator for unsampled areas can be modeled as follows:

$$\hat{\mu}_{i*} = x_{i*}^{T}\hat{\beta}$$

with $i*$ are the unsampled subdistricts in this study (Padureso sub-district, Batuwarno sub-district, and Lebakbarang sub-district).

The sampled and unsampled sub-districts will be grouped based on the auxiliary variables so that the cluster for each sub-district can be identified. The auxiliary variables used are selected variables that have met the assumptions of sample adequacy and non-multicollinearity first. The next step to be done in the sampled sub-districts is to average the random area effects per known cluster. Then the average of the random area effect per cluster will be entered into the prediction model as the estimator of the random area effect. The average random area effect per cluster is formulated in the following equation:

$$\overline{\hat{\mathbf{u}}}_{\mathbf{c}} = \frac{1}{m_c}\sum\nolimits_{i=1}^{m_c}\hat{\mathbf{u}}_{\mathbf{i}} \quad (12)$$

with

m_c: number of sub-districts sampled in the c-th cluster

$\overline{\hat{\mathbf{u}}}_{\mathbf{c}}$: the average random effect area in the c-th cluster

$\hat{\mathbf{u}}_{\mathbf{i}}$: random effect area in the i-th sample

The average random effect area is used as additional information in areas where there are no samples in the corresponding cluster. Thus, the EBLUP estimator for unsampled areas can be formulated as follows:

$$\hat{\mu}_{i*c} = \mathbf{x}_{i*c}^{T}\hat{\boldsymbol{\beta}} + \overline{\hat{\mathbf{u}}}_{\mathbf{c}} \quad (13)$$

with $i * c$ are the unsampled subdistricts in the c-th cluster and $\overline{\hat{\mathbf{u}}}_{\mathbf{c}}$ is the average of random effect area in the c-th cluster.

The quality of the resulting estimates can be evaluated based on the Relative Standard Error (RSE) value. The RSE value for the Multivariate EBLUP method is obtained by comparing the square root value of the MSE to the estimated value of the response variable, expressed as a percentage, according to the following formula:

$$\mathrm{RSE}(\theta_i) = \frac{\sqrt{\mathrm{MSE}(\theta_i)}}{\theta_i} \times 100\%,\ i = 1, \ldots, m \quad (14)$$

According to BPS (2020), decisions regarding the accuracy of an estimate with RSE conditions $\leq$25% the resulting data is accurate (and can be used), condition 25%$<$ RSE $\leq$ 50% needs to be careful if the data will be used, and the condition RSE $>$ 50% data is considered inaccurate. The greater the RSE value, the more the estimator value differs significantly from the real parameter value.

2.8. Research Stages

The stages of research using the Multivariate EBLUP method and with the addition of cluster information are as follows:

1. Prepare response variable data from National Socio-Economic Survey (Susenas) March 2020 data and auxiliary variable data from Village Potential Podes 2020 data for each sub-district in Central Java Province.
2. Prepare the direct estimation results for the response variable of average household food and non-food expenditures that have been obtained from the results of the March 2020 National Socio-Economic Survey (Susenas) processing, namely 573 sub-districts out of a total of 576 sub-districts in Central Java Province.

3. Test the correlation between the response variables average household expenditure on food and average household expenditure on non-food with Pearson Correlation.

   The Pearson Correlation test hypothesis is as follows:

$H_0 : \rho = 0\ (no\ correlation)$
$H_1 : \rho \neq 0\ (there\ is\ a\ correlation)$

with the Pearson correlation coefficient formula as follows:

$$r = \frac{m\sum_{i=1}^{m} y_{1i}\ y_{2i} - (\sum_{i=1}^{m} y_{1i})(\sum_{i=1}^{m} y_{2i})}{\sqrt{m\sum_{i=1}^{m} y_{1i}^2 - (\sum_{i=1}^{m} y_{1i})^2}\ \sqrt{m\sum_{i=1}^{m} y_{2i}^2 - (\sum_{i=1}^{m} y_{2i})^2}} \quad (15)$$

To test the significance of the correlation, the t-test is used with the following formula:

$$t = \frac{r\sqrt{m-2}}{\sqrt{1-r^2}} \quad (16)$$

where:

m = sample size
r = the computed correlation coefficient being tested for significance.

The *t*-distribution formula for obtaining the appropriate *t*-value for testing the significance of the correlation coefficient r is given by Equation (16). Then, the results of Equation (16) are compared to the *t*-table values with degrees of freedom $(m-2)$. If $t \geq t\ table$, then H_0 will be rejected or if the p-value is less than α which is set at 0.05.

4. In the sampled area, the SAE area-level model was built to estimate parameters through the Multivariate EBLUP method, namely by:
   a. Estimating the variance component $\boldsymbol{\delta}$ using the REML method through the Fisher scoring iteration procedure, according to Equation (10). The estimation process was conducted with the help of open-source R software version 4.1.3, using the package "msaeDB".
   b. Estimating $\hat{\boldsymbol{\beta}}$ where $\hat{\boldsymbol{\beta}} = (\mathbf{X}^T\hat{\boldsymbol{\Omega}}^{-1}\mathbf{X})^{-1}\mathbf{X}^T\hat{\boldsymbol{\Omega}}^{-1}\mathbf{y}$
   c. Perform the selection of auxiliary variables using the stepwise method
   d. Estimating the average household expenditure on food and non-food ($\hat{\boldsymbol{\mu}}$) in each sampled sub-district using the selected auxiliary variables according to Equation (11)
   e. Calculate the RSE values of EBLUP-FH Multivariate on the average of household expenditure on food and non-food for each sub-district according to Equation (14)
5. Perform the estimation process on non-sampled sub-districts using the Multivariate EBLUP method by adding cluster information with the K-Medoids technique, preceded by the following steps:
   a. Checking the assumption of sample adequacy (KMO value) and detecting multicollinearity.
   b. Apply the Z-Score approach to standardize the auxiliary variables used in the clustering procedure.
   c. Determination of the optimum number of clusters using the silhouette method.
   d. In the sampled area, the known components $\hat{\mathbf{u}}_i$ are averaged in each cluster according to Equation (12).
   e. Estimating the average household expenditure on food and non-food in the non-sampled area using the EBLUP-FH Multivariate method by adding cluster information $(\hat{\mu}_{i*c})$ according to Equation (13). The estimation process uses R software with the "msaeDB" package and "msaefhns" function.

6. Analyzing the results of estimating the average household expenditure on food and non-food at the sub-district level in Central Java Province.

2.9. Data Source

This research uses secondary data from the Central Bureau of Statistics (BPS) as follows:

1. Average monthly household expenditure on food and non-food data for 573 sub-districts in Central Java Province, sourced from the March 2020 National Socio-Economic Survey (Susenas) raw data using the direct estimation method. This data is used as response variables.
2. Data on facilities, infrastructure, and other auxiliary variables available in each sub-district in Central Java Province were sourced from processing Village Potential (Podes) 2020 raw data.

This research is a case study for all sub-districts (576 sub-districts) in the districts/cities of Central Java Province in 2020. The National Socio-Economic Survey (Susenas) and Podes data used are aggregated data for each sub-district in Central Java Province. The processing in this study was carried out using the open-source software R version 4.1.3.

2.10. Research Variables

The variables used in this study include response variables and auxiliary variables. The response variable used is the average monthly food and non-food consumption expenditure of households in the *i*-th sub-districts, sourced from the March 2020 National Socio-Economic Survey (SUSENAS) data. Meanwhile, auxiliary variables in each sub-district are obtained from PODES data in the 2020 Central Java Province. The determination of the auxiliary variables in this study is based on factors that affect the average household food and non-food consumption expenditure. The 40 candidates for auxiliary variables are shown in Appendix A, Table A1. Meanwhile, the significant auxiliary variables included in the model are presented in Table 2.

Table 2. Selected Significant Auxiliary Variables.

Variables	Names of Variables	Source
(1)	(2)	(3)
Y_1	Average household expenditure on food (IDR)	Susenas March 2020
Y_2	Average household expenditure on non-food items (IDR)	Susenas March 2020
X_1	Number of families using electricity (PLN and Non-PLN)	PODES 2020
X_3	Number of elementary school/islamic elementary school	PODES 2020
X_4	Number of junior high school/islamic junior high school	PODES 2020
X_7	Number of academies/colleges	PODES 2020
X_{12}	Number of polyclinics/treatment centers	PODES 2020
X_{13}	Number of physician practices	PODES 2020
X_{15}	Number of midwife practices	PODES 2020
X_{16}	Number of village health posts	PODES 2020
X_{23}	Number of fabric/weaving micro and small industries	PODES 2020
X_{26}	Number of food and beverage micro and small industries	PODES 2020
X_{27}	Number of other small micro industries	PODES 2020
X_{29}	Number of markets with permanent buildings	PODES 2020
X_{30}	Number of markets with semi-permanent buildings	PODES 2020
X_{32}	Number of minimarket/supermarket	PODES 2020
X_{34}	Number of restaurants/restaurants	PODES 2020
X_{37}	Number of lodgings	PODES 2020

3. Results

In Section 3, the study's results are introduced along with a general overview of welfare problems in Central Java Province, Indonesia. For both the sub-districts sampled for the March 2020 Susenas and those not sampled, the findings from the estimation of the average household expenditure on food and non-food items will be provided. Maps of distribution, graphs, and boxplots of RSE values will be used to compare the results between the direct estimation and the EBLUP-FH Multivariate method for the 573 sampled sub-districts. In addition, the EBLUP-FH Multivariate method's findings for the estimation of non-sampled sub-districts are shown in this section.

3.1. *Overview of Central Java Province*

In 2020, Central Java had an economic share of 8.55 percent (Figure 1), which was the fourth largest contributor to the national economy, after DKI Jakarta (17.55 percent), East Java (14.58 percent), and West Java (13.22 percent). However, all levels of society did not equally enjoy a high share of Central Java's economy. It was reflected in the percentage of poverty which ranked as the second highest in Java after Yogyakarta, or ranked 13th nationally, with a poverty, percentage of 11.41 percent.

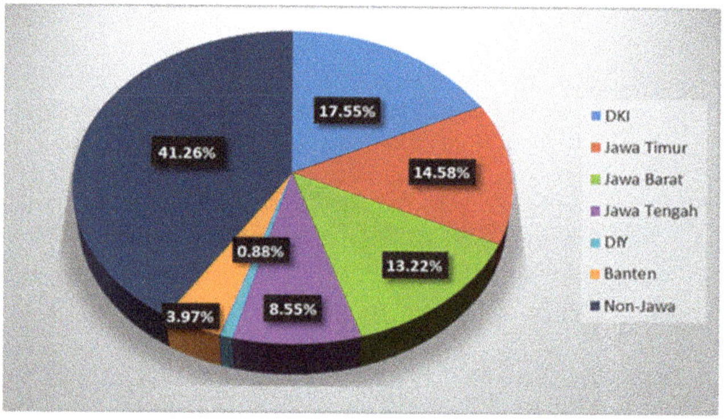

Figure 1. Share of the economy in Indonesia in 2020. Source: Central Bureau of Statistics.

When the poverty rate is broken down by district/city, 23 out of 29 districts in Central Java have a poverty rate above the national rate (Figure 2). Meanwhile, the poverty rates in the six cities in Central Java are far below the national rate. The calculation of poverty cannot be separated from the indicator of average household expenditure on both food and non-food items.

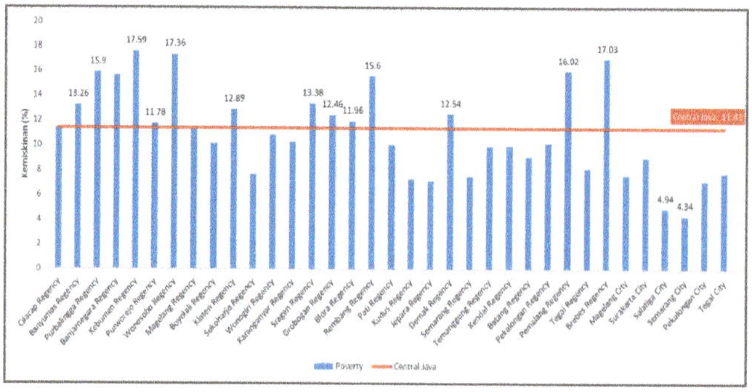

Figure 2. Poverty Percentage in Central Java Province by District/City in 2020. Source: Central Bureau of Statistics.

3.2. Direct Estimation

The March 2020 National Socio-Economic Survey sampling design was used to get the direct estimates for the average household expenditure on food and non-food items. According to the sampling plan in Appendix B Table A2, parameters are estimated at the district or city level using a two-stage, one-phase sampling method. Direct estimation of average household expenditure on food and non-food can only be conducted in areas sampled in the March 2020 National Socio-Economic Survey (Susenas). In total, Central Java has 576 sub-districts. Out of these sub-districts, only 573 sub-districts were sampled in the March 2020 National Socio-Economic Survey (Susenas). The results of the direct estimation calculation were not obtained for the Padureso sub-district in the Kebumen district, the Batuwarno sub-district in the Wonogiri district, and the Lebakbarang sub-district in the Pekalongan district because these three sub-districts were not sampled in the March 2020 National Socio-Economic Survey (Susenas).

Using the direct estimation method to estimate the average household expenditure on food at the subdistrict level, the difference in expenditure figures between sub-districts is significant. Figure 3 shows the map of the estimated results for the average household expenditure on food per sub-district based on the direct estimation method. Wonogiri District's Paranggupito Subdistrict has the lowest average household food expenditure of IDR 796,888. The sub-district of Banyumanik in the city of Semarang has the highest average household expenditures on food, at IDR 3,324,899. The median of average household food expenditure is IDR 1,668,801, indicating that 50 percent of sub-districts have average household food expenditures that are less than or equal to IDR 1,668,801.

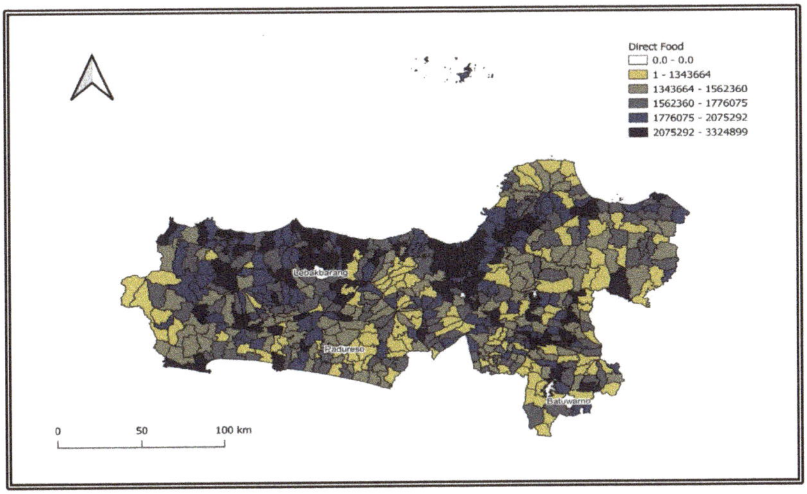

Figure 3. Map of Estimation of Average Household Expenditure on Food at the Subdistrict Level in Central Java Province using the Direct Estimation Method.

The average household expenditure on non-food items varies greatly across subdistricts, according to direct estimates (Figure 4). Geyer sub-district in Grobogan District has the lowest average household expenditure on non-food items at IDR 486,601. In line with food expenditure, the sub-district of Banyumanik in Semarang City has the highest average value of non-food household expenditure at IDR 7,680,844.

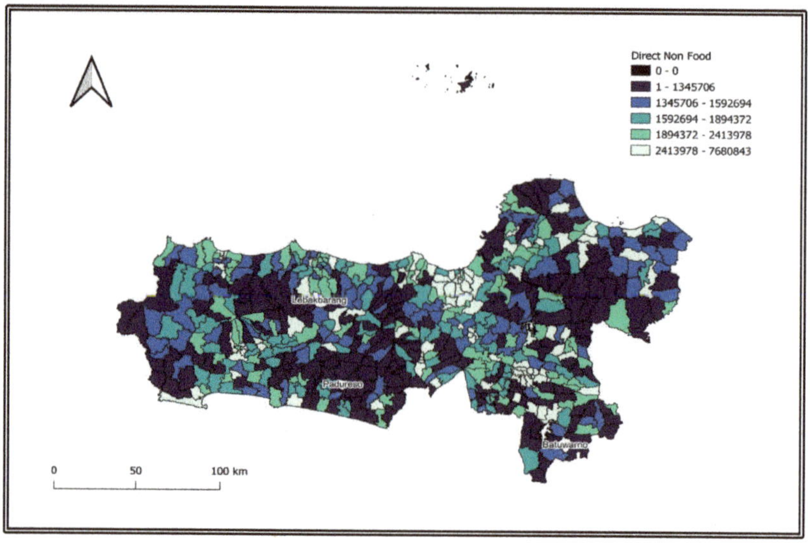

Figure 4. Map of Estimation of Average Household Expenditure on Non-Food at the Subdistrict Level in Central Java Province using the Direct Estimation Method.

It can be seen from Figures 3 and 4 that sub-districts with high average household food expenditure also tend to have high average household non-food expenditure. It demonstrates a correlation between the average household's food expenditure and other expenditures.

3.3. Multivariate Empirical Best Linear Unbiased Prediction (EBLUP) Modeling

3.3.1. Correlation Test of Response Variables

According to the results of the Pearson Correlation test in Equations (15) and (16), the p-value is less than 0.05, indicating that there is a correlation between the two response variables employed in the study. The correlation coefficient between the two response variables is 0.6216, which falls within the strong correlation range (De Vaus [25]). Therefore, the Multivariate Fay–Herriot EBLUP model can be applied to the variable that represents the average household expenditures for food and non-food in 2020 in Central Java.

3.3.2. Selection of Auxiliary Variables

After obtaining the results of the direct estimation of household expenditure at the sub-district level, estimation is carried out using the EBLUP-FH method. However, before estimating EBLUP-FH, the selection of auxiliary variables is first carried out based on the correlation value and its significance to the direct estimation. The selection of auxiliary variables was carried out using the stepwise method with a significance level of five percent. From the initial 40 candidate auxiliary variables, 13 significant auxiliary variables were generated for Multivariate EBLUP modeling of average household expenditure data for food (Y_1), the number of families using electricity (X_1), number of elementary/islamic elementary school (X_3), number of junior high school / Islamic junior high school (X_4), number of polyclinics/medical centers (X_{12}), number of doctor's offices (X_{13}), number of midwife practice sites (X_{15}), number of village health posts (X_{16}), number of small medium industry (IMK) from fabric/weaving (X_{23}), total IMK of food and beverages (X_{26}), number of other of small medium industry (X_{27}), number of markets with permanent buildings (X_{29}), number of markets with semi-permanent buildings (X_{30}), and number of inns (X_{37}).

Meanwhile, for Multivariate EBLUP modeling of average household expenditure data for non-food (Y_2), eight significant auxiliary variables were generated, namely the number of families using electricity (X_1), the number of junior high schools/Islamic junior high schools (X_4), number of universities/colleges (X_7), number of polyclinics/medical centers (X_{12}), number of doctor's offices (X_{13}), number of markets with permanent buildings (X_{29}), number of minimarkets/supermarkets (X_{32}), and number of restaurants/eateries (X_{34}).

3.3.3. Fay–Herriot EBLUP Estimation for the Sampled Area

The results of estimating the regression coefficients of 13 auxiliary variables and 8 selected auxiliary variables can be seen in Tables 3 and 4. The results of the modeling of the average household expenditure data for food and non-food in Tables 3 and 4 are then used to estimate the small area of the average household expenditure variables for food and non-food in all sampled sub-districts of the National Socio-Economic Survey (Susenas) in March 2020.

Table 3. Modeling Results of Average Household Expenditure on Food Data Using Multivariate EBLUP.

Estimator	Value of Coefficient	t-Value	*p*-Value
(1)	(2)	(3)	(4)
$\hat{\beta}_0$	1.774×10^6	34.7640	0.0000 *
$\hat{\beta}_1$	1.068×10^1	3.0020	0.0028 *
$\hat{\beta}_3$	-6.817×10^3	−3.0360	0.0025 *
$\hat{\beta}_4$	-1.041×10^4	−4.1980	0.0000 *
$\hat{\beta}_{12}$	1.879×10^4	2.6870	0.0074 *
$\hat{\beta}_{13}$	1.042×10^4	4.3360	0.0000 *
$\hat{\beta}_{15}$	8.603×10^3	3.3290	0.0009 *
$\hat{\beta}_{16}$	-7.513×10^3	−2.1250	0.0340 *
$\hat{\beta}_{23}$	1.493×10^2	2.9280	0.0035 *
$\hat{\beta}_{26}$	6.808×10^1	2.6260	0.0089 *
$\hat{\beta}_{27}$	-7.358×10^1	−2.1930	0.0287 *
$\hat{\beta}_{29}$	-2.940×10^4	−3.2270	0.0013 *
$\hat{\beta}_{30}$	-2.465×10^4	−3.0150	0.0027 *
$\hat{\beta}_{37}$	2.183×10^3	2.2320	0.0260 *

* Indicates that the variable is significant in the model.

Table 4. Modeling Results of Average Household Expenditure on Non-Food Using Multivariate EBLUP.

Estimator	Value of Coefficient	t-Value	*p*-Value
(1)	(2)	(3)	(4)
$\hat{\beta}_0$	1.827×10^6	22.4620	0.0000 *
$\hat{\beta}_1$	1.328×10^1	2.2190	0.0269 *
$\hat{\beta}_4$	-1.900×10^4	−4.6490	0.0000 *
$\hat{\beta}_7$	-3.573×10^4	−3.2110	0.0014 *
$\hat{\beta}_{12}$	3.600×10^4	2.8400	0.0047 *
$\hat{\beta}_{13}$	1.887×10^4	3.8800	0.0001 *
$\hat{\beta}_{29}$	-3.893×10^4	−2.4420	0.0149 *
$\hat{\beta}_{32}$	1.087×10^4	2.9080	0.0038 *
$\hat{\beta}_{34}$	7.059×10^3	3.7660	0.0002 *

* Indicates that the variable is significant in the model.

Figures 5 and 6 below show a comparison of the results of direct estimation and the results of Multivariate EBLUP estimation for each variable of average household expenditure on food and non-food. Figures 5 and 6 show that the results of estimating the average household expenditure on food and non-food using the Multivariate EBLUP method tend to be lower than the results of the direct estimate for the 573 sampled sub-districts.

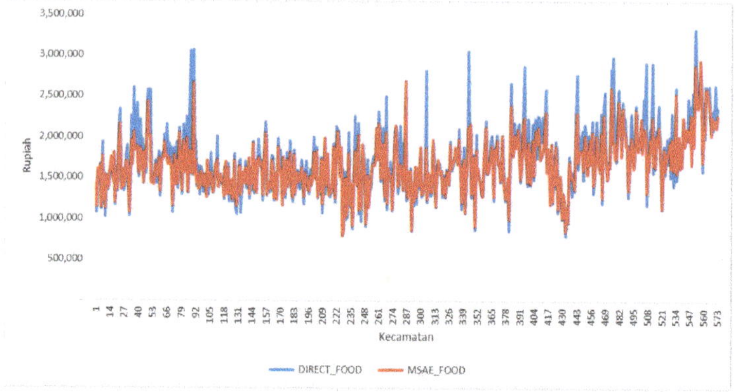

Figure 5. Estimation of Average Household Expenditure on Food at the Subdistrict Level in Central Java Province Using the Direct Estimation Method and the Multivariate EBLUP Method.

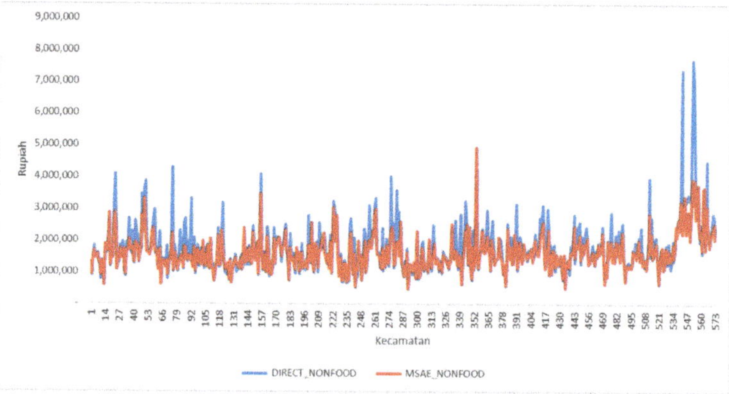

Figure 6. Estimation of Average Household Expenditure on Non-Food at the Subdistrict Level in Central Java Province Using the Direct Estimation Method and the Multivariate EBLUP Method.

After estimating the regression coefficients, the RSE values of the direct and indirect estimate results (EBLUP-FH Multivariate) were compared. Figures 7 and 8 show the RSE values of the direct estimator and the EBLUP-FH Multivariate estimate for average household expenditure on food and non-food in the sampled sub-districts of Central Java.

Figure 7 demonstrates that the Multivariate EBLUP model provides a lower RSE value for the average household expenditure variable for food and non-food than the direct estimation. The RSE value of the Multivariate EBLUP model is less than 25 percent in all Central Java sub-districts.

Based on the boxplot in Figure 8, we can see that the results of the direct estimation of the average household expenditure variable for food and non-food at the sub-district level have a wider RSE range than the Multivariate EBLUP method. Although there are still outliers in the RSE value of the direct estimation and the Multivariate EBLUP model on the average household expenditure variable for non-food, the outliers in the Multivariate EBLUP model are significantly fewer in number and close to the tail of the boxplot. It can be concluded that the Multivariate EBLUP method produces a smaller level of diversity than the direct estimation method.

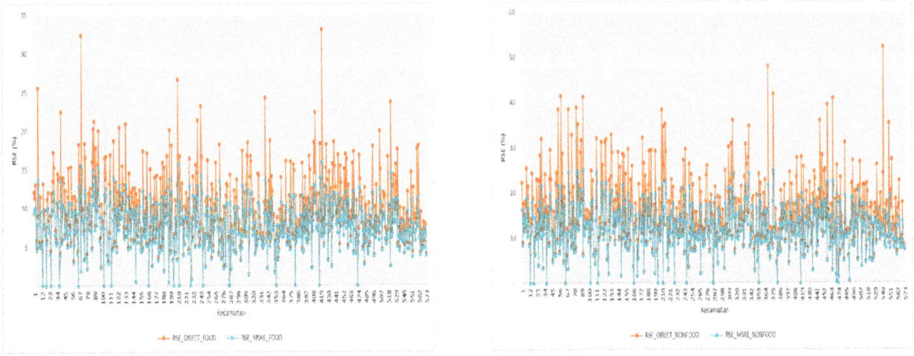

(a) (b)

Figure 7. RSE (%) of Direct Estimation and Multivariate EBLUP Model for Average Household Expenditure Variables at Subdistrict Level in Central Java: (**a**) for food; (**b**) for non-food.

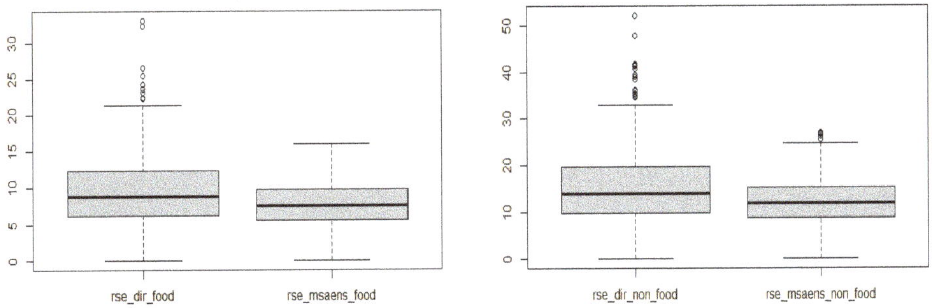

(a) (b)

Figure 8. Boxplot of RSE (%) of Direct Estimation and Multivariate EBLUP Model for Average District Level Household Expenditure Variables in Central Java: (**a**) for food; (**b**) for non-food.

3.3.4. Estimation of Non-Sampled Subdistricts

The estimation of average household expenditure on food and non-food in non-sampled sub-districts of the National Socio-Economic Survey (Susenas) March 2020, was carried out by utilizing non-hierarchical clustering information using the K-Medoids cluster technique. This clustering process uses selected auxiliary variables for each response variable so that later clusters will be formed for modeling average household expenditure on food and clusters for modeling average household expenditure on non-food. Before further analysis is carried out using the K-Medoids cluster method, standardization is first carried out using the Z-Score method for each auxiliary variable used in clustering.

The next step is to check the assumption of sample adequacy by calculating the Kaiser-Meyer-Olkin (KMO) value. The processing results produced a KMO value of 0.72 and 0.82 for each auxiliary variable used in modeling average household expenditure on food and non-food, respectively. It can be concluded that the number of samples is sufficient or has adequately represented the population, allowing for further analysis.

Detection of multicollinearity is also carried out on auxiliary variables using the Variance Inflation Factor (VIF) value. The VIF values of thirteen auxiliary variables for the average household expenditure on food (Y_1) and eight auxiliary variables for the average household expenditure on non-food (Y_2) are shown in Tables 5 and 6 below.

Table 5. VIF Values of Thirteen Auxiliary Variables for Average Household Expenditure on Food.

Variables	Value of VIF
(1)	(2)
X_1	5.5327
X_3	1.2035
X_4	3.8324
X_{12}	2.7109
X_{13}	2.8847
X_{15}	2.6079
X_{16}	1.6935
X_{23}	1.0362
X_{26}	1.0561
X_{27}	1.0496
X_{29}	1.4295
X_{30}	1.1257
X_{37}	1.0251

Table 6. VIF Values of the Eight Auxiliary Variables for Average Household Expenditure on Non-Food.

Variables	Value of VIF
(1)	(2)
X_1	5.0259
X_4	3.3379
X_7	1.4979
X_{12}	2.8600
X_{13}	3.7910
X_{29}	1.4054
X_{32}	2.5572
X_{34}	2.3163

Based on the results in Tables 5 and 6, the VIF value of the selected auxiliary variables for each average household expenditure response variable is less than 10. This means that there is no multicollinearity between the auxiliary variables. After the two cluster assumptions are met, the two groups of auxiliary variables will be used in cluster formation using the K-Medoids Cluster technique. The clustering process was carried out on all 576 sub-districts in Central Java for each group of auxiliary variables. The determination of the number of clusters in K-Medoids is based on the average silhouette method shown in Figure 9.

Based on Figure 9, it can be seen that the highest average silhouette value is in the number of clusters of two clusters, both for the average food and non-food expenditure. As a result, this study will employ up to two clusters in grouping sub-districts using the K-Medoids Cluster method. In the average household expenditure group for food, cluster 1 consists of 380 sub-districts, and cluster 2 consists of 196 sub-districts. Meanwhile, cluster 1 in the non-food average household expenditure group consists of 260 sub-districts, and cluster 2 consists of 316 sub-districts. The characteristics of cluster 2 are generally those sub-districts with greater education and health infrastructure than cluster 1.

After the sub-district clusters are formed, the next step is to use the known components of random area effects per cluster and then average them per cluster. Then the average of the random area effects per cluster will be entered into the Multivariate EBLUP model as an estimator of the random area effects of the non-sampled sub-districts in the March 2020 National Socio-Economic Survey (Susenas). Estimates of average household expenditure on food and non-food in unsampled sub-districts resulting from Multivariate EBLUP modeling with the addition of cluster information are shown in Tables 7 and 8.

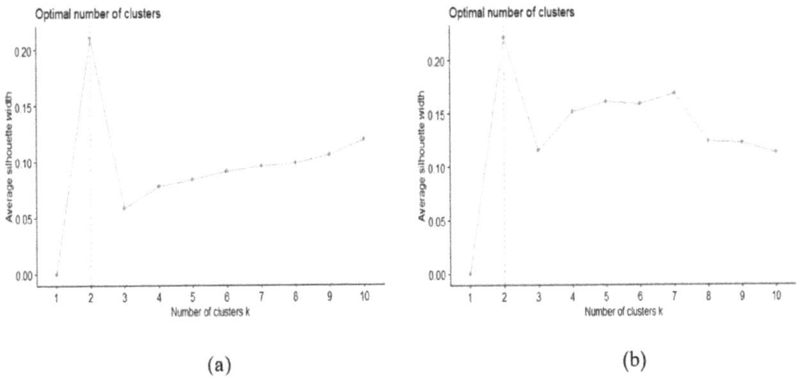

Figure 9. Determination of the Optimal Number of Clusters by the Average Silhouette Method (**a**) Optimal number of Clusters for Average Food Expenditure (**b**) Optimal number of Clusters for Average Non-Food Expenditure.

Table 7. Average household expenditure on food in non-sampled sub-districts.

Sub-Districts	Average Value of Household Expenditure on Food in Non-Sampled Sub-Districts (IDR)	Cluster
(1)	(2)	(3)
Padureso	1,550,241	1
Batuwarno	1,574,599	1
Lebakbarang	1,540,425	1

Table 8. Average household Expenditure on non-food in non-sampled sub-districts.

Sub-Districts	Average Value of Household Expenditure on Non-Food in Non-Sampled Sub-Districts (IDR)	Cluster
(1)	(2)	(3)
Padureso	1,470,115	2
Batuwarno	1,455,223	2
Lebakbarang	1,416,978	1

3.4. Mapping of Estimates of Average Subdistrict Level Household Expenditure from Multivariate EBLUP Modeling Results

The mapping of the estimation of the average household expenditure per sub-district is conducted based on the results of the estimation of the average sub-district level household expenditure obtained from the Multivariate EBLUP modeling with the addition of cluster information for sampled and non-sampled sub-districts. Based on Figure 10, it can be seen that the color gradation reflects the high and low average household expenditure on food in each sub-district in Central Java. Sub-districts with high average household expenditure on food include Laweyan, Pasar Kliwon, Jebres, and Banjarsari in Surakarta City; Argomulyo, Tingkir, and Sidomukti in Salatiga City; West Pekalongan, East Pekalongan, South Pekalongan, and North Pekalongan in Pekalongan City; South Tegal, East Tegal, West Tegal, and Margadana in Tegal City; Talun, Doro, Bojong, Wonopringgo, Kedungwuni, Buaran, Tirto, and Wiradesa in Pekalongan District; Patikraja, Purwokerto Selatan, West Purwokerto Barat, East Purwokerto, and North Purwokerto in Banyumas District; Bumijawa, Bojong, Balapulang, Slawi, Talang, and Kramat in Tegal District; and almost all sub-districts in Semarang City.

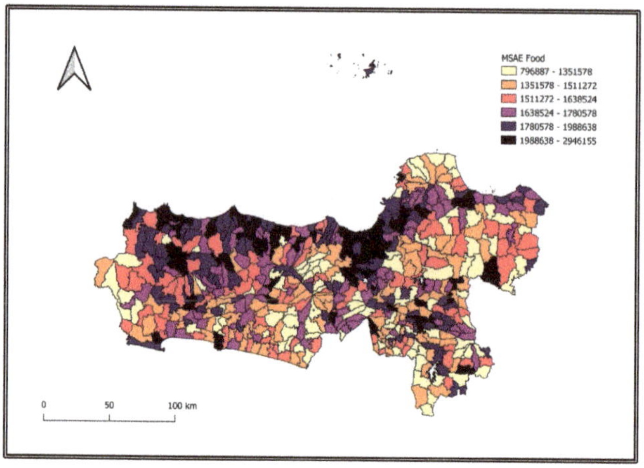

Figure 10. Map of Estimation of Average Household Expenditure on Food at Subdistrict Level in Central Java using the Multivariate EBLUP Method.

Figure 10 also shows sub-districts with low average household expenditure on food, including sub-districts Paranggupito, Giritontro, Karangtengah, Tirtomoyo, Baturetno, Eromoko, Manyaran, Kismantoro, Bulukerto, and Jatipurno in Wonogiri Regency; Kedungjati, Geyer, Kradenan, Ngaringan, and Tanggungharjo in Grobogan Regency; Kayen, Pucakwangi, Tlogowungu, and Dukuhseti in Pati Regency; and Bulu, Tlogomulyo, Kaloran, Ngadirejo, Jumo, Candiroto, Bejen, Tretep, and Wonoboyo in Temanggung Regency.

Sub-districts with high average household expenditure on non-food items are generally located in urban areas, including South Magelang, Central Magelang, and North Magelang in Magelang city; Laweyan, Serengan, Pasar Kliwon, Jebres, and Banjarsari in Surakarta city; Argomulyo, Tingkir, Sidomukti, and Sidorejo sub-districts in Salatiga city; West Pekalongan, East Pekalongan, and North Pekalongan in Pekalongan city; South Tegal, East Tegal, and West Tegal in Tegal city; and almost all sub-districts in Semarang city (Figure 11). Meanwhile, sub-districts with low average food expenditure also tend to have low average non-food expenditure.

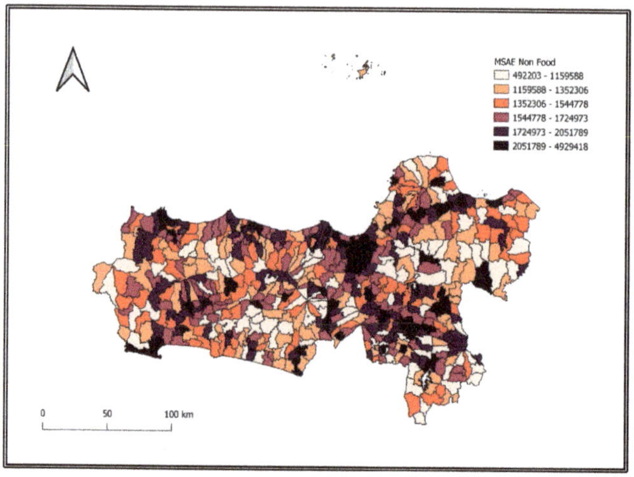

Figure 11. Map of Estimation of Average Household Expenditure on Non-Food at the Sub-district Level in Central Java using the Multivariate EBLUP Method.

4. Discussion

The results of the estimation of the average household expenditure on food and non-food at the sub-district level in Central Java from the EBLUP-Fay–Herriot Multivariate model produced a better level of diversity than the direct estimation results. It can be seen from the comparison between the Relative Standard Error (RSE) value between direct estimation and the EBLUP Multivariate model for each sub-district in Central Java. Many outliers are still found in the box plot of the direct estimation results RSE value, and the RSE value is greater than 25 percent. Meanwhile, the EBLUP-Fay–Herriot Multivariate SAE results can significantly reduce the number of outliers in the RSE value. There are not even outliers at all in the RSE value of the EBLUP Multivariate estimation results for the average household expenditure variable for food in each sub-district. This result is in line with studies about EBLUP Multivariate that show the effectiveness of the EBLUP Multivariate method in producing estimates down to the smallest area level (sub-district). The EBLUP multivariate method outperforms direct estimation based on the survey design.

For the three sub-districts that were not sampled in the March 2020 National Socio-Economic Survey (Susenas), the average household expenditure on food and non-food was estimated by adding cluster information to the EBLUP-Fay–Herriot Multivariate. Table 6 shows that the estimated average household expenditure on food in Padureso sub-district is IDR 1,550,241, in Batuwarno sub-district it is IDR 1,574,599, and in Lebakbarang sub-district it is IDR 1,540,425. These three sub-districts are all members of cluster 1 for the average food expenditure variable group. Meanwhile, the estimated average household expenditure on non-food items in the three non-sampled sub-districts is lower than the value of food expenditure, namely IDR 1,470,115 in Padureso, IDR 1,455,223 in Batuwarno, and IDR 1,416,978 in Lebakbarang.

The Multivariate EBLUP estimation with the addition of cluster information can be used to estimate average household expenditure data down to the sub-district level, which can then be used as an indicator to categorize sub-districts in a region based on expenditure groupings. The estimated data can also be used as an indication or a reference in identifying priority regions to get targeted locations in programs for reducing poverty or improving community welfare. Through direct estimation of the survey design, it is impossible to collect statistics on average household expenditures down to the sub-district level. It is because the BPS survey has a limited budget and people to survey. This issue can be solved by using small area estimation using the EBLUP Multivariate approach and adding cluster information for areas not sampled in the survey. As a result, local government's activities are more effective and focused since data is available down to the small area (subdistrict) level.

For future research, the use of the EBLUP Fay–Herriot Multivariate model can be applied to other data that has a strong correlation. If the research is conducted in areas that have different geographical characteristics, researchers can also develop the Fay–Herriot Multivariate model by adding spatial and time aspects. The auxiliary variables used can be differentiated in each research area because the influence of variables can be different in different areas, so it is expected that the estimation model formed will be better and more accurate. In addition, other clustering methods can also be used as alternatives in estimating unsampled areas, such as the Fuzzy K-Means non-hierarchical cluster method, Fuzzy K-Medoids, or hierarchical cluster methods.

5. Conclusions

The EBLUP-Fay–Herriot Multivariate method can improve the parameter estimates generated by the direct estimation method since it yields lower levels of variance (RSE) when estimating average household expenditure on food and non-food at the sub-district level for the sampled sub-districts in Central Java Province, Indonesia. For the sub-districts in Central Java Province that were not sampled from the March 2020 Susenas, the application of the EBLUP-Fay–Herriot multivariate method with the addition of K-Medoids cluster information can be done to estimate the average household expenditure for food and non-food at the sub-district level. The RSE value of all sub-districts from the EBLUP-Fay–Herriot Multivariate estimation is also below 25 percent, so the estimation results are reliable and provide a good level of diversity.

This research is expected to contribute significantly to multivariate modeling of the small area estimation level area. Additionally, it is envisaged that regional governments will use the information on average household expenditure at the sub-district level that results from the estimation using the Multivariate EBLUP-FH approach to design and implement programs relating to welfare and poverty. Because of the limited number of samples and budget, BPS, as the official statistics provider, is unable to provide this data down to the sub-district level.

Author Contributions: Writing (original draft), A.D., I.G. and T.T. All authors have read and agreed to the published version of the manuscript.

Funding: This research was supported by the Acceleration of Associate Professor Research (RPLK) Padjadjaran University 2022 Number 2203/UN6.3.1/PT.00/2022 and The APC was funded by DRPM of Padjadjaran University.

Data Availability Statement: Not applicable.

Conflicts of Interest: The authors declare no conflict of interest.

Appendix A

Table A1. All Candidate Auxiliary Variables that Will Be Selected for EBLUP Multivariate Model.

No.	Variable Notation	Data	Source
(1)	(2)	(3)	(4)
		Response Variable	
1	Y_1	Average household food consumption expenditure at sub-district level (IDR)	SUSENAS March 2020
2	Y_2	Average household non-food consumption expenditure at sub-district level (IDR)	SUSENAS March 2020
		Auxiliary variables	
	Population		
3	X_1	Number of families using electricity (PLN and Non-PLN)	PODES 2020
4	X_2	Number of house buildings in slums	PODES 2020
	Education		
5	X_3	Number of elementary/islamic elementary Schools	PODES 2020
6	X_4	Number of junior high/islamic junior high Schools	PODES 2020
7	X_5	Number of high schools/islamic high schools	PODES 2020
8	X_6	Number of vocational schools	PODES 2020
9	X_7	Number of universities/colleges	PODES 2020
	Health		
10	X_8	Number of maternity hospitals	PODES 2020
11	X_9	Number of health centers with inpatient care	PODES 2020
12	X_{10}	Number of health centers without inpatient care	PODES 2020

Table A1. *Cont.*

No.	Variable Notation	Data	Source
(1)	(2)	(3)	(4)
13	X_{11}	Number of auxiliary health centers	PODES 2020
14	X_{12}	Number of polyclinics/treatment centers	PODES 2020
15	X_{13}	Number of doctor's offices	PODES 2020
16	X_{14}	Number of maternity homes	PODES 2020
17	X_{15}	Number of midwife practice sites	PODES 2020
18	X_{16}	Number of village health posts (poskesdes)	PODES 2020
19	X_{17}	Number of village maternity clinics (Polindes)	PODES 2020
20	X_{18}	Number of pharmacies	PODES 2020
21	X_{19}	Number of specialty medicine/herbal shops	PODES 2020
	Economy (Industry)		
22	X_{20}	Number of small and medium industries (IMK) of leather	PODES 2020
23	X_{21}	Number of small and medium industries (IMK) of wood	PODES 2020
24	X_{22}	Number of small and medium industries (IMK) of precious metals or metal materials	PODES 2020
25	X_{23}	Number of small and medium industries (IMK) of fabric/weaving	PODES 2020
26	X_{24}	Number of small and medium industries (IMK) of pottery/ceramics/stone	PODES 2020
27	X_{25}	Number of small and medium industries (IMK) from rattan/bamboo, grass, pandanus, etc.	PODES 2020
28	X_{26}	Number of small and medium industries (IMK) of food and beverages	PODES 2020
29	X_{27}	Number of other small and medium industries (IMK)	PODES 2020
	Economy (Other than Industry)		
30	X_{28}	Number of shop groups	PODES 2020
31	X_{29}	Number of markets with permanent buildings	PODES 2020
32	X_{30}	Number of markets with semi-permanent buildings	PODES 2020
33	X_{31}	Number of markets without buildings	PODES 2020
34	X_{32}	Number of minimarkets/supermarkets	PODES 2020
35	X_{33}	Number of shops/grocery stores	PODES 2020
36	X_{34}	Number of restaurants/dining houses	PODES 2020
37	X_{35}	Number of food and beverage stalls	PODES 2020
38	X_{36}	Number of hotels	PODES 2020
39	X_{37}	Number of lodgings	PODES 2020
	Economy (Financial Inclusiveness)		
40	X_{38}	Number of state-owned commercial banks	PODES 2020
41	X_{39}	Number of private commercial banks	PODES 2020
42	X_{40}	Number of rural banks	PODES 2020

Appendix B

Table A2. Two Stage One Phase Sampling for March 2020 National Socio-Economic Survey.

Phase	Unit	The Number of Units of the-h Strata		Sampling Method	Possibilities for Sample Selection	Sampling Fraction
		Population	Sample			
1	Census Block	V_{th}	v'_{th}	PPS-with replacement	$\frac{N_{thf}}{N_{th}}$	$v'_{th}\frac{N_{thf}}{N_{th}}$
		v'_{th}	v_{th}	Systematic	$\frac{1}{v'_{th}}$	$\frac{v_{th}}{v'_{th}}$
2	Household	$N^{up}{}_{thf}$	$\overline{n}$	Systematic	$\frac{1}{N^{up}{}_{thf}}$	$\frac{\overline{n}}{N^{up}{}_{thf}}$

with:

V_{th} : number of census blocks in the h-th strata of the t-th district
v'_{th} : 40% of the total census block in the h-th strata of the t-th district
v_{th} : number of samples of the March Susenas census blocks in the h-th strata of the t-th district
N_{th}: total household load of the h-th strata of the t-th district SP2020 data
N_{thf}: total load of households in the f-th census block, h-th stratum, t-th district SP2020
$N^{up}{}_{thf}$: the number of household contents in the f-th updated census block, h-th stratum, t-th district
$\overline{n}$: number of household samples in each census block

If there are $\boldsymbol{M}$ sub-districts in a population and $\boldsymbol{m}$ sub-districts are sampled randomly, and household expenditure $\boldsymbol{y_{ij}}$ is available for each j-th household in $\boldsymbol{i}$ sub-district, then the average household expenditure of a sub-district is calculated by the formula:

$$\overline{y}_i = \frac{\sum_{j=i}^{n_i} w_{ij} y_{ij}}{\sum_{j=i}^{n_i} w_{ij}} \quad , i = 1, \ldots, m \; ; \quad j = 1, \ldots, n_i$$

with:

$\overline{y}_i$: the average expenditure of households in the $\boldsymbol{i}$-th sub-district
y_{ij} : total expenditure of the j-th household in the $\boldsymbol{i}$-th sub-district
w_{ij}: the weighting factor of the j-th household in the i-th sub-district obtained from the March Susenas sampling design
n_i: the number of households in the $\boldsymbol{i}$-th sub-district
m: number of the sub-districts

References

1. Sekhampu, T.J.; Niyimbanira, F. Analysis of the Factors Influencing Household Expenditure In A South African Township. *Int. Bus. Econ. Res. J.* **2013**, *12*, 279. [CrossRef]
2. Irawan, P.B.; Usman, H. *Official Statistics: Sosial Kependudukan Dasar*; Media: Bogor, Indonesia, 2016.
3. Kurnia, A.; Notodiputro, K.A. Eb-Eblup Mse Estimator on Small Area Estimation with Application to BPS Data. In Proceedings of the First International Conference on Mathematics and Statistics (ICoMS-1), Bandung, Indonesia, 19–21 June 2006; pp. 1–6.
4. Rao, J.N.K.; Molina, I. *Small Area Estimation*, 2nd ed.; John Wiley & Sons: New York, NY, USA, 2015.
5. Ghosh, M.; Rao, J.N.K. Small area estimation: An appraisal. *Stat. Sci.* **1994**, *9*, 55–76. [CrossRef]
6. Fay, R.E., III; Herriot, R.A. Estimates of Income for Small Places: An Application of James-Stein Procedures to Census Data. *J. Am. Stat. Assoc.* **1979**, *74*, 269. [CrossRef]
7. Nurizza, W.A. *Penerapan Model Fay-Heriot Multivariat Pada Small Area Estimation (Studi Simulasi Pengeluaran Rumah Tangga per Kapita di Indonesia Tahun 2017) [Skripsi]*; STIS: Jakarta, Indonesia, 2018.
8. Ghosh, M. Small area estimation: Its evolution in five decades. *Stat. Transit. New Ser.* **2020**, *21*, 1–22. [CrossRef]
9. Benavent, R.; Morales, D. Multivariate Fay-Herriot models for small area estimation. *Comput. Stat. Data Anal.* **2016**, *94*, 372–390. [CrossRef]
10. BPS. Pengeluaran per Kapita, Sirusa. 2021. Available online: https://sirusa.bps.go.id/sirusa/index.php/indikator/197 (accessed on 1 June 2022).
11. Rao, J.N.K. Some Recent Advances in Model- Based Small Area Estimation. *Surv. Methodol.* **1999**, *25*, 175–186.

12. Saei, A.; Chambers, R. *Small Area Estimation: A Review of Methods Based on the Application of Mixed Models;* University of Southampton: Highfield, UK, 2003.
13. Ginanjar, I.; Iaeng, M.; Wulandary, S.; Toharudin, T. Empirical Best Linear Unbiased Prediction Method with K-Medoids Cluster for Estimate Per Capita Expenditure of Sub-District Level. *IAENG Int. J. Appl. Math.* **2022**, *52*, 3.
14. Anisa, R.; Kurnia, A.; Indahwati, I. Cluster Information of Non-Sampled Area In Small Area Estimation. *IOSR J. Math.* **2014**, *19*, 15–19. [CrossRef]
15. Nuryadin, H.; Susetyo, B.; Sadik, K. Application of Small Area Estimation of Multivariate Fay-Herriot Model for The Average of Per Capita Expeniture in Village Level. *Int. J. Sci. Eng.* **2017**, *8*, 1673–1676.
16. Patel, A.; Singh, P. New Approach for K-mean and K-medoids Algorithm. *Int. J. Comput. Appl. Technol. Res.* **2012**, *2*, 1–5. [CrossRef]
17. Sangga, V.A.P. Perbandingan Algoritma K-Means dan Algoritma K-Medoids dalam Pengelompokan Komoditas Peternakan di Provinsi Jawa Tengah Tahun 2015. *Tugas Akhir Jur. Stat. Fak. Mat. dan Ilmu Pengetah. Alam Univ. Islam Inndonesia Yogyakarta* **2018**, *53*, 1689–1699.
18. Rao, J.N.K. *Small Area Estimation;* Wiley: Hoboken, NJ, USA, 2003.
19. Desiyanti, A.; Toharudin, T.; Suparman, Y. The Implementation of Empirical Best Linear Unbiased Prediction-Fay Herriot (EBLUP-FH) on the Estimation of Average per Capita Expenditure at District Level in West Sumatra Province in 2019. *J. Math. Comput. Sci.* **2022**, *12*. [CrossRef]
20. Amaliana, L.; Fithriani, I.; Siswantining, T. Pendugaan Mean Squared Error (Mse) Pada Model Fay-Herriot Small Area Estimation (Sae). *Pros. Semin. Nas. Mat. Dan Pembelajarannya* **2017**, *9*, 205–212.
21. Nurizza, W.A.; Ubaidillah, A. A comparative study of multivariate Fay-Herriot model for small area estimation in various sample sizes. *IOP Conf. Ser. Earth Environ. Sci.* **2019**, *299*, 12027. [CrossRef]
22. Pfeffermann, D. New important developments in small area estimation. *Stat. Sci.* **2013**, *28*, 40–68. [CrossRef]
23. Ubaidillah, A. Simultaneous Equation Models for Small Area Estimation. Ph.D. Thesis, Bogor Agricultural University, Bogor, Indonesia, 2017. [CrossRef]
24. Patterson, H.D.; Thompson, R. Recovery of Inter-Block Information when Block Sizes are Unequal. *Biometrika* **1971**, *58*, 545. [CrossRef]
25. De Vaus, D. *Surveys in Social Research*, 5th ed.; Allen and Unwin: Crows Nest, NSW, Australia, 2002.

mathematics

Article

Privacy Protection Practice for Data Mining with Multiple Data Sources: An Example with Data Clustering

Pauline O'Shaughnessy *,† and Yan-Xia Lin †

School of Mathematics and Applied Statistics, University of Wollongong, Wollongong, NSW 2522, Australia
* Correspondence: poshaugh@uow.edu.au; Tel.: +61-02-4221-4241
† These authors contributed equally to this work.

Abstract: In the age of data, data mining provides feasible tools with which to handle large datasets consisting of data from multiple sources. However, there is limited research on retrieving statistical information from data when data are confidential and cannot be shared directly. In this paper, we address this problem and propose a framework for performing data analysis using data from multiple sources without revealing true values for privacy purposes. The proposed framework includes three steps. First, data custodians individually mask data before publishing; then, the masked data collection is used to reconstruct the density function of the original dataset, from which resampled values are generated; last, existing data mining techniques are applied directly to the resampled data. This framework utilises the technique of reconstructing an original density function from noise-masked data using the moment-based density estimation method, which plays an essential role. Simulation studies show that the proposed framework performs well; analysis results from the resampled data are comparable to those of the original data when the density of the original data is estimated well. The proposed framework is demonstrated in data clustering analysis using the example of a real-life Australian soybean dataset. Results from the k-means algorithms with two and three fitted clusters are presented to show that cluster analysis using resampled data can well replicate that of the original data.

Keywords: data masking; multiplicative noise; data mining; sample size calculation

MSC: 68P27; 92B15

Citation: O'Shaughnessy, P.Y.; Lin, Y.-X. Privacy Protection Practice for Data Mining with Multiple Data Sources: An Example with Data Clustering. *Mathematics* **2022**, *10*, 4744. https://doi.org/10.3390/math10244744

Academic Editors: Niansheng Tang and Shen-Ming Lee

Received: 28 October 2022
Accepted: 9 December 2022
Published: 14 December 2022

1. Introduction

With the explosive evolution of information technology and computer science, it is easier and less expensive to collect and store data, and the databases containing this information are often massive. While technological evolution makes access to voluminous data feasible, it also brings many challenges in how to turn big data into big knowledge. Data mining is a key component in big data analytics. It is an inductive process for extracting hidden and potentially useful patterns and information without a priori hypotheses, where traditional hypothesis-driven methods, such as online analytic processing and most statistical methods, fall short [1]. This feature makes data mining techniques ideal when hypotheses are difficult to determine or define.

Given its nature, big data can consist of data from multiple sources, and require a sophisticated information systems for storage and access, often being stored off-site or in systems managed by a third party (e.g., cloud storage). When the control of data access is no longer in the hands of the data owners, there are potential threats to data security. In practice, data access control protocols are implemented to secure data privacy [2]. One of the more extreme ways is to indiscriminately restrict public access to data. This method is often chosen by the data owners for data containing sensitive commercial values. Access restriction provides reasonable data security in this case, as it solely relies on the safekeeping of datasets [3]. However, data access restriction is usually not an optimal solution, as it is restrictive for general data use and data sharing.

The main interest in data privacy research is to develop methods for protecting data privacy that also allow the preservation of statistical information. This topic has been studied separately in the fields of statistics (statistical disclosure) and computer science (privacy-preserving data mining and privacy-enhancing technologies) [4]. Torra and Navarro-Abrribas [5] provided an overview of the existing data privacy methods, categorised by the types of data and the types of analyses applied to these data. They summarised that when data are published for a general purpose, masking (statistics) and anonymisation (computer science) are the two available methods which can be used to protect the privacy of the data values. Masking and anonymisation methods systematically transform datasets prior to release. They can be classified into three categories: perturbative, non-perturbative and synthetic data generators. Perturbative methods alter data values by introducing predetermined errors, including noise addition or multiplication, substitution, rank swapping, etc. Non-perturbative methods generally refer to data generalisation and suppression, which make data less detailed. Synthetic data generators replace original data with values generated from an underlying model, ideally retaining the desired statistical information of the original data.

Data privacy simultaneously requires that data values are well protected from disclosure and that statistical inference is accurate about the population of interest [4]. Figure 1 demonstrates these two processes for a set of data published for a general purpose. (i) Data protecting techniques are used by data providers to protect original data values to ensure a certain level of privacy protection before publicly releasing datasets. (ii) Once the protected data are available to the general public, suitable procedures are then performed to retrieve the statistical information of the unpublished, original data.

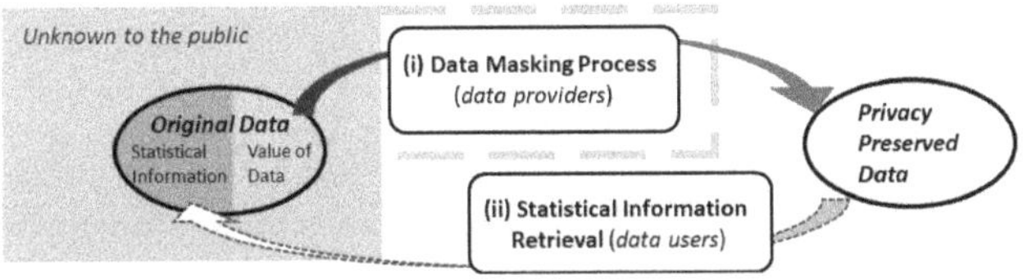

Figure 1. Overview of the data privacy process. The grey area is unavailable to the public for privacy purposes. Information regarding the data masking process performed by data providers can be made partially available to the public.

Current data privacy research focuses on developing methods of ensuring a desirable amount of disclosure with some guarantee on the utility loss for a given statistic (process (i) in Figure 1). An overview of practical privacy protection methods and their applications can be found in [6]. However, there is very limited work on investigating the statistical information retrieval process ((ii) in Figure 1), i.e., how to apply various statistical techniques to a privacy-protected dataset to obtain inferential results other than that considered by the utility loss. Consider the following scenario. Data collection consists of data collected independently from K institutions. Due to the issue of data sensitivity, all institutions require a guarantee of a certain level of privacy protection upon releasing data. Meanwhile, all of them are interested in the statistical inference given by the clustering analysis using the entire data collection. To the best of our knowledge, there is no literature on discussing how to apply existing data mining techniques, particularly clustering analysis, directly to published protected data from multiple data sources when the original data values are not accessible. This topic is the focus of this paper.

Note that there exists a strand of research within the data mining community that addresses privacy issues, namely, privacy-preserving data mining. Privacy-preserving data mining involves modifying existing data mining algorithms to ensure the privacy of the outcomes of algorithms. Reference [7] gives a detailed review of these methods and discusses developments in this area. The focus of privacy-preserving data mining is on the protection of the outcomes of algorithms, not the data themselves [8], which is a fundamentally different situation from the confidentiality-related privacy issues discussed in this paper. Furthermore, privacy-preserving data mining methods generally require access to original data and need to be customised depending on the analysis. This is different from the problem of the original data being inaccessible, which is discussed in this paper; therefore, we will not consider these privacy-preserving data mining methods.

This paper proposes a framework for data clustering analysis, assuming that the underlying true data are confidential and that it is impossible to directly share data between multiple data sources. In this framework, confidential quantitative data are firstly protected using the noise-multiplicative masking method. Then, the density function of the original data are reconstructed from the noise-protected data using the moment-based density estimation method. Resampled values are then drawn from the reconstructed density and analysed directly for modelling and inferential results.

The paper is organised as follows. In Section 2, we introduce the multiplicative noise masking method for data value protection and the moment-based density function reconstruction for statistical information retrieval. We also introduce an application of the Kolmogorov–Smirnov test for determining the sample size in the context of the reconstructed density function. This is the basic knowledge required for the clustering analysis discussed in this paper. The proposed framework and its performance evaluation through simulations are presented in Section 3. In Section 4, we present the application of the framework to a real-life dataset and evaluate it empirically.

2. Data Publishing and Information Retrieval

Let X be a random variable. Sometimes, we also call it the data population. Assume that there are K institutions. Each of them independently and randomly draws a sample from the population X. Denote $\boldsymbol{x}^{(k)} = \{x_i^{(k)}\}_{i=1}^{N_k}$, as the data collected by the kth institution, where N_k is the size of sample and $k = 1, \cdots, K$. We merge those datasets and form a large sample from the population X. This paper assumes that the K institutions want to carry out clustering analysis based on the large sample. However, all institutions consider their data confidential and do not wish to share them with others without any privacy protection measures in place.

In current data privacy literature, information retrieval is often treated as a part of the data masking strategy. Depending on the parameters of interest and the methods used for data analysis, a specific data masking method is chosen not only for data value protection but also for obtaining reasonable estimates for the parameters. For example, in differential privacy [9], which is a widely-used data privacy mechanism, a zero-mean Laplace noise is used to ensure the unbiased estimation of a group sum, and the infinity divisibility property of the Laplace distribution is utilised to achieve a certain level of privacy when running queries [9–12]. A differential privacy mechanism ensures that no single observation is identifiable from differentiating queries. However, in practice, the level of perturbation needed to ensure a statistically level of privacy protection often is high, which leads to a low statistical utility. Additionally, when the parameter of interest is no longer the sum, the masking techniques or noise distributions must be customised accordingly [13]. Currently, there is no discussion on how to retrieve the accurate statistical information beyond simple statistics in the differential privacy framework, when a dataset is masked and published for general use and the intended analyses are unspecified. Simply applying cluster analysis to masked data protected by a differential privacy mechanism cannot guarantee the results from masked values represent those from the original values.

In this section, we propose a general framework for perturbing data values for privacy, then retrieving relevant statistical information by reconstructing the density function of original data. The basic idea is motivated by Fisher's likelihood principle, which is arguably one of his greatest contributions to the foundation of statistical science. It states that the likelihood function contains all the evidence in a data sample relevant to model parameters [14]. The likelihood principle implies that statistical information is fully stored in the density function, and data are a representation of the density function. If we can reconstruct the original density function from masked data, we can generate a new dataset from the reconstructed density function, and this new dataset will contain the same statistical information as the original data. Here we discuss the details relevant to the two data privacy processes described in Figure 1, specifically for the general framework for masking and analysing data from multiple data sources.

2.1. Data Masking and Reconstructing the Density Function

2.1.1. Data Masking at Publishing

Data masking protects data by altering values at the individual observation level. Given that data mining techniques are traditionally performed at the individual data level, we only consider the data masking methods that allow for releasing the protected individual data. In particular, we propose to use the multiplicative noise method in this framework, which has desirable properties for masking a wild range of datasets. The multiplicative noise method can be applied to both numerical and categorical data. In addition, the multiplicative noise method provides uniform protection in terms of the coefficient of variation of the noise. This means that the required variation of noise to achieve a desirable level of certainty in estimation does not depend on the values of data, providing an effective way of using small variance for noise distribution to significantly alter large-value data, especially in datasets with large spreads [15].

To protect the values of $\mathbf{x}^{(k)}$ for $k = 1, \cdots, N_K$, firstly, data owners agree on an appropriate random noise C, which is independent of X. Then, each data owner selects a random sample $\{c_i^{(k)}\}$ from the noise population C; a new dataset $\mathbf{x}^{*(k)} = \{x_i^{*(k)}\} = \{x_i^{(k)} c_i^{(k)}\}$ is calculated for the kth institution and can be released to others.

Note that all data owners are required to use the same random noise C to mask their data. Data owners often choose to release certain characteristics of the noise distribution, C, i.e., the shape of the distribution or moment information, etc. (shown as the dashed line around (i) data masking process in Figure 1). When this partial information about the noise distribution is known to the public, the values of $\{x_i^{(k)}\}$ will still be well protected and unable to be recovered from $\{x_i^{*(k)}\}$. For the relevant discussion, see [15].

2.1.2. Reconstructing Density Function

After masked data are publicly available, we use the masked data to reconstruct the density function of the original data in order to accurately obtain the data's statistical information. In practice, there is often no additional information about the underlying distribution beyond actual observations. A robust estimation method with less prior information on reference density is preferred, even though it may be computationally expensive. References [16–18] were the first to independently introduce the fundamental methods for estimating the density function of original data from masked data for a single variable. Lin and Krivitsky [19] gave a detailed review and pointed out that the algorithms proposed in the first three papers have several technical problems, including non-convergence and slow computation. These problems are pronounced in skewed data. Lin [18] exclusively discussed density estimation using a moment-based polynomial approach for noise-multiplied data. This research showed that, for a random variable X with a density function defined on a finite interval $[a, b]$, the density function of X can be approximated by

$$f_{X,P}(x) = \sum_{p=0}^{P} a_p(x) \frac{\mu_{X^*}(p)}{\mu_C(p)},$$

with an appropriate integer P, where $X^* = XC$ is the masked random variable, noise C is the independent multiplicative random variable, $\mu_{X^*}(p) = E(X^{*p})$, and $\mu_C(p) = E(C^p)$. $a_p(x)$ is a continuous polynomial function of x.

Lin [18] also pointed out that, given the noise-multiplied data $\{x_i^*\}_{i=1}^N$ and sample moments' information on the multiplicative noise C, $f_{X,P}(x)$ can be empirically approximated by

$$f_{X,P|\{x_i^*,c_i\}}(x) = \sum_{p=0}^{P} a_p(x) \frac{\overline{(X^*)^p}}{\overline{C^p}}, \quad (1)$$

where $\overline{(X^*)^p} = \sum_{i=1}^N (x_i^*)^p / N$ and $\overline{C^p} = \sum_{i=1}^N c_i^p / N$ are the empirical pth moment for masked data X^* and noise distribution C, respectively. This means that we can use the moment information about the masked data and the noise distribution to reconstruct the density function of the original data. Lin [20] subsequently developed a computational algorithm and built an R package called `MaskDensityBM` using the moment-based density estimation method. In this study, we used the method proposed by Lin [18] and utilised the existing software packages for density reconstruction. After reconstructing the density function, we can generate resamples to perform analysis.

2.2. Determining Sample Size for Resampled Data

Since the original data are confidential, we cannot directly use the data for clustering analysis. Our approach uses a sample drawn from the constructed density function (sometimes called the simulated data or resampled data below) to replace the original data to avoid this problem. Based on the approach we propose, the quality of clustering analysis will rely on two factors. One factor is the closeness of the reconstructed density function to the actual density function. We applied the R package `MaskDensityBM` [20] to determine the reconstructed density function. The other factor is the size of the sample drawn from the reconstructed density function, which ensures the statistical information of the reconstructed density can be well retrieved.

We assume that the reconstructed density function captures the main characterises of the density function of the original data. Even under a perfect scenario, the outputs of data analysis given by the original data and those of the simulated data are likely different if the size of the simulated data is small. The main reason is that when the size of the resamples is too small, the information on certain characteristics of the distribution may be missing from the simulated samples, especially in the two tail-end regions. Even if the size of the simulated data is the same as that of the original data, due to randomness in data generating process, there is no guarantee that the set of simulated data has a similar density to the original data.

We suggest an analytic solution to determine an appropriate data size through a sequence of Kolmogorov–Smirnov tests. Denote $\{x_i\}_{i=1}^N$ as the set of the underlying original data with a sample size of N; $\hat{f}_{X,N}$ is the estimated smoothed density function determined by the original data. Let $\{\tilde{x}_i\}_{i=1}^M$ be a set of resampled data with a size of M. Verifying if the smoothed density function given by $\{\tilde{x}_i\}_{i=1}^M$ is statistically equivalent to $\hat{f}_{X,N}$ is the same as checking whether the empirical cumulative probability distribution function given by $\{\tilde{x}_i\}_{i=1}^M$ is close to the cumulative probability distribution determined by $\hat{f}_{X,N}$. The hypotheses are defined as:

$$H_0 : \hat{F}_{\tilde{X}} = \hat{F}_{X,N}$$

and

$$H_1 : \hat{F}_{\tilde{X}} \neq \hat{F}_{X,N} \,,$$

where $\hat{F}_{\tilde{X}}$ is the empirical cumulative function given by the simulated data $\{\tilde{x}_i\}_{i=1}^M$ and $\hat{F}_{X,N}$ is the cumulative distribution related to $\hat{f}_{X,N}$. The test statistic is

$$D_M = \max_{1 \le i \le M} \left\{ \left| \hat{F}_{X,N}(\tilde{x}_{(i)}) - \frac{i-1}{M} \right| \right\}, \quad (2)$$

where $\tilde{x}_{(i)}$ represents the ith ordered values in the dataset $\{\tilde{x}_i\}_{i=1}^{M}$. A small D_M suggests similarity between the smoothed density function of the original data and the empirical density of the resamples. We considered 0.007 as a critical value for this test and solved for M.

Example 1. *We generated 1000 data from a random variable X following a mixture of normal distributions with density function*

$$f_X = 0.25 \times N(0, 1^2) + 0.75 \times N(4, 2^2)\,. \tag{3}$$

Using Criterion (2), the resampled data with a size of 37,000 has a sufficiently small D_M (=0.0056), and the smoothed density function of the resampled data is shown to be a reasonable estimation of the density of the original data (Figure 2).

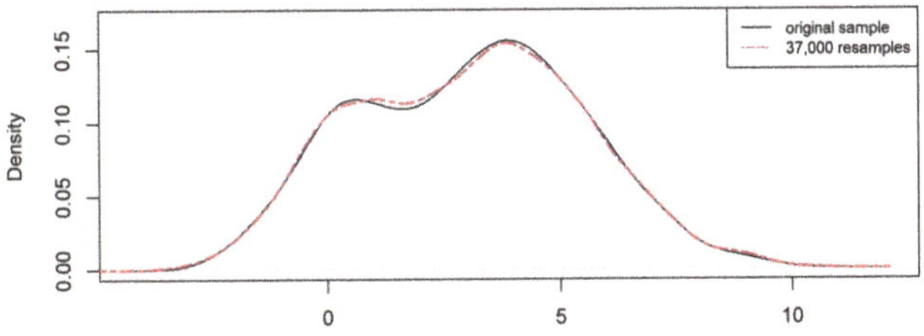

Figure 2. The plots of the smoothed density functions given by $\{x_i\}$ (solid line) for $i = 1, \ldots, 1000$ and a set of resampled values $\{\tilde{x}_i\}$ determined by $D_M < 0.007$ (dash line).

Figure 3 illustrates the relationship between sample size and the information lost, measured by D_M. We generated 500 samples of 1000 data from the model in (3); then we calculated D_M for the resampled data with various sizes of 300, 700, 1000, 3000, 6000, and 12,000. The larger size of resampled data preserves the information of the cumulative distribution of the density function in (3) better with a smaller mean of D_M. It also shows that the variations of the test statistics are much larger in the resampled data with smaller sizes.

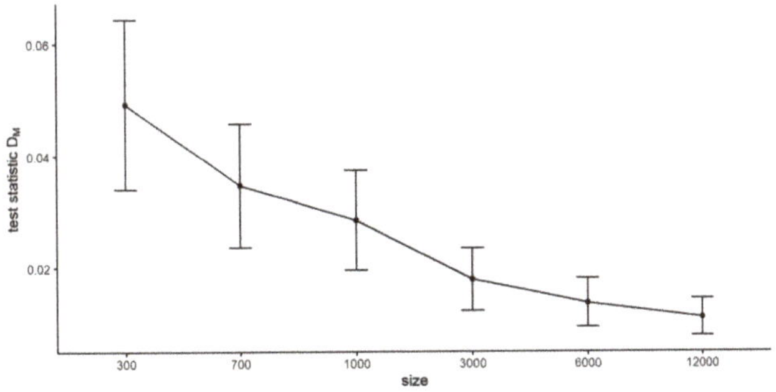

Figure 3. Relationship between D_M and the size of the resampled data for M = 300, 700, 1000, 3000, 6000, and 12,000. The bars extend to one standard deviation above and below the average D_M values from 500 simulation samples.

3. Proposing a Framework and Simulation Studies

In this section, we propose a general framework for publishing data for general use and retrieving statistical information by generating resamples using reconstructed density functions. We consider all data from the K institutions as a whole. Let $\sum_{k=1}^{K} N_k = N$ be the total number of observations from the K institutions and $\mathbf{x} = \{\mathbf{x}^{(1)}, \ldots, \mathbf{x}^{(K)}\} = \{x_j\}$ for $j = 1, \ldots, N$ be a collection of N original data from the K institutions.

Framework for publishing and mining data from multiple data sources:

(i) Publishing data masking:

(a) Data owners across the K institutions agree on an appropriate noise distribution C. Then, information about the noise distribution and parameter values are released to the public;

(b) For the kth institution, independently generate a sample $\{c_i^{(k)}\}_{i=1}^{N_k}$ from C, and produce a masked dataset $\mathbf{x}^{*(\mathbf{k})} = \{x_i^{(k)} c_i^{(k)}\}$;

(c) Each institution publishes the masked data $\mathbf{x}^{*(k)}$ separately. Considering $\mathbf{x}^* = \{\mathbf{x}^{*(1)}, \ldots, \mathbf{x}^{*(K)}\}$, this new collection $\mathbf{x}^*$ with sample size of N is the masked data of the original collection $\mathbf{x}$.

(ii) Generating simulated samples:

(a) Calculate the moments of the masked data $\mathbf{x}^*$ and the noise C;

(b) Reconstruct the density function of the original data $\mathbf{x}$ based on the masked data collection $\mathbf{x}^*$ using the moment-based estimation method implemented in the `R` package `MaskDensityBM`;

(c) Generate a large set of resampled data $\tilde{\mathbf{x}} = \{\tilde{x}_i\}$ from the reconstructed density function. Use these data to replace the original data $\mathbf{x}$ for retrieving the statistical information of $\mathbf{X}$. The size of the simulated data M can be determined iteratively and must satisfy the $D_M < 0.007$ criterion (2).

(iii) Analysing resampled data:
Apply a data mining technique directly to the resampled data $\tilde{\mathbf{x}}$ to obtain statistical information about the original data.

This framework covers several possible practical scenarios. If data owners want to combine their data with those of others to perform data analysis, they will need to follow all three steps, starting with masking their data (i). If a data owner is only interested in publishing his data but still wants to allow others to perform analysis, only Step (i) needs to be followed to release the masked data and the relevant information on the noise distribution. If a masked data collection $\mathbf{x}$ and relevant information about the noise distribution are already available, data users can start from the resampled data generation (ii).

3.1. Simulation Study

To evaluate the performance of the proposed framework, we conducted a simulation study under four different scenarios for cluster analysis, each representing different compositions of locations of means and proportions of samples. First, we present a short introduction to clustering. Cluster analysis or clustering is the task of grouping a set of objects so that objects in the same group (called a "cluster") are more similar to each other than to those in other groups. K-means, introduced by MacQueen [21], is a classic and still-popular algorithm for clustering analysis in data mining.

The K-means algorithm is a special case of the expectation-maximization (EM) algorithm for Gaussian mixture analysis, which decides cluster assignment based on posterior probabilities. Bishop [22] demonstrated that in the limit, the EM algorithm for the Gaussian mixture reduces to the K-mean result. In general, mixture model analysis aims to identify individual base distributions, which are used to form a mixture distribution for the underlying mixture model. Those individual base distributions are usually unimodal probability distributions. If the centres of those unimodal probability distributions can be identified with statistical significance, these centres are considered to be the centres of clusters. In other words, if we can sufficiently estimate the mixture distribution of data, we can use the EM algorithm for the clustering exercises using the mixture distribution. In this study, we used the commonly used `R` software `mclust` [23] (k-means clustering analysis tool) to carry out clustering analysis.

The simulation settings considered in this paper represent factors relevant to cluster analysis, which are how close the means are to each other and the proportions of the sizes of clusters. Let X be the random variable of the sample data; the four simulation settings are given as follows.

Setting 1. Two-group unequal proportions with a large difference in means: $f_X = 0.25 \times N(0,1^2) + 0.75 \times N(6,2^2)$.
Setting 2. Two-group equal proportions with a large difference in means: $f_X = 0.5 \times N(0,1^2) + 0.5 \times N(6,2^2)$.
Setting 3. Two-group equal proportions with close means: $f_X = 0.5 \times N(0,1^2) + 0.5 \times N(4,2^2)$.
Setting 4. Three-group equal proportions with two close means and one large mean: $f_X = 1/3 \times N(0,1^2) + 1/3 \times N(6,2^2) + 1/3 \times N(10,2^2)$.

We generated 400 Monte Carlo simulations for each simulation setting; each simulation sample contained 900 data. For each simulation, we reconstructed the density function then generated $M = 18,000$ resampled data. We ensured that the sample size criterion $D_M < 0.007$ (2) was satisfied in all simulations so that the density of the resampled data was close to that of the original data. Both sample data and resampled data were then analysed using the `R` function `kmeans` for the cluster analysis results.

The performance of the proposed framework was evaluated in terms of estimation accuracy and variation for cluster analysis, under the condition that the cumulative density of resampled sample estimates that of the original sample well. For estimation accuracy, we examined the sampling bias, which is the average value of the differences in cluster means between the resampled data and sample data. To examine the estimation variability, we considered two measures, the sampling standard deviation (s.d.) and the coefficient of variation (CV). Sampling standard deviation is the standard deviation of the cluster means of the resamples, and CV measures the dispersion of the estimation by taking the ratio of the sampling standard deviation and sampling cluster means. We also included the root mean-square error (RMSE), which is the root average of the sum of the square of differences in cluster means between resampled values and sample data. RMSE can be used to directly compare the performance of the proposed method under different simulation settings.

Table 1 shows the results from the Monte Carlo simulations for different simulation settings, with various compositions of mean locations and cluster sizes. In terms of estimation accuracy, average biases were relatively small for all simulation settings, and better performance was achieved from the settings with equal proportions between clusters (Settings 2 and 3). Setting 4, with a smaller cluster size, is slightly more biased than others, possibly due to the reduced quality of fit from a smaller cluster size.

Estimation variability was relatively stable across different simulation settings. The slightly larger sampling standard deviation in Setting 4 indicates that estimation variations elevated when the original cluster sizes are small. Coefficients of variations are generally larger for smaller clusters with low means. This is consistent with the stable sampling standard deviation results, as the CV is the ratio between standard deviation and means; i.e., when the standard deviations are similar, smaller CVs are caused by smaller means.

Results of RMSE, which measures the dispersion of cluster means between resampled values and original sample data, can be used directly to compare the performance of the proposed framework for the four different settings. The most ideal scenario, Setting 2, with two groups of equal cluster sizes and a large difference in cluster means, has the smallest RMSE. This means that the dispersion is smallest and the proposed framework's performance was best in Setting 2. Equal cluster size and larger clusters also contribute to low dispersion (smaller RMSE). Dispersion was elevated in the case of smaller cluster sizes (Setting 4), which is consistent with the conclusion observed from the measure for estimation accuracy.

Table 1. Monte Carlo simulation results comparing the cluster analysis results from the resampled data to those of the sample data under four simulation settings, including average bias, sampling standard deviation (s.d.), coefficient of variation (CV), and root mean-square error of the estimation differences (RMSE).

		Average Bias	Sampling s.d.	CV	RMSE
Setting 1	Cluster 1 mean = 0	0.044	0.105	0.162	0.873
	Cluster 2 mean = 6	0.037	0.083	0.013	0.733
Setting 2	Cluster 1 mean = 0	-0.009	0.056	0.325	0.182
	Cluster 2 mean = 6	0.019	0.093	0.015	0.386
Setting 3	Cluster 1 mean = 0	-0.026	0.055	0.268	0.525
	Cluster 2 mean = 4	0.015	0.108	0.023	0.298
Setting 4	Cluster 1 mean = 0	-0.034	0.073	0.330	0.682
	Cluster 2 mean = 4	0.050	0.173	0.035	1.003
	Cluster 3 mean = 10	0.061	0.138	0.013	1.221

4. Real-Life Data Application

This section illustrates how to implement the framework proposed in Section 2.1 for data clustering and apply it to a real dataset. We applied the proposed framework to the Australian soybean dataset (more information on the study design and the data download link are available at http://three-mode.leidenuniv.nl/, accessed on 1 October 2021) [24], which contains data for 58 different genotypes of soybeans collected from eight experiments for six different soybean attributes. In the dataset, the 58 different lines (genotypes) of soybeans are 43 Australian lines and 15 other lines, of which 12 are from the US. Line 1–40 are local Australian selections from Mamloxi (CPI 172) and Avoyelles (CPI 15939).

In this example, we considered that each genotype of soybean is owned by a data provider and clustered the soybean genotypes based on the attribute seed size. The total number of data providers was 58, and there were 8 data points from each of the providers (genotype). The total number of observations for seed-size data N is $58 \times 8 = 464$. Each provider wants to know which cluster his/her data belongs to, when there is no access to the actual values of data from other providers. In particular, they are interested in which clusters their data can be classified into if there are two or three clusters.

Following the framework proposed in Section 3, all 58 data providers first agree on a noise distribution C. Assume that the probability density function of C is

$$f_C = 0.6 \times Uni(2,5) + 0.4 \times Uni(4,6).$$

Then, the data providers independently mask their raw seed-size data using the multiplicative noises C and publish their own masked values to create a collection of masked data for see size from 58 data providers. Figure 4 plots the masked data of seed size against the original values, showing the effectiveness of data masking. A given masked value corresponds to a large range of possible values of original data. This indicates that it is hard to accurately estimate the values of the original data from the masked values.

The second step is to reconstruct the density function of the original data based on the masked data and the information of the noise distribution C to generate resampled data. We applied the R package `MaskDensityBM` to the masked data collection and obtained the estimated density function associated with the set of the original seed-size data. The density function of the original seed size and its reconstructed density function are presented in Figure 5, which shows that the reconstructed density function preserves the two-mode feature and follows the pattern of the original density reasonably well. Then, the resampled data were generated from the reconstructed density function. The sample size required to satisfy the $D_M < 0.007$ criterion is 1856, approximately four times the original sample size of 464.

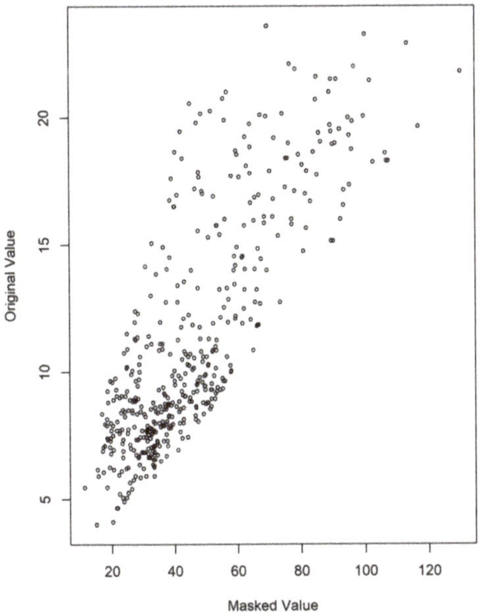

Figure 4. The scatter plot of the masked values and the original values for seed size.

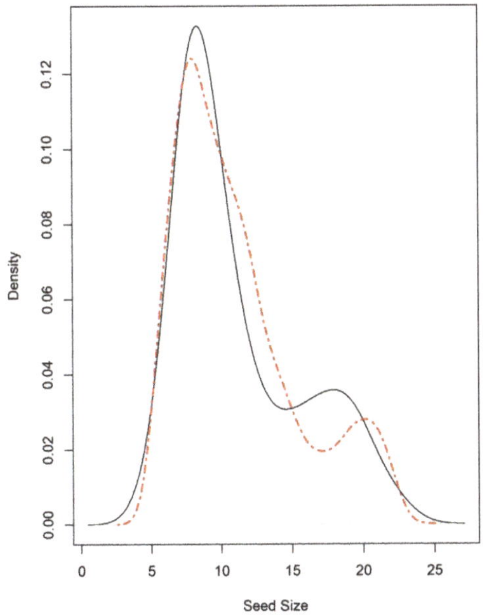

Figure 5. The plot of smoothed original density function (solid line) and reconstructed density function from 1856 simulated samples (dotted line).

We fitted both datasets—the resampled soybean seed-size data and the original data—using the k-means clustering analysis tool in R. We obtained the outputs of clustering analysis for $k = 2$ and 3 clusters. The outputs are given in Table 2. For $k = 2$, centres from the two datasets are similar to each other, having similar standard deviations. A higher cluster mean in the resampled data was observed, though the difference in means was not statistically significant. This is consistent with what we observe in Figure 5; the reconstructed density for the resampled data has a second mode at larger seed-size values. A similar conclusion can be drawn for the $k = 3$ output, except that the larger mean only occurs in the last cluster of the resampled dataset, and there are two groups with a significant difference in means. However, this is not a surprise, as the density plot suggests that the original data are more likely to have two clusters (not three), so the k-means with $k = 3$ clusters may not fit the data well. Furthermore, the clusters show similar allocation (in proportion) between the two datasets for both $k = 2$ clusters, but not as good of a fit for $k = 3$ clusters.

Table 2. Comparison of outputs of the clustering analysis from the resampled dataset and original dataset. Here, the results include cluster mean, cluster standard deviation (s.d.), cluster size, and its corresponding proportion.

	Number of Clusters $k = 2$	
	Resampled data	**Original data**
Cluster centre (*s.d.*)	8.882 (2.111 #) 17.631 (2.709)	8.686 (1.837) 17.503 (2.530)
Cluster size (*proportion*)	1412 (76.1%) 444 (23.9%)	335 (72.2%) 129 (27.8%)
	Number of Clusters $k = 3$	
	Resampled data	**Original data**
Cluster centre (*s.d.*)	7.650 * (1.235) 11.896 (1.457) 18.942 * (1.949)	7.901 (1.253) 12.016 (1.526) 18.476 (1.980)
Cluster size (*proportion*)	902 (48.6%) 633 (34.1%) 321 (17.3%)	256 (55.2%) 108 (23.3%) 100 (21.6%)

* Sample means are statistically different between groups at the 5% significance level. # Sample standard deviations are statistically different between groups at the 5% significance level. Details of statistics and associated p values for comparing group means and variances in given in Table A1 in Appendix A.

We conclude that the resamples generated from reconstructed density can produce statistically equivalent results of the original data. However, this may not be guaranteed when the model fit is not appropriate. The analysis results from resampled data must be used with caution, as they depend not only on the quality of the reconstructed density, but also on the appropriate use of a data analysis technique for making inferences about the population parameter of interest.

5. Closing Remarks

The issues of data privacy are currently receiving widespread and significant attention. In general, methods for the statistical analysis of confidential data should be different from traditional methods. This paper proposes a data clustering analysis method for scenarios where data are independently collected from various data sources. These data are confidential and cannot be shared across data sources directly. The approach proposed is supported by the technique of reconstructing density functions based on noise-multiplied data. The method ensures that an original density function can be closely approached by the reconstructed density function. Therefore, we can retrieve accurate statistical information of the original data from the samples generated from its reconstructed density function. We detailed the application of the approach to a real-life dataset, assuming that the data have privacy issues.

The proposed framework is feasible in practice. Few traditional data analysis R tools can be directly applied for confidential data analysis due to privacy issues. The sample generated from the reconstructed density function plays the role of a "bridge", linking the confidential data and the existing R tools. The proposed approach brings great convenience to realistic data analysis practices when data privacy is of concern, avoiding the need to develop special R tools for data analysis.

The framework developed in this paper is not limited to cluster analysis. Its applications extend to a broad range of data mining analyses. This paper only focuses on univariate data. However, we can apply the framework of the approach to multivariate data once a technique of reconstructing joint density function based on multivariate masked data is available. This technique for multivariate density estimation is under development and will be introduced soon in another paper.

Author Contributions: Conceptualization, P.O. and Y.-X.L.; methodology, Y.-X.L.; software, Y.-X.L. and P.O.; validation, P.O.; writing, P.O. and Y.-X.L. All authors have read and agreed to the published version of the manuscript.

Funding: This research received no external funding.

Institutional Review Board Statement: Not applicable.

Informed Consent Statement: Not applicable.

Data Availability Statement: Not applicable.

Conflicts of Interest: The authors declare no conflict of interest.

Appendix A

It is important to evaluate the accuracy of the clustering analysis results from the resampled values. We compared the analysis outcomes to examine whether the clustering groups in the resampled and original data have statistically equal means and variances. We firstly tested the spread of the data from each allocated group using a F test of equal variance between the resampled data and original data groups. Depending on the F test result, either a pooled or unpooled t test was then used to test whether group means between the resampled data and the original data are statistically equivalent; for the groups with statistically different variance (p values from F test less than 0.05), an unpaired unpooled t test was performed to test the difference in group means, assuming a difference in group variances. Otherwise, an unpaired pooled t test was performed for the groups with statistically equivalent variance ($p > 0.05$ in F test of equal variance) in the resampled data and in the original data.

Table A1. Test statistics and associated p values for comparing the cluster means (t-tests) and cluster standard deviations (F tests) between the resampled and original Australian soybean data.

	F Tests for Equal Variance		*t* Tests for Equal Means	
	F Statistic	p	T Statistic	p
Number of clusters k = 2	1.3206	0.0018	1.7041	0.0889
	1.1465	0.3554	0.4793	0.6318
Number of clusters k = 3	0.9684	0.734	−2.8607	0.004
	0.9116	0.5046	−0.7856	0.4324
	0.9689	0.8236	2.0799	0.03814

Table A1 includes the test statistics and p values from the relevant F tests and t-tests to compare the cluster variances and cluster means between the resampled and original Australian soybean data. The equal-variance tests (F tests) show that the allocated groups in the resampled and original data have nonsignificant difference (similar) variances, except for the first group in the cluster analysis with two clusters. The equal-mean tests (t tests) for the cluster analysis with two clusters are non-significant, suggesting that the resampled data and the original data produce the same groups means. However, when the model fit is less appropriate (cluster analysis with three clusters), two groups show a significant difference in cluster means between the resamples and the original data.

References

1. Zhao, C.-M.; Luan, J. Data mining: Going beyond traditional statistics. *New Dir. Institutional Res.* **2006**, *131*, 7–16. [CrossRef]
2. Colombo, P.; Ferrari, E. Access control technologies for Big Data management systems: literature review and future trends. *Cybersecurity* **2019**, *2*, 1–13. [CrossRef]
3. Bertino, E.; Ghinita, G.; Kamra, A. Access Control for Databases: Concepts and Systems. *Found. Trends® Databases* **2011**, *3*, 4–7.
4. Torra, V. *Data Privacy: Foundations, New Developments and the Big Data Challenge*; Springer International: Cham, Switzerland, 2017.
5. Torra, V.; Navarro-Arribas, G. Big Data Privacy and Anonymization. In *Proceedings of the Privacy and Identity Management. Facing up to Next Steps. Privacy and Identity 2016*; IFIP Advances in Information and Communication Technology; Springer: New York, NY, USA, 2016.
6. Templ, M. *Statistical Disclosure Control for Microdata: Methods and Applications in R*; Springer International: Cham, Switzerland, 2017; pp. 99–132.
7. Aldeen, Y.; Sallen, M.; Razzqque, M. A comprehensive review on privacy preserving data mining. *Springerplus* **2015**, *4*, 1–36. [CrossRef] [PubMed]
8. Sachan, A.; Roy D.; Arun, P.V. An analysis of privacy preservation techniques in data mining. *Adv. Comput. Inf. Technol.* **2013**, *3*, 119–128.
9. Dwork, C. Differential privacy. In Proceedings of the 33rd International Colloquium on Automata, Languages and Programming, Venice, Italy, 10–14 July 2006; pp. 1–12.
10. McSherry, F.; Talwar, K. Mechanism Design via Differential Privacy. In Proceedings of the 48th Annual IEEE Symposium on Foundations of Computer Science, Providence, RI, USA, 20–23 October 2007; pp. 94–103.
11. Ács G.; Castelluccia, C. I Have a DREAM! (DiffeRentially privatE smArt Metering). *Inf. Hiding* **2011**, *6958*, 118–132.
12. Dwork, C.; Roth, A. The algorithmic foundations of differential privacy. *Found. Trends Theor. Comput. Sci.* **2014**, *9*, 211–407. [CrossRef]
13. Bambauer, Y.; Jane, R.; Muralidhar, K.; Sarathy, R. Fool's Gold: An Illustrated Critique of Differential Privacy. *Vanderbilt J. Entertain. Technol. Law* **2014**, *16*, 13–47.
14. Fisher, R. On the Mathematical Foundations of Theoretical Statistics. *Philos. Trans. R. Soc. A* **1922**, *222*, 594–604.
15. Nayak, T. K.; Sinha, B.; Zayatz, L. Statistical properties of multiplicative noise masking for confidentiality protection. *J. Off. Stat.* **2011**, *27*, 527–541.
16. Agrawal, R.; Srikant, R. Privacy-preserving data mining. *ACM Sigmod Rec.* **2000**, *29*, 439–450. [CrossRef]
17. Kargupta, H.; Datta, S.; Wang, Q.; Sivakumar, K. On the privacy preserving properties of random data perturbation techniques. In Proceedings of the Third IEEE International Conference on Data Mining, Washington, DC, USA, 19–22 November 2003; pp. 99–106.
18. Lin, Y.X. Density approximant based on noise multiplied data. In Proceedings of the International Conference on Privacy in Statistical Databse, Ibiza, Spain, 17–19 September 2014; Lecture Notes in Computer Science Series; pp. 89–104.
19. Lin, Y.X.; Krivitsky, P. Reviewing methods for estimating density function based masked data. In Proceedings of the International Conference on Privacy in Statistical Databse, Valencia, Spain, 26–28 September 2018; Lecture Notes in Computer Science Series; pp. 231–246.
20. Lin, Y.X. Mining the Statistical Information of Confidential Data from Noise-Multiplied Data. In Proceedings of the 3rd IEEE International Conference on Big Data Intelligence and Computing, Orlando, FL, USA, 6–11 November 2017.
21. MacQueen, J. Some methods for classification and analysis of multivariate observations. In Proceedings of the Fifth Berkeley Symposium on Mathematical Statistics and Probability, Berkeley, CA, UAS, 21 June – 18 July, 1965 Volume 1: Statistics.
22. Biship, C. *Pattern Recognition and Machine Learning*; Springer: Berlin/Heidelberg, Germany, 2006; p. 423.
23. Scrucca, L.; Fop, M; Murphy, T.B.; Raftery, A. mclust 5: Clustering, classification and density estimation using Gaussian finite mixture models. *R J.* **2016**, *8*, 289–317. [CrossRef] [PubMed]
24. Shorter, R.; Byth, D.; Mungomery, V. Genotype by environment interactions and environmental adaptation. ii. Assessment of environmental contributions. *Aust. J. Agric. Res.* **1977**, *28*, 223–235. [CrossRef]

mathematics

Article

Model Selection for High Dimensional Nonparametric Additive Models via Ridge Estimation

Haofeng Wang [1,2], Hongxia Jin [2], Xuejun Jiang [2,*] and Jingzhi Li [3]

1 Department of Mathematics, Harbin Institute of Technology, Harbin 150001, China
2 Department of Statistics and Data Science, Southern University of Science and Technology, Shenzhen 518055, China
3 Department of Mathematics, Southern University of Science and Technology, Shenzhen 518055, China
* Correspondence: jiangxj@sustech.edu.cn

Abstract: In ultrahigh dimensional data analysis, to keep computational performance well and good statistical properties still working, nonparametric additive models face increasing challenges. To overcome them, we introduce a methodology of model selection for high dimensional nonparametric additive models. Our approach is to propose a novel group screening procedure via nonparametric smoothing ridge estimation (GRIE) to find the importance of each covariate. It is then combined with the sure screening property of GRIE and the model selection property of extended Bayesian information criteria (EBIC) to select the suitable sub-models in nonparametric additive models. Theoretically, we establish the strong consistency of model selection for the proposed method. Extensive simulations and two real datasets illustrate the outstanding performance of the GRIE-EBIC method.

Keywords: model selection; nonparametric additive models; nonparametric smoothing; ridge estimation

MSC: 62H12; 62J12

Citation: Wang, H.; Jin, H.; Jiang, X.; Li, J. Model Selection for High Dimensional Nonparametric Additive Models via Ridge Estimation. *Mathematics* **2022**, *10*, 4551. http://doi.org/10.3390/math10234551

Academic Editors: Niansheng Tang and Shen-Ming Lee

Received: 2 November 2022
Accepted: 28 November 2022
Published: 1 December 2022

1. Introduction

With the advances in information technology, high-dimensional data exists in various fields such as biology, chemistry, economics, finance, genetics, neuroscience, etc. A common assumption of sparse is that only a few features are truly related to the response. Following that, plenty of variable selection approaches based on regularized M-estimation have been developed, which include but are not limited to Lasso by [1], SCAD by [2], Dantzig selector by [3], and MCP by [4]. However, there always exist two limitations in the above-penalized methods. One is the big burden for computation, and the other is the unstable performance for variable selection in high-dimensional situations [5].

To avoid the mentioned limitations, correlation ranking becomes one of the most popular ways to rapidly reduce the dimensionality of feature space. Fan and Lv [6] proposed the sure independence screening (SIS) by utilizing the marginal Pearson correlation between predictor and response for gaussian linear regression. Fan et al. [7] extended the idea of Pearson correlation ranking to marginal smooth estimation strength ranking and proposed the nonparametric independence screening (NIS) method. Meanwhile, Zhu et al. [8] considered the marginal correlation between the predictor and the conditional cumulative density function of response and developed the model-free screening method. However, in practice, there exist strong correlations between the predictors, which may lead to important predictors being jointly correlated to the response. Hence, the marginal correlation ranking process may miss some important variables. To decrease the effect of correlation between the predictors, some forward variable screening methods based on the prediction rankings were introduced. Wang [9] ranked the residuals of the predictor and proposed the forward regression (FR) algorithm. Cheng et al. [10] applied the forward regression to high dimensional varying coefficient models and proposed the forward-BIC screening method. Zhong et al. [11] further extended the forward regression to ultrahigh-dimensional nonparametric additive models. Based on the cumulative divergence (CD), Zhou et al. [12] proposed a forward screening procedure that considered the joint effects among covariates in the feature screening process.

Next, let us turn to the specific model. In this paper, we are interested in the model of nonlinear regression. It is well known that if there exists extensive nonlinear independence between response and predictors, traditional (partial) linear models can not detect nonlinear independence. Although the nonlinear regression could capture the nonlinear independence accurately, the nonlinear regression suffers from the curse of dimensionality and heavy computational burden in high dimensions. To model them simplify, here, we consider the nonparametric additive models. The nonparametric additive models were introduced by Hastie and Tibshirani [13], which are defined as follows,

$$y = \sum_{j=1}^{p_n} m_j(x_j) + \epsilon, \tag{1}$$

where y is the response variable, x_j is the covariate, m_j is an unknown function with $j = 1, \ldots, p_n$, and ϵ is the random error. Obviously, this additive combination of univariate functions could detect the nonlinear independence easily, but their good statistical properties and high computational performance only belong to low dimensions. For ultrahigh dimensions, to keep them working well, one of the most popular methods is the two-stage approach. Its main idea is to perform model selection in a fast and efficient way while retaining all the important features in the reduced feature space and then refitting the reduced models. In the following paper, we focus on the methodology of model selection for ultrahigh nonparametric additive models. In that field, the last decade has seen a growing trend toward smooth-group penalized methods, see [14–17]. Whereas the above methods may involve some tuning parameters, which bring a heavy computational burden and unstable results in high dimensions. A forward feature selection procedure, proposed by [11] for ultrahigh dimensional nonparametric additive models, does not involve any initial parameters. In addition, model-free methods have been developed recently. Based on the cumulative divergence (CD), Zhou et al. [12] proposed a forward screening procedure that considered the joint effects among covariates in the feature screening process. These two above methods screen the remaining candidate indexes into the sub-models through forwarding procedures. This kind of forward-searching algorithm also leads to a high computational burden. Furthermore, under previous studies' correlation assumption, they ignored that the predictors are often correlated for high-dimensional feature space. In detail, the unimportant covariate x_ℓ corresponding to $m_\ell \equiv 0$ in the nonparametric additive models (1) may have a strong correlation with the residual $y - \sum_{j \in \mathcal{M}} m_j(x_j)$ given index set $\mathcal{M} \subseteq \{1, \ldots, p_n\}$, which implies that their methodologies may screen quite a few unimportant features into the sub-models.

To improve these limitations, first, our approach is to propose a group screening procedure via nonparametric smoothing ridge estimation (GRIE), motivated by the theoretical property and outstanding simulation performance of the ridge estimator in [18]. The core idea of GRIE is to get the importance of each covariate by combining the ridge estimator and group contribution. Its details are as follows. We begin with fitting the ridge regression by B-spline smoothing and then treating the spline basis corresponding to each covariate as a group. Next, we evaluate the group contribution of covariates by the magnitude of group estimators. Lastly, we sort the importance of the covariates by the group contribution in descending order. To further conduct model selection, we propose the refined GRIE-EBIC method mixing GRIE and the extended Bayesian information criteria (EBIC) in [19]. The GRIE-EBIC method is used to search for the predictor with the most group contributions by EBIC.

Compared with other feature selection methods for nonparametric additive models, the GRIE-EBIC method has the following advantages: (1) the joint correlation among covariates is considered, and the strong marginal correlation assumption between response and important predictors is relaxed; (2) simple calculation with lower computational complexity; (3) strong consistency for feature screening, and it implies that the true features can be extracted accurately with probability tending to one, which does not exist in other stepwise feature screening methods, such as forward additive regression in [11], forward screening in [12], etc.

The rest of the paper is organized as follows. In Section 2, we introduce the GRIE screening procedure, the GRIE-EBIC method, and its algorithm. In Section 3, we establish the sure screening property of the GRIE screening procedure and the strong consistency of screening by the GRIE-EBIC. In Section 4, we present the performance of our proposed algorithm through simulation studies. In Section 5, we apply our methodology to fit two real datasets to further illustrate the performance of our proposed method. The first is based on Boston housing, while the second is related to *Arabidopsis thaliana* gene data. A conclusion is given in Section 6. The proofs are in Appendix A.

Notation. *Let* $\mathbf{A}$ *be* m *by* l *matrix,* $\mathbf{M}$ *be any subset of* $\{1, 2, \ldots, l\}$ *with any positive integers of* m *and* l*, and then* $\mathbf{A_M}$ *be the submatrix of* $\mathbf{A}$ *formed by column indexes in* $\mathbf{M}$*. We write* $\lambda_{\min}(\mathbf{A})$ *and* $\lambda_{\max}(\mathbf{A})$ *to denote the minimum and maximum eigenvalues of a symmetric matrix* $\mathbf{A}$*, separately. We write* $\mathbf{I}_m$ *as the identity matrix. We defined* $\mathbf{P}_{\lambda,\mathbf{A}} = \mathbf{A}(\mathbf{A}^\top\mathbf{A} + \lambda\mathbf{I}_m)^{-1}\mathbf{A}^\top$*, where* λ *is some positive constant,* $\mathbf{A}^\top$ *represents the transpose of matrix* $\mathbf{A}$*, and here* $\mathbf{A}$ *is the column full rank* $l \times m$ *matrix with* $m \leq l$*. When* $\lambda = 0$*,* $\mathbf{P_A} = \mathbf{A}(\mathbf{A}^\top\mathbf{A})^{-1}\mathbf{A}^\top$*, which is the projection onto column space of* $\mathbf{A}$*. Otherwise,* $\mathbf{e}_i = (0, \ldots, 0, 1, 0, \ldots, 0)^\top$ *is the unit vector, which has zeros everywhere, except in the ith position. For vector* $\mathbf{a} \in \mathbb{R}^n$*, the* L^2 *norm of* $\mathbf{a} = (a_1, a_2, \ldots, a_n)^\top$ *is captured by* $\|\mathbf{a}\|_2 = \sqrt{\mathbf{a}^\top\mathbf{a}}$*.*

2. Methodology

Suppose we have the random sample $\{(y_i, x_{i,1}, \ldots, x_{i,p_n}) : i = 1, \ldots, n\}$, which is generated from the population model (1). Then the nonparametric additive model can be rewritten as:

$$y_i = \sum_{j=1}^{p_n} m_j(x_{i,j}) + \epsilon_i, \quad i = 1, \ldots, n. \tag{2}$$

Without loss generality, we assume that the mean response is zero. For identification of the model, we further assume the mean of each additive function is zero, i.e., $Em_j(x_{i,j}) = 0$ for $j = 1, \ldots, p_n$. We note that all of the response variables are centralized to satisfy the above assumption during a real application. Here, the variance of the additive function $\mathrm{Var}(m_j(x_j))$ is used to distinguish the importance of the covariate. Thus, we let x_j be the important predictor if $\mathrm{Var}(m_j(x_j)) > 0$; otherwise x_j is the redundant predictor. Then we define the index set of the important predictors as $\mathbf{S} = \{j : \mathrm{Var}(m_j(x_j)) > 0, j = 1, \ldots, p_n\}$.

Next, we use B-spline basis functions to approximate $m_j(\cdot)$. Let us assume $x_j \in [0, 1]$ for $j = 1, \ldots, p_n$, $\bar{\phi} = \{\phi_k\}_{k=0}^{q}$ be a knot sequence such that $0 = \phi_0 < \phi_1 < \ldots < \phi_q = 1$, and $\mathcal{S}(\ell, \bar{\phi})$ are the space of polynomial splines of order ℓ with knot sequence $\bar{\phi}$. $\mathcal{S}(\ell, \bar{\phi})$ is a κ_n–dimensional linear space with $\kappa_n = q + \ell$. For any $m_j(x_j), j = 1, \ldots, p_n$, there exists the unique vector $\boldsymbol{\theta}_j^*$ to satisfy

$$m_j(x_j) \approx \sum_{t=1}^{\kappa_n} \theta_{jt} B_t(x_j) = \mathbf{B}(x_j)^\top \boldsymbol{\theta}_j^*, \tag{3}$$

where $\mathbf{B}(x_j) = (B_1(x_j), \ldots, B_{\kappa_n}(x_j))^\top$ and $\boldsymbol{\theta}_j^* = (\theta_{j1}^*, \ldots, \theta_{j\kappa_n}^*)^\top$. Let $\mathbf{w}_i = (\mathbf{w}_{i,1}^\top, \ldots, \mathbf{w}_{i,p_n}^\top)^\top$ with $\mathbf{w}_{i,j} = \mathbf{B}(x_{i,j})$, $\mathbf{W} = (\mathbf{w}_1, \ldots, \mathbf{w}_n)^\top$ and $\mathbf{Y} = (y_1, \ldots, y_n)^\top$. Based on the approximation of (3), model (2) becomes

$$y_i = \mathbf{w}_i^\top \boldsymbol{\theta}^* + \epsilon_i^*, i = 1, \ldots, n, \tag{4}$$

where $\boldsymbol{\theta}^* = (\boldsymbol{\theta}_1^{*\top}, \ldots, \boldsymbol{\theta}_{p_n}^{*\top})^\top$ and $\epsilon_i^* = \sum_{j=1}^{p_n} m_j(x_{i,j}) - \mathbf{w}_i^\top \boldsymbol{\theta}^* + \epsilon_i$. Under model (4), the ridge estimator minimizes the following loss

$$\|\mathbf{Y} - \mathbf{W}\boldsymbol{\theta}\|_2^2 + \lambda\|\boldsymbol{\theta}\|_2^2,$$

where λ is a positive constant. Then $\hat{\boldsymbol{\theta}}$ admits

$$\hat{\boldsymbol{\theta}} = \mathbf{W}^\top(\mathbf{W}\mathbf{W}^\top + \lambda\mathbf{I}_n)^{-1}\mathbf{Y}, \tag{5}$$

where $\mathbf{I}_n$ is the $n \times n$ identity matrix. For linear regression, Wang and Leng [18] considered the effect of each entry of $\boldsymbol{\theta}$, and showed that the ridge estimator achieves screening consistency. Notice that $\mathrm{Var}(m_j(x_j)) \approx \boldsymbol{\theta}_j^{*\top} E(\mathbf{w}_j \mathbf{w}_j^\top) \boldsymbol{\theta}_j^*$. Different from linear regression, we need to consider the group contribution of $\boldsymbol{\theta}_j^*$. By the boundedness of $E(\mathbf{w}_{i,j}\mathbf{w}_{i,j}^\top)$ from assumption A4(i), we use $\|\boldsymbol{\theta}_j^*\|_2$ to evaluate the group contribution. Similar to the results in [18], the ridge estimator $\hat{\boldsymbol{\theta}}$ provides the ranking order of the group contribution in $\boldsymbol{\theta}^*$ with $P(\|\hat{\boldsymbol{\theta}}_j\|_2 > \|\hat{\boldsymbol{\theta}}_k\|_2) \to 1$ if $j \in \mathbf{S}, k \in \mathbf{S}^c$ (see Theorem 1).

One natural screening method is to sort $\{\|\hat{\boldsymbol{\theta}}_j\|_2^2\}$ in decreasing order, and select its top m indexes, denoted as $\mathcal{F}_m = \{i_1, i_2, i_3, \ldots, i_m\}, 1 \le m \le p_n$. This screening process is referred to as the "GRIE" screening procedure. We define $\mathcal{G} = \{\mathcal{F}_m : m = 1, \ldots, p_n\}$, $\mathcal{A} = \{m : \mathbf{S} \subseteq \mathcal{F}_m, 1 \le m \le p_n\}$. Further, to get a more accurate result of model selection, i.e., searching d_n, which is the minimum item in the set $\mathcal{A}$. At that time, $\mathcal{F}_{d_n}$ is a set with the shortest length in $\mathcal{G}$ that contains important variable set $\mathbf{S}$. With the definition of $\mathcal{G}$, we have $\mathbf{S} \subseteq \mathcal{F}_{p_n}$. Then $\mathcal{F}_{d_n}$ is not an empty set. In summary, we want to find $\mathcal{F}_{d_n}$ from $\mathcal{G}$.

It is well known that the extended Bayesian information criteria (EBIC) have appealing theoretical properties and outstanding numerical performance for model selection. Let $\mathbf{W}_{\mathcal{T}} = (\mathbf{W}_j, j \in \mathcal{T})$ for any subset of $\mathcal{T} \subset \{1, \ldots, p_n\}$. The formula of the EBIC for the sub-model $(\mathbf{Y}, \mathbf{W}_{\mathcal{T}})$ is given by

$$EBIC(\mathcal{T}) = \log(RSS(\mathcal{T})/n) + \{\kappa_n |\mathcal{T}| \log(n) + 2\gamma \log f(|\mathcal{T}|)\}/n, \tag{6}$$

where γ is the preset positive constant, $RSS(\mathcal{T}) = \|\mathbf{Y} - \mathbf{W}_{\mathcal{T}} \hat{\boldsymbol{\theta}}_{\mathcal{T}}\|_2^2$ is the sum of squared residuals (RSS), and $f(|\mathcal{T}|) = C_{p_n \kappa_n}^{|\mathcal{T}|\kappa_n}$ is the combination number.

For a linear model, Wang [9] showed that $EBIC(\mathcal{F}_m) < EBIC(\mathcal{F}_{m-1})$ if $i_m \in \mathbf{S}$. Based on this property of EBIC and the preserving rank property of GRIE screening procedure (see Theorem 1), we propose the following Algorithm 1 for the model selection of (1).

Algorithm 1 GRIE-EBIC algorithm.

Initialization: Input $(\mathbf{W}, \mathbf{Y})$, $RSS_0 = \|\mathbf{Y}\|_2^2, n, p_n, \lambda, \kappa_n, \gamma, L$.
Step (i): Compute the GRIE screening procedure
1: Calculate ridge estimator $\hat{\boldsymbol{\theta}} = \mathbf{W}^\top(\mathbf{W}\mathbf{W}^\top + \lambda \mathbf{I}_n)^{-1}\mathbf{Y}$;
2: Sort $\{\|\hat{\boldsymbol{\theta}}_j\|_2, j = 1, \ldots, p_n\}$ in decreasing order and select the top n index set which is denoted by $\mathcal{F}_n = \{i_1, i_2, i_3, \ldots, i_n\}$;
Step (ii): Direct decreasing solution path
3: For $k = 1, \ldots, n$, do
3.1: Let $\hat{\mathbf{S}}_k = \{i_1, \ldots, i_k\}$ and compute the sum of squared residuals
$RSS_k = \|\mathbf{Y} - \mathbf{W}_{\hat{\mathbf{S}}_k}(\mathbf{W}_{\hat{\mathbf{S}}_k}^\top \mathbf{W}_{\hat{\mathbf{S}}_k})^{-1}\mathbf{W}_{\hat{\mathbf{S}}_k}^\top \mathbf{Y}\|_2^2$;
3.2: Compute EBIC: $EBIC_k = \log(RSS_k/n) + \{\kappa_n k \log(n) + 2\gamma \log f(k)\}/n$;
3.3: If $k \ge L+1$ and $EBIC_k > \cdots > EBIC_{k-L}$, compute $K = k - L$ and stop;
4: Compute the difference of the EBIC to obtain the decreasing solution path
$\mathcal{I} = \{k : EBIC_k - EBIC_{k-1} < 0, k = 1, 2, \ldots, K\}$;
5: Find the decreasing index set $\hat{\mathbf{S}}_* = \{i_k : k \in \mathcal{I}\}$;
Step (iii): Forward decreasing solution path
6: Compute $RSS_* = \|\mathbf{Y} - \mathbf{W}_{\hat{\mathbf{S}}_*}(\mathbf{W}_{\hat{\mathbf{S}}_*}^\top \mathbf{W}_{\hat{\mathbf{S}}_*})^{-1}\mathbf{W}_{\hat{\mathbf{S}}_*}^\top \mathbf{Y}\|_2^2$ and
$EBIC_* = \log(RSS_*/n) + \{\kappa_n |\hat{\mathbf{S}}_*| \log(n) + 2\gamma \log f(|\hat{\mathbf{S}}_*|)\}/n$;
7: For $\ell \in \mathcal{F}_n \backslash \hat{\mathbf{S}}_*$, do
Let $\hat{\mathbf{S}}_{*\ell} = \hat{\mathbf{S}}_* \cup \{\ell\}$, compute $RSS_{*\ell} = \|\mathbf{Y} - \mathbf{W}_{\hat{\mathbf{S}}_{*\ell}}(\mathbf{W}_{\hat{\mathbf{S}}_{*\ell}}^\top \mathbf{W}_{\hat{\mathbf{S}}_{*\ell}})^{-1}\mathbf{W}_{\hat{\mathbf{S}}_{*\ell}}^\top \mathbf{Y}\|_2^2$ and
$EBIC_{*\ell} = \log(RSS_{*\ell}/n) + \{\kappa_n |\hat{\mathbf{S}}_{*\ell}| \log(n) + 2\gamma \log f(|\hat{\mathbf{S}}_{*\ell}|)\}/n$;
8: Find decreasing solution path $\hat{\mathbf{S}} = \hat{\mathbf{S}}_* \cup \{\ell : EBIC_{*\ell} - EBIC_* < 0, \ell \in \mathcal{F}_n \backslash \hat{\mathbf{S}}_*\}$;
Output final index set $\hat{\mathbf{S}}$.

In step (ii) of the GRIE-EBIC algorithm, we search the important covariates from the top n predictor space $\mathcal{F}_n$. Based on Theorem 1, GRIE has the consistency of preserving order in sorting. The higher the index position of the variable in $\mathcal{F}_{p_n}$, the more likely it is to be an important variable. To speed up the calculation, we set a stopping rule for screening when the EBIC value increases for L times continuously. To improve the robustness of the GRIE-EBIC algorithm, in step (iii), we add the further forward screening process.

3. Asymptotic Properties

3.1. Assumptions

To establish the asymptotic properties of our proposed method, we give the following notations and assumptions. Let $\mathbf{\Sigma} = E(\mathbf{w}\mathbf{w}^\top)$, $\mathbf{Z} = \mathbf{W}\mathbf{\Sigma}^{-1/2}$, $\mathbf{z} = \mathbf{\Sigma}^{-1/2}\mathbf{w}$, and $t_n = p_n\kappa_n$, where $\mathbf{w} = (\mathbf{w}_1^\top, \ldots, \mathbf{w}_{p_n}^\top)^\top$ with $\mathbf{w}_j = \mathbf{B}(x_j)$. We use $\mathbf{\Sigma}_\mathcal{T} = E(n^{-1}\mathbf{W}_\mathcal{T}^\top\mathbf{W}_\mathcal{T})$. $\mathcal{H}_r$ denotes a space of functions whose d-th order derivative is Hölder continuous of order v, i.e., $\mathcal{H}_r = \{h(z) : |h^{(d)}(a') - h^{(d)}(a)| \leq C|a' - a|^v, a, a' \in [0,1]\}$, where $h^{(d)}(\cdot)$ is the d-th derivative of $h(\cdot)$ and $r = d + v$. If $v = 1$, $h^{(d)}(\cdot)$ is Lipschitz continuous. Let s_n be the cardinality of $\mathbf{S}$. The following assumptions are required:

A1 Assume $\mathbf{z}$ has a spherically symmetric distribution, and there exists some positive c_1 and C_1 such that

$$P(\lambda_{\min}({t_n}^{-1}\mathbf{Z}\mathbf{Z}^\top) \leq c_1^{-1} \text{ or } \lambda_{\max}({t_n}^{-1}\mathbf{Z}\mathbf{Z}^\top) > c_1) \leq 2\exp(-C_1 n).$$

A2 Assume there exists some positive constant C_* such that, for any $a \in R$,

$$\max_{i=1,\ldots,n} E\{\exp(a\varepsilon_i)|\mathbf{x}_i\} \leq \exp(C_* a^2/2).$$

A3 Assume that (i) there exists some $r \geq 2$ such that $m_j \in \mathcal{H}_r$ and $\kappa_n = O(n^{1/(2r+1)})$ for any $j \in \mathbf{S}$; (ii) $\sum_{j\in\mathbf{S}} E|m_j(x_j)|^2 \leq c_2 s_n$; (iii) $\lambda_{\max}(\mathbf{\Sigma})/\lambda_{\min}(\mathbf{\Sigma}) \leq c_3 n^\tau$, where c_2, c_3 are some positive constants and $\tau \geq 0$.

A4 (i) $c_4^{-1}\kappa_n^{-1} \leq \lambda_{\min}(E(\mathbf{B}(x_j)\mathbf{B}(x_j)^\top)) \leq \lambda_{\max}(E(\mathbf{B}(x_j)\mathbf{B}(x_j)^\top)) \leq c_4\kappa_n^{-1}$ for some positive constant c_4; (ii) $\min_{j\in\mathbf{S}}\{E|m_j(x_j)|^2\}^{1/2} \geq d_n$ for some positive sequence $d_n \to 0$; (iii) $\frac{\kappa_n^{r-1/2} d_n}{n^{2\tau} s_n \sqrt{\log n}} \to \infty$, $\log(t_n) = o\left(\frac{d_n^2 n^{1-4\tau}}{\kappa_n^2 s_n^2 \log n}\right)$.

A5 (i) $\mathrm{Var}(y_1) = O(\kappa_n s_n^2 n^{3\tau}\log(n))$; (ii) For any integer N with $s_n < N \leq s_n \log n$, there exists positive constant $c_6 > 0$ such that

$$\frac{c_6 n^{-\tau}}{\kappa_n} \leq \lambda_{\min}(\mathbf{\Sigma}_\mathcal{T}) \tag{7}$$

holds uniformly in $\mathcal{T} \subset \mathcal{F}_n$ satisfying $|\mathcal{T}| \leq N$ and $\mathbf{S} \subset \mathcal{T}$.

Assumptions A1 and A3(iii) are like Assumptions 1 and 3 of [18]. Assumption A2 is the same as Assumption A3 of [11], which means that the random error follows the sub-Gaussian distribution. Assumption A3(i) is a common assumption in the literature for the polynomial spline basis, A3(ii) gives the upper bound of all signals, and A3(iii) gives the upper bound of the condition number. In addition, Assumption A3(ii)–(iii) are implied by Assumption A2 in [11]. Assumption A4(i) and a stronger assumption $\mathrm{Var}(y_1) = O(1)$ than A5(i), which is also imposed in [11] for achieving the consistency of variable selection. They also assumed A5(ii) holds. Assumptions A4(ii) and (iii) give the lower bound and upper bound of the minimal signal and dimensionality of the design matrix $\mathbf{W}$.

3.2. Main Theorems

Theorem 1. *If Assumptions A1–A4 hold, then*

$$P\left(\min_{j\in\mathbf{S}} \|\hat{\boldsymbol{\theta}}_j\|_2 > \max_{j\in\mathbf{S}^c} \|\hat{\boldsymbol{\theta}}_j\|_2\right) \to 1.$$

Alternatively, we can choose a sub-model $\mathcal{F}_{d_n}$ with $d_n = O(n^{\iota})$ for some $0 < \iota < 1$ such that

$$P(\mathbf{S} \subset \mathcal{F}_{d_n}) \to 1.$$

Theorem 1 states the consistency of preserving order in sorting, i.e., $\hat{\boldsymbol{\theta}}$ could totally separate the unimportant and important variables with a probability tending to 1. For the linear models, Theorem 1 is in line with Theorem 2 in [18], which is the special case of our theorem.

Theorem 2. *If Assumptions A1–A5 hold, then*

$$P(\hat{\mathbf{S}} = \mathbf{S}) \to 1.$$

The screening methods in [7,11,12] adopted a forward selection algorithm, which means the later results are affected by the results of the previous steps. This not only brings a heavy computation burden but also results in overfitting results for screening with $P(\mathbf{S} \subseteq \hat{\mathbf{S}}) \to 1$. Compared with this result, Theorem 2 gives strong consistency of screening with $P(\hat{\mathbf{S}} = \mathbf{S}) \to 1$.

4. Simulations

In this section, we investigate the finite sample performance of our proposed method and compare our method with the following two procedures: forward additive regression (FAR) in [11] and cumulative divergence-based forward regression (C-FS) in [12]. We choose $\lambda = 1$, $L = 5$ (suggested by [10]), $\gamma = 0.5$ (suggested by [20]), and $\kappa_n = \lfloor n^{1/5} \rfloor + 2$ (suggested by [11]) for the GRIE-EBIC algorithm, where κ_n is the dimension of B-spline basis space and $\lfloor n^{1/5} \rfloor$ is the greatest integer less than $n^{1/5}$.

Three specific criteria are adopted to evaluate the performance of variable selection for the additive model (1). True positive (TP) is the number of the true variables that are considered true variables in the selected model, and false positive (FP) is the number of the noise variables that are misclassified as true variables in the selected model. Combining TP and FP, they reflect the accuracy of variable selection methods in the selected sub-models. In addition, we select time as the third criterion to reflect the efficiency of variable selection by different methods. It is easy to find that our proposed method, GRIE, is more efficient than FAR and C-FS in computation since their complexities of calculation are $O(n^2 p_n \kappa_n)$, $O(n^3 p_n)$, and $O(T n^3 p_n)$, respectively, where T is the number of repetitions for the bootstrap procedure in the C-FS method. The comparison of computation complexities highlights the time efficiency of GRIE in the calculation, which will be further demonstrated by simulation results in Tables 1 and 2.

The following examples perform the effect from different dimensions and correlations between any two covariates with each other by the above three procedures. Given two different dimensions and three different correlations between any two predictors with each other, the considered error followed the standard normal $N(0,1)$ and Chi-square $0.5\chi_2^2$. In each example, we generate 100 random samples, each consisting of $n = 300$. The data generation procedures are implemented by the R package "MASS" generating the random covariates, errors, and response variables. The details are as follows: (1) "rnorm": simulated from a multivariate normal distribution; (2) "mvrnorm": simulated from a multivariate normal distribution; (3) "rchisqure": simulated from a multi Chi-square distribution; (4) "runif": simulated from a uniform distribution.

Example 1. *We generated n samples from the following nonparametric additive model:*

$$y = m_1(x_1) + m_2(x_2) + m_3(x_3) + m_4(x_4) + \epsilon,$$

where $m_1(x) = 0.75\exp(x)$, $m_2(x) = x^2$, $m_3(x) = 3\sin(x)$, $m_4(x) = 2x$, and $(x_1, x_2, \ldots, x_{p_n})^{\top}$ follows a multinormal distribution $N(0, \boldsymbol{\Sigma})$. In this example, given $\boldsymbol{\Sigma} = (\sigma_{ij})$

under the following two cases: (1) *Autoregressive (AR) structure,* $\sigma_{ij} = \rho^{|i-j|}$*;* (2) *Compound symmetry (CS) structure, namely, if* $i \neq j$*,* $\sigma_{ij} = \rho$*, else* $\sigma_{ij} = 1$*. Here, we set the parameter* ρ *used to control the strength of correlation between any two predictors with each other at different values of* 0.3, 0.6, *and* 0.9.

Table 1. Average number of true positive (TP), false positive (FP), and calculation time over 100 repetitions and their robust standard deviations (in parentheses) of Example 1 with $\epsilon \sim N(0,1)$.

ρ	Approach	$p_n = 500$			$p_n = 1000$		
		TP	**FP**	**Time (s)**	**TP**	**FP**	**Time (s)**
				AR Structure			
0.3	FAR	4.00 (0.00)	0.00 (0.00)	83.19 (9.80)	4.00 (0.00)	0.00 (0.00)	166.26 (18.65)
	C-FS	3.20 (0.40)	5.21 (2.96)	16.18 (5.38)	3.34 (0.48)	11.44 (5.38)	39.64 (14.35)
	GRIE	4.00 (0.00)	0.00 (0.00)	2.37 (0.28)	3.99 (0.10)	0.01 (0.10)	3.56 (0.77)
0.6	FAR	4.00 (0.00)	0.00 (0.00)	82.06 (9.77)	4.00 (0.00)	0.00 (0.00)	168.16 (20.51)
	C-FS	3.71 (0.46)	4.81 (2.39)	16.57 (4.28)	3.70 (0.46)	9.33 (4.88)	34.61 (12.24)
	GRIE	3.99 (0.10)	0.00 (0.00)	2.40 (0.35)	3.98 (0.14)	0.03 (0.30)	3.43 (0.72)
0.9	FAR	3.17 (0.60)	0.00 (0.00)	81.34 (9.48)	3.09 (0.60)	0.00 (0.00)	168.70 (18.62)
	C-FS	3.14 (0.51)	2.44 (1.72)	10.63 (3.01)	3.14 (0.53)	4.43 (2.96)	19.14 (6.78)
	GRIE	3.71 (0.46)	0.20 (0.40)	2.22 (0.40)	3.70 (0.46)	0.21 (0.43)	3.45 (0.76)
				CS Structure			
0.3	FAR	4.00 (0.00)	0.00 (0.00)	83.60 (10.17)	4.00 (0.00)	0.00 (0.00)	165.38 (19.00)
	C-FS	3.45 (0.52)	4.96 (2.97)	16.11 (5.23)	3.33 (0.47)	11.69 (6.24)	39.98 (16.38)
	GRIE	4.00 (0.00)	0.09 (0.90)	2.30 (0.39)	4.00 (0.00)	0.02 (0.20)	3.57 (0.72)
0.6	FAR	4.00 (0.00)	0.00 (0.00)	84.24 (10.26)	4.00 (0.00)	0.01 (0.10)	166.92 (18.64)
	C-FS	3.74 (0.44)	5.05 (2.98)	16.82 (5.26)	3.61 (0.55)	10.26 (5.25)	36.73 (13.38)
	GRIE	4.00 (0.00)	0.23 (2.30)	2.35 (0.37)	4.00 (0.00)	0.11 (0.62)	3.41 (0.74)
0.9	FAR	3.03 (0.67)	0.00 (0.00)	85.57 (11.01)	2.79 (0.70)	0.00 (0.00)	166.02 (18.65)
	C-FS	2.63 (0.65)	4.48 (3.47)	13.35 (6.08)	2.56 (0.67)	9.70 (5.93)	32.23 (15.07)
	GRIE	3.89 (0.31)	1.47 (7.62)	2.21 (0.35)	3.79 (0.41)	3.16 (17.90)	3.44 (0.77)

Table 2. Average numbers of true positive (TP), false positive (FP), and calculation time over 100 repetitions and their robust standard deviations (in parentheses) of Example 1 with $\epsilon \sim 0.5\chi_2^2$.

ρ	Approach	$p_n = 500$			$p_n = 1000$		
		TP	**FP**	**Time (s)**	**TP**	**FP**	**Time (s)**
				AR Structure			
0.3	FAR	4.00 (0.00)	0.00 (0.00)	79.30 (11.14)	4.00 (0.00)	0.00 (0.00)	165.38 (22.09)
	C-FS	3.27 (0.45)	5.38 (3.00)	16.43 (5.40)	3.33 (0.47)	11.24 (4.85)	39.44 (12.59)
	GRIE	4.00 (0.00)	0.00 (0.00)	2.40 (0.36)	3.99 (0.10)	0.00 (0.00)	3.33 (0.68)
0.6	FAR	4.00 (0.00)	0.00 (0.00)	79.19 (12.07)	4.00 (0.00)	0.00 (0.00)	163.64 (23.37)
	C-FS	3.70 (0.46)	4.42 (2.53)	15.60 (4.49)	3.77 (0.42)	9.56 (4.29)	35.74 (11.14)
	GRIE	3.99 (0.10)	0.01 (0.10)	2.31 (0.33)	3.98 (0.14)	0.03 (0.30)	3.42 (0.67)
0.9	FAR	3.09 (0.68)	0.00 (0.00)	80.28 (10.89)	3.01 (0.72)	0.00 (0.00)	163.88 (22.78)
	C-FS	3.10 (0.48)	2.28 (1.56)	10.15 (2.86)	3.15 (0.50)	4.26 (2.20)	19.12 (5.44)
	GRIE	3.71 (0.46)	0.23 (0.51)	2.28 (0.32)	3.78 (0.42)	0.16 (0.39)	3.33 (0.67)
				CS Structure			
0.3	FAR	4.00 (0.00)	0.00 (0.00)	80.28 (9.59)	4.00 (0.00)	0.00 (0.00)	164.25 (19.31)
	C-FS	3.51 (0.52)	5.10 (2.99)	16.50 (5.68)	3.36 (0.48)	10.87 (4.98)	37.91 (13.02)
	GRIE	4.00 (0.00)	0.00 (0.00)	2.31 (0.34)	3.98 (0.14)	0.34 (3.30)	3.38 (0.66)
0.6	FAR	4.00 (0.00)	0.00 (0.00)	80.12 (11.56)	4.00 (0.00)	0.01 (0.10)	165.41 (20.04)
	C-FS	3.72 (0.49)	4.71 (2.57)	16.04 (4.68)	3.68 (0.49)	9.79 (5.39)	36.12 (14.41)
	GRIE	3.99 (0.10)	0.00 (0.00)	2.31 (0.29)	4.00 (0.00)	0.11 (0.65)	3.40 (0.70)

Table 2. *Cont.*

ρ	Approach	$p_n = 500$			$p_n = 1000$		
		TP	**FP**	**Time (s)**	**TP**	**FP**	**Time (s)**
0.9	FAR	3.00 (0.79)	0.03 (0.17)	79.62 (11.60)	2.85 (0.78)	0.02 (0.14)	164.90 (19.25)
	C-FS	2.73 (0.66)	4.40 (2.81)	13.56 (4.91)	2.69 (0.63)	10.82 (5.99)	35.72 (15.68)
	GRIE	3.94 (0.24)	3.13 (16.94)	2.28 (0.35)	3.82 (0.39)	3.63 (18.13)	3.30 (0.72)

Tables 1–4 summarize the results for the additive model in Example 1. Under the setting of $\rho = 0.3$ and 0.6, except for C-FS, our proposed method and FAR method could identify all important features and keep the FP value close to zero in both AR and CS structures. Even so, the FAR method has the longest calculation time among the three methods. Furthermore, when there exists strong correlations between covariates ($\rho = 0.9$), the performances of all three methods are worse at identifying important variables, especially for FAR and C-FS methods. Under this situation, compared with the other two methods, our method has the highest TP and shortest cost time. To perform the stability of our model, we report the empirical probabilities of each important covariate and all important covariates are retained for 100 replications in Tables 3 and 4, where $\mathcal{P}_j$ and $\mathcal{P}_{\text{all}}$ are the empirical probabilities of each important covariate and all important covariates being retained in the selected sub-model, respectively. Following Tables 3 and 4, $\mathcal{P}_{\text{all}}$ is below 0.3 for FAR and C-FS, while the $\mathcal{P}_{\text{all}}$ of GRIE is at least 0.70. In addition, the $\mathcal{P}_{\text{j}}$'s of our method is the best among the three methods in high-dimensional settings. Hence, we conclude that our proposed GRIE method performs robustly in the model selection of nonparametric additive models under high-dimension settings.

Table 3. The empirical probabilities of each important covariate and all important covariates being retained for 100 replications in Example 1 with $\epsilon \sim N(0,1)$.

ρ	Approach	$p_n = 500$					$p_n = 1000$				
		$\mathcal{P}_1$	$\mathcal{P}_2$	$\mathcal{P}_3$	$\mathcal{P}_4$	$\mathcal{P}_{\text{all}}$	$\mathcal{P}_1$	$\mathcal{P}_2$	$\mathcal{P}_3$	$\mathcal{P}_4$	$\mathcal{P}_{\text{all}}$
						AR Structure					
0.3	FAR	1.00	1.00	1.00	1.00	1.00	1.00	1.00	1.00	1.00	1.00
	C-FS	1.00	0.20	1.00	1.00	0.20	1.00	0.34	1.00	1.00	0.34
	GRIE	1.00	1.00	1.00	1.00	1.00	1.00	0.99	1.00	1.00	0.99
0.6	FAR	1.00	1.00	1.00	1.00	1.00	1.00	1.00	1.00	1.00	1.00
	C-FS	1.00	0.71	1.00	1.00	0.71	0.98	0.72	1.00	1.00	0.70
	GRIE	1.00	0.99	1.00	1.00	0.99	1.00	0.98	1.00	1.00	0.98
0.9	FAR	0.80	0.49	0.97	0.91	0.28	0.82	0.42	0.98	0.87	0.23
	C-FS	0.50	0.67	0.97	1.00	0.21	0.50	0.67	0.97	1.00	0.22
	GRIE	0.83	0.88	1.00	1.00	0.71	0.79	0.91	1.00	1.00	0.70
						CS Structure					
0.3	FAR	1.00	1.00	1.00	1.00	1.00	1.00	1.00	1.00	1.00	1.00
	C-FS	0.99	0.46	1.00	1.00	0.46	1.00	0.33	1.00	1.00	0.33
	GRIE	1.00	1.00	1.00	1.00	1.00	1.00	1.00	1.00	1.00	1.00
0.6	FAR	1.00	1.00	1.00	1.00	1.00	1.00	1.00	1.00	1.00	1.00
	C-FS	0.93	0.81	1.00	1.00	0.74	0.88	0.73	1.00	1.00	0.64
	GRIE	1.00	1.00	1.00	1.00	1.00	1.00	1.00	1.00	1.00	1.00
0.9	FAR	0.63	0.57	0.98	0.85	0.24	0.58	0.49	0.91	0.81	0.16
	C-FS	0.11	0.62	0.97	0.93	0.05	0.12	0.53	0.97	0.94	0.07
	GRIE	0.93	0.96	1.00	1.00	0.89	0.87	0.92	1.00	1.00	0.79

Table 4. The empirical probabilities of each important covariate and all important covariates being retained for 100 replications in Example 1 with $\epsilon \sim 0.5\chi_2^2$.

ρ	Approach	$p_n = 500$					$p_n = 1000$				
		$\mathcal{P}_1$	$\mathcal{P}_2$	$\mathcal{P}_3$	$\mathcal{P}_4$	$\mathcal{P}_{\text{all}}$	$\mathcal{P}_1$	$\mathcal{P}_2$	$\mathcal{P}_3$	$\mathcal{P}_4$	$\mathcal{P}_{\text{all}}$
		AR Structure									
0.3	FAR	1.00	1.00	1.00	1.00	1.00	1.00	1.00	1.00	1.00	1.00
	C-FS	1.00	0.27	1.00	1.00	0.27	1.00	0.33	1.00	1.00	0.33
	GRIE	1.00	1.00	1.00	1.00	1.00	1.00	0.99	1.00	1.00	0.99
0.6	FAR	1.00	1.00	1.00	1.00	1.00	1.00	1.00	1.00	1.00	1.00
	C-FS	1.00	0.70	1.00	1.00	0.70	0.99	0.78	1.00	1.00	0.77
	GRIE	1.00	0.99	1.00	1.00	0.99	1.00	0.99	1.00	0.99	0.98
0.9	FAR	0.81	0.47	0.95	0.86	0.28	0.82	0.45	0.94	0.80	0.26
	C-FS	0.42	0.70	0.98	1.00	0.17	0.53	0.65	0.97	1.00	0.21
	GRIE	0.82	0.89	1.00	1.00	0.71	0.84	0.94	1.00	1.00	0.78
		CS Structure									
0.3	FAR	1.00	1.00	1.00	1.00	1.00	1.00	1.00	1.00	1.00	1.00
	C-FS	0.99	0.52	1.00	1.00	0.52	0.99	0.37	1.00	1.00	0.36
	GRIE	1.00	1.00	1.00	1.00	1.00	1.00	0.98	1.00	1.00	0.98
0.6	FAR	1.00	1.00	1.00	1.00	1.00	1.00	1.00	1.00	1.00	1.00
	C-FS	0.93	0.79	1.00	1.00	0.74	0.92	0.76	1.00	1.00	0.69
	GRIE	1.00	0.99	1.00	1.00	0.99	1.00	1.00	1.00	1.00	1.00
0.9	FAR	0.54	0.65	0.97	0.84	0.28	0.55	0.55	0.94	0.81	0.24
	C-FS	0.12	0.66	0.97	0.98	0.09	0.14	0.61	0.97	0.97	0.08
	GRIE	0.97	0.97	1.00	1.00	0.94	0.88	0.94	1.00	1.00	0.82

Example 2. *In this example, we consider a linear model with a group structure given by*

$$y = \sum_{i=1}^{p_n} \beta_i x_i + \epsilon$$

with the predictors being generated by the following process

$$\begin{cases} x_i = z_1 + z + w_i, & \forall\, i = 1, 3, \\ x_i = z_2 + z + w_i, & \forall\, i = 2, 4, \\ x_5, \ldots, x_{p_n} \overset{\text{i.i.d}}{\sim} N(0,1), & \end{cases}$$

where $w_1, \ldots, w_4 \overset{\text{i.i.d}}{\sim} U(0,1)$, $z_1, z_2 \overset{\text{i.i.d}}{\sim} U(0,1)$ *and the common component* $z \sim N(0, \delta^2)$. *The variance parameter* δ *is set at different values of* 0.4, 0.6, *and* 0.8 *to control the strength of the group structure. The true value of the coefficients are* $\beta_i = 3$ *with* $i = 1, \ldots, 4$ *and* $\beta_i = 0$ *with* $i = 5, \ldots, p_n$.

We also conducted simulations with the normal errors and chi-square errors for Example 2 and found that the performances of the two errors in this example were very close. Therefore, we omitted the results of chi-square errors to save space. In the following, we only report the results from the normal errors in Tables 5 and 6. We find that the FAR's performance is the worst for identifying important features with the increase in correlations between groups, the performances of C-FS and our method GRIE also become worse when δ is over 0.6, while GRIE performs better even if there exists a strong correlation among covariates. The above phenomena can be further explained by Table 6. When δ is over 0.6, there is no longer an overwhelming empirical probability of screening important covariates for FAR and C-FS, which results in a decrease in TP and $\mathcal{P}_{\text{all}}$ values. However, our proposed method is still relatively robust to different values of δ in terms of TP and $\mathcal{P}_{\text{all}}$.

Table 5. Average numbers of true positive (TP), false positive (FP), and calculation time over 100 repetitions and their robust standard deviations (in parentheses) of Example 2 with $\epsilon \sim N(0,1)$.

δ	Approach	$p_n = 500$			$p_n = 1000$		
		TP	FP	Time (s)	TP	FP	Time (s)
0.4	FAR	4.00 (0.00)	0.59 (0.51)	81.85 (10.28)	3.98 (0.20)	0.57 (0.50)	168.16 (20.16)
	C-FS	4.00 (0.00)	5.32 (2.97)	18.74 (5.35)	4.00 (0.00)	11.40 (5.37)	42.87 (15.18)
	GRIE	4.00 (0.00)	0.04 (0.24)	2.41 (0.36)	4.00 (0.00)	0.06 (0.34)	3.59 (0.64)
0.6	FAR	3.94 (0.28)	1.09 (0.49)	80.25 (9.06)	3.86 (0.49)	1.07 (0.48)	164.35 (18.90)
	C-FS	4.00 (0.00)	6.05 (2.88)	19.32 (5.19)	4.00 (0.00)	12.11 (5.37)	43.61 (14.17)
	GRIE	4.00 (0.00)	0.17 (0.49)	2.33 (0.34)	4.00 (0.00)	0.18 (0.54)	3.43 (0.63)
0.8	FAR	3.66 (0.73)	1.26 (0.50)	80.04 (9.10)	3.68 (0.72)	1.22 (0.54)	164.05 (18.76)
	C-FS	3.81 (0.42)	5.88 (2.82)	18.62 (5.41)	3.85 (0.36)	12.13 (5.18)	42.92 (13.12)
	GRIE	3.95 (0.22)	0.38 (0.72)	2.37 (0.34)	3.89 (0.31)	0.27 (0.63)	3.45 (0.75)

Table 6. The empirical probabilities of each important covariate and all important covariates being retained for 100 replications in Example 2 with $\epsilon \sim N(0,1)$.

δ	Approach	$p_n = 500$					$p_n = 1000$				
		$\mathcal{P}_1$	$\mathcal{P}_2$	$\mathcal{P}_3$	$\mathcal{P}_4$	$\mathcal{P}_{\text{all}}$	$\mathcal{P}_1$	$\mathcal{P}_2$	$\mathcal{P}_3$	$\mathcal{P}_4$	$\mathcal{P}_{\text{all}}$
0.4	FAR	1.00	1.00	1.00	1.00	1.00	1.00	1.00	0.99	0.99	0.99
	C-FS	1.00	1.00	1.00	1.00	1.00	1.00	1.00	1.00	1.00	1.00
	GRIE	1.00	1.00	1.00	1.00	1.00	1.00	1.00	1.00	1.00	1.00
0.6	FAR	0.99	0.99	0.98	0.98	0.95	0.96	0.98	0.97	0.95	0.92
	C-FS	1.00	1.00	1.00	1.00	1.00	1.00	1.00	1.00	1.00	1.00
	GRIE	1.00	1.00	1.00	1.00	1.00	1.00	1.00	1.00	1.00	1.00
0.8	FAR	0.92	0.91	0.91	0.92	0.81	0.90	0.92	0.93	0.93	0.83
	C-FS	0.93	0.97	0.96	0.95	0.82	0.94	0.97	0.97	0.97	0.85
	GRIE	1.00	1.00	0.97	0.98	0.95	0.97	1.00	0.95	0.97	0.89

5. Real Data

5.1. Boston Housing Data

We use the Boston housing dataset to further illustrate the performance of our proposed method. The dataset contains the MEDV (median value of owner-occupied homes) in 506 U.S. census tracts of Boston from the 1970 census and 13 other variables that explain the variation in housing value. The 13 explaining variables are RM (average number of rooms per dwelling), AGE (proportion of owner-occupied units built prior to 1940), RAD (index of accessibility to radial highways), TAX (full-value property-tax rate per 10,000), PTRATIO (pupil-teacher ratio by town), B ($1000(\text{Bk}-0.63)^2$, Bk is the proportion of blacks by town), LSTAT (lower status of the population), CRIM (per capita crime rate by town), ZN (proportion of residential land zoned for lots over 25,000 square footage), INDUS (proportion of non-retail business acres per town), CHAS (Charles River dummy variable), NOX (nitric oxides concentration parts per 10 million), and DIS (weighted distances to five Boston employment centers). To simplify notation, we denote the covariates RM, AGE, RAD, TAX, PTRATIO, B, LSTAT, CRIM, ZN, INDUS, CHAS, NOX, and DIS as $x_1, \ldots, x_{13}$. To study the relationship between MEDV and the above 13 variables, we consider the following nonparametric addition models:

$$y = \sum_{j=1}^{13} m_j(x_j) + \epsilon, \tag{8}$$

where y is the log(MEDV). In order to extend the above model to the setting of high-dimensional data, followed by [21], we generate artificial variables x_j to add noise variables, which is defined as follows.

$$x_j = \frac{Z_j + 2W}{3},$$

for $j = 14, \ldots, 1000$ into (8), where $Z_{14}, \ldots, Z_{1000} \overset{i.i.d}{\sim} N(0,1)$, and $W \sim U(0,1)$.

We use FAR, C-FS, and GRIE to identify important variables in the above additive model (8) with the full dataset. The results are as follows.

(i) Under FAR, 3 covariates $\{x_1, x_7, x_8\}$ are selected, denoted by "model (A_1)".
(ii) Under GRIE, we receive 6 covariates $\{x_1, x_5, x_6, x_7, x_8, x_{12}\}$, denoted by "model (B_1)".
(iii) Under C-FS, there are 15 covariates chosen. They are $\{x_1, x_2, x_3, x_4, x_5, x_6, x_7, x_8, x_9, x_{12}, x_{13}, x_{156}, x_{377}, x_{737}, x_{859}\}$, denoted by "model (C_1)".

The above three sub-models have such a nest relation with $A_1 \subseteq B_1 \subseteq C_1$, and we want to investigate which model is best for fitting this dataset. The nondegenerative Vuong test in [22] is considered here to compare two nested models, and its null hypothesis is that the two models are equivalent. We first compare model (A_1) with model (B_1) by the Vuong test, and its p-value $= 0.001$, which leads to the rejection of the null hypothesis. This indicates model (B_1) is better than model (A_1) since (A_1) is nested in (B_1). We also compare model (B_1) with model (C_1), and its corresponding p-value of the Vuong test equals 0.981, which indicates models (B_1) and (C_1) are equivalent since the null hypothesis is not rejected in this situation. However, model (B_1) has a smaller model size than model (C_1). Therefore, model (B_1) is more suitable than model (C_1) for fitting the Boston housing dataset to be the best working model, which indicates that GRIE performs the best in identifying the important variables among the above three variable selection methods.

To further demonstrate our results, we compare FAR, C-FS, and GRIE through their prediction errors. Toward this end, we randomly select 100 validation sets, with each of which the full sample is randomly partitioned into the training and validation sets with the size ratio 4 : 1. The training sets are for variable section, and the validation sets are for the estimation of the prediction error. We centralize the response variable y and choose the cubic splines $\kappa_n = 3$ to approximate the additive function. The average numbers of model size, the number of selected noise variables (SNV), and adjusted mean prediction errors (A-PE) are used to evaluate the performance of the three methods. All the results are reported in Table 7.

Table 7. Average numbers of model size, the number of SNV, and A-PE over 100 repetitions and their robust standard deviations (in parentheses) of Boston Housing Data.

Approach	Model Size	SNV	A-PE
FAR	2.10 (0.30)	0.00 (0.00)	0.052 (0.011)
C-FS	19.26 (5.39)	8.71 (5.10)	0.047 (0.012)
GRIE	5.07 (0.95)	0.00 (0.00)	0.043 (0.010)

From Table 7, we have that: (1) The model sizes of our method, GRIE, and FAR are both smaller than C-FS, but the A-PE of FAR is the largest among the three methods, which means that FAR may fail to identify some important variables. To verify it, we report the frequency for 13 real covariates being selected over 100 replications in Table 8. Table 8 shows that RM and LSTAT are selected by all methods in each repetition. Except for the FAR method, PTRATIO, B, and CRIM can be selected by GRIE and C-FS with high frequency. It is seen that the pupil–teacher ratio, the proportion of blacks, and the per capita crime rate are the key factors affecting housing prices. However, FAR misses the above important variables. (2) For the value of SNV, both our method, GRIE, and FAR are 0, which means that they can successfully exclude all artificial variables.

In summary, compared with C-FS and FAR, our method has the smallest A-PE, the smallest SNV, and a simple model, which implies our method has better performance in feature screening under high-dimensional settings.

Table 8. The frequency for 13 real covariates being selected over 100 replications for Boston Housing Data.

Variable	FAR	C-FS	GRIE
RM	100	100	100
AGE	0	99	0
RAD	0	60	6
TAX	0	59	7
PTRATIO	0	100	68
B	0	92	99
LSTAT	100	100	100
CRIM	10	100	80
ZN	0	97	0
INDUS	0	22	0
CHAS	0	26	0
NOX	0	100	47
DIS	0	100	0

5.2. *Arabidopsis thaliana* Gene Data

We now turn to *Arabidopsis thaliana* gene data to illustrate the screening performance of our method. This dataset was developed by Wille et al. (2004) [23], who detected modules of closely connected isoprenoid genes in *Arabidopsis thaliana*. It is available on the website https://www.ncbi.nlm.nih.gov/pmc/articles/PMC545783 (accessed on 16 November 2022), which is composed of 834 genes from 58 different pathways in 118 samples. Chen et al. [24] found that GGPPS11 played an essential role in the generation of GGPP, which is the common precursor of several biologically important compounds (such as carotenoids, chlorophylls, and gibberellins), in Arabidopsis. Our goal is to identify the remaining 833 genes' effects on the expression value of gene GGPPS11.

Followed by Wille et al. [23], the downloaded data $R = \{y, x_1, \ldots, x_{833}\}$ were converted to permille data by taking $1000R$. To get the original dataset, we model $0.001R$ here and consider the corresponding nonparametric additive models:

$$y = \sum_{j=1}^{833} m_j(x_j) + \epsilon, \qquad (9)$$

where y is the expression value of gene GGPPS11, and $\{x_1, \ldots, x_{833}\}$ are the expression values of the remaining 833 genes. Next, we adopt the above additive model on the full dataset to identify the important variables by the three mentioned methods. The results are given as follows:

(i) Under FAR, we get one gene $\{x_{72}\}$, denoted by"model (A_2)";
(ii) Under GRIE, three genes $\{x_{140}, x_{571}, x_{560}\}$ are chosen, denoted by "model (B_2)";
(iii) Under C-FS, there nine genes were chosen, which are $\{x_{72}, x_{105}, x_{191}, x_{476}, x_{510}, x_{517}, x_{554}, x_{658}, x_{800}\}$, and it is denoted by "model (C_2)".

Again, using the nondegenerative Vuong test from Liao and Shi [22], we compare models (A_2) and (B_2). The corresponding p-value of the test is 0.012, indicating that the above two models are not equivalent at the 5% significance level. Then, we also compare models (B_2) with (C_2), and the p-value is 0. Hence, models (B_2) and (C_2) are not equivalent at the 5% significance level.

Lastly, similarly to the first real data case, we compare FAR, C-FS, and GRIE through their prediction errors. Again, we randomly divide the full dataset into the training and validation sets with a ratio of 4:1 and repeat this process 100 times. Here, we also centralize the response variable y and set $\kappa_n = 3$. For this real data, we consider the average numbers of model size and A-PE to evaluate the performance of the three models. The results are shown in Table 9. Thus, we conclude that our proposed method has the smallest model size with the strongest ability for prediction and outstanding performance in identifying important covariates compared with the other two methods.

Table 9. Average numbers of model size, A-PE over 100 repetitions, and their robust standard deviations (in parentheses) of *Arabidopsis thaliana* gene data.

Approach	Model Size	A-PE
FAR	1.00 (0.00)	0.289 (0.099)
C-FS	10.15 (3.34)	0.282 (0.181)
GRIE	1.76 (1.18)	0.276 (0.093)

6. Conclusions

In this paper, we propose a novel variable screening screener (GRIE) for high-dimensional nonparametric additive models, which is a combination of the nonparametric smoothing ridge estimation and the group information. We note that our paper is one of the first to focus on the free marginal correlation assumption. Without the marginal correlation assumption, the proposed screener can totally separate the unimportant and important variables with a probability tending to one. Compared with iterative sure independence screening and forward screening, the proposed screener could essentially eliminate the computational burden and achieve strong, sure screening consistency. Furthermore, it allows the covariates to be strongly correlated and performs better than its alternative competitors. For these reasons, combining the strong, sure screening property of GRIE with the model selection property of EBIC, we propose the GRIE-EBIC method to further eliminate the noise variables and improve the accuracy of model selection. Theoretically, we establish the strong consistency of model selection for the GRIE-EBIC method, which reveals that our proposed method achieves the ideal model selection results.

We conclude this paper with a discussion of directions for future research. One direction to consider is nonparametric additive models with interaction effects between covariates, which are defined as

$$E(y \mid \mathbf{x}) = \sum_{1 \le j < k \le p_n} m_{j,k}(x_j, x_k),$$

where x_j is the jth element of $\mathbf{x}$. They are the generalization of linear models with two-way interaction effects [25] that are more flexible for capturing the intersection between covariates. One potential approach may be to use the tensor splines bases to approximate each nonparametric function $m_{j,k}(\cdot,\cdot)$. The other direction is to study how to apply our methodology in the nonparametric generalized additive models [26,27]. The nonparametric generalized additive models admits

$$G\{E(y \mid \mathbf{x})\} = \sum_{j=1}^{p_n} m_j(x_j),$$

where x_j is the jth elements of $\mathbf{x}$, and $G(\cdot)$ is the link function. Since the nonparametric smoothing ridge estimation has outstanding performance in nonparametric additive models, its performance in generalized additive models may be worth investigating.

Author Contributions: Conceptualization, X.J. and J.L.; methodology, H.W. and X.J.; software, H.W. and H.J.; resources, J.L.; data curation, H.J.; writing—original draft preparation, H.W.; supervision, X.J.; funding acquisition, X.J. and J.L. All authors have read and agreed to the published version of the manuscript.

Funding: The work of Jiang is partially supported by the National Natural Science Foundation of China (11871263), and the Shenzhen Sci-Tech Fund No. JCYJ20210324104803010. The work of Li was partially supported by the NSF of China No. 11971221, Guangdong NSF Major Fund No. 2021ZDZX1001, the Shenzhen Sci-Tech Fund No. RCJC20200714114556020.

Institutional Review Board Statement: Not applicable.

Informed Consent Statement: Not applicable.

Data Availability Statement: The Boston housing dataset is available in the R package "MASS". *Arabidopsis thaliana* gene data are available on the website https://www.ncbi.nlm.nih.gov/pmc/articles/PMC545783 (accessed on 16 November 2022).

Acknowledgments: We would like to acknowledge the editor and four referees for their valuable comments and suggestions which leads to a substantial improvement of this article.

Conflicts of Interest: The authors declare no conflict of interest.

Appendix A

Now we give technical proofs of our theorems. To streamline our arguments, we introduce some notations and technical lemmas. Define $\mathbf{v} = (v_1, \ldots, v_n)^\top$ with $v_i = \sum_{j=1}^{p_n} m_j(x_{i,j}) - \mathbf{w}_i^\top \boldsymbol{\theta}^*$. Denoted by $\xi_i = \mathbf{e}_i^\top \mathbf{W}^\top (\mathbf{W}\mathbf{W}^\top)^{-1} \mathbf{W}\boldsymbol{\theta}^*$, $\eta_i = \mathbf{e}_i^\top \mathbf{W}^\top (\mathbf{W}\mathbf{W}^\top + \lambda \mathbf{I}_n)^{-1} \boldsymbol{\varepsilon}$ with $\boldsymbol{\varepsilon} = (\epsilon_1, \ldots, \epsilon_n)^\top$, and $\zeta_i = \mathbf{e}_i^\top \mathbf{W}^\top (\mathbf{W}\mathbf{W}^\top + \lambda \mathbf{I}_n)^{-1} \mathbf{v}$.

Lemma A1. *UnderAssumptions A1 and A3, the following conclusions hold*

(i) *for $C > 0$ and any fixed vector $\mathbf{b}$ with $\|\mathbf{b}\|_2 = 1$, there exists constants c_1' and c_2' with $0 < c_1' < 1 < c_2'$ such that*

$$P(\mathbf{b}^\top \mathbf{P}_{\lambda,\mathbf{W}^\top} \mathbf{b} < c_1' \frac{n^{1-\tau}}{t_n} \text{ or } \mathbf{b}^\top \mathbf{P}_{\lambda,\mathbf{W}^\top} \mathbf{b} > c_2' \frac{n^{1+\tau}}{t_n}) \leq 4\exp(-Cn);$$

(ii) *for any $C > 0$, there exists positive constant $M > 0$ such that*

$$P(|\mathbf{e}_i^\top \mathbf{P}_{\lambda,\mathbf{W}^\top} \mathbf{e}_j| > \frac{M n^{1+\tau-\alpha}}{t_n \sqrt{\log n}}) = O\{\exp\big(-C \frac{n^{1-2\alpha}}{2\log n}\big)\}$$

holds for any $0 \leq \alpha < 1/2$ and $1 \leq i \neq j \leq t_n$;

(iii) *for any $1 \leq i \leq t_n$, the following inequality*

$$P(\|(\mathbf{W}\mathbf{W}^\top + \lambda \mathbf{I}_n)^{-1} \mathbf{W}\mathbf{e}_i\|_2^2 > c_2' c_1 c_3 \kappa_n n^{1+2\tau} t_n^{-2}) \leq 3\exp(-C_1 n)$$

holds.

Proof of Lemma A1. Similar to proof of Theorem 3 in [18], we can show that Lemma A1 holds. □

Lemma A2. *Under Assumptions A1–A4, the following conclusions hold*

(i) $d_n \kappa_n^r \to \infty$ *and* $d_n n^{1/2-2\tau} / \sqrt{\log n} \to \infty$;

(ii) $\|\mathbf{v}\|_2 \leq c_n s_n n^{1/2} \kappa_n^{-r}$ *for some* $c_n > 0$, $\|\boldsymbol{\theta}_j^*\|_2 \geq 0.5 c_4^{-1/2} \kappa_n^{1/2} \min_{j \in \mathbf{S}} \{E|m_j(x_j)|^2\}^{1/2}$, *and* $\sum_{j \in \mathbf{S}} \|\boldsymbol{\theta}_j^*\|_2^2 \leq 3 c_2 c_4 s_n \kappa_n$;

(iii) $P(|\eta_i| \geq \sqrt{c_2' c_1 c_3 C_* d_n (\log n)^{-1/2} n^{1-\tau} t_n^{-1}}) \leq 2\exp(-c_0 \kappa_n^{-1} d_n^2 n^{1-4\tau} / \log n)$ *for some constant* $c_0 > 0$;

(iv) $P(|\zeta_i| \geq \sqrt{c_2' c_1 c_3 c_n s_n \kappa_n^{1/2-r} n^{1+\tau} t_n^{-1}}) \leq 3\exp(-C_1 n)$.

Proof of Lemma A2. (i) It follows that Lemma A2(i) holds by Assumptions A3 and A4.

(ii) By Assumption A3 (i) and Corollary 6.21 of [28], we can obtain

$$\sup_{x,j} |m_j(x) - \mathbf{B}(x)^\top \boldsymbol{\theta}_j^*| \leq c_n \kappa_n^{-r}, \tag{A1}$$

and

$$
\begin{aligned}
& \left|\{E|\mathbf{B}(x_j)^\top \boldsymbol{\theta}_j^*|^2\}^{1/2} - \{E|m_j(x_j)|^2\}^{1/2}\right| \\
= & \frac{\left|E|\mathbf{B}(x_j)^\top \boldsymbol{\theta}_j^*|^2 - E|m_j(x_j)|^2\right|}{\{E|\mathbf{B}(x_j)^\top \boldsymbol{\theta}_j^*|^2\}^{1/2} + \{E|m_j(x_j)|^2\}^{1/2}} \\
\le & \frac{\sup_{x,j}|m_j(x) - \mathbf{B}(x)^\top \boldsymbol{\theta}_j^*|\{E|m_j(x_j)| + E|\mathbf{B}(x_j)^\top \boldsymbol{\theta}_j^*|\}}{\{E|\mathbf{B}(x_j)^\top \boldsymbol{\theta}_j^*|^2\}^{1/2} + \{E|m_j(x_j)|^2\}^{1/2}} = O(\kappa_n^{-r}).
\end{aligned}
$$

This combined with $\min_{j\in\mathbf{S}}\{E|m_j(x_j)|^2\}^{1/2} \ge d_n$, $d_n\kappa_n^r \to \infty$ in Lemma A2(i), and

$$
\|\boldsymbol{\theta}_j^*\|_2^2 \ge \lambda_{\max}^{-1}(E(\mathbf{B}(x_j)\mathbf{B}(x_j)^\top))E|\mathbf{B}(x_j)^\top \boldsymbol{\theta}_j^*|^2 \ge c_4^{-1}\kappa_n(E|\mathbf{B}(x_j)^\top \boldsymbol{\theta}_j^*|^2)
$$

by noticing $\lambda_{\max}(E(\mathbf{B}(x_j)\mathbf{B}(x_j)^\top)) \le c_4\kappa_n^{-1}$, yields that

$$
\|\mathbf{v}\|_2 = O(s_n n^{1/2}\kappa_n^{-r}) \text{ and } \|\boldsymbol{\theta}_j^*\|_2 \ge 0.5c_4^{-1/2}\kappa_n^{1/2}\{E|m_j(x_j)|^2\}^{1/2}
$$

for any $j \in \mathbf{S}$. By (A1) and $\lambda_{\min}(E(\mathbf{B}(x_j)\mathbf{B}(x_j)^\top)) \ge c_4^{-1}\kappa_n^{-1}$, we have

$$
\begin{aligned}
\|\boldsymbol{\theta}_j^*\|_2^2 & \le \lambda_{\min}^{-1}(E(\mathbf{B}(x_j)\mathbf{B}(x_j)^\top))E|\mathbf{B}(x_j)^\top \boldsymbol{\theta}_j^*|^2 \\
& \le 2c_4\kappa_n\{E|\mathbf{B}(x_j)^\top \boldsymbol{\theta}_j^* - m_j(x_j)|^2 + E|m_j(x_j)|^2\} \\
& = O(\kappa_n^{1-2r}) + 2c_4\kappa_n E|m_j(x_j)|^2.
\end{aligned}
$$

It follows from assumption A3(i)-(ii) that

$$
\sum_{j\in\mathbf{S}} \|\boldsymbol{\theta}_j^*\|_2^2 \le O(s_n\kappa_n^{1-2r}) + 2c_4\kappa_n \sum_{j\in\mathbf{S}} E|m_j(x_j)|^2 \le 3c_2c_4s_n\kappa_n.
$$

(iii) It is noticed that

$$
\eta_i = \mathbf{e}_i^\top \mathbf{W}^\top(\mathbf{W}\mathbf{W}^\top + \lambda\mathbf{I}_n)^{-1}\boldsymbol{\varepsilon} = \|(\mathbf{W}\mathbf{W}^\top + \lambda\mathbf{I}_n)^{-1}\mathbf{W}\mathbf{e}_i\|_2\mathbf{a}^\top\boldsymbol{\varepsilon}, \tag{A2}
$$

where

$$
\mathbf{a} = (\mathbf{W}\mathbf{W}^\top + \lambda\mathbf{I}_n)^{-1}\mathbf{W}\mathbf{e}_i / \|(\mathbf{W}\mathbf{W}^\top + \lambda\mathbf{I}_n)^{-1}\mathbf{W}\mathbf{e}_i\|_2.
$$

Using Lemma A1, for some $C_1 > 0$, we have

$$
P(\mathbf{a}^\top\mathbf{P}_{\lambda,\mathbf{W}^\top}\mathbf{a} > c_2'\frac{n^{1+\tau}}{t_n}) \le 4\exp(-C_1 n)
$$

and

$$
P(\|(\mathbf{W}\mathbf{W}^\top + \lambda\mathbf{I}_n)^{-1}\mathbf{W}\mathbf{e}_i\|_2^2 > c_2'c_1c_3\kappa_n n^{1+2\tau}t_n^{-2}) \le 3\exp(-C_1 n). \tag{A3}
$$

By Assumption A2 and Proposition 3 of [4], we obtain

$$
P(\|\mathbf{P}_{\mathbf{a}}\boldsymbol{\varepsilon}\|_2^2 > C_*h(t)) \le (1+t)^{1/2}\exp(-t/2)
$$

for any $t > 2$, where

$$
h(t) = \frac{(1+t)}{\{1 - 2/(\exp(t/2)\sqrt{1+t} - 1)\}^2}.
$$

Let $\chi_n = 0.9\kappa_n^{-1}d_n^2n^{1-4\tau}/\log n$. We have $h(\chi_n) \le \kappa_n^{-1}d_n^2n^{1-4\tau}/\log n$ for sufficient large n since $d_n\kappa_n^{-1/2}n^{1/2-2\tau}/\sqrt{\log n} \to \infty$. Therefore, there exists some positive constant $c_0 < 0.45$ such that

$$
\begin{aligned}
P(|\mathbf{a}^\top \boldsymbol{\varepsilon}| > C_*^{1/2} d_n \kappa_n^{-1/2} n^{1/2-2\tau}/\sqrt{\log n}) &= P(\|\mathbf{P}_{\mathbf{a}}\boldsymbol{\varepsilon}\|_2^2 > C_* \kappa_n^{-1} d_n^2 n^{1-4\tau}/\log n) \\
&\leq P(\|\mathbf{P}_{\mathbf{a}}\boldsymbol{\varepsilon}\|_2^2 > C_* h(\chi_n)) \\
&\leq (1+\chi_n)^{1/2} \exp(-\chi_n/2) \\
&\leq \exp(-c_0 \kappa_n^{-1} d_n^2 n^{1-4\tau}/\log n)
\end{aligned}
$$

for sufficient large n. This, combined with (A2) and (A3), leads to

$$
P(|\eta_i| \geq \sqrt{c_2' c_1 C_* c_3} d_n (\log n)^{-1/2} n^{1-\tau} t_n^{-1}) \leq 2\exp(-c_0 \kappa_n^{-1} d_n^2 n^{1-4\tau}/\log n).
$$

(iv) From Lemmas A2(ii) and (A3), we have

$$
P(|\zeta_i| \geq \sqrt{c_2' c_1 c_3 c_n \kappa_n^{1/2-r} n^{1+\tau} t_n^{-1} s_n}) \leq 3\exp(-C_1 n).
$$

This completes the proof of Lemma A2. □

Proof of Theorem 1. From the definition of $\hat{\boldsymbol{\theta}}_j$ in (5), we have

$$
\begin{aligned}
\hat{\boldsymbol{\theta}}_j &= \mathbf{W}_j^\top (\mathbf{W}\mathbf{W}^\top + \lambda \mathbf{I}_n)^{-1} \mathbf{Y} \\
&= \mathbf{W}_j^\top (\mathbf{W}\mathbf{W}^\top + \lambda \mathbf{I}_n)^{-1} \mathbf{W}\boldsymbol{\theta}^* + \mathbf{W}_j^\top (\mathbf{W}\mathbf{W}^\top)^{-1} \mathbf{v} + \mathbf{W}_j^\top (\mathbf{W}\mathbf{W}^\top + \lambda \mathbf{I}_n)^{-1} \boldsymbol{\varepsilon} \\
&\equiv \tilde{\boldsymbol{\theta}}_j + \mathbf{E}_{1,j} + \mathbf{E}_{2,j}.
\end{aligned}
$$

Next, we divide the proof into four parts.
Part (I): In this part, we establish the upper bound of $\max_{j \in \mathbf{S}^c} \|\mathbf{E}_{1,j} + \mathbf{E}_{2,j}\|_2$.
By noticing $\|\mathbf{E}_{2,j}\|_2 \leq \kappa_n^{1/2} \max_{1 \leq i \leq t_n} |\eta_i|$, we have

$$
\begin{aligned}
P(\max_{1\leq j \leq p_n} \|\mathbf{E}_{2,j}\|_2 \geq \frac{c\kappa_n^{1/2} d_n n^{1-\tau}}{t_n \sqrt{\log n}}) &\leq P(\max_{1 \leq i \leq t_n} |\eta_i| \geq \frac{c d_n n^{1-\tau}}{t_n \sqrt{\log n}}) \\
&\leq \sum_{i=1}^{t_n} P(|\eta_i| \geq \frac{c d_n n^{1-\tau}}{t_n \sqrt{\log n}}).
\end{aligned}
$$

It follows from Lemma A2 that, for some constants c and c_0,

$$
\begin{aligned}
P(\max_{1\leq j \leq p_n} \|\mathbf{E}_{2,j}\|_2 \geq \frac{c\kappa_n^{1/2} d_n n^{1-\tau}}{t_n \sqrt{\log n}}) &\leq 2t_n \exp(-c_0 \kappa_n^{-1} d_n^2 n^{1-4\tau} (\log n)^{-1}) \\
&\leq \exp(-0.5 c_0 \kappa_n^{-1} d_n^2 n^{1-4\tau} (\log n)^{-1}),
\end{aligned}
$$

where the last inequality holds due to $\log(t_n) = o(\kappa_n^{-1} d_n^2 n^{1-4\tau} (\log n)^{-1})$. Similarly, by Lemma A2, $\|\mathbf{E}_{1,j}\|_2 \leq \kappa_n^{1/2} \max_{1 \leq i \leq t_n} |\zeta_i|$, and Bonferroni's inequality, there exists some constant c_* such that

$$
P(\max_{1\leq j \leq p_n} \|\mathbf{E}_{1,j}\|_2 \geq \frac{c_* \kappa_n^{1-r} n^{1+\tau} s_n}{t_n}) \leq 3t_n \exp(-C_1 n) \leq 3\exp(-0.5 C_1 n).
$$

By noticing $\kappa_n^{r-1/2} d_n / (n^{2\tau} s_n \sqrt{\log n}) \to \infty$, we obtain

$$
P(\max_{1\leq j \leq p_n} \|\mathbf{E}_{1,j} + \mathbf{E}_{2,j}\|_2 \geq \frac{(c + c_*)\kappa_n^{1/2} d_n n^{1-\tau}}{t_n \sqrt{\log n}}) \leq 2\exp(-0.5 c_0 \kappa_n^{-1} d_n^2 n^{1-4\tau} (\log n)^{-1}). \tag{A4}
$$

Part (II): In this part, we establish the upper bound of $\max_{j \in \mathbf{S}^c} \|\tilde{\boldsymbol{\theta}}_j\|_2$. For $1 \leq j \leq t_n$, there exists index set $\mathcal{M}_j \subseteq \{1, \ldots, t_n\}$ such that $\boldsymbol{\theta}_j = \boldsymbol{\theta}_{\mathcal{M}_j}$, where $\boldsymbol{\theta}_{\mathcal{M}_j}$ is the sub-vector of $\boldsymbol{\theta}$ formed by all components with indexes in $\mathcal{M}_j$. Denoted by $\mathcal{M} = \cup_{j \in \mathbf{S}} \mathcal{M}_j$ and

$\boldsymbol{\theta} = (\theta_1, \ldots, \theta_{t_n})^\top$ with $t_n = p_n \kappa_n$. By Cauchy–Schwarz's inequality, Lemma A2(ii), and Assumption A4(ii), we obtain that

$$\begin{aligned} \|\tilde{\boldsymbol{\theta}}_j\|_2 &\leq \sqrt{\kappa_n} \max_{i \in \mathcal{M}_j} \Big| \sum_{k \in \mathcal{M}} \mathbf{e}_i^\top \mathbf{P}_{\lambda, \mathbf{W}^\top} \mathbf{e}_k \theta_k^* \Big| \\ &\leq \sqrt{s_n \kappa_n^2} \|\boldsymbol{\theta}^*\|_2 \max_{1 \leq i \neq k \leq t_n} |\mathbf{e}_i^\top \mathbf{P}_{\lambda, \mathbf{W}^\top} \mathbf{e}_k| \\ &\leq \sqrt{3 c_2 c_4 s_n^2 \kappa_n^3} \max_{1 \leq i \neq k \leq t_n} |\mathbf{e}_i^\top \mathbf{P}_{\lambda, \mathbf{W}^\top} \mathbf{e}_k| \end{aligned}$$

for $j \in \mathbf{S}^c$, where c_2 and c_4 are defined in Assumptions A3 and A4. It follows from Lemma A1 and Bonferroni inequalities that, for some constants $M, C_1 > 0$,

$$\begin{aligned} P\Big(\max_{1 \leq i \neq k \leq t_n} |\mathbf{e}_i^\top \mathbf{P}_{\lambda, \mathbf{W}^\top} \mathbf{e}_k| > \frac{M n^{1+\tau-\alpha}}{t_n \sqrt{\log n}} \Big) &\leq \sum_{1 \leq i \neq k \leq t_n} P\Big(|\mathbf{e}_i^\top \mathbf{P}_{\lambda, \mathbf{W}^\top} \mathbf{e}_k| > \frac{M n^{1+\tau-\alpha}}{t_n \sqrt{\log n}} \Big) \\ &= O\Big\{ \exp\Big(2 \log t_n - C_1 \frac{n^{1-2\alpha}}{2 \log n} \Big) \Big\}, \end{aligned}$$

holds for any $0 \leq \alpha < 1/2$. By taking $n^\alpha = d_n^{-1} \kappa_n s_n n^{2\tau}$ and assumption $\log(t_n) = o\big(\frac{d_n^2 n^{1-4\tau}}{\kappa_n^2 s_n^2 \log n} \big)$ in A4 (iii), we can obtain

$$\begin{aligned} P\Big(\max_{j \in \mathbf{S}^c} \|\tilde{\boldsymbol{\theta}}_j\|_2 > \frac{\sqrt{3 c_2 c_4 \kappa_n} M n^{1-\tau} d_n}{t_n \sqrt{\log n}} \Big) &\leq O\Big\{ \exp\Big(2 \log t_n - C_1 \frac{d_n^2 n^{1-4\tau}}{2 \kappa_n^2 s_n^2 \log n} \Big) \Big\} \\ &= O\Big\{ \exp\Big(- C_1 \frac{d_n^2 n^{1-4\tau}}{3 \kappa_n^2 s_n^2 \log n} \Big) \Big\}. \end{aligned} \quad \text{(A5)}$$

Part (III): In this part, we establish the lower bound of $\min_{j \in \mathbf{S}} \|\tilde{\boldsymbol{\theta}}_j\|_2$. From the triangle inequality, we have

$$\begin{aligned} &\min_{j \in \mathbf{S}} \|\tilde{\boldsymbol{\theta}}_j\|_2 \\ &= \min_{j \in \mathbf{S}} \|\mathbf{W}_j^\top (\mathbf{W}\mathbf{W}^\top + \lambda \mathbf{I}_n)^{-1} \mathbf{W}_j \boldsymbol{\theta}_j^* + \sum_{k \neq j, k \in \mathbf{S}} \mathbf{W}_j^\top (\mathbf{W}\mathbf{W}^\top + \lambda \mathbf{I}_n)^{-1} \mathbf{W}_k \boldsymbol{\theta}_k^* \|_2 \\ &\geq \min_{j \in \mathbf{S}} \|\mathbf{W}_j^\top (\mathbf{W}\mathbf{W}^\top + \lambda \mathbf{I}_n)^{-1} \mathbf{W}_j \boldsymbol{\theta}_j^* \|_2 - \max_{j \in \mathbf{S}} \| \sum_{k \neq j, k \in \mathbf{S}} \mathbf{W}_j^\top (\mathbf{W}\mathbf{W}^\top + \lambda \mathbf{I}_n)^{-1} \mathbf{W}_k \boldsymbol{\theta}_k^* \|_2 \\ &\equiv I_{n,1} - I_{n,2}. \end{aligned}$$

With the same arguments as (A5), we can establish that

$$P\Big(I_{n,2} > \frac{\sqrt{3 c_2 c_4 \kappa_n} M n^{1-\tau} d_n}{t_n \sqrt{\log n}} \Big) = O\Big\{ \exp\Big(- C_1 \frac{d_n^2 n^{1-4\tau}}{3 \kappa_n^2 s_n^2 \log n} \Big) \Big\}. \quad \text{(A6)}$$

Applying equality $(a+b)^2 \geq a^2/2 - b^2$ and Jensen's inequality, we can obtain

$$\begin{aligned} &\|\mathbf{W}_j (\mathbf{W}\mathbf{W}^\top + \lambda \mathbf{I}_n)^{-1} \mathbf{W}_j \boldsymbol{\theta}_j^* \|_2^2 \\ &= \sum_{i \in \mathcal{M}_j} \Big(\sum_{k \in \mathcal{M}_j} \mathbf{e}_i^\top \mathbf{P}_{\lambda, \mathbf{W}^\top} \mathbf{e}_k \theta_k^* \Big)^2 \\ &\geq \sum_{i \in \mathcal{M}_j} (\mathbf{e}_i^\top \mathbf{P}_{\lambda, \mathbf{W}^\top} \mathbf{e}_i)^2 |\theta_i^*|^2 / 2 - \sum_{i \in \mathcal{M}_j} \Big(\sum_{k \in \mathcal{M}_j, k \neq i} \mathbf{e}_i^\top \mathbf{P}_{\lambda, \mathbf{W}^\top} \mathbf{e}_k \theta_k^* \Big)^2 \\ &\geq \min_{i \in \mathcal{M}_j} (\mathbf{e}_i^\top \mathbf{P}_{\lambda, \mathbf{W}^\top} \mathbf{e}_i)^2 \|\boldsymbol{\theta}_j^*\|_2^2 / 2 - \kappa_n \sum_{i \in \mathcal{M}_j} \sum_{k \in \mathcal{M}_j, k \neq i} (\mathbf{e}_i^\top \mathbf{P}_{\lambda, \mathbf{W}^\top} \mathbf{e}_k)^2 |\theta_k^*|^2 \\ &\geq \min_{i \in \mathcal{M}_j} (\mathbf{e}_i^\top \mathbf{P}_{\lambda, \mathbf{W}^\top} \mathbf{e}_i)^2 \|\boldsymbol{\theta}_j^*\|_2^2 / 2 - \kappa_n^2 \|\boldsymbol{\theta}_j^*\|_2^2 \max_{i, k \in \mathcal{M}_j, i \neq k} (\mathbf{e}_i^\top \mathbf{P}_{\lambda, \mathbf{W}^\top} \mathbf{e}_k)^2. \end{aligned}$$

Thus,

$$I_{n,1}^2 \geq \min_{j\in\mathbf{S}} \|\boldsymbol{\theta}_j\|_2^2 \{ \min_{i\in\mathcal{M}} (\mathbf{e}_i^\top \mathbf{P}_{\lambda,\mathbf{W}^\top}\mathbf{e}_i)^2/2 - \kappa_n^2 \max_{i,k\in\mathcal{M},i\neq k} (\mathbf{e}_i^\top \mathbf{P}_{\lambda,\mathbf{W}^\top}\mathbf{e}_k)^2 \}.$$

Lemma A1, $s_n\kappa_n = o(n)$ and Bonferroni inequalities give that, for some constants c_1', M, α and $C_1 > 0$,

$$\begin{aligned} P\big(\min_{i\in\mathcal{M}} \mathbf{e}_i^\top \mathbf{P}_{\lambda,\mathbf{W}^\top}\mathbf{e}_i \leq \frac{c_1' n^{1-\tau}}{t_n}\big) &\leq \sum_{i\in\mathcal{M}} P\big(\mathbf{e}_i^\top \mathbf{P}_{\lambda,\mathbf{W}^\top}\mathbf{e}_i \leq \frac{c_1' n^{1-\tau}}{t_n}\big) \\ &\leq 4n\exp(-C_1 n) \end{aligned}$$

and

$$\begin{aligned} P\big(\max_{i,k\in\mathcal{M},i\neq k} |\mathbf{e}_i^\top \mathbf{P}_{\lambda,\mathbf{W}^\top}\mathbf{e}_k| \geq \frac{Mn^{1+\tau-\alpha}}{t_n\sqrt{\log n}}\big) &\leq \sum_{i,k\in\mathcal{M},i\neq k} P\big(\mathbf{e}_i^\top \mathbf{P}_{\lambda,\mathbf{W}^\top}\mathbf{e}_k \geq \frac{Mn^{1+\tau-\alpha}}{t_n\sqrt{\log n}}\big) \\ &\leq O\{n\exp\big(-C_1\frac{n^{1-2\alpha}}{2\log n}\big)\} \end{aligned}$$

holds for any $0 \leq \alpha < 1/2$. Denoted by

$$\mathbf{A}_1 = \{ \min_{i\in\mathcal{M}} \mathbf{e}_i^\top \mathbf{P}_{\lambda,\mathbf{W}^\top}\mathbf{e}_i \leq \frac{c_1' n^{1-\tau}}{t_n} \},\ \mathbf{A}_2 = \{ \max_{i,k\in\mathcal{M},i\neq k} |\mathbf{e}_i^\top \mathbf{P}_{\lambda,\mathbf{W}^\top}\mathbf{e}_k| \geq \frac{Mn^{1+\tau-\alpha}}{t_n\sqrt{\log n}} \},$$

and

$$\mathbf{A}_3 = \{ \min_{i\in\mathcal{M}} (\mathbf{e}_i^\top \mathbf{P}_{\lambda,\mathbf{W}^\top}\mathbf{e}_i)^2/2 - \kappa_n^2 \max_{i,k\in\mathcal{M},i\neq k} (\mathbf{e}_i^\top \mathbf{P}_{\lambda,\mathbf{W}^\top}\mathbf{e}_k)^2 > \frac{|c_1'|^2 n^{2-2\tau}}{3t_n^2} \}.$$

By taking $\alpha = 2\tau + \log_n(\kappa_n)$, we have

$$P(\mathbf{A}_3) \geq P(\mathbf{A}_1^c \cap \mathbf{A}_2^c) \geq 1 - P(\mathbf{A}_1) - P(\mathbf{A}_2) = 1 - O\{n\exp\big(-C_1\frac{n^{1-2\tau}}{2\kappa_n^2\log n}\big)\}. \tag{A7}$$

It is obvious that $\min_{j\in\mathbf{S}} \|\boldsymbol{\theta}_j\|_2^2 \geq 0.25c_4^{-1}\kappa_n d_n^2$ from Lemma A2(ii) and Assumption A4(ii). This, combined with (A7), yields that

$$P\big(I_{n,1}^2 \geq \frac{|c_1'|^2 c_4^{-1}\kappa_n d_n^2 n^{2-2\tau}}{12t_n^2}\big) \geq 1 - O\{n\exp\big(-C_1\frac{n^{1-2\tau}}{2\kappa_n^2\log n}\big)\}. \tag{A8}$$

Similar to (A7), we can obtain

$$P\big(\min_{j\in\mathbf{S}} \|\tilde{\boldsymbol{\theta}}_j\|_2 \geq \frac{c_1' c_4^{-1/2}\kappa_n^{1/2} d_n n^{1-\tau}}{12t_n}\big) \geq 1 - O\{\exp\big(-C_1\frac{d_n^2 n^{1-4\tau}}{3\kappa_n^2 s_n^2\log n}\big)\} \tag{A9}$$

by combing (A6) and (A8).

Part (IV): In this part, we show that

$$P\big(\min_{j\in\mathbf{S}} \|\hat{\boldsymbol{\theta}}_j\|_2 > \max_{j\in\mathbf{S}^c} \|\hat{\boldsymbol{\theta}}_j\|_2\big) \to 1. \tag{A10}$$

Similar to (A7), by $\hat{\boldsymbol{\theta}}_j = \tilde{\boldsymbol{\theta}}_j + \mathbf{E}_{1,j} + \mathbf{E}_{2,j}$, (A4) and (A9), we can show that

$$\begin{aligned} &P\big(\min_{j\in\mathbf{S}} \|\hat{\boldsymbol{\theta}}_j\|_2 \geq \frac{c_1' c_4^{-1/2}\kappa_n^{1/2} d_n n^{1-\tau}}{13t_n}\big) \\ &\geq P\big(\min_{j\in\mathbf{S}} \|\tilde{\boldsymbol{\theta}}_j\|_2 - \max_{1\leq j\leq p_n} \|\mathbf{E}_{1,j} + \mathbf{E}_{2,j}\|_2 \geq \frac{c_1' c_4^{-1/2}\kappa_n^{1/2} d_n n^{1-\tau}}{14t_n}\big) \end{aligned}$$

$$\geq 1 - O\{\exp\big(-C_1\frac{d_n^2 n^{1-4\tau}}{3\kappa_n^2 s_n^2 \log n}\big) + \exp\big(-\frac{c_0 d_n^2 n^{1-4\tau}}{2\kappa_n \log n}\big)\}. \quad \text{(A11)}$$

Denote by $\mathbf{A}_4 = \{\max_{1\leq j\leq p_n} \|\mathbf{E}_{1,j} + \mathbf{E}_{2,j}\|_2 \geq \frac{(c+c_*)\kappa_n^{1/2} d_n n^{1-\tau}}{t_n\sqrt{\log n}}\}$, $\mathbf{A}_5 = \{\max_{j\in\mathbf{S}^c} \|\tilde{\boldsymbol{\theta}}_j\|_2 > \frac{\sqrt{3c_2c_4\kappa_n} M n^{1-\tau} d_n}{t_n\sqrt{\log n}}\}$, and

$$\mathbf{A}_6 = \{\max_{1\leq j\leq p_n} \|\mathbf{E}_{1,j} + \mathbf{E}_{2,j}\|_2 + \max_{j\in\mathbf{S}^c} \|\tilde{\boldsymbol{\theta}}_j\|_2 \geq \frac{(c + c_* + \sqrt{3c_2c_4})\kappa_n^{1/2} d_n n^{1-\tau}}{t_n\sqrt{\log n}}\}.$$

Since $\mathbf{A}_6 \cap \mathbf{A}_5^c \subseteq \mathbf{A}_4$, by (A4) and (A5), we have

$$\begin{aligned} P(\mathbf{A}_6) &= P(\mathbf{A}_6 \cap \mathbf{A}_5) + P(\mathbf{A}_6 \cap \mathbf{A}_5^c) \\ &\leq P(\mathbf{A}_5) + P(\mathbf{A}_4) \\ &= O\{\exp\big(-\frac{c_0 d_n^2 n^{1-4\tau}}{2\kappa_n \log n}\big) + \exp\big(-C_1\frac{d_n^2 n^{1-4\tau}}{3\kappa_n^2 s_n^2 \log n}\big)\}. \end{aligned}$$

Using $\max_{j\in\mathbf{S}^c} \|\hat{\boldsymbol{\theta}}_j\|_2 \leq \max_{1\leq j\leq p_n} \|\mathbf{E}_{1,j} + \mathbf{E}_{2,j}\|_2 + \max_{j\in\mathbf{S}^c} \|\tilde{\boldsymbol{\theta}}_j\|_2$, we obtain that

$$\begin{aligned} &P\big(\max_{j\in\mathbf{S}^c} \|\hat{\boldsymbol{\theta}}_j\|_2 < \frac{(c + c_* + \sqrt{3c_2c_4})\kappa_n^{1/2} d_n n^{1-\tau}}{t_n\sqrt{\log n}}\big) \\ &\geq P\big(\max_{j\in\mathbf{S}^c} \|\tilde{\boldsymbol{\theta}}_j\|_2 + \max_{1\leq j\leq p_n} \|\mathbf{E}_{1,j} + \mathbf{E}_{2,j}\|_2 < \frac{(c + c_* + \sqrt{3c_2c_4})\kappa_n^{1/2} d_n n^{1-\tau}}{t_n\sqrt{\log n}}\big) \\ &\geq 1 - O\{\exp\big(-\frac{c_0 d_n^2 n^{1-4\tau}}{2\kappa_n \log n}\big) + \exp\big(-C_1\frac{d_n^2 n^{1-4\tau}}{3\kappa_n^2 s_n^2 \log n}\big)\}. \end{aligned} \quad \text{(A12)}$$

Notice that $\frac{d_n^2 n^{1-4\tau}}{\kappa_n^2 s_n^2 \log n} \to \infty$ and $(c + c_* + \sqrt{3c_2c_4})/\sqrt{\log n} \ll c_1' c_4^{-1}/13$ for sufficient large n. This, combined with (A11) and (A12), establishes (A10). The proof is completed. □

Proof of Theorem 2. We divide the proof into two parts.

Part (I) to show that $P(\hat{\mathbf{S}}_* = \mathbf{S}) \to 1$; Part (II) to show that $P(\hat{\mathbf{S}} = \hat{\mathbf{S}}_*) \to 1$.

Part (I): Step (i) It is noticed that $\mathbf{Y} = \mathbf{W}_\mathbf{S}\boldsymbol{\theta}_\mathbf{S}^* + \mathbf{v} + \boldsymbol{\varepsilon}$ and $\mathbf{P}_{\mathbf{W}_{\hat{\mathbf{S}}_k}} - \mathbf{P}_{\mathbf{W}_{\hat{\mathbf{S}}_{k-1}}} = \mathbf{P}_{\widetilde{\mathbf{W}}_{i_k}}$ with $\widetilde{\mathbf{W}}_{i_k} = (\mathbf{I}_n - \mathbf{P}_{\mathbf{W}_{\hat{\mathbf{S}}_{k-1}}})\mathbf{W}_{i_k}$. For $i_k \in \mathbf{S}$, we obtain that

$$\begin{aligned} RSS_{k-1} - RSS_k &= \mathbf{Y}^\top(\mathbf{I}_n - \mathbf{P}_{\mathbf{W}_{\hat{\mathbf{S}}_{k-1}}})\mathbf{Y} - \mathbf{Y}^\top(\mathbf{I}_n - \mathbf{P}_{\mathbf{W}_{\hat{\mathbf{S}}_k}})\mathbf{Y} \\ &= \|\mathbf{P}_{\widetilde{\mathbf{W}}_{i_k}}(\mathbf{W}_\mathbf{S}\boldsymbol{\theta}_\mathbf{S}^* + \mathbf{v} + \boldsymbol{\varepsilon})\|_2^2 \\ &\geq \|\mathbf{P}_{\widetilde{\mathbf{W}}_{i_k}}\mathbf{W}_\mathbf{S}\boldsymbol{\theta}_\mathbf{S}^*\|_2^2/2 - \|\mathbf{P}_{\widetilde{\mathbf{W}}_{i_k}}(\mathbf{v} + \boldsymbol{\varepsilon})\|_2^2. \end{aligned} \quad \text{(A13)}$$

Next, let us deal with the above two terms separately. Denoted by $\mathcal{T}_k = (\mathbf{S} \cup \hat{\mathbf{S}}_{k-1}) \setminus \{i_k\}$. We have

$$\begin{aligned} \|\mathbf{P}_{\widetilde{\mathbf{W}}_{i_k}}\mathbf{W}_\mathbf{S}\boldsymbol{\theta}_\mathbf{S}^*\|_2^2 &= \|(\mathbf{P}_{\mathbf{W}_{\hat{\mathbf{S}}_k}} - \mathbf{P}_{\mathbf{W}_{\hat{\mathbf{S}}_{k-1}}})\mathbf{W}_\mathbf{S}\boldsymbol{\theta}_\mathbf{S}^*\|_2^2 \\ &\geq \inf_{\mathbf{t}} \|\mathbf{P}_{\mathbf{W}_{\hat{\mathbf{S}}_k}}\mathbf{W}_\mathbf{S}\boldsymbol{\theta}_\mathbf{S}^* - \mathbf{W}_{\hat{\mathbf{S}}_{k-1}}\mathbf{t}\|_2^2 \\ &\geq \inf_{\mathbf{a}} \|\mathbf{P}_{\mathbf{W}_{\hat{\mathbf{S}}_k}}\mathbf{W}_{i_k}\boldsymbol{\theta}_{i_k}^* - \mathbf{W}_{\mathcal{T}_k}\mathbf{a}\|_2^2. \end{aligned}$$

From $\mathbf{P}_{\mathbf{W}_{\hat{\mathbf{S}}_k}}\mathbf{W}_{i_k} = \mathbf{W}_{i_k}$, Lemma A2, Assumption A4(ii), and $i_k \in \mathbf{S}$, we can obtain

$$\begin{aligned}\min_{i_k\in\mathbf{S}} \|\mathbf{P}_{\widetilde{\mathbf{W}}_{i_k}}\mathbf{W}_{\mathbf{S}}\boldsymbol{\theta}^*_{\mathbf{S}}\|_2^2 &\geq \min_{i_k\in\mathbf{S}} \|\boldsymbol{\theta}^*_{i_k}\|_2^2\|(\mathbf{I}_n - \mathbf{P}_{\mathbf{W}_{\mathcal{T}_k}})\mathbf{W}_{i_k}\|_2^2 \\ &\geq 0.25c_4^{-1}\kappa_n d_n^2 \min_{i_k\in\mathbf{S}} \|(\mathbf{I}_n - \mathbf{P}_{\mathbf{W}_{\mathcal{T}_k}})\mathbf{W}_{i_k}\|_2^2. \end{aligned} \tag{A14}$$

From Theorem 1, we have conclusion $|\mathcal{T}_k \cup \{i_k\}| = O(s_n)$ holding for $\forall\, i_k \in \mathbf{S}$ with probability tending to one. This, combined with Assumption A5, yields that

$$\lambda_{\min}(n^{-1}\mathbf{W}_{\mathcal{T}}^\top\mathbf{W}_{\mathcal{T}}) \geq 0.5c_6 n^{-\tau}\kappa_n^{-1} \tag{A15}$$

with probability going to one, where $\mathbf{W}_{\mathcal{T}} = (\mathbf{W}_{\mathcal{T}_k}, \mathbf{W}_{i_k})$. It follows from $\lambda_{\max}\{(\mathbf{W}_{i_k}^\top\mathbf{W}_{i_k})^{-1}\}$ $\leq \lambda_{\max}\{\mathbf{W}_{\mathcal{T}}^\top\mathbf{W}_{\mathcal{T}}\}$ and (A15) that

$$\min_{i_k\in\mathbf{S}} \|\mathbf{P}_{\widetilde{\mathbf{W}}_{i_k}}\mathbf{W}_{\mathbf{S}}\boldsymbol{\theta}^*_{\mathbf{S}}\|_2^2 \geq 2\mu_0 d_n^2 n^{1-\tau} \tag{A16}$$

with $\mu_0 = 0.0625c_4^{-1}c_6$.

Following Lemma A2, we have that

$$\begin{aligned}\|\mathbf{P}_{\widetilde{\mathbf{W}}_{i_k}}(\mathbf{v}+\boldsymbol{\varepsilon})\|_2^2 &= 2\|\mathbf{P}_{\widetilde{\mathbf{W}}_{i_k}}\mathbf{v}\|_2^2 + 2\|\mathbf{P}_{\widetilde{\mathbf{W}}_{i_k}}\boldsymbol{\varepsilon}\|_2^2 \\ &\leq 2\|\mathbf{v}\|_2^2 + 2\|\mathbf{P}_{\widetilde{\mathbf{W}}_{i_k}}\boldsymbol{\varepsilon}\|_2^2 \\ &= O(n\kappa_n^{-2r}) + 2\|\mathbf{P}_{\widetilde{\mathbf{W}}_{i_k}}\boldsymbol{\varepsilon}\|_2^2.\end{aligned}$$

From Assumption A2 and Proposition 3 of [4], we have

$$P(\|\mathbf{P}_{\widetilde{\mathbf{W}}_{i_k}}\boldsymbol{\varepsilon}\|_2^2 > \frac{\kappa_n C_*(1+t)}{\{1-2/(\exp(t/2)\sqrt{1+t}-1)\}^2}). \leq (1+t)^{1/2}\exp(-\kappa_n t/2)$$

By taking $t = \log p_n + \log n - 1$ and applying Bonferroni inequalities, we can obtain

$$\begin{aligned}P(\max_{i_k\in\mathbf{S}} \|\mathbf{P}_{\widetilde{\mathbf{W}}_{i_k}}\boldsymbol{\varepsilon}\|_2^2 > \beta_n) &\leq \sum_{i_k\in\mathbf{S}} P(\|\mathbf{P}_{\widetilde{\mathbf{W}}_{i_k}}\boldsymbol{\varepsilon}\|_2^2 > \beta_n) \\ &\leq \sum_{i_k\in\mathbf{S}} \sqrt{\log p_n + \log n}\exp\{-\kappa_n(\log p_n + \log n - 1)/2\} \\ &= O(s_n\sqrt{\log p_n})\exp\{-\kappa_n(\log p_n + \log n - 1)/2\} \\ &\to 0,\end{aligned}$$

where

$$\beta_n = \frac{\kappa_n C_*(\log p_n + \log n - 1)}{\{1-2/(\exp((\log p_n + \log n - 1)/2)\sqrt{\log p_n + \log n} - 1)\}^2}.$$

Therefore, we establish that

$$\max_{i_k\in\mathbf{S}} \|\mathbf{P}_{\widetilde{\mathbf{W}}_{i_k}}\boldsymbol{\varepsilon}\|_2^2 = o_P\{\kappa_n(\log p_n + \log n)\}. \tag{A17}$$

By $\kappa_n^{r-1/2}d_n/n^{2\tau} \to \infty$ and $\log(t_n) = o(\frac{d_n^2 n^{1-4\tau}}{\kappa_n^2 s_n^2 \log n})$ in Assumption A4(ii), we obtain

$$\|\mathbf{P}_{\widetilde{\mathbf{W}}_{i_k}}(\mathbf{v}+\boldsymbol{\varepsilon})\|_2^2 = o_P(d_n^2 n^{1-\tau}).$$

This, combined with (A13) and (A16), yields that

$$\min_{i_k \in \mathbf{S}} \{RSS_{k-1} - RSS_k\} \geq \mu_0 d_n^2 n^{1-\tau}$$

with probability going to one. Applying the inequality $\log(1+x) \geq \min\{\log 2, 0.5x\}$ for $x > 0$, we obtain that

$$\begin{aligned} \log(RSS_{k-1}) - \log(RSS_k) &= \log\{1 + (RSS_{k-1} - RSS_k)/RSS_k\} \\ &\geq 0.5(RSS_{k-1} - RSS_k)/RSS_k \\ &\geq 0.5\mu_0 d_n^2 n^{1-\tau}/RSS_k, \end{aligned}$$

This combined with $n^{-1}RSS_k \leq n^{-1}\|\mathbf{Y} - \bar{\mathbf{Y}}_n\|_2^2 \to \mathrm{Var}(y_1)$ with $\bar{\mathbf{Y}}_n = n^{-1}\sum_{i=1}^n y_i$, leads to

$$\min_{i_k \in \mathbf{S}} \{\log(RSS_{k-1}) - \log(RSS_k)\} \geq 0.4\mu_0 d_n^2 n^{-\tau}/\mathrm{Var}(y_1).$$

Noticing that $\log(t_n) = o(\frac{d_n^2 n^{1-4\tau}}{\kappa_n^2 s_n^2 \log n})$ and $\mathrm{Var}(y_1) = O(\kappa_n s_n^2 n^{3\tau} \log(n))$ and $\log(f(k+1)) - \log(f(k)) = O\{\kappa_n \log(p_n)\}$, we can obtain

$$\begin{aligned} EBIC_{k-1} - EBIC_k &\geq 0.4\mu_0 d_n^2 n^{-\tau}/\mathrm{Var}(y_1) - n^{-1}\big[\log(n) + \gamma\{\log(f(k+1) - \log(f(k))\}\big] \\ &\geq 0.4\mu_0 d_n^2 n^{-\tau}/\mathrm{Var}(y_1) - n^{-1}O\{\log(n) + \gamma\kappa_n \log(p_n)\} \\ &> 0. \end{aligned}$$

Therefore, for $i_k \in \mathbf{S}$, the conclusion

$$EBIC_k < EBIC_{k-1} \tag{A18}$$

holds uniformly with probability going to one.

Step (ii): Let k_0 be an integer satisfying $\mathbf{S} \not\subset \hat{\mathbf{S}}_{k_0-1}$ and $\mathbf{S} \subset \hat{\mathbf{S}}_{k_0}$. We prove that

$$\min_{1 \leq j \leq L} \{EBIC_{k_0+j} - EBIC_{k_0+j-1}\} > 0,$$

By $\log(1+x) \leq x$ and $\log\left\{\frac{f(k_0+j)}{f(k_0+j-1)}\right\} = O\{\kappa_n \log(p_n)\}$, we have

$$EBIC_{k_0+j-1} - EBIC_{k_0+j} \leq \frac{RSS_{k_0+j-1} - RSS_{k_0+j}}{RSS_{k_0+j}} - \left[\kappa_n \log n + \gamma\kappa_n \log(p_n)\right]/n.$$

With the same arguments as (A17), we can show that

$$\max_{1 \leq j \leq L} (RSS_{k_0+j-1} - RSS_{k_0+j}) = \max_{1 \leq j \leq L} \|(\mathbf{P}_{\mathbf{W}_{\hat{\mathbf{S}}_{k_0+j}}} - \mathbf{P}_{\mathbf{W}_{\hat{\mathbf{S}}_{k_0+j-1}}})\varepsilon\|_2^2 = o_P\{\kappa_n(\log p_n + \log n)\}.$$

From (26) in [10], we have $n^{-1}RSS_{k_0+l} = E\epsilon_1^2 + o_P(1)$. Furthermore, $E\epsilon_1^2 = O(1)$ from assumption A2. Thus

$$P(\max_{1 \leq j \leq L} \{EBIC_{k_0+j-1} - EBIC_{k_0+j}\} < 0) \to 1. \tag{A19}$$

Combination of (A18) and (A19) leads to $P(\hat{\mathbf{S}}_* = \mathbf{S}) \to 1$.

Part (II): Similar to step (ii) in Part (I), we can show that

$$\min_{l \in \mathcal{F} \backslash \hat{\mathbf{S}}_{*\ell}} \{EBIC_{*\ell} - EBIC_*\} > 0,$$

with probability tending to one. This leads to $P(\hat{\mathbf{S}} = \hat{\mathbf{S}}_*) \to 1$. The proof is completed. □

References

1. Tibshirani, R. Regression shrinkage and selection via the lasso. *J. R. Stat. Soc. Ser. B Stat. Methodol.* **1996**, *58*, 267–288. [CrossRef]
2. Fan, J.; Li, R. Variable selection via nonconcave penalized likelihood and its oracle properties. *J. Am. Stat. Assoc.* **2001**, *96*, 1348–1360. [CrossRef]
3. Candes, E.; Tao, T. The Dantzig selector: Statistical estimation when p is much larger than n. *Ann. Stat.* **2007**, *35*, 2313–2351.
4. Zhang, C.H. Nearly unbiased variable selection under minimax concave penalty. *Ann. Stat.* **2010**, *38*, 894–942. [CrossRef]
5. Fan, J.; Samworth, R.; Wu, Y. Ultrahigh dimensional feature selection: Beyond the linear model. *J. Mach. Learn. Res.* **2009**, *10*, 2013–2038.
6. Fan, J.; Lv, J. Sure independence screening for ultrahigh dimensional feature space. *J. R. Stat. Soc. Ser. B (Stat. Methodol.)* **2008**, *70*, 849–911. [CrossRef]
7. Fan, J.; Feng, Y.; Song, R. Nonparametric independence screening in sparse ultra-high-dimensional additive models. *J. Am. Stat. Assoc.* **2011**, *106*, 544–557. [CrossRef]
8. Zhu, L.; Li, L.; Li, R.; Zhu, L. Model-free feature screening for ultrahigh-dimensional data. *J. Am. Stat. Assoc.* **2011**, *106*, 1464–1475. [CrossRef]
9. Wang, H. Forward regression for ultra-high dimensional variable screening. *J. Am. Stat. Assoc.* **2009**, *104*, 1512–1524. [CrossRef]
10. Cheng, M.Y.; Honda, T.; Zhang, J.T. Forward variable selection for sparse ultra-high dimensional varying coefficient models. *J. Am. Stat. Assoc.* **2016**, *111*, 1209–1221. [CrossRef]
11. Zhong, W.; Duan, S.; Zhu, L. Forward additive regression for ultrahigh dimensional nonparametric additive models. *Stat. Sin.* **2020**, *30*, 175–192. [CrossRef]
12. Zhou, T.; Zhu, L.; Xu, C.; Li, R. Model-free forward screening via cumulative divergence. *J. Am. Stat. Assoc.* **2020**, *115*, 1393–1405. [CrossRef] [PubMed]
13. Hastie, T.; Tibshirani, R. *Generalized Additive Models*; Chapman and Hall: New York, NY, USA, 1990.
14. Meier, K.; Van de Geer, S.; Bühlmann, P. Minimax optimal rates of estimation in high dimensional additive models. *Ann. Stat.* **2009**, *47*, 3779–3821.
15. Gregory, K.; Mammen, E.; Wahl, M. Statistical inference in sparse high-dimensional additive models. *Ann. Stat.* **2021**, *49*, 1514–1536. [CrossRef]
16. Lu, J.; Kolar, M.; Liu, H. Kernel meets sieve: Post-regularization confidence bands for sparse additive model. *J. Am. Stat. Assoc.* **2020**, *115*, 2084-2099. [CrossRef]
17. Bai, R.; Moran, G.; Antonelli, J.; Cheng, Y.; Boland, M. Spike-and-slab group lassos for grouped regression and sparse generalized additive models. *J. Am. Stat. Assoc.* **2022**, *117*, 184–197. [CrossRef]
18. Wang, X.; Leng, C. High dimensional ordinary least squares projection for screening variables. *J. R. Stat. Soc. Ser. B Stat. Methodol.* **2016**, *78*, 589–611. [CrossRef]
19. Chen, J.; Chen, Z. Extended Bayesian information criteria for model selection with large model spaces. *Biometrika* **2008**, *95*, 759–771. [CrossRef]
20. Chen, J.; Chen, Z. Extended BIC for small-n-large-P sparse GLM. *Stat. Sin.* **2012**, *22*, 555–574. [CrossRef]
21. Fan, J.; Ma, Y.; Dai, W. Nonparametric independence screening in sparse ultra-high-dimensional varying coefficient models. *J. Am. Stat. Assoc.* **2014**, *109*, 1270–1284. [CrossRef]
22. Liao, Z.; Shi, X. A nondegenerate Vuong test and post selection confidence intervals for semi/nonparametric model. *Quant. Econ.* **2020**, *11*, 983–1017. [CrossRef]
23. Wille, A.; Zimmermann, P.; Vranová, E.; Fürholz, A.; Laule, O.; Bleuler, S.; Hennig, L.; Prelić, A.; Von Rohr, P.; Thiele, L.; et al. Sparse graphical Gaussian modeling of the isoprenoid gene network in *Arabidopsis thaliana*. *Genome Biol.* **2004**, *5*, R92. [CrossRef] [PubMed]
24. Chen, Q.; Fan, D.; Wang, G. Heteromeric geranyl (geranyl) diphosphate synthase is involved in monoterpene biosynthesis in Arabidopsis flowers. *Mol. Plant* **2015**, *8*, 1434–1437. [CrossRef] [PubMed]
25. Hao, N.; Zhang, H. A note on high-dimensional linear regression with interactions. *Am. Stat.* **2017**, *71*, 291–297. [CrossRef]
26. Hastie, T.; Tibshirani, R. Generalized additive models: Some applications. *J. Am. Stat. Assoc.* **1987**, *82*, 371–386. [CrossRef]
27. Horowitz, J. Nonparametric estimation of a generalized additive model with an unknown link function. *Econometrica* **1987**, *69*, 499–513. [CrossRef]
28. Schumaker, L.L. *Spline Functions: Basic Theory*; Cambridge University Press: Cambridge, UK, 2007.

mathematics

MDPI

Article

Intelligent Multi-Strategy Hybrid Fuzzy K-Nearest Neighbor Using Improved Hybrid Sine Cosine Algorithm

Chengfeng Zheng [1], Mohd Shareduwan Mohd Kasihmuddin [1,*], Mohd. Asyraf Mansor [2], Ju Chen [1] and Yueling Guo [1]

1 School of Mathematical Sciences, Universiti Sains Malaysia, Penang 11800, Malaysia
2 School of Distance Education, Universiti Sains Malaysia, Penang 11800, Malaysia
* Correspondence: shareduwan@usm.my; Tel.: +60-4-6534769

Abstract: The sine and cosine algorithm is a new simple and effective population optimization method proposed in recent years that has been studied in many works of literature. Based on the basic principle of the sine and cosine algorithm, this paper fully studies the main parameters affecting the performance of the sine and cosine algorithm, integrates the reverse learning algorithm, adds an elite opposition solution and forms the hybrid sine and cosine algorithm (hybrid SCA). Combined with the fuzzy k-nearest neighbor method and the hybrid SCA, this paper numerically simulates two-class datasets and multi-class datasets, obtains a large number of numerical results and analyzes the results. The hybrid SCA FKNN proposed in this paper has achieved good accuracy in classification and prediction results under 10 different types of data sets. Compared with SCA FKNN, LSCA FKNN, BA FKNN, PSO FKNN and SSA FKNN, the prediction accuracy is significantly improved. In the Wilcoxon signed rank test with SCA FKNN and LSCA FKNN, the zero hypothesis (significance level 0.05) is rejected and the two classifiers have a significantly different accuracy.

Keywords: meta learning; data classification; hybrid sine and cosine algorithm; Wilcoxon signed rank test; multiple application scenario datasets

MSC: 68T07; 68T27; 68T20

Citation: Zheng, C.; Kasihmuddin, M.S.M.; Mansor, M.A.; Chen, J.; Guo, Y. Intelligent Multi-Strategy Hybrid Fuzzy K-Nearest Neighbor Using Improved Hybrid Sine Cosine Algorithm. *Mathematics* **2022**, *10*, 3368. https://doi.org/10.3390/math10183368

Academic Editors: Niansheng Tang and Shen-Ming Lee

Received: 8 August 2022
Accepted: 5 September 2022
Published: 16 September 2022

1. Introduction

The swarm intelligence algorithm (SI) has gained attention from many researchers in various field of sciences. SI is currently being used to provide solutions to various optimization problems. Several applications of swarm intelligence include material technology [1–3], biological system modeling [3], train assembly, high-performance graphics card [4], path planning [5] and robot control [6,7]. SI is based on the collective behavior of the elements that self-organize in order to get exposed with the solution of the optimization problem. Examples of popular SI algorithms include particle swarm optimization (PSO) [8], artificial bee colony (ABC) [9], gravitational search algorithm (GSA) [10] and whale optimization algorithm (WOA) [11]. One of the main challenges in SI is the lack of profound theoretical analysis, which requires a solid mathematical foundation that includes a proper analysis that assesses the robustness, computational complexity and parameter setting. All of these analyses are required to ensure that SI can avoid converging to a local minimum solution. Note that the local minimum solution will affect the optimality of the solution to the respective optimization problem.

The sine cosine algorithm (SCA) [12] is a new SI algorithm proposed by Mirjalili in 2016. SCA was inspired by a mathematical model of the sine cosine function used to make the oscillation of the solution converge towards the optimal solution. The random and adaptive parameters in the algorithm have the ability to balance both exploration and exploitation during solution searching. Several advantages of SCA include very few parameters, easy implementation, a simple structure, a fast convergence speed, strong parallelism and universality and a better performance in practical applications. Therefore, it has attracted extensive attention from scholars in recent years.

In [13], a SCA with nonlinear decreasing conversion parameters was proposed. The change in parameter r1 is controlled by a parabolic function and exponential function, respectively. The experimental results show that the adjustment of parameter r1 by the exponential function can better balance the global and local exploration of the solution. The study in [14] proposed a method of combining quantum computing with SCA by using quantum bits, rotating gates and a non-gate, where each gate has their own specialization in exploring the solution. The proposed SCA was reported to be very effective and accurate. The study in [15] introduces the method of reverse learning to generate reverse solutions for the current individual, which expands the exploration of solution space. The study in [16] proposed a hybrid gray wolf with SCA that uses the sine cosine update formula to improve the moving direction and speed of the head wolf. By combining the benefit of SCA, the hybrid algorithm improves drastically in terms of exploration and exploitation. Another interesting work by [17] was carried out, where SCA was combined with a differential evolution algorithm (DEA). In this context, SCA was reported to help DEA jump out from the local optimal solution region. However, the application of the SCA in the above literature failed to classify a more general dataset. The test of the robust metaheuristics depends on the ability of the algorithm to classify non-bias datasets.

In 2017, Rizk M and Rizk-Allah [18] proposed a sine cosine algorithm (MOSCA) based on a multi-orthogonal search strategy to solve engineering design problems. The proposed MOSCA improves the defects of unbalanced exploration and premature convergence of the conventional SCA. MOSCA utilizes SCA during the exploration phase and uses a multi-orthogonal search strategy to find the optimal solution in the search space. MOSCA was reported to obtain a better speed of convergence with a higher solution accuracy. In another development, Elaziz et al. [15] proposed SCA based on reverse learning (OBSCA). A reverse learning strategy is an important method used to enhance the performance of the stochastic optimization algorithm. By selecting the value of the objective function according to greedy selection at the current solution and reverse solution, OBSCA enhances the diversity of the population and improves the ability of the algorithm to approach the global optimal solution. This experiment highlights the robustness of OBSCA in terms of convergence.

In 2017, Songjin and Wen [19] proposed an improved SCA (ISCA) for solving high-dimensional optimization problems. Inspired by PSO, the ISCA algorithm introduces inertia weight to improve the convergence accuracy and increase the convergence speed of the SCA. At the same time, it adopts a reverse learning strategy to generate initial individuals to improve the diversity and reconciliation quality of the population. The experimental results showed that, compared with the basic SCA, ISCA has a better optimization performance in a high-dimensional test function. In 2018, Nenavath and Jatoth [20] proposed a hybrid SCA-DE algorithm based on differential evolution to solve optimization problems and target tracking problems. The experimental results show that the hybrid SCA-DE algorithm has a higher convergence accuracy and faster convergence speed than basic SCA. In 2021, Wu et al. [21] proposed a LSCA method and FKNN method to solve biomedical problems. Compared with other methods, the proposed LSCA obtained acceptable results but the accuracy of this method still requires improvement.

In this paper, we capitalize on the mathematical properties of the SCA to balance the global and local exploration of the algorithm during the searching process. This can be achieved by adaptively changing the amplitude of the sine function and cosine function until the SCA converges towards the global optimal solution. In addition, reverse learning will be used to provide a jump mechanism to the SCA so that it can avoid a potential unwanted local solution. Both methods will be integrated into a fuzzy k-nearest neighbor (FKNN) that has the capability to classify real life datasets. Thus, the contributions of this paper are as follows:

1. In this paper, reverse learning will be implemented into an SCA model to form a hybrid SCA. In this context, the adaptive weight coupled with the reverse learning alter the position of the solution towards the global solution.
2. The proposed hybrid SCA will be implemented into a fuzzy k-nearest neighbor (SCA-FKNN). In this context, the proposed SCA-FKNN has the ability to avoid local convergence by jumping out of the current non-optimal solution.
3. The performance of the proposed SCA-FKNN will be tested using various real life datasets. SCA-FKNN will be evaluated according to the various performance metrics, such as accuracy, precision, sensitivity, specificity, Mathews correlation coefficient and Wilcoxon signed rank test. In addition, the proposed SCA-FKNN will be compared with the existing conventional state-of-the-art classifier.

The rest of this paper is organized as follows. Section 2 introduces in detail the content of the SCA model and FKNN classifier. Section 3 presents in detail the process of forming the hybrid SCA FKNN model based on the SCA model and FKNN classifier by adding a parameter adjustment and reverse learning mechanism. Section 4 introduces and analyzes 10 different data sets and evaluation indicators. Section 5 shows the prediction and classification results of 10 types of data sets under five models with extensive comparison analysis. Section 6 describes conclusions and further research.

2. Background

2.1. Sine Cosine Algorithm

The sine cosine algorithm is an algorithm based on the mathematical characteristics of sin and cos. It updates individuals through the changes in sine and cosine functions. In SCA, it is assumed that, in j-dimensional space, the population size is n, and that, in each iteration, the location update mode of the i-th individual is

$$X_i^j(t+1) = \begin{cases} X_i^j(t) + r_1 \times \sin(r_2) \times \left| r_3 X_{best}^j - X_i^j(t) \right| & r_4 < 0.5 \\ X_i^j(t) + r_1 \times \cos(r_2) \times \left| r_3 X_{best}^j - X_i^j(t) \right| & r_4 \geq 0.5 \end{cases} \quad (1)$$

where X_i^j is the position of the i-th individual in the j dimension of the t iteration; $X_{best,j}$ is the optimal position in the j dimension of the position X_i of the i-th individual; r_2, r_3 and r_4 are random numbers subject to uniform distribution, $r_2 \in [0, 2\pi]$, $r_3 \in [0, 2]$ and $r_4 \in [0, 1]$; r_1 is the control parameter.

$$r_1 = a * (1 - \frac{t}{MaxFEs}) \quad (2)$$

where $MaxFEs$ represents the maximum number of iterations and a is a constant number and is equal to 2.

The fluctuation amplitude of $r_1 \times \sin(r_2)$ and $r_1 \times \cos(r_2)$ (sine and cosine parameters) gradually attenuates with the increase in iteration times. Its values are in the range of $(1, 2]$ and $[-2, -1)$. The algorithm performs a global search in the solution space, and the algorithm performs a local development in the range of $[-1, 1]$. The SCA algorithm flow is shown in Figure 1.

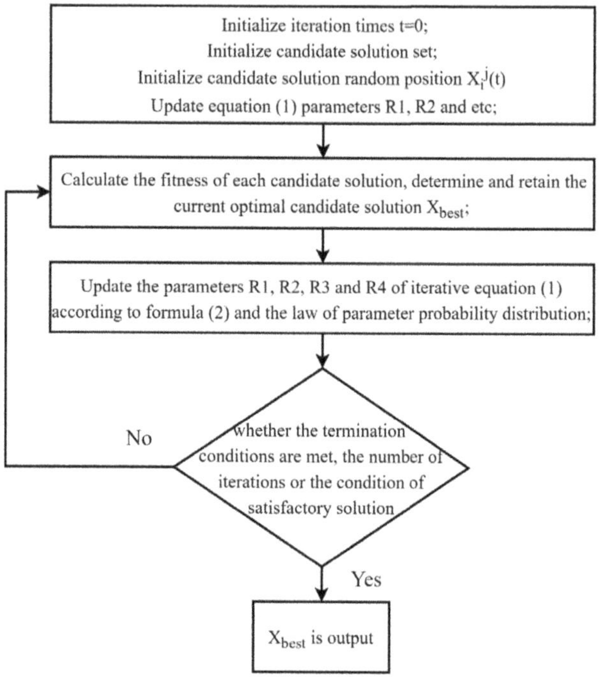

Figure 1. The flow chart of SCA.

2.2. *Fuzzy K-Nearest Neighbors (FKNN)*

As one of the simplest classifiers, KNN mainly infers the class of the sample according to the classes of the K training samples closest to the sample to be classified. The default of this method is that each of the k samples have the same weight, which is not the case. The KNN algorithm (nearest neighbor method) was first proposed by Covcr and Hart in 1967. Many researchers have conducted in-depth theoretical research and development due to the low error rate of the nearest neighbor method, which makes it one of the important methods of pattern classification.

The FKNN algorithm (fuzzy k-nearest neighbor algorithm) was proposed by Keller et al. in 1985 [22]. He assigned different weighting coefficients to k-nearest neighbors, and then used the fuzzy decision-making method to calculate the class label with the largest coefficient as the category of test data. Because the weight coefficient based on distance is used, the recognition effect is improved. Nevertheless, the selection of fuzzy k-nearest neighbor parameter K has a great impact on the recognition effect. Choosing appropriate parameters plays an important role in improving the accuracy of the classification.

A fuzzy KNN algorithm is proposed based on the KNN algorithm. This method has the advantages of a high calculation accuracy and no data input assumption. It is a relatively mature classifier. For data sets, the membership of each member data to each class is calculated by Equation (3).

$$U_{i,k} = \begin{cases} 0.51 + \left(\frac{n_k}{K}\right) \cdot 0.49, k = Y_k \\ \left(\frac{n_k}{K}\right) \cdot 0.49, k \neq Y_k \end{cases} \quad (3)$$

where $i = 1, 2, 3 \ldots N$ represents the i-th training sample and N represents the number of all training samples. $k = 1, 2, 3 \ldots M$, where k represents the k-th class, and M denotes the number of classes. $U_{i,k}$ represents the member level of the i-th sample to the k-th class. K represents the present number of nearest neighbors, Y_k represents the class of the

i-th training sample and n_k represents the number of the i-th training sample's neighbors belonging to the k-class among the nearest K neighbors. Note that membership should meet the following:

$$U_k(x) = \frac{\sum_{j-1}^{K} U_{I_j,k}\left(x - x_{I_j}\right)^{\frac{2}{m-1}}}{\sum_{j-1}^{K}\left(x - x_{I_j}\right)^{\frac{2}{m-1}}} \tag{4}$$

where x stands for the test sample, $U_k(x)$ represents the test sample weight to the k-class, $j = 1, 2, \ldots K$ represents the test sample's j-th nearest neighbor, I_j represents the i index corresponding to the j-th nearest neighbor in the training samples, $U_{I_j,k}$ is the membership degree, which is calculated by Equation (3), and $x - x_{I_j}$ represents the distance measurement. m stands for fuzzy strength, which is used to control the weight of each neighbor in the membership calculation, and its range is $[1, \infty]$.

$$C(x) = \arg\max_k U_k(x) \tag{5}$$

The calculation steps of FKNN are as follows in Figure 2.

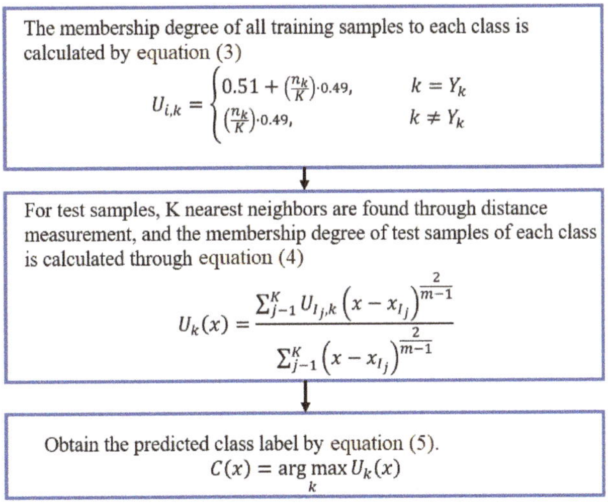
The membership degree of all training samples to each class is calculated by equation (3)
$U_{i,k} = \begin{cases} 0.51 + \left(\frac{n_k}{K}\right) \cdot 0.49, & k = Y_k \\ \left(\frac{n_k}{K}\right) \cdot 0.49, & k \neq Y_k \end{cases}$
For test samples, K nearest neighbors are found through distance measurement, and the membership degree of test samples of each class is calculated through equation (4)
$U_k(x) = \frac{\sum_{j-1}^{K} U_{I_j,k}\left(x - x_{I_j}\right)^{\frac{2}{m-1}}}{\sum_{j-1}^{K}\left(x - x_{I_j}\right)^{\frac{2}{m-1}}}$
Obtain the predicted class label by equation (5).
$C(x) = \arg\max_k U_k(x)$

Figure 2. The flow chart of FKNN.

The above FKNN solved the problem of multivariate classification and distance weight, and the SCA will deal with the problem of a low search efficiency of the optimal solution after the distance weight.

3. The Proposed Method

At the end of the iteration, SCA will conduct a small neighborhood search near the current global optimal location and constantly try to update the optimal solution. If the search process is far from the theoretical optimal solution, it is difficult for the algorithm to converge to the global optimal solution in a short time. Therefore, the current research papers are roughly divided into two ways to improve the convergence speed and accuracy of SCA. One way is to improve the convergence speed of SCA by changing Equation (1). The other is to improve the accuracy of SCA by adding reverse learning.

In the parameter adjustment mechanism, reference [23] has introduced the adaptive weight coefficient parameter adjustment mechanism, and this mechanism has achieved good results in solving the problem of jumping out of local convergence. Based on the parameter adjustment mechanism and combined with reverse learning, this paper forms an improved version of the sine and cosine algorithm with multiple strategies.

The combination of the swarm intelligence algorithm, lion swarm algorithm and reverse learning strategy further expands the search scope of the group, thus improving the problems of a slow convergence speed and insufficient accuracy of the group.

3.1. The Weight Factor

In this part, an adaptive weight w is used, which makes the individual position have a great impact on the individual moving direction and distance in the algorithm and effectively improves the ability of algorithm development. The value of w^{t+1} in the latter iteration is 100 times that of the previous iteration w^t, with an obvious step search. The mathematical model [23] of w is

$$w = \mu \times \sinh\left(1 - 20\frac{t}{MaxFEs}\right)^8 \tag{6}$$

where μ is the weight factor; in most cases, the value of μ is 0.5. Adding the weight parameter w to the sine cosine algorithm in Equation (1), we obtain:

$$X_i^j(t+1) = \begin{cases} w(X_i^j(t) + r_1 \times \sin(r_2) \times \left|r_3 X_{best}^j - X_i^j(t)\right|) & r_4 < 0.5 \\ w(X_i^j(t) + r_1 \times \cos(r_2) \times \left|r_3 X_{best}^j - X_i^j(t)\right|) & r_4 \geq 0.5 \end{cases} \tag{7}$$

3.2. Reverse Learning

In SCA, the individuals of the population only rely on the current optimal solution to update their own state, so the algorithm is likely to fall into the local optimal state, resulting in the algorithm being unable to find a satisfactory solution. At this time, it is necessary to carry out a local mutation operation on the individual, and the individual reflects on the previous learning situation with the current learning results so as to increase the probability of escaping from the local area. The formula of reflective learning is

$$X_i^* = X_i^s + \omega \otimes (X_i^s - X_i^t) \tag{8}$$

where X_i^s represents the position of individual i in the t-th iteration; X_i^* represents the position after executing Equation (7); X_i^* represents the new position generated through the reflection process; ω represents a learning factor, $\omega \in [-1, 1]$; $\otimes$ indicates dot multiplication.

In order to prevent too much randomness in the process of reflection, the learning factor was compared with ω. At the same time, in order to avoid the degradation of the learning ability and enhance the convergence of the algorithm, greedy learning was used to select the best algorithm according to the learning status before and after reflection.

$$\omega = C^{(-t/MaxFEs)} \times \cos(r_5) \tag{9}$$

where r_5 is a random number on $[0, \pi]$; C is a constant, and the effect is better when $C = 100$.

In order to reduce the possibility of the algorithm deviating from the global optimal position, the evaluation of excellent algorithms is strengthened. It is very necessary to search the space around the volume, and this improvement can improve the efficiency of the algorithm and the ability to explore new solutions. This paper integrates the strategy of elite reverse learning into SCA. The information of the elite population was used to search the space of elite individuals and their reverse solutions.

The specific operations [24] were as follows:

1. The individuals in the population were arranged after the implementation of formula $fitness$, where 10% of the excellent individuals were selected to form the elite population $\mathbb{X}_{best}$;
2. Individual $X_{best}^i \in \mathbb{X}_{best}$ boundary $[lb_j^i, ub_j^i]$ and the dynamic boundary $[min(lb_j^i), max(ub_j^i)]$ were calculated;

3. The dynamic elite reverse population $\mathbb{X}'_{best}$ of individual X^i_{best} was generated according to Equation (10);
4. If the reverse population $\mathbb{X}'_{best}$ exceeded the limit of dynamic boundary $[min(lb^i_j), max(ub^i_j)]$, it was replaced by a new individual randomly generated in the boundary;
5. The top 50% from $[\mathbb{X}_{best}, \mathbb{X}'_{best}]$ was selected for the next generation according to $fitness$;
6. Steps 2 and 5 were cycled until the stop condition was reached, and the algorithm ended.

The elite inverse solution was set in d-dimensional space. $X'_{best} = (x'_1, x'_2, \cdots, x'_D)$ is the inverse solution of the elite individual. $X_{best} = (x_1, x_2, \cdots, x_D)$ is the inverse solution of the current population. The inverse solution is defined as

$$x'_i = k(lb_i + ub_i) - x_i \tag{10}$$

where $k \in [0, 1]$ is a random number subject to uniform distribution. Multiple inverse solutions of the elite individual can be generated by using this coefficient.

The generated elite inverse solution increases the useful information of the population converging to the global optimum, strengthens the exploration of the neighborhoods around the optimal individual and improves the local development ability of the algorithm.

3.3. The Proposed Hybrid SCA FKNN Model

In this paper, the $Fitness_i$ is equal to ACC. ACC represents the accuracy of FKNN classification, which is obtained by k-cross-validation. In this paper, five-fold validation was used. After combining hybrid SCA and FKNN, the pseudocode of the hybrid SCA FKNN is shown in Algorithm 1. Figures 3 and 4 show the operation flow of the whole hybrid SCA FKNN method in detail.

Algorithm 1 The hybrid SCA-FKNN.

```
while t < MaxFEs do
  update r1, r2, r3, r4
  w_t = μ * sinh(1 − 20 t/MaxFEs)^8
  if r4 < 0.5 then
    X_i^s = w_t(X_i(t) + r1 × sin(r2) × |r3 X_best − X_i(t)|)
    X_i^* = X_i^s + ω ⊗ (X_i^s − X_i^t)
    if f(X_i^s) > BF then
      if f(X_i^s) < f(X_i^*) then
        X_i^{t+1} = X_i^*
        X_best = X_i^{t+1}
        BF = f(X_i^*)
      else
        X_i^{t+1} = X_i^s
        X_best = X_i^{t+1}
        BF = f(X_i^*)
      end if
    end if
    for i=1 to SupN do
      generate random k, X'_i(t+1) = k(lb + ub) − X_i(t+1)
    end for
    put all X'_i into train dataset as elite opposition solutions
  else
    X_i^s = w_t(X_i(t) + r1 × cos(r2) × |r3 X_best − X_i(t)|)
    As the up,the same progress
  end if
end while
```

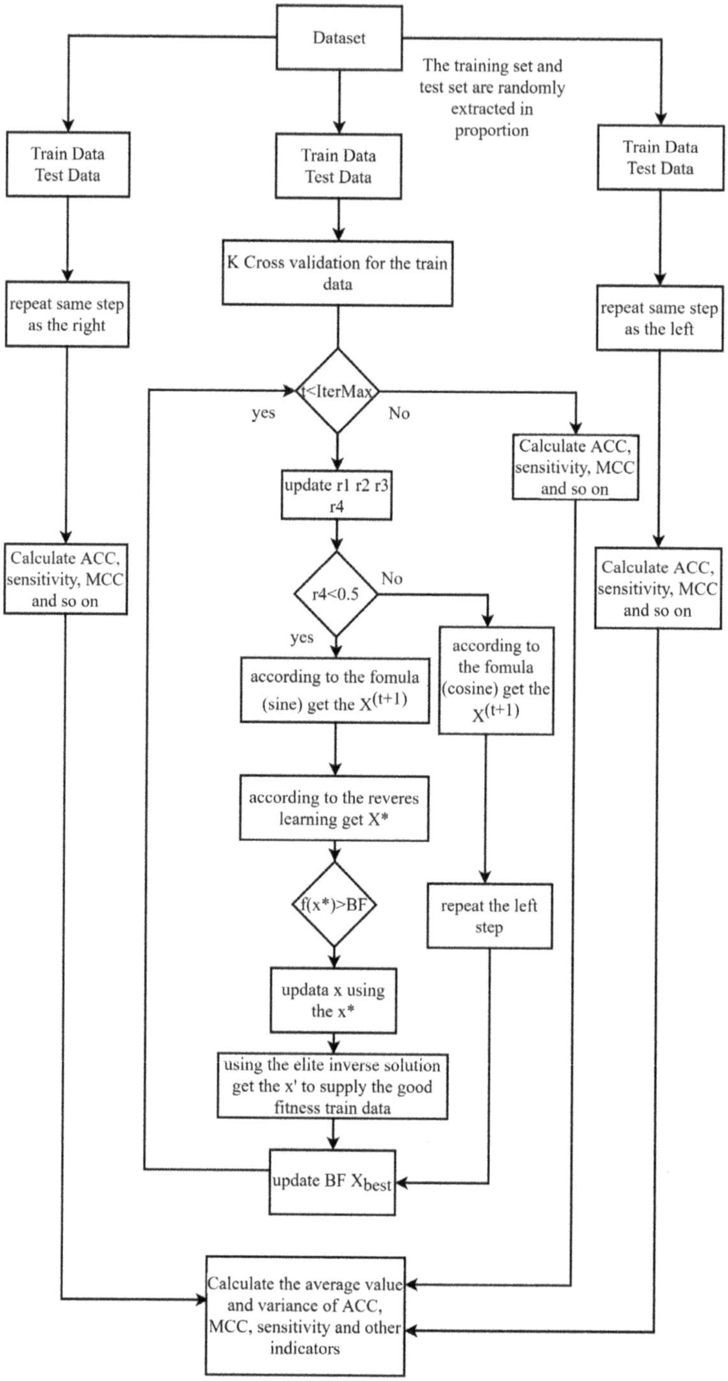

Figure 3. The flow chart of the hybrid SCA FKNN.

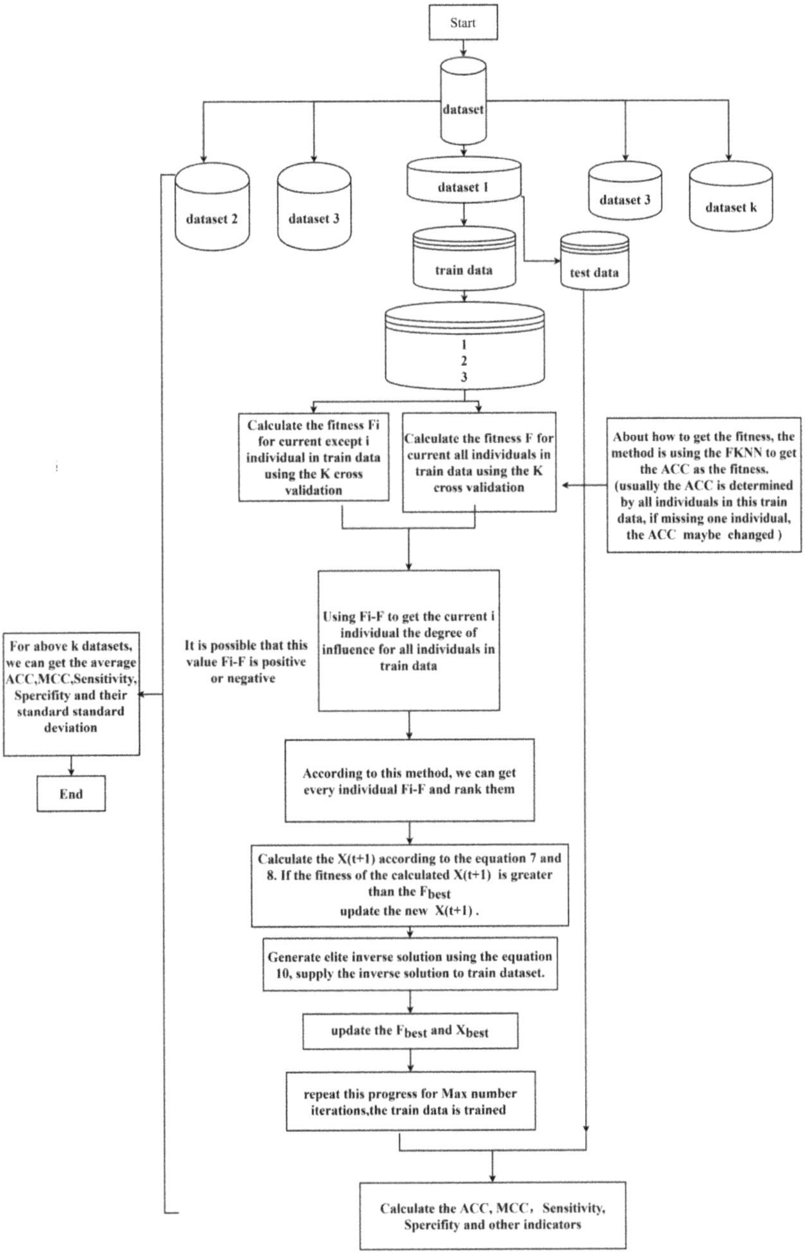

Figure 4. Numerical simulation diagram of the whole process.

4. Experiment and Discussion

4.1. Experiment Setup

In this section, the components of the experiment will be described in detail. The purpose of this experiment is to illustrate that the hybrid SCA FKNN method proposed in this paper can be used in two or more types of data sets and can achieve good numerical results, with strong adaptability and accuracy. In order to ensure the reproducibility of the experiment, the experimental setup will be shown below.

4.2. Benchmark Datasets

The datasets used in this paper were all open source datasets; for details of the datasets used in this paper, please visit this website: https://archive.ics.uci.edu/ml/index.php (accessed on 30 April 2022). For all datasets, the feature was normalized to $[-1, 1]$ using maximum and minimum normalization. In order to better show the numerical results of the method proposed in this paper, this paper focused on the numerical experiments on two-class data sets and multi-class data sets.

In order to reflect the wide adaptability of the methods proposed in this paper, this paper selected 10 kinds of data sets from different application scenarios and different data types. The 10 kinds of data sets involve a variety of use scenarios with practical life significance, such as medical treatment, daily necessities, automobiles, etc. From Tables 1 and 2, it can be seen that the sample size, characteristics and categories of the 10 types of data sets cover different levels. This paper verifies the effectiveness of the method proposed in this paper from various angles according to different conditions and different use scenarios of the data sets.

Table 1. The two-class-dataset-related information.

	Categories	Samples	Features	Positive	Negative
Bupa	2	345	6	145	200
Hepatitis	2	155	19	32	123
SPECT	2	267	22	212	55

Table 2. The multi-class-dataset-related information.

Datasets	Categories	Samples	Feartures	Positive	Negative
Caesarian section classification dataset	2	80	4	34	46
Indian liver patient dataset (ILPD)	2	583	10	415	167
Glass identification dataset	7	214	9	69 (class 1)	145 (other classes except positive)
User knowledge modeling dataset	4	403	5	102 (class 1)	301 (other classes except positive)
Breast tissue dataset	6	106	9	20 (class 1)	86 (other classes except positive)
Car dataset	4	1728	6	1209 (class 1)	519 (other classes except positive)
QCM sensor alcohol dataset	5	125	15	24 (class 3)	101 (other classes except positive)

For two-class data sets, this paper considered the following three data sets. The basic situation of these three data sets is shown in Table 1. Table 1 describes the indicators, such as the number of data label categories, data scale and data feature quantity, of the following three datasets.

For multi-classes datasets, in order to further verify the effectiveness of the method proposed in this paper, this paper retrieved the following eight types of data sets on the open data platform of the University of California for numerical experiments. The contents of the relevant data sets are described in Table 2. These data sets involve multiple areas of life, which is more convincing for verifying the effectiveness of the method. The relevant data categories range from the least to the most, and the diversity of data features ranges from small sample data to large sample data.

Table 2 describes the basic information of seven multi-category data sets, including the category, sample number, feature number and number of positive samples and negative samples. For example, the caesarian section classification dataset, Indian liver patient dataset (ILPD), glass identification dataset, user knowledge modeling dataset, car dataset and QCM sensor alcohol dataset. The content of data sets covers all aspects of real life, with a wider range and more complex data types. There are both large sample data sets and small sample data sets, and both multi-feature data sets and a small number of feature data sets.

4.3. Performance Metrics

The evaluation indicators used in numerical experiments include the classification accuracy (ACC), sensitivity, precision, specificity and Matthews correlation coefficient (MCC). Sensitivity refers to the ability of the model to identify positive examples. Precision indicates samples with positive prediction results. These are positive cases. The specificity measurement model is the ability to identify negative examples. The measurement range of MCC is $[-1, 1]$, and the other is $[0, 1]$. The larger the evaluation indicator is, the better the performance of the model under this indicator.

For multi-class datasets, the corresponding concerned data categories are taken as positive categories and other categories are taken as negative categories. The data sets were calculated to obtain the values of relevant evaluation indicators, such as the accuracy (ACC), sensitivity, precision, specificity and Matthews correlation coefficient (MCC).

Standard classification indicators, such as the accuracy (ACC), sensitivity, precision, specificity and Matthews correlation coefficient (MCC), were used in the experiment. According to [25–27], the true positive (TP) is the number of positive instances of correct classification, the false negative (FN) is the number of positive instances of incorrect classification, the true negative (TN) is the number of negative instances of correct classification and the false positive (FP) is the number of positive instances of incorrect classification. The basic configuration matrix of TP, FN, TN and FP is shown in Table 3.

Table 3. The Basic Confusion Matrix.

Basic Confusion Matrix		**Predicted Class**	
		Positive	**Negative**
Actual Class	**Positive**	True Positive (TP)	False Negative (FN)
	Negative	False Positive (FP)	True Negative (TN)

By referring to the papers [25–27], this paper lists the evaluation indicators of accuracy (ACC), sensitivity, precision, specificity and Matthews correlation coefficient (MCC) as follows:

$$ACC = \frac{TP + TN}{TP + TN + FN + FP} \tag{11}$$

$$Precision = \frac{TP}{TP + FP} \tag{12}$$

$$Sensitivity = \frac{TP}{TP + FN} \tag{13}$$

$$Specificity = \frac{TN}{FP + TN} \tag{14}$$

$$MCC = \frac{TP \cdot TN - FP \cdot FN}{\sqrt{(TP+FP)(TP+FN)(TN+FP)(TN+FN)}} \quad (15)$$

The above evaluation indicators can comprehensively evaluate the performance of the proposed model.

4.4. Baseline Methods

In order to verify the hybrid SCA FKNN model, a large number of data experiments were conducted to verify the effectiveness of the proposed method. Firstly, in the first part, this paper tested two classes of data sets, and made a numerical comparison of nine metaheuristic-based algorithms (LSCA [21], SCA [12], PSO [28], SSA [29], SA [30], BA [31], CGSCA [32], mSCA [33] and CESCA [34]), fixing their $M = 2$ and $K = 3$ to verify the advantages of execution data results, respectively. In order to ensure the fairness of the numerical experiment, the experiment was repeated five times on the same machine. Based on the repeated experiment, the average value and standard deviation of the model were analyzed. Each experiment included five cross validation results. The average value of five cross validations was taken for performance evaluation.

4.5. Experimental Design

All numerical experiments were calculated by MATLAB 2017. All experiments were conducted on the same equipment, and 8 GB ram Intel Core i5 (Intel) equipped with windows 11 (Microsoft, Redmond, WA, USA) was used as a workstation to avoid the impact of experimental hardware during the simulation process.

5. Results and Discussion

5.1. Numerical Results for Two-Classes Datasets

For the following three types of two-class datasets, the hybrid SCA FKNN method proposed in this paper will be compared and analyzed with eight metaheuristic algorithms. The superior performance of hybrid SCA FKNN in the evaluation metrics fully shows the advantages of the proposed method, and further verifies the effectiveness of the method.

5.1.1. Experimental Results on the Bupa Dataset

The numerical results of the hybrid SCA FKNN compared with other models in the Bupa dataset are shown in Table 4. This paper carried out 10 repeated numerical experiments, and the average value and standard deviation of the 10 repeated experiments are listed in Table 4. It can be seen that the hybrid SCA FKNN model proposed in this paper achieves the best results among the four evaluation indicators. The hybrid SCA FKNN model proposed in this paper observes better results on ACC, which are approximately 8.4–25.1% higher than the comparison models. Although the standard deviation of LSCA-FKNN is lower than that of hybrid SCA FKNN in most cases, the numerical results of hybrid SCA FKNN are significantly better than LSCA FKNN in terms of average evaluation index values.

In order to show the overall benchmarking analysis results of each model, Figure 5 draws a bar graph of the performance of each model, draws the average value of 10 repeated experiments of each model and adds the standard deviation of repeated experiments as the error line. Figure 5 is a visual display of Table 4. As shown in Figure 5, except for precision, good results have been achieved in sensitivity, specificity and MCC. It can be clearly seen from the figure that the hybrid SCA FKNN method has better numerical results and stronger stability.

Table 4. Results of the hybrid FKNN and comparison models on the Bupa dataset. (Bold indicates the best in comparison method).

Algorithm	Metric	ACC	Precision	Sensitivity	Specificity	MCC
Hybrid SCA-FKNN	avg	**0.7799**	**0.7015**	**0.6412**	**0.8791**	**0.4728**
	std	**0.0143**	**0.0284**	**0.0299**	**0.0283**	**0.0303**
LSCA-FKNN	avg	0.6232	0.6674	0.5687	0.8393	0.2465
	std	0.0199	0.0338	0.0175	0.0177	0.0367
SCA-FKNN	avg	0.6175	0.5494	0.4645	0.7968	0.2946
	std	0.0383	0.0439	0.0487	0.0178	0.0546
PSO-FKNN	avg	0.6686	0.6531	0.4851	0.8047	0.3105
	std	0.0266	0.0344	0.0379	0.0231	0.0472
BA-FKNN	avg	0.6056	0.5600	0.4693	0.7121	0.1920
	std	0.0292	0.0479	0.0423	0.0292	0.0694
SSA-FKNN	avg	0.6377	0.5862	0.5667	0.6923	0.2601
	std	0.0586	0.0069	0.1233	0.0327	0.0895
SA-FKNN	avg	0.6721	0.6444	0.4511	0.8087	0.3131
	std	0.0142	0.0340	0.0128	0.0415	0.0279
CGSCA-FKNN	avg	0.6600	0.6486	0.4711	0.7981	0.2939
	std	0.0193	0.0356	0.0195	0.0308	0.0382

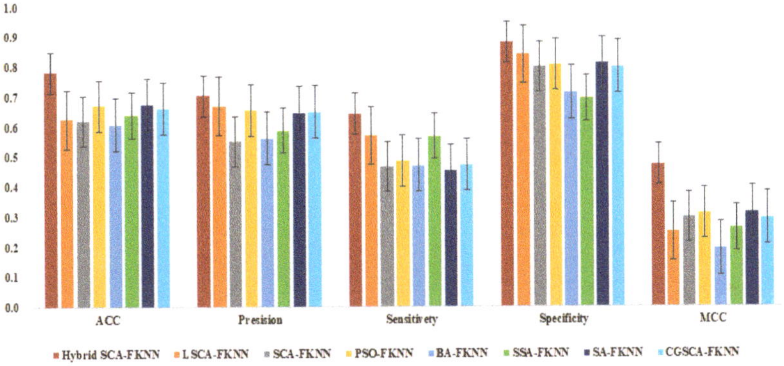

Figure 5. Classification performance of each model on the Bupa dataset.

5.1.2. Experimental Results on the Hepatitis Dataset

As reflected in the above table on the Bupa dataset, Table 5 shows the benchmarking results between the hepatitis dataset and other model methods. It can be seen that the hybrid SCA FKNN model proposed in this paper achieves the best results among the three evaluation indicators.In terms of sensitivity and precision, the hybrid SCA FKNN performs worse than BA FKNN and CGSCA FKNN, but significantly better than their numerical results in terms of ACC, specificity and MCC. The hybrid SCA FKNN model proposed in this paper observes better results on ACC, which are approximately 15.2–19.6% higher than the comparison models.

Similarly, in order to further visualize the comparison of the five types of evaluation indicators, Figure 6 shows the performance of each model more intuitively. For this data set, the data size of the positive samples is small, at only 32 data, so it has a great impact on the sensitivity and MCC. In general, the hybrid SCA FKNN model has competitive advantages.

Table 5. Results of the hybrid-FKNN and comparison models on the hepatitis dataset. (Bold indicates the best in comparison method).

Algorithm	Metric	ACC	Precision	Sensitivity	Specificity	MCC
Hybrid SCA-FKNN	avg	**0.9465**	0.3638	0.4072	**0.9392**	**0.4342**
	std	**0.0569**	0.0937	0.0845	**0.0312**	**0.0945**
LSCA-FKNN	avg	0.8191	0.4566	0.3760	0.9192	0.3276
	std	0.0296	0.0874	0.0676	0.0303	0.0648
SCA-FKNN	avg	0.8051	0.4236	0.3512	0.9167	0.3009
	std	0.0323	0.1061	0.0745	0.0301	0.0875
PSO-FKNN	avg	0.7742	0.4641	0.3376	0.9217	0.3118
	std	0.0378	0.0969	0.0727	0.0230	0.0788
BA-FKNN	avg	0.8172	0.4333	**0.4692**	0.8305	0.3593
	std	0.0233	0.0702	**0.0903**	0.0267	0.0812
SSA-FKNN	avg	0.8750	0.2975	0.3333	0.9333	0.3846
	std	0.0432	0.0379	0.1925	0.0087	0.0098
SA-FKNN	avg	0.8076	0.4115	0.3280	0.9097	0.2771
	std	0.0242	0.0913	0.0751	0.0266	0.0797
CGSCA-FKNN	avg	0.8033	**0.5533**	0.3944	0.9067	0.3744
	std	0.0199	**0.0740**	0.0666	0.0266	0.0582

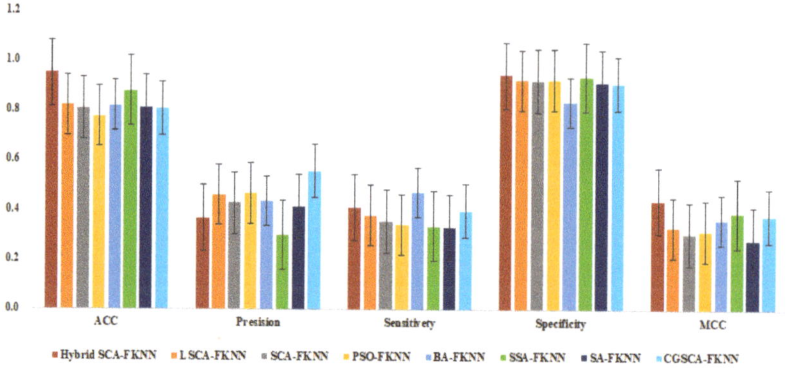

Figure 6. Classification performance of each model on the hepatitis dataset.

ACC is an index used to describe the accuracy of the model. The higher the value of ACC, the better the prediction result of the model. For the current hepatitis dataset, Table 5 is obtained according to the comparison with the numerical results in paper [21]. As shown in Table 5 and Figure 6, the hybrid-FKNN model proposed in this paper obtains better results in ACC, which are approximately 15.2–19.6% higher than the comparison model. However, its variance is high and its stability is poor. The data results are greatly affected by random data sampling.

5.1.3. Experimental Results on the SPECT Dataset

Similarly, Table 6 shows the benchmarking results of the SPECT dataset and other model methods on the evaluation indicators of ACC, sensitivity, precision and MCC. In terms of sensitivity and precision, the hybrid SCA FKNN performs worse than BA FKNN and LSCA FKNN. BA FKNN has a high sensitivity and low specificity, and there is a significant difference in its ability to recognize positive cases and negative cases. However, in terms of ACC, specification and MCC, it is significantly better than their numerical results.

Table 6. Results of the hybrid-FKNN and comparison models on the SPECT dataset. (Bold indicates the best in comparison method).

Algorithm	Metric	ACC	Precision	Sensitivity	Specificity	MCC
Hybrid SCA-FKNN	avg	**0.8936**	**0.8620**	0.7157	**0.5220**	**0.4436**
	std	**0.0195**	**0.0845**	0.0610	**0.0227**	**0.0605**
LSCA-FKNN	avg	0.7593	0.8538	0.8730	0.4094	0.2588
	std	0.0191	0.0187	0.0357	0.0561	0.0656
SCA-FKNN	avg	0.7297	0.7953	0.8601	0.3427	0.1759
	std	0.0449	0.0283	0.0278	0.0707	0.0718
PSO-FKNN	avg	0.7615	0.8405	0.8541	0.3866	0.2079
	std	0.0351	0.0216	0.0308	0.0637	0.0975
BA-FKNN	avg	0.7585	0.7098	**0.9270**	0.1049	0.0259
	std	0.0287	0.0064	**0.0164**	0.0493	0.0702
SSA-FKNN	avg	0.6471	0.5455	0.8571	0.4443	0.3228
	std	0.0899	0.0951	0.0825	0.0673	0.0943
SA-FKNN	avg	0.7658	0.8195	0.8920	0.2891	0.1031
	std	0.0164	0.0176	0.0234	0.1013	0.0637
CGSCA-FKNN	avg	0.7546	0.8497	0.8330	0.4308	0.2034
	std	0.0229	0.0140	0.0238	0.0587	0.0709

Figure 7 vividly shows the performance of various models on different evaluation indicators. It can be seen from the figure that the sensitivity, specificity and MCC indicators of the model vary greatly, which may be due to the small number of negative samples, at only 55 negative samples. Cross validation has a great impact on the sensitivity and MCC. It can be seen from the figure that the hybrid SCA FKNN method is quite competitive in obtaining numerical results on SPECT data sets.

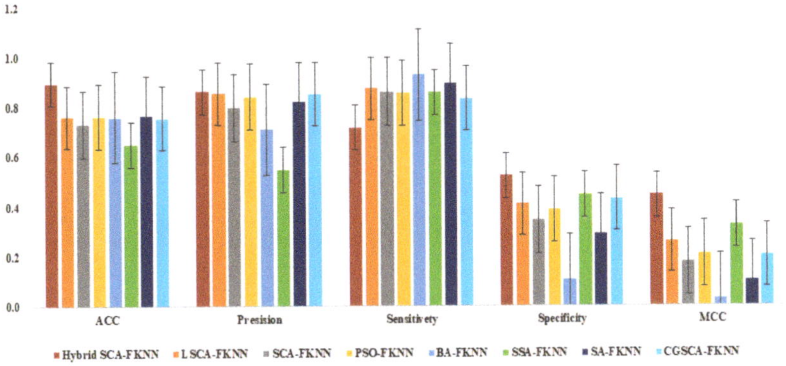

Figure 7. Classification performance of each model on the SPECT dataset.

For the current SPECT dataset, Table 6 is also obtained by the hybrid SCA FKNN. As shown in Table 6, the hybrid-FKNN model obtains better results in ACC, which are approximately 12.1–14.3% higher than the comparison models. As shown in Figure 7, except for sensitivity and precision, the best results were also achieved in specificity and MCC. However, satisfactory results have been achieved in sensitivity and precision. The numerical results are quite competitive.

In order to further verify the effectiveness of the proposed method, the standard is attached in Appendix A, which concerns the experimental results obtained in hepatitis, Bupa and SPECT datasets under the conditions of different maximum cycle test times and different cross validation numbers for researchers' reference.

5.2. Numerical Results for Multi-Classes Datasets

For the above seven different application scenarios and different types of data sets, the following data results are obtained in this paper. As shown in Table 7, for multi-class datasets, the data prediction accuracy is between 0.65–0.90, and the hybrid-SCA FKNN method can still achieve good results. It has good data prediction results for datasets with multiple or few characteristics, and multiple or few samples. This method is more adaptable.

Table 7. Results of the hybrid-FKNN on multi-class datasets.

Datasets	Metric	ACC	Precision	Sensitive	Specificity	MCC
Caesarian section classification dataset	Avg	0.7026	0.7197	0.8336	0.7049	0.4694
	Std	0.0901	0.0500	0.0160	0.0927	0.0747
Indian Liver Patient Dataset (ILPD)	Avg	0.7953	0.7876	0.8255	0.3788	0.1621
	Std	0.0342	0.0379	0.0853	0.0541	0.0437
Glass Identification Dataset	Avg	0.7827	0.9016	0.9526	0.8347	0.4734
	Std	0.0355	0.0501	0.0376	0.0751	0.1037
User Knowledge Modeling Dataset	Avg	0.8606	0.9545	0.9709	0.9185	0.9042
	Std	0.0267	0.0408	0.0163	0.0864	0.0319
Breast Tissue Dataset	Avg	0.6554	0.9667	0.8883	0.9770	0.6969
	Std	0.0727	0.0577	0.0459	0.1443	0.1163
Car Dataset	Avg	0.8807	0.9188	0.9973	0.9823	0.8312
	Std	0.0916	0.0612	0.0716	0.0982	0.1616
QCM sensor Alcohol Dataset	Avg	0.9043	0.8501	0.8568	0.8477	0.8562
	Std	0.0939	0.0838	0.0719	0.0973	0.1008

In order to better demonstrate the effectiveness of the method proposed in this paper, this paper compares the numerical results of the above seven different data sets calculated by the LSCA FKNN [21], SCA FKNN [12], PSO FKNN [28], BA FKNN [31] and SSA FKNN [29] methods. The relevant numerical comparison results are shown in Tables 8–14. From the five evaluation indicators, the hybrid SCA FKNN method proposed in this paper achieved good numerical results under seven datasets.

For the current caesarian section classification dataset, Table 8 is also obtained from hybrid SCA FKNN. As shown in Table 8, the hybrid SCA FKNN model achieved better results in ACC, sensitivity and MCC, which were approximately 5.2–21.7% higher than the comparison model in ACC.

For the Indian liver patient dataset (ILPD), Table 9 shows the data results obtained by the hybrid SCA FKNN method and other numerical models. As shown in Table 9, the hybrid SCA FKNN model achieved better results in ACC, precision, specificity and MCC, which were approximately 10.9–23.2% higher than the comparison model in ACC.

Table 8. Results of the hybrid-FKNN and comparison models on the caesarian section classification dataset. (Bold indicates the best in comparison method).

Algorithm	Metric	ACC	Precision	Sensitivity	Specificity	MCC
Hybrid SCA-FKNN	avg	**0.7026**	0.7197	**0.8336**	0.7049	**0.4694**
	std	**0.0901**	0.0500	**0.0160**	0.0927	**0.0747**
LSCA-FKNN	avg	0.6677	0.8148	0.5741	0.7095	0.3923
	std	0.0955	0.1197	0.0986	0.0965	0.1295
SCA-FKNN	avg	0.6667	0.6766	0.6349	**0.7333**	0.3626
	std	0.0722	0.2384	0.0755	**0.0882**	0.0414
PSO-FKNN	avg	0.6675	**0.8194**	0.7505	0.7250	0.4045
	std	0.0701	**0.1138**	0.1220	0.0992	0.0939
BA-FKNN	avg	0.5625	0.5361	0.7424	0.2500	0.2655
	std	0.0625	0.0804	0.0957	0.0443	0.0995
SSA-FKNN	avg	0.5775	0.6528	0.5370	0.5952	0.2381
	std	0.0523	0.0241	0.0656	0.0591	0.0817

Table 9. Results of the hybrid-FKNN and comparison models on the Indian liver patient dataset (ILPD). (Bold indicates the best in comparison method).

Algorithm	Metric	ACC	Precision	Sensitivity	Specificity	MCC
Hybrid SCA-FKNN	avg	**0.7953**	**0.7876**	0.8255	**0.3788**	**0.1621**
	std	**0.0342**	**0.0379**	0.0853	**0.0541**	**0.0437**
LSCA-FKNN	avg	0.6912	0.6961	0.9856	0.1078	0.0712
	std	0.0191	0.0123	0.0220	0.0309	0.0257
SCA-FKNN	avg	0.6455	0.7440	0.8882	0.2058	0.1038
	std	0.0222	0.0732	0.0964	0.0821	0.0674
PSO-FKNN	avg	0.7173	0.7187	**0.9967**	0.0963	0.0953
	std	0.0139	0.0162	**0.0058**	0.0107	0.0641
BA-FKNN	avg	0.7108	0.7209	0.9534	0.0865	0.0532
	std	0.0085	0.0076	0.0034	0.0012	0.0125
SSA-FKNN	avg	0.7092	0.7215	0.9695	0.0502	0.0644
	std	0.0028	0.0140	0.0277	0.0457	0.0112

Table 10. Results of the hybrid-FKNN and comparison models on the glass dataset. (Bold indicates the best in comparison method).

Algorithm	Metric	ACC	Precision	Sensitivity	Specificity	MCC
Hybrid SCA-FKNN	avg	**0.7827**	**0.9016**	**0.9526**	**0.8347**	0.4734
	std	**0.0355**	**0.0501**	**0.0376**	**0.0751**	0.1037
LSCA-FKNN	avg	0.6589	0.5961	0.6759	0.7618	0.4242
	std	0.0355	0.2470	0.1530	0.0546	0.1972
SCA-FKNN	avg	0.6654	0.6078	0.8614	0.7028	0.5339
	std	0.0355	0.0453	0.0558	0.0337	0.0394
PSO-FKNN	avg	0.6047	0.6429	0.6923	0.7727	0.4587
	std	0.0968	0.0415	0.0994	0.0646	0.0950
BA-FKNN	avg	0.5349	0.3333	0.5000	0.6429	0.3187
	std	0.1005	0.0907	0.0874	0.0707	0.0587
SSA-FKNN	avg	0.7209	0.7778	0.9091	0.6875	**0.6209**
	std	0.0880	0.0128	0.1905	0.1168	**0.2040**

Table 11. Results of the hybrid-FKNN and comparison models on the user modeling dataset hamdi tolga dataset. (Bold indicates the best in comparison method).

Algorithm	Metric	ACC	Precision	Sensitivity	Specificity	MCC
Hybrid SCA-FKNN	avg	**0.8606**	**0.9545**	**0.9709**	0.9185	0.9042
	std	**0.0267**	**0.0408**	**0.0163**	0.0864	0.0319
LSCA-FKNN	avg	0.7901	0.9286	0.9286	**0.9808**	0.9093
	std	0.0317	0.0299	0.0469	**0.0127**	0.0388
SCA-FKNN	avg	0.7977	0.9107	0.9639	0.9678	**0.9143**
	std	0.0744	0.0233	0.0313	0.0138	**0.0400**
PSO-FKNN	avg	0.7713	0.8860	0.9434	0.9444	0.8876
	std	0.0681	0.0218	0.0246	0.0059	0.0395
BA-FKNN	avg	0.5179	0.6324	0.5404	0.8189	0.3828
	std	0.0890	0.1101	0.3625	0.1877	0.2242
SSA-FKNN	avg	0.8025	0.9437	0.7593	0.9541	0.7018
	std	0.0377	0.0150	0.0590	0.0153	0.0629

Table 12. Results of the hybrid-FKNN and comparison models on the breast tissues dataset. (Bold indicates the best in comparison method).

Algorithm	Metric	ACC	Precision	Sensitivty	Specificity	MCC
Hybrid SCA-FKNN	avg	0.6554	**0.9667**	**0.8883**	**0.9770**	**0.6969**
	std	0.0727	**0.0577**	**0.0459**	**0.1443**	**0.1163**
LSCA-FKNN	avg	0.5397	0.8667	0.6389	0.9333	0.6154
	std	0.0727	0.2309	0.1273	0.1155	0.2682
SCA-FKNN	avg	0.5373	0.7500	0.8167	0.9024	0.6471
	std	0.0550	0.0012	0.1243	0.0117	0.0937
PSO-FKNN	avg	0.5238	0.6583	0.8333	0.7500	0.5677
	std	0.0991	0.0366	0.0787	0.0605	0.0879
BA-FKNN	avg	0.4928	0.5843	0.6875	0.6742	0.4731
	std	0.0727	0.0473	0.0887	0.0751	0.0949
SSA-FKNN	avg	**0.6667**	0.9487	0.8196	0.6667	0.5657
	std	**0.0825**	0.0888	0.0239	0.0774	0.0865

Table 13. Resultsof the hybrid-FKNN and comparison models on the car dataset. (Bold indicates the best in comparison method).

Algorithm	Metric	ACC	Precision	Sensitivity	Specificity	MCC
Hybrid SCA-FKNN	avg	**0.8807**	0.9188	0.9973	**0.9823**	**0.8312**
	std	**0.0916**	0.0612	0.0716	**0.0982**	**0.1616**
LSCA-FKNN	avg	0.8691	0.9450	0.9467	0.8388	0.7922
	std	0.0161	0.0372	0.0289	0.1106	0.0454
SCA-FKNN	avg	0.8168	0.8789	0.9559	0.9428	0.7818
	std	0.0134	0.0095	0.0057	**0.0271**	0.0110
PSO-FKNN	avg	0.7645	0.7718	**0.9977**	0.3179	0.4601
	std	0.0159	0.0964	**0.0434**	0.0530	0.0064
BA-FKNN	avg	0.7107	0.7342	0.9468	0.6591	0.6596
	std	0.0859	0.1090	0.0350	0.1100	0.1226
SSA-FKNN	avg	0.8618	**0.9461**	0.8816	0.8307	0.6653
	std	0.0854	**0.0939**	0.0269	0.0819	0.0945

Table 14. Results of the hybrid-FKNN and comparison models on the QCM sensor alcohol dataset. (Bold indicates the best in comparison method).

Algorithm	Metric	ACC	Precision	Sensitivity	Specificity	MCC
Hybrid SCA-FKNN	avg	**0.9043**	**0.8501**	**0.8568**	0.8477	**0.8562**
	std	**0.0939**	**0.0838**	**0.0719**	0.0973	**0.1008**
LSCA-FKNN	avg	0.7600	0.7917	0.8327	0.8189	0.7269
	std	0.0367	0.0908	**0.0823**	0.0925	0.1415
SCA-FKNN	avg	0.7702	0.7333	0.7333	**0.8841**	0.7479
	std	0.0693	0.0887	0.1082	**0.0275**	0.1270
PSO-FKNN	avg	0.4400	0.5095	0.6656	0.6794	0.2208
	std	0.0400	0.0744	0.0672	0.0531	0.0580
BA-FKNN	avg	0.3067	0.6567	0.2611	0.7804	0.3568
	std	0.0231	0.0333	0.0674	0.0756	0.0632
SSA-FKNN	avg	0.8133	0.6640	0.7714	0.8682	0.6117
	std	0.1007	0.0856	0.0960	0.0304	0.1126

For the glass dataset, Table 10 shows the data results obtained by the hybrid SCA FKNN method and other numerical models. As shown in Table 10, the hybrid SCA FKNN model achieved better results in ACC, precision, sensitivity specificity and MCC, which were approximately 8.6–46.3% higher than the comparison model in ACC.

For the user modeling dataset hamdi tolga dataset, Table 11 shows the data results obtained by the hybrid SCA FKNN method and other numerical models. As shown in Table 11, the hybrid SCA FKNN model achieved better results in ACC, precision, sensitivity and specificity, which were approximately 7.2–66.2% higher than the comparison model in ACC.

For the breast tissues dataset, Table 12 shows the data results obtained by the hybrid SCA FKNN method and other numerical models. As shown in Table 12, the hybrid SCA FKNN model achieved better results in precision, sensitivity specificity and MCC, which were slightly lower than SSA-FKNN and higher than the comparison model in ACC.

For the car dataset, Table 13 shows the data results obtained by the hybrid SCA FKNN method and other numerical models. As shown in Table 13, the hybrid SCA FKNN model achieved better results in ACC, specificity and MCC, which were approximately 1.3–8.6% higher than the comparison model in ACC.

For the QCM sensor alcohol dataset, Table 14 shows the data results obtained by the hybrid SCA FKNN method and other numerical models. As shown in Table 14, the hybrid SCA FKNN model achieved better results in ACC, precision, sensitivity and MCC, which were twice as large as the results of PSO FKNN and BA FKNN in ACC.

In order to better verify the method proposed in this paper, this paper analyzed the operation process of the five data sets. The change in best fitness can analyze the convergence of the data running process. If the best fitness does not change during the cycle, the data prediction results do not change in general. If a few cycles are used, the best fitness will not change, indicating that the method has a faster convergence speed.

From Figure 8, it can be seen that the optimal fitness will start to be in a stable state at approximately 12–23 iterations; that is, in the next cycle, the data of the training set will not be optimized, and the method will be in a convergent state. As shown in Figure 8, after the first iteration, the best fitness of the current training set will be obtained, and the current best fitness will not be equal to 0. The value of this best fitness gradually stabilizes with the increase in the number of iterations, but it does not start from 0. For the car dataset, QCM sensor alcohol dataset and glass identification dataset, the best fitness converges quickly and converges to a stable value at approximately the 10th iteration. For the ILPD and the breast tissue dataset, it also converges to a stable value at approximately the 15th iteration.

With the increase in the number of iterations, the best fitness gradually increases on the car dataset. When the number of iterations reaches 15, the best fitness gradually stabilizes to 0.8543. With the update and optimization of the car training dataset, the data prediction result of the car test set reaches 0.8514. For the QCM sensor alcohol dataset, when the number of iterations reaches 10, the optimal fitness reaches a stable state at 0.8400, and the data prediction result of the QCM sensor alcohol test set reaches 0.8520. For the glass identification dataset, when the number of iterations reaches 12, the optimal fitness reaches a stable state at 0.7256, and the data prediction result of the glass identification test set reaches 0.7364. The classification accuracies of the above three data sets in the cycle process, best fitness and test data sets are roughly the same, which shows that this method can find convergent data points in the simulation process effectively and obtain more accurate results.

For the ILPD, when the number of iterations reaches 20, the optimal fitness reaches a stable state at 0.7256, and the data prediction result of the ILPD test set reaches 0.6609. For the breast tissue dataset, when the number of iterations reaches 15, the optimal fitness reaches a stable state at 0.7256, and the data prediction result of the breast tissue test set reaches 0.6475. For the above two datasets, although the accuracy of the method is slightly lower than that of best fitness, the method achieves better results in precision and stability.

According to Figure 8, it can be clearly seen that the method proposed in this paper has a good convergence effect and achieves the purpose of prediction results when fewer cycles are required.

For further experiments, and to compare the results of LSCA-FKNN and SCA-FKNN for all 10 datasets, this paper will run Wilcoxon signed rank test hybrid SCA FKNN. The null hypothesis is that there is no difference between the accuracy of the two classifiers. As shown in the accuracy results of this paper, we reject the null hypothesis (significance level

0.05), and accept that the two classifiers have significantly different accuracies. This result confirms the advantages of hybrid SCA FKNN.

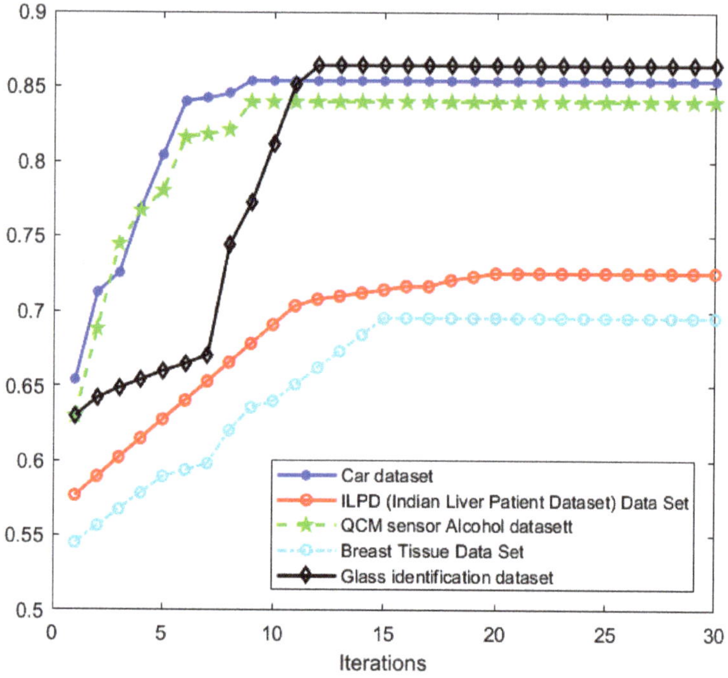

Figure 8. The process of best fitness change with increasing number of iterations on multi-class dataset.

6. Conclusions

The hybrid SCA FKNN algorithm is proposed in this paper based on the improved SCA algorithm combined with reverse learning and an FKNN classifier. It is a further combination of the swarm intelligence algorithm and classifier. This method is a multi-strategy hybrid algorithm that further optimizes the sine cosine algorithm, makes it easier to jump out of local convergence and obtains more accurate numerical solutions. In the process of implementing hybrid SCA into FKNN, this paper mainly uses the FKNN classifier to calculate the prediction accuracy by cross validation as the current best fitness to iteratively optimize the training dataset in order to obtain a more accurate classification. This way, the training set population can be optimized until the training set cannot be optimized any more and the numerical value converges, which can greatly improve the the accuracy of the numerical results. After comparing the numerical results of the hybrid SCA FKNN method with five other methods in 10 data sets, and through the Wilcoxon signed rank test with SCA-FKNN and LSCA-FKNN, the numerical results were significantly improved.

In the next step, we will further consider logic mining to improve the method [27,35–38] and integrate multiple patterns to optimize swarm intelligence algorithms and obtain a more efficient method. In the process of using FKNN to calculate fitness, this method repeatedly calculates the location distance, requires a lot of numerical calculations and takes a large amount of time. The next step is to consider a more efficient classifier to reduce the time cost. In the next step, we will further optimize the model in combination with spiritual Gaussian mutation [39] to improve the accuracy.

Author Contributions: C.Z.: conceptualization, methodology, software, data curation, writing—original draft preparation; M.S.M.K.: supervision, visualization, investigation, review; M.A.M.: review, editing, supervision; J.C.: writing, validation; Y.G.: review, editing. All authors have read and agreed to the published version of the manuscript.

Funding: This research is fully funded and supported by Universiti Sains Malaysia, Short Term Grant, 304/PMATHS/6315655.

Institutional Review Board Statement: Not applicable.

Informed Consent Statement: Not applicable.

Data Availability Statement: Please refer to data availability statements in the UC Irvine Machine Learning Repository at https://archive.ics.uci.edu/ml/ (accessed on 30 April 2022).

Acknowledgments: We would like to acknowledge "Universiti Sains Malaysia, Short Term Grant, 304/PMATHS/6315655" for the support and funding.

Conflicts of Interest: The authors declare no conflict of interest.

Abbreviations

Notation	Explanation
Hybrid SCA	The hybrid algorithm proposed based on the sine cosine algorithm and reverse learning
SCA	Sine cosine algorithm
LSCA	The linear population size reduction sine and cosine algorithm
PSO	Particle swarm optimization
BA	Bat algorithm
SSA	Sparrow search algorithm
SA	Salp swarm algorithm
CGSCA	Cauchy and Gaussian sine cosine optimization
FKNN	Fuzzy k-nearest neighbor

Appendix A

Table A1. Numerical results for three two-class datasets in different MaxFEs when $K = 5$-fold cross-validation.

MaxFEs	Datasets	Metric	ACC	Precision	Sensitive	Specificity	MCC
5	Hepatitis dataset	avg	0.8280	0.5417	0.2142	0.9583	0.2426
		std	0.0660	0.1021	0.1241	0.0417	0.1102
	Bupa dataset	avg	0.6663	0.6245	0.4947	0.7913	0.2985
		std	0.0366	0.0625	0.0949	0.0367	0.0738
	SPECT dataset	avg	0.5934	0.5667	0.7164	0.4515	0.1978
		std	0.1287	0.1115	0.2763	0.1400	0.2842
10	Hepatitis dataset	avg	0.8017	0.6667	0.2564	0.9420	0.2785
		std	0.0501	0.0946	0.0943	0.1004	0.0954
	Bupa dataset	avg	0.6979	0.7000	0.5122	0.8364	0.372
		std	0.0483	0.0486	0.0643	0.0303	0.0514
	SPECT dataset	avg	0.5934	0.5515	0.7655	0.4344	0.2248
		std	0.1077	0.0973	0.1998	0.1534	0.2218
20	Hepatitis dataset	avg	0.8526	0.5833	0.4500	0.9472	0.4149
		std	0.0412	0.0174	0.0500	0.0273	0.0540
	Bupa dataset	avg	0.7576	0.6500	0.5909	0.8409	0.4429
		std	0.0582	0.0284	0.0299	0.0283	0.0303
	SPECT dataset	avg	0.6127	0.5681	0.7524	0.4601	0.2353
		std	0.1038	0.0951	0.0999	0.0706	0.0937

Table A2. Numerical results for three two-class datasets in different-fold cross-validation when $MaxFEs = 5$.

Fold Cross-Validation	Datasets	Metric	ACC	Precision	Sensitive	Specificity	MCC
K = 3	Hepatitis dataset	avg	0.8065	0.5000	0.2001	0.9872	0.2418
		std	0.0559	0.1421	0.0854	0.0222	0.1120
	Bupa dataset	avg	0.6338	0.6775	0.5295	0.8276	0.3751
		std	0.0692	0.1268	0.1104	0.0599	0.1517
	SPECT dataset	avg	0.6617	0.6553	0.7456	0.5931	0.3701
		std	0.1165	0.0998	0.2663	0.1623	0.2376
K = 5	Hepatitis dataset	avg	0.7957	0.5222	0.2762	0.9338	0.2673
		std	0.0186	0.1347	0.1288	0.0426	0.0877
	Bupa dataset	avg	0.6663	0.6245	0.495	0.7913	0.2985
		std	0.0366	0.0625	0.0949	0.0367	0.0738
	SPECT dataset	avg	0.5934	0.5667	0.7164	0.4515	0.1978
		std	0.1287	0.1115	0.2763	0.1400	0.2842
K = 8	Hepatitis dataset	avg	0.8065	0.7222	0.2050	0.9725	0.3000
		std	0.0645	0.2546	0.0556	0.0242	0.0343
	Bupa dataset	avg	0.6717	0.6310	0.4786	0.8075	0.3033
		std	0.0544	0.0938	0.0879	0.0456	0.1204
	SPECT dataset	avg	0.5826	0.5176	0.8714	0.4172	0.3164
		std	0.1134	0.2038	0.1384	0.2307	0.1509

References

1. Wang, C.-N.; Yang, F.-C.; Nguyen, V.T.T.; Nguyen, Q.M.; Huynh, N.T.; Huynh, T.T. Optimal design for compliant mechanism flexure hinges: Bridge-type. *Micromachines* **2021**, *12*, 1304. [CrossRef] [PubMed]
2. Nguyen, T.V.; Huynh, N.-T.; Vu, N.-C.; Kieu, V.N.; Huang, S.-C. Optimizing compliant gripper mechanism design by employing an effective bi-algorithm: fuzzy logic and anfis. *Microsyst. Technol.* **2021**, *27*, 3389–3412. [CrossRef]
3. Chau, N.L.; Dao, T.-P.; Nguyen, V.T.T. Optimal design of a dragonfly-inspired compliant joint for camera positioning system of nanoindentation tester based on a hybrid integration of jaya-anfis. *Math. Probl. Eng.* **2018**, *2018*, 8546095. [CrossRef]
4. Liu, H.; Wen, Z.; Cai, W. Fastpso: Towards efficient swarm intelligence algorithm on GPUs. In Proceedings of the ICPP 2021: 50th International Conference on Parallel Processing, Lemont, IL, USA, 9–12 August 2021.
5. Du, Y.; Chen, W.; Fan, B. Research and application of swarm intelligence algorithm in path planning. *Electron. Meas. Technol.* **2016**, *39*, 65–70.
6. Duan, H.; Qiao, P. Pigeon-inspired optimization: A new swarm intelligence optimizer for air robot path planning. *Int. J. Intell. Comput. Cybern.* **2014**, *7*, 24–37. [CrossRef]
7. Xu, H.; Guan, H.; Liang, A.; Yan, X. A multi-robot pattern formation algorithm based on distributed swarm intelligence. In Proceedings of the 2010 Second International Conference on Computer Engineering and Applications, Bali, Indonesia, 19–21 March 2010; IEEE: Piscataway, NJ, USA, 2010; Volume 1, pp. 71–75.
8. Verma, O.P.; Gupta, S.; Goswami, S.; Jain, S. Opposition based modified particle swarm optimization algorithm. In Proceedings of the 2017 8th International Conference on Computing, Communication and Networking Technologies (ICCCNT), Delhi, India, 3–5 July 2017; IEEE: Piscataway, NJ, USA, 2017; pp. 1–6.
9. Wang, X.; Li, Z.Y.; Xu, G.Y.; Yan, W. Artificial bee colony algorithm based on chaos local search operator. *J. Comput. Appl.* **2012**, *32*, 1033–1036. [CrossRef]
10. Xu, Y.; Zhou, J.; Xue, X.; Fu, W.; Li, C. An adaptively fast fuzzy fractional order pid control for pumped storage hydro unit using improved gravitational search algorithm. *Energy Convers. Manag.* **2016**, *111*, 67–78. [CrossRef]
11. Kaveh, A.; Dadras, A. A novel meta-heuristic optimization algorithm: Thermal exchange optimization. *Adv. Eng. Softw.* **2017**, *110*, 69–84. [CrossRef]
12. Mirjalili, S. Sca: A sine cosine algorithm for solving optimization problems. *Knowl. Based Syst.* **2016**, *96*, 120–133. [CrossRef]
13. Yong, L.I.U, Liang, M.A. Sine cosine algorithm with nonlinear decreasing conversion parameter. *Comput. Eng. Appl.* **2017**, *53*, 1–5.
14. Cong, C.; Liang, M.; Yong, L.; School, B. Quantum sine cosine algorithm for function optimization. *Appl. Res. Comput.* **2017**, *34*, 3214–3218.
15. Abd Elaziz, M.; Oliva, D.; Xiong, S. An improved opposition-based sine cosine algorithm for global optimization. *Expert Syst. Appl. Int. J.* **2017**, *90*, 484–500. [CrossRef]
16. Singh, N.; Singh, S.B. A novel hybrid gwo-sca approach for optimization problems. *Eng. Sci. Technol. Int. J.* **2017**, *20*, 1586–1601. [CrossRef]

17. Abd Elaziz, M.E.; Ewees, A.A.; Oliva, D.; Duan, P.; Xiong, S. A hybrid method of sine cosine algorithm and differential evolution for feature selection. In Proceedings of the international Conference on Neural Information Processing, Long Beach, CA, USA, 4–9 December 2017; Springer: Cham, Switzerland, 2017; pp. 145–155.
18. Rizk-Allah, R.M. Hybridizing sine cosine algorithm with multi-orthogonal search strategy for engineering design problems. *J. Comput. Des. Eng.* **2017**, *5*, 249–273. [CrossRef]
19. Long, W.; Wu, T.; Liang, X.; Xu, S. Solving high-dimensional global optimization problems using an improved sine cosine algorithm. *Expert Syst. Appl.* **2019**, *123*, 108–126. [CrossRef]
20. Nenavath, H.; Jatoth, R.K. Hybridizing sine cosine algorithm with differential evolution for global optimization and object tracking. *Appl. Soft Comput.* **2018**, *62*, 1019–1043. [CrossRef]
21. Wu, S.; Mao, P.; Li, R.; Cai, Z.; Chen, X. Evolving fuzzy k-nearest neighbors using an enhanced sine cosine algorithm: Case study of lupus nephritis. *Comput. Biol. Med.* **2021**, *135*, 104582. [CrossRef]
22. Keller, J.M.; Gray, M.R.; Givens, J.A. A fuzzy k-nearest neighbor algorithm. *IEEE Trans. Syst. Man Cybern.* **1985**, *4*, 580–585. [CrossRef]
23. Lin, J.; He, Q. Mixed strategy to improve sine cosine algorithm. *Appl. Res. Comput.* **2020**, *37*, 6.
24. Wachowiak, M.P.; Smolíková, R.; Zheng, Y.; Zurada, J.M.; Elmaghraby, A.S. An approach to multimodal biomedical image registration utilizing particle swarm optimization. *Evol. Comput. IEEE Trans.* **2004**, *8*, 289–301. [CrossRef]
25. Faris, H.; Mafarja, M.M.; Heidari, A.A.; Aljarah, I.; Fujita, H. An efficient binary salp swarm algorithm with crossover scheme for feature selection problems. *Knowl.-Based Syst.* **2018**, *154*, 43–67. [CrossRef]
26. Jha, K.; Saha, S. Incorporation of multimodal multiobjective optimization in designing a filter based feature selection technique. *Appl. Soft Comput.* **2021**, *98*, 106823. [CrossRef]
27. Kasihmuddin, M.S.M.; Jamaludin, S.Z.M.; Mansor, M.A.; Wahab, H.A.; Ghadzi, S.M.S. Supervised learning perspective in logic mining. *Mathematics* **2020**, *10*, 915. [CrossRef]
28. Yang, G. A modified particle swarm optimizer algorithm. In Proceedings of the 2007 8th International Conference on Electronic Measurement and Instruments, Warsaw, Poland, 1–3 May 2007; IEEE: Piscataway, NJ, USA, 2007; Volume 2, pp. 675–679.
29. Xue, J.; Shen, B. A novel swarm intelligence optimization approach: Sparrow search algorithm. *Syst. Sci. Control. Eng. Open Access J.* **2020**, *8*, 22–34. [CrossRef]
30. Mirjalili, S.; Gandomi, A.H.; Mirjalili, S.Z.; Saremi, S.; Faris, H.; Mirjalili, S.M. Salp swarm algorithm: A bio-inspired optimizer for engineering design problems. *Adv. Eng. Softw.* **2017**, *114*, 163–191. [CrossRef]
31. Mirjalili, S.; Mirjalili, S.M.; Yang, X.S. Binary bat algorithm. *Neural Comput. Appl.* **2014**, *25*, 663–681. [CrossRef]
32. Kumar, N.; Hussain, I.; Singh, B.; Panigrahi, B. Single sensor-based mppt of partially shaded pv system for battery charging by using cauchy and gaussian sine cosine optimization. *IEEE Trans. Energy Convers.* **2017**, *32*, 983–992. [CrossRef]
33. Gupta, S.; Deep, K. A hybrid self-adaptive sine cosine algorithm with opposition based learning. *Expert Syst. Appl.* **2019**, *119*, 210–230. [CrossRef]
34. Wsa, B.; Zq, B.; Aahc, D.; Hc, E.; Ht, F.; Yt, A. Double adaptive weights for stabilization of moth flame optimizer: Balance analysis, engineering cases, and medical diagnosis. *Knowl.-Based Syst.* **2020**, *214*, 106728.
35. Jamaludin, S.Z.M.; Romli, N.A.; Kasihmuddin, M.S.M.; Baharum, A.; Mansor, M.A.; Marsani, M.F. Novel logic mining incorporating log linear approach. *J. King Saud-Univ. -Comput. Inf. Sci.* **2022**. [CrossRef]
36. Jamaludin, S.Z.M.; Kasihmuddin, M.S.M.; Ismail, A.I.M.; Mansor, M.A.; Basir, M.F.M. Energy based logic mining analysis with hopfield neural network for recruitment evaluation. *Entropy* **2020**, *23*, 40. [CrossRef]
37. Zamri, N.E.; Mansor, M.A.; Kasihmuddin, M.S.M.; Alway, A.; Jamaludin, S.Z. .M.; Alzaeemi, S.A. Amazon employees resources access data extraction via clonal selection algorithm and logic mining approach. *Entropy* **2020**, *22*, 596. [CrossRef]
38. Alway, A.; Zamri, N.E.; Kasihmuddin, M.S.M.; Mansor, A.; Sathasivam, S. Palm oil trend analysis via logic mining with discrete hopfield neural network. *Pertanika J. Sci. Technol.* **2020**, *28*, 967–981.
39. Zhou, W.; Wang, P.; Heidari, A.A.; Zhao, X.; Chen, H. Spiral gaussian mutation sine cosine algorithm: Framework and comprehensive performance optimization. *Expert Syst. Appl.* **2022**, *209*, 118372. [CrossRef]

mathematics

Review

Randomized Response Techniques: A Systematic Review from the Pioneering Work of Warner (1965) to the Present

Truong-Nhat Le [1], Shen-Ming Lee [2], Phuoc-Loc Tran [3] and Chin-Shang Li [4,*]

1 Faculty of Mathematics and Statistics, Ton Duc Thang University, Ho Chi Minh City, Vietnam; letruongnhat@tdtu.edu.vn
2 Department of Statistics, Feng Chia University, Taichung 40724, Taiwan; smlee@mail.fcu.edu.tw
3 Department of Mathematics, College of Natural Science, Can Tho University, Can Tho 900000, Vietnam; tploc@ctu.edu.vn
4 School of Nursing, The State University of New York, Buffalo, NY 14214, USA
* Correspondence: csli2003@gmail.com or chinshan@buffalo.edu

Abstract: The randomized response technique is one of the most commonly used indirect questioning methods to collect data on sensitive characteristics in survey research covering a wide variety of statistical applications including, e.g., behavioral science, socio-economic, psychological, epidemiology, biomedical, and public health research disciplines. After nearly six decades since the technique was invented, many improvements of the randomized response techniques have appeared in the literature. This work provides several different aspects of improvements of the original randomized response work of Warner, as well as statistical methods used in the RR problems.

Keywords: indirect questioning; non-randomized response technique; randomized response technique; sensitive attribute; statistical methods

MSC: 62F12; 62F15; 62J12

Citation: Le, T.-N.; Lee, S.-M.; Tran, P.-L.; Li, C.-S. Randomized Response Techniques: A Systematic Review from the Pioneering Work of Warner (1965) to the Present. *Mathematics* **2023**, *11*, 1718. https://doi.org/10.3390/math11071718

Academic Editor: Christophe Chesneau

Received: 12 January 2023
Revised: 24 March 2023
Accepted: 1 April 2023
Published: 3 April 2023

1. Introduction to Randomized Response Techniques

Sample surveys are commonly used to collect data for studies in a wide range of statistical applications such as behavioral science, socio-economic, psychological, epidemiological, biomedical, and public health research disciplines. Mail surveys, telephone surveys, and personal interviews (face-to-face interviews) are the commonly used traditional data-collection methods; see, e.g., [1]. The data collected from these surveys are used to estimate and make statistical inferences about the unknown population parameters of interest, e.g., the population proportion of individuals with a certain property appearing in most related research, the population honest response rate [2,3], and the sensitivity level of a question of interest; in other words, the population proportion of individuals considering the question of interest to be sensitive [4–6]. Because of that, researchers and practitioners are particularly interested in the reliability of collected data (e.g., non-response rate and dishonest answer rate) in studies using sample surveys, but more so while the topics of investigation involve, e.g., threatening, embarrassing, stigmatizing, highly personal, and even incriminating issues. The aforementioned issues are collectively referred to as sensitive characteristics (attributes, behaviors, features, traits). For example, people consider abortion behavior, cheating on examinations, discrimination, domestic violence, drug use, gambling, illegal income, plagiarism, political opinions, sexual behavior, tax evasion, and other illicit behaviors to be sensitive. Refer to [7] for a more detailed classification of the three types of sensitive questions.

Research on sensitive issues is increasingly receiving the attention of many researchers, practitioners, and social organizations. For instance, in the study by Krumpal and Voss [8], the General Social Survey (Allgemeine Beölkerungsumfrage der Sozialwissenschaften—ALLBUS) in Germany asked respondents whether they have committed tax evasion and shoplifting, dodged fares, or driven drunk. In the United States, the National Survey on Drug Use and Health (NSDUH) and the General Social Survey (GSS) routinely require surveyees to self-report on sensitive issues, e.g., sexual habits or drug use. The Taiwan Social Change Survey (TSCS) conducted face-to-face interviews about sexual orientation [9,10], the presidential election [11], monthly income [12], and extramarital relationships [13,14]. Estimating the prevalence of such sensitive features is of great importance in helping researchers to build scientific knowledge and recommend necessary strategies to the authorities.

It is widely accepted that most survey participants consider the aforementioned issues to be secret, shameful, and even illegal. Then, when participating in surveys that use traditional data-collection methods including, e.g., computer-assisted self-interviewing or telephone interviewing and self-administered questionnaires with paper and pencil, to avoid being stigmatized by society or punished by the government, and to leave a good impression on others, survey respondents tend to ignore sensitive questions, which causes a non-response bias problem, or they answer these sensitive questions according to socially desirable behaviors and attitudes, which causes a social desirability bias problem. See, e.g., [7,15,16]. For example, a student is directly asked a question about a socially undesirable behavior: "Have you ever cheated on examinations?". Naturally, regardless of whether she/he has ever cheated on examinations or not, it is more likely she/he may deny it. Refer to [17] for more information on this sensitive topic. Or, in a validation study by Preisendörfer and Wolter [18], where the researchers knew the true answers in advance, 42 percent (face-to-face interviews) and 33 percent (mail survey) of respondents did not admit that they had been convicted. Likewise, van der Heijden et al. [19] conducted a face-to-face interview, and 75 percent of respondents who committed welfare or unemployment benefits fraud denied doing so. As another real example, Hsieh and Perri [20] pointed out that the proportion of non-heterosexual subjects present in a community is generally underestimated if respondents have to answer sensitive questions directly. In contrast, respondents tend to present themselves positively by displaying behaviors and attitudes that conform to social norms, such as engaging in charitable activities, volunteering, and eating healthily. See, e.g., [1]. In general, socially desirable attributes are over-reported while socially undesirable attributes are under-reported when data are collected by direct interrogation methods. Therefore, the quality of data collected through direct questions on such topics is not guaranteed. As a result, collected data may produce inaccurate estimated results and invalid inferences about the sensitive behavior under investigation.

In an effort to reduce potential bias due to social desirability response and non-response and thereby improve the reliability of data gathered from responses to sensitive questions for better estimation of the population proportion of individuals who have a sensitive characteristic, various indirect questioning techniques (IQTs) have been proposed by, e.g., [21–24]. Among them, some commonly used techniques are the randomized response (RR) technique (RRT) [25], the unmatched count technique—also called the item count technique—unmatched block design, or block total response [26,27], and the triangular model (TRM) and crosswise model (CWM) [28], which are two of the non-randomized response (NRR) techniques (NRRTs). These techniques have been developed to ensure anonymity as well as minimize the feelings of jeopardy for survey respondents when answering sensitive questions. That is what motivates them to answer honestly sensitive questions.

Blair et al. [29] provided an excellent review of the RRTs and classified them into mirrored question, forced response, disguised response, and unrelated question techniques. Among these techniques, Sungkawichai et al. [30] extended the classical forced RRT by using an arbitrary random variable. Tian and Tang [31] also presented another classification for the RRTs. Interested readers may also refer to the monographs on the RRTs and other alternative IQTs by [21,32–37] for comprehensive reviews. Tian and Tang [31] contributed an excellent monograph to the NRRT until 2013. Next, we present a review of RRTs from the work of Warner [25] to the present.

2. Warner's Randomized Response Design and Some Direct Extensions

The first version of the RRT, conceived by Warner [25] in 1965, is to increase the response rate and eliminate dishonest responses for the estimation of the proportion of individuals in a population bearing some sensitive attribute. The main idea of the RRT is to add random noise to respondents' answers for the protection of their privacy. Specifically, according to the idea of Warner [25], two questions were designed: a sensitive question of interest and its complementary question. That is why the original design of [25] is also known as a "related-question RR design". For example,

A : Have you ever had a one-night stand through a dating website or mobile app (with probability p of selecting this question).

$\overline{\mathbf{A}}$: Have you never had a one-night stand through a dating website or mobile app (with probability $1-p$ of selecting this question).

Suppose we wish to estimate the proportion θ of people belonging to a sensitive group, called group A. A simple random sample of size n is selected from the population. Each surveyee uses the outcome generated by a randomization device, e.g., spinners, dice, or random number generators, which is not observed by the interviewer, to determine which question to honestly answer "Yes" or "No" to. The interviewee responds to statements **A** and $\overline{\mathbf{A}}$ with probabilities p and $1-p$, respectively. Let n_1 be the number of individuals responding "Yes". The parameter θ is estimated based on the indirect responses of all individuals via the maximum likelihood (ML) estimator $\widehat{\theta}_W = \frac{p-1}{2p-1} + \frac{n_1}{n(2p-1)}$ with $\mathrm{Var}(\widehat{\theta}_W) = \frac{\theta(1-\theta)}{n} + \frac{p(1-p)}{n(2p-1)^2}$ as long as $p \neq 0.5$. $\widehat{\theta}_W$ is then an unbiased estimator of θ and used to replace θ to obtain an estimator of $\mathrm{Var}(\widehat{\theta}_W)$. See Appendix A.1. Because the surveyor does not know which question has been answered by the interviewee, the respondent can feel more comfortable with answering sensitive questions without fear of personal privacy being revealed. It makes the respondent more likely to give an honest response to the sensitive question in case she/he carries that sensitive characteristic. In fact, a validation study by Lensvelt-Mulders et al. [38] showed that, for sensitive questions, the RRT yields a more valid estimation of prevalence in comparison to other methods.

Despite solving many of the problems posed earlier, the original RR design of Warner [25] has certain limitations. For example, Warner's model does not work for $p = 0.5$. However, the inefficiency of Warner's model is its most serious limitation when compared with the design of *direct questioning* (DQ), which is clearly demonstrated in Tian and Tang [31]. The variance of the estimator $\widehat{\theta}$ of θ by the DQ design is $\mathrm{Var}(\widehat{\theta}) = \frac{\theta(1-\theta)}{n}$, based on the binomial distribution with parameters n and θ. Using the RR design of Warner [25] induces the extra variance, $\frac{p(1-p)}{n(2p-1)^2}$, which is the variance due to the randomization device, compared to $\mathrm{Var}(\widehat{\theta})$. Accordingly, $\widehat{\theta}_W$ is less efficient than $\widehat{\theta}$. During nearly six decades of efforts to overcome these limitations and improve computational efficiency, quite a few alternative RR models have been proposed and empirically applied. For instance, just to name a few, Horvitz et al. [39] and Greenberg et al. [40] combined a sensitive question of interest and another question that is innocuous and completely unrelated to the sensitive topic to propose an unrelated-question RR design. Chaudhuri and Mukerjee [41] introduced optional RRTs. Bhargava and Singh [42] introduced a modified randomization device for the RR design of [25]. Kim and Warde [43] proposed a stratified RR design of [25].

Abbasi et al. [44] proposed a partial RRT to gather reliable sensitive data for the estimation of the proportion of a population in a ranked set sampling scheme using auxiliary information. The authors provided respondents the option of both "direct" and "randomized" responses for the sensitive question in order to increase their confidence/co-operation. Zapata et al. [45] proposed an electronic randomization device, which is able to directly produce a response when utilized by a respondent. The proposed randomization device builds upon the model of Warner [25] by utilizing a variation on the spinner approach. However, instead of a physical spinner, they have developed a model, which utilizes the Python programming language to electronically replicate the functionality of a spinner with the selection of a button, with the user simply being requested to choose either a "Red" or "Green" button depending on his/her status of possessing a sensitive characteristic.

3. Some Aspects Extended from Warner's Randomized Response Design

3.1. Unrelated-Question Randomized Response Design

Motivated by the case where the model of Warner [25] does not work when $p = 0.5$, Horvitz et al. [39] and Greenberg et al. [40] modified Warner's method by incorporating a non-sensitive question within a sensitive question. Along with that, some respondents find the questions in the design of [25] sensitive or uncomfortable to answer even if a randomization device is used. Two questions in the unrelated-question design, for example, are given as follows:

A : Have you ever had a one-night stand through a dating website or mobile app (with probability p of selecting this question).

C : Were you born between January and September (with probability $1 - p$ of selecting this question).

Again, each respondent selected in the sample uses a device such as a deck of cards to determine the question to which she/he responds. Let c_0 be the true proportion of individuals with non-sensitive characteristic. If c_0 is known, [39,40] proposed the unbiased estimator $\widehat{\theta}_{U_1} = \frac{n_1/n-(1-p)c_0}{p}$ for θ. In the case where c_0 is unknown, they considered two independent samples of sizes n_1^* and n_2^* with $n = n_1^* + n_2^*$. In each sample, the above procedure is carried out. Assume that the probabilities of selecting the designed sensitive question in the samples of sizes n_1^* and n_2^* are p_1 and p_2, respectively, with $p_1 \neq p_2$. They proposed the unbiased estimator $\widehat{\theta}_{U_2} = \frac{(1-p_2)m_1/n_1^*-(1-p_1)m_2/n_2^*}{p_1-p_2}$ for θ, where m_1 and m_2 are the numbers of respondents who answer "Yes" in the first and second samples, respectively. Because the modified method boosts the degree of privacy, it may receive greater cooperation from respondents. According to Edgell et al. [46], compared to the RRT of Warner [25], the unrelated-question RRT is much more statistically efficient and becomes even more so when the population parameters of the non-sensitive question are known. To assess whether respondents would honestly respond to the non-sensitive question, even if it could be interpreted as socially undesirable when paired with a sensitive question, the researchers conducted a study using an unrelated-question RRT. Shaw and Chaudhuri [47] utilized the approach of the inverse hypergeometric trial to improve the revised unrelated characteristics model device of Chaudhuri and Shaw [48]. Lee et al. [14] introduced a data-collection method for survey on sensitive issues in which both the unrelated-question RRT and the DQ design are combined. They proposed two new methods for estimating the proportion of respondents possessing the sensitive attribute under a missing data setup.

3.2. Some Kind of Two-Stage Randomized Response Design

In 1990, Mangat and Singh [49] proposed a two-stage RR procedure in which two randomization devices, R_1 and R_2, are used. In the first stage, each survey participant is asked to use the randomization device R_1, such as a well-shuffled deck of cards, to select one from the following two statements:

A : I belong to group A.

C : go to the randomization device R_2.

The two statements are selected with probabilities p_0 and $1 - p_0$, respectively. In the second stage, the design of Warner [25] is used. An unbiased estimator of θ is shown as $\widehat{\theta}_{MS} = \frac{n_1/n-(1-p_0)(1-p)}{2p-1+2p_0(1-p)}$ with $\mathrm{Var}(\widehat{\theta}_{MS}) = \frac{\theta(1-\theta)}{n} + \frac{(1-p)(1-p_0)\{1-(1-p)(1-p_0)\}}{n\{2p-1+2p_0(1-p)\}^2}$. It is shown that compared to the RR design of Warner [25], the two-stage RR design is more efficient.

Mangat [50] proposed another RR model in which each interviewee is asked to respond "Yes" if she/he were in the sensitive group; she/he is guided to utilize the device of Warner [25] otherwise. It is shown that the RR design of Mangat [50] is more efficient in comparison to the RR designs of Warner [25] and Mangat and Singh [49]. Specially, for this RR design, an unbiased estimator of θ and its variance are given by $\widehat{\theta}_M = \frac{n_1/n-(1-p)}{p}$ with $\text{Var}(\widehat{\theta}_M) = \frac{\lambda_M(1-\lambda_M)}{np^2}$, respectively, where, $\lambda_M = \theta + (1-p)(1-\theta)$. According to the unrelated-question model of Horvitz et al. [39] and the model of Mangat and Singh [49], Chang and Liang [51] conducted a new two-stage unrelated RR design. Gjestvang and Singh [52] adjusted the parameters of the randomization device to propose a more efficient RR model than the models of [25,49,50] to refine the two-stage randomization. Huang [3] used the two-stage RR procedure to improve efficiency of the RR procedure of [25]. Recently, Chang et al. [2] utilized logistic regression to estimate the prevalence of a sensitive feature with a categorical or quantitative explanatory variable.

A new two-stage unrelated RR model was proposed by Vishwakarma et al. [53] to estimate the mean number of individuals in a given population who have a rare sensitive attribute by using Poisson probability distribution, when the proportion of rare non-sensitive unrelated attribute is known and unknown.

3.3. The Generalized Randomized Response Design of Christofides and Some Direct Extensions

In 2003, Christofides [54] provided the generalized RR (GRR) design of a single sensitive question to let respondents have more than two response options and be more protective toward their privacy. It is shown that the GRR design is more efficient in comparison to the RR design of Warner [25]. Let a respondent have one of the sensitive and non-sensitive attributes. If the respondent had the sensitive attribute, let her/him remember the number $L+1$; otherwise, let her/him remember the number 0. Next, she/he utilizes a randomization device to generate a random integer from 1 to L with probability distribution $\boldsymbol{P} = (P_1, P_2, \ldots, P_L)$, where $\sum_{j=1}^{L} P_j = 1$. This number is not reported directly to the surveyor. If the respondent had the sensitive attribute, she/he only provides the answer how far this number is away from $L+1$; otherwise, provide the answer how far this number is away from 0.

Assume that Y_i, $i = 1, 2, \ldots, n$, is respondent i taking the value $L+1$ if having the sensitive attribute and 0 otherwise. T_i is a random integer generated by respondent i using the randomization device to obtain the value j with probability $P_j = P(T_i = j)$, $j = 1, 2, \ldots, L$. Assume that θ is the population proportion of the sensitive trait. Y_i has the Bernoulli distribution with probability $\theta = P(Y_i = L+1)$ and probability $1-\theta = P(Y_i = 0)$, denoted by $Y_i \sim (L+1) \times B(1,\theta)$, where $B(1,\theta)$ denotes the Bernoulli distribution of a random variable taking the value 1 with probability θ and 0 with probability $1-\theta$. See Figure 1 of Lee et al. [55] for illustration of the probability mass functions (pmfs) for Y_i and T_i, respectively. From the GRR design of Christofides [54], the ith respondent reports how far Y_i is away from T_i. Thus, this respondent only provides the value of $D_i = |Y_i - T_i|$, whose pmf is $P(D_i = d) = (1-\theta)P_d + \theta P_{L+1-d}$, $i = 1, 2, \ldots, n$, $d = 1, 2, \ldots, L$. Christofides [54] obtained the expectation of D_i, $\text{E}(D_i) = \text{E}(T_i) + \theta(L+1-2\text{E}(T_i))$, and took $\overline{D} = \sum_{j=1}^{n} D_j/n$ to replace $\text{E}(D_i)$. Because the expectation of T_i is known, $\widehat{\theta}_C = \frac{\overline{D}-\text{E}(T_i)}{L+1-2\text{E}(T_i)}$ is used as an estimator of θ. Similarly, it is easy to verify the variance of D_i as $\text{Var}(D_i) = \text{Var}(T_i) + \theta(1-\theta)(L+1-2\text{E}(T_i))^2$. Hence, Christofides [54] showed $\text{Var}(\widehat{\theta}_C) = \frac{\theta(1-\theta)}{n} + \frac{\text{Var}(T_i)}{n(L+1-2\text{E}(T_i))^2}$. See Appendix A.2. θ can be replaced by $\widehat{\theta}_C$ to obtain an estimator of $\text{Var}(\widehat{\theta}_C)$. The first and second terms of $\text{Var}(\widehat{\theta}_C)$ are the variance because of random sampling and the variance due to the randomization procedure, respectively. If choosing suitable values for $P_1, P_2, \ldots, P_L$ such that $\frac{\text{Var}(T_i)}{n(L+1-2\text{E}(T_i))^2} < \frac{p(1-p)}{n(2p-1)^2}$, then $\widehat{\theta}_C$ is more efficient than $\widehat{\theta}_W$. When $n \to \infty$, $\widehat{\theta}_C$ is asymptotically normally distributed, and, hence, interval estimation can be performed. When $L = 2$, $P_1 = p$ (and $P_2 = 1-p$) and, hence, this GRR model is reduced to the RR model of Warner [25]. Furthermore, when $L \geq 3$, the mean squared error of $\widehat{\theta}_C$ is smaller in comparison to that of $\widehat{\theta}_W$ [54].

Christofides [54] also showed that $\mathrm{Var}(\widehat{\theta}_C)$ can be reduced by multiple use of the randomization device. In this instance, individual i is asked to use the randomization device m_i times. The m_i repetitions of the procedure must be independent of each other. Let T_{ij} be the number produced by individual i using the randomization device at the jth time. Suppose that $D_{ij} = |Y_i - T_{ij}|$ is the reported number. Define $\widehat{\theta}_{m.} = \frac{\overline{D}_{m.} - \mathrm{E}(T)}{L+1-2\mathrm{E}(T)}$, where $\overline{D}_{m.} = (\sum_{i=1}^{n} m_i)^{-1} \sum_{i=1}^{n} \sum_{j=1}^{m_i} D_{ij}$. Assume that T has the same distribution as the T_{ij}'s, $j = 1, 2, \ldots, m_i$, $i = 1, 2, \ldots, n$. $\widehat{\theta}_{m.}$ is shown to be an unbiased estimator of θ with

$$\mathrm{Var}(\widehat{\theta}_{m.}) = \frac{\sum_{i=1}^{n} {m_i}^2}{(\sum_{i=1}^{n} m_i)^2}\theta(1-\theta) + \frac{1}{\sum_{i=1}^{n} m_i} \frac{\mathrm{Var}(T)}{[L+1-2\mathrm{E}(T)]^2}.$$

In the special case where when $m_i = m$, $i = 1, 2, \ldots, n$, i.e., each respondent is asked to use the randomization device m times,

$$\mathrm{Var}(\widehat{\theta}_{m.}) = \frac{\theta(1-\theta)}{n} + \frac{\mathrm{Var}(T)}{mn[L+1-2\mathrm{E}(T)]^2}.$$

Thus, when $m_i = m$, $i = 1, 2, \ldots, n$, $\mathrm{Var}(\widehat{\theta}_{m.})$ is then smaller via multiple use of the randomization device in comparison to $\mathrm{Var}(\widehat{\theta}_C) = \frac{\theta(1-\theta)}{n} + \frac{\mathrm{Var}(T)}{n[L+1-2\mathrm{E}(T)]^2}$ in Christofides [54].

Christofides [54] proposed an improved modification of the RR design of Warner [25] to estimate an unknown proportion of population bearing a sensitive characteristic in a given community. Chaudhuri [56] presented methods to estimate an unknown population proportion of a sensitive attribute when RR data of Christofides [57] are available from unequal probability samples. Christofides [58] extended the GRR model of Christofides [54] to the case of stratified sampling. Christofides [57] extended the GRR model of [54] by proposing an RRTthat allows for estimation of the population proportion of subjects with two sensitive attributes simultaneously. Lee et al. [59] proposed a special model of the GRR version of Christofides [57], called a simple model. They also proposed a so-called crossed model that is more efficient compared to the simple model. Perri et al. [60] applied the crossed model to investigate the phenomena of the induced abortion and illegal immigration simultaneously in Calabria, Italy and also attested to the fact that the crossed model is more efficient.

3.4. *Sensitive Characteristics with More Than One Category*

It is in the RR model of Warner [25] supposed that every individual in a population is in either the sensitive group or the non-sensitive group, and the population proportion of subjects in the sensitive group is estimated by a survey. Abul-Ela et al. [61] improved the RR design of Warner [25] for the trichotomous population with at least one sensitive group. Hsieh et al. [9] extended the GRR design [54] to the case where there are more than two categories and estimated the proportion of each category by employing the ML method. Hsieh and Lukusa [10] used the ML method and Bayesian approach to estimate the proportion of each group in a trichotomous population. The population with ℓ ($\ell \geq 3$) related mutually exclusive groups, with at least one and at most $\ell - 1$ of them being sensitive, was also extended by, e.g., Hsieh et al. [9] and Liu and Chow [62]. Recently, Hsieh et al. [12] provided the two-stage multilevel RRT based on an extension of the GRR design in [9] to collect the monthly income data.

3.5. *Simultaneous Study of Multiple Sensitive Characteristics*

Some works have estimated the population proportion of two sensitive features simultaneously. Barksdale [63] proposed some RRTs to collect data for analysis to investigate two sensitive dichotomous traits. Drane [64] explored the problem of testing independence between two sensitive dichotomous characteristics by utilizing repeated applications of various RRTs for single attribute. Fox and Tracy [65] estimated the correlation between two sensitive traits. Christofides [57] introduced an RRT to estimate the proportion of subjects with two sensitive attributes simultaneously. Lee et al. [59] extended the RR design in [25] to capture two sensitive characteristics. Afterwards, Ewemooje [66] improved the procedure to estimate the population proportion of two sensitive features at a time by utilizing equal probabilities of protection on the randomization devices. It has been shown that the proposed model is more efficient compared to the model of Lee et al. [59] in some cases. Ewemooje and Amahia [67,68] extended the work of Mangat [50] to propose new and more efficient estimators of the population proportion of respondents bearing two related sensitive traits in survey sampling. Batool and Shabbir [69] considered the problem of estimating the several proportions of two inter-dependent sensitive attributes prevailing in a given population. Xu et al. [70] proposed a new, unique unrelated-question RR model, where each card contains two questions, either both questions on the sensitive characteristics or both questions on the unrelated characteristics. Chung et al. [71] implemented the RRT with multiple sensitive traits and utilized a Bayesian approach to estimate covariance matrices with incomplete information. Chu et al. [72] proposed a new statistical method to combine the RRT, probit modeling, and Bayesian analysis to analyze large-scale online surveys of multiple binary RRs. Recently, Hsieh and Perri [20] provided a logistic regression extension for the RR *simple* and *crossed models* to discuss two related sensitive attributes in [59].

3.6. Randomized Response Techniques for Quantitative Sensitive Data

Greenberg et al. [73] extended the RRT of reducing respondent bias in obtaining answers to sensitive questions from a situation where the response is categorical to that in which the response is quantitative. Gupta et al. [74] estimated the expected mean of the stigmatized variable by using an optional RR sampling. By using double sampling, Grewal et al. [75] estimated the expected mean of a sensitive quantitative variable. Hussain and Shabbir [76] provided an unbiased estimator of the population mean of a sensitive quantitative variable based on multiple selections of numbers from a scrambling distribution to confound the actual response on a sensitive variable with some unrelated variable. Hsieh et al. [12] estimated the personal monthly mean income by using a two-stage multilevel RRT with proportional odds (PO) models.

Hussain et al. [77] proposed a new RR model to estimate the population total of a sensitive variable of quantitative nature. To achieve the objective, they introduced additive scrambling mechanism when sample is drawn through probability proportional to size sampling scheme. Gupta et al. [78] proposed an optional enhanced trust (OET) quantitative RRT model to mitigates the effect of respondents' lack of trust by allowing them who do not trust the traditional additive RRT model to use an alternative scrambling technique. They utilized a combined measure of respondent privacy and model efficiency to demonstrate both theoretically and empirically that the proposed OET model is superior to the traditional model of Warner [79].

3.7. Applications of Randomized Response Techniques to Real Data

Applications of RRTs to real data related to sensitive topics can be found in various works, such as illegitimacy of offspring [40], drug use [72,80–82], incidence of induced abortions [60,62,83,84], fraudulent acts [19,85–88], racism [89,90], sexual behavior [2,9,10,20,55,91–93], cheating in examinations [94], monthly income [12], illegal immigration [95], and conservation [23,24]. In recent years, many researchers have been attracted to using RRTs to collect data on fraudulent behaviors during the COVID-19 pandemic. For example, Mieth et al. [96] used indirect questions to provide prevalence estimates for personal hygiene behavior during the early stages of the COVID-19 pandemic in Germany in 2020. Reiber et al. [97] conducted a survey on intimate partner violence during the COVID-19 pandemic, along with various other studies.

Striegel et al. [98] estimated the prevalence of doping and illicit drug abuse. They used a two-sided z-test to compare the anonymous standardized questionnaire and RRT results with the respective official German National Anti-Doping Agency data on the prevalence of doping. Christiansen et al. [99] measured the prevalence of doping in recreational sport by using the RRT. Mielecka-Kubień and Toniszewski [100] estimated the prevalence of illicit drug use among high school students living in the Silesian voivodship (Poland) by using either the RRTs of forced response design or the Liu-Chow method [101]. Burgstaller et al. [102] argued that the RRT and list experiments would validate and improve prevalence estimates of undeclared work that is defined as a taxable and essentially legal economic activity, but that is not intentionally reported to the relevant authority. They considered an undeclared work case in Germany to demonstrate the strengths and weaknesses of conventional surveys. Furthermore, readers can refer to [22,32] for more studies using IQT for real data.

3.8. *Statistical Methods for Randomized Response Data*

The two well-known estimation methods, frequentist and Bayesian, in statistics have been applied by several authors RR data.

3.8.1. Frequentist Methods

After collecting data through RR designs, estimation and statistical inference of unknown population parameters of interest, such as the proportion of sensitive characteristics, honest response rate, and sensitivity level of questions, can be carried out. In the frequentist approach, the commonly used classical methods are the ML method and method of moments (MM). A common problem with these two methods is that the estimated parameter value may be out of the true parameter space. For example, the estimate of the proportion of a sensitive feature may fall outside the interval $[0, 1]$; see, e.g., [20,33,103]. In addition, the calculation of ML estimates is sometimes more complicated and requires numerical methods. The expectation–maximization (EM) method [104] can be used to address this issue; see, e.g., [22,105–107]. Specifically, Bourke and Moran [105] presented the particular applicability of the EM algorithm in obtaining ML estimates of proportions where the sensitive data are collected by using an RR design. They considered two kinds of RR designs: related-question [25] and unrelated-question [40] designs. van den Hout and Kooiman [107] developed a fast and straightforward EM algorithm to obtain ML estimates of the parameters of a linear regression model with categorical covariates subject to RR. Groenitz [22] derived a general EM algorithm to obtain general ML estimates of the parameters of a logistic regression model. Recently, to obtain an efficient estimator of the proportion of a sensitive characteristic and to investigate the association between the sensitive characteristic or latent variable and an observed binary variable, Lee et al. [106] proposed a combination of Warner's RRT [25] and a latent class model. An EM algorithm is proposed to estimate the model parameters. However, the EM method also has its own weaknesses, such as its tendency to fail to converge to the true value; see, e.g., [108].

3.8.2. Bayesian Method

Some authors have suggested using the Bayesian method to deal with the weaknesses and improve the efficiency of previous estimation methods in cases where some prior information on parameters is available. The major references on the RRT in the Bayesian framework are listed below. Winkler and Franklin [84] proposed a seminal work in which the Bayesian approach was used to analyze RR data. Hussain et al. [109], Migon and Tachibana [110], and a bunch of other authors then used the Bayesian method to estimate the population proportion of a sensitive trait in Warner's RR design [25]. Pitz [111] used a Bayesian analysis of the model of Fidler and Kleiknecht [112] to give a more useful estimation when the sample size is not large or the response proportions are extreme. O'hagan [113] employed a non-parametric approach to derive Bayes linear estimators.

Oh [114] and Unnikrishnan and Kunte [115] used the Bayesian method through a Gibbs sampling algorithm to estimate parameters of interest by introducing latent variables to an RR model. Bar-lev et al. [103] presented a common conjugate prior structure for some RR models. Hussain and Shabbir [116] used a stratified random sampling protocol and the Bayesian method to estimate the population proportion of a sensitive feature. Song and Kim [117] addressed the Bayesian formulation of two types of Poisson regression models for RR sum score variables under the self-protection assumption. Adepetun and Adewara [118] utilized both Kumaraswamy and generalised beta prior distributions to propose the Bayesian estimators of the population proportion of a stigmatized characteristic when data were obtained via the RRT of Kim and Warde [43]. Groenitz [119] proposed a design method for multiple-choice sensitive features and provided the Bayesian method combined with Gibbs sampling and Markov chain Monte Carlo (MCMC) to estimate the population proportions of multichotomous sensitive features. Song and Kim [120] employed the RRT to propose a Bayesian estimation of the rate of a rare sensitive trait. Mehta and Aggarwal [4] and Narjis and Shabbir [5] provided Bayesian estimation of a sensitivity level and the population proportion of a sensitive attribute of optional unrelated-question RR models.

Recently, Nandram and Yu [108] introduced a Bayesian analysis of spare counts gathered from the unrelated-question design. More recently, Hsieh and Lukusa [10] implemented a Bayesian framework for multilevel RR data and compared the Bayesian method with the ML method for estimating the population proportion of individuals aged 18–54 years who self-reported as bisexual and homosexual among Taiwanese. Hsieh and Perri [20] proposed a Gibbs sampling algorithm to estimate the population proportion of the sensitive characteristic θ. They compared, in connection with the GRR data-collection model of [54], the MM, ML, and Bayesian methods for the estimation of the population proportion of non-heterosexuals aged 20 years or older for the Taiwanese population, gender groups, and age groups. Specifically, suppose that $\{(D_i, Y_i) : i = 1, 2, \ldots, n\}$ are available. The joint pmf of (D_i, Y_i) is given by $P(D_i = d_i, Y_i = y_i) = \left(P_{L+1-d_i}\theta\right)^{I(y_i=L+1)}\left(P_{d_i}(1-\theta)\right)^{I(y_i=0)}$, where $I(\cdot)$ is an indicator function. Given $\mathcal{D}^* = \{(d_i, y_i) : i = 1, 2, \ldots, n\}$, the likelihood function can be obtained as $\mathcal{L}^*(\theta|\mathcal{D}^*) = \theta^{\sum_{i=1}^n I(y_i=L+1)}(1-\theta)^{\sum_{i=1}^n I(y_i=0)}\prod_{i=1}^n P_{L+1-d_i}^{I(y_i=L+1)} P_{d_i}^{I(y_i=0)}$. Thus, given that a beta prior distribution with parameters α_1 and α_2, denoted by $\theta \sim \text{Beta}(\alpha_1, \alpha_2)$, is assigned to θ, [20] derived the conditional posterior distribution of θ given $\mathcal{D}^*$ as $\theta|\mathcal{D}^* \sim \text{Beta}(\alpha_1 + \sum_{i=1}^n I(y_i = L+1), \alpha_2 + \sum_{i=1}^n I(y_i = 0))$. However, in practice, through the GRR design of [54], only $\boldsymbol{d} = (d_1, d_2, \ldots, d_n)$ can be obtained, so, [20] treated $\boldsymbol{Y} = (Y_1, Y_2, \ldots, Y_n)$ as latent variables to derive the conditional distribution of Y_i given θ and $D_i = d_i$. The probability of $Y_i = L+1$ given θ and $D_i = d_i$ is $p(\theta, d_i) = P(Y_i = L+1|\theta, D_i = d_i) = \frac{P_{L+1-d_i}\theta}{P_{L+1-d_i}\theta + P_{d_i}(1-\theta)}$, $i = 1, 2, \ldots, n$. The conditional distribution of Y_i given θ and $D_i = d_i$ is then a Bernoulli distribution with probability $p(\theta, d_i)$ of $Y_i = L+1$ and probability $1 - p(\theta, d_i)$ of $Y_i = 0$, denoted by $Y_i|\theta, D_i = d_i \sim (L+1) \times B(1, p(\theta, d_i)), i = 1, 2, \ldots, n$.

Chung et al. [71] used a Bayesian approach to estimate covariance matrices with incomplete information in a population with multiple sensitive characteristics. According to the idea of Hsieh and Perri [20], Lee et al. [55] used the Bayesian estimation method through data augmentation and MCMC to estimate the prevalence of the population possessing the sensitive attribute and the distribution of a categorical or quantitative variable in each of the non-sensitive and sensitive groups. The deviance information criterion and marginal likelihood are employed to select a suitable model to describe the association of the sensitive characteristic with the auxiliary random variable in this work. Chu et al. [72] combined the RRT, probit modeling, and Bayesian approach to analyze large-scale online surveys of multiple binary RRs.

In 2023, Ewemooje et al. [82] proposed a new Bayesian estimation method for Alternative Tripartite RRTs to gain the proportion of individuals belonging to a sensitive character. The proposed Bayesian estimators used the Kumaraswamy and the generalized beta prior distributions. A comparison of the classical technique and Bayesian method is provided in [82].

3.9. Use of Auxiliary Information in Randomized Response Problems

3.9.1. Regression Models for Randomized Response Data

In sample surveys on sensitive topics, besides sensitive information of interest collected by IQTs, information on some auxiliary variables is also obtained. The data of these auxiliary variables are collected by using direct questioning techniques (DQTs). Using these auxiliary variables reasonably to improve computational efficiency is an important issue that has received the attention of several authors. The following is a brief summary of the use of auxiliary variables in sensitive variable research.

In 1983, Maddala [81] employed a logit model to investigate the relationships between auxiliary variables and randomized response survey data through the RR design of Warner [25]. The author obtained ML model parameter estimates using the Newton–Raphson iterative procedure. An estimate of the asymptotic covariance matrix was shown. This logit model was then illustrated for the first time in real data by Kerkvliet [121] in the study of college students' cocaine use at two public universities in the United States that were surveyed in 1989. Scheers and Dayton [94] established a theory for an extension of the RR design of [25] and a covariate extension of the unrelated-question RR design of Greenberg et al. [40]. They showed that if the relationship between the covariates and the sensitive population proportions is correctly specified, the covariate RR model is relatively more efficient. In 1996, van der Heijden and van Gils [87] presented the model where the response variable is subject to the RR design of Boruch [122] or Kuk [123]. van den Hout et al. [88] discussed univariate and multivariate logistic regression where response variables are subject to RR.

van den Hout and Kooiman [107] derived the likelihood of the linear regression model with categorical covariates subject to RR. They developed a fast and straightforward EM algorithm to obtain ML estimates of the regression parameters. Cruyff et al. [124] provided a review of regression procedures for RR data, including the univariate and multivariate logistic regression models, PO regression model, item response model, and self-protective responses. Blair et al. [29] presented how their developed multivariate logistic regression techniques were employed to analyze data collected from the four RR designs: mirrored question, forced response, disguised response, and unrelated question. Hsieh et al. [85,86] and recently Chang et al. [2] estimated the prevalence of a sensitive characteristic with a categorical or quantitative explanatory variable by fitting logistic regression.

Let Y be the answer to a sensitive question, $\mathbf{Z}$ a vector of covariates that are always observed, and $\mathbf{X}$ another covariate vector that may be missing on some subjects. Assume that $\mathbf{W}$ is a surrogate for $\mathbf{X}$ and independent of Y given $\mathbf{X}$ and $\mathbf{Z}$. Let $Y = 1$ and $Y = 0$ denote answering "Yes" and "No", respectively, to the sensitive question. Now consider the following logistic regression model:

$$P(Y = 1|\mathbf{X}, \mathbf{Z}, \mathbf{W}) = H(\beta_0 + \boldsymbol{\beta}_1^T\mathbf{X} + \boldsymbol{\beta}_2^T\mathbf{Z}) = H(\boldsymbol{\beta}^T\mathcal{X}),$$

where $H(u) = 1/(1 + \exp(-u))$ and $\boldsymbol{\beta} = (\beta_0, \boldsymbol{\beta}_1^T, \boldsymbol{\beta}_2^T)^T$ is a vector of unknown parameters for $\mathcal{X} = (1, \mathbf{X}^T, \mathbf{Z}^T)^T$. Under the RRT, Y is not observable. Let Y^0 denote the binary response to the sensitive question based on some RRT, such as [25,40,42,49]. The probability of Y^0 given $\mathbf{X}$ and $\mathbf{Z}$ can then be expressed as follows:

$$P(Y^0 = 1|\mathbf{X}, \mathbf{Z}) = kH(\boldsymbol{\beta}^T\mathcal{X}) + s, \tag{1}$$

where k and s are known constants in different RRTs. For example, $k = 2p - 1$ and $s = 1 - p$ in Warner's RRT [25]; $k = p$ and $s = (1 - p)c$ in the RRT proposed by Greenberg et al. [40], where p is the probability of selecting the sensitive question and c is the probability of selecting the innocuous question to answer "Yes".

Most recently, Groenitz [22] used logistic regression for the analysis of direct data on the covariates and indirect data on the sensitive variable. The author derived a general algorithm for the ML estimation and a general procedure for variance estimation. Ronning [125] analyzed effects of RR with respect to some binary dependent variable on the estimation of the probit model. Hsieh and Perri [95] proposed a logistic regression extension for analyzing the factors that influence two sensitive variables when data are collected by the RR simple and crossed models.

3.9.2. Missing Data in Randomized Response Problems

Most works on RR data assume that the data are observable. That means the data used in these works are assumed to be fully observed. This assumption is sometimes difficult to achieve in practice. Hsieh et al. [85] developed two semiparametric approaches to estimate the parameters of logistic regression for RR data with missing covariates. After that, Hsieh et al. [86] utilized a logistic regression model for analyzing RR data with covariates missing at random (MAR). Hsieh et al. [13] combined the unrelated-question RRT of Greenberg et al. [40] and the related-question RRT of Warner [25] to address the issue of an innocuous question in the unrelated-question RR design. They utilized logistic regression with missing data to estimate the prevalence of the sensitive characteristic. Lee et al. [14] combined both the unrelated-question RRT of [40] and the DQT under a missing data setting to propose a data-collection method for surveys of sensitive issues. Recently, Hsieh et al. [12] employed PO regression on the two-stage multilevel RRT of [9] to investigate the monthly income when some covariates are MAR.

Let δ indicate whether $\boldsymbol{X}$ is observed ($\delta = 1$) or not ($\delta = 0$). Assume that $\boldsymbol{W}$ is a possible surrogate of $\boldsymbol{X}$ such that $\boldsymbol{W}$ is dependent on $\boldsymbol{X}$ and independent of Y^0 given $\boldsymbol{X}$ and $\boldsymbol{Z}$. Hsieh et al. [85,86] assumed that the missing mechanism is missing at random (MAR) [126], i.e., the probability of $\boldsymbol{X}$ being observed, the selection probability $P(\delta = 1|Y^0, \boldsymbol{X}, \boldsymbol{Z}, \boldsymbol{W}) = \pi(Y^0, \boldsymbol{Z}, \boldsymbol{W})$, depends on $(Y^0, \boldsymbol{Z}, \boldsymbol{W})$, but not on $\boldsymbol{X}$. The validation data set consists of $\{(Y_i^0, \boldsymbol{X}_i, \boldsymbol{Z}_i, \boldsymbol{W}_i, \delta_i = 1) : i = 1, 2, \ldots, n\}$, and the non-validation data set includes $\{(Y_i^0, \boldsymbol{Z}_i, \boldsymbol{W}_i, \delta_i = 0) : i = 1, 2, \ldots, n\}$. Let $\boldsymbol{v}_1, \boldsymbol{v}_2, \ldots, \boldsymbol{v}_g$ denote the distinct values of the $\boldsymbol{V}_i$'s, where $\boldsymbol{V}_i = (\boldsymbol{Z}_i, \boldsymbol{W}_i)$. For $\boldsymbol{v} \in \{\boldsymbol{v}_1, \boldsymbol{v}_2, \ldots, \boldsymbol{v}_g\}$ and $y^0 = 0, 1$, $\pi(y^0, \boldsymbol{v})$ is estimated by

$$\widehat{\pi}(y^0, \boldsymbol{v}) = \frac{\sum_{i=1}^n \delta_i I(Y_i^0 = y^0, \boldsymbol{V}_i = \boldsymbol{v})}{\sum_{i=1}^n I(Y_i^0 = y^0, \boldsymbol{V}_i = \boldsymbol{v})}.$$

To estimate $\boldsymbol{\beta}$, Hsieh et al. [86] proposed the Horvitz and Thompson-type weighted estimating equations [127] as follows:

$$\boldsymbol{U}_w(\boldsymbol{\beta}, \widehat{\boldsymbol{\pi}}) = \frac{1}{\sqrt{n}} \sum_{i=1}^n \left\{ \frac{\delta_i}{\widehat{\pi}(Y_i^0, \boldsymbol{V}_i)} \mathcal{X}_i A_i(\boldsymbol{\beta}) \left[Y_i^0 - [kH(\boldsymbol{\beta}^T \mathcal{X}_i) + s] \right] \right\} = \boldsymbol{0},$$

where $\widehat{\boldsymbol{\pi}} = (\widehat{\pi}(Y_1^0, \boldsymbol{V}_1), \widehat{\pi}(Y_2^0, \boldsymbol{V}_2), \ldots, \widehat{\pi}(Y_n^0, \boldsymbol{V}_n))$,

$$A_i(\boldsymbol{\beta}) = \frac{kH(\boldsymbol{\beta}^T \mathcal{X}_i)[1 - H(\boldsymbol{\beta}^T \mathcal{X}_i)]}{(kH(\boldsymbol{\beta}^T \mathcal{X}_i) + s)(1 - kH(\boldsymbol{\beta}^T \mathcal{X}_i) - s)}. \quad (2)$$

Hsieh et al. [86] also proposed to model $\pi(Y_i^0, \boldsymbol{V}_i)$ with logistic regression with known parameters or unknown parameters to discuss the efficiency problem.

Multiple imputation (MI) is another statistical technique to deal with the missing data. Lee et al. [128] and Stoklosa et al. [129] proposed generating imputed data by applying the MI scheme developed by Wang and Chen [130] in different areas. One can estimate the parameters of the RR regression model in (1) by utilizing the empirical conditional distribution function (CDF) as follows:

$$\widehat{F}(\boldsymbol{x}|Y_i^0, \boldsymbol{V}_i) = \sum_{r=1}^{n} \left\{ \frac{\delta_r I(Y_r^0 = Y_i^0, \boldsymbol{V}_r = \boldsymbol{V}_i)}{\sum_{j=1}^{n} I(Y_j^0 = Y_i^0, \boldsymbol{V}_j = \boldsymbol{V}_i)} \right\} I(\boldsymbol{X}_r \leq \boldsymbol{x}). \tag{3}$$

A unified estimate for the MI procedure proposed by Rubin [131] is the average of estimates obtained from all imputed data sets. Given the number of imputations M, the MI approach is summarized as follows:

Step 1. For missing $\boldsymbol{X}_i$ ($\delta_i = 0$), generate $\widetilde{\boldsymbol{X}}_{vi}$ from the empirical CDF $\widehat{F}(\boldsymbol{x}|Y_i^0, \boldsymbol{V}_i)$ in (3), $v = 1, 2, \ldots, M$.

Step 2. Let $\widehat{\boldsymbol{\beta}}_v$ denote the solution to the following estimating equations:

$$\begin{aligned} \boldsymbol{U}_v(\boldsymbol{\beta}) = & \frac{1}{\sqrt{n}} \sum_{i=1}^{n} \Big\{ \delta_i \mathcal{X}_i A_i(\boldsymbol{\beta}) \Big[Y_i^0 - [kH(\boldsymbol{\beta}^T \mathcal{X}_i) + s] \Big] \\ & + (1 - \delta_i) \widetilde{\mathcal{X}}_{vi} \widetilde{A}_{vi}(\boldsymbol{\beta}) \Big[Y_i^0 - [kH(\boldsymbol{\beta}^T \widetilde{\mathcal{X}}_{vi}) + s] \Big] \Big\} \\ = & \, \boldsymbol{0}, \end{aligned} \tag{4}$$

where $\widetilde{\mathcal{X}}_{vi} = (1, \boldsymbol{X}_{vi}^T, \boldsymbol{Z}_i^T)^T$ and is used to replace $\mathcal{X}_i$ in $A_i(\boldsymbol{\beta})$ in (2) to denote $\widetilde{A}_{vi}(\boldsymbol{\beta})$.

Step 3. The MI estimate of $\boldsymbol{\beta}$ is $\widehat{\boldsymbol{\beta}}_{m1} = \sum_{v=1}^{M} \widehat{\boldsymbol{\beta}}_v / M$.

Lee et al. [128] provided the second MI-type method as in Fay [132] to estimate $\boldsymbol{\beta}$. In step 2, one can define the following estimating function:

$$\boldsymbol{U}_{m2}(\boldsymbol{\beta}) = \frac{1}{M} \sum_{v=1}^{M} \boldsymbol{U}_v(\boldsymbol{\beta}).$$

Let $\widehat{\boldsymbol{\beta}}_{m2}$ denote the solution to the estimating equations $\boldsymbol{U}_{m2}(\boldsymbol{\beta}) = \boldsymbol{0}$. The asymptotic properties of the two MI estimators, $\widehat{\boldsymbol{\beta}}_{m1}$ and $\widehat{\boldsymbol{\beta}}_{m2}$, and their corresponding asymptotic variance estimators still need to be established.

In the above discussion, we considered all the elements of $\boldsymbol{X}$ to be missing simultaneously. In practice, the elements of $\boldsymbol{X}$ may be missing simultaneously or separately in the RR regression model. Now consider $\boldsymbol{X}_i = (\mathtt{X}_{1i}^T, \mathtt{X}_{2i}^T)^T$, where $\mathtt{X}_{1i}$ and $\mathtt{X}_{2i}$ may be missing simultaneously or separately.

Define the missingness statuses of the data as follows. For $i = 1, 2, \ldots, n$, $\delta_{i1} = 1$ if both $\mathtt{X}_{1i}$ and $\mathtt{X}_{2i}$ are observed; 0 otherwise. $\delta_{i2} = 1$ if $\mathtt{X}_{1i}$ is missing and $\mathtt{X}_{2i}$ is observed; 0 otherwise. $\delta_{i3} = 1$ if $\mathtt{X}_{1i}$ is observed and $\mathtt{X}_{2i}$ is missing; 0 otherwise. $\delta_{i4} = 1$ if both $\mathtt{X}_{1i}$ and $\mathtt{X}_{2i}$ are missing; 0 otherwise. Assume that $\mathtt{W}_1$ and $\mathtt{W}_2$ are the possible surrogates of $\mathtt{X}_1$ and $\mathtt{X}_2$, respectively, such that $\mathtt{W}_1$ and $\mathtt{W}_2$ are dependent on $\mathtt{X}_1$ and $\mathtt{X}_2$ and independent of Y^0 given $\boldsymbol{X}$ and $\boldsymbol{Z}$. Let $\boldsymbol{W} = (\mathtt{W}_1^T, \mathtt{W}_2^T)^T$. Under the assumption of MAR mechanism [126] of $\mathtt{X}_1$ and $\mathtt{X}_2$, the selection probability model is assumed as follows:

$$P(\delta_{ij} = 1|Y_i^0, \mathtt{X}_{1i}, \mathtt{X}_{2i}, \boldsymbol{Z}_i, \boldsymbol{W}_i) = \pi_j(Y_i^0, \boldsymbol{V}_i), \; j = 1, 2, 3, 4, \tag{5}$$

where $\boldsymbol{V}_i = (\boldsymbol{Z}_i^T, \boldsymbol{W}_i^T)^T$ and $\sum_{j=1}^{4} \pi_j(Y_i^0, \boldsymbol{V}_i) = 1$. $\pi_j(Y_i^0, \boldsymbol{V}_i)$'s are the nuisance parameters and unknown, although it may be specified at design stage in some applications.

Lee et al. [133] proposed two different types of MI methods for the estimation of the parameters of the logistic regression model with covariates missing separately or simultaneously. Their approaches, which are based on the ideas of [130,132], involve a two-step procedure instead of the three-step procedure as in the traditional MI approaches, in order to reduce the computing time, and are more efficient in estimation. These estimation methods can also be applied to the RRT. For example, one can use the first approach of [133] in the RRT below.

Consider the following empirical CDFs of X_{1i}, given (X_{2i}, Y_i^0, V_i), X_{2i}, given (X_{1i}, Y_i^0, V_i), and $\boldsymbol{X}_i$ given (Y_i^0, V_i):

$$\widetilde{F}_{X_{1i}}(x_1|X_{2i}, Y_i^0, V_i) = \sum_{k=1}^{n}\left(\frac{\delta_{k1} I(Y_k^0 = Y_i^0, X_{2k} = X_{2i}, V_k = V_i)}{\sum_{s=1}^{n}\delta_{s1} I(Y_s^0 = Y_i^0, X_{2s} = X_{2i}, V_s = V_i)}\right) I(X_{1k} \leq x_1),$$

$$\widetilde{F}_{X_{2i}}(x_2|X_{1i}, Y_i^0, V_i) = \sum_{k=1}^{n}\left(\frac{\delta_{k1} I(Y_k^0 = Y_i^0, X_{1k} = X_{1i}, V_k = V_i)}{\sum_{s=1}^{n}\delta_{s1} I(Y_s^0 = Y_i^0, X_{1s} = X_{1i}, V_s = V_i)}\right) I(X_{2k} \leq x_2),$$

$$\widetilde{F}_{\boldsymbol{X}_i}(\boldsymbol{x}|Y_i^0, V_i) = \sum_{k=1}^{n}\left(\frac{\delta_{k1} I(Y_k^0 = Y_i^0, V_k = V_i)}{\sum_{s=1}^{n}\delta_{s1} I(Y_s^0 = Y_i^0, V_s = V_i)}\right) I(\boldsymbol{X}_k \leq \boldsymbol{x}),$$

respectively. The two steps of the MI method are given as follows:

Step 1. ***Imputation:*** Generate the vth imputed ("completed") data set, $v = 1, 2, \ldots, M$, based on the missingness status of $\boldsymbol{X}_i = (X_{1i}^T, X_{2i}^T)^T, i = 1, 2, \ldots, n$.

(i) If $\delta_{i1} = 1$, keep the values of X_{1i} and X_{2i}, and define $\mathcal{X}_i = (1, X_{1i}^T, X_{2i}^T, \boldsymbol{Z}_i^T)^T$ for all v.

(ii) If $\delta_{i2} = 1$, keep the value of X_{2i}, and generate $\widetilde{X}_{1iv}$ from $\widetilde{F}_{X_{1i}}(x_1|X_{2i}, Y_i^0, V_i)$ to impute the missing value of X_{1i}, and define $\widetilde{\mathcal{X}}_{2iv} = (1, \widetilde{X}_{1iv}^T, X_{2i}^T, \boldsymbol{Z}_i^T)^T$.

(iii) If $\delta_{i3} = 1$, keep the value of X_{1i}, and generate $\widetilde{F}_{X_{2i}}(x_2|X_{1i}, Y_i^0, V_i)$ to impute the missing value of X_{2i}, and define $\widetilde{\mathcal{X}}_{3iv} = (1, X_{1i}^T, \widetilde{X}_{2iv}^T, \boldsymbol{Z}_i^T)^T$.

(iv) If $\delta_{i4} = 1$, generate $\widetilde{X}_{1iv}$ and $\widetilde{X}_{2iv}$ from $\widetilde{F}_{\boldsymbol{X}_i}(\boldsymbol{x}|Y_i^0, V_i)$ to impute the missing values of X_{1i} and X_{2i}, and define $\widetilde{\mathcal{X}}_{4iv} = (1, \widetilde{X}_{1iv}^T, \widetilde{X}_{2iv}^T, \boldsymbol{Z}_i^T)^T$.

Step 2. ***Analysis:*** Solve the following estimating equations:

$$\boldsymbol{U}_M(\boldsymbol{\beta}) = \frac{1}{\sqrt{n}}\sum_{i=1}^{n}\Bigg\{\delta_{i1}\mathcal{X}_i A_i(\boldsymbol{\beta})\Big(Y_i^0 - [kH(\boldsymbol{\beta}^T\mathcal{X}_i) + s]\Big) + \frac{1}{M}\sum_{j=2}^{4}\sum_{v=1}^{M}\delta_{ij}\widetilde{\mathcal{X}}_{jiv}\widetilde{A}_{jiv}(\boldsymbol{\beta})\Big(Y_i^0 - [kH(\boldsymbol{\beta}^T\widetilde{\mathcal{X}}_{jiv}) + s]\Big)\Bigg\} = \boldsymbol{0},$$

to obtain the MI estimate of $\boldsymbol{\beta}$, where

$$A_i(\boldsymbol{\beta}) = \frac{kH^{(1)}(\boldsymbol{\beta}^T\mathcal{X}_i)}{[kH(\boldsymbol{\beta}^T\mathcal{X}_i) + s][1 - kH(\boldsymbol{\beta}^T\mathcal{X}_i) - s]},$$

$$\widetilde{A}_{jiv}(\boldsymbol{\beta}) = \frac{kH^{(1)}(\boldsymbol{\beta}^T\widetilde{\mathcal{X}}_{jiv})}{[kH(\boldsymbol{\beta}^T\widetilde{\mathcal{X}}_{jiv}) + s][1 - kH(\boldsymbol{\beta}^T\widetilde{\mathcal{X}}_{jiv}) - s]},$$

with $H^{(1)}(\cdot) = H(\cdot)[1 - H(\cdot)]$. In Step 1, the aforementioned empirical CDFs are utilized to generate imputed data sets by using the complete-case data. δ_{ij}s are employed to identify exactly the partitioned covariate vector without missing observations that are used as the information for the empirical CDFs. More specifically, when $\delta_{i2} = 1$ ($\delta_{i3} = 1$), one can employ the condition from the observed X_{2i} (X_{1i}), Y_i^0, and V_i to generate a set of values to impute the missing values of X_{1i} (X_{2i}). When $\delta_{i4} = 1$, i.e., X_{1i} and X_{2i} missing simultaneously, the condition from Y_i^0 and V_i is utilized to generate a set of values to impute the missing values of X_{1i} and X_{2i}. Therefore, the estimation is more efficient. The estimation method can reduce computing time because it only uses two steps to solve the estimating equations once. The asymptotic properties of the MI estimators need to be established, along with the estimation of their variances.

3.9.3. Investigation of Influence of a Sensitive Trait on a Non-Sensitive Variable

In general, the aforementioned studies evaluate the influences of auxiliary variables on sensitive variables of interest. However, there has not been any work evaluating the association of a sensitive variable with auxiliary variables of interest, i.e., whether or not some random variable of interest on the research subjects depends on the sensitive characteristic. Therefore, motivated by the issue, Lee et al. [55] proposed mixture models for assessing the dependency relationship. Auxiliary information includes a univariate categorical variable, a univariate quantitative variable, and a multivariate quantitative variable to examine in turn. They proposed the Bayesian method through data augmentation and MCMC to estimate the prevalence of the population possessing the sensitive feature and the distribution of a categorical or quantitative variable in each of the non-sensitive and sensitive groups. Moreover, they employed three Bayesian model selection criteria to choose the most suitable one among the proposed models to explore the association of the sensitive variable with a multivariate auxiliary variable in simulation studies. Finally, the two Bayesian model selection criteria, deviance information criterion [134], and marginal likelihood [135] were utilized to choose a more suitable model for the univariate auxiliary variable case.

It is difficult to study empirically sexual behaviors due to their sensitive nature. Accurate estimation of the prevalence and frequency of sexual behaviors is difficult using standard techniques, refer to, e.g., [20,92]. There are various works analyzing the efficacy of the RRT, and more generally IQTs, to accomplish honest self-reporting about sexual behaviors, compared to traditional survey techniques. Refer to, e.g., [92], for more detailed discussions. The sensitive issue of a one-night stand was also mentioned in some materials, including, e.g., Wentland and Reissing [136] and Kaspar et al. [137]. However, the number of research works on this behavior is quite modest. A study on this topic can help researchers, managers, and society have a more complete view of this sexual behavior of young people. Lee et al. [55] applied their proposed methodology to study the influence of the response to the sensitive question, "Have you ever had a one-night stand through a dating site or mobile app?", on each of the response to the statement, "I am considering finding a one-night stand through a dating site or mobile app", the response to the question, "How many significant others have you had?", and "the sum of scores of responses to six internet dating experience questions" by using the data set collected from the survey study of sexuality of freshmen at Feng Chia University in Taiwan in 2016.

Recently, Lee et al. [106] proposed a combination of Warner's RRT [25] and a latent class model to provide a more efficient estimation of the proportion of a sensitive characteristic and to investigate the association between the sensitive characteristic or latent variable and an observed binary variable. The concept of the relationship between the sensitive characteristic variable and other variables in [55] was extended by employing the RR design of [25] to collect sensitive characteristic information. Let Y be the answer to the sensitive question and $\mathbf{Z}$ an observed vector of k dichotomous variables with values 0 and 1. In Warner's RRT [25], p is the probability of selecting the sensitive question and Y^0 is a binary outcome, where $Y^0 = 1$ and $Y^0 = 0$ denote answering "Yes" and "No", respectively. Based on a latent variable model, it is assumed that under the group to which an individual is known to belong, the corresponding observed/manifest variables are independent. Therefore, assume that $Z_1, Z_2, \ldots, Z_k$ given Y are independent. Let $P(Y = 1) = \theta$ and $P(Z_s = 1|Y = y) = \alpha_{ys}$, $y = 0, 1$, $s = 1, 2, \ldots, k$. Lee et al. [106] provided the joint probability distribution of $Y^0, Z_1, Z_2, \ldots, Z_k$ as follows:

$$
\begin{aligned}
&P(Y^0 = 1, Z_1 = z_1, Z_2 = z_2, \ldots, Z_k = z_k) \\
&= P(Y^0 = 1, Z_1 = z_1, Z_2 = z_2, \ldots, Z_k = z_k|Y = 1)P(Y = 1) \\
&\quad + P(Y^0 = 1, Z_1 = z_1, Z_2 = z_2, \ldots, Z_k = z_k|Y = 0)P(Y = 0) \\
&= p\theta \prod_{s=1}^{k} \alpha_{1s}^{z_s}(1 - \alpha_{1s})^{1-z_s} + (1 - p)(1 - \theta) \prod_{s=1}^{k} \alpha_{0s}^{z_s}(1 - \alpha_{0s})^{1-z_s}
\end{aligned}
$$

and

$$\begin{aligned}
&P(Y^0 = 0, Z_1 = z_1, Z_2 = z_2, \ldots, Z_k = z_k) \\
&= P(Y^0 = 0, Z_1 = z_1, Z_2 = z_2, \ldots, Z_k = z_k | Y = 1) P(Y = 1) \\
&\quad + P(Y^0 = 0, Z_1 = z_1, Z_2 = z_2, \ldots, Z_k = z_k | Y = 0) P(Y = 0) \\
&= (1-p)\theta \prod_{s=1}^{k} \alpha_{1s}^{z_s} (1-\alpha_{1s})^{1-z_s} + p(1-\theta) \prod_{s=1}^{k} \alpha_{0s}^{z_s} (1-\alpha_{0s})^{1-z_s}.
\end{aligned}$$

For obtaining the RR data and k-variate dichotomous data of responses to DQ, Ref. [106] proposed an EM algorithm to estimate θ, α_{1s}, and α_{0s}, $s = 1, 2, \ldots, k$. They estimated the variances of estimators using the bootstrap method. An analytic expression for the asymptotic variance still needs to be established. However, the k-variate data of response to DQ are often not dichotomous. For example, "I think online dating is very new/modern" is DQ, and there are five response options: "very consistent", "almost consistent", "fairly consistent", "a bit consistent" and "very inconsistent". Therefore, one can extend the case of k-variate dichotomous responses to DQ in [106] to the case of k-variate multiple responses to DQ. Define $P(Z_s = r | Y = y) = \alpha_{ys,r}$, $r = 1, 2, \ldots, B_s$, with $\sum_{r=1}^{B_s} \alpha_{ys,r} = 1$, where $y = 0, 1$. Under the assumption that $Z_1, Z_2, \ldots, Z_k$ given Y are independent, one can express the joint probability distribution of $Y^0, Z_1, Z_2, \ldots, Z_k$ as follows:

$$P(Y^0 = 1, Z_1 = z_1, Z_2 = z_2, \ldots, Z_k = z_k) = p\theta \prod_{s=1}^{k} \prod_{r=1}^{B_s} \alpha_{1s,r}^{I(z_s=r)} + (1-p)(1-\theta) \prod_{s=1}^{k} \prod_{r=1}^{B_s} \alpha_{0s,r}^{I(z_s=r)}$$

and

$$P(Y^0 = 0, Z_1 = z_1, Z_2 = z_2, \ldots, Z_k = z_k) = (1-p)\theta \prod_{s=1}^{k} \prod_{r=1}^{B_s} \alpha_{1s,r}^{I(z_s=r)} + p(1-\theta) \prod_{s=1}^{k} \prod_{s=1}^{B_s} \alpha_{0s,r}^{I(z_s=r)}.$$

To estimate these parameters $\theta, \alpha_{1s,r}$, and $\alpha_{0s,r}$, $s = 1, 2, \ldots, k$, $r = 1, 2, \ldots, B_s$, a procedure must be developed. One can consider an EM algorithm or the Newton–Raphson method to solve unbiased estimating equations for these parameters and, hence, estimate the variances of their estimators. Another way to estimate these parameters is to use the Bayesian approach, which involves combining the MCMC/Gibbs sampler to generate samples from the posterior distribution of these parameters.

3.10. Statistical Software: Packages and Modules for Randomized Response Data

Some authors have used statistical software to perform analysis of data from randomized surveys. For instance, Hox and Lensvelt-Mulders [138] presented a way to analyze the relations between RR estimates and explanatory variables by using standard structural equation modeling software, `Mplus`. Sehra [139] provided `SAS` code to perform analysis of data gathered from a two-stage additive optional RR model. Jann [140] presented the `Stata` module **rrlogit** to fit logistic regression to RR data. `R` software is also commonly used in RR data analysis. Tian and Tang [31] provided numerous `R` programs to illustrate their analysis in a monograph. Moreover, some other researchers have developed `R` packages for estimation with RR surveys. Some of them are mentioned as follows. Blair et al. [29] developed the `R` package **rr** to perform regression analyses of sensitive data under some standard RR designs. They also provided tools to conduct power analysis for designing RR items. Heck and Moshagen [141] developed the `R` package **RRreg** to conduct correlation and regression analysis of RR data, simple univariate analysis, bivariate correlations including RR variables, logistic regression with an RR variable, and linear regression with RR variables as predictors. Rueda et al. [142] developed the `R` package **RRTCS** to perform point and interval estimation of linear parameters with data collected from RR surveys under complex sampling designs. Fox et al. [143] extended the existing implementations by providing generalized regression tools for multiple-group RR designs in the R package **GLMMRR**.

3.11. Non-Randomized Response Techniques

In RR surveys, respondents use a randomization device such as a coin or a deck of cards to generate an outcome that influences the required scrambled answer. However, running a random experiment can be cumbersome and expensive. This has led to the development of NRRTs in recent years. In contrast to RR surveys, in NRR surveys, respondents use an independent non-sensitive question such as their birthday in the questionnaire to obtain their answer to a sensitive question indirectly. In NRR surveys, respondents are expected to give the same response to the questions that are repeated. Some of the more common NRRTs are reviewed below.

3.11.1. Some Common Non-Randomized Response Models

Hidden sensitivity model (HSM): In 2007, Tian et al. [144] proposed a non-randomized HSM to investigate the association between two sensitive binary questions. For example, they considered two variables $X_1, X_2 \in \{0,1\}$, where $X_1 = 1$ if using drugs and $X_2 = 1$ if having AIDS. This technique is called the HSM because the truthful sensitive attributes of all respondents are hidden. Before Tian et al. [144], for example, Fox and Tracy [65] estimated the correlation between two sensitive questions. Christofides [57] provided an RRT for two sensitive characteristics simultaneously. However, all of these models require the use of randomization devices.

CWM and TRM: In 2008, Yu et al. [28] introduced two NRRTs—the CWM and TRM—for a single sensitive question with binary options. Of which, the CWM can be viewed as a non-randomized version of the original RR model of Warner [25]. However, compared to the original Warner's RR model, the CWM has several advantages, including, e.g., better reproducibility of results and increased cooperation from respondents due to its perceived lower invasiveness. Let X be the sensitive attribute. In these models, X has two categories. For instance, $X \in \{1,0\}$ with $X = 1$ if having sensitive characteristics and $X = 0$ otherwise. In 2009, Tan et al. [145] showed that the non-randomized TRM has higher relative efficiency and better degree of privacy protection compared to the Warner's RR model [25]. In 2020, Hoffmann et al. [146] conducted a study to compare directly the validity of the CWM and TRM and contrast their performance with a conventional DQ approach.

Multi-category response model (MCRM): In 2009, Tang et al. [147] developed a non-randomized MCRM for surveys with a single categorical sensitive question. This model is suitable for the case of the sensitive variable X with k categories: $X \in \{1,2,\ldots,k\}, k \geq 2$. For example, let $X \in \{1,2,3\}$ with $X = 1$ if having never violated traffic laws; $X = 2$ if having ever violated traffic laws once or twice; and $X = 3$ if having violated traffic laws three or more times. A requirement for this model is that at least one value of X, say $X = 1$, is non-sensitive.

Diagonal model (DM): In 2014, Groenitz [148] proposed a survey technique, called a DM, for multi-categorical sensitive variables. The DM is an NRR method to avoid using any randomization device and, hence, reduce the complexity and costs of surveys. That at least one category of the sensitive variable be non-sensitive is not required in the DM. Consequently, one can even apply the DM to attributes, such as income, which are sensitive as a whole.

Parallel model (PM): In 2014, Tian [149] introduced another NRRT, the PM that is a non-randomized version of the randomized unrelated-question model. He explored the asymptotic properties of the ML estimator and its modified version for the proportion of interest. Theoretical comparisons have shown that the PM is generally more efficient than the CWM and TRM for most possible parameter ranges. Additionally, he developed Bayesian methods to analyze survey data gathered from the PM.

By using direct and indirect questions, Perri et al. [150] proposed a procedure to detect the presence of liars in sensitive surveys that allows researchers to evaluate the impact of untruthful responses on the estimation of the prevalence of a sensitive attribute. They first introduced the theoretical framework, then applied the proposal to the RR method of Warner [25], the unrelated question model [40], the item count technique, the CWM, and the TRM.

3.11.2. Statistical Methods for Non-Randomized Response Models

In 2009, Tian et al. [151] proposed the Bayesian NRR models for surveys including one and two sensitive questions. They derived the exact posterior distributions and their explicit posterior moments, as well as posterior modes via the EM algorithm. They also presented an approach to generate independent and identically-distributed posterior samples for the CWM and TRM, respectively. For the HSM, Tian et al. [144] presented the Bayesian analysis under a conjugate Dirichlet prior as well as some other prior structures. In 2011, Tian et al. [152] developed the formula for determining the sample size required for the non-randomized TRM. This formula was designed to help researchers determine the optimal sample size for a given survey design and level of desired precision.

In 2014, Tang et al. [93] considered a non-randomized TRM to test the equality of the proportions of individuals with a sensitive feature between two independent populations. They derived the Wald, score, and likelihood ratio (LR) tests. They also developed the formulae for determining the sample size. In 2015, Groenitz [119] introduced Bayesian estimation for the DM in [148]. In 2019, Tian et al. [153] developed hidden logistic regression according to the non-randomized PM in Tian [149] to study the relationships between non-sensitive covariates and a sensitive binary response variable. Groenitz [22] developed a general approach for logistic regression analysis with direct data on the covariates and indirect data on the sensitive variable that covers many NRRTs to generate the indirect data. Groenitz [22] derived a general algorithm for the ML estimation and a general procedure for variance estimation.

3.11.3. Real Data with Non-Randomized Response Models

Various applications of NRR designs have appeared in the literature. For instance, Tian et al. [144] described how the non-randomized HSM can be utilized to assess the association between "sex exchange for drugs or money" and "HIV status". Tang et al. [147] illustrated how their NRR method is used to estimate the distribution of the attribute, "number of sex partners", in the population of Korean adolescents. Tang et al. [93] applied a TRM to conduct a simple questionnaire survey to test whether the proportions of college students who had homosexual experience were equal for men and women. The equality of the proportions of college students who had homosexual experience for males and females were examined by the Wald, score, and LR tests. Hoffmann et al. [146] conducted an experimental comparison of the CWM and TRM.

Hoffmann et al. [146] conducted a study on Xenophobia and opposition to reception of refugees in Germany. In a paper-pencil survey of 1,382 students, they estimated prevalence of the two sensitive features, xenophobia and rejection of further refugee admissions, and one non-sensitive control trait with a known prevalence (the first letter of respondents' surnames). They showed that NRRTs provide more valid prevalence estimates for socially undesirable characteristics compared to conventional DQ. The CWM was particularly able to successfully control for the influence of social desirability bias, and outperformed the TRM, presumably because of the favorable influence of the response symmetry found in the CWM but not the TRM. They also found that the sensitivity of two questions was contingent on respondents' political orientation, and that the CWM provided the most valid estimates for respondents for whom these questions were most sensitive. According to these results, they recommended the use of the CWM over the TRM or DQ for highly sensitive topics in a survey's target population. Recently, Chang et al. [2] and Lee et al. [55] studied the experience of one-night stands among freshmen at Feng Chia University in Taiwan in 2016. They used an NRR design via the concept of Warner's RR model [25] and Christofides GRR model [54], respectively. Groenitz [22] re-presented real data on the sales of gas stations in

Germany with the sensitive characteristic sales (with categories low, medium and high) to demonstrate the applicability of the developed general framework. Perri et al. [150] used the CWM and the TM to collect the data and to investigate the problem of racism among students at the University of Calabria, Italy, in 2016, and the phenomenon of workplace mobbing. They showed the estimates for the prevalence of the sensitive attributes under study and evaluated the impact of the liars on the reliability of the final results.

3.11.4. Some Extensions of the Non-Randomized Response Models

Extended crosswise model (ECRM): In the CRM, the sample is not split into multiple groups. Heck et al. [154] introduced the ECRM, where respondents are randomly assigned to two groups. The ECRM not only guarantees the same statistical efficiency as the CRM but also can enable researchers to detect respondents' non-compliance with instructions.

Dual NRR model and alternating NRR model: Wu and Tang [155] proposed the dual NRRT and the alternating NRRT to actively account for deception in the TRM. In the former, the sample is split into two groups, with two different non-sensitive questions. In the latter, although the sample is also split into two groups, only one non-sensitive question is used. Both the two methods have been argued to provide more accurate estimates than the TRM.

Cheating detection triangular model (CDTM): To improve upon the previous IQTs, Meisters et al. [156] proposed the new CDTM. Similar to the cheating detection model of Clark and Desharnais [157], it includes a mechanism for detecting instruction non-adherence and, similar to the TRM, it utilizes simplified instructions to improve respondents' understanding of the procedure. Based on their results, the CDTM appears to be the best choice among the investigated IQTs.

4. Conclusions

We have systematically reviewed the RRT-related works, from the pioneering work of Warner (1965) [25] to the present, according to their respective aspects and to the best of our knowledge. It includes several developments in RR designs as well as statistical methods used in the problems of interest in this field. In each respect, instead of introducing all related works, we re-introduced typical and pioneering works. A more complete view of the evolution of the RRT can be found in the monographs listed in the References.

Author Contributions: Ideas, S.-M.L. and C.-S.L.; writing—original draft preparation, T.-N.L. and P.-L.T.; writing—review and editing, C.-S.L. and S.-M.L.; supervision, S.-M.L. and C.-S.L. All authors have read and agreed to the published version of the manuscript.

Funding: Lee's research was supported by Ministry of Science and Technology (MOST) Grant of Taiwan, ROC, MOST-109-2118-M-035-002-MY3.

Data Availability Statement: Not applicable.

Conflicts of Interest: The authors declare no conflict of interest.

Appendix A

Appendix A.1. Expectation and Variance of $\widehat{\theta}_W$ in the Model of Warner [25]

Let λ denote the probability of answering "Yes". Then, $\lambda = P(Yes) = P(A)P(Yes|A) + P(\overline{A})P(Yes|\overline{A}) = \theta p + (1-\theta)(1-p)$. Let n_1 be the number of individuals responding "Yes". n_1 then follows the binomial distribution with parameters n and λ. Its expectation and variance are given by

$$\begin{aligned} \mathrm{E}(n_1) &= n(\theta p + (1-\theta)(1-p)), \\ \mathrm{Var}(n_1) &= n(\theta p + (1-\theta)(1-p))[1-(\theta p + (1-\theta)(1-p))] \\ &= n\left(-\theta^2(2p-1)^2 + \theta(2p-1)^2 + p(1-p)\right). \end{aligned}$$

$\widehat{\theta}_W = \frac{p-1}{2p-1} + \frac{n_1}{(2p-1)n}$ is then an unbiased estimator of θ because

$$\begin{aligned}\mathrm{E}(\widehat{\theta}_W) &= \frac{p-1}{2p-1} + \frac{\mathrm{E}(n_1)}{(2p-1)n} \\ &= \frac{p-1}{2p-1} + \frac{n(\theta p + (1-\theta)(1-p))}{(2p-1)n} \\ &= \frac{p-1}{2p-1} + \frac{1-p+\theta(2p-1)}{2p-1} \\ &= \theta.\end{aligned}$$

Moreover, we can get

$$\begin{aligned}\mathrm{Var}(\widehat{\theta}_W) &= \frac{\mathrm{Var}(n_1)}{(2p-1)^2 n^2} \\ &= \frac{n(-\theta^2(2p-1)^2 + \theta(2p-1)^2 + p(1-p))}{(2p-1)^2 n^2} \\ &= \frac{-\theta^2(2p-1)^2 + \theta(2p-1)^2 + p(1-p)}{(2p-1)^2 n} \\ &= \frac{\theta(1-\theta)}{n} + \frac{1}{4n}\left[\frac{1}{(2p-1)^2} - 1\right] \\ &= \frac{\theta(1-\theta)}{n} + \frac{p(1-p)}{n(2p-1)^2}.\end{aligned}$$

Appendix A.2. Expectation and Variance of $\widehat{\theta}_C$ in the Model of Christofides [54]

Now, each sampled person is provided with a randomization device that is used to generate the integers $1, 2, \ldots, L$ with probabilities $P_1, P_2, \ldots, P_L$, respectively. Using the randomization device, the individual generates one of these L numbers and reports how far the generated number is away from $L+1$ if she/he had the sensitive characteristic or from 0 otherwise.

Let Y_i take on the value $L+1$ if individual i had the sensitive characteristic and the value 0 if not. Clearly $P(Y_i = L+1) = \theta$ and $P(Y_i = 0) = 1-\theta$. Let T_i be the integer produced by individual i using the randomization device. The reported number is then $D_i = |Y_i - T_i|$ whose pmf is given by

$$P(D_i = d) = (1-\theta)P_d + \theta P_{L+1-d}, \quad d = 1, 2, \ldots, L.$$

Direct calculation shows that

$$\begin{aligned}\mathrm{E}(D_i) &= \sum_{d=1}^{L} dP(D_i = d) \\ &= \sum_{d=1}^{L} d[(1-\theta)P_d + \theta P_{L+1-d}] \\ &= \sum_{d=1}^{L} dP_d + \theta \sum_{d=1}^{L} d(P_{L+1-d} - P_d).\end{aligned}$$

Because

$$\begin{aligned}\sum_{d=1}^{L} d(P_{L+1-d}-P_d) &= (P_L-P_1)+2(P_{L-1}-P_2)+\cdots+L(P_1-P_L)\\ &= (L-1)P_1+(L-3)P_2+(L-5)P_3+\cdots+(L-(2L-1))P_L\\ &= (L+1-2)P_1+(L+1-4)P_2+(L+1-6)P_3+\cdots+(L+1-(2L))P_L\\ &= (L+1)\sum_{d=1}^{L}P_d-2P_1-4P_2-\cdots-2LP_L\\ &= (L+1)\times 1-2(P_1+2P_2+\cdots+LP_L)\\ &= L+1-2\sum_{d=1}^{L}dP_d,\end{aligned}$$

it can yield

$$\begin{aligned}\mathrm{E}(D_i) &= \sum_{d=1}^{L}dP_d+\theta\left(L+1-2\sum_{d=1}^{L}dP_d\right)\\ &= \mathrm{E}(T_i)+\theta(L+1-2\mathrm{E}(T_i)).\end{aligned}$$

Similarly, one can obtain

$$\begin{aligned}\mathrm{E}(D_i^2) &= \sum_{d=1}^{L}d^2P(D_i=d)\\ &= \sum_{d=1}^{L}d^2((1-\theta)P_d+\theta P_{L+1-d})\\ &= \sum_{d=1}^{L}d^2P_d+\theta\sum_{d=1}^{L}d^2(P_{L+1-d}-P_d).\end{aligned}$$

We have

$$\begin{aligned}&\sum_{d=1}^{L}d^2(P_{L+1-d}-P_d)\\ &= (P_L-P_1)+2^2(P_{L-1}-P_2)+\cdots+L^2(P_1-P_L)\\ &= (L^2-1)P_1+((L-1)^2-2^2)P_2+((L-2)^2-3^2)P_3+\cdots+((L-(L-1))^2-L^2)P_L\\ &= (L+1)(L-1)P_1+(L+1)(L-3)P_2+(L+1)(L-5)P_3+\cdots+(L+1)(L-(2L-1))P_L\\ &= (L+1)[(L-1)P_1+(L-3)P_2+(L-5)P_3+\cdots+(L-(2L-1))P_L]\\ &= (L+1)[(L+1-2)P_1+(L+1-4)P_2+(L+1-6)P_3+\cdots+(L+1-2L)P_L]\\ &= (L+1)\left[(L+1)\sum_{d=1}^{L}P_d-2P_1-4P_2-6P_3-\cdots-2LP_L\right]\\ &= (L+1)\left[L+1-2\sum_{d=1}^{L}dP_d\right].\end{aligned}$$

Thus,

$$\begin{aligned}
\mathrm{E}(D_i^2) &= \sum_{d=1}^{L} d^2 P_d + \theta \sum_{d=1}^{L} d^2 (P_{L+1-d} - P_d) \\
&= \sum_{d=1}^{L} d^2 P_d + \theta \left\{ (L+1) \left[L+1-2\sum_{d=1}^{L} dP_d \right] \right\} \\
&= \mathrm{E}(T_i^2) + \theta\{(L+1)[L+1-2\mathrm{E}(T_i)]\}.
\end{aligned}$$

Accordingly,

$$\begin{aligned}
&\mathrm{Var}(D_i) \\
&= \mathrm{E}(D_i^2) - (\mathrm{E}(D_i))^2 \\
&= \mathrm{E}(T_i^2) + \theta\{(L+1)[L+1-2\mathrm{E}(T_i)]\} - \{\mathrm{E}(T_i) + \theta[L+1-2\mathrm{E}(T_i)]\}^2 \\
&= \mathrm{Var}(T_i) + \theta\{(L+1)[L+1-2\mathrm{E}(T_i)]\} - 2\mathrm{E}(T_i)\theta[L+1-2\mathrm{E}(T_i)] - \{\theta[L+1-2\mathrm{E}(T_i)]\}^2 \\
&= \mathrm{Var}(T_i) + \theta(1-\theta)[L+1-2\mathrm{E}(T_i)]^2.
\end{aligned}$$

Let $\overline{D} = \frac{1}{n}\sum_{i=1}^{n} D_i$ and define the estimator

$$\widehat{\theta}_C = \frac{\overline{D} - \mathrm{E}(T_i)}{L+1-2\mathrm{E}(T_i)},$$

provided that $L+1-2\mathrm{E}(T_i) \neq 0$. Then,

$$\begin{aligned}
\mathrm{E}(\widehat{\theta}_C) &= \frac{\mathrm{E}(\overline{D}) - \mathrm{E}(T_i)}{L+1-2\mathrm{E}(T_i)} \\
&= \frac{\mathrm{E}(D_i) - \mathrm{E}(T_i)}{L+1-2\mathrm{E}(T_i)} \\
&= \frac{\mathrm{E}(T_i) + \theta[L+1-2\mathrm{E}(T_i)] - \mathrm{E}(T_i)}{L+1-2\mathrm{E}(T_i)} \\
&= \theta,
\end{aligned}$$

and

$$\begin{aligned}
\mathrm{Var}(\widehat{\theta}_C) &= \frac{\mathrm{Var}(\overline{D})}{[L+1-2\mathrm{E}(T_i)]^2} \\
&= \frac{\mathrm{Var}(D_i)}{n[L+1-2\mathrm{E}(T_i)]^2} \\
&= \frac{\mathrm{Var}(T_i) + \theta(1-\theta)[L+1-2E(T_i)]^2}{n[L+1-2\mathrm{E}(T_i)]^2} \\
&= \frac{\theta(1-\theta)}{n} + \frac{\mathrm{Var}(T_i)}{n[L+1-2E(T_i)]^2}.
\end{aligned}$$

References

1. Rueda, M.; Cobo, B.; Perri, P.F. Randomized response estimation in multiple frame surveys. *Int. J. Comput. Math.* **2020**, *97*, 189–206. [CrossRef]
2. Chang, P.C.; Pho, K.H.; Lee, S.M.; Li, C.S. Estimation of parameters of logistic regression for two-stage randomized response technique. *Comput. Stat.* **2021**, *36*, 2111–2133. [CrossRef]
3. Huang, K.C. A Survey technique for estimating the proportion and sensitivity in a dichotomous finite population. *Stat. Neerl.* **2004**, *58*, 75–82. [CrossRef]
4. Mehta, S.; Aggarwal, P. Bayesian estimation of sensitivity level and population proportion of a sensitive characteristic in a binary optional unrelated question RRT model. *Commun. Stat.-Theory Methods* **2018**, *47*, 4021–4028. [CrossRef]

5. Narjis, G.; Shabbir, J. Bayesian analysis of optional unrelated question randomized response models. *Commun. Stat.-Theory Methods* **2021**, *50*, 4203–4215. [CrossRef]
6. Sihm, J.S.; Chhabra, A.; Gupta, S.N. An optional unrelated question RRT model. *Involve* **2016**, *9*, 195–209. [CrossRef]
7. Tourangeau, R.; Yan, T. Sensitive questions in surveys. *Psychol. Bull.* **2007**, *133*, 859–883. [CrossRef]
8. Krumpal, I.; Voss, T. Sensitive questions and trust: Explaining respondents' behavior in randomized response surveys. *SAGE Open* **2020**, 1–17. [CrossRef]
9. Hsieh, S.H.; Lee, S.M.; Tu, S.H. Randomized response techniques for a multi-level attribute using a single sensitive question. *Stat. Pap.* **2018**, *59*, 291–306. [CrossRef]
10. Hsieh, S.H.; Lukusa, M.T.W. Comparison of estimators for multi-level randomized response data: Evidence from a case of sexual identity. *Field Methods* **2021**, *33*, 85–103. [CrossRef]
11. Hsieh, S.H.; Tu, S.H.; Lee, S.M.; Wang, C.W. Application of the randomized response technique in the 2012 presidential election of Taiwan. *Surv. Res.-Method Appl.* **2016**, *35*, 81–109.
12. Hsieh, S.H.; Lee, S.M.; Li, C.S. A two-stage multilevel randomized response technique with proportional odds models and missing covariates. *Sociol. Methods Res.* **2022**, *51*, 439–467. [CrossRef]
13. Hsieh, S.H.; Lee, S.M.; Li, C.S.; Tu, S.H. An alternative to unrelated randomized response techniques with logistic regression analysis. *Stat. Method. Appl.* **2016**, *25*, 601–621. [CrossRef] [PubMed]
14. Lee, S.M.; Peng, T.C.; Tapsoba, J.D.D.; Hsieh, S.H. Improved estimation methods for unrelated question randomized response techniques. *Commun. Stat.-Theory Methods* **2017**, *46*, 8101–8112. [CrossRef]
15. Hyman, H. Do they tell the truth? *Public Opin. Q.* **1944**, *8*, 557–559. [CrossRef]
16. Tourangeau, R.; Rips, L.J.; Rasinski, K. *The Psychology of Survey Response*, 1st ed.; Cambridge University Press: Cambridge, UK, 2000.
17. Kerkvliet, J. Cheating by economics students: A comparison of survey results. *J. Econ. Educ.* **1994**, *25*, 121–133. [CrossRef]
18. Preisendörfer, P.; Wolter, F. Who is telling the truth? A validation study on determinants of response behavior in surveys. *Public Opin. Q.* **2014**, *78*, 126–146. [CrossRef]
19. van der Heijden, P.G.M.; van Gils, G.; Bouts, J.A.N.; Hox, J.J. A comparison of randomized response, computer-assisted self-interview, and face-to-face direct questioning: Eliciting sensitive information in the context of welfare and unemployment benefit. *Sociol. Methods Res.* **2000**, *28*, 505–537. [CrossRef]
20. Hsieh, S.H.; Perri, P.F. Estimating the proportion of non-heterosexuals in Taiwan using Christofides' randomized response model: A comparison of different estimation methods. *Soc. Sci. Res.* **2021**, *93*, 102475. [CrossRef]
21. Chaudhuri, A.; Christofides, T.C. *Indirect Questioning in Sample Surveys;* Springer: Berlin/Heidelberg, Germany, 2013.
22. Groenitz, H. Logistic regression analyses for indirect data. *Commun. Stat.-Theory Methods* **2018**, *47*, 3838–3856. [CrossRef]
23. Ibbett, H.; Jones, J.P.; St. John, F.A. Asking sensitive questions in conservation using randomised response techniques. *Biol. Conserv.* **2021**, *260*, 109191. [CrossRef] [PubMed]
24. Nuno, A.; John, F.A.S. How to ask sensitive questions in conservation: A review of specialized questioning techniques. *Biol. Conserv.* **2015**, *189*, 5–15. [CrossRef]
25. Warner, S.L. Randomized response: A survey technique for eliminating evasive answer bias. *J. Am. Stat. Assoc.* **1965**, *60*, 63–69. [CrossRef] [PubMed]
26. Dalton, D.R.; James, C.W.; Catherine, M.D. Using the unmatched count technique (UCT) to estimate base rates for sensitive behavior. *Pers. Psychol.* **1994**, *47*, 817–827. [CrossRef]
27. Droitcour, J.; Caspar, R.A.; Hubbard, M.L.; Parsley, T.L.; Visscher, W.; Ezzati, T.M. The item count technique as a method of indirect questioning: A review of its development and a case study application. In *Measurement Errors in Surveys*; Biemer, P.P., Groves, R.M., Lyberg, L.E., Mathiowetz, N.A., Sudman, S., Eds.; Wiley: New York, NY, USA, 1991; pp. 185–210.
28. Yu, J.W.; Tian, G.L.; Tang, M.L. Two new models for survey sampling with sensitive characteristic: Design and analysis. *Metrika* **2008**, *67*, 251–263. [CrossRef]
29. Blair, G.; Imai, K.; Zhou, Y.Y. Design and analysis of the randomized response technique. *J. Am. Stat. Assoc.* **2015**, *110*, 1304–1319. [CrossRef]
30. Sungkawichai, T.; Thongsata, P.; Paka, T.; Laoharenoo, A.; Vatiwutipong, P. Forced randomized response protocol using arbitrary random variable. *Curr. Appl. Sci. Technol.* **2023**, *23*, 1–10. [CrossRef]
31. Tian, G.L.; Tang, M.L. *Incomplete Categorical Data Design: Non-Randomized Response Techniques for Sensitive Questions in Surveys;* Chapman & Hall/CRC: Boca Raton, FL, USA, 2013.
32. Arnab, R. *Survey Sampling Theory and Applications;* Academic Press: Cambridge, MA, USA, 2017.
33. Chaudhuri, A.; Mukerjee, R. *Randomized Response: Theory and Techniques;* CRC Press: New York, NY, USA, 1988.
34. Chaudhuri, A. *Randomized Response and Indirect Questioning Techniques in Surveys;* Chapman & Hall/CRC: Boca Raton, FL, USA, 2011.
35. Chaudhuri, A.; Christofides, T.C.; Rao, C.R. Data Gathering, analysis and protection of privacy through randomized response techniques: Qualitative and quantitative human traits. In *Handbook of Statistics 34;* Chaudhuri, A., Christofides, T.C., Rao, C.R., Eds.; Elsevier: Amsterdam, The Netherlands, 2016; pp. 29–41.
36. Fox, J.A. *Randomized Response and Related Methods: Surveying Sensitive Data;* Sage Publication: Thousand Oaks, CA, USA, 2016.

37. Tracy, D.S.; Mangat, N.S. Some developments in randomized response sampling during the last decade—A follow up of review by Chauduri and Mukerjee. *J. Appl. Stat. Sci.* **1996**, *4*, 147–158.
38. Lensvelt-Mulders, G.J.L.M.; Van Der Heijden, P.G.M.; Laudy, O.; Van Gils, G. A validation of a computer-assisted randomized response survey to estimate the prevalence of fraud in social security. *J. R. Stat. Soc. Ser. A* **2006**, *169*, 305–318. [CrossRef]
39. Horvitz, D.G.; Shah, B.V.; Simmons, W.R. The unrelated question randomized response model. *Proc. Soc. Stat. Sect. Am. Stat. Assoc.* **1967**, *62*, 65–72.
40. Greenberg, B.G.; Abul-Ela, A.L.A.; Simmons, W.R.; Horvitz, D.G. The unrelated question randomized response model: Theoretical framework. *J. Am. Stat. Assoc.* **1969**, *64*, 520–539. [CrossRef]
41. Chaudhuri, A.; Mukerjee, R. Optionally randomized response techniques. *Calcutta Stat. Assoc. Bull.* **1985**, *34*, 225–230. [CrossRef]
42. Bhargava, M.; Singh, R. A modified randomization device for Warner's model. *Statistica* **2000**, *60*, 315–322.
43. Kim, J.M.; Warde, W.D. A stratified Warner's randomized response model. *J. Stat. Plan. Inference* **2004**, *120*, 155–165. [CrossRef]
44. Abbasi, A.M.; Shad, M.Y.; Ahmed, A. On partial randomized response model using ranked set sampling. *PLoS ONE* **2022**, *17*, e0277497. [CrossRef]
45. Zapata, Z.; Sedory, S.A.; Singh, S. An innovative improvement in Warner's randomized response device for evasive answer bias. *J. Stat. Comput. Simul.* **2023**, *93*, 298–311. [CrossRef]
46. Edgell, S.E.; Duchan, K.L.; Himmelfarb, S. An empirical test of the unrelated question randomized response technique. *Bull. Psychon. Soc.* **1992**, *30*, 153–156. [CrossRef]
47. Shaw, P.; Chaudhuri, A. Further improvements on unrelated characteristic models in randomized response techniques. *Commun. Stat.-Theory Methods* **2022**, *51*, 7305–7321. [CrossRef]
48. Chaudhuri, A.; Shaw, P. Generating randomized response by inverse Bernoullian trials in unrelated characteristics model. *Model Assist. Stat. Appl.* **2016**, *11*, 235–245.
49. Mangat, N.S.; Singh, R. An alternative randomized response procedure. *Biometrika* **1990**, *77*, 439–442. [CrossRef]
50. Mangat, N.S. An improved randomized response strategy. *J. R. Stat. Soc. Ser. B-Stat. Methodol.* **1994**, *56*, 93–95. [CrossRef]
51. Chang, H.J.; Liang, D.H. A two-stage unrelated randomized response procedure. *Aust. N. Z. J. Stat.* **1996**, *38*, 43–51.
52. Gjestvang, C.R.; Singh, S. A new randomized response model. *J. R. Stat. Soc. Ser. B-Stat. Methodol.* **2006**, *68*, 523–530. [CrossRef]
53. Vishwakarma, G.K.; Kumar, A.; Kumar, N. Two-stage unrelated randomized response model to estimate the prevalence of a sensitive attribute. *Comput. Stat.* **2023**, 1–26. [CrossRef]
54. Christofides, T.C. A generalized randomized response technique. *Metrika* **2003**, *57*, 195–200. [CrossRef]
55. Lee, S.M.; Le, T.N.; Tran, P.L.; Li, C.S. Investigating the association of a sensitive attribute with a random variable using the Christofides generalised randomised response design and Bayesian methods. *J. R. Stat. Soc. Ser. C* **2022**, *71*, 1471–1502. [CrossRef]
56. Chaudhuri, A. Christofides' randomized response technique in complex sample surveys. *Metrika* **2004**, *60*, 223–228. [CrossRef]
57. Christofides, T.C. Randomized response technique for two sensitive characteristics at the same time. *Metrika* **2005**, *62*, 53–63. [CrossRef]
58. Christofides, T.C. Randomized response in stratified sampling. *J. Stat. Plan. Infer.* **2005**, *128*, 303–310. [CrossRef]
59. Lee, C.S.; Sedory, S.A.; Singh, S. Estimating at least seven measures of qualitative variables from a single sample using randomized response technique. *Stat. Probab. Lett.* **2013**, *83*, 399–409. [CrossRef]
60. Perri, P.F.; Pelle, E.; Stranges, M. Estimating induced abortion and foreign irregular presence using the randomized response crossed model. *Soc. Indic. Res.* **2016**, *129*, 601–618. [CrossRef]
61. Abul-Ela, A.L.A.; Greenberg, G.G.; Horvitz, D.G. A multi-proportions randomized response model. *J. Am. Stat. Assoc.* **1967**, *62*, 990–1008. [CrossRef]
62. Liu, P.T.; Chow, L.P. The efficiency of the multiple trial randomized response technique. *Biometrika* **1976**, *32*, 607–618. [CrossRef]
63. Barksdale, W.B. New Randomized Response Techniques for Control of Non-Sampling Errors in Surveys. Ph.D. Dissertation, University of North Carolina, Chapel Hill, NC, USA, 1971. [CrossRef]
64. Drane, W. On the theory of randomized responses to two sensitive questions. *Commun. Stat.-Theory Methods* **1976**, *5*, 565–574. [CrossRef]
65. Fox, J.A.; Tracy, P.E. Measuring associations with randomized response. *Soc. Sci. Res.* **1984**, *13*, 188–197.
66. Ewemooje, O.S. Estimating two sensitive characters with equal probabilities of protection. *Cogent Math.* **2017**, *4*, 1319607. [CrossRef]
67. Ewemooje, O.S.; Amahia, G.N. Improved randomized response technique for two sensitive attributes. *Afr. Stat.* **2015**, *10*, 839–852. [CrossRef]
68. Ewemooje, O.S.; Amahia, G.N. Improving the efficiency of randomized response technique for two sensitive characters. *FUTA J. Res. Sci.* **2016**, *12*, 65–72. [CrossRef]
69. Batool, F.; Shabbir, J. A two-stage design for multivariate estimation of proportions. *Commun. Stat.-Theory Methods* **2016**, *45*, 5412–5426.
70. Xu, T.; Sedory, S.A.; Singh, S. Two sensitive characteristics and their overlap with two questions per card. *Biom. J.* **2021**, *63*, 1688–1705.
71. Chung, R.S.W.; Chu, A.M.Y.; So, M.K.P. Bayesian randomized response technique with multiple sensitive attributes: The case of information systems resource misuse. *Ann. Appl. Stat.* **2018**, *12*, 1969–1992. [CrossRef]

72. Chu, A.M.Y.; Omori, Y.; So, H.Y.; So, M.K.P. A multivariate randomized response model for sensitive binary data. *Econom. Stat.* **2022**, 1–20. [CrossRef]
73. Greenberg, B.G.; Kuebler, R.R., Jr.; Abernathy, J.R.; Horvitz, D.G. Application of the randomized response technique in obtaining quantitative data. *J. Am. Stat. Assoc.* **1971**, *66*, 243–250. [CrossRef]
74. Gupta, S.; Gupta, B.; Singh, S. Estimation of sensitivity level of personal interview survey questions. *J. Stat. Plan. Inference* **2002**, *100*, 239–247. [CrossRef]
75. Grewal, I.S.; Bansal, M.L.; Singh, S. Estimation of population mean of a stigmatized quantitative variable using double sampling. *Statistica* **2003**, *63*, 79–88. [CrossRef]
76. Hussain, Z.; Shabbir, J. Estimation of mean of a sensitive quantitative variable. *J. Stat. Res.* **2007**, *41*, 83–92. [CrossRef]
77. Hussain, Z.; Shakeel, S.; Cheema, S.A. Estimation of stigmatized population total: A new additive quantitative randomized response model. *Commun. Stat.-Theory Methods* **2022**, *51*, 8741–8753.
78. Gupta, S.; Zhang, J.; Khalil, S.; Sapra, P. Mitigating lack of trust in quantitative randomized response technique models. *Commun. Stat.-Simul. Comput.* **2022**, 1–9.
79. Warner, S.L. The linear randomized response model. *J. Am. Stat. Assoc.* **1971**, *366*, 884–888. [CrossRef]
80. Goodstadt, M.S.; Gruson, V. The randomized response technique: A test on drug use. *J. Am. Stat. Assoc.* **1975**, *70*, 814–818. [CrossRef]
81. Maddala, G.S. *Limited-Dependent and Qualitative Variables in Econometrics*; Cambridge University Press: Cambridge, UK, 1983.
82. Ewemooje, O.S.; Adeniyi, I.O.; Adediran, A.A.; Molefe, W.B.; Adebola, F.B. Bayesian estimation in alternative tripartite randomized response techniques. *Sci. Afr.* **2023**, *19*, e01584. [CrossRef]
83. Abernathy, J.R.; Greenberg, B.G.; Horvitz, D.G. Estimates of induced abortion in urban North Carolina. *Demography* **1970**, *7*, 19–29. [CrossRef]
84. Winkler, R.L.; Franklin, L.A. Warner's randomized response model: A Bayesian approach. *J. Am. Stat. Assoc.* **1979**, *74*, 207–214. [CrossRef]
85. Hsieh, S.H.; Lee, S.M.; Shen, P.S. Semiparametric analysis of randomized response data with missing covariates in logistic regression. *Comput. Stat. Data Anal.* **2009**, *53*, 2673–2692. [CrossRef]
86. Hsieh, S.H.; Lee S.M.; Shen, P.S. Logistic regression analysis of randomized response data with missing covariates. *J. Stat. Plan. Inference* **2010**, *140*, 927–940. [CrossRef]
87. van der Heijden, P.G.M.; van Gils, G. Some logistic regression models for randomized response data. In *Statistical Modelling, Proceedings of the 11th International Workshop on Statistical Modelling, Orvieto, Italy, 15–19 July 1996*; Forcina, A., Marchetti, G.M., Hatzinger, R., Falmacci, G., Eds.; Graphos: Città di Castello, Italy, 1996; pp. 341–348.
88. van den Hout, A.; van der Heijden, P.G.M.; Gilchrist, R. The logistic regression model with response variables subject to randomized response. *Comput. Stat. Data Anal.* **2007**, *51*, 6060–6069. [CrossRef]
89. Krumpal, I. Estimating the prevalence of xenophobia and anti-Semitism in Germany: A comparison of randomized response and direct questioning. *Soc. Sci. Res.* **2012**, *41*, 1387–1403. [CrossRef]
90. Ostapczuk, M.; Musch, J.; Mashagen, M. A randomized-response investigation of the education effect in attitudes towards foreigners. *Eur. J. Soc. Psychol.* **2009**, *39*, 920–931. [CrossRef]
91. Arnab, R.; Mothupi, T. Randomized response techniques: A case study of the risky behaviors' of students of a certain University. *Model Assist. Stat. Appl.* **2015**, *10*, 421–430. [CrossRef]
92. Rueda, M.M.; Cobo, B.; López-Torrecillas, F. Measuring inappropriate sexual behavior among university students: Using the randomized response technique to enhance self-reporting. *Sex. Abus.* **2020**, *32*, 320–334. [CrossRef] [PubMed]
93. Tang, M.L.; Wu, Q.; Tian, G.L.; Guo, J.H. Two-sample non randomized response techniques for sensitive questions. *Commun. Stat.-Theory Methods* **2014**, *43*, 408–425. [CrossRef]
94. Scheers, N.J.; Dayton, C.M. Covariate randomized response models. *J. Am. Stat. Assoc.* **1988**, *83*, 969–974. [CrossRef]
95. Hsieh, S.H.; Perri, P.F. A logistic regression extension for the randomized response simple and crossed models: Theoretical results and empirical evidence. *Sociol. Methods Res.* **2022**, *51*, 1244–1281. [CrossRef]
96. Mieth, L.; Mayer, M.M.; Hoffmann, A.; Buchner, A.; Bell, R. Do they really wash their hands? Prevalence estimates for personal hygiene behaviour during the COVID-19 pandemic based on indirect questions. *BMC Public Health* **2021**, *21*, 12. [CrossRef]
97. Reiber, F.; Bryce, D.; Ulrich, R. Self-protecting responses in randomized response designs: A survey on intimate partner violence during the coronavirus disease 2019 pandemic. *Sociol. Methods Res.* **2022**, 1–32. [CrossRef]
98. Striegel, H.; Ulrich, R.; Simon, P. Randomized response estimates for doping and illicit drug use in elite athletes. *Drug Alcohol Depend.* **2010**, *106*, 230–232. [CrossRef]
99. Christiansen, A.V.; Frenger, M.; Chirico, A.; Pitsch, W. Recreational athletes' use of performance-enhancing substances: Results from the first European randomized response technique survey. *Sport. Med.-Open* **2023**, *9*, 1. [CrossRef]
100. Mielecka-Kubień, Z.; Toniszewski, M. Estimation of illicit drug use among high school students in the Silesian voivodship (Poland) with the use of the randomized response technique. *Math. Popul. Stud.* **2022**, *29*, 47–57. [CrossRef]

101. Liu, P.T.; Chow, L.P. A new discrete quantitative randomized response model. *J. Am. Stat. Assoc.* **1976**, *71*, 72–73. [CrossRef]
102. Burgstaller, L.; Feld, L.P.; Pfeil, K. Working in the shadow: Survey techniques for measuring and explaining undeclared work. *J. Econ. Behav. Organ.* **2022**, *200*, 661–671. [CrossRef]
103. Bar-Lev, S.K.; Bobovich, E.; Boukai, B. A common conjugate prior structure for several randomized response models. *Test* **2003**, *12*, 101–113. [CrossRef]
104. Dempster, A.P.; Laird, N.M.; Rubin, D.B. Maximum likelihood from incomplete data via the EM algorithm. *J. R. Stat. Soc. Ser. B-Stat. Methodol.* **1977**, *39*, 1–22.
105. Bourke, P.D.; Moran, M.A. Estimating proportions from randomized response data using the EM algorithm. *J. Am. Stat. Assoc.* **1988**, *83*, 964–968. [CrossRef]
106. Lee, S.M.; Tran, P.L.; Le, T.N.; Li, C.S. Prediction of a sensitive feature under indirect questioning via Warner's randomized response technique and latent class model. *Mathematics* **2023**, *11*, 345. [CrossRef]
107. van den Hout, A.; Kooiman, P. Estimating the linear regression model with categorical covariates subject to randomized response. *Comput. Stat. Data Anal.* **2006**, *50*, 3311–3323. [CrossRef]
108. Nandram, B.; Yu, Y. Bayesian analysis of sparse counts obtained from the unrelated question design. *Int. J. Stat. Probab.* **2019**, *8*, 66–84. [CrossRef]
109. Hussain, Z.; Shabbir, J.; Riaz, M. Bayesian estimation using Warner's randomized response model through simple and mixture prior distributions. *Commun. Stat.-Simul. Comput.* **2011**, *40*, 147–164. [CrossRef]
110. Migon, H.S.; Tachibana, V.M. Bayesian approximations in randomized response model. *Comput. Stat. Data Anal.* **1997**, *24*, 401–409. [CrossRef]
111. Pitz, G.F. Bayesian analysis of random response models. *Psychol. Bull.* **1980**, *87*, 209–212. [CrossRef]
112. Fidler, D.S.; Kleinknecht, R.E. Randomized response versus direct questioning: Two data-collection methods for sensitive information. *Psychol. Bull.* **1977**, *84*, 1045–1049. [CrossRef]
113. O'Hagan, A. Bayes linear estimators for randomized response models. *J. Am. Stat. Assoc.* **1987**, *82*, 580–585. [CrossRef]
114. Oh, M.S. Bayesian analysis of randomized response models: A Gibbs sampling approach. *J. Korean Stat. Soc.* **1994**, *23*, 463–482.
115. Unnikrishnan, N.K.; Kunte, S. Bayesian analysis for randomized response models. *Sankhyā Indian J. Stat. (Ser. B)* **1999**, *61*, 422–432.
116. Hussain, Z.; Shabbir, J. Bayesian estimation of population proportion in Kim and Warde mixed randomized response technique. *Electron. J. Appl. Stat. Anal.* **2012**, *5*, 213–225.
117. Song, J.J.; Kim, J.M. Bayesian analysis of randomized response sum score variables. *Commun. Stat.-Theory Methods* **2012**, *41*, 1875–1884. [CrossRef]
118. Adepetun, A.O.; Adewara, A.A. Bayesian analysis of Kim and Warde randomized response technique using alternative priors. *Am. J. Comput. Appl. Math.* **2014**, *4*, 130–140.
119. Groenitz, H. Using prior information in privacy-protecting survey designs for categorical sensitive variables. *Stat. Pap.* **2015**, *56*, 167–189. [CrossRef]
120. Song, J.J.; Kim, J.M. Bayesian estimation of rare sensitive attribute. *Commun. Stat.-Simul. Comput.* **2017**, *64*, 4154–4160. [CrossRef]
121. Kerkvliet, J. Estimating a logit model with randomized data: The case of cocaine use. *Aust. N. Z. J. Stat.* **1994**, *36*, 9–20. [CrossRef]
122. Boruch, R.F. Assuring confidentiality of responses in social research: A note on strategies. *Am. Sociol.* **1971**, *6*, 308–311.
123. Kuk, A.Y.C. Asking sensitive questions indirectly. *Biometrika* **1990**, *77*, 436–438. [CrossRef]
124. Cruyff, M.J.; Böckenholt, U.; Van Der Heijden, P.G.; Frank, L.E. A review of regression procedures for randomized response data, including univariate and multivariate logistic regression, the proportional odds model and item response model, and self-protective responses. In *Handbook of Statistics 34*; Chaudhuri, A., Christofides, T.C., Rao, C.R., Eds.; Elsevier: Amsterdam, The Netherlands, 2016; pp. 287–315.
125. Ronning, G. Randomized response and the binary probit model. *Econ. Lett.* **2005**, *86*, 221–228. [CrossRef]
126. Rubin, D.B. Inference and missing data. *Biometrika* **1976**, *63*, 581–592. [CrossRef]
127. Horvitz, D.G.; Thompson, D.J. A generalization of sampling without replacement from a finite universe. *J. Am. Stat. Assoc.* **1952**, *47*, 663–685. [CrossRef]
128. Lee, S.M.; Lukusa, T.M.; Li, C.S. Estimation of a zero-inflated Poisson regression model with missing covariates via nonparametric multiple imputation methods. *Comput. Stat.* **2020**, *35*, 725–754. [CrossRef]
129. Stoklosa, J.; Lee, S.M.; Hwang, W.H. Closed population capture–recapture models with measurement error and missing observations in covariates. *Stat. Sin.* **2019**, *29*, 589–610. [CrossRef]
130. Wang, D.; Chen, S.X. Empirical likelihood for estimating equations with missing values. *Ann. Stat.* **2009**, *37*, 490–517. [CrossRef]
131. Rubin, D.B. Multiple imputations in sample surveys-a phenomenological Bayesian approach to nonresponse. In *Proceedings of the Survey Research Methods Section of the American Statistical Association*; American Statistical Association: Alexandria, VA, USA, 1978; Volume 1, pp. 20–34.
132. Fay, R.E. Alternative paradigms for the analysis of imputed survey data. *J. Am. Stat. Assoc.* **1996**, *91*, 490–498. [CrossRef]
133. Lee, S.M.; Le, T.N.; Tran, P.L.; Li, C.S. Estimation of logistic regression with covariates missing separately or simultaneously via multiple imputation methods. *Comput. Stat.* **2022**, 1–35. [CrossRef]

134. Spiegelhalter, D.J.; Best, N.; Carlin, B.; van der Linde, A. Bayesian measures of model complexity and fit. *J. R. Stat. Soc. Ser. B-Stat. Methodol.* **2002**, *64*, 583–639. [CrossRef]
135. Chib, S. Marginal likelihood from the Gibbs output. *J. Am. Stat. Assoc.* **1995**, *90*, 1313–1321. [CrossRef]
136. Wentland, J.J.; Reissing, E. Casual sexual relationships: Identifying definitions for one night stands, booty calls, fuck buddies, and friends with benefits. *Can. J. Hum. Sex.* **2014**, *23*, 167–177. [CrossRef]
137. Kaspar, K.; Buß, L.V.; Rogner, J.; Gnambs, T. Engagement in one-night stands in Germany and Spain: Does personality matter? *Pers. Individ. Differ.* **2016**, *92*, 74–79. [CrossRef]
138. Hox, J.; Lensvelt-Mulders, G. Randomized response analysis in Mplus. *Struct. Equ. Model.* **2004**, *11*, 615–620. [CrossRef]
139. Sehra, S. Two-Stage Optional Randomized Response Models. Master's Thesis, The University of North Carolina, Greensboro, NC, USA, 2008.
140. Jann, B. RRLOGIT: Stata Module to Estimate Logistic Regression for rAndomized Response Data. 2011. Available at Research Papers in Economics (RePEc). Available online: https://ideas.repec.org/c/boc/bocode/s456203.html (accessed on 12 May 2011).
141. Heck, D.W.; Moshagen, M. RRreg: An R package for correlation and regression analyses of randomized response data. *J. Stat. Softw.* **2018**, *85*, 1–29. [CrossRef]
142. Rueda, M.D.M.; Cobo, B.; Arcos, A. RRTCS: An R package for randomized response techniques in complex surveys. *Appl. Psychol. Meas.* **2016**, *40*, 78–80. [CrossRef]
143. Fox, J.P.; Klotzke, K.; Veen, D. Generalized linear randomized response modeling using GLMMRR. *arXiv* **2021**, arXiv:2106.10171.
144. Tian, G.L.; Yu, J.W.; Tang, M.L.; Geng, Z. A new non-randomized model for analyzing sensitive questions with binary outcomes. *Statist. Med.* **2007**, *26*, 4238–4252. [CrossRef]
145. Tan, M.T.; Tian, G.L.; Tang, M.L. Sample surveys with sensitive questions: A nonrandomized response approach. *Am. Stat.* **2009**, *63*, 9–16. [CrossRef]
146. Hoffmann, A.; Meisters, J.; Musch, J. On the validity of non-randomized response techniques: An experimental comparison of the crosswise model and the triangular model. *Behav. Res. Methods* **2020**, *52*, 1768–1782. [CrossRef] [PubMed]
147. Tang, M.L.; Tian, G.L.; Tang, N.S.; Liu, Z.Q. A new non-randomized multicategory response model for surveys with a single sensitive question: Design and analysis. *J. Kor. Statist. Soc.* **2009**, *38*, 339–349. [CrossRef]
148. Groenitz, H. A new privacy-protecting survey design for multichotomous sensitive variables. *Metrika* **2014**, *77*, 211–224. [CrossRef]
149. Tian, G.L. A new non-randomized response model: The parallel model. *Stat. Neerl.* **2014**, *68*, 293–323. [CrossRef]
150. Perri, P.F.; Manoli, E.; Christofides, T.C. Assessing the effectiveness of indirect questioning techniques by detecting liars. *Stat. Pap.* **2022**, 1–24. [CrossRef]
151. Tian, G.L.; Yuen, K.C.; Tang, M.L.; Tan, M.T. Bayesian non-randomized response models for survey with sensitive questions. *Stat. Interface* **2009**, *2*, 13–25.
152. Tian, G.L.; Tang, M.L.; Liu, Z.; Tan, M.; Tang, N.S. Sample size determination for the non-randomized triangular model for sensitive questions in a survey. *Statist. Meth. Med. Res.* **2011**, *20*, 159–173. [CrossRef]
153. Tian, G.L.; Liu, Y.; Tang, M.L. Logistic regression analysis of non-randomized response data collected by the parallel model in sensitive surveys. *Aust. N. Z. J. Stat.* **2019**, *61*, 134–151. [CrossRef]
154. Heck, D.W.; Hoffmann, A.; Moshagen, M. Detecting nonadherence without loss in efficiency: A simple extension of the crosswise model. *Behav. Res. Methods* **2018**, *50*, 1895–1905. [CrossRef]
155. Wu, Q.; Tang, M.L. Non-randomized response model for sensitive survey with noncompliance. *Stat. Methods Med. Res.* **2016**, *25*, 2827–2839. [CrossRef] [PubMed]
156. Meisters, J.; Hoffmann, A.; Musch, J. A new approach to detecting cheating in sensitive surveys: The cheating detection triangular model. *Sociol. Methods Res.* **2022**, 1–31. [CrossRef]
157. Clark, S.J.; Desharnais, R.A. Honest answers to embarrassing questions: Detecting cheating in the randomized response model. *Psychol. Methods* **1998**, *3*, 160–168. [CrossRef]

MDPI
St. Alban-Anlage 66
4052 Basel
Switzerland
www.mdpi.com

Mathematics Editorial Office
E-mail: mathematics@mdpi.com
www.mdpi.com/journal/mathematics